S0-BZB-501

COPYRIGHT GEORGE PHILIP LTD

OXFORD

DESK
REFERENCE
ATLAS

REF

OXFORD

DESK
REFERENCE
ATLAS

PROPERTY OF ALUMNI LIBRARY
WENTWORTH INSTITUTE OF TECHNOLOGY

FOURTH EDITION

CONTENTS

REF *AES4248*
912
.G461

2001

WORLD STATISTICS

vi–ix	Countries
x–xi	Cities
xii–xv	Physical
xvi	Climate

THE EARTH IN FOCUS

2–3	The Universe and Solar System
4–5	The Changing Earth
6–7	Earthquakes and Volcanoes
8–9	Water and Ice
10–11	Weather and Climate
12–13	Landforms and Vegetation
14–15	Population
16–17	Languages and Religions
18–19	Agriculture and Industry
20–21	Trade and Commerce
22–23	Transport and Travel
24–27	International Organizations
28–29	Regions in the News
30–32	World Flags

Cartography by Philip's

Text
Keith Lye

Picture Acknowledgements
Courtesy of NPA Group, Edenbridge, UK 1
Image Bank /Lionel Brown 10
Rex Features /Sipa 6, 24
Still Pictures 26, /Anne Piantanida 8,
/Chris Caldicott 16, /Mark Edwards 18, 20,
/Hartmut Schwarzbach 14, 22, /Luke White 4
Tony Stone Images /Kevin Kelley 2, /Art Wolfe 12

Copyright © 2001 George Philip Limited
Fourth edition 2001

George Philip Limited,
a division of Octopus Publishing Group Limited,
2–4 Heron Quays, London E14 4JP

Published in North America by
Oxford University Press, Inc.,
198 Madison Avenue,
New York, N.Y. 10016

www.oup-usa.org/atlas

Oxford is a registered trademark of
Oxford University Press

All rights reserved. No part of this publication
may be reproduced, stored in a retrieval system,
or transmitted, in any form or by any means,
electronic, mechanical, photocopying, recording,
or otherwise, without the prior permission of
the publisher.

*Library of Congress Cataloging-in-Publication
Data available*

ISBN 0–19–521792–6

Printing (last digit): 9 8 7 6 5 4 3 2 1

Printed in Hong Kong

WORLD MAPS

1	General Reference	54–55	Northwest Africa
2–3	Northern Hemisphere	56–57	Central Africa
4–5	Southern Hemisphere	58–59	Southern Africa
6–7	Europe	60–61	Australia
8–9	Scandinavia	62–63	Southeast Australia
10–11	British Isles	64–65	New Zealand, Central
12–13	France		and Southwest Pacific
14–15	Germany and Benelux	66–67	North America
16–17	Central Europe	68–69	Eastern Canada
18–19	Spain and Portugal	70–71	Western Canada
20–21	Italy and the Adriatic	72–73	Northeast USA
22–23	Greece and the Balkans	74–75	Southeast USA
24–25	Eastern Europe	76–77	North central USA
26–27	Asia	78–79	Southern USA
28–29	Western Russia and	80–81	Northwest USA
	Central Asia	82–83	Southwest USA
30–31	Eastern Siberia	84–85	Mexico
32–33	Japan	86–87	Caribbean and Central
34–35	China		America
36–37	Southeast Asia	88–89	South America
38–39	Philippines and Eastern	90–91	South America –
	Indonesia		Northwest
40–41	Eastern India, Bangladesh and	92–93	South America –
	Burma		Northeast
42–43	Western India and Pakistan	94–95	South America –
44–45	Iran, the Gulf and Afghanistan		South
46–47	The Middle East and Turkey	96	Antarctica
48–49	Arabia and the Horn of Africa		
50–51	Africa		
52–53	Northeast Africa	97–160	**Index to World Maps**

WORLD STATISTICS – COUNTRIES

Listed below are the principal countries of the world; the more important territories are also included. If a territory is not completely independent, then the country it is associated with is named. The area figures give the total area of land, inland water, and ice. Annual income is the GNP per capita. The figures are the latest available: usually 1998.

Country / Territory	Area (1,000 sq km)	Area (1,000 sq mi)	Population (1,000s)	Capital City	Annual Income US$
Afghanistan	652	252	26,511	Kabul	800
Albania	28.8	11.1	3,795	Tirana	810
Algeria	2,382	920	32,904	Algiers	1,550
Andorra	0.45	0.17	49	Andorra La Vella	18,000
Angola	1,247	481	13,295	Luanda	340
Argentina	2,767	1,068	36,238	Buenos Aires	8,970
Armenia	29.8	11.5	3,968	Yerevan	480
Australia	7,687	2,968	18,855	Canberra	20,300
Austria	83.9	32.4	7,613	Vienna	26,850
Azerbaijan	86.6	33.4	8,324	Baku	490
Azores (Portugal)	2.2	0.87	238	Ponta Delgada	–
Bahamas	13.9	5.4	295	Nassau	20,100
Bahrain	0.68	0.26	683	Manama	7,660
Bangladesh	144	56	150,589	Dhaka	350
Barbados	0.43	0.17	265	Bridgetown	7,890
Belarus	207.6	80.1	10,697	Minsk	2,200
Belgium	30.5	11.8	9,832	Brussels	25,380
Belize	23	8.9	230	Belmopan	2,700
Benin	113	43	6,369	Porto-Novo	380
Bhutan	47	18.1	1,906	Thimphu	1,000
Bolivia	1,099	424	9,724	La Paz/Sucre	1,000
Bosnia-Herzegovina	51	20	4,601	Sarajevo	1,720
Botswana	582	225	1,822	Gaborone	3,600
Brazil	8,512	3,286	179,487	Brasília	4,570
Brunei	5.8	2.2	333	Bandar Seri Begawan	24,000
Bulgaria	111	43	9,071	Sofia	1,230
Burkina Faso	274	106	12,092	Ouagadougou	240
Burma (= Myanmar)	677	261	51,129	Rangoon	1,200
Burundi	27.8	10.7	7,358	Bujumbura	140
Cambodia	181	70	10,046	Phnom Penh	280
Cameroon	475	184	16,701	Yaoundé	610
Canada	9,976	3,852	28,488	Ottawa	20,020
Canary Is. (Spain)	7.3	2.8	1,494	Las Palmas/Santa Cruz	–
Cape Verde Is.	4	1.6	515	Praia	1,060
Central African Republic	623	241	4,074	Bangui	300
Chad	1,284	496	7,337	Ndjaména	230
Chile	757	292	15,272	Santiago	4,810
China	9,597	3,705	1,299,180	Beijing	750
Colombia	1,139	440	39,397	Bogotá	2,600
Comoros	2.2	0.86	670	Moroni	370
Congo	342	132	3,167	Brazzaville	690
Congo (Dem. Rep. of the)	2,345	905	49,190	Kinshasa	110
Costa Rica	51.1	19.7	3,711	San José	2,780
Croatia	56.5	21.8	4,960	Zagreb	4,520
Cuba	111	43	11,504	Havana	1,560

Country / Territory	Area (1,000 sq km)	Area (1,000 sq mi)	Population (1,000s)	Capital City	Annual Income US$
Cyprus	9.3	3.6	762	Nicosia	13,000
Czech Republic	78.9	30.4	10,500	Prague	5,040
Denmark	43.1	16.6	5,153	Copenhagen	33,260
Djibouti	23.2	9	552	Djibouti	1,200
Dominica	0.75	0.29	87	Roseau	3,010
Dominican Republic	48.7	18.8	8,621	Santo Domingo	1,770
Ecuador	284	109	13,319	Quito	1,530
Egypt	1,001	387	64,210	Cairo	1,290
El Salvador	21	8.1	6,739	San Salvador	1,850
Equatorial Guinea	28.1	10.8	455	Malabo	1,500
Eritrea	94	36	4,523	Asmara	200
Estonia	44.7	17.3	1,647	Tallinn	3,390
Ethiopia	1,128	436	61,841	Addis Ababa	100
Fiji	18.3	7.1	883	Suva	2,110
Finland	338	131	5,077	Helsinki	24,110
France	552	213	58,145	Paris	24,940
French Guiana (France)	90	34.7	130	Cayenne	6,000
French Polynesia (France)	4	1.5	268	Papeete	10,800
Gabon	268	103	1,612	Libreville	3,950
Gambia, The	11.3	4.4	1,119	Banjul	340
Georgia	69.7	26.9	5,777	Tbilisi	930
Germany	357	138	76,962	Berlin/Bonn	25,850
Ghana	239	92	20,564	Accra	390
Greece	132	51	10,193	Athens	11,650
Grenada	0.34	0.13	83	St George's	3,170
Guadeloupe (France)	1.7	0.66	365	Basse-Terre	9,200
Guatemala	109	42	12,222	Guatemala City	1,640
Guinea	246	95	7,830	Conakry	540
Guinea-Bissau	36.1	13.9	1,197	Bissau	160
Guyana	215	83	891	Georgetown	770
Haiti	27.8	10.7	8,003	Port-au-Prince	410
Honduras	112	43	6,846	Tegucigalpa	730
Hong Kong (China)	1.1	0.40	6,336	–	23,670
Hungary	93	35.9	10,531	Budapest	4,510
Iceland	103	40	274	Reykjavik	28,010
India	3,288	1,269	1,041,543	New Delhi	430
Indonesia	1,905	735	218,661	Jakarta	680
Iran	1,648	636	68,759	Tehran	1,770
Iraq	438	169	26,339	Baghdad	2,400
Ireland	70.3	27.1	4,086	Dublin	18,340
Israel	27	10.3	5,321	Jerusalem	15,940
Italy	301	116	57,195	Rome	20,250
Ivory Coast (Côte d'Ivoire)	322	125	17,600	Yamoussoukro	700
Jamaica	11	4.2	2,735	Kingston	1,680
Japan	378	146	128,470	Tokyo	32,380
Jordan	89.2	34.4	5,558	Amman	1,520
Kazakstan	2,717	1,049	19,006	Astana	1,310
Kenya	580	224	35,060	Nairobi	330
Korea, North	121	47	26,117	Pyŏngyang	1,000
Korea, South	99	38.2	46,403	Seoul	7,970

Country / Territory	Area (1,000 sq km)	Area (1,000 sq mi)	Population (1,000s)	Capital City	Annual Income US$
Kuwait	17.8	6.9	2,639	Kuwait City	22,700
Kyrgyzstan	198.5	76.6	5,403	Bishkek	350
Laos	237	91	5,463	Vientiane	330
Latvia	65	25	2,768	Riga	2,430
Lebanon	10.4	4	3,327	Beirut	3,560
Lesotho	30.4	11.7	2,370	Maseru	570
Liberia	111	43	3,575	Monrovia	1,000
Libya	1,760	679	6,500	Tripoli	6,700
Lithuania	65.2	25.2	3,935	Vilnius	2,440
Luxembourg	2.6	1	377	Luxembourg	43,570
Macau (China)	0.02	0.006	656	Macau	16,000
Macedonia (F.Y.R.O.M.)	25.7	9.9	2,157	Skopje	1,290
Madagascar	587	227	16,627	Antananarivo	260
Madeira (Portugal)	0.81	0.31	253	Funchal	–
Malawi	118	46	12,458	Lilongwe	200
Malaysia	330	127	21,983	Kuala Lumpur	3,600
Maldives	0.30	0.12	283	Malé	1,230
Mali	1,240	479	12,685	Bamako	250
Malta	0.32	0.12	366	Valletta	9,440
Martinique (France)	1.1	0.42	362	Fort-de-France	10,700
Mauritania	1,030	412	2,702	Nouakchott	410
Mauritius	2.0	0.72	1,201	Port Louis	3,700
Mexico	1,958	756	107,233	Mexico City	3,970
Micronesia, Fed. States of	0.70	0.27	110	Palikir	1,800
Moldova	33.7	13	4,707	Chişinău	410
Mongolia	1,567	605	2,847	Ulan Bator	400
Morocco	447	172	31,559	Rabat	1,250
Mozambique	802	309	20,493	Maputo	210
Namibia	825	318	2,437	Windhoek	1,940
Nepal	141	54	24,084	Katmandu	210
Netherlands	41.5	16	15,829	Amsterdam/The Hague	24,760
Netherlands Antilles (Neths)	0.99	0.38	203	Willemstad	11,500
New Caledonia (France)	18.6	7.2	195	Nouméa	11,400
New Zealand	269	104	3,662	Wellington	14,700
Nicaragua	130	50	5,261	Managua	390
Niger	1,267	489	10,752	Niamey	190
Nigeria	924	357	105,000	Abuja	300
Norway	324	125	4,331	Oslo	34,330
Oman	212	82	2,176	Muscat	7,900
Pakistan	796	307	162,409	Islamabad	480
Panama	77.1	29.8	2,893	Panama City	3,080
Papua New Guinea	463	179	4,845	Port Moresby	890
Paraguay	407	157	5,538	Asunción	1,760
Peru	1,285	496	26,276	Lima	2,460
Philippines	300	116	77,473	Manila	1,050
Poland	313	121	40,366	Warsaw	3,900
Portugal	92.4	35.7	10,587	Lisbon	10,690
Puerto Rico (US)	9	3.5	3,836	San Juan	9,000
Qatar	11	4.2	499	Doha	17,100
Réunion (France)	2.5	0.97	692	Saint-Denis	4,800

Country / Territory	Area (1,000 sq km)	Area (1,000 sq mi)	Population (1,000s)	Capital City	Annual Income US$
Romania	238	92	24,000	Bucharest	1,390
Russia	17,075	6,592	155,096	Moscow	2,300
Rwanda	26.3	10.2	10,200	Kigali	230
St Lucia	0.62	0.24	177	Castries	3,410
St Vincent & Grenadines	0.39	0.15	128	Kingstown	2,420
Samoa	2.8	1.1	171	Apia	1,020
São Tomé & Príncipe	0.96	0.37	151	São Tomé	280
Saudi Arabia	2,150	830	20,697	Riyadh	9,000
Senegal	197	76	8,716	Dakar	530
Sierra Leone	71.7	27.7	5,437	Freetown	140
Singapore	0.62	0.24	3,000	Singapore	30,060
Slovak Republic	49	18.9	5,500	Bratislava	3,700
Slovenia	20.3	7.8	2,055	Ljubljana	9,760
Solomon Is.	28.9	11.2	429	Honiara	750
Somalia	638	246	9,736	Mogadishu	600
South Africa	1,220	471	43,666	C. Town/Pretoria/ Bloemfontein	2,880
Spain	505	195	40,667	Madrid	14,080
Sri Lanka	65.6	25.3	19,416	Colombo	810
Sudan	2,506	967	33,625	Khartoum	290
Surinam	163	63	497	Paramaribo	1,660
Swaziland	17.4	6.7	1,121	Mbabane	1,400
Sweden	450	174	8,560	Stockholm	25,620
Switzerland	41.3	15.9	6,762	Bern	40,080
Syria	185	71	17,826	Damascus	1,020
Taiwan	36	13.9	22,000	Taipei	12,400
Tajikistan	143.1	55.2	7,041	Dushanbe	350
Tanzania	945	365	39,639	Dodoma	210
Thailand	513	198	63,670	Bangkok	2,200
Togo	56.8	21.9	4,861	Lomé	330
Trinidad & Tobago	5.1	2	1,484	Port of Spain	4,430
Tunisia	164	63	9,924	Tunis	2,050
Turkey	779	301	66,789	Ankara	3,160
Turkmenistan	488.1	188.5	4,585	Ashkhabad	1,630
Uganda	236	91	26,958	Kampala	320
Ukraine	603.7	233.1	52,558	Kiev	850
United Arab Emirates	83.6	32.3	1,951	Abu Dhabi	18,220
United Kingdom	243.3	94	58,393	London	21,400
United States of America	9,373	3,619	266,096	Washington, DC	29,340
Uruguay	177	68	3,274	Montevideo	6,180
Uzbekistan	447.4	172.7	26,044	Tashkent	870
Vanuatu	12.2	4.7	206	Port-Vila	1,270
Venezuela	912	352	24,715	Caracas	350
Vietnam	332	127	82,427	Hanoi	330
Virgin Is. (US)	0.34	0.13	135	Charlotte Amalie	12,500
Western Sahara	266	103	228	El Aaiún	300
Yemen	528	204	13,219	Sana	300
Yugoslavia	102.3	39.5	10,761	Belgrade	2,300
Zambia	753	291	12,267	Lusaka	330
Zimbabwe	391	151	13,123	Harare	610

WORLD STATISTICS – CITIES

Listed below are all the cities with more than 600,000 inhabitants (only cities with more than 1 million inhabitants are included for Brazil, China, and India). The figures are taken from the most recent censuses and surveys, and are in thousands. As far as possible the figures are for the metropolitan area, e.g. greater New York or Mexico City.

Population (1,000s)	Population (1,000s)	Population (1,000s)	Population (1,000s)
Afghanistan	Ottawa–Hull 1,022	**Dominican Republic**	Vishakhapatnam 1,052
Kabul 1,565	Edmonton 885	Santo Domingo 2,135	Varanasi 1,026
Algeria	Calgary 831	Santiago. 691	Ludhiana. 1,012
Algiers 2,168	Québec 693	**Ecuador**	**Indonesia**
Oran 916	Winnipeg. 677	Guayaquil 1,973	Jakarta 11,500
Angola	Hamilton 643	Quito 1,487	Surabaya 2,701
Luanda 2,418	**Chile**	**Egypt**	Bandung 2,368
Argentina	Santiago 5,067	Cairo. 9,900	Medan. 1,910
Buenos Aires 11,256	**China**	Alexandria 3,431	Semarang 1,366
Córdoba. 1,208	Shanghai 15,082	El Gîza 2,144	Palembang 1,352
Rosario. 1,118	Beijing. 12,362	Shubra el Kheima 834	Tangerang. 1,198
Mendoza 773	Tianjin. 10,687	**El Salvador**	Ujung Pandang 1,092
La Plata 642	Hong Kong (SAR)* . . . 6,502	San Salvador 1,522	Bandar Lampung. 832
San Miguel de	Chongqing 3,870	**Ethiopia**	Malang 763
Tucumán 622	Shenyang. 3,860	Addis Ababa. 2,112	Padang 721
Armenia	Wuhan 3,520	**France**	**Iran**
Yerevan. 1,248	Guangzhou 3,114	Paris 9,319	Tehran. 6,750
Australia	Harbin. 2,505	Lyon 1,262	Mashhad 1,964
Sydney 3,770	Nanjing. 2,211	Marseille 1,087	Esfahan 1,221
Melbourne 3,217	Xi'an 2,115	Lille 959	Tabriz 1,166
Brisbane 1,489	Chengdu 1,933	Bordeaux. 696	Shiraz 1,043
Perth. 1,262	Dalian 1,855	Toulouse 650	Ahvaz. 828
Adelaide 1,080	Changchun 1,810	**Georgia**	Qom 780
Austria	Jinan 1,660	Tbilisi 1,300	Bakhtaran 666
Vienna. 1,595	Taiyuan 1,642	**Germany**	**Iraq**
Azerbaijan	Qingdao 1,584	Berlin 3,470	Baghdad 3,841
Baku 1,720	Fuzhou, Fujian 1,380	Hamburg 1,706	Diyala. 961
Bangladesh	Zibo 1,346	Munich 1,240	As Sulaymaniyah 952
Dhaka. 6,105	Zhengzhou 1,324	Cologne. 964	Arbil. 770
Chittagong 2,041	Lanzhou 1,296	Frankfurt 651	Al Mawsil 664
Khulna 877	Anshan 1,252	Essen 616	**Ireland**
Belarus	Fushun 1,246	Dortmund. 600	Dublin 952
Minsk 1,700	Kunming 1,242	**Ghana**	**Israel**
Belgium	Changsha 1,198	Accra. 949	Tel Aviv-Yafo. 1,502
Brussels. 948	Hangzhou. 1,185	**Greece**	**Italy**
Bolivia	Nanchang 1,169	Athens 3,097	Rome 2,775
La Paz. 1,126	Shijiazhuang 1,159	**Guatemala**	Milan 1,369
Santa Cruz. 767	Guiyang. 1,131	Guatemala 1,167	Naples 1,067
Brazil	Ürümqi. 1,130	**Guinea**	Turin 962
São Paulo 16,417	Jilin 1,118	Conakry 1,508	Palermo. 698
Rio de Janeiro 9,888	Tangshan. 1,110	**Haiti**	Genoa 678
Salvador 2,211	Qiqihar 1,104	Port-au-Prince 1,255	**Ivory Coast**
Belo Horizonte 2,091	Baotou 1,033	**Honduras**	**(Côte d'Ivoire)**
Fortaleza. 1,965	Hefei. 1,000	Tegucigalpa 813	Abidjan 2,500
Brasília 1,821	**Colombia**	**Hungary**	**Jamaica**
Curitiba 1,476	Bogotá 6,004	Budapest. 1,885	Kingston 644
Recife 1,346	Cali 1,985	**India**	**Japan**
Pôrto Alegre 1,288	Medellín 1,970	Mumbai (Bombay) . . . 12,572	Tokyo–
Manaus 1,157	Barranquilla 1,157	Kolkata 10,916	Yokohama. 26,836
Belém 1,144	Cartagena 812	Delhi. 7,207	Osaka 10,601
Goiânia. 1,004	**Congo**	Chennai (Madras) . . . 5,361	Nagoya 2,152
Bulgaria	Brazzaville 937	Hyderabad 4,280	Sapporo 1,757
Sofia 1,116	**Congo (Dem. Rep. of the)**	Bangalore 4,087	Kyoto 1,464
Burkina Faso	Kinshasa 1,655	Ahmadabad 3,298	Kobe 1,424
Ouagadougou 690	Lubumbashi 851	Pune 2,485	Fukuoka 1,285
Burma (Myanmar)	Mbuji-Mayi. 806	Kanpur 2,111	Kawasaki. 1,203
Rangoon. 2,513	**Costa Rica**	Nagpur 1,661	Hiroshima. 1,109
Cambodia	San José 1,220	Lucknow. 1,642	Kitakyushu 1,020
Phnom Penh 920	**Croatia**	Surat 1,517	Sendai 971
Cameroon	Zagreb 931	Jaipur 1,514	Chiba 857
Douala 1,200	**Cuba**	Coimbatore 1,136	Sakai. 803
Yaoundé. 800	Havana 2,241	Vadodara 1,115	Kumamoto 650
Canada	**Czech Republic**	Indore. 1,104	Okayama 616
Toronto 4,344	Prague. 1,209	Patna. 1,099	**Jordan**
Montréal. 3,337	**Denmark**	Madurai 1,094	Amman. 1,300
Vancouver 1,831	Copenhagen. 1,362	Bhopal. 1,064	Az-Zarqā 609

	Population (1,000s)
Kazakstan	
Almaty	1,150
Kenya	
Nairobi	2,000
Mombasa	600
Korea, North	
Pyŏngyang	2,639
Hamhung	775
Chŏngjin	754
Chinnampo	691
Korea, South	
Seoul	11,641
Pusan	3,814
Taegu	2,449
Inchon	2,308
Taejŏn	1,272
Kwangju	1,258
Ulsan	967
Sŏngnam	869
Puch'on	779
Suwŏn	756
Latvia	
Riga	846
Lebanon	
Beirut	1,900
Libya	
Tripoli	1,083
Madagascar	
Antananarivo	1,053
Malaysia	
Kuala Lumpur	1,145
Mali	
Bamako	800
Mauritania	
Nouakchott	735
Mexico	
Mexico City	15,048
Guadalajara	2,847
Monterrey	2,522
Puebla	1,055
León	872
Ciudad Juárez	798
Tijuana	743
Culiacán Rosales	602
Mexicali	602
Moldova	
Chişinău	700
Mongolia	
Ulan Bator	627
Morocco	
Casablanca	3,079
Rabat-Salé	1,344
Fès	735
Marrakesh	621
Mozambique	
Maputo	2,000
Netherlands	
Amsterdam	1,101
Rotterdam	1,076
The Hague	694
New Zealand	
Auckland	997
Nicaragua	
Managua	864
Nigeria	
Lagos	10,287
Ibadan	1,365
Ogbomosho	712
Kano	657
Norway	
Oslo	714

	Population (1,000s)
Pakistan	
Karachi	9,863
Lahore	5,085
Faisalabad	1,875
Peshawar	1,676
Gujranwala	1,663
Rawalpindi	1,290
Multan	1,257
Hyderabad	1,107
Paraguay	
Asunción	945
Peru	
Lima–Callao	6,601
Callao	638
Arequipa	620
Philippines	
Manila	9,280
Quezon City	1,989
Davao	1,191
Caloocan	1,023
Cebu	662
Poland	
Warsaw	1,638
Lódz	825
Kraków	745
Wroclaw	642
Portugal	
Lisbon	2,561
Oporto	1,174
Romania	
Bucharest	2,060
Russia	
Moscow	9,233
St Petersburg	4,883
Nizhniy Novgorod	1,425
Novosibirsk	1,400
Yekaterinburg	1,300
Samara	1,200
Omsk	1,200
Chelyabinsk	1,100
Kazan	1,100
Ufa	1,100
Volgograd	1,003
Perm	1,000
Rostov	1,000
Voronezh	908
Saratov	895
Krasnoyarsk	869
Togliatti	689
Simbirsk	678
Izhevsk	654
Krasnodar	645
Vladivostok	632
Yaroslavl	629
Khabarovsk	618
Saudi Arabia	
Riyadh	1,800
Jedda	1,500
Mecca	630
Senegal	
Dakar	1,571
Singapore	
Singapore	3,104
Somalia	
Mogadishu	1,000
South Africa	
Cape Town	2,350
East Rand	1,379
Johannesburg	1,196
Durban	1,137
Pretoria	1,080

	Population (1,000s)
West Rand	870
Port Elizabeth	853
Vanderbijlpark– Vereeniging	774
Spain	
Madrid	3,029
Barcelona	1,614
Valencia	763
Sevilla	719
Zaragoza	607
Sri Lanka	
Colombo	1,863
Sudan	
Omdurman	1,267
Khartoum	925
Khartoum North	879
Sweden	
Stockholm	1,744
Göteborg	775
Switzerland	
Zürich	1,175
Bern	942
Syria	
Aleppo	1,591
Damascus	1,549
Homs	644
Taiwan	
Taipei	2,653
Kaohsiung	1,405
Taichung	817
Tainan	700
Tanzania	
Dar-es-Salaam	1,361
Thailand	
Bangkok	5,572
Togo	
Lomé	590
Tunisia	
Tunis	1,827
Turkey	
Istanbul	7,490
Ankara	3,028
Izmir	2,333
Adana	1,472
Bursa	1,317
Konya	1,040
Gaziantep	930
Icel	908
Antalya	734
Diyarbakir	677
Kocaeli	661
Urfa	649
Kayseri	648
Manisa	641
Uganda	
Kampala	773
Ukraine	
Kiev	2,630
Kharkiv	1,555
Dnipropetrovsk	1,147
Donetsk	1,088
Odesa	1,046
Zaporizhzhya	887
Lviv	802
Kryvyy Rih	720
United Kingdom	
London	8,089
Birmingham	2,373
Manchester	2,353
Liverpool	852
Glasgow	832

	Population (1,000s)
Sheffield	661
Nottingham	649
Newcastle	617
United States	
New York	16,329
Los Angeles	12,410
Chicago	7,668
Philadelphia	4,949
Washington, DC	4,466
Detroit	4,307
Houston	3,653
Atlanta	3,331
Boston	3,240
Dallas	2,898
Minneapolis–St Paul	2,688
San Diego	2,632
St Louis	2,536
Phoenix	2,473
Baltimore	2,458
Pittsburgh	2,402
Cleveland	2,222
San Francisco	2,182
Seattle	2,180
Tampa	2,157
Miami	2,025
Newark	1,934
Denver	1,796
Portland (Or.)	1,676
Kansas City (Mo.)	1,647
Cincinnati	1,581
San Jose	1,557
Norfolk	1,529
Indianapolis	1,462
Milwaukee	1,456
Sacramento	1,441
San Antonio	1,437
Columbus (Oh.)	1,423
New Orleans	1,309
Charlotte	1,260
Buffalo	1,189
Salt Lake City	1,178
Hartford	1,151
Oklahoma	1,007
Jacksonville (Fl.)	665
Omaha	663
Memphis	614
Uruguay	
Montevideo	1,378
Uzbekistan	
Tashkent	2,107
Venezuela	
Caracas	2,784
Maracaibo	1,364
Valencia	1,032
Maracay	800
Barquisimeto	745
Vietnam	
Ho Chi Minh City	4,322
Hanoi	3,056
Haiphong	783
Yemen	
Sana	972
Yugoslavia	
Belgrade	1,137
Zambia	
Lusaka	982
Zimbabwe	
Harare	1,189
Bulawayo	622

* SAR = Special Administrative Region of China

WORLD STATISTICS – PHYSICAL

Under each subject heading, the statistics are listed by continent. The figures are in size order beginning with the largest, longest, or deepest, and are rounded as appropriate. Both metric and imperial measurements are given. The lists are complete down to the > mark; below this mark they are selective.

Land and Water

	km²	miles²	%
The World	509,450,000	196,672,000	–
Land	149,450,000	57,688,000	29.3
Water	360,000,000	138,984,000	70.7
Asia	44,500,000	17,177,000	29.8
Africa	30,302,000	11,697,000	20.3
North America	24,241,000	9,357,000	16.2
South America	17,793,000	6,868,000	11.9
Antarctica	14,100,000	5,443,000	9.4
Europe	9,957,000	3,843,000	6.7
Australia & Oceania	8,557,000	3,303,000	5.7
Pacific Ocean	179,679,000	69,356,000	49.9
Atlantic Ocean	92,373,000	35,657,000	25.7
Indian Ocean	73,917,000	28,532,000	20.5
Arctic Ocean	14,090,000	5,439,000	3.9

Seas

Pacific Ocean	km²	miles²
South China Sea	2,974,600	1,148,500
Bering Sea	2,268,000	875,000
Sea of Okhotsk	1,528,000	590,000
East China & Yellow	1,249,000	482,000
Sea of Japan	1,008,000	389,000
Gulf of California	162,000	62,500
Bass Strait	75,000	29,000

Atlantic Ocean	km²	miles²
Caribbean Sea	2,766,000	1,068,000
Mediterranean Sea	2,516,000	971,000
Gulf of Mexico	1,543,000	596,000
Hudson Bay	1,232,000	476,000
North Sea	575,000	223,000
Black Sea	462,000	178,000
Baltic Sea	422,170	163,000
Gulf of St Lawrence	238,000	92,000

Indian Ocean	km²	miles²
Red Sea	438,000	169,000
The Gulf	239,000	92,000

Mountains

Europe		m	ft
Elbrus	Russia	5,642	18,510
Mont Blanc	France/Italy	4,807	15,771
Monte Rosa	Italy/Switzerland	4,634	15,203
Dom	Switzerland	4,545	14,911
Liskamm	Switzerland	4,527	14,852
Weisshorn	Switzerland	4,505	14,780
Taschorn	Switzerland	4,490	14,730
Matterhorn/Cervino	Italy/Switzerland	4,478	14,691
Mont Maudit	France/Italy	4,465	14,649
Dent Blanche	Switzerland	4,356	14,291
>Nadelhorn	Switzerland	4,327	14,196
Grandes Jorasses	France/Italy	4,208	13,806
Jungfrau	Switzerland	4,158	13,642
Barre des Ecrins	France	4,103	13,461
Gran Paradiso	Italy	4,061	13,323
Piz Bernina	Italy/Switzerland	4,049	13,284

Europe (cont.)		m	ft
Eiger	Switzerland	3,970	13,025
Monte Viso	Italy	3,841	12,602
Grossglockner	Austria	3,797	12,457
Wildspitze	Austria	3,772	12,382
Monte Disgrazia	Italy	3,678	12,066
Mulhacén	Spain	3,478	11,411
Pico de Aneto	Spain	3,404	11,168
Marmolada	Italy	3,342	10,964
Etna	Italy	3,340	10,958
Zugspitze	Germany	2,962	9,718
Musala	Bulgaria	2,925	9,596
Olympus	Greece	2,917	9,570
Triglav	Slovenia	2,863	9,393
Monte Cinto	France (Corsica)	2,710	8,891
Gerlachovka	Slovak Republic	2,655	8,711
Torre de Cerredo	Spain	2,648	8,688
Galdhöpiggen	Norway	2,468	8,100
Hvannadalshnúkur	Iceland	2,119	6,952
Kebnekaise	Sweden	2,117	6,946
Ben Nevis	UK	1,343	4,406

Asia		m	ft
Everest	China/Nepal	8,850	29,035
K2 (Godwin Austen)	China/Kashmir	8,611	28,251
Kanchenjunga	India/Nepal	8,598	28,208
Lhotse	China/Nepal	8,516	27,939
Makalu	China/Nepal	8,481	27,824
Cho Oyu	China/Nepal	8,201	26,906
Dhaulagiri	Nepal	8,172	26,811
Manaslu	Nepal	8,156	26,758
Nanga Parbat	Kashmir	8,126	26,660
Annapurna	Nepal	8,078	26,502
Gasherbrum	China/Kashmir	8,068	26,469
Broad Peak	China/Kashmir	8,051	26,414
Xixabangma	China	8,012	26,286
Kangbachen	India/Nepal	7,902	25,925
Jannu	India/Nepal	7,902	25,925
Gayachung Kang	Nepal	7,897	25,909
Himalchuli	Nepal	7,893	25,896
Disteghil Sar	Kashmir	7,885	25,869
Nuptse	Nepal	7,879	25,849
Khunyang Chhish	Kashmir	7,852	25,761
Masherbrum	Kashmir	7,821	25,659
Nanda Devi	India	7,817	25,646
Rakaposhi	Kashmir	7,788	25,551
Batura	Kashmir	7,785	25,541
Namche Barwa	China	7,756	25,446
Kamet	India	7,756	25,446
Soltoro Kangri	Kashmir	7,742	25,400
Gurla Mandhata	China	7,728	25,354
>Trivor	Pakistan	7,720	25,328
Kongur Shan	China	7,719	25,324
Tirich Mir	Pakistan	7,690	25,229
K'ula Shan	Bhutan/China	7,543	24,747
Pik Kommunizma	Tajikistan	7,495	24,590
Demavend	Iran	5,604	18,386
Ararat	Turkey	5,165	16,945
Gunong Kinabalu	Malaysia (Borneo)	4,101	13,455
Yu Shan	Taiwan	3,997	13,113
Fuji-San	Japan	3,776	12,388

Africa		m	ft
Kilimanjaro	Tanzania	5,895	19,340
Mt Kenya	Kenya	5,199	17,057
Ruwenzori	Uganda/Congo (D. Rep.)	5,109	16,762
Ras Dashan	Ethiopia	4,620	15,157

Africa (cont.)		m	ft
Meru	Tanzania	4,565	14,977
Karisimbi	Rwanda/Congo (D. Rep.)	4,507	14,787
Mt Elgon	Kenya/Uganda	4,321	14,176
Batu	Ethiopia	4,307	14,130
Guna	Ethiopia	4,231	13,882
Toubkal	Morocco	4,165	13,665
Irhil Mgoun	Morocco	4,071	13,356
Mt Cameroon	Cameroon	4,070	13,353
Amba Ferit	Ethiopia	3,875	13,042
Pico del Teide	Spain (Tenerife)	3,718	12,198
Thabana Ntlenyana	Lesotho	3,482	11,424
Emi Koussi	Chad	3,415	11,204
Mt aux Sources	Lesotho/South Africa	3,282	10,768
Mt Piton	Réunion	3,069	10,069

Oceania		m	ft
Puncak Jaya	Indonesia	5,029	16,499
Puncak Trikora	Indonesia	4,750	15,584
Puncak Mandala	Indonesia	4,702	15,427
Mt Wilhelm	Papua New Guinea	4,508	14,790
Mauna Kea	USA (Hawaii)	4,205	13,796
Mauna Loa	USA (Hawaii)	4,169	13,681
Mt Cook (Aoraki)	New Zealand	3,753	12,313
Mt Balbi	Solomon Is.	2,439	8,002
Orohena	Tahiti	2,241	7,352
Mt Kosciuszko	Australia	2,237	7,339

North America		m	ft
Mt McKinley (Denali)	USA (Alaska)	6,194	20,321
Pierre Elliott Trudeau	Canada	5,959	19,551
Citlaltepetl	Mexico	5,700	18,701
Mt St Elias	USA/Canada	5,489	18,008
Popocatepetl	Mexico	5,452	17,887
Mt Foraker	USA (Alaska)	5,304	17,401
Ixtaccihuatl	Mexico	5,286	17,342
Lucania	Canada	5,227	17,149
Mt Steele	Canada	5,073	16,644
Mt Bona	USA (Alaska)	5,005	16,420
Mt Blackburn	USA (Alaska)	4,996	16,391
Mt Sanford	USA (Alaska)	4,940	16,207
Mt Wood	Canada	4,848	15,905
Nevado de Toluca	Mexico	4,670	15,321
Mt Fairweather	USA (Alaska)	4,663	15,298
Mt Hunter	USA (Alaska)	4,442	14,573
Mt Whitney	USA	4,418	14,495
Mt Elbert	USA	4,399	14,432
Mt Harvard	USA	4,395	14,419
Mt Rainier	USA	4,392	14,409
Blanca Peak	USA	4,372	14,344
Longs Peak	USA	4,345	14,255
Tajumulco	Guatemala	4,220	13,845
Grand Teton	USA	4,197	13,770
Mt Waddington	Canada	3,994	13,104
Mt Robson	Canada	3,954	12,972
Chirripó Grande	Costa Rica	3,837	12,589
Mt Assiniboine	Canada	3,619	11,873
Pico Duarte	Dominican Rep.	3,175	10,417

South America		m	ft
Aconcagua	Argentina	6,960	22,834
Bonete	Argentina	6,872	22,546
Ojos del Salado	Argentina/Chile	6,863	22,516
Pissis	Argentina	6,779	22,241
Mercedario	Argentina/Chile	6,770	22,211
Huascaran	Peru	6,768	22,204
Llullaillaco	Argentina/Chile	6,723	22,057
Nudo de Cachi	Argentina	6,720	22,047
Yerupaja	Peru	6,632	21,758
N. de Tres Cruces	Argentina/Chile	6,620	21,719
Incahuasi	Argentina/Chile	6,601	21,654
Cerro Galan	Argentina	6,600	21,654
Tupungato	Argentina/Chile	6,570	21,555

South America (cont.)		m	ft
Sajama	Bolivia	6,542	21,463
Illimani	Bolivia	6,485	21,276
Coropuna	Peru	6,425	21,079
Ausangate	Peru	6,384	20,945
Cerro del Toro	Argentina	6,380	20,932
Siula Grande	Peru	6,356	20,853
Chimborazo	Ecuador	6,267	20,561
Cotapaxi	Ecuador	5,896	19,344
Pico Colon	Colombia	5,800	19,029
Pico Bolivar	Venezuela	5,007	16,427

Antarctica		m	ft
Vinson Massif		4,897	16,066
Mt Kirkpatrick		4,528	14,855
Mt Markham		4,349	14,268

Ocean Depths

Atlantic Ocean	m	ft
Puerto Rico (Milwaukee) Deep	9,220	30,249
Cayman Trench	7,680	25,197
Gulf of Mexico	5,203	17,070
Mediterranean Sea	5,121	16,801
Black Sea	2,211	7,254
North Sea	660	2,165
Baltic Sea	463	1,519

Indian Ocean	m	ft
Java Trench	7,450	24,442
Red Sea	2,635	8,454
Persian Gulf	73	239

Pacific Ocean	m	ft
Mariana Trench	11,022	36,161
Tonga Trench	10,882	35,702
Japan Trench	10,554	34,626
Kuril Trench	10,542	34,587
Mindanao Trench	10,497	34,439
Kermadec Trench	10,047	32,962
New Guinea Trench	9,140	29,987
Peru–Chile Trench	8,050	26,410

Arctic Ocean	m	ft
Molloy Deep	5,608	18,399

Land Lows

		m	ft
Dead Sea	Asia	−411	−1,348
Lake Assal	Africa	−156	−512
Death Valley	North America	−86	−282
Valdés Peninsula	South America	−40	−131
Caspian Sea	Europe	−28	−92
Lake Eyre North	Oceania	−16	−52

Rivers

Europe		km	miles
Volga	Caspian Sea	3,700	2,300
Danube	Black Sea	2,850	1,770
Ural	Caspian Sea	2,535	1,575
Dnepr (Dnipro)	Black Sea	2,285	1,420
Kama	Volga	2,030	1,260
Don	Black Sea	1,990	1,240
Petchora	Arctic Ocean	1,790	1,110
Oka	Volga	1,480	920
Belaya	Kama	1,420	880

Europe (cont.)		km	miles
Dnister (Dniester)	Black Sea	1,400	870
Vyatka	Kama	1,370	850
Rhine	North Sea	1,320	820
North Dvina	Arctic Ocean	1,290	800
Desna	Dnepr (Dnipro)	1,190	740
Elbe	North Sea	1,145	710
Wisla	Baltic Sea	1,090	675
Loire	Atlantic Ocean	1,020	635
West Dvina	Baltic Sea	1,019	633

Asia		km	miles
Yangtze	Pacific Ocean	6,380	3,960
Yenisey–Angara	Arctic Ocean	5,550	3,445
Huang He	Pacific Ocean	5,464	3,395
Ob–Irtysh	Arctic Ocean	5,410	3,360
Mekong	Pacific Ocean	4,500	2,795
Amur	Pacific Ocean	4,400	2,730
Lena	Arctic Ocean	4,400	2,730
Irtysh	Ob	4,250	2,640
Yenisey	Arctic Ocean	4,090	2,540
Ob	Arctic Ocean	3,680	2,285
Indus	Indian Ocean	3,100	1,925
Brahmaputra	Indian Ocean	2,900	1,800
Syrdarya	Aral Sea	2,860	1,775
Salween	Indian Ocean	2,800	1,740
Euphrates	Indian Ocean	2,700	1,675
Vilyuy	Lena	2,650	1,645
Kolyma	Arctic Ocean	2,600	1,615
Amudarya	Aral Sea	2,540	1,575
Ural	Caspian Sea	2,535	1,575
Ganges	Indian Ocean	2,510	1,560
Si Kiang	Pacific Ocean	2,100	1,305
Irrawaddy	Indian Ocean	2,010	1,250
Tarim–Yarkand	Lop Nor	2,000	1,240
Tigris	Indian Ocean	1,900	1,180
Angara	Yenisey	1,830	1,135
Godavari	Indian Ocean	1,470	915
Sutlej	Indian Ocean	1,450	900
Yamuna	Indian Ocean	1,400	870

Africa		km	miles
Nile	Mediterranean	6,670	4,140
Congo	Atlantic Ocean	4,670	2,900
Niger	Atlantic Ocean	4,180	2,595
Zambezi	Indian Ocean	3,540	2,200
Oubangi/Uele	Congo (Dem. Rep.)	2,250	1,400
Kasai	Congo (Dem. Rep.)	1,950	1,210
Shaballe	Indian Ocean	1,930	1,200
Orange	Atlantic Ocean	1,860	1,155
Cubango	Okavango Swamps	1,800	1,120
Limpopo	Indian Ocean	1,600	995
Senegal	Atlantic Ocean	1,600	995
Volta	Atlantic Ocean	1,500	930
Benue	Niger	1,350	840

Australia		km	miles
Murray–Darling	Indian Ocean	3,750	2,330
Darling	Murray	3,070	1,905
Murray	Indian Ocean	2,575	1,600
Murrumbidgee	Murray	1,690	1,050

North America		km	miles
Mississippi–Missouri	Gulf of Mexico	6,020	3,740
Mackenzie	Arctic Ocean	4,240	2,630
Mississippi	Gulf of Mexico	3,780	2,350
Missouri	Mississippi	3,780	2,350
Yukon	Pacific Ocean	3,185	1,980
Rio Grande	Gulf of Mexico	3,030	1,880
Arkansas	Mississippi	2,340	1,450
Colorado	Pacific Ocean	2,330	1,445
Red	Mississippi	2,040	1,270

North America (cont.)		km	miles
Saskatchewan	Lake Winnipeg	1,940	1,205
Snake	Columbia	1,670	1,040
Churchill	Hudson Bay	1,600	990
Ohio	Mississippi	1,580	980
Brazos	Gulf of Mexico	1,400	870
St Lawrence	Atlantic Ocean	1,170	730

South America		km	miles
Amazon	Atlantic Ocean	6,450	4,010
Paraná–Plate	Atlantic Ocean	4,500	2,800
Purus	Amazon	3,350	2,080
Madeira	Amazon	3,200	1,990
São Francisco	Atlantic Ocean	2,900	1,800
Paraná	Plate	2,800	1,740
Tocantins	Atlantic Ocean	2,750	1,710
Paraguay	Paraná	2,550	1,580
Orinoco	Atlantic Ocean	2,500	1,550
Pilcomayo	Paraná	2,500	1,550
Araguaia	Tocantins	2,250	1,400
Juruá	Amazon	2,000	1,240
Xingu	Amazon	1,980	1,230
Ucayali	Amazon	1,900	1,180
Marañón	Amazon	1,600	990
Uruguay	Plate	1,600	990
Magdalena	Caribbean Sea	1,540	960

Lakes

Europe		km²	miles²
Lake Ladoga	Russia	17,700	6,800
Lake Onega	Russia	9,700	3,700
Saimaa system	Finland	8,000	3,100
Vänern	Sweden	5,500	2,100
Rybinskoye Reservoir	Russia	4,700	1,800

Asia		km²	miles²
Caspian Sea	Asia	371,800	143,550
Lake Baykal	Russia	30,500	11,780
Aral Sea	Kazak./Uzbek.	28,687	11,086
Tonlé Sap	Cambodia	20,000	7,700
Lake Balqash	Kazakstan	18,500	7,100
Lake Dongting	China	12,000	4,600
Lake Ysyk	Kyrgyzstan	6,200	2,400
Lake Orumiyeh	Iran	5,900	2,300
Lake Koko	China	5,700	2,200
Lake Poyang	China	5,000	1,900
Lake Khanka	China/Russia	4,400	1,700
Lake Van	Turkey	3,500	1,400
Lake Ubsa	China	3,400	1,300

Africa		km²	miles²
Lake Victoria	East Africa	68,000	26,000
Lake Tanganyika	Central Africa	33,000	13,000
Lake Malawi/Nyasa	East Africa	29,600	11,430
Lake Chad	Central Africa	25,000	9,700
Lake Turkana	Ethiopia/Kenya	8,500	3,300
Lake Volta	Ghana	8,500	3,300
Lake Bangweulu	Zambia	8,000	3,100
Lake Rukwa	Tanzania	7,000	2,700
Lake Mai-Ndombe	Congo (D. Rep.)	6,500	2,500
Lake Kariba	Zambia/Zimbabwe	5,300	2,000
Lake Mobutu	Uganda/Congo (D. Rep.)	5,300	2,000
Lake Nasser	Egypt/Sudan	5,200	2,000
Lake Mweru	Zambia/Congo (D. Rep.)	4,900	1,900
Lake Cabora Bassa	Mozambique	4,500	1,700
Lake Kyoga	Uganda	4,400	1,700
Lake Tana	Ethiopia	3,630	1,400
Lake Kivu	Rwanda/Congo (D. Rep.)	2,650	1,000
Lake Edward	Uganda/Congo (D. Rep.)	2,200	850

Australia		km²	miles²
Lake Eyre	Australia	8,900	3,400
Lake Torrens	Australia	5,800	2,200
Lake Gairdner	Australia	4,800	1,900

North America		km²	miles²
Lake Superior	Canada/USA	82,350	31,800
Lake Huron	Canada/USA	59,600	23,010
Lake Michigan	USA	58,000	22,400
Great Bear Lake	Canada	31,800	12,280
Great Slave Lake	Canada	28,500	11,000
Lake Erie	Canada/USA	25,700	9,900
Lake Winnipeg	Canada	24,400	9,400
Lake Ontario	Canada/USA	19,500	7,500
Lake Nicaragua	Nicaragua	8,200	3,200
Lake Athabasca	Canada	8,100	3,100
Smallwood Reservoir	Canada	6,530	2,520
Reindeer Lake	Canada	6,400	2,500
Nettilling Lake	Canada	5,500	2,100
Lake Winnipegosis	Canada	5,400	2,100
Lake Nipigon	Canada	4,850	1,900
Lake Manitoba	Canada	4,700	1,800

South America		km²	miles²
Lake Titicaca	Bolivia/Peru	8,300	3,200
Lake Poopo	Peru	2,800	1,100

Islands

Europe		km²	miles²
Great Britain	UK	229,880	88,700
Iceland	Atlantic Ocean	103,000	39,800
Ireland	Ireland/UK	84,400	32,600
Novaya Zemlya (North)	Russia	48,200	18,600
West Spitzbergen	Norway	39,000	15,100
Novaya Zemlya (South)	Russia	33,200	12,800
Sicily	Italy	25,500	9,800
Sardinia	Italy	24,000	9,300
North-east Spitzbergen	Norway	15,000	5,600
Corsica	France	8,700	3,400
Crete	Greece	8,350	3,200
Zealand	Denmark	6,850	2,600

Asia		km²	miles²
Borneo	South-east Asia	744,360	287,400
Sumatra	Indonesia	473,600	182,860
Honshu	Japan	230,500	88,980
Sulawesi (Celebes)	Indonesia	189,000	73,000
Java	Indonesia	126,700	48,900
Luzon	Philippines	104,700	40,400
Mindanao	Philippines	101,500	39,200
Hokkaido	Japan	78,400	30,300
Sakhalin	Russia	74,060	28,600
Sri Lanka	Indian Ocean	65,600	25,300
Taiwan	Pacific Ocean	36,000	13,900
Kyushu	Japan	35,700	13,800
Hainan	China	34,000	13,100
Timor	Indonesia	33,600	13,000
Shikoku	Japan	18,800	7,300
Halmahera	Indonesia	18,000	6,900
Ceram	Indonesia	17,150	6,600
Sumbawa	Indonesia	15,450	6,000
Flores	Indonesia	15,200	5,900
Samar	Philippines	13,100	5,100
Negros	Philippines	12,700	4,900
Bangka	Indonesia	12,000	4,600
Palawan	Philippines	12,000	4,600
Panay	Philippines	11,500	4,400
Sumba	Indonesia	11,100	4,300
Mindoro	Philippines	9,750	3,800

Asia (cont.)		km²	miles²
Buru	Indonesia	9,500	3,700
Bali	Indonesia	5,600	2,200
Cyprus	Mediterranean	3,570	1,400

Africa		km²	miles²
Madagascar	Indian Ocean	587,040	226,660
Socotra	Indian Ocean	3,600	1,400
Réunion	Indian Ocean	2,500	965
Tenerife	Atlantic Ocean	2,350	900
Mauritius	Indian Ocean	1,865	720

Oceania		km²	miles²
New Guinea	Indon./Papua NG	821,030	317,000
New Zealand (South)	New Zealand	150,500	58,100
New Zealand (North)	New Zealand	114,700	44,300
Tasmania	Australia	67,800	26,200
New Britain	Papua NG	37,800	14,600
New Caledonia	Pacific Ocean	19,100	7,400
Viti Levu	Fiji	10,500	4,100
Hawaii	Pacific Ocean	10,450	4,000
Bougainville	Papua NG	9,600	3,700
Guadalcanal	Solomon Is.	6,500	2,500
Vanua Levu	Fiji	5,550	2,100
New Ireland	Papua NG	3,200	1,200

North America		km²	miles²
Greenland	Atlantic Ocean	2,175,600	839,800
Baffin Is.	Canada	508,000	196,100
Victoria Is.	Canada	212,200	81,900
Ellesmere Is.	Canada	212,000	81,800
Cuba	Cuba	110,860	42,800
Newfoundland	Canada	110,680	42,700
Hispaniola	Atlantic Ocean	76,200	29,400
Banks Is.	Canada	67,000	25,900
Devon Is.	Canada	54,500	21,000
Melville Is.	Canada	42,400	16,400
Vancouver Is.	Canada	32,150	12,400
Somerset Is.	Canada	24,300	9,400
Jamaica	Caribbean Sea	11,400	4,400
Puerto Rico	Atlantic Ocean	8,900	3,400
Cape Breton Is.	Canada	4,000	1,500

South America		km²	miles²
Tierra del Fuego	Argentina/Chile	47,000	18,100
Falkland Is. (East)	Atlantic Ocean	6,800	2,600
South Georgia	Atlantic Ocean	4,200	1,600
Galapagos (Isabela)	Pacific Ocean	2,250	870

WORLD STATISTICS – CLIMATE

For each city, the top row of figures shows total rainfall in inches whilst the bottom row shows the average temperature in ° Fahrenheit. The total annual rainfall and average annual temperature are given at the end of the rows.

	Jan.	Feb.	Mar.	Apr.	May	June	July	Aug.	Sept.	Oct.	Nov.	Dec.	Total
Europe													
Berlin, Germany	1.8	1.6	1.3	1.7	1.9	2.6	2.9	2.7	1.9	1.9	1.8	1.7	23.7
Altitude 180 feet	30	32	39	48	57	63	66	64	59	48	41	34	48
London, UK	2.1	1.6	1.5	1.5	1.8	1.8	2.2	2.3	1.9	2.2	2.5	1.9	23.3
16 ft	39	41	45	48	54	61	64	63	59	52	46	41	52
Málaga, Spain	2.4	2.0	2.4	1.8	1.0	0.2	0	0.1	1.1	2.5	2.5	2.4	18.7
108 ft	54	55	61	63	66	84	77	79	73	68	61	55	66
Moscow, Russia	1.5	1.5	1.4	1.5	2.1	2.3	3.5	2.8	2.3	1.8	1.9	2.1	24.6
512 ft	9	14	25	43	55	61	64	63	54	43	30	19	39
Paris, France	2.2	1.8	1.4	1.7	2.2	2.1	2.3	2.5	2.2	2.0	2.0	2.0	24.4
246 ft	37	39	46	52	59	64	66	63	64	54	45	39	53
Rome, Italy	2.8	2.4	2.2	2.0	1.8	1.5	0.6	0.8	2.5	3.9	5.1	3.7	29.3
56 ft	46	48	52	57	64	72	77	77	72	63	55	50	61
Asia													
Bangkok, Thailand	0.3	0.8	1.4	2.3	7.8	6.3	6.3	6.9	12.0	8.1	2.6	0.2	55
7 ft	79	82	84	86	84	84	82	82	82	82	79	77	82
Bombay (Mumbai), India	0.1	0.1	0.1	<0.1	0.7	19.1	24.3	13.4	10.4	2.5	0.5	0.1	71.4
36 ft	75	75	79	82	86	84	81	81	81	82	81	79	80
Ho Chi Minh, Vietnam	0.6	0.1	0.5	1.7	8.7	13.0	12.4	10.6	13.2	10.6	4.5	2.2	78.1
30 ft	79	81	84	86	84	82	82	82	81	81	81	79	82
Hong Kong, China	1.3	1.8	2.9	5.4	11.5	15.5	15.0	14.2	10.1	4.5	1.7	1.2	85.2
108 ft	61	59	64	72	79	82	82	82	81	77	70	64	73
Tokyo, Japan	1.9	2.9	4.2	5.3	5.8	6.5	5.6	6.0	9.2	8.2	3.8	2.2	61.6
20 ft	37	39	45	55	63	70	77	79	73	63	52	43	58
Africa													
Cairo, Egypt	0.2	0.2	0.2	0.1	0.1	<0.1	0	0	<0.1	<0.1	0.1	0.2	1.1
1,380 ft	55	59	64	70	77	82	82	82	79	75	68	59	71
Cape Town, South Africa	0.6	0.3	0.7	1.9	3.1	3.3	3.5	2.6	1.7	1.2	0.7	0.4	20
56 ft	70	70	68	63	57	55	54	55	57	61	64	66	62
Lagos, Nigeria	1.1	1.8	4.0	5.9	10.6	18.1	11.0	2.5	5.5	8.1	2.7	1.0	72.4
10 ft	81	82	84	82	82	79	77	77	79	79	82	82	81
Nairobi, Kenya	1.5	2.5	4.9	8.3	6.2	1.8	0.6	0.9	1.2	2.1	4.3	3.3	37.8
5,970 ft	66	66	66	66	64	61	61	61	64	66	64	64	64
Australia, New Zealand & Antarctica													
Christchurch, New Zealand	2.2	1.7	1.9	1.9	2.6	2.6	2.7	1.9	1.8	1.7	1.9	2.2	25.1
33 ft	61	61	57	54	48	43	43	45	48	54	57	61	53
Darwin, Australia	15.2	12.3	10.0	3.8	0.6	0.1	<0.1	0.1	0.5	2	4.7	9.4	58.7
98 ft	84	84	84	84	82	79	77	79	82	84	86	84	83
Mawson, Antarctica	0.4	1.2	0.8	0.4	1.7	7.1	0.2	1.6	0.1	0.8	0	0	14.3
46 ft	32	23	14	7	5	3	0	0	−1	9	23	30	12
Sydney, Australia	3.5	4.0	5.0	5.3	5.0	4.6	4.6	3.0	2.9	2.8	2.9	2.9	46.5
138 ft	72	72	70	64	59	54	54	55	59	64	66	70	63
North America													
Anchorage, Alaska, USA	0.8	0.7	0.6	0.4	0.5	0.7	1.6	2.6	2.6	2.2	1.0	0.9	14.6
131 ft	12	18	23	36	45	54	57	55	48	36	23	12	35
Kingston, Jamaica	0.9	0.6	0.9	1.2	4.0	3.5	1.5	3.6	3.9	7.1	2.9	1.4	31.5
112 ft	77	77	77	79	79	82	82	82	81	81	79	79	80
Los Angeles, USA	3.1	3.0	2.8	1.0	0.4	0.1	<0.1	<0.1	0.2	0.6	1.2	2.6	15
312 ft	55	57	57	61	63	66	70	72	70	64	61	57	63
Mexico City, Mexico	0.5	0.2	0.4	0.8	2.1	4.7	6.7	6.0	5.1	2.0	0.7	0.3	29.5
7,574 ft	12	13	16	18	19	19	17	18	18	16	14	13	16
New York, N. Y., USA	3.7	3.8	3.6	3.2	3.2	3.3	4.2	4.3	3.4	3.5	3.0	3.6	42.8
315 ft	30	30	37	50	61	68	73	73	70	59	45	36	53
Vancouver, Canada	6.1	4.5	4.0	2.4	2.0	1.8	1.3	1.6	2.6	4.5	5.9	7.2	43.8
46 ft	37	41	43	48	54	59	63	63	57	50	43	39	50
South America													
Antofagasta, Chile	0	0	0	<0.1	<0.1	0.1	0.2	0.1	<0.1	0.1	<0.1	0	0.6
308 ft	70	70	68	64	61	59	57	57	59	61	64	66	63
Buenos Aires, Argentina	3.1	2.8	4.3	3.5	3.0	2.4	2.2	2.4	3.1	3.4	3.3	3.9	37.4
89 ft	73	73	70	63	55	48	50	52	55	59	66	72	61
Lima, Peru	0.1	<0.1	<0.1	<0.1	0.2	0.2	0.3	0.3	0.3	0.1	0.1	<0.1	1.7
394 ft	73	75	75	72	66	63	63	61	63	64	66	70	68
Rio de Janeiro, Brazil	4.9	4.8	5.1	4.2	3.1	2.1	1.6	1.7	2.6	3.1	4.1	5.4	42.8
200 ft	79	77	75	72	70	70	70	70	70	72	73	77	74

THE EARTH IN FOCUS

> Landsat image of the
San Francisco Bay area.
The narrow entrance to
the bay (crossed by the
Golden Gate Bridge)
provides an excellent
natural harbor. The
San Andreas Fault runs
parallel to the coastline.

THE UNIVERSE & SOLAR SYSTEM

RECENT ESTIMATES SUGGEST that around 12,5000 million years ago, the Universe was created in a huge explosion known as the "Big Bang." In the first 10^{-24} of a second the Universe expanded rapidly and the basic forces of nature, radiation and subatomic particles, came into being. The Universe has been expanding ever since. Traces of the original "fireball" of radiation can still be detected, and most scientists accept the Big Bang theory of the origin of the Universe.

> The Lagoon Nebula is a huge cloud of dust and gas. Hot stars inside the nebula make the gas glow red.

The Nearest Stars ▼

The 20 nearest stars, excluding the Sun, with their distance from Earth in light-years.*

Proxima Centauri	4.25
Alpha Centauri A	4.3
Alpha Centauri B	4.3
Barnard's Star	6.0
Wolf 359	7.8
Lalande 21185	8.3
Sirius A	8.7
Sirius B	8.7
UV Ceti A	8.7
UV Ceti B	8.7
Ross 154	9.4
Ross 248	10.3
Epsilon Eridani	10.7
Ross 128	10.9
61 Cygni A	11.1
61 Cygni B	11.1
Epsilon Indi	11.2
Groombridge 34 A	11.2
Groombridge 34 B	11.2
L789-6	11.2

A light year equals approximately 5,900 billion miles [9,500 billion km].

GALAXIES

Almost a million years passed before the Universe cooled sufficiently for atoms to form. When a billion years had passed, the atoms had begun to form proto-galaxies, which are masses of gas separated by empty space. Stars began to form within the protogalaxies, as particles were drawn together, producing the high temperatures necessary to bring about nuclear fusion. The formation of the first stars brought about the evolution of the protogalaxies into galaxies proper, each containing billions of stars.

Our Sun is a medium-sized star. It is

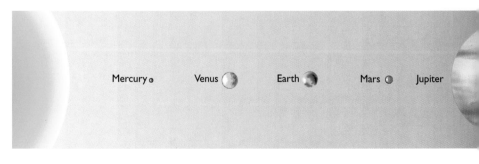

Mercury ·   Venus ◐   Earth ◑   Mars ○   Jupiter

PLANETARY DATA

	Mean distance from Sun (million miles)	Mass (Earth = 1)	Period of orbit (Earth years)	Period of rotation (Earth days)	Equatorial diameter (miles)	Escape velocity (miles/sec)	Number of known satellites
Sun	–	332,946	–	25.38	865,000	383.7	–
Mercury	36.2	0.06	0.241	58.67	3,031	2.65	0
Venus	66.9	0.8	0.615	243.0	7,521	6.44	0
Earth	93.0	1.0	1.00	0.99	7,926	6.95	1
Mars	141.2	0.1	1.88	1.02	4,217	3.13	2
Jupiter	483.4	317.8	11.86	0.41	88,730	37.0	16
Saturn	886.8	95.2	29.46	0.42	74,500	22.1	20
Uranus	1,784.8	14.5	84.01	0.45	31,763	13.2	15
Neptune	2,797.8	17.2	164.79	0.67	30,775	14.5	8
Pluto	3,662.5	0.002	248.54	6.38	1,430	0.68	1

one of the billions of stars that make up the Milky Way galaxy, which is one of the millions of galaxies in the Universe.

THE SOLAR SYSTEM

The Solar System lies toward the edge of the Milky Way galaxy. It consists of the Sun and other bodies, including planets (together with their moons), asteroids, meteoroids, comets, dust and gas, which revolve around it.

The Earth moves through space in three distinct ways. First, with the rest of the Solar System, it moves around the center of the Milky Way galaxy in an orbit that takes 200 million years.

As the Earth revolves around the Sun once every year, its axis is tilted by about 23.5 degrees. As a result, first the northern and then the southern hemisphere lean toward the Sun at different times of the year, causing the seasons experienced in the mid latitudes.

The Earth also rotates on its axis every 24 hours, causing day and night. The movements of the Earth in the Solar System determine the calendar. The length of a year – one complete orbit of the Earth around the Sun – is 365 days, 5 hours, 48 minutes and 46 seconds. Leap years prevent the calendar from becoming out of step with the solar year.

> The diagram below shows the planets around the Sun. The sizes of the planets are relative but the distances are not to scale. Closest to the Sun are dense rocky bodies, known as the terrestrial planets. They are Mercury, Venus, Earth, and Mars. Jupiter, Saturn, Uranus, and Neptune are huge balls of gas. Pluto is a small, icy body.

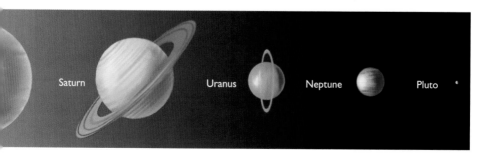

Saturn   Uranus   Neptune   Pluto

THE CHANGING EARTH

THE SOLAR SYSTEM was formed around 4.7 billion years ago, when the Sun, a glowing ball of gases, was created from a rotating disk of dust and gas. The planets were then formed from material left over after the creation of the Sun.

After the Earth formed, around 4.6 billion years ago, lighter elements rose to the hot surface, where they finally cooled to form a hard shell, or crust. Denser elements sank, forming the partly liquid mantle, the liquid outer core, and the solid inner core.

EARTH HISTORY

The oldest known rocks on Earth are around 4 billion years old. Natural processes have destroyed older rocks. Simple life forms first appeared on Earth around 3.5 billion years ago, though rocks formed in the first 4 billion years of Earth history contain little evidence of life. But

> Fold mountains, such as the Himalayan ranges which are shown above, were formed when two plates collided and the rock layers between them were squeezed upward into loops or folds.

rocks formed since the start of the Cambrian period (the first period in the Paleozoic era), about 590 million years ago, are rich in fossils. The study of fossils has enabled scientists to gradually piece together the long and complex story of life on Earth.

THE PLANET EARTH

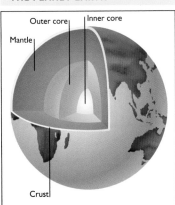

Outer core | Inner core
Mantle
Crust

CRUST The continental crust has an average thickness of 22–25 miles [35–40 km]; the oceanic crust averages 4 miles [6 km].

MANTLE 1,800 miles [2,900 km] thick. The top layer is solid, resting on a partly molten layer called the asthenosphere.

OUTER CORE 1,300 miles [2,100 km] thick. It consists mainly of molten iron and nickel.

INNER CORE (DIAMETER) 840 miles [1,350 km]. It is mainly solid iron and nickel.

ELEMENTS

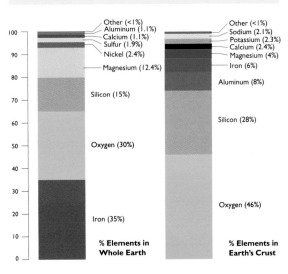

% Elements in Whole Earth

- Other (<1%)
- Aluminum (1.1%)
- Calcium (1.1%)
- Sulfur (1.9%)
- Nickel (2.4%)
- Magnesium (12.4%)
- Silicon (15%)
- Oxygen (30%)
- Iron (35%)

% Elements in Earth's Crust

- Other (<1%)
- Sodium (2.1%)
- Potassium (2.3%)
- Calcium (2.4%)
- Magnesium (4%)
- Iron (6%)
- Aluminum (8%)
- Silicon (28%)
- Oxygen (46%)

> The Earth contains about 100 elements, but eight of them account for 99% of the planet's mass. Iron makes up 35% of the Earth's mass, but most of it is in the core. The most common elements in the crust – oxygen and silicon – are often combined with one or more of the other common crustal elements, to form a group of minerals called silicates. The mineral quartz, which consists only of silicon and oxygen, occurs widely in such rocks as granites and sandstones.

PLATE BOUNDARIES

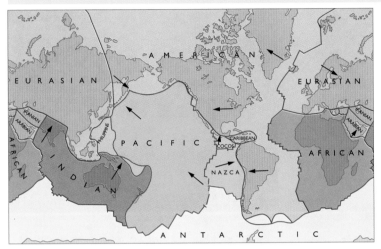

> The Earth's lithosphere is divided into six huge plates and several small ones. Ocean ridges, where plates are moving apart, are called constructive plate margins. Ocean trenches, where plates collide, are subduction zones. These are destructive plate margins. The map shows the main plates and the directions in which they are moving.

——— Plate boundaries

→ Direction of plate movements

PACIFIC Major plates

THE DYNAMIC EARTH

The Earth's surface is always changing because of a process called plate tectonics. Plates are blocks of the solid lithosphere (the crust and outer mantle), which are moved around by currents in the partly liquid mantle. Around 250 million years ago, the Earth contained one super-continent called Pangaea. Around 180 million years ago, Pangaea split into a northern part, Laurasia, and a southern part, Gondwanaland. Later, these huge continents, in turn, also split apart and the continents drifted to their present positions. Ancient seas disappeared and mountain ranges, such as the Himalayas and Alps, were pushed upward.

PLATE TECTONICS

In the early 1900s, two scientists suggested that the Americas were once joined to Europe and Africa. Together they proposed the theory of continental drift to explain the similarities between rock structures on both sides of the Atlantic. But no one could offer an explanation as to how the continents moved.

Evidence from the ocean floor in the 1950s and 1960s led to the theory of plate tectonics, which suggested that the lithosphere is divided into large blocks, or plates. The plates are solid, but they rest on the partly molten asthenosphere, within the mantle. Long ridges on

the ocean floor were found to be the edges of plates which were moving apart, carried by currents in the asthenosphere. As the plates moved, molten material welled up from the mantle to fill the gaps. But at the ocean trenches, one plate is descending beneath another along what is called a subduction zone. The descending plate is melted and destroyed. This crustal destruction at subduction zones balances the creation of new crust along the ridges. Transform faults, where two plates are moving alongside each other, form another kind of plate edge.

GEOLOGICAL TIME SCALE

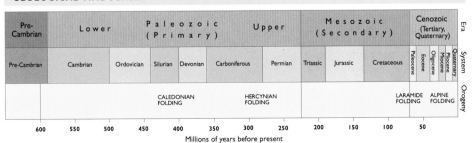

Pre-Cambrian	Lower	Paleozoic (Primary)			Upper		Mesozoic (Secondary)			Cenozoic (Tertiary, Quaternary)	Era
Pre-Cambrian	Cambrian	Ordovician	Silurian	Devonian	Carboniferous	Permian	Triassic	Jurassic	Cretaceous	Paleocene / Eocene / Oligocene / Pliocene / Pliocene / Quaternary	System
			CALEDONIAN FOLDING		HERCYNIAN FOLDING				LARAMIDE FOLDING	ALPINE FOLDING	Orogeny

600 550 500 450 400 350 300 250 200 150 100 50

Millions of years before present

5

EARTHQUAKES & VOLCANOES

PLATE TECTONICS HELP us to understand such phenomena as earthquakes, volcanic eruptions, and mountain building.

EARTHQUAKES

Earthquakes can occur anywhere, but they are most common near the edges of plates. They occur when intense pressure breaks the rocks along plate edges, making the plates lurch forward.

Year	Location	Mag.	Deaths
1906	San Francisco, USA	8.3	503
1906	Valparaiso, Chile	8.6	22,000
1908	Messina, Italy	7.5	83,000
1915	Avezzano, Italy	7.5	30,000
1920	Gansu, China	8.6	180,000
1923	Yokohama, Japan	8.3	143,000
1927	Nan Shan, China	8.3	200,000
1932	Gansu, China	7.6	70,000
1934	Bihar, India/Nepal	8.4	10,700
1935	Quetta, Pakistan	7.5	60,000
1939	Chillan, Chile	8.3	28,000
1939	Erzincan, Turkey	7.9	30,000
1960	Agadir, Morocco	5.8	12,000
1964	Anchorage, Alaska	8.4	131
1968	North-east Iran	7.4	12,000
1970	North Peru	7.7	66,794
1976	Guatemala	7.5	22,778
1976	Tangshan, China	8.2	255,000
1978	Tabas, Iran	7.7	25,000
1980	El Asnam, Algeria	7.3	20,000
1980	South Italy	7.2	4,800
1985	Mexico City, Mexico	8.1	4,200
1988	North-west Armenia	6.8	55,000
1990	North Iran	7.7	36,000
1993	Maharashtra, India	6.4	30,000
1994	Los Angeles, USA	6.6	51
1995	Kobe, Japan	7.2	5,000
1997	North-east Iran	7.1	2,400
1998	Takhar, Afghanistan	6.1	4,200
1998	Rostaq, Afghanistan	7.0	5,000
1999	Izmit, Turkey	7.4	15,000
2001	Gujrat, India	7.9	20,000

Major Earthquakes since 1900 ▼

> The earthquake that struck Kobe in January 1995 was the worst one experienced in Japan since 1923. Japan lies alongside subduction zones.

> The section between the Pacific and Indian oceans shows a subduction zone under the American plate, with spreading ocean ridges in the Atlantic and Indian oceans. East Africa may one day split away from the rest of Africa as plate movements pull the Rift Valley apart.

Earthquakes are common along the mid-ocean ridges, but they are a long way from land and cause little damage. Other earthquakes occur near land in subduction zones, such as those that encircle much of the Pacific Ocean. These earthquakes often trigger off powerful sea waves, called tsunamis. Other earthquakes occur along transform faults, such as the San Andreas fault in California, a boundary between the North American and Pacific plates. Movements along this fault cause periodic disasters, such as the earthquakes in San Francisco (1906) and Los Angeles (1994).

VOLCANOES & MOUNTAINS

Volcanoes are fueled by magma (molten rock) from the mantle. Some volcanoes, such as in Hawaii, lie above "hot spots" (sources of heat in the mantle). But most volcanoes occur either along the ocean ridges or above subduction zones, where

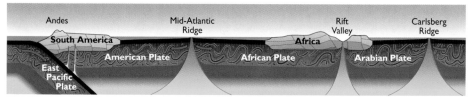

EARTHQUAKES

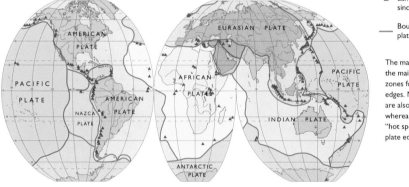

1976 ○	Selected major earthquakes & dates
▦	Mobile land areas
▦	Submarine zones of mobile land areas
▢	Stable land platforms
▢	Submarine extensions of land platforms
▢	Mid-oceanic volcanic ridges
▢	Oceanic platforms

VOLCANOES

▲	Land volcanoes active since 1700
——	Boundaries of tectonic plates

The maps show that the main earthquake zones follow plate edges. Most volcanoes are also in these zones, whereas some lie over "hot spots," far from plate edges.

magma is produced when the descending plate is melted.

Volcanic mountains are built up gradually by runny lava flows or by exploded volcanic ash. Fold mountains occur when two plates bearing land areas collide and the plate edges are buckled upward into fold mountain ranges. Plate movements also fracture rocks and block mountains are formed when areas of land are pushed upward along faults or between parallel faults. Blocks of land sometimes sink down between faults, creating deep, steep-sided rift valleys.

> Volcanoes occur when molten magma reaches the surface under pressure through long vents. "Quiet" volcanoes emit runny lava (called pahoehoe). Explosive eruptions occur when the magma is sticky. Explosive gases shatter the magma into ash, which is hurled upward into the air.

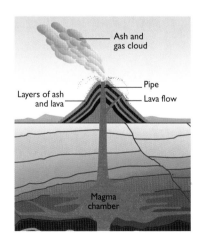

Ash and gas cloud

Pipe

Layers of ash and lava

Lava flow

Magma chamber

PROPERTY OF ALUMNI LIBRARY
WENTWORTH INSTITUTE OF TECHNOLOGY

WATER & ICE

A VISITOR FROM outer space might be forgiven for naming our planet "Water" rather than "Earth," because water covers more than 70% of its surface. Without water, our planet would be as lifeless as the Moon. Through the water cycle, fresh water is regularly supplied from the sea to the land. Most geographers divide the world's water into four main oceans: the Pacific, the Atlantic, the Indian and the Arctic. Together the oceans contain 97.2% of the world's water.

The water in the oceans is constantly on the move, even, albeit extremely slowly, in the deepest ocean trenches. The greatest movements of ocean water occur in the form of ocean currents. These are marked, mainly wind blown

> Ice breaks away from the ice sheet of Antarctica, forming flat-topped icebergs. Researchers fear that warmer weather is melting Antarctica's ice sheets at a dangerous rate, after large chunks of the Larsen ice shelf and the Ronne ice shelf broke away in 1997 and 1998, respectively.

EXPLANATION OF TERMS

GLACIER A body of ice that flows down valleys in mountain areas. It is usually narrow and hence smaller than ice caps or ice sheets.

ICE AGE A period of Earth history when ice sheets spread over large areas. The most recent Ice Age began about 1.8 million years ago and ended 10,000 years ago.

ICEBERG A floating body of ice in the sea. About eight-ninths of the ice is hidden beneath the surface of the water.

ICE SHEET A large body of ice. During the last Ice Age, ice sheets covered large parts of the northern hemisphere.

OCEAN The four main oceans are the Pacific, the Atlantic, the Indian and the Arctic. Some

people classify a fifth southern ocean, but others regard these waters as extensions of the Pacific, Atlantic, and Indian oceans.

OCEAN CURRENTS Distinct currents of water in the oceans. Winds are the main causes of surface currents.

SEA An expanse of water, but smaller than an ocean.

JANUARY TEMPERATURE AND OCEAN CURRENTS

(Northern Hemisphere – Winter)

ACTUAL SURFACE
TEMPERATURE

°F
86
68
50
32
14
-4
-22
-40

OCEAN CURRENTS
Cold Warm Speed (knots)
←-- ←-- Less than 0.5
←— ←— 0.5 – 1.0
←— ←— Over 1.0

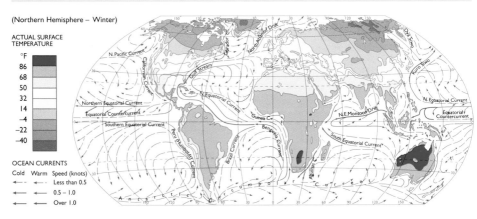

CROSS-SECTION OF ANTARCTICA

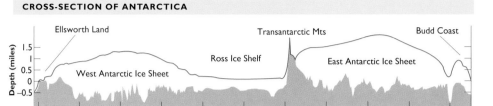

movements of water on or near the surface. Other dense, cold currents creep slowly across the ocean floor. Warm and cold ocean currents help to regulate the world's climate by transferring heat between the tropics and the poles.

ICE

About 2.15% of the world's water is locked in two large ice sheets, several smaller ice caps and glaciers. The world's largest ice sheet covers most of Antarctica. The ice is up to 15,750 ft [4,800 m] thick and it represents 70% of the world's fresh water. The volume of ice is about nine times greater than that contained in the world's other ice sheet in Green-land. Besides these ice sheets, smaller ice caps are found in northern Canada, Iceland, Norway, and Spitzbergen, and

in several valley glaciers in numerous mountain areas.

Reports in the early 21st century sugg-ested global warming had begun to melt polar and glacier ice. If all the world's ice melted, sea level could rise by 330 ft [100 m], flooding islands and coastal areas and displacing tens of millions of people.

> This section across Antarctica shows the concealed land areas in brown, with the top of the ice in blue. The section is divided into the West and East Antarctic Ice Sheets. The vertical scale has been exaggerated.

Composition of Seawater ▾

The principal components of seawater, by percentage, excluding the elements of water itself:

Chloride (Cl)	55.04%	Potassium (K)	1.10%
Sodium (Na)	30.61%	Bicarbonate (HCO₃)	0.41%
Sulfate (SO₄)	7.69%	Bromide (Br)	0.19%
Magnesium (Mg)	3.69%	Strontium (Sr)	0.04%
Calcium (Ca)	1.16%	Fluorine (F)	0.003%

The oceans contain virtually every other element, the more important ones being lithium, rubidium, phosphorus, iodine and barium.

JULY TEMPERATURE AND OCEAN CURRENTS

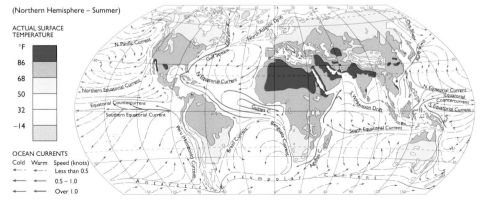

(Northern Hemisphere – Summer)

ACTUAL SURFACE
TEMPERATURE

°F
86
68
50
32
−14

OCEAN CURRENTS
Cold Warm Speed (knots)
←--   ←--   Less than 0.5
←—   ←—   0.5 – 1.0
←—   ←—   Over 1.0

WEATHER & CLIMATE

WEATHER IS A description of the day-to-day state of the atmosphere. Climate, on the other hand, is weather in the long term: the seasonal pattern of temperature and precipitation averaged over time.

In some areas, the weather is so stable and predictable that a description of the weather is much the same as a statement of the climate. But in parts of the mid latitudes, the weather changes from hour to hour. Changeable weather is caused mainly by low air pressure systems, called cyclones or depressions, which form along the polar front where warm subtropical air meets cold polar air.

The main elements of weather and

LIGHTNING

Lightning is a flash of light in the sky caused by a discharge of electricity in the atmosphere. Lightning occurs within cumulonimbus clouds during thunderstorms. Positive charges build up at the top of the cloud, while negative charges build up at the base. The charges are finally discharged as an electrical spark. Sheet lightning occurs inside clouds, while cloud to ground lightning is usually forked. Thunder occurs when molecules along the lightning channel expand and collide with cool molecules.

climate are temperature and rainfall. Temperatures vary because the Sun heats the Earth unequally, with the most intense heating around the Equator. Unequal heating is responsible for the general circulation of the atmosphere and the main wind belts.

Rainfall occurs when warm air containing invisible water vapor rises. As the rising air cools, the capacity of the air to hold water vapor decreases and so the water vapor condenses into droplets of water or ice crystals, which collect together to form raindrops or snowflakes.

> Lightning occurs in clouds and also between the base of clouds and the ground. Lightning that strikes the ground can kill people or start forest fires.

> The rainfall map shows areas affected by tropical storms, which are variously called hurricanes, tropical cyclones, willy willies, and typhoons. Strong polar winds bring blizzards in winter.

ANNUAL RAINFALL

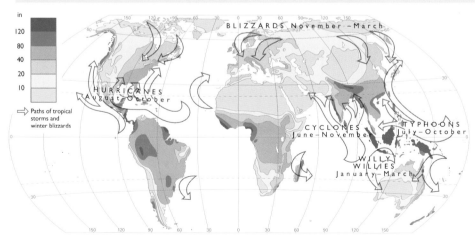

in
120
80
40
20
10

⇨ Paths of tropical storms and winter blizzards

BLIZZARDS November–March
HURRICANES August–October
CYCLONES June–November
TYPHOONS July–October
WILLY WILLIES January–March

10

GLOBAL WARMING

The Earth's climates have changed many times during its history. Around 11,000 years ago, much of the northern hemisphere was buried by ice. Some scientists believe that the last Ice Age may not be over and that ice sheets may one day return. Other scientists are concerned that air

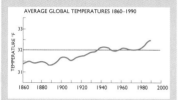

AVERAGE GLOBAL TEMPERATURES 1860–1990

pollution may be producing an opposite effect – a warming of the atmosphere. Since 1900, average world temperatures have risen by about 0.9°F [0.5°C] and increases are likely to continue. Global warming is the result of an increase in the amount of carbon dioxide in the atmosphere, caused by the burning of coal, oil, and natural gas, together with deforestation. Short-wave radiation from the Sun passes easily through the atmosphere. But, as the carbon dioxide content rises, more of the long-wave radiation that returns from the Earth's surface is absorbed and trapped by the carbon dioxide. This creates a "greenhouse effect," which will change the world's climates with, perhaps, disastrous environmental consequences.

CLIMATE

The world contains six main climatic types: hot and wet tropical climates; dry climates; warm temperate climates; cold temperate climates; polar climates; and mountain climates. These regions are further divided according to the character and amount of precipitation and special features of the temperature, notably seasonal variations. Regions with temperate climates include Mediterranean areas with hot, dry summers and mild, moist winters. Because of its large size, the United States experiences a range of climates, from temperate on the east and west coasts, to dry in the interior.

CLIMATIC REGIONS

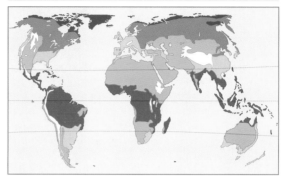

▨ Tropical Climate (hot & wet)

▨ Dry Climate (desert & steppe)

☐ Temperate Climate (warm & wet)

▨ Continental Climate (cold & wet)

■ Polar Climate (very cold & wet)

☐ Mountainous Areas (where altitude affects climate types)

WORLD CLIMATIC RECORDS

Highest Recorded Temperature
Al Aziziyah, Libya: 136.4°F [58°C] on 13 September 1922

Highest Mean Annual Temperature
Dallol, Ethiopia: 94°F [34.4°C] from 1960–66

Lowest Mean Annual Temperature
Polus, Nedostupnosti, Pole of Cold, Antarctica: −72°F [−57.8°C]

Lowest Recorded Temperature (outside poles)
Verkhoyansk, Siberia, Russia: −90°F [−68°C] on 6 February 1933

Windiest Place
Commonwealth Bay, Antarctica: gales often exceed 200 mph [320 km/h]

Longest Heatwave
Marble Bar, Western Australia: 162 days over 94°F [38°C], 23 October 1923 to 7 April 1924

Driest Place
Calama, northern Chile: no recorded rainfall in 400 years to 1971

Wettest Place (average)
Tututendo, Colombia: mean annual rainfall 463 in [11,770 mm]

Wettest Place (24 hours)
Cilaos, Réunion, Indian Ocean: 73.6 in [1,870 mm] from 15–16 March 1952

Wettest Place (12 months)
Cherrapunji, Meghalaya, northeast India: 1,040 in [26,470 mm], August 1860 to 1861. Cherrapunji also holds the record for rainfall in one month: 115 in [2,930 mm] in July 1861

Heaviest Hailstones
Gopalganj, central Bangladesh: up to 2.25 lbs [1.02 kg] in April 1986, which killed 92 people

Heaviest Snowfall (continuous)
Bessans, Savoie, France: 68 in [1,730 mm] in 19 hours over the period 5–6 April 1969

Heaviest Snowfall (season/year)
Paradise Ranger Station, Mt Rainier, Washington, USA: 1,224 in [31,102 mm] fell from 19 February 1971 to 18 February 1972

11

LANDFORMS & VEGETATION

THE CLIMATE LARGELY determines the nature of soils and vegetation types throughout the world. The studies of climate and plant and animal communities are closely linked. For example, tropical climates are divided into tropical forest and tropical grassland climates. The tropical forest climate, which is hot and rainy throughout the year, is ideal for the growth of forests that contain more than half of the world's known plant and animal species. But tropical grassland, or savanna, climates have a marked dry season. As a result, the forest gives way to grassland, with scattered trees.

CLIMATE & SCENERY

The climate also helps to shape the land. Frost action in cold areas splits boulders apart, while rapid temperature changes in hot deserts make rock surfaces peel away like the layers of an onion. These are examples of mechanical weathering.

Chemical weathering usually results from the action of water on rocks. For example, rainwater containing dissolved carbon dioxide is a weak acid, which reacts with limestone. This chemical process is responsible for the erosion of the world's most spectacular caves.

Running water and glaciers play a major part in creating scenery, while in

> The tropical broadleaf forests are rich in plant and animal species. The extinction of many species because of deforestation is one of the great natural disasters of our time.

NATURAL VEGETATION

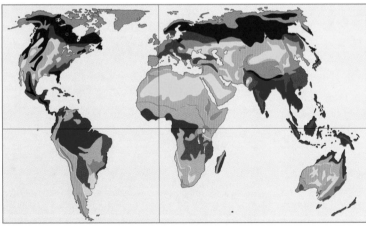

> Human activities, especially agriculture, have greatly modified plant and animal communities throughout the world. As a result, world vegetation maps show the natural "climax vegetation" of regions – that is, the kind of vegetation that would grow in a particular climatic area, had that area not been affected by human activities. For example, the climax vegetation of western Europe is broadleaf, deciduous forest, but most of the original forest, together with the animals which lived in it, was destroyed long ago.

- ▨ Tundra & mountain vegetation
- ▧ Needleleaf evergreen forest
- ▧ Broadleaf deciduous forest
- ▨ Mixed needleleaf evergreen & broadleaf deciduous trees
- ▨ Mid-latitude grassland
- ▨ Semidesert scrub land
- ▨ Evergreen broadleaf & deciduous trees & scrub
- ▨ Desert
- ▨ Tropical grassland (savanna)
- ▨ Tropical broadleaf & monsoon rain forest
- ▨ Subtropical broadleaf & needleleaf forest

DESERTIFICATION AND DEFORESTATION

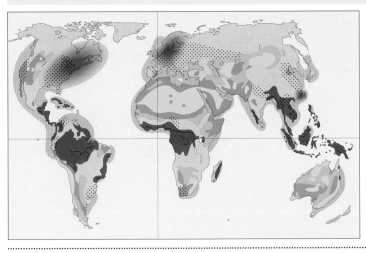

Pollution

- ☐ Polluted seas
- ▧ Main areas of sulfur & nitrogen emissions
- ▦ Areas of acid rain

Desertification

- ☐ Existing deserts
- ▨ Areas with a high risk of desertification
- ▩ Areas with a moderate risk of desertification

Deforestation

- ▪ Former areas of rain forest
- ■ Existing rain forest

dry areas, wind-blown sand is a powerful agent of erosion. Most landforms seem to alter little in one person's lifetime. But geologists estimate that natural forces remove an average of 1.4 in [3.5 cm] from land areas every 1,000 years. Over millions of years, these forces reduce mountains to flat plains.

HUMAN INTERFERENCE

Climate also affects people, though air conditioning and central heating now make it possible for us live in comfort almost anywhere in the world.

However, human activities are damaging our planet. Pollution is poisoning rivers and seas, while acid rain, caused by air pollution, is killing trees and acidifying lakes. The land is also harmed by such things as nuclear accidents and the dumping of toxic wastes.

Some regions have been overgrazed or so intensively farmed that once fertile areas have been turned into barren deserts. The clearance of tropical forests means that some plant and animal species are disappearing before scientists have had a chance to study them.

MOULDING THE LAND

Powerful forces inside the Earth buckle rock layers to form fold mountain ranges. But even as they rise, the forces of erosion wear them away. On mountain slopes, water freezes in cracks in rocks. Because ice occupies more space than the equivalent amount of water, this "frost action" shatters rocks, and the fragments tumble downhill. Some end up on or inside moving glaciers. Other rocks are carried away by running water. The glaciers and streams not only transport rock fragments, but they also wear out valleys and so add to their load. The eroded material breaks down into fragments of sand, silt and mud, much of which reaches the sea, where it piles up on the sea floor in layers. These layers eventually become compacted into sedimentary rocks, such as sandstones and shales. These rocks may eventually be squeezed up again by a plate collision to form new fold mountains, so completing a natural cycle of mountain building and destruction.

MAJOR FACTORS AFFECTING WEATHERING

	WEATHERING RATE		
	SLOW		**FAST**
Mineral solubility	low (e.g. quartz)	moderate (e.g. feldspar)	high (e.g. calcite)
Rainfall	low	moderate	heavy
Temperature	cold	temperate	hot
Vegetation	sparse	moderate	lush
Soil cover	bare rock	thin to moderate soil	thick soil

Weathering is the breakdown and decay of rocks in situ. It may be mechanical (physical), chemical or biological.

POPULATION

THE ADVENT OF agriculture around 10,000 years ago had a great impact on human society. People abandoned their nomadic way of life and settled in farming villages. With plenty of food, some people were able to pursue jobs unconnected with farming. These developments eventually led to rapid social changes, including the growth of early cities and the emergence of civilization.

THE POPULATION EXPLOSION

The social changes had a major effect on the world's population, which rose from around 8 million in 8000 BC, to about 300 million by AD 1000. The rate of population increase then began to accelerate further, passing the 1 billion mark in the 19th century, the 2 billion mark in the 1920s, and the 4 billion mark in the 1970s.

Today the world has a population of more than 6 billion and experts forecast that it will reach around 11 billion by 2200. However, they then predict that it will stabilize at this level or even begin to decline. Most of the expected increase will occur in developing countries in Africa, Asia, and Latin America.

> Many cities in India, such as Mumbai (formerly called Bombay), have grown so quickly that they lack sufficient jobs and homes for their populations. As a result, slums now cover large areas.

POPULATION PYRAMIDS

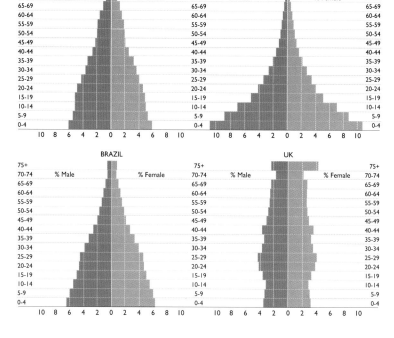

> The population pyramids compare the average age structures for the world with those of three countries at varying stages of development. Kenya, a developing country, had, until recently, one of the world's highest annual rates of population increase. As a result, a high proportion of Kenyans are aged under 15. Brazil has a much more balanced economy than Kenya's, and a lower rate of population increase. This is reflected in a higher proportion of people aged over 40. The UK is a developed country with a low rate of population growth, 0.3% per year between 1985–95, much lower than the world average of 1.6%. The UK has a far higher proportion of people over 60 years old.

The World's Largest Cities ▾

Early in the 21st century, for the first time ever, the majority of the world's population live in cities. Below is a list of the 20 largest cities (in thousands) based on latest available figures.

1	Tokyo, *Japan*	26,836
2	São Paulo, *Brazil*	16,417
3	New York, *USA*	16,329
4	Shanghai, *China*	15,082
5	Mexico City, *Mexico*	15,048
6	Bombay (Mumbai), *India*	12,572
7	Los Angeles, *USA*	12,410
8	Beijing, *China*	12,362
9	Seoul, *South Korea*	11,641
10	Jakarta, *Indonesia*	11,500
11	Buenos Aires, *Argentina*	11,256
12	Calcutta, *India*	10,916
13	Tianjin, *China*	10,687
14	Osaka, *Japan*	10,601
15	Lagos, *Nigeria*	10,287
16	Cairo, *Egypt*	9,900
17	Rio de Janeiro, *Brazil*	9,888
18	Karachi, *Pakistan*	9,863
19	Paris, *France*	9,319
20	Manila, *Philippines*	9,280

This population explosion has been caused partly by better medical care, which has reduced child mortality and increased the average life expectancy at birth throughout the world. But it has also created problems. In some developing countries, nearly half of the people are children. They make no contribution to the economy, but they require costly education and health services. In richer countries, the high proportion of retired people is also a strain on the economy.

In the 21st century, for the first time in 10,000 years, the majority of people are no longer forced to rely on farming for their livelihood. Instead, nearly half of them live in cities where many of them enjoy a high standard of living. But rapid urbanization also creates problems, especially in the developing world, with the growth of slums and an increase in homelessness and crime.

POPULATION BY CONTINENT

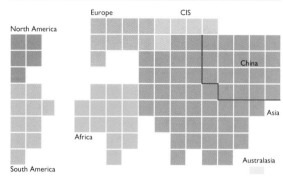

> The cartogram shows the populations of the continents in a diagrammatic way, with each square representing 1% of the world's population. For example, North America is represented by five squares, which means that it contains about 5% of the world's population, while Asia, the most populous continent even excluding the Asian part of the former USSR, is represented by 56 squares (China accounting for 19 of these). By contrast, Australasia is represented by less than half of a square because it contains only 0.45% of the world's population.

WORLD DEMOGRAPHIC EXTREMES

Fastest growing population; average annual % growth (1992–2000)		Slowest growing population; average annual % growth (1992–2000)	
1	Nigeria ... 5.09	1	Kuwait ... -1.39
2	Afghanistan ... 4.21	2	Ireland ... -0.24
3	Ivory Coast ... 3.54	3	St Kitts & Nevis ... -0.22
4	Oman ... 3.52	4	Bulgaria ... -0.13
5	Syria ... 3.51	5	Latvia ... -0.10

Youngest populations; % aged under 15 years (1996)		Oldest populations; % aged over 65 years (1996)	
1	West Bank/Gaza ... 51.7	1	Sweden ... 17.3
2	Uganda ... 48.6	2	Italy ... 16.1
3	Benin ... 48.4	3	Greece ... 15.9
=	Niger ... 48.4	=	Norway ... 15.9
5	Zambia ... 48.2	5	Belgium ... 15.8

Highest urban populations; % of population in urban areas (1996)		Lowest urban populations; % of population in urban areas (1996)	
1	Singapore ... 100.0	1	Bhutan ... 6.0
=	Bermuda ... 100.0	=	Rwanda ... 6.0
3	Macau ... 99.0	3	Burundi ... 8.0
4	Kuwait ... 97.0	4	Ethiopia ... 13.0
5	Hong Kong ... 95.0	=	Uganda ... 13.0

Most male populations; number of men per 100 women (1997)		Fewest male populations; number of men per 100 women (1997)	
1	Qatar ... 193.3	1	Latvia ... 84.3
2	United Arab Emirates ... 176.4	2	Ukraine ... 86.8
3	Bahrain ... 133.7	3	Russia ... 88.0
4	Saudi Arabia ... 125.1	5	Estonia ... 88.7
5	Oman ... 113.4	4	Belarus ... 88.8

Languages & Religions

All people belong to one species, *Homo sapiens*, but within that species is a great diversity of cultures. Two of the main factors that give people an identity and sense of kinship with their neighbors are language and religion.

Definitions of languages vary and as a result estimates of the total number of languages in existence range from about 3,000 to 6,000. Many languages are spoken only by a small number of people. Papua New Guinea, for example, has only 4.2 million people but 869 languages.

The world's languages are grouped into families, of which the Indo-European is the largest. Indo-European languages are spoken in a zone stretching from

> Religion is a major force in Southeast Asia. About 94% of the people in Thailand are Buddhists, and more than 40% of men over the age of 20 spend some time, if only a few weeks, serving as Buddhist monks. Confucianism, Islam, Hinduism, and Christianity are also practiced in Thailand.

THE WORLD'S LANGUAGES

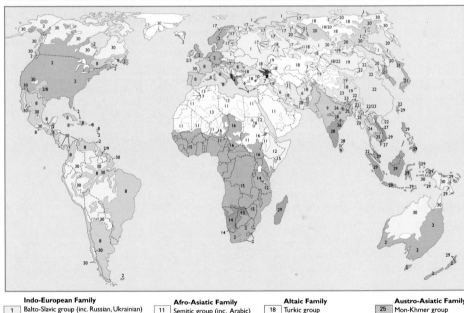

Indo-European Family

1	Balto-Slavic group (inc. Russian, Ukrainian)
2	Germanic group (inc. English, German)
3	Celtic group
4	Greek
5	Albanian
6	Iranian group
7	Armenian
8	Romance group (inc. Spanish, Portuguese, French, Italian)
9	Indo-Aryan group (inc. Hindi, Bengali, Urdu, Punjabi, Marathi)
10	**Caucasian Family**

Afro-Asiatic Family

11	Semitic group (inc. Arabic)
12	Kushitic group
13	Berber group

14	**Khoisan Family**
15	**Niger-Congo Family**
16	**Nilo-Saharan Family**
17	**Uralic Family**

Altaic Family

18	Turkic group
19	Mongolian group
20	Tungus-Manchu group
21	Japanese & Korean

Sino-Tibetan Family

22	Sinitic (Chinese) languages
23	Tibetic-Burmic languages

| 24 | **Tai Family** |

Austro-Asiatic Family

25	Mon-Khmer group
26	Munda group
27	Vietnamese

| 28 | **Dravidian Family** (inc. Telugu, Tamil) |

| 29 | **Austronesian Family** (inc. Malay-Indonesian) |

| 30 | **Other Languages** |

NATIVE SPEAKERS

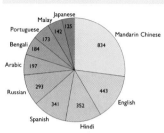

> The chart shows the native speakers of major languages in millions. Mandarin Chinese is the language of 834 million, as compared with English, which has 443 million speakers. However, many other people speak English as a second language.

Religious Adherents ▾	
The world's major religions, with the number of adherents in millions (latest available year)	
Christian	1,669
Roman Catholic	952
Protestant	337
Orthodox	162
Anglican	70
Other Christian	148
Muslim	945
Sunni	841
Shia	104
Hindu	663
Buddhist	312
Chinese folk	172
Ethnic/local	92
Jewish	18
Sikh	17

> Most languages have alphabetic systems of writing. The Greek alphabet uses some letters from the Roman alphabet, such as the A and B. Russians use the Cyrillic alphabet, which is based partly on Roman and partly on Greek letters. The Cyrillic alphabet is also used for Bulgarian and some central Asian languages. Serbs use either the Cyrillic or the Roman alphabet to write Serbo-Croat.

Europe, through southwestern Asia into the Indian subcontinent. In addition, during the period of European colonization, they spread throughout North and South America and also to Australia and New Zealand. Today about two-fifths of the world's people speak an Indo-European language, as compared with one-fifth who speak a language belonging to the Sino-Tibetan language.

The Sino-Tibetan language family includes Chinese, which is spoken as a first language by more people than any other. English is the second most important first language, but it is more important than Chinese in international affairs and business, because so many people speak it as a second language.

RELIGIONS

Christianity is the religion of about a third of the world's population. Other major religions include Buddhism, Islam, Hinduism, Judaism, Chinese folk religions and traditional tribal religions.

Religion is a powerful force in human society, establishing the ethics by which people live. It has inspired great music, painting, architecture and literature, yet at the same time religion and language have contributed to conflict between people throughout history. Even today, the cause of many of the conflicts around the world are partly the result of linguistic and religious differences.

ALPHABETS

The Greek Alphabet

Α	Β	Γ	Δ	Ε	Ζ	Η	Θ	Ι	Κ	Λ	Μ	Ν	Ξ	Ο	Π	Ρ	Σ	Τ	Υ	Φ	Χ	Ψ	Ω
A	V/B	G	D	E	Z	E	TH	I	K	L	M	N	X	O	P	R	S	T	Y	F	CH	PS	O

The Cyrillic Alphabet

А	Б	В	Г	Д	Е	Ё	Ж	З	И	Й	К	Л	М	Н	О	П	Р	С	Т	У	Ф	Х	Ц	Ч	Ш	Щ	Ю	Я
A	B	V	G	D	E	YO	ZH	Z	I	Y	K	L	M	N	O	P	R	S	T	U	F	KH	TS	CH	SH	SHCH	YU	YA

17

AGRICULTURE & INDUSTRY

BECAUSE IT SUPPLIES so many basic human needs, agriculture is the world's leading economic activity. But its relative importance varies from place to place. In most developing countries, agriculture employs more people than any other activity. For example, the diagram at the bottom of this page shows that more than 90% of the people of Nepal are employed in farming.

Many farmers in developing countries live at subsistence level, producing barely enough to supply the basic needs of their families. Alongside the subsistence sector, some developing countries produce one or two cash crops that they export. Dependence on cash crops is precarious: when world commodity prices fall, the country is plunged into financial crisis.

In developed countries, by contrast, the proportion of people engaged in agriculture has declined over the last 200

> The cultivation of rice, one of the world's most important foods, is still carried out by hand in many areas. But the introduction of new strains of rice has greatly increased yields.

years. Yet, by using farm machinery and scientific methods, notably the selective breeding of crops and animals, the production of food has soared. For example, although agriculture employs only 3% of its workers, the United States is one of the world's top food producers.

INDUSTRIALIZATION

The Industrial Revolution began in Britain in the late 18th century and soon spread to mainland Europe and other parts of the world. Industries first arose in areas with supplies of coal, iron ore and cheap water power. But later, after oil and gas came into use as industrial fuels, factories could be set up almost anywhere.

The growth of manufacturing led to an increase in the number of industrial cities. The flight from the land was accompanied by an increase in efficiency in agriculture. As a result, manufacturing replaced agriculture as the chief source of

EMPLOYMENT

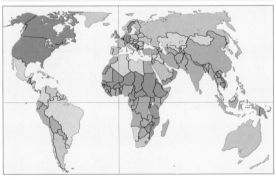

The number of workers employed in manufacturing for every 100 workers engaged in agriculture (latest available year)

- Under 10
- 10 – 50
- 50 – 100
- 100 – 200
- 200 – 500
- Over 500

DIVISION OF EMPLOYMENT

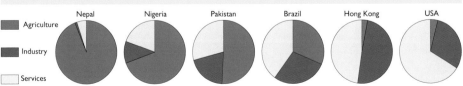

- Agriculture
- Industry
- Services

Nepal Nigeria Pakistan Brazil Hong Kong USA

18

PATTERNS OF PRODUCTION

> The table shows how the economy breaks down (in terms of the Gross Domestic Product for 1997) in a selection of industrialized countries. Agriculture remains important in some countries, though its percentage share has steadily declined since the start of the Industrial Revolution. Industry, especially manufacturing, accounts for a higher proportion, but service industries account for the greatest percentage of the GDP in most developed nations. The figures for Manufacturing are shown separately from Industry because of their importance in the economy.

Country	Agriculture	Industry (excl. manufacturing)	Manufacturing	Services
Australia	3%	24%	12%	61%
Austria	1%	24%	14%	61%
Brazil	10%	28%	18%	44%
Denmark	4%	7%	20%	69%
Finland	5%	3%	28%	64%
France	2%	20%	13%	65%
Germany	1%	8%	24%	67%
Greece	17%	13%	23%	47%
Hungary	4%	24%	14%	58%
Ireland	8%	7%	3%	82%
Italy	3%	8%	21%	68%
Japan	1%	28%	19%	52%
Kuwait	0%	46%	9%	45%
Mexico	4%	18%	17%	61%
Netherlands	3%	21%	12%	64%
Norway	2%	24%	10%	64%
Singapore	0%	29%	17%	54%
Sweden	3%	8%	28%	61%
UK	2%	8%	23%	67%
USA	3%	10%	20%	67%

income and employment in industrialized countries, and rapidly widened the wealth gap between them and the poorer non-industrialized countries whose economies continued to rely on agriculture.

SERVICE INDUSTRIES

Eventually, the manufacturing sector became so efficient that it could supply most of the things that people wanted to buy. Trade between industrialized countries also increased, so widening the choice for consumers in the developed world. These factors led to a further change in the economies of developed countries, namely a reduction in the relative importance of manufacturing and the growth of the service sector.

Service industries include such activities as government, transport, insurance, finance, and even the writing of computer software. In the United States, service industries now account for about two-thirds of the Gross National Product (GNP), while in Japan they account for just over half. But the wealth of both countries still rests on their massive industrial production.

AGRICULTURE

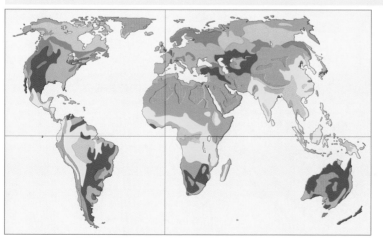

Predominant type of farming or land use

- Nomadic herding
- Hunting, fishing, & gathering
- Subsistence agriculture
- Commercial ranching
- Commercial livestock & grain farming
- Urban areas
- Forestry
- Unproductive land

19

TRADE & COMMERCE

TRADE HAS ALWAYS been an important human activity. It has widened the choice of goods available in any country, lowered prices and generally raised living standards. People regard any growth of world trade as a sign that the world economy is healthy, whereas a decline indicates a world recession.

Exports and imports are of two main kinds. Visible imports and exports include primary products, such as food and manufactures. Invisible imports and exports include services, such as banking, insurance, interest on loans, and money spent by tourists.

World trade, both visible and invisible, is dominated by the 29 members of the OECD (Organization for Economic Development), which includes the world's top trading nations, namely the United States, Japan, Germany, France, Italy and the United Kingdom, as well as Australia, New Zealand, Canada and Mexico. Hungary, Poland and South Korea joined in 1996.

> The new port of the historic Italian city of Ravenna is linked to the Adriatic Sea by a canal. The port has large oil refining and petrochemical industries.

CHANGING EXPORTS

From the late 19th century to the 1950s, primary products, including farm products, minerals, natural fibers, timber and, in the latter part of this period, oil

DEBT AND AID

International debtors and the development aid they receive (latest available year)

The provision of aid by rich countries to developing countries is part of international politics. But the grants made to developing countries are often dwarfed by the burden of debt which the countries are expected to repay. In 1990, the debts of Mozambique, one of the world's poorest countries, were estimated to be 75 times its entire earnings from exports.

Debt, US$ per capita
Aid, US$ per capita

$5,014

2,750
2,500
2,250
2,000
1,750
1,500
1,250
1,000
750
500
250
0

India
Tanzania
Sierra Leone
Guinea Bissau
Nigeria
Madagascar
Mozambique
Laos
Egypt
Honduras
Zambia
Papua New Guinea
Mauritania
Ivory Coast
Jordan
Ecuador
Congo
Jamaica
Nicaragua
Israel
Panama

50
100
<200
$391

	The World's Largest Businesses ▼	
	The world's largest businesses in 1997 by sales, in billions of US$.	
1	General Motors, *USA*	168.4
2	Ford Motor, *USA*	147.0
3	Mitsui, *Japan*	144.9
4	Mitsubishi, *Japan*	140.2
5	Itochu, *Japan*	135.5
6	Royal Dutch/Shell Group, *UK/Neths*	128.2
7	Marubeni, *Japan*	124.0
8	Exxon, *USA*	119.4
9	Summitomo, *Japan*	119.3
10	Toyota Motor, *Japan*	108.7
11	Wal-Mart Stores, *USA*	106.1
12	General Electric, *USA*	79.2
13	Nissho Iwai, *Japan*	78.9
14	Nippon Telegraph/Telephone, *Japan*	78.3
15	Intl. business Machines, *USA*	75.9
16	Hitachi, *Japan*	75.7
17	AT&T, *USA*	74.5
18	Nippon Life Insurance, *Japan*	72.6
19	Mobil, *USA*	72.3
20	Daimler-Benz, *Germany*	71.6

TRADED PRODUCTS

The character of world trade has greatly changed in the last 50 years. While primary products were once the leading commodities, world trade is now dominated by manufactured products. Cars are the single most valuable traded product, followed by vehicle parts and engines. The next most valuable goods are high-tech products such as data processing (computer) equipment, telecommunications equipment, and transistors. Other items include aircraft, paper and board, trucks, measuring and control instruments, and electrical machinery. Trade in most manufactured products is dominated by the OECD countries. For example, the leading vehicle exporter is Japan, which became the world's leading car manufacturer in the 1980s. The United States, Germany, the United Kingdom, France and Japan lead in the production of data processing equipment.

and natural gas, dominated world trade.

Many developing countries still remain dependent on exporting mineral ores, fossil fuels, or farm products such as cocoa or coffee whose prices fluctuate according to demand. But today, manufactured goods are the most important commodities in world trade. The OECD nations lead the world in exporting manufactured goods, but they are being challenged by a group of "tiger economies" in eastern Asia, notably Singapore, Hong Kong, and Taiwan. Other rapidly industrializing countries in Asia include Thailand, Malaysia, and the Philippines. Despite a recession in the late 1990s, these countries, with their generally low labor costs, are able to produce manufactured goods that compete with similar goods made in the Western world.

Private companies carry on most of the world's trade. The small proportion handled by governments decreased recently with the collapse of Communist regimes in eastern Europe and the former Soviet Union.

SHARE OF WORLD TRADE

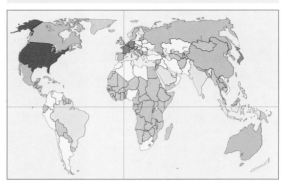

Percentage share of total world exports by value (1999)

- Over 10%
- 5 – 10%
- 1 – 5%
- 0.5 – 1%
- 0.1 – 0.5%
- Under 0.1%

DEPENDENCE ON TRADE

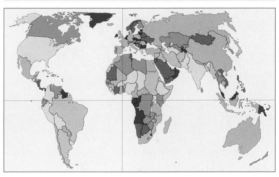

Value of exports as a percentage of Gross Domestic Product (1997)

- Over 50% GDP
- 40 – 50% GDP
- 30 – 40% GDP
- 20 – 30% GDP
- 10 – 20% GDP
- Under 10% GDP

Trade in Oil ▾

Major world trade in oil in millions of tons (1997)

Middle East to Asia (not Japan) 294.4	Mexico to USA 68.0
Middle East to Japan 218.1	W. Africa to W. Europe 40.1
Middle East to W. Europe 187.9	Western Europe to USA 32.9
S. and C. America to USA 132.1	Middle East to Africa 32.0
N. Africa to W. Europe 97.9	Middle East to South and Central America 27.8
CIS to Western Europe 90.8	
Middle East to USA 86.9	CIS to Central Europe 31.8
Canada to USA 72.7	Middle East to Central Europe 19.3
West Africa to USA 68.3	Total world trade 1,978.9

Transport & Travel

About 200 years ago, most people never traveled far from their birthplace. But adventurous travelers can now reach almost any part of the world.

Transport is concerned with moving goods and people around by land, water and air. Land transport was once laborious, and was dependent on pack animals or animal-drawn vehicles. But during the Industrial Revolution, railroads played a vital role in moving bulky materials and equipment required by factories. They were also important in the opening up and development of remote areas around the world in North and South America, Africa, Asia and Australia.

Today, however, motor vehicles have taken over many of the functions once served by railroads. Unlike railroads, motor vehicles provide a door-to-door service and modern trucks can carry large loads. In the United States, however, the long distances between cities means that railroads still carry about 35% of the domestic freight traffic, with trucks accounting for just 25% (compared to 90% in Britain). However, automobiles account for more than 76% of intercity passenger traffic.

> *Traffic jams and vehicle pollution have affected cities throughout the world. Many of Bangkok's beautiful old canals have been filled in to provide extra roads to cope with the enormous volume of traffic in the city.*

TRAVEL & TOURISM

Sea transport, which now employs huge bulk grain carriers, oil tankers and container ships, still carries most of the world's trade. But since the late 1950s, fewer passengers have traveled overseas by sea, because air travel is so much faster, though many former ocean liners now operate successfully as cruise ships.

Air travel has played a major part in the rapid growth of the tourist industry,

AIR TRAVEL

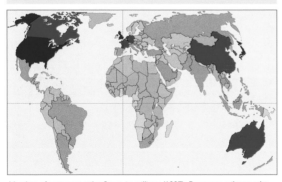

Number of passenger miles flown, in millions (1997). Passenger miles are the number of passengers (both international and domestic) multiplied by the distance flown by each passenger from airport of origin.

■ Over 60,000   ▨ 6,000 – 30,000   ▢ 300 – 600
■ 30,000 – 60,000   □ 600 – 6,000   ▨ Under 300

The World's Busiest Airports ▼	
Total number of passengers, in thousands (1997)	
1 O'Hare Intl., *Chicago*	70,295
2 Hartsfield Atlanta Int., *Atlanta*	68,206
3 Dallas/Fort Worth Int., *Dallas*	60,489
4 Los Angeles Intl., *Los Angeles*	60,143
5 Heathrow, *London*	57,975
6 Haneda, *Tokyo*	49,302
7 San Francisco Intl., *San Francisco*	40,500
8 Frankfurt/Main, *Frankfurt*	40,263
9 Kimpo Intl., *Seoul*	36,757
10 Charles de Gaulle, *Paris*	35,294
11 Denver Intl., *Denver*	34,973
12 Miami Intl., *Miami*	34,533
13 Schiphol, *Amsterdam*	31,570
14 Metro Wayne County, *Detroit*	31,521
15 John F. Kennedy Intl., *New York*	31,229

The Longest Rail Networks ▾

Extent of rail network, in thousands of miles (latest available year)

1	USA	151.2
2	Russia	54.1
3	India	39.1
4	China	35.2
5	Germany	25.4
6	Argentina	21.3
7	France	19.8
8	Mexico	16.5
9	South Africa	16.1
10	Poland	14.5

which accounted for 7.5% of world trade by the 1990s. Travel and tourism have greatly increased people's understanding and knowledge of the world, especially in the OECD countries, which account for about 8% of world tourism.

Some developing countries have large tourist industries which have provided employment and led to improvements in roads and other facilities. In some cases, tourism plays a vital role in the economy. For example, in Kenya, tourism provides more income than any other activity apart from the production and sale of tea and coffee. However, too many tourists can damage fragile environments, such as the wildlife and scenery in national parks, and also harm local cultures.

THE IMPORTANCE OF TOURISM

Nations receiving the most from tourism, millions of US$ (1996)

1	USA	64,400
2	Spain	28,400
3	France	28,200
4	Italy	27,300
5	UK	20,400
6	Austria	15,100
7	Germany	13,200
8	Hong Kong	11,200
9	China	10,500
10	Switzerland	9,900

Fastest growing tourist destinations, % change in receipts (1994–95)

1	South Korea	49%
2	Czech Republic	27%
3	India	21%
4	Russia	19%
5	Philippines	18%
6	Turkey	17%
7	Thailand	15%
8	Poland	13%
9	China	12%
10	Israel	12%

Number of tourist arrivals, millions (1996)

1	France	66,800
2	USA	49,038
3	Spain	43,403
4	Italy	34,087
5	UK	25,960
6	China	23,770
7	Poland	19,514
8	Mexico	18,667
9	Canada	17,610
10	Czech Republic	17,400

Overseas travelers to the USA, thousands (1997)

1	Canada	13,900
2	Mexico	12,370
3	Japan	4,640
4	UK	3,350
5	Germany	1,990
6	France	1,030
7	Taiwan	885
8	Venezuela	860
9	South Korea	800
10	Brazil	785

THE WORLD'S VEHICLES

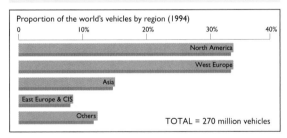

Proportion of the world's vehicles by region (1994)

TOTAL = 270 million vehicles

CAR OWNERSHIP

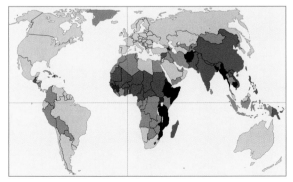

Number of people per car (1998)

- ■ Over 1,000
- ■ 500 – 1,000
- ■ 100 – 500
- ■ 25 – 100
- ▢ 5 – 25
- ▢ Under 5

Two-thirds of the world's vehicles are found in the developed countries of Europe and North America. Car ownership is also high in Australia and New Zealand, as well as in Japan, the world's leading car exporter. Car transport is the most convenient form of passenger travel, but air pollution caused by exhaust fumes is a serious problem in many large cities.

23

INTERNATIONAL ORGANIZATIONS

IN THE LATE 1980s, people rejoiced at the collapse of Communist regimes in eastern Europe and the former Soviet Union, because this brought to an end the Cold War, a long period of hostility between East and West. But hope of a new era of peace was shattered when ethnic and religious rivalries led to civil war in Yugoslavia and in parts of the former Soviet Union.

In order to help maintain peace, many governments have formed international organizations to increase cooperation. Some, such as NATO (North Atlantic

> In the early 1990s, the United Nations peacekeeping mission worked to end the civil war in Bosnia-Herzegovina and also to bring aid to civilians affected by the fighting.

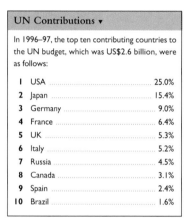

UN Contributions ▾

In 1996–97, the top ten contributing countries to the UN budget, which was US$2.6 billion, were as follows:

1	USA	25.0%
2	Japan	15.4%
3	Germany	9.0%
4	France	6.4%
5	UK	5.3%
6	Italy	5.2%
7	Russia	4.5%
8	Canada	3.1%
9	Spain	2.4%
10	Brazil	1.6%

Treaty Organization), are defense alliances, while others aim to encourage economic and social cooperation. Some organizations such as the Red Cross are non-governmental organizations, or NGOs.

UNITED NATIONS

The United Nations, the principal international organization, was formed in October 1945 and now has 188 member countries. The only independent nations that are not members are Switzerland, Taiwan, and the Vatican City.

THE UNITED NATIONS

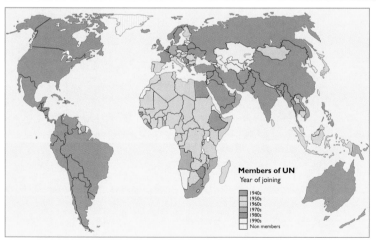

Members of UN
Year of joining

1940s
1950s
1960s
1970s
1980s
1990s
Non members

> The membership of the UN had risen from 51 in 1945 to 188 by the end of 2000. The first big period of expansion came in the 1960s when many former colonies achieved their independence. The membership again expanded rapidly in the 1990s when new countries were formed from the former Soviet Union and Yugoslavia. The most recent addition, Palau, is a former US trust territory in the Pacific Ocean and joined in 1994.

The United Nations was formed at the end of World War II to promote peace, international cooperation and security, and to help solve economic, social, cultural, and humanitarian problems. It promotes human rights and freedom and is a forum for negotiations between nations.

The main organs of the UN are the General Assembly, the Security Council, the Economic and Social Council, the Trusteeship Council, the International Court of Justice and the Secretariat.

The UN also operates 14 specialized agencies concerned with particular issues, such as agriculture, education, working conditions, communications and health. For example, UNICEF (the United Nations International Children's Fund), established in 1946 to deliver postwar relief to children, now aims to provide basic health care to children and mothers worldwide. The ILO (International Labor Organization) seeks to improve working conditions, while the FAO (Food and Agricultural Organization) aims at improving the production and distribution of food. The WTO (World Trade Organization) was set up as recently as January 1995 to succeed GATT (General Agreements on Tariffs and Trade).

THE UNITED NATIONS

THE GENERAL ASSEMBLY is the meeting of all member nations every September under a newly-elected president to discuss issues affecting development, peace, and security.

THE SECURITY COUNCIL has 15 members, of which five are permanent. It is responsible for maintaining international peace.

THE SECRETARIAT consists of the staff and employees of the UN, including the Secretary-General (appointed for a five-year term), who is the UN's chief administrator.

THE ECONOMIC & SOCIAL COUNCIL works with the specialized agencies to implement UN policies on improving living standards, health, cultural and educational cooperation.

THE TRUSTEESHIP COUNCIL was designed to bring several dependencies to independence. This work is now complete.

THE INTERNATIONAL COURT OF JUSTICE, or World Court, deals with legal problems and helps to settle disputes. Its headquarters are at The Hague, in the Netherlands.

UN DEPARTMENTS

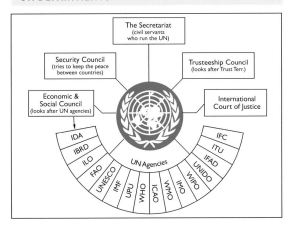

The Secretariat (civil servants who run the UN)

Security Council (tries to keep the peace between countries)

Trusteeship Council (looks after Trust Terr.)

Economic & Social Council (looks after UN agencies)

International Court of Justice

IDA
IBRD
ILO
FAO
UNESCO
IMF
UPU
OHM
ICAO
WMO
IMO
WIPO
UNIDO
IFAD
ITU
IFC

UN Agencies

UN PEACEKEEPING MISSIONS

The United Nations tries to resolve international disputes in several ways. It sends unarmed observer missions to monitor cease-fires or supervise troop withdrawals, and the Security Council members also send peacekeeping forces.

The first of these forces was sent in 1948 to supervise the cease-fire between Arabs and Jews in disputed parts of Palestine and, since then, it has undertaken more than 30 other missions. The "Blue Berets," as the 25,650 UN troops are called, must be impartial in any dispute

and they can fire only in self-defense. Hence, they can operate only with the support of both sides, which leaves them open to criticism when they are unable to prevent violence by intervening.

By the mid-1990s, the UN was involved in 15 world conflicts, was policing the boundary in partitioned Cyprus, and was seeking to enforce a peace agreement in Angola after 20 years of civil war. Other UN missions were in Tajikistan, Georgia, the Israeli-occupied Golan Heights, Haiti, Kuwait, southern Lebanon, the India–

Pakistan border, Liberia, Mozambique, Western Sahara and the former Yugoslavia. A force known as UNPROFOR (UN Protection Force) had been operating in Bosnia-Herzegovina and, by 1995, it accounted for 60% of the total UN peacekeeping budget. In February 1996, the Secretary-General of the UN approved the setting up of a new force, the United Nations Mission in Bosnia-Herzegovina (UNMIBH). Its main objective was to help create the right climate for the elections held in September 1996.

cludes the countries of East and Southeast Asia, as well as North America, plus Australia, New Zealand and Chile. APEC aims to create a free trade zone by 2020.

Together the United States, Canada and Mexico form NAFTA (North American Free Trade Agreement), which aims at eliminating trade barriers within 15 years of its foundation on 1 January 1994. Other economic groupings link the countries of Latin America.

Another economic group with more limited aims is OPEC (Organization of Petroleum Exporting Countries). It works to unify policies concerned with the sale of petroleum on world markets.

The central aim of the Colombo Plan is to provide economic development assistance for South and Southeast Asia.

ECONOMIC ORGANIZATIONS

Over the last 40 years, many countries have joined common markets aimed at eliminating trade barriers and encouraging the free movement of workers and capital.

> The European Parliament, one of the branches of the EU, consists of 626 members. The number of members for each country is based mainly on population.

The best known of these is the European Union. Other organizations include ASEAN (the Association of Southeast Asian Nations), which aims at reducing trade barriers between its ten members: Brunei, Burma, Cambodia, Indonesia, Laos, Malaysia, the Philippines, Singapore, Thailand, and Vietnam.

APEC (the Asia-Pacific Cooperation Group) was founded in 1989 and in-

OTHER ORGANIZATIONS

Some organizations exist for consultation on matters of common interest. The Commonwealth of Nations grew out of the links created by the British Empire, while the OAS (Organization of American States) works to increase understanding throughout the Western hemisphere. The OAU (Organization of

THE EUROPEAN UNION

At the end of World War II (1939–45), many Europeans wanted to end the ancient emnities that had caused such destruction and rebuild the shattered continent. It was in this mood that Belgium, France, West Germany, Italy, Luxembourg and the Netherlands signed the Treaty of Paris in 1951. This set up the European Coal and Steel Community (ECSC), the forerunner of the European Union.

In 1957, through the Treaty of Rome, the same six countries created the European Economic Community (EEC) and the European Atomic Community (EURATOM). In 1967, the ECSC, the EEC and EURATOM merged to form the single European Community (EC).

Another economic group, the European Free Trade Association (EFTA), was set up in 1960 by seven countries: Austria, Denmark, Norway, Portugal, Sweden, Switzerland and the United Kingdom. However, Denmark, Ireland and the UK left to become members of the EC in 1973, followed by Greece in 1981, Spain and Portugal in 1986, and Austria, Finland and Sweden in 1995. The expansion of the EC to 15 members left EFTA with just four members: Iceland, Liechtenstein, Norway and Switzerland.

In 1993, following the signing of the Maastricht Treaty, the EC was reconstituted as the European Union (EU). The aims of the EU include economic and monetary union, a single currency for all 15 countries, and closer cooperation on foreign and security policies and also on home affairs. This step has led to a debate. Some people would like the EU to develop into a federal Europe, but others fear that this would lead to a loss of national identity. On January 1, 1999, 11 EU countries adopted the euro as their official currency, although euro coins and notes would not to come into use until January 1, 2002. On January 1, 2001, Greece also adopted the euro, leaving only Denmark, Sweden, and the United Kingdom outside the euro zone.

AUSTRALIA'S NEW ROLE

Most of the people who settled in Australia between 1788 and the mid-20th century came from the British Isles. However, the strong ties between Australia and Britain were weakened after Britain joined the European Community in 1973. Since 1973, many Australians have argued that their world position has changed and that they are part of a Pacific community of nations, rather than an extension of Europe. Some want closer integration with ASEAN, the increasingly powerful economic group formed by seven Southeast Asian nations. But in 1995, the prime minister of Malaysia, Dr Mahathir Mohamad, argued that Australia could not be regarded as Asian until at least 70% of its people were of ethnic Asian origin.

African Unity) has a similar role in Africa, while the Arab League is made up of Arabic-speaking North African and Middle Eastern states. The CIS (Commonwealth of Independent States) was formed in 1991 to maintain links between 12 of the former 15 republics in the Soviet Union.

NORTH–SOUTH DIVIDE

The deepest division in the world today is the divide between rich and poor nations. In international terms, this is called the North–South divide, because the North contains most of the world's developed countries, while the developing countries lie mainly in the South. The European Union recognizes this division and gives special trading terms to more than 60 former European dependencies, which form the ACP (African, Caribbean and Pacific) states. One organization containing a majority of developing countries is the Non-Aligned Movement. This Movement was created in 1961 during the Cold War as a political bloc allied neither to the East nor to the West. However, the aims of the 113 members who attended the movement's 11th gathering in 1995 were concerned mainly with economic matters. The 113 countries between them produce only about 7% of the world's gross output and they can speak for the poorer South.

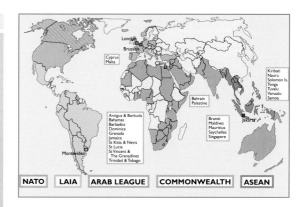

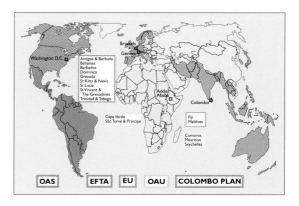

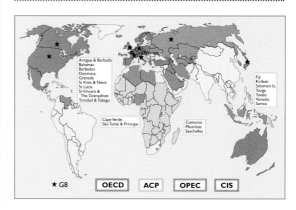

> The maps above show the membership of major international organizations. One important grouping shown on the bottom map is the Group of Eight (often called "G8"). This group of eight leading industrial nations (comprising Canada, France, Germany, Italy, Japan, Russia, the United Kingdom and the United States) holds periodic meetings to discuss major problems, such as world recessions.

27

REGIONS IN THE NEWS

THE BREAK-UP OF YUGOSLAVIA

> The former Yugoslavia, a federation of six republics, split apart in 1991–92. Fearing Serb domination, Croatia, Slovenia, Macedonia and Bosnia-Herzegovina declared themselves independent. This left two states,' Serbia and Montenegro, to continue as Yugoslavia. The presence in Croatia and Bosnia-Herzegovina of Orthodox Christian Serbs, Roman Catholic Croats and Muslims led to civil war and "ethnic cleansing." In 1995, the war ended when the Dayton Peace Accord affirmed Bosnia-Herzegovina as a single state partitioned into a Muslim-Croat Federation and a Serbian Republic. But the status of Kosovo, a former autonomous Yugoslav region, remained unresolved. Kosovo's autonomy was abolished in 1989 and Albanian-speaking, Muslim Kosovars came under direct Serbian rule. From 1995, support grew for the rebel Kosovo Liberation Army. War broke out, and NATO launched an offensive in 1999 that led to the withdrawal of Serbian troops from Kosovo. In 2000, President Slobodan Milosevic, whose policies were considered to be the cause of much of the ethnic conflict, was defeated in elections.

Population Breakdown ▼

Population totals and the proportion of ethnic groups (1995)

Yugoslavia **10,881,000**
  Serb 63%, Albanian 17%, Montenegrin 5%,
  Hungarian 3%, Muslim 3%
Serbia.. 6,017,200
  Kosovo 2,045,600
  Vojvodina 2,121,800
Montenegro 696,400

Bosnia-Herzegovina **4,400,000**
  Muslim 49%, Serb 31%, Croat 17%

Croatia **4,900,000**
  Croat 78%, Serb 12%

Slovenia................................. **2,000,000**
  Slovene 88%, Croat 3%, Serb 2%

Macedonia (F.Y.R.O.M.) **2,173,000**
  Macedonian 64%, Albanian 22%, Turkish 5%,
  Romanian 3%, Serb 2%

International borders — · — · —
Republic boundaries — · — · —
Province boundaries — — — — —
Line of the Dayton Peace Accord ———
Muslim– Croat Federation
Serbian Republic

> Since its establishment in 1948, the State of Israel has seldom been out of the news. During wars with its Arab neighbors in 1948–49, 1956, 1967 and 1973, it occupied several areas. The largest of the occupied territories, the Sinai peninsula, was returned to Egypt in 1979 following the signing of an Egyptian–Israeli peace treaty. This left three Israeli-occupied territories: the Gaza Strip, the West Bank bordering Jordan, and the Golan Heights, a militarily strategic area overlooking southwestern Syria.

Despite the peace agreement with Egypt, conflict continued in Israel with the PLO (Palestine Liberation Organization), which claimed to represent Arabs in Israel and Palestinians living in exile. Finally, on 13 September 1993 Israel officially recognized the PLO, and Yasser Arafat, leader of the PLO, renounced terrorism and recognized the State of Israel. This led to an agreement signed by both sides in Washington, DC. In May 1994, limited Palestinian self-rule was established in the Gaza Strip and in parts of the occupied West Bank. A Palestinian National Authority (PNA) was created and took over from the Israeli military administration when Israeli troops withdrew from the Gaza Strip and the city of Jericho. On 1 July 1994 the Palestinian leader, Yasser Arafat, stepped on to Palestinian land for the first time in 25 years.

Many people hoped that these developments would eventually lead to the creation of a Palestinian state, which would coexist in peace with its neighbor Israel. But groups on both sides sought to undermine the peace process. In November 1995, a right-wing Jewish student assassinated the Israeli prime minister, Yitzhak Rabin, who was succeeded by Símon Peres.

In 1996, a right-wing coalition led by Binyamin Netanyahu was elected to power. Peace talks with the PLO were halted, but, in 1999, the Labor Party leader Ehud Barak was elected prime minister. Barak revived negotiations with the PLO and Middle Eastern leaders aimed at exchanging "land for peace". But agreement, especially on the status of Jerusalem, proved elusive and fighting broke out in 2000. In 2001, Barak was defeated in elections by the right-wing Ariel Sharon.

Population Breakdown ▾

Population totals and the proportion of ethnic groups (1995)

Israel **5,696,000**
Jewish 82%, Arab Muslim 14%, Arab
Christian 3%, Druse 2%
West Bank 973,500
Palestinian Arab 97% (Arab Muslim 85%,
Christian 8%, Jewish 7%)
Gaza Strip 658,200
Arab Muslim 98%

Jordan **5,547,000**
Arab 99% (Palestinian Arab 50%)

Syria **14,614,000**
Arab 89%, Kurdish 6%

THE NEAR EAST

—·—·— 1949 Armistice Line

------- 1974 Cease-fire Lines (Golan Heights)

Efrata ● Main Jewish settlements in the West Bank and Gaza Strip

Halhul □ Main Palestinian Arab towns in the West Bank and Gaza Strip
– under Palestinian control since May 1994 (Gaza and Jericho)
and 28 September 1995 (West Bank)

WORLD FLAGS

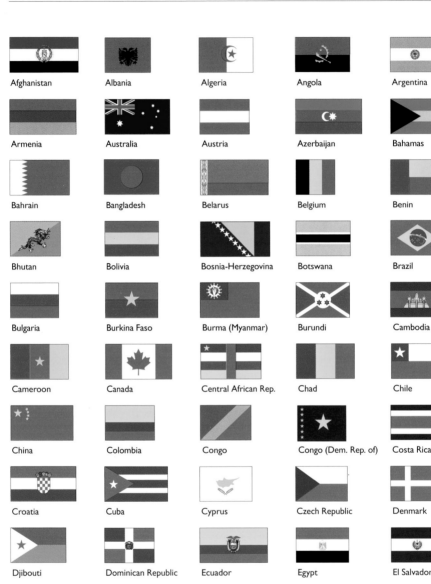

Afghanistan	Albania	Algeria	Angola	Argentina
Armenia	Australia	Austria	Azerbaijan	Bahamas
Bahrain	Bangladesh	Belarus	Belgium	Benin
Bhutan	Bolivia	Bosnia-Herzegovina	Botswana	Brazil
Bulgaria	Burkina Faso	Burma (Myanmar)	Burundi	Cambodia
Cameroon	Canada	Central African Rep.	Chad	Chile
China	Colombia	Congo	Congo (Dem. Rep. of)	Costa Rica
Croatia	Cuba	Cyprus	Czech Republic	Denmark
Djibouti	Dominican Republic	Ecuador	Egypt	El Salvador
Equatorial Guinea	Eritrea	Estonia	Ethiopia	Finland
France	Gabon	Georgia	Germany	Ghana

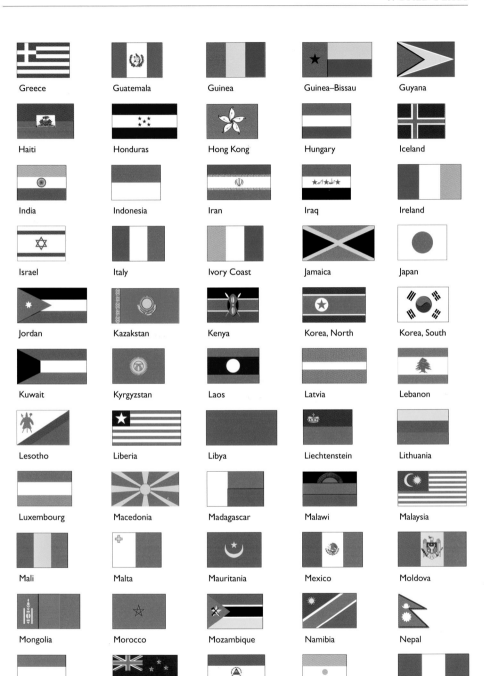

Greece	Guatemala	Guinea	Guinea–Bissau	Guyana
Haiti	Honduras	Hong Kong	Hungary	Iceland
India	Indonesia	Iran	Iraq	Ireland
Israel	Italy	Ivory Coast	Jamaica	Japan
Jordan	Kazakstan	Kenya	Korea, North	Korea, South
Kuwait	Kyrgyzstan	Laos	Latvia	Lebanon
Lesotho	Liberia	Libya	Liechtenstein	Lithuania
Luxembourg	Macedonia	Madagascar	Malawi	Malaysia
Mali	Malta	Mauritania	Mexico	Moldova
Mongolia	Morocco	Mozambique	Namibia	Nepal
Netherlands	New Zealand	Nicaragua	Niger	Nigeria

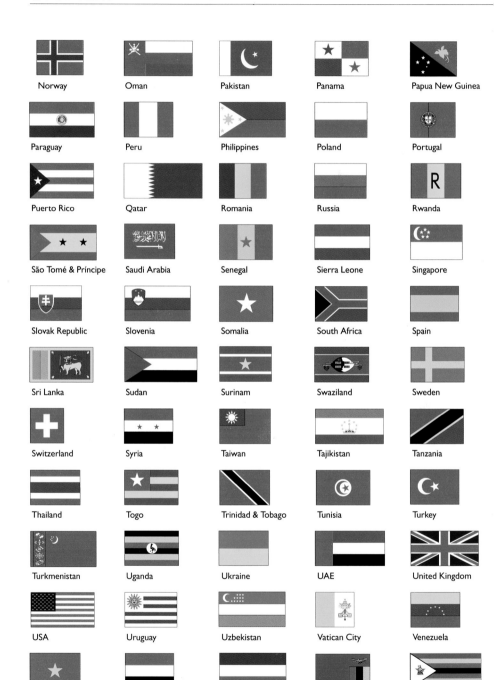

Norway	Oman	Pakistan	Panama	Papua New Guinea
Paraguay	Peru	Philippines	Poland	Portugal
Puerto Rico	Qatar	Romania	Russia	Rwanda
São Tomé & Príncipe	Saudi Arabia	Senegal	Sierra Leone	Singapore
Slovak Republic	Slovenia	Somalia	South Africa	Spain
Sri Lanka	Sudan	Surinam	Swaziland	Sweden
Switzerland	Syria	Taiwan	Tajikistan	Tanzania
Thailand	Togo	Trinidad & Tobago	Tunisia	Turkey
Turkmenistan	Uganda	Ukraine	UAE	United Kingdom
USA	Uruguay	Uzbekistan	Vatican City	Venezuela
Vietnam	Yemen	Yugoslavia	Zambia	Zimbabwe

WORLD MAPS — GENERAL REFERENCE

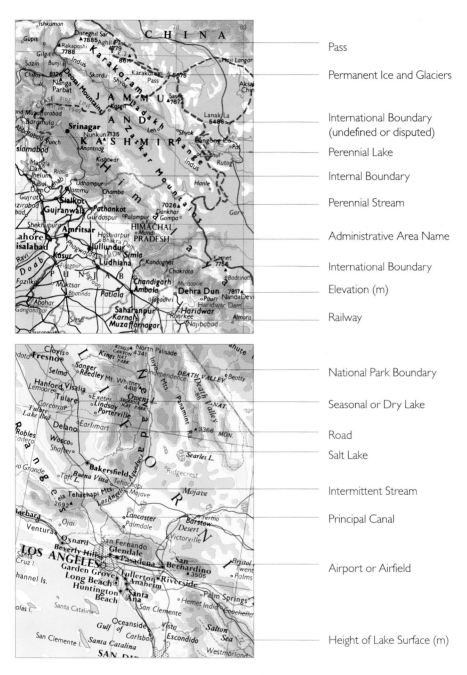

Pass

Permanent Ice and Glaciers

International Boundary
(undefined or disputed)

Perennial Lake

Internal Boundary

Perennial Stream

Administrative Area Name

International Boundary

Elevation (m)

Railway

National Park Boundary

Seasonal or Dry Lake

Road

Salt Lake

Intermittent Stream

Principal Canal

Airport or Airfield

Height of Lake Surface (m)

Settlements

Settlement symbols and type styles vary
according to the scale of each map and
indicate the importance of towns rather
than specific population figures.

All distances measured through the centre
of the map are correct for scale

• Capital cities

PROJECTION CENTRED ON LONDON

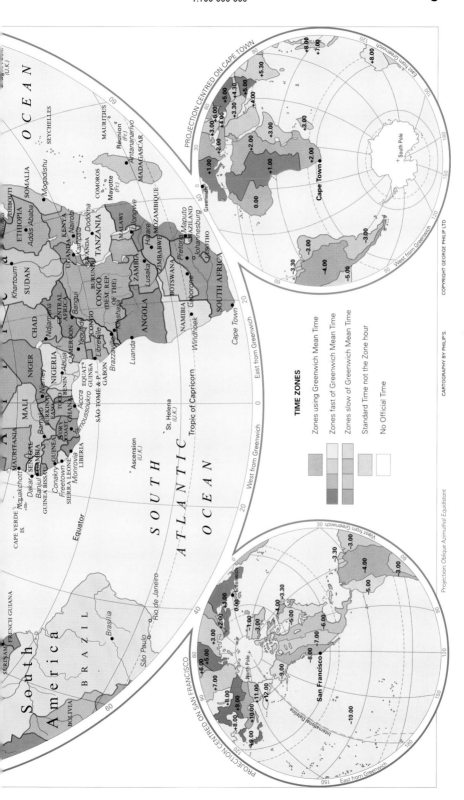

TIME ZONES

Zones using Greenwich Mean Time

Zones fast of Greenwich Mean Time

Zones slow of Greenwich Mean Time

Standard Time not the Zone hour

No Official Time

PROJECTION CENTRED ON CAPE TOWN

PROJECTION CENTRED ON SAN FRANCISCO

Projection: Oblique Azimuthal Equidistant

CARTOGRAPHY BY PHILIP'S.

COPYRIGHT GEORGE PHILIP LTD

PROJECTION CENTRED ON THE ANTIPODES OF LONDON

All distances measured through the centre of the map are correct for scale

• Capital cities

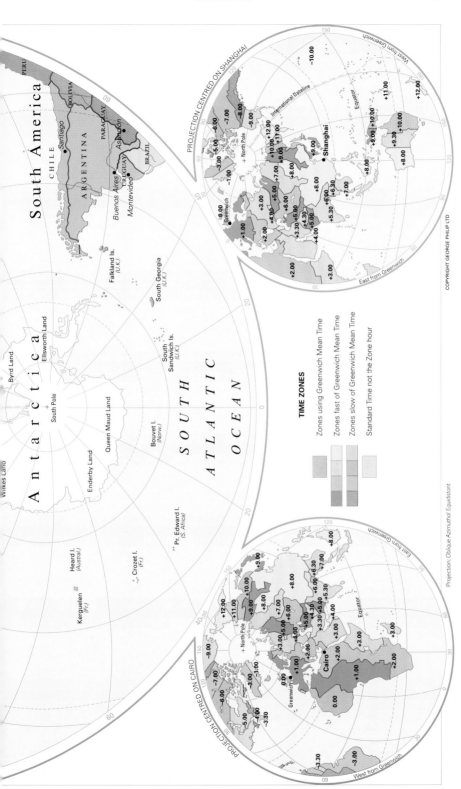

PROJECTION CENTRED ON SHANGHAI

West from Greenwich

−10.00

International Dateline

+11.00

+12.00

150

150

120

90

Equator

Shanghai

+8.00

+10.00

+10.00

+9.30

+8.00

−8.00

−7.00

−6.00

−5.00

−3.00

−1.00

+ North Pole

+10.00 +12.00

+11.00

+9.00

+9.00

+8.00

+7.00

+8.00

+6.30

+6.00

+5.30

+7.00

Greenwich

0.00

−1.00

+1.00

+2.00

+3.00

+4.00

+5.00

+6.00

+3.30 +5.30

+5.00

+4.00

60

40

30

East from Greenwich

+2.00

+3.00

South America

PERU

BOLIVIA

CHILE

ARGENTINA

PARAGUAY

Santiago

Asunción

URUGUAY

Buenos Aires

Montevideo

BRAZIL

60

40

Falkland Is.
(U.K.)

South Georgia
(U.K.)

South
Sandwich Is.
(U.K.)

20

A n t a r c t i c a

Byrd Land

Ellsworth Land

South Pole

Queen Maud Land

Enderby Land

Wilkes Land

S O U T H

A T L A N T I C

O C E A N

Bouvet I.
(Norw.)

** Pr. Edward I.
(S. Africa)

* Crozet I.
(Fr.)

Heard I.
(Austral.)

Kerguelen
(Fr.)

0

TIME ZONES

Zones using Greenwich Mean Time

Zones fast of Greenwich Mean Time

Zones slow of Greenwich Mean Time

Standard Time not the Zone hour

COPYRIGHT GEORGE PHILIP LTD

Projection: Oblique Azimuthal Equidistant

PROJECTION CENTRED ON CAIRO

East from Greenwich

120

120

90

+9.00

+10.00

+8.00

+7.00

+8.00

+6.00 +6.30

+7.00

+6.00

+5.30

Equator

60

+12.00

+11.00

+9.00

+8.00

+7.00

+6.00

+5.00

+4.00

+4.30

+5.00

+3.30 +5.00

+4.00

30

+3.00

+ North Pole

+3.00 +5.00

+2.00

+1.00

+2.00

Cairo

+2.00

+3.00

+2.00

−9.00

−7.00

−1.00

Greenwich

0.00

+1.00

−6.00

−5.00

−4.00

−3.30

0.00

+3.00

−1.00

−3.00

−3.30

60

30

0

West from Greenwich

−3.00

I: 20 000 000

100   0   100   200   300   400   500 miles

100 0   200   400   600   800 km

C

Ob

60

Murmansk

White Sea

Arkhangelsk

D

FINLAND

N. Dvina

Nizhniy Tagil

Kotlas

Perm

Yekaterinburg

55

L. Onega

Kirov

R U S S I A

Chelyabinsk

Vyborg L. Ladoga

Vologda

Ufa

Magnitogorsk

ST. PETERBURG

Rybinsk Res.

Kostroma

Kazan

E

ESTONIA

Tallinn

L. Chudskoye

Yaroslavl

Ivanovo

Nizhniy Novgorod

Simbirsk

Samara

Orenburg

L A T V I A

Riga

MOSCOW

Penza

Volga

Uralsk

50

W. Dvina

Smolensk

Tula

Saratov

Ural

ITHUANIA

Kaunas

Vitebsk

Orel

Tambov

K A Z A K S T A N

ningrad

Vilnius

Mogilev

Minsk

Kursk

Voronezh

B E L A R U S

Gomel

Chernigov

Volgograd

Atyraū

F

N

Brest

Pripet

Zhitomir

Kiev

Dnieper

Kharkov

Don

Astrakhan

45

varsaw

Lublin

Lvov

U K R A I N E

Donetsk

Caspian Sea

EP.

Dniester

Dnepropetrovsk

Taganrog

Rostov

Krivoy Rog

Zaporozhye

Bug

Kherson

Stavropol

G

Debrecen

MOLDOVA

Kishinev

Nikolayev

Makhachkala

Cluj-Napoca

Odessa

Krasnodar

R O M A N I A

Galați

Crimea

Timișoara

Brașov

GEORGIA

Tbilisi

AZERBAIJAN

Baku

Ploiești

Sevastopol

40

rade

Bucharest

Constanța

Black   Sea

ARMENIA

Yerevan

Araks

iș

Danube

Varna

Samsun

VIA

Sofia

Bosporus

Erzurum

Tabriz

BULGARIA

Plovdiv

T U R K E Y

H

EDONIA

Skopje

ISTANBUL

Diyarbakır

IRAN

Thessaloniki

Bursa

Ankara

35

EECE

Kayseri

A   s   i   a

IRAQ

İzmir

Konya

Adana

Euphrates

Tigris

Patrai

Athens

Antalya

S Y R I A

Aleppo

Baghdad

J

Rhodes

CYPRUS

Nicosia

Aegean Sea

Crete

CARTOGRAPHY BY PHILIPS.

10   11   12   13   14   15

11   12   13   14   15   16   17   18   19

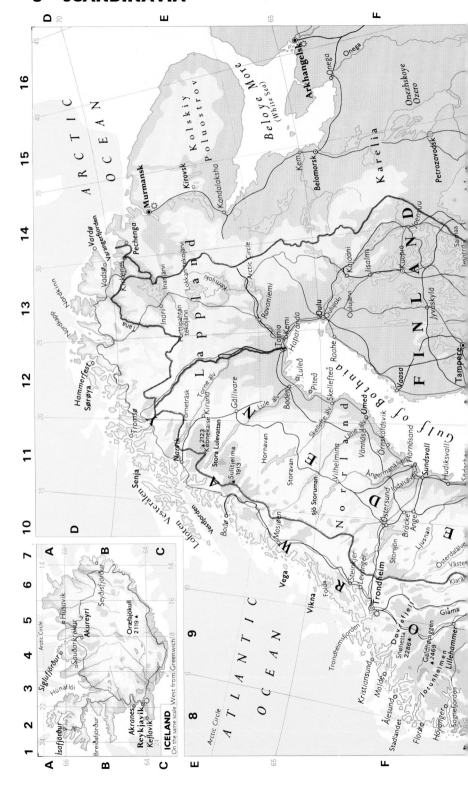

ARCTIC OCEAN

Murmansk

Kolskiy Poluostrov

Beloye More
(White Sea)

Arkhangelsk

Onega

Onega

Onezhskoye
Ozero

Kirovsk

Kandaksha

Kem

Belomorsk

Karelia

Petrozavodsk

Vardø
Vadsø
Varangerfjorden
Pechenga
Kirkenes
Nordkinn
Nordkapp
Hammerfest
Sørøya

Inari
Inarijärvi
Lokka
Lokan tekojärvi
Portipahtan
tekojärvi
Tana

Kemijoki

Arctic Circle

Rovaniemi

Kemijärvi
Kuusamo
Suhana

FINLAND

Kajaani
Iisalmi
Kuopio
Jyväskylä

Tampere

Tornio
Tornio
Haparanda
Kemi
Oulu
Oulujoki
Oulujärvi

Vaasa

Gulf of Bothnia

Luleå
Piteå
Boden
Kalix älv

Skellefte älv
Skellefteå
Raahe

Ornsköldsvik

Umeå
Umeå älv
Vännäs

Härnösand

Sundsvall
Indalsälven

Hudiksvall

Torne älv
Ometräsk
Kiruna
Kebnekaise ▲2123
Gällivare

Lule älv

Hornavan

Storavan

Sorsele

Sjö Storuman

Storuman

Stora Lulevattan

Sulitjelma
1913

Tromsø
Senja
Narvik

Lofoten
Vesterålen
Vestfjorden

Bodø
Mosjøen

Mo i Rana

Vega

Vikna

Folda

Steinkjer
Levanger

Trondheim

Trondheimsfjorden

Kristiansund

Molde

Ålesund
Stadlandet

Florø
Høyanger
Sognefjorden

Dovrefjell
Snøhetta
2286▲
Galdhøpiggen
2469 ▲
Jotunheimen

Lillehammer

Glåma

Östersund

Storsjön

Bräcke
Ange

Ljusnan

Österdalälven
Västerdalälven

Klarälv

Storjön

NORRLAND

Gulf of Bothnia

ATLANTIC OCEAN

Arctic Circle

Lappland

ICELAND
On the same scale   West from Greenwich 18

Ísafjörður
Siglufjörður
Húsavík
Sauðárkrókur
Akureyri
Seyðisfjörður
Öræfajökull
2119 ▲
Húnaflói
Breiðafjörður
Akranes
Reykjavik
Keflavík

Arctic Circle

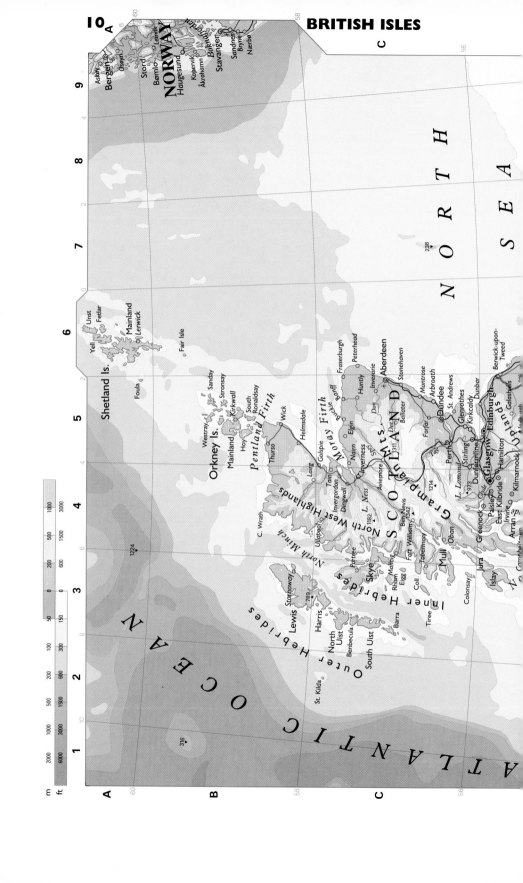

NORWAY

Askøy
Bergen
Osøyri
Stord
Bømlo
Leirvik
Bokn
Haugesund
Kopervik
Åkrehamn
Stavanger
Sandnes
Bryne
Nærbø

N O R T H   S E A

238

Shetland Is.

Unst
Fetlar
Yell
Mainland
Lerwick

Fair Isle

Foula

Berwick-upon-Tweed

Fraserburgh
Peterhead

Aberdeen
Stonehaven
Montrose
Arbroath
Dundee
St. Andrews

Huntly
Inverurie
Elgin
Nairn
Don
Forfar
Ballater
1181
Dee

Westray
Sanday
Stronsay
Kirkwall
South Ronaldsay
Hoy
Mainland

Orkney Is.

Pentland Firth

Wick
Helmsdale
Thurso

C. Wrath

1224

Golspie
Tain
Invergordon
Dingwall
Ullapool

Moray Firth

Buckie
Banff

Loch Ness
Inverness
Aviemore
Ben Nevis
1342
Fort William
Tobermory

S C O T L A N D

Grampian Mts.
1214
1311

North West Highlands

Perth
Stirling
Dunfermline
Glasgow
Hamilton
973
Paisley
Greenock
Kilmarnock
East Kilbride
Irvine
Dalkeith

Edinburgh
Galashiels
Glenrothes
Kirkcaldy
Dunbar

Southern Uplands

Stornoway
Lewis
789
Harris
North Uist
Benbecula
South Uist
Barra

Outer Hebrides

St. Kilda

Portree
Skye
Rhum
Eigg
Coll
Tiree
Mull
Oban

Inner Hebrides

Jura
Islay
Colonsay

Arran
N. Campbeltown

North Minch

A T L A N T I C   O C E A N

316

m ft
2000 6000
1000 3000
500 1500
200 600
100 300
50 150
0 0
0 0
150 50
600 200
1500 500
3000 1000

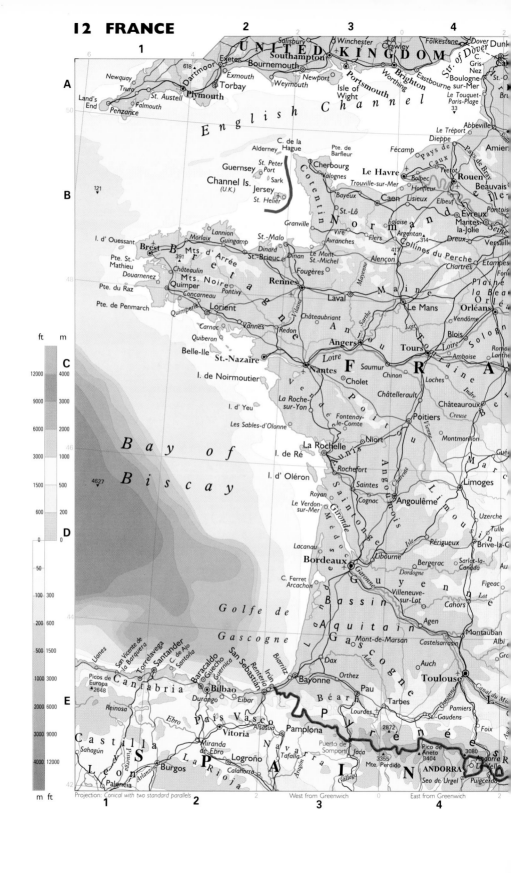

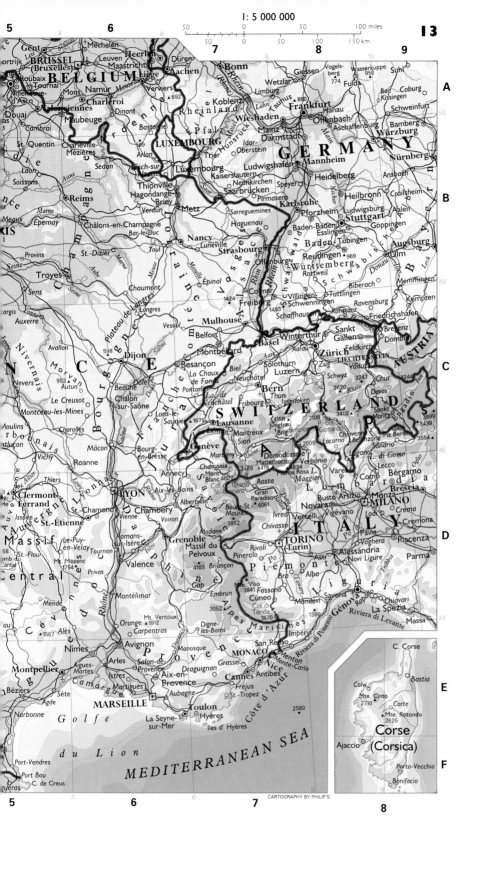

1 : 5 000 000

50   0   50   100 miles

50   0   50   100   150 km

5   6   7   8   9

A

Gent Schelde Mechelen Heerlen Düren Bonn Giessen Vogels- Wasserkuppe
Leuven Maastricht Aachen berg 950
ortrijk Leie BRUSSEL Liège Verviers Limburg Wetzlar 774 Fulda Suhl
(Bruxelles) Namur Koblenz Lahn Taunus 880
Roubaix BELGIUM 692 Rheinland- Frankfurt Hanau Schweinfurt
Tournai Mons Charleroi Dinant Bastogne Pfalz Wiesbaden Offenbach Aschaffenburg Bamberg Coburg Bad
d'Ascq Maubeuge Ardennes Mainz Darmstadt Würzburg Kissingen
Cambrai Charleville- LUXEMBOURG Trier Idar- GERMANY
St-Quentin Mézières Anon Oberstein Mannheim Nürnberg
Laon Sedan Esch-sur- Luxembourg Ludwigshafen Heidelberg Ansbach
Soissons Aisne Thionville Kaiserslautern Speyer

B

Reims Hagondange Saarbrücken Neunkirchen Karlsruhe Pforzheim Ludwigsburg Crailsheim
Briey Metz Pirmasens Baden-Baden Stuttgart Aalen
Châlons-en-Champagne Sarreguemines Esslingen Göppingen
Épernay Bar-le-Duc Verdun Haguenau Baden Tübingen Augsburg
Provins Nancy Lunéville Strasbourg Württemberg Reutlingen 969 Ulm
Troyes Chaumont Épinal Offenburg Rottweil Schwäbische Donau Memmingen
Sens Langres Freiburg Villingen Tuttlingen Ravensburg Kempten
1424 1493 Schwenningen Biberach
Auxerre Vesoul Belfort Schaffhausen Konstanz Friedrichshafen

C

Avallon Dijon Montbéliard Basel Winterthur Sankt Bregenz
598 Besançon Aarau Zürich Gallen Dornbirn Austria
Nevers Beaune La Chaux Biel Solothurn Zug Feldkirch
902 Autun de Fonds Neuchâtel Luzern Schwyz Chur 3244
Dole Pontarlier 3620 Rhein Davos
Le Creusot Charolles Lac de Fribourg 3402 Sankt 3899
Montceau-les-Mines Neuchâtel Thun Interlaken 2108 Moritz 3439
Mâcon Lons-le- 4158 Jungfrau P. del San Bellinzona 3554
Saunier 1679 SWITZERLAND Brig Simplon Gottardo Locarno L. di Como

D

Vichy Bourg- Montreux 2005 Sondrio
Roanne en-Bresse Genève Sion Verbánia L.
Thiers Annecy Martigny Domodóssola Maggiore Varese Como
Clermont- Aix-les-Bains Mont 2489 4478 Matterhorn Monte Rosa Lecco Bérgamo
Ferrand Blanc 4634 Brescia
St-Chamond Chamonix Col du Grand Aosta Busto Arsizio Monza MILANO
LYON Albertville St-Bernard Gran Novara Vigevano Crema
Issoire Chambéry Paradiso Ivrea Vercelli Lodi Cremona
St-Étienne Vienne Voiron 3852 Chivasso Pavia
Grenoble Maurice TORINO Po Voghera Piacenza
Massif Le-Puy- Romans- Modane (Turin) Alessandria Parma
en-Velay sur-Isère Massif du Rivoli Asti Novi Ligure
Pelvoux Pinerolo Po Piemonte
St-Flour Mt. Mézenc Privas 4103 Briançon Bra Alba
1754 Valence Gap Liguria
Central

E

Cevennes Montélimar Mt. Viso Cúneo Mondovì Savona Gènova Chiávari
1567 Alès Orange 1912 3841 Fossano La Spezia Massa
Mende Carpentras Digne- Col di 1386 Riviera di Levante
Nîmes Mt. Ventoux les-Bains Tenda Imperia
Avignon Manosque San Remo Riviera di Ponente
Montpellier Arles Salon-de- Draguignan Grasse MONACO Menten
Aigues- Provence Aix-en- Cannes Nice Monte-Carlo
Béziers Mortes Istres Provence Antibes
Sète Camargue Martigues Aubagne Fréjus St-Tropez Côte d'Azur
Agde MARSEILLE Toulon Hyères
Narbonne Golfe La Seyne- Iles d'Hyères 2580
sur-Mer

F

Port-Vendres du Lion MEDITERRANEAN SEA
Port Bou
C. de Creus

CARTOGRAPHY BY PHILIP'S.

5   6   7   8

Inset — Corse (Corsica):

C. Corse
Calvi Bastia
Mte. Cinto Corte
2710 Mte. Rotondo E
2625
Corse
(Corsica)
Ajaccio F
Porto-Vecchio
Bonifacio

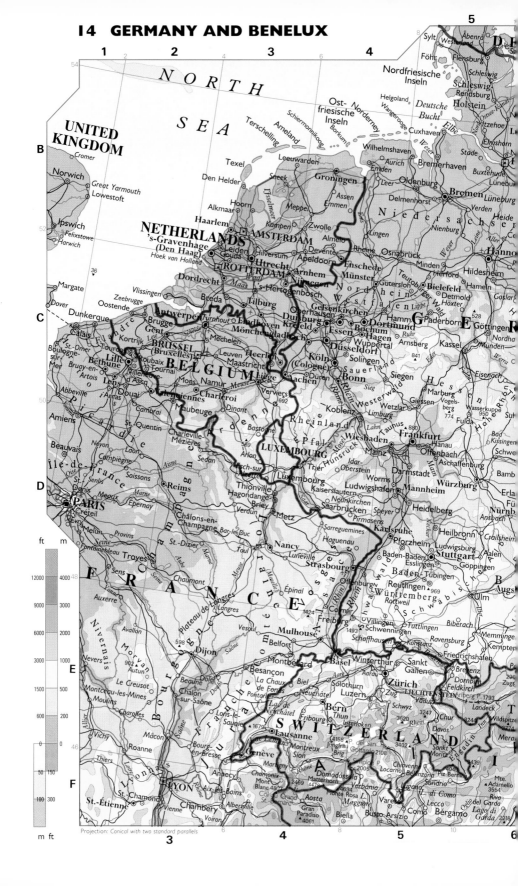

5

1   2   3   4

Sylt   Westerland   Abenra   D F

Föhr   Flensburg

Nordfriesische   Schleswig
Inseln   Rendsburg
Helgoland   Deutsche   Holstein
Ost-   Norderney   Bucht   Itzehoe
friesische   Wangerooge   Cuxhaven   Elbe
Inseln   Borkum   Elmshorn

NORTH

SEA

Schiermonnikoog   Wilhelmshaven   Stade   HE

Ameland   Aurich   Bremerhaven   Buxtehude   Lüneburg
Terschelling   Leeuwarden   Emden   Oldenburg   Verden   Lüneburg

UNITED
KINGDOM   Cromer

Norwich

Great Yarmouth
Lowestoft

Ipswich
Felixstowe
Harwich

Margate

Dover   Dunkerque

Calais
Boulogne-
sur-
Mer

Texel   Den Helder   Sneek   Groningen   Leer   Delmenhorst   **Bremen**

Hoorn   Assen   N   i   e   d   e   r   s   a   c   h   s   e   Hanno

Alkmaar   Meppel   Emmen   Lingen   Nienburg   Heide   Verden
Haarlem   Kampen   Zwolle   Rheine   Osnabrück   Minden   Hameln   Hildesheim

NETHERLANDS   **AMSTERDAM**   Almelo   Deventer   Enschede   Münster   Gütersloh   Herford   Detmold
's-Gravenhage   Leiden   Hilversum   Apeldoorn   **Bielefeld**   Höxter
(Den Haag)   Gouda   Utrecht   Arnhem   Nijmegen   N   o   r   d   Paderborn   Göttingen
Hoek van Holland   **ROTTERDAM**   's-Hertogenbosch   r   h   e   i   n   Kassel
Dordrecht   Maas   Gelsenkirchen   Hamm

Vlissingen   Breda   Tilburg   Oberhausen   Dortmund
Zeebrugge   Antwerpen   Turnhout   Eindhoven   Duisburg   Krefeld   Essen   Bochum   Hagen   Münden
Oostende   Brugge   Gent   Mönchengladbach   Düsseldorf   Wuppertal   Arnsberg

St.-Omer   Kortrijk   **BRUSSEL**   Mechelen   Heerlen   **Köln**   Solingen
Tourcoing   (Bruxelles)   Leuven   Maastricht   (Cologne)   Siegen   Marburg   Eisenach
Lille   Roubaix   **BELGIUM**   Liège   Aachen   Bonn   S   a   u   e   r   Giessen   Wasserkuppe
Béthune   d'Ascq   Tournai   Mons   Namur   Düren   W   e   s   t   e   r   w   a   l   d   Wetzlar   950
Lens   Valenciennes   Charleroi   Verviers   Koblenz   Limburg   Fulda
Douai   Maubeuge   Dinant   R   h   e   i   n   l   a   n   d   Wiesbaden   Frankfurt
Abbeville   Arras   Cambrai   Bastogne   P   f   a   l   z   Mainz   Hanau
Amiens   St.-Quentin   Charleville-   **LUXEMBOURG**   Hunsrück   Offenbach   Aschaffenburg
Beauvais   Mézières   Arlon   Trier   Idar-   Darmstadt
Noyon   Laon   Sedan   Esch-sur-   Oberstein   Worms   Würzburg
Compiègne   Soissons   Thionville   Luxembourg   Ludwigshafen   Mannheim
St.-   Aisne   Hagondange   Kaiserslautern   Speyer   Heidelberg
Senlis   Reims   Briey   Neunkirchen   Erla
PARIS   Marne   Épernay   Verdun   Metz   Saarbrücken   Pirmasens   Ansbach   Nürnb
Créteil   Châlons-en-   Sarreguemines   Karlsruhe
Evry   Champagne   Bar-le-Duc   Haguenau   Pforzheim   Ludwigsburg   Crailsheim
Melun   Provins   Toul   Nancy   Baden-Baden   Heilbronn   Stuttgart   Aalen
Fontainebleau   Lunéville   Strasbourg   Esslingen   Göppingen   Augs
Seine   Troyes   **F R A N C E**   Baden-   Tübingen   Ulm
Sens   Chaumont   Offenburg   Reutlingen   Württemberg
Auxerre   Langres   Épinal   Colmar   Freiburg   Rottweil   Biberach
Avallon   Plateau de Langres   Vesoul   Villingen   Tuttlingen   Memmingen
Nevers   Dijon   Saône   Belfort   Schwenningen   Ravensburg   Kempten
Le Creusot   Beaune   Dole   Montbéliard   Basel   Schaffhausen   Konstanz   Friedrichshafen
Autun   Chalon-   Besançon   Biel   Winterthur   Sankt   Bregenz
Montceau-les-Mines   sur-Saône   La Chaux-   Solothurn   Aarau   **Zürich**   Gallen   Dornbirn
Moulins   Charolles   Pontarlier   de Fonds   Neuchâtel   Luzern   Zug   **LIECHTENSTEIN**   Feldkirch   Landeck
Vichy   Mâcon   Lac de   Fribourg   Schwyz   Vaduz
Roanne   Bourg-   Neuchâtel   **Bern**   Chur   Wildspitz
Thiers   en-Bresse   Thun   Interlaken   Davos
LYON   Aix-les-Bains   Lausanne   **SWITZERLAND**   Sankt   Engadin
St.-Étienne   Chambéry   Genève   Montreux   Sion   Jungfrau   Moritz
Vienne   Albertville   Annecy   Martigny   Brig   Gottardo   Mera
Voiron   Mont   Chamonix   Matterhorn   Domodossola   Locarno   Bellinzona   Adamello
Blanc   Col du Grand   Monte Rosa   Verbania   Lugano   Riva
St.-Bernard   Aosta   Maggiore   Como   Lecco   Lago di
Gran   Busto Arsizio   Bérgamo   Garda
Paradiso   Biella

B

C

D

E

F

ft	m
12000	4000
9000	3000
6000	2000
3000	1000
1500	500
600	200
0	0
	150
50	300
100	

m ft

Projection: Conical with two standard parallels

3   6   4   8   5   10   6

1: 5 000 000

50 0 50 100 miles
50 0 50 100 150 km

BALTIC SEA

Zatoka
Gdańska

A

ARK
Næstved
Møn
Lolland
Falster
Nakskov
Nykøbing
Rødbyhavn
Gedser
Fehmarn
Rügen
Sassnitz
Darłowo
Kołobrzeg
Koszalin
Słupsk
Lębork
Wejherowo
Rumia Gdynia
Sopot
Gdańsk
Tczew
329
Elbląg
Malbork
54
Mecklenburger
Bucht
Wismar
Stralsund
Greifswald
Usedom
Wolin
Świnoujście
Białogard
Szczecinek
Bytów
Chojnice
Świecie
Starogard
Gdański
Kwidzyn
Iława

G
Schwerin
Mecklenburg
Stettiner
Haff
Police
Goleniów
Szczecin
Stargard
Szczeciński
Wałcz
Piła
Bydgoszcz
Chełmno
Grudziądz
Brodnica
Toruń
Rypin

B

Güstrow
Neubrandenburg
Neustrelitz
Müritz-
see
Brandenburg
Wittenberge
Neuruppin
Oranienburg
Eberswalde-
Finow
Schwedt
Choszczno
Gorzów
Wielkopolski
Noteć
Inowrocław
Włocławek
Płock
Kutno

Stendal
Rathenow
BERLIN
Potsdam
Fürstenwalde
Frankfurt
Świebodzin
Międzychód
Nowy Tomyśl
Poznań
Gniezno
Września
Koło
Łęczyca

P O L A N D

sburg
Magdeburg
Luckenwalde
Brandenburg
Zielona
Góra
Kościan
Śrem
Konin
Turek
52

Salzwedel
Wittenberg
Dessau
Anhalt
Bernburg
Cottbus
Forst
Nowa Sól
Leszno
Krotoszyn
Ostrów
Wielkopolski
Kalisz
Sieradz
Zduńska
Wola
Łódź
Pabianice

M A N Y
Halle
Torgau
Lauchhammer
Żary
Żagań
Głogów
Lubin
Wieluń
Piotrków
Trybunalski

Merseburg
Leipzig
Riesa
Hoyerswerda
Bolesławiec
Oleśnica
Radomsko

Naumburg
Meissen
Bautzen
Zgorzelec
Legnica
Wrocław
Kluczbork
Częstochowa

C

Weimar
Gera
Sachsen
Dresden
Görlitz
Jelenia Góra
Świdnica
Oława
Opole
Myszków
Zawiercie

Zwickau
Chemnitz
Děčín
Liberec
Wałbrzych
Dzierżoniów
Tarnowskie
Góry
Zabrze Bytom
Sosno-
wiec

Greiz
Reichenbach
Plauen
Erzgebirge
Teplice
Ústí nad
Labem
Jablonec
Mladá
Boleslav
Trutnov
Kłodzko
Nysa
Gliwice
Katowice
Tychy
Oświęcim

Hof
Karlovy Vary
Kladno
Hradec
Králové
Raciborz
Karviná
Bielsko-
Biała

Bayreuth
Cheb
Beroun
PRAHA
(Prague)
Kolín
Pardubice
Opava
Ostrava
Havířov
Cieszyn

Weiden
Plzeň
Příbram
C Z E C H R E P.
Sumperk
Frýdek-
Místek
Žywie

652
Amberg
Klatovy
Písek
Tábor
Jihlava
Vyškov
Olomouc
Prostějov
Přerov
Zlín

D

Regensburg
Böhmerwald
Strakonice
České
Budějovice
Jindřichův
Hradec
Třebíč
Brno
Bielé Karpaty
Trenčín
Banská Bystrica

Straubing
Deggendorf
Passau
Gmünd
Znojmo
Hodonín
SLOVAK REP
Prievidza
Topoľčany
Zvolen

MÜNCHEN
(Munich)
Braunau
Ried
Linz
Krems
Stockerau
WIEN
(Vienna)
Bratislava
Nitra
Levice
48

Chiemsee
Salzburg
Gmunden
Wels
Steyr
Amstetten
Sankt
Pölten
Baden
Wiener
Neustadt
Neusiedler
See
Sopron
Győr
Nové
Zámky
Komárno
Vác

A U S T R I A
Kufstein
Bad Ischl
Eisenerz
Kapfenberg
Szombathely
Mosonmagyaróvár
Tatabánya
Esztergom
BUDAPEST

bruck
Salzach
Bad Gastein
Bruck an der Mur
Pápa
Székesfehérvár

I T A L Y
Gross Glockner
Lienz
Kärnten
Wolfsberg
Graz
Steiermark
Veszprém
Balaton
Siófok
Dunaújváros

E

Karnische Alpen
Villach
Klagenfurt
Maribor
Zalaegerszeg
Nagykanizsa
Kaposvár
Szekszárd
Kalocsa
Baja

H U N G A R Y

Triglav
Kranj
Celje
Varaždin
Koprivnica
Pécs
Mohács

Ljubljana
SLOVENIA
Zagreb
Bjelovar
Virovitica
Drava
46

East from Greenwich
CARTOGRAPHY BY PHILIP'S.

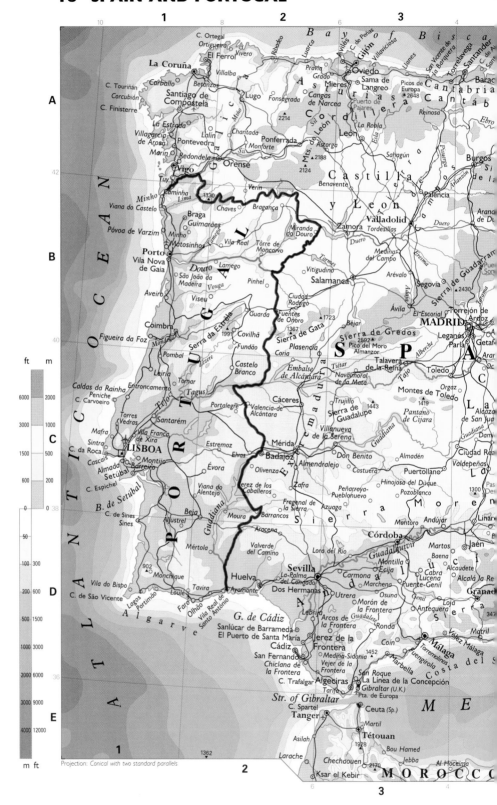

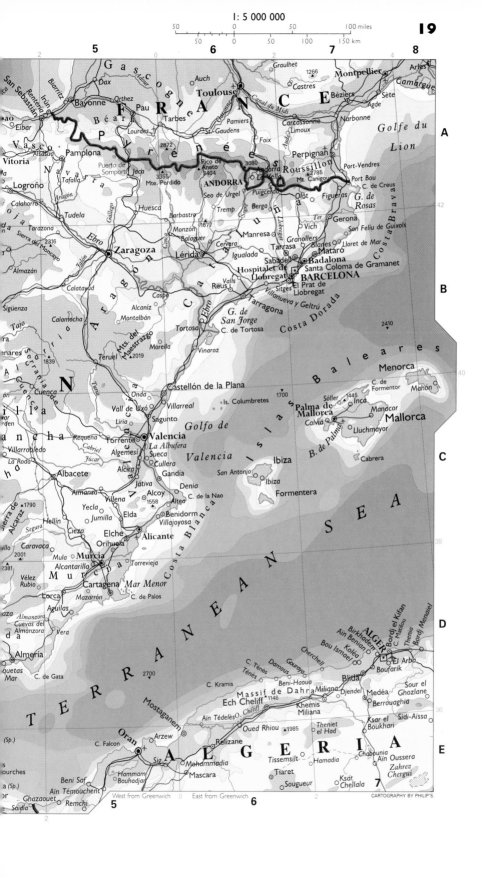

1: 5 000 000

CARTOGRAPHY BY PHILIP'S.

East from Greenwich

Projection: Conical with two standard parallels

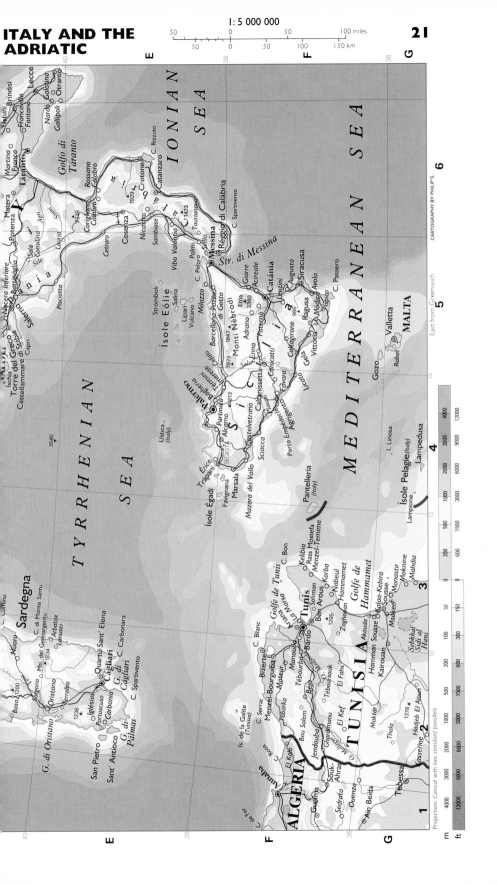

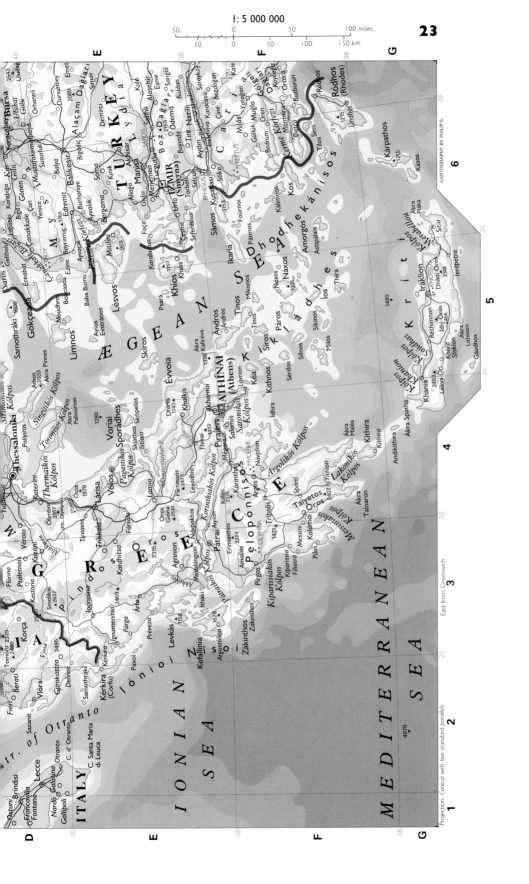

1: 5 000 000

50   0   50   100 miles
50   0   50   100   150 km

CARTOGRAPHY BY PHILIP'S.

Projection: Conical with two standard parallels

East from Greenwich

ITALY

Ostuni
Brindisi
Francavilla
Fontana   Galatina
Lecce
Gallipoli
Nardò
C. Santa Maria
di Leuca
Str. of Otranto
C. d'Otranto

MEDITERRANEAN SEA

IONIAN SEA

Vlora
Sazani
Fieri
Berati
Gjirokastra
Debina
Samothraki
Kérkira
(Corfu)
Paxoí
Levkás
Kefallinía
Zákinthos
Zákinthos
Ithaki
Argostólion
Párga
Igoumenitsa
Préveza
Naípaktos
Mesolóngion
Agrínion
Amaliás
Pírgos
Kipárissia
Filiatrá
Pílos
Kalámai
Messíni
Kiparissía

GREECE

Pindos Oros

Peloponnísos

Ioánnina
Trikkala
Kardhítsa
Lárisa
Vólos
Lamía
Levádhia
Khalkís
Thívai
Kórinthos
Argos
Náfplion
Trípolis
Spárti
Kalámai
Taíyetos Oros
Akra Maléa
Kíthira
Andikíthira

ATHÍNAI (Athens)
Piraiévs
Salamís
Mégara

Korç
Tómorrit 2379
Vlora

ALBANIA
Korça

Flórina
Ptolemaís
Kastoría
Kozáni
Véroia
Katerini
Thessaloníki
Poliyiros
Athos
Sithonía

Toronaíos Kólpos
Sinaitikós Kólpos
Thermaïkós Kólpos
Pagasitikós Kólpos
Voriai Sporádhes
Skíathos
Skópelos
Skíros
Samothráki
Límnos
Lésvos
Khíos
Psará
Ikaría
Sámos
Pátmos
Náxos
Páros
Mílos
Síkinos
Íos
Thíra
Amorgós
Astipálaia
Kos
Tílos
Sími
Kárpathos
Kásos

ÆGEAN SEA

Kikládhes

Dhodhekánisos

Ródhos (Rhodes)

TURKEY

Kerkeçu
Bursa
Ulubat Gölü
Uluabat
Orhaneli
Dursunbey
Sinav
Emet
Kütahya
Demirci
Gediz
Eşme
Simav
Kula
Alaşehir
Saṛhisar
Balıkesir
Edremit
Bergama
Soma
Akhisar
Manisa
Turgutlu
Salihli
Ödemiş
Tire
Aydın
Nazilli
Ayvalık
Mitilíni
Foça
Karaburun
Çeşme
Sevrihisar
Urla
İZMIR (Smyrna)
Menemen
Seferihisar
Kuşadası
Söke
Aydın
Karacasu
Tavas
Muğla
Yatağan
Milas
Bodrum
Güllük
Oren
Marmaris
Köyceğiz
Dalaman
Fethiye

Karia

Akra Pinnes
Kassándra

Samothráki 1600
Gökçeada
Bozcaada
Kaz Daği
Baba Burnu
Çanakkale
Gelibolu
Çan
Biga
Bandırma
Gönen
Susurluk
Karabiga

Thásos
Móudhros

G
F
E
D

6   5   4   3   2   1

1 : 10 000 000

100   50   0   50   100   150   200 miles
100   0   100   200   300 km

1. Karachey-Cherkessia
2. Kabardino-Balkaria
3. North Ossetia
4. Ingushetia

Projection: Conic with two standard parallels 30

35 East from Greenwich

CARTOGRAPHY BY PHILIP'S

m   4000   2000   1000   400   200   0   200   600   1000   2000   4000
ft   12 000   6000   3000   1200   600   0   600   3000   6000   12 000

C   B   A

0   20   40   60   80

ARCTIC

GREENLAND

Svalbard

ICELAND   Arctic Circle

D

Barents Sea   Novaya Zemlya

Kara Sea

ATLANTIC

UNITED KINGDOM

NORWAY

Murmansk

Vorkuta

Ob   Salekhard

R U

OCEAN

North Sea

SWEDEN

FINLAND

White Sea   Arkhangelsk

LONDON

PARIS

FRANCE

GERMANY

Berlin

ST. PETERSBURG

E

Warsaw

Prague

Vienna

Nizhniy Novgorod

MOSCOW

Kazan

Perm

Ufa

Yekaterinburg   Irtysh

Chelyabinsk

Omsk

E u r o p e

ITALY

Rome

Belgrade

UKRAINE

Volga

Samara

Astana

Pavlodar

Karaganda

Athens

Danube

Black Sea

Odessa

Don

Rostov

Volgograd

Astrakhan

K A Z A K S T A N

F

ISTANBUL

GEORGIA

Caspian Sea

Aral Sea

Syrdarya

L. Balkhash

Bursa

Ankara

Izmir

Konya

TURKEY

Yerevan

Tbilisi

AZERBAIJAN

UZBEKISTAN

Alma Ata

Nicosia

CYPRUS

Beirut

Adana

ARMENIA

Baku

Tashkent

Bishkek

KYRGYZSTAN

LEBANON

Aleppo

Tabriz

TURKMENISTAN

Samarkand

Kashi

G

LIBYA

Alexandria

ISRAEL

SYRIA

Damascus

Mosul

Euphrates

Ashkhabad

Mashhad

TAJIKISTAN

Dushanbe

JAMMU & KASHMIR

CAIRO

Jerusalem

Amman

JORDAN

Baghdad

Tigris

IRAN

TEHRĀN

Eşfahān

Herāt

Kābul

Islamabad

Suez

IRAQ

Basra

Kuwait

AFGHANISTAN

Qandahār

Faisalabad

Lahore

EGYPT

Nile

Aswān

KUWAIT

Shīrāz

Zāhedān

PAKISTAN

DELHI

New Delhi

SAUDI

BAHRAIN

Riyadh

QATAR

Manāmah

Doha

The Gulf

G. of Oman

Jaipur

Lucknow

H

Port Sudan

Medina

Jedda

Mecca

ARABIA

Abu Dhabi

UNITED ARAB EMIRATES

Muscat

KARACHI

Indus

Kanpur

Varan

I N D I

SUDAN

Khartoum

ERITREA

Ahmadabad

Vadodara

Indore

Bhopal

Nag

Surat

Sana'

Aden

YEMEN

G. of Oman

Arabian

MUMBAI (Bombay)

Pune

Hyder

DJIBOUTI

G. of Aden

Socotra (Yemen)

Sea

J

A

Addis Ababa

ETHIOPIA

SOMALI

REP.

Lakshadweep Is. (India)

Bangalore

CH (Ma

UGANDA

f

L. Victoria

KENYA

Madurai

Mogadishu

Equator

Colombo

S

K

CONGO (DEM. REP. OF THE)

Nairobi

r

MALDIVES

Male

I N D I A N   O

TANZANIA

Mombasa

i

c

Dar es Salaam

SEYCHELLES

a

L

ZAMBIA

MALAWI

Aldabra Is. (Seychelles)

Amirante Is. (Seychelles)

Victoria

Chagos Arch. (U.K.)

Projection: *Bonne* 30

6   40   7   8   50 Hanoi ● Capital Cities   9   60   10   70 East from Greenwich   80   11

1:67 000 000

| 200 | 0 | 200 | 400 | 600 | 800 | 1000 | 1200 miles |
| 200 | 0 | 400 | 800 | 1200 | 1600 | 2000 km |

B   C   D

OCEAN

naya
olya
New
Siberian
Is.
Wrangel I.
ALASKA
(U.S.A.)

Laptev Sea

Bering
Sea
Aleutian Is.
(U.S.A.)
50

Khatanga
Verkhoyansk
Gizhiga
Okhotsk
Magadan
Petropavlovsk-
Kamchatskiy

A S I A
Lena
Sea of
Okhotsk
40

Yakutsk

Sakhalin

Komsomolsk

E

Angara
Krasnoyarsk
Bratsk
L. Baikal
Chita
Khabarovsk
Yuzhno-
Sakhalinsk

Kuril Is.
40

irsk
vokuznetsk
Irkutsk
Ulan Ude
Blagoveshchensk
Hailar
Qiqihar
Vladivostok
Hokkaidō
Sapporo

F

Ürümqi
Ulan Bator
Harbin
Changchun
Jilin
Sea of
Japan
Honshū
TŌKYŌ
30

Hami
M O N G O L I A
SHENYANG
Anshan
NORTH
KOREA
P'yongyang
Yokohama
JAPAN

Yumen
Baotou
Jinzhou
Daljan
SEOUL
Kyoto
Nagoya
Osaka

G

Lanzhou
BEIJING
TIANJIN
SOUTH
Pusan
KOREA
Hiroshima
Kitakyushū
Bonin Is.
(Japan)

Taiyuan
Jinan
Yellow
Sea

C H I N A
Xi'an
Jinan
Hwang-ho
East
Volcano Is.
(Japan)
Tropic of Cancer
20

T
Chengdu
Wuhan
Nanjing
SHANGHAI
China
Ryukyu Is.

Lhasa
Yangtze
Changsha
HANGZHOU
Nanchang
Fuzhou
Sea

Thimphu
BHUTAN
CHONGQING
Taipei
TAIWAN

du
BANGLADESH
Kunming
GUANGZHOU
HONG KONG
H

a
DACCA
BURMA
(MYANMAR)
Chittagong
Si Kiang
Macau
GUAM
(U.S.A.)

TTA
Hanoi
Haiphong
Hainan
Luzon
FED. STATES
OF MICRONESIA

Bay of
Bengal
LAOS
Vientiane
VIETNAM
MANILA
PHILIPPINES
PALAU
J

Andaman Is.
(India)
Rangoon
THAILAND
BANGKOK
Cebu
Mindanao

Nicobar Is.
(India)
CAMBODIA
Phnom Penh
Ho Chi Minh
City
Palawan
Sulu
Sea
Davao
Zamboanga

G. of
Thailand
South China Sea
Celebes
Sea
Manado
Halmahera
K

Str. of Malacca
Medan
PEN.
MALAYSIA
Kuala Lumpur
BRUNEI
SABAH
Bandar Seri Begawan
IRIAN
JAYA

AN
M A L A Y S I A
SINGAPORE
SARAWAK
Ceram
Ambon

Sumatra
Borneo
Celebes
I N D O N E S I A
Banda
Sea
L

Palembang
Banjarmasin
Ujung Pandang
Arafura Sea

JAKARTA
Semarang
Surabaya
Java Sea
Flores
Timor
Timor Sea
AUSTRALIA

Bandung
Java
Sumba

CARTOGRAPHY BY PHILIP'S.

2   13   14   15   16   17

PACIFIC

OCEAN

D   E

9

CARTOGRAPHY BY PHILIP'S.

80

8

70

East from Greenwich

7

60

Projection: Conical Orthomorphic with two standard parallels

40

F

G

6

Sym
Maksimkin Yar
Bogotol
Chulym

Loptok
Belyy Yar
Chuym
Kolpashevo
Mariinsk
Kemerovo
Leninsk-Kuznetskiy
Novo-
kuznetsk
GORNO-ALTAY
Belukha
4506

Ket
Ob
Molchanovo
Anzhero Sudzhensk
Kiselevsk
Prokopyevsk
Gorno-Altaysk
(Oirot-Tura)

Narym
Kargat
Tomsk
Topki
Belovo

Kargasok
Kolpashevo
Tara
Kargat
Barabinsk
Novosibirsk
Cherepanovo
Biysk
Aleisk
Rubtsovsk
Zmeinogorsk

Tyukalinsk
Om
Barabinsk
Kainsk
Kamen
Barnaul
Khrebet Tarabagatay

Kurgan
Petropavl
Omsk
Isilkul
Ekibastuz
Semey

Chelyabinsk
Kopeysk
Kustanay
Astana
Temirtau
Karaghandy
1565

KAZAKHSTAN

Pavlodar

URUMQI

5445

XINJIANG

CHINA

K. Pobedy
7439

Almaty
ALMATY

KYRGYZSTAN
7495

TAJIKISTAN
Dushanbe

UZBEKISTAN

Tashkent

Samarkand

TURKMENISTAN

Ashgabat

AFGHANISTAN

Herat

Mashhad
331.6

IRAN

Tehran

Esfahan

Baku
996

AZERBAIJAN

GEORGIA

ARMENIA

Tbilisi

Yerevan

Tabriz

TURKEY

Erzurum
5165

Black Sea

Volgograd

Astrakhan

Rostov

Baghdad

IRAQ

m   ft
600

400

200

0

200

600

1200

3000

6000

12 000

4000

2000

1000

400

200

0

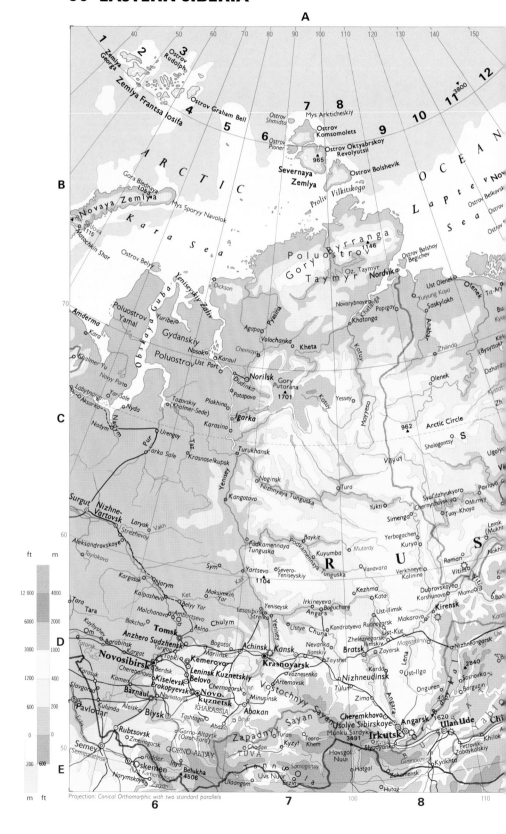

A

40 50 60 70 80 90 100 110 120 130 140 150

1 2 3 4 5 6 7 8 9 10 11 12

Zemlya
Georga
Zemlya Frantsa Iosifa
Ostrov
Rudolph.
Ostrov Graham Bell

3800

B

ARCTIC OCEAN

Ostrov
Shmidta
Mys Arkticheskiy
Ostrov
Komsomolets
Ostrov
Pioner
Ostrov Oktyabrskoy
Revolyutsii
965
Severnaya
Zemlya
Ostrov Bolshevik

Laptev Nov

Gora Blednaya
1053
Novaya Zemlya
Mys Sporyy Navolok
Proliv Vilkitskogo
Ostrov Belkov
Ostr

Sedova
1115
Matochkin Shar
Ostrov Belyy
Kara Sea
Poluostrov
Goryu Ostrov 146
Byrranga
Taymyr
Oz. Taymyr
Nordvik
Ostrov Bolshoy
Begichev
Ust Olenek
Yurung Kaya
Saskylakh
Olenek
Tit-Ar
Bu

70

Amderma
Poluostrov
Yamal
Yeniseyskiy Zaliv
Dickson
Pyasina
Novorybnoye
Khatanga
Popigay
Anabar
Zhilinda
Dzhard

Khalmer Yu
Kara
Obskaya Guba
Yuribey
Gydanskiy
Agapa
Volochanka
Kheta
Kotuy
Olenek
Kystat
Zh

Novy Porto
Nosok
Karaul
Poluostrov
Ust Port
Norilsk
Gory
Putorana
1701
Yessey
Mogyeto
962 Arctic Circle
S
Ugoly

C

Labytnangi
Aksarka
Yar Sale
Nyda
Tazovskiy
(Khalmer-Sede)
Plakhino
Potapovo
Dudinka
Kotuy
Olenek

Nadym
Nagym
Pur
Urengoy
Tarko Sale
Taz
Karasino
Igarka
Krasnoselkupsk
Turukhansk
Viluy
Shologontsy
S

Surgut
Nizhne-
Vartovsk
Laryak
Vakh
Strezhevoy
Yenisey
Noginsk
Nizhnyaya Tunguska
Tura
Yukti
Syul'dzhyukyoro
Chernyshovskiy
Mirnyy
Tuoy-Khaya
Pavlov
Vi

60

Aleksandrovskoye
Taylakova
Sym
Podkamennaya
Tunguska
Baykit
Podkamennaya
Tunguska
Kuyumba
Mutoray
Vanavara
Yerbogachen
Kurya
Roman
Vitim
Lensk
(Mukht
Nokht

ft m

12 000 4000

6000 2000

3000 1000

1200 400

600 200

0 0

200 600

50

m ft

Kargasok
Narym
Belyy Yar
Yartsevo
Severo-
Yeniseyskiy
1104
R U S
Verkhneye
Kalinino

Tara Tara
Kalpashevo
Ket
Maksimkin
Yar
Lesosibirsk
Strelka
Yeniseysk
Irkineyeva
Boguchany
Kezhma
Kata
Ust-Ilimsk
Korshunovo
Dubrovskoye
Mamo
Bod

Kurbyshev
Om
Barabinsk
Molchanovo
Ambortsevo
Asino
Chulym
Ustye Chuna
Angara
Nevanka
Kondratyevo Rudnogorsk
Makarovo
Ust-Kut
Kirensk

Tatarsk
Bakchar
Tomsk
Anzhero Sudzhensk
Bogotol
Marilinsk
Achinsk
Kansk
Ilanskiy
Zheleznogorsk
Tayshet
Zayarsk
Magistralnyy
Nizhneangarsk

D

Novosibirsk
Berdsk
Topki
Kemerovo
Leninsk Kuznetskiy
Belovo
Krasnoyarsk
Artemovsk
Tulun
Zima
Karda
Bratsk
Ust-Ilga
Onguren
2840
Sosnovka

Kargat
Cherepanovo
Kiselevsk
Chernogorsk
Minusinsk
Vostochnyy
Tulun
Nizhneudinsk
452
Barguzin

Slavgorod
Kamen
Prokopyevsk
Novo-
kuznetsk
Naoatayst
Abakan
KHAKASSIA
Beya
Sayan
Cheremkhovo
1620
Munku Sardyk
Ulan Ude
Chi

Pavlodar
Barnaul
Biysk
Kulunda
Aleisk
Tashtagol
Abaza
Zapadnyy
Sayan
Turan
Toora-
Khem
Usolye Sibirskoye
3491
Angarsk
Irkutsk
Kyrer

Rubtsovsk
Zmeinogorsk
Gorno-Altaysk
(Oirot-Tura)
Chadan
Kyzyl
TUVA
Munku Sardyk
Slyudyanka
Petrovsk-
Zabaykalskiy
Khilok

Semey
(Semipalatinsk)
Oskemen
Belukha
4506
Inya
Narymskoye
Ust Kamenogorsk
Narymskaya
Ulaangom
Uvs Nuur
Erzin
Hovsgol
Nuur
Hatgal
Samagaltay
Zakamensk
Gusinoozersk
Kyakhta
Hutag

Projection: Conical Orthomorphic with two standard parallels

SOUTHERN HONSHU, KYUSHU AND SHIKOKU

SEA OF JAPAN

PACIFIC

Sea of Okhotsk

HOKKAIDO

SAPPORO

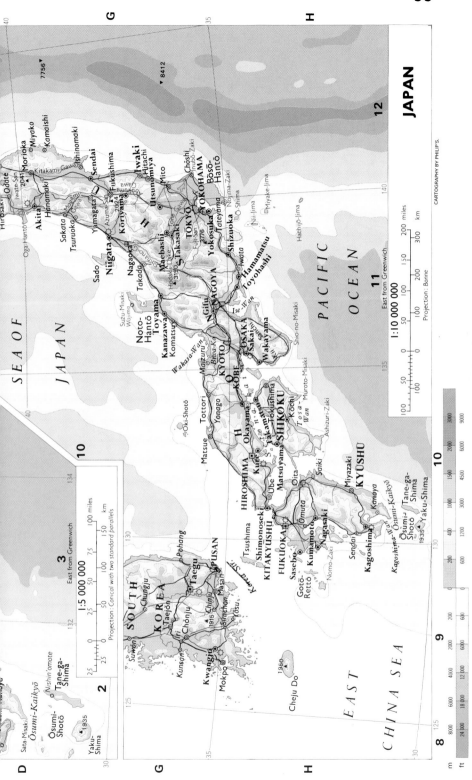

JAPAN

12

CARTOGRAPHY BY PHILIP'S.

1:10 000 000

East from Greenwich

Projection: Bonne

0   50   100   150   200 miles
0   100 200   300   km

11

PACIFIC

OCEAN

SEA OF

JAPAN

1:5 000 000

East from Greenwich

0   25   50   75   100 miles
25   50   100 150 km

Projection: Conical with two standard parallels

3

2

SOUTH

KOREA

PUSAN

Seoul

EAST

CHINA SEA

KYŪSHŪ

SHIKOKU

HIROSHIMA

OSAKA

KYOTO

KOBE

NAGOYA

TOKYO

YOKOHAMA

Sendai

Akita

Niigata

10

9

8

m   ft
24 000
8000   18 000
6000   12 000
4000
2000   6000
1000   3000
600   2000
400   1200
200   600
0   0

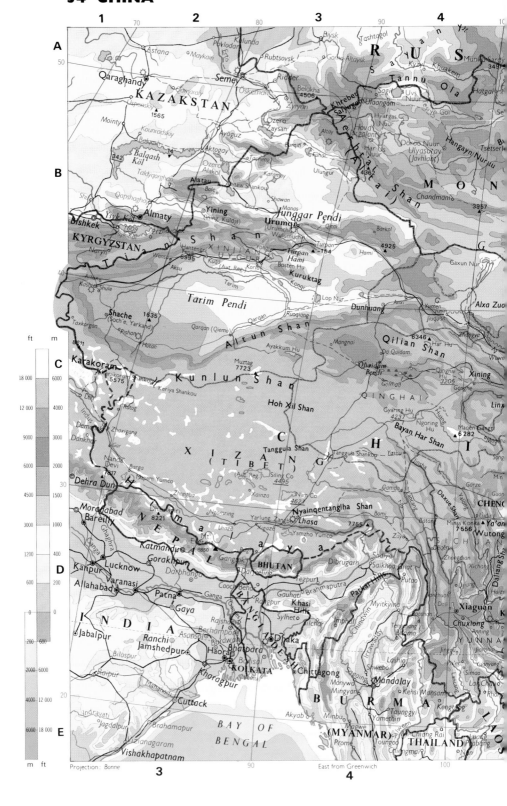

Projection: Bonne

East from Greenwich

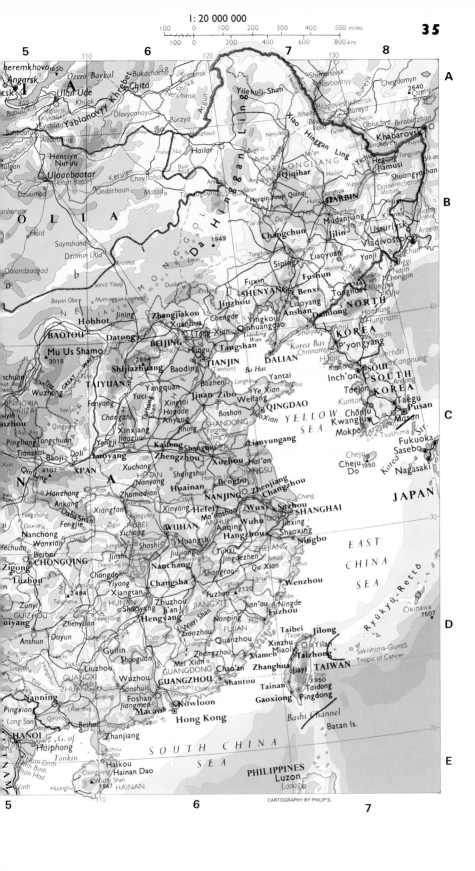

CARTOGRAPHY BY PHILIP'S.

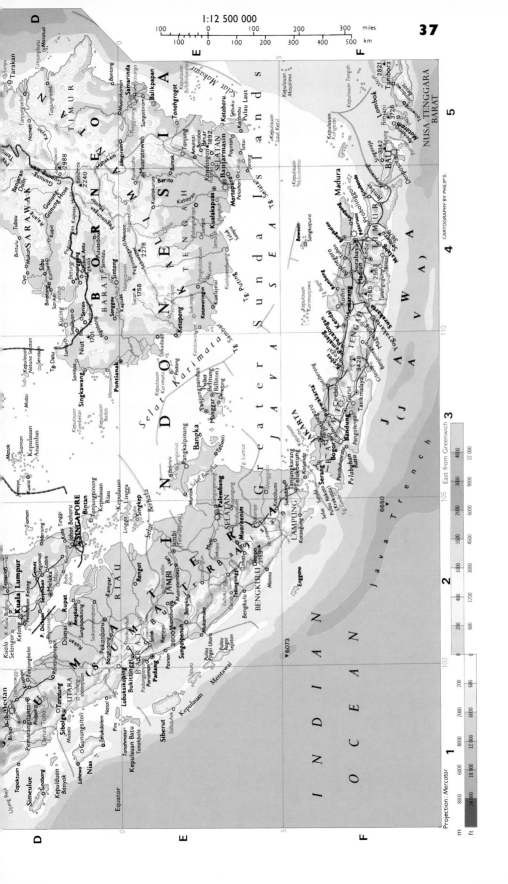

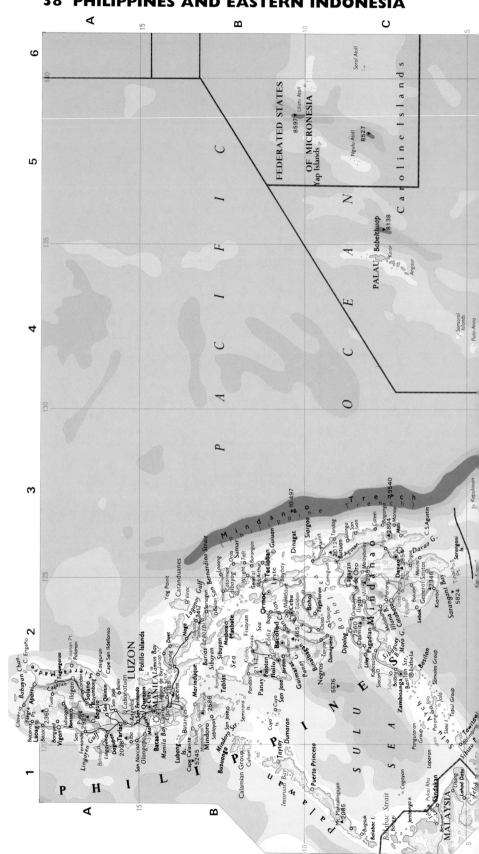

PACIFIC OCEAN

FEDERATED STATES
OF MICRONESIA
Yap Islands

Sorol Atoll

Ulithi Atoll 8597

Ngulu Atoll 8527

Caroline Islands

PALAU Babelthuap 8138
Koror
Angaur

Sonsorol
Islands

Pulo-Anna

Philippine Trench

Mindanao Trench 10,497

9540

Kepulauan

PHILIPPINE SEA

LUZON

MANILA

Polillo Islands

Lingayen Gulf

Babuyan Chan.

C. Engaño

Aparri
Laoag
Vigan

Baguio

San Fernando
Tarlac

Angeles
Quezon City
Bataan
Manila Bay

Mindoro

Batangas

Lubang Is.

Calamian Group

Mindoro Str.

Busuanga

Puerto Princesa

PHILIPPINES

Calavite

Marinduque
Tablas
Masbate
Panay
Iloilo
Negros
Bacolod
Cebu
Bohol
Dumaguete
Tagbilaran

Samar
Tacloban
Leyte

Catanduanes

Legaspi

Bicol

Sorsogon

San Bernardino Strait

Dinagat
Siargao

Surigao
Butuan

Cagayan de Oro

Mindanao

Davao
Davao G.

C. S. Agustin

Sarangani Pt.

Zamboanga

Basilan

Jolo

SULU SEA

MALAYSIA

Sandakan

Balabac Strait

Tawitawi

1:12 500 000

100   0   100   200   300 miles
100 0 100 200 300 400 500 km

PAPUA NEW GUINEA

Equator

I R I A N J A Y A

Pegunungan Maoke
Pegunungan Sudirman

Puncak Jaya 5029
Puncak Trikora 4750

Merauke

A R A F U R A   S E A

CARTOGRAPHY BY PHILIP'S

East from Greenwich

Projection Mercator

Teluk Cenderawasih

Yapen
Biak

Kepulauan Mapia

Halmahere

Morotai

Ternate
Tidore

Obi

Misool

Waigeo

Salawati

Jazirah Doberai
3100

S E R A M   S E A

Seram
Wahai
3019

Buru
2429 Namlea
5888

Ambon

Kep. Bacan
4370

B A N D A   S E A

MALUKU
7440

Kepulauan Kai

Kepulauan Aru
Wokam

Trangan
Tanimbar
Yamdena

Kepulauan Tanimbar

Kep. Sula

Kepulauan Banggai

SULAWESI
(CELEBES)

UTARA

Manado 2022

TENGAH
3311

SELATAN
Ujung Pandang

TENGGARA
Kendari

Buton
Muna

Kabaena

F L O R E S   S E A

Lesser Sunda Islands

Flores
Ende

Sumbawa
Bima

Sumba
Waingapu

Sawu Sea

Kupang
Roti

TIMOR TIMUR
2920

Wetar

Alor

C E L E B E S
S E A

Kepulauan Sangihe

Kepulauan Talaud

I N D O N E S I A

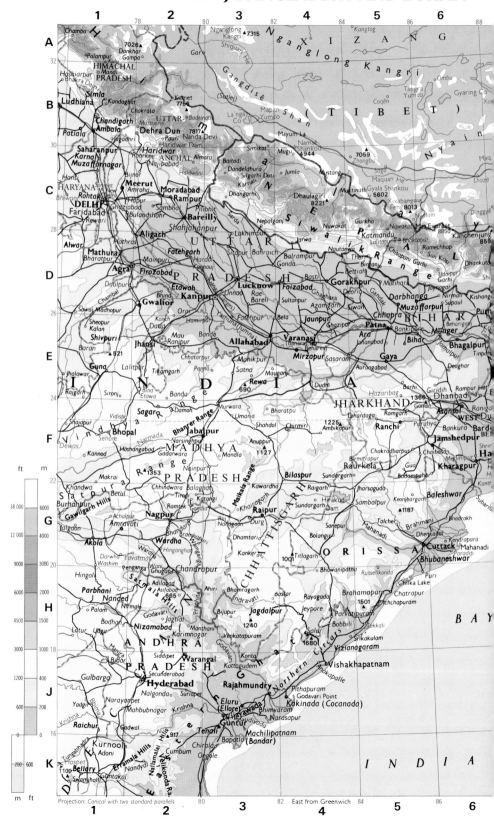

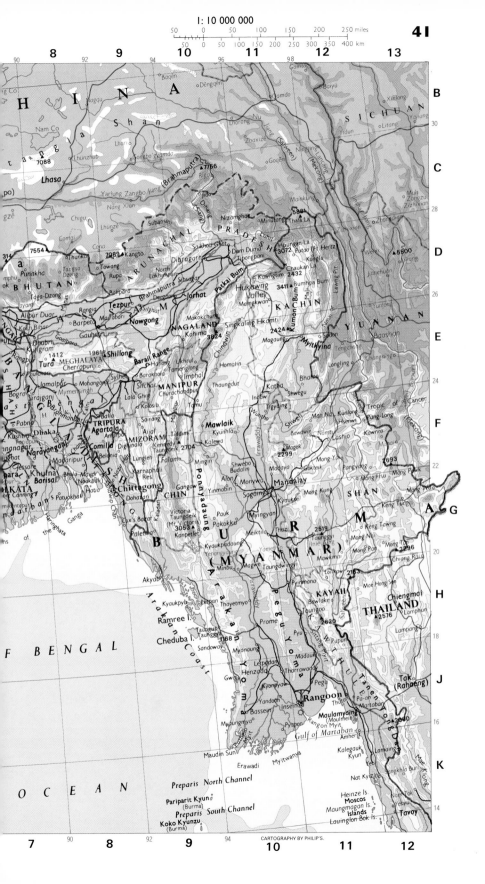

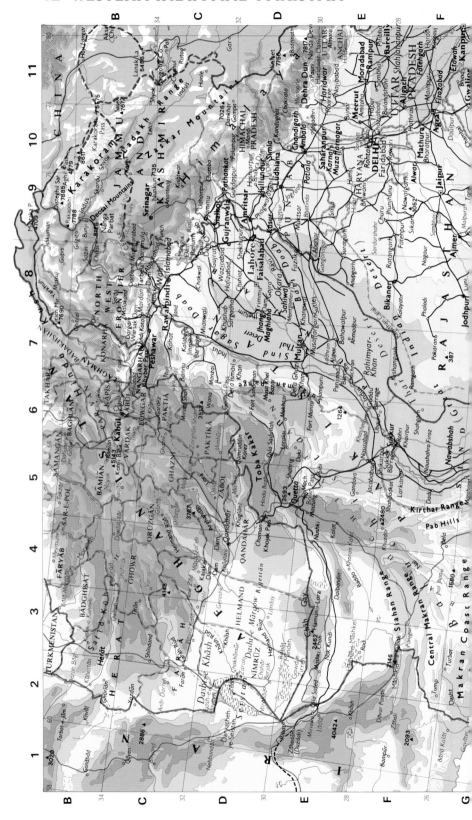

1:10 000 000

CARTOGRAPHY BY PHILIP'S.

Continuation Southwards on same scale

Projection: Conical with two standard parallels

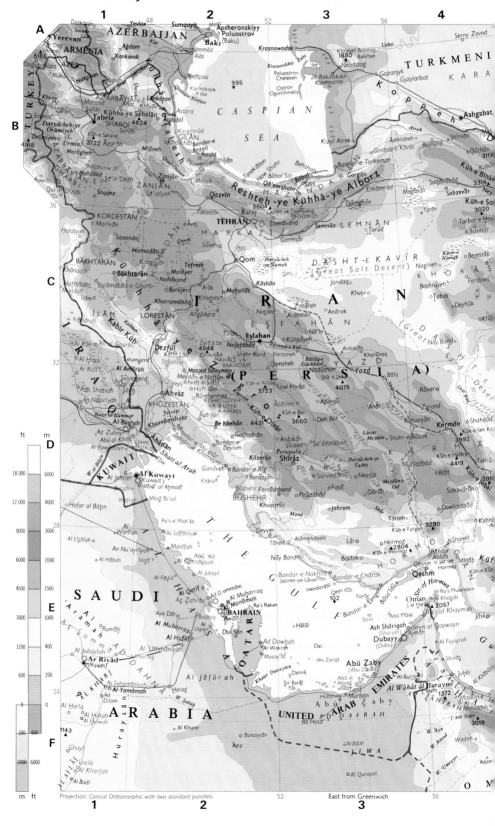

Projection: Conical Orthomorphic with two standard parallels   East from Greenwich

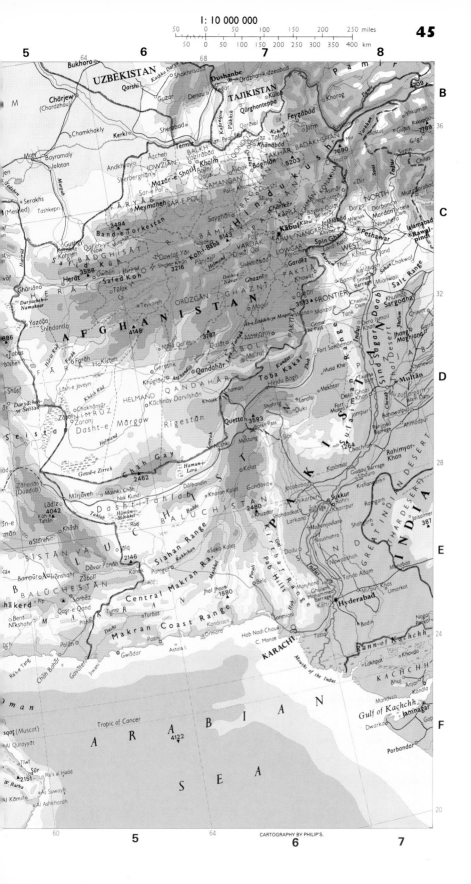

1: 10 000 000

50   0   50   100   150   200   250 miles

50   0   50   100   150   200   250   300   350   400 km

UZBEKISTAN

TAJIKISTAN

Bukhoro
Chärjew
(Chardzhou)
Qarshi
Shakhrisabz
Denou
Guzar
Sherobod
Termiz
Dushanbe
Ordzhonikidzeabad
Hisor
Qürghonteppa
Külob
Khorog
Pamir

Mary
Bayramaly
Iolotan
Kerki
Andkhvoy
Sheberghan
Aqcheh
Mazār-e Sharif
Kholm
BALKH
Vozirabad
Feyzābād
Jorm
Qondöz
Khānābād
TAKHAR
BADAKHSHĀN
Chitrāl
Gilgit

Chamkhakly
Serakhs
Tashkepri
(Meshed)
Gushgy
Kohneh
SAR-E-POL
Sar-e Pol
SAMANGĀN
Pol-e Khomri
Boyni
Dowshi
Baghlān
Qara
Asmār
Dargal
Darband
Mardan
Peshāwar
Rawal-
pindi
Islāmābād

Meymaneh
FĀRYĀB
Band-e Torkestān
BĀDGHISĀT
Dowlat Yār
Kohi-Bābā
Panjāb
Charīkār
Kābul
NANGARHĀR
Jalālābād
Spin Ghar
WEST

Herāt
Owbeh
Safed Koh
GHŌR
Shahrak
Diwal Qol
VARDAK
LOWGAR
Gardēz
PAKTIĀ
Khowst
Bannu
Salt Range
Sargodha

HERĀT
Ghūriāno
Daryācheh-ye
Namaksar
Yazdān
Shindand
Tevvareh
ORŪZGĀN
GHAZNĪ
Ghazni
Mogor
Moqor
Qalāt
PAKTĪKĀ
Manzari
Pass
Fort Sandeman
INDIA

Ḥokrteh
FĀRĀH
Farah
Gereshk
Qandahār
Māruf
Toba Kakar
Hindu Bagh
Quetta
Kalat
Mirpur

Lāsh-e Joveyn
Chakhānsūr
ZābolNIMRUZ
Zaranj
Dasht-e Margow
HELMAND
Rigestān
Bolan Pass
Sukkur
KARACHI

SEISTĀN
BALŪCHESTĀN
Baluchistan
Siahan Range
Central Makran Range
Makran Coast Range
Gwādar
Karāchi
Hyderabad
Mouths of the Indus

ARABIAN SEA

Tropic of Cancer

OMAN
sqat (Muscat)
Al Qurayyāt
Sūr
Ra's al Hadd

Gulf of Kachchh
Jamnagar
Porbandar
KACHCHH

CARTOGRAPHY BY PHILIP'S.

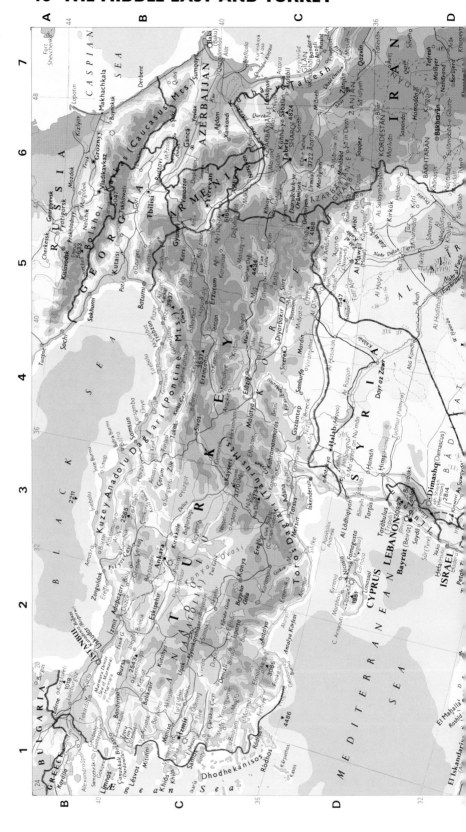

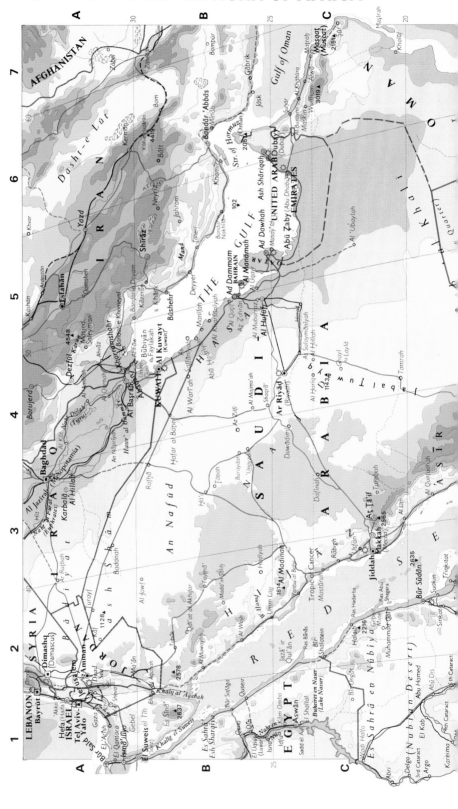

1: 15 000 000

100 0 100 200 300 400 miles
100 0 100 200 300 400 500 600 km

49

CARTOGRAPHY BY PHILIP'S.

Projection: Sonson-Flamsteed's Sinusoidal

East from Greenwich

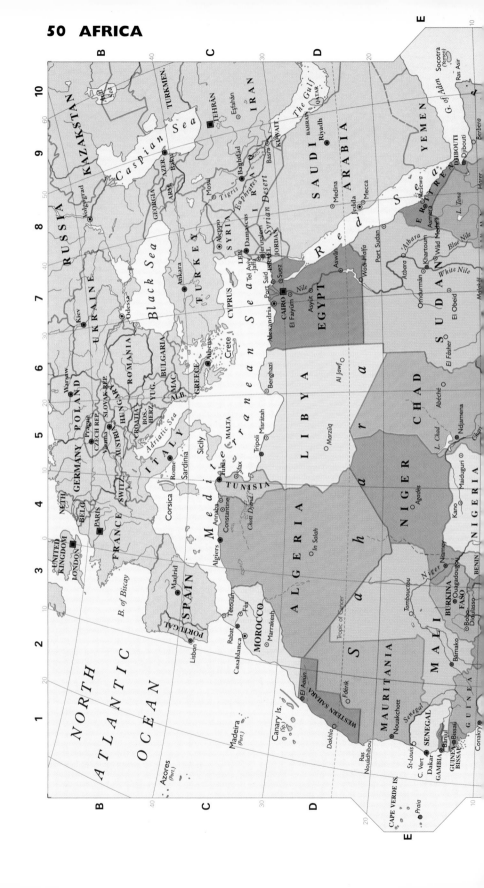

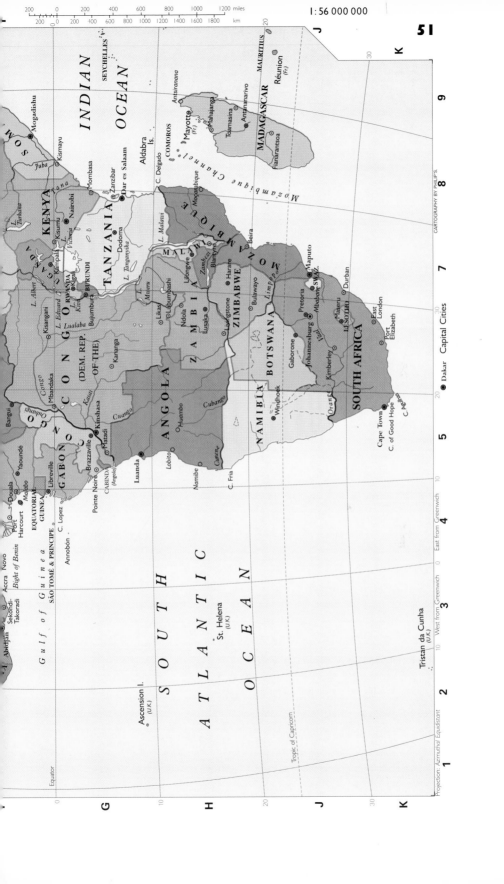

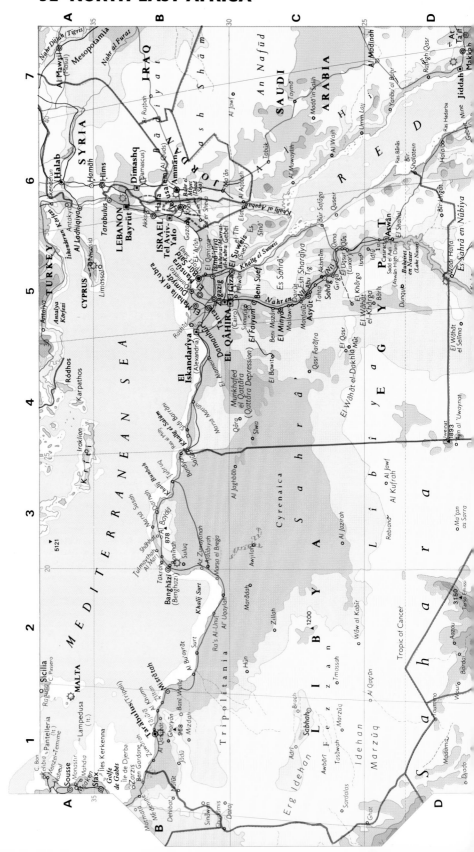

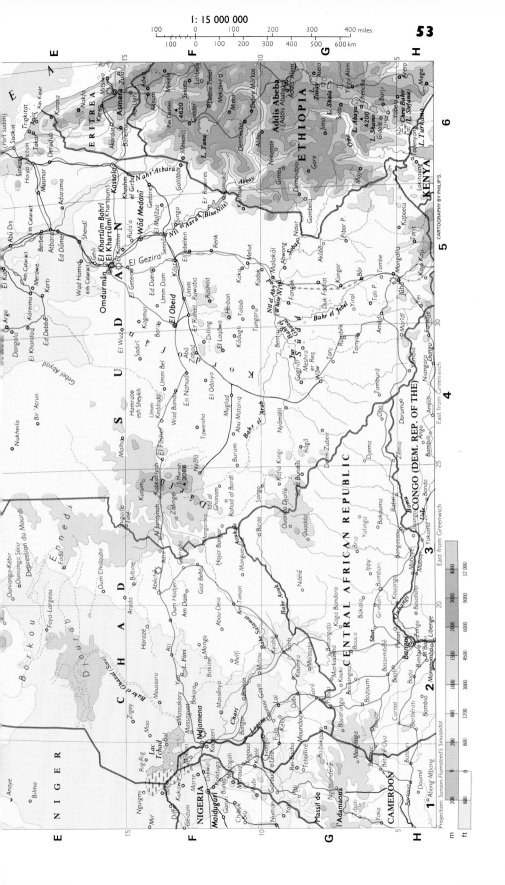

1: 15 000 000

100   0   100   200   300   400 miles
100   0   100   200   300   400   600 km

CARTOGRAPHY BY PHILIP'S.

Projection: Sanson-Flamsteed's Sinusoidal

m   ft

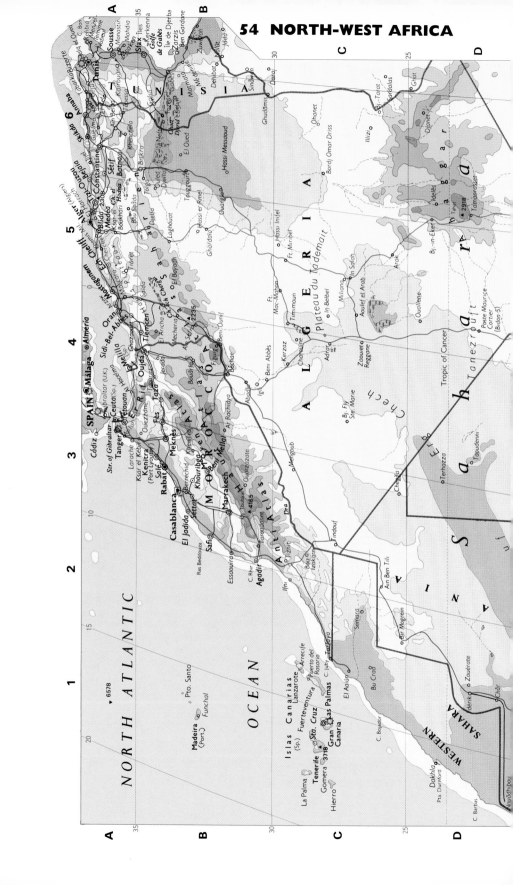

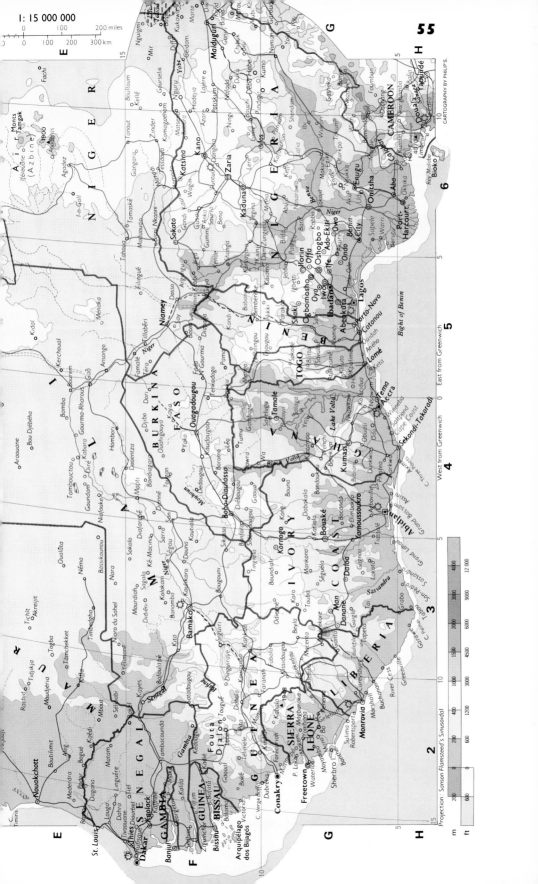

1 : 15 000 000

100   200 miles

0   100   200
0   200   300 km

CARTOGRAPHY BY PHILIP'S

Projection : Sanson Flamsteed's Sinusoidal

m
ft

200   0   200   400   600   1000   1500   2000   3000   4000
600   0   600   1200   3000   4500   6000   9000   12 000

1   10   2   15   3   20   4

A

N I G E R

Tanout · Boultoum · Nguigmi · Zigey · Bahr el Ghazal (Soro) · Arada · Biltine · Shigaibo · Tiné

Gangara · 15 · Kellé · Mir · Rig-Rig · Mao · Moussoro · Abéché · Adré · Al Junaynah

Zinder · Gourselik · Bosso · Diffa · Lac Tchad · Bol · Massakory · Yao · Haraze · Oum Hadjer · Am Guereda · Zalingei

Tessaoua · Kamaguenam · Nguru · Yobé · Kukawa · Makari · Massaguet · Bokoro · L. Fitri · Am Dam · Goz Beida · Mongororo

Matsena · Bebura · Hadejia · Lajere · Dikwa · Kousseri · Ndjamena (Fort Lamy) · Mongo · Bitkine · Abou-Deïa · Hajar Bangar · Rahad al B

B

Kano · Azare · Maiduguri · Konduga · Bama · Madagali · Chari · Massenya · Melfi · Am-Timan · Mangueigne · Birao · Ouanda Djall

Dangora · Ning · Potiskum · Nafada · Goniri · Meroua · Yagoua · Bongor · Boussa · Miltou · Bahr Salamat · Sarh · Ndélé · Ouadda

Lere · Bauchi · Duku · Biu · Mubi · Kolélé · Fianga · Léré · Gounou Gaya · Lai · Kéla · Koumra · Bakouma

Jos · Lame · Pindiga · Deba Habe · Numan · Garoua · Pala · Doba · Goré · Baibokoum · Marcounda · Batangafo · Kaga Bandoro · Bria · Yalinga

Kafanchan · Bogoro · Kumo · Rei Bouba · Moundou · Tcholliré · Papou · Bocaranga · Kouki · Bossangoa · Bouca · Bakala · Ippy

C

Oturkpo · Takum · Massif de · Ngaoundéré · l'Adamaoua · Meiganga · Bozoum · Sibut · Grimari · Bambari · Bakouma

Makurdi · Gashaka · Nkambe · Banyo · Tibati · Baboua · Bossembélé · Kouanga · Bangassou

Wum · Bamenda · Foumban · Yoko · Bouar · Carnot · Rossel · Boali · Zongo · Bosobolo · Mobaye · Ouango · Bomu

Mamfe · Bali · Dschang · Bafia · Bertoua · Batouri · Boda · Berbérati · Bimbo · Bangui · Oubangi · Mobayi · Yakoma

D

CAMEROON · Yaoundé · Doumé · Abong Mbang · Nola · Mongoumba · Libenge · Busingo · Gemena · Monveda · Aketi

Calabar · Kumba · Nkongsamba · Nanga-Eboko · Yokadouma · Bambio · M'Baiki · Budjala · Lisala · Bumba · Congo · Busu-Djanoa

Mont Cameroun · Douala · Sanaga · Edéa · M'Balmayo · Sangmélima · Djoum · Lomié · Bomboma · Bongandango · Basankusa · Yahuma

4070 · Limbe · Bioko (Fernando Póo) · Kribi · Campo · Ambam · Bitam · Oyem · Minvoul · Souanke · Moloundou · Dongou · Impfondo · Lulonga · Bolomba · Befale · Djoluo · Isang

E

EQUATORIAL GUINEA · Cabo San Juan · Mbini · Evinayong · Mvadi · Ousye · Belinga · Makokou · Mekambo · Ouesso · Bomongo · Bokote · Boende · Opa

Libreville · Cocobeach · Mitzic · Makoua · Rukp · Mbandaka · Ingende · Irebu · Bokungu · Lomela

Owendo · Kango · Njolé · Booué · GABON · Kellé · Owanda · Ewo · Mosaka · Lukolela · Lac Tumba · Kiri · Monkoto · CONGO

Port-Gentil · Lambaréné · Lastoursville · Okondja · Okoyo · Gamboma · Inongo · Lokolama · Loto · (DEM. REP. OF)

C. Lopez · Ogooué · Fougamou · Koula-Moutou · Franceville · Djambala · L. Mai-Ndombe · Mushie · Kutu · Dekese · Kole · Lodja

Omboué · Iguéla · Moabi · Ndendé · Tchibanga · Mossendjo · Zanaga · Bolobo · Kwamouth · Bandundu · Oshwe · Lukenie · Talo · Lusam

F

Setté Cama · Nyanga · Kibangou · Komono · Sibiti · Mindouli · Kinkala · Brazzaville · Masi-Manimba · Basongo · Idiofa · Mweka · Bena Dibele

Mayumba · Kouilou · Loubomo · Madingou · Luozi · Kinshasa · Kenge · Kikwit · Charlesville · Luebo · Demba · Dimbele

Pointe Noire · Tshela · Madimba · Kasangulu · Gungu · Makumbi · Kananga · Mbu

CABINDA · Cacongo · Mbanza Ngungu · Matadi · Maquela · Popokabaka · Feshi · Kumzumba · Dibaya

Cabinda · Boma · Soyo · Nqoqi · do-Zombo · Kasongo Lunda · Tshikapa · Luiza · Luilu

ATLANTIC · Mbanza Congo · Damba · Sanza Pombo · Kahemba · Luachimo · Luremo · Camissombo · Lucapa · Kapanga

Nzeto · Uige · N'Gage · Camabatela · Caúngula · Capaia · Sandoa

OCEAN · Ambriz · Caxito · Quibaxe · Lubalo · Chiluage · Saurimo · Kai

Luanda · Pta. das Palmeirinhas · Ndalatando · Quela · Malanje · Cacôlo

Muxima · Dondo · Calulo · Cambundi-Catembo · Muconda · Dilolo · Mutsha

G

Gunza · Gabela · A N G O L A · Luau · Luacano

Sumbe · Andulo

ft · m

12 000 · 4000

9000 · 3000

6000 · 2000

4500 · 1500

3000 · 1000

1200 · 400

600 · 200

0 · 0

200 · 600

m · ft

1: 15 000 000

100   0   100   200   300   400 miles
100   0   100   200   300   400   500   600 km

5   6   7   8

A

Omdurmân   El Khartûm Bahrî
El Khartûm
(Khartoum)   Kassala   Akordat   Keren   Mitsiwa   Dahlak Kebir
El Kamlin   Khashm   Adi Ugri   Asmera   Zula
El Wuz   Rufa'a   el Girba   Barentu   ERITREA   Mersa Fatma
El Odaiya   Sodiri   El Geteina   Nahr Atbara   Adwa   Edd
Hamrat   Kagmar   Gedaref   Aksum
esh Sheykh   Wâd Medanî   15
T Fâsher   Umm   Ed Dueim   El Mâfâza   Ras Dashen   Mekele   -116
Keddada   Umm Bel   Bara   Sennâr   4620
Wad Banda   Umm Dam   Gallâbât   Gonder   Sekota
En Nahud   Abû   Umm Ruwaba   Metema   B
El Obeid   Kôsti   Debre   Lalibela
Zabad   Er Rahad   Singa   L. Tana   Tabor   Tendaho
Taweisha   Dilling   El Jebelein   Er Roseires   Mekele
Abu Matariq   Heiban   Renk   Mota   Dese
Muglad   El Laqâwa   Dembecha   Debre Markos
Bahr el 'Arab   Kâdugli   Kaka   Alibo   Ankober   10
Talodi   Kodok   Nekemte   Gedo   Addis Abeba
Nyâmlêll   Tungaru   Malakâl   Gimbi   Addis Alem   Awash
Bentiu   Ntl el Abyad   Abwong   Dembidolo   ETHIOPIA   Asela
Gogrial   White Nile   Fangak   Gore   Jima   L. Ziway
Mesha   Bahr el Ghazal   Nasir   Gambela   L. Shala
er Req   Wâw   Duk Fadiat   Akôbo   Sodo   Goba
Tonj   Rumbêk   Omo   L. Abaya   4307
Tamburâ   Yirol   Bôr   Kongor   Maji   Yirga Alem   Ginir
Amadi   Tali P   Tombe   L. Shamo   Chencha
Mongalla   Kapoeta   Lotagipi   Gidale   Burji
Yambio   Yei   Juba   Swamp   Jarso   Negele
Maridî   Kaja Kaji   Torit   Todenyang   Chew Bahir   Arero   C
Nimule   Lokitaung   (L. Stefanie)   Mega   El Niybo
Faradje   Kitgum   L. Turkana   Moyale
Gulu   Moroto   (L. Rudolf)   El Wak
Aru   Kabarega   Lira   Lodwar   Buna
Mahagi   Falls   Masindi   Mt Elgon   South Horr   Wajir   D
Djugu   UGANDA   Soroti   4321   Kitale   Marsabit   Habaswein   Dif
Bunia   L. Albert   Hoima   L. Kyoga   Tororo   Eldoret   Nyahururu   Isiolo
Beni   Ft Portal   Mubende   Kakamega   Meru
Ruwenzori   Kasese   Jinja   Nakuru   Nyeri   5199   Garissa
5109   Kampala   Kisumu   Kericho   Naivasha   Murang'a   Kitui
Equator   Lufoy   Entebbe   Kisii   Karungu   Thika   0
L. Edward   Masaka   Nairobi   Machakos   Lamu
L. George   Mbarara   L.   Musoma   Loliondo   Magadi   Konza   Garsen
Rutshuru   Kabale   Bukoba   Victoria   Nyahanga   Natron   Makindu   Kibwezi   Formosa
Goma   Ukerewe   Geita   Kilimanjaro   Bay
RWANDA   Kigali   I.   Mwanza   5895   Malindi
Bukavu   Butare   Ngudu   Arusha   Moshi   Taveta   Voi
Mwenga   Uvira   Lake   Manyara   Same
Lac Kivu   Kahama   Eyasi   Mbulu   Mombasa
BURUNDI   Fizi   Kibondo   Bukene   Kilindini
Bujumbura   Nzega   Singida   Kondoa   Korogwe   Tanga
Uvinza   Kasulu   Usoke   Tabora   Lushoto   Pemba I.   5
Kabambare   Kigoma-Ujiji   Kaliua   Manyoni   Kibaya   Handeni
Kongolo   773   Kibwesa   Mpanda   Dodoma   Sadani   Zanzibar
Kabalo   Karema   Rungwa   Mpwapwa   Bagamoyo   Zanzibar I.
Ankoro   Moba   TANZANIA   Iloa   Morogoro   Dar-es-Salaam
Kiambi   Kipili   Sumbawanga   Gt Ruaha   Kisiju
Manono   Molira   L.   Kipembawe   Rufiji   Utete   Mafia I.
Mitwaba   Pweto   Rukwa   Chunya   Mohoro   Kilwa Kivinje
Kilwa   Chiengi   Mbeya   Iringa   Mahenge   Liwale
L. Upemba   L. Mweru   Mbala   Tukuyu   Njombe   Lindi
Kamwamba   Mweru   Rasa   Kasama   L. Nyasa   Nachingwea   Mtwara   10
Kawambwa   Swamp   Isoka   Songea   Tunduru   Mikindani   Cabo
ZAMBIA   Luwingu   Karonga   Manda   Masasi   Newala   Delgado
Likasi   L. Chambeshi   MALAWI   Mbamba Bay   Ruvuma   Moçimboa
Mambilima   Mansa   Bangweulu   Nkhata Bay   da Praia   Palma
Falls   Livingstonia

CARTOGRAPHY BY PHILIP'S.

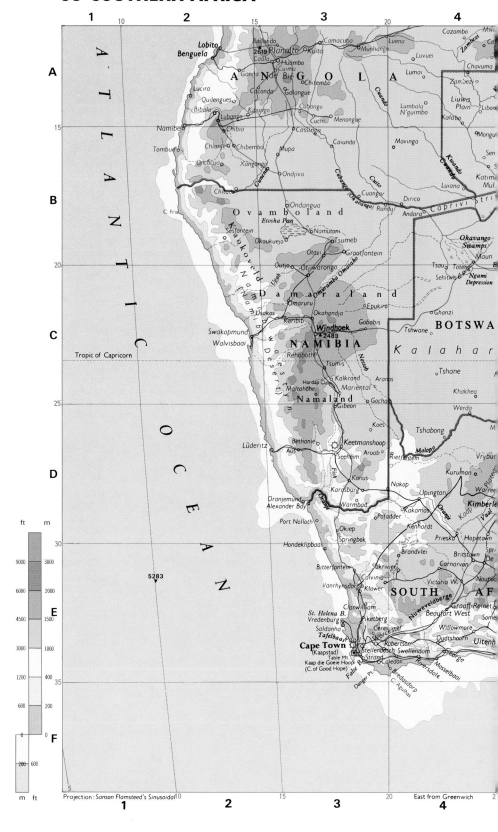

58 SOUTHERN AFRICA

ANGOLA

Lobito
Benguela
Bailundo
Planalto
Camacupa
Munhango
Luena
Cazombo
Mwi
Cadla
Kuito
2619
Zambezi
Caala
Huambo
Cuima
Ganda
Nde
Bie
Chitembo
Luvuei
Chavuma
Zambezi
Lucira
Caconda
Galangue
Lumai
Quilengues
Kubango
Cubango
Cuchi
Menongue
Lumbala N'guimbo
Liuwa Plain
Libon
Bibala
Lubango
Mavinga
Kalabo
Mongu
Namibe
Chibia
Cassinga
Caiundo
Kaundu
Sen
Tombua
Chianje
Chibemba
Mupa
Cubango (Okavango)
Katim Mul
Onbcua
Xangongo
Ondjiva
Cuito
Cuangar
Luiana
Katim Mul
Chitado
Cunene
Cuangar
Dirico
Andara
Capriv
Stri
C. Fria
Ovamboland
Ondangua
Rundu
Okavango Swamps
Sesfontein
Etosha Pan
Namutoni
Tsau
Totes
Maun
Okaukuejo
Tsumeb
Sehitwe
Ngami Depression
Otavi
Grootfontein
Outjo
Otjiwarongo
Omuramba Omatako
Tsu
Ghanzi
BOTSWA
Omaruru
Okahandja
Epukiro
Swakopmund
Karibib
Windhoek 2483
Gobabis
Tshwane
Usakos
NAMIBIA
Rehoboth
Kalahar
Walvisbaai
Tsumis
Nasob
Tsane
Tropic of Capricorn
Kalkrand
Aranos
Khakhea
Hardap Dam
Mariental
Maltahöhe
Gibeon
Gocha
Werda
Namaland
Koes
Tshabong
M
Bethanie
Keetmanshoop
Molop
Vrybu
Lüderitz
Aus
Seeheim
Aroab
Rietfontein
Kuruman
Kimberle
Kanus
Nakop
Upington
Warre
Karasburg
Kakamas
Oranjemund
Warmbad
Pofadder
Kenhardt
Prieska
Hopetown
Alexander Bay
Orange
Kaap
Vaal
Port Nolloth
Okiep
Kakamas
Brandvlei
Britstown
Spr
Springbok
Hondeklipbaai
Sakrivier
Carnarvon
De
Bitterfontein
Calvinia
Victoria W.
Noupo
Vanrhynsdorp
Klawer
SOUTH
AF
Nuweveldberge
Graaff-Reinet
Clanwilliam
Beaufort West
Some
St. Helena B.
Piketberg
Ceres
Witlowmore
Vredenburg
Worcester
Oudtshoorn
Uitenh
Saldanha
Paarl
Robertson
George
Tafelbaai
Stellenbosch
Swellendam
Mosselbaai
Cape Town (Kaapstad)
Strand
Caledon
Riversdale
Table Mt. B.
Kaap die Goeie Hoop (C. of Good Hope)
False B.
Danger Pt.
Bredasdorp
C. Agulhas

A T L A N T I C   O C E A N

5283

Projection: Sanson Flamsteed's Sinusoidal

East from Greenwich

ft	m
9000	3000
6000	2000
4500	1500
3000	1000
1200	400
600	200
0	0
200	600

m   ft

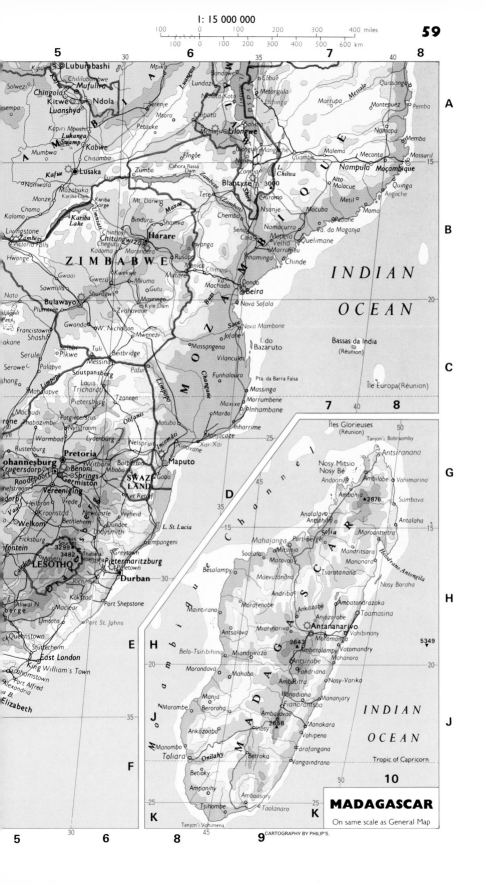

1:15 000 000

100   0   100   200   300   400 miles
100 0 100 200 300 400 500 600 km

59

INDIAN

OCEAN

Bassas da India
(Réunion)

Île Europa(Réunion)

Îles Glorieuses
(Réunion)

Tanjon'i Bobraomby

Antsiranana

Nosy Mitsio
Nosy Bé

Andoany   Ambilobe   Vohimarina

Ambanja   ▲2876   Sambava

Analalava
Antsohihy   Antalaha

Sofia   Maroantsetra

Mahajanga   Port-Berge   Mandritsara

Mitsinjo   Mananara

Soalala   Marovoay

Tsaratanana

Besalampy   Maevatanana   Nosy Boraha

Andriba

Maintirano   Morafenobe   Ankazobe   Ambatondrazaka

Anjozorobe   Toamasina

Antsalova   Miarinarivo   Antananarivo

▲2643   Moramanga   Vohibinany

Belo-Tsiribihina   Miandrivazo   Ambatolampy   Vatomandry

Antsirabe   Mahanoro   5349

Morondava   Mahabo   Ambositra

Manja   Fandriana   Nosy-Varika

Beroroha   Ifanadiana   Mananjary

Morombe   Ambalavao   Fianarantsoa

▲2658   Manakara

Ankazoabo   Ihosy

Manombo   Vohipeno

Toliara   Onilahy   Betroka   Farafangana

Manombo   Vangaindrano

Betioky   Tropic of Capricorn

Ampanihy

Ambaosary   Taolanaro

Tsihombe

Tanjon'i Vohimena

INDIAN

OCEAN

MADAGASCAR

On same scale as General Map

CARTOGRAPHY BY PHILIP'S.

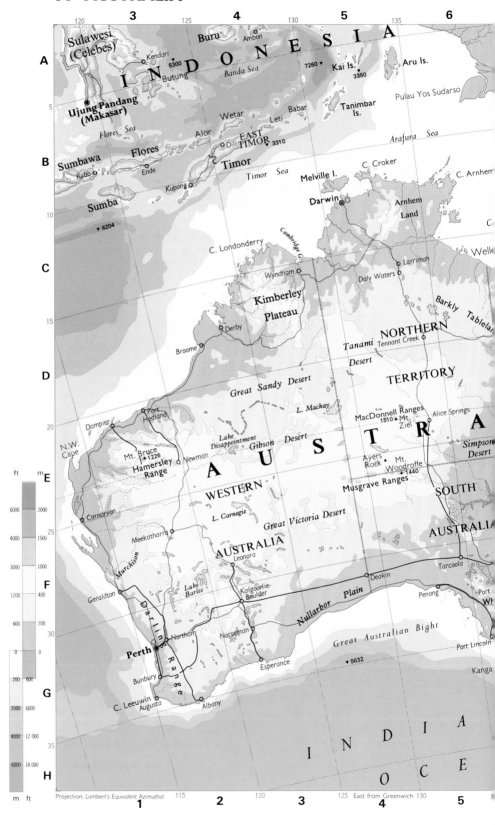

Sulawesi
(Celebes)

Buru

Ambon

I N D O N E S I A

Kendari

Butung

5300

Banda Sea

7260 ▾

Kai Is.

3350

Aru Is.

Pulau Yos Sudarso

Ujung Pandang
(Makasar)

Wetar

Leti

Babar

Tanimbar
Is.

Arafura Sea

Flores Sea

Alor

EAST
TIMOR

Dili

3310

C. Croker

C. Arnhem

Sumbawa

Flores

Timor

Melville I.

Sumba

Baba

Ende

Kupang

Timor Sea

Darwin

Arnhem
Land

6204

C. Londonderry

Cambridge G.

C. Larrimah

We

Wyndham

Daly Waters

Barkly Tablela

Kimberley
Plateau

NORTHERN

Derby

Tanami

Tennant Creek

Broome

Desert

TERRITORY

Great Sandy Desert

L. Mackay

MacDonnell Ranges

Alice Springs

Port
Hedland

1510 ▲ Mt.
Ziel

A

Dampier

Lake
Disappointment

Gibson Desert

U

S

T

R

Simpson
Desert

N.W.
Cape

Mt. Bruce
▲ 1226
Hamersley
Range

Newman

Ayers
Rock ▲

Mt.
Woodroffe
▲ 1440

Carnarvon

WESTERN

Musgrave Ranges

SOUTH

L. Carnegie

Great Victoria Desert

AUSTRALIA

Meekatharra

AUSTRALIA

Murchison

Leonora

Tarcoola

Lake
Barlee

Geraldton

Kalgoorlie-
Boulder

Deakin

Penong

Port

Darling Range

Northam

Norseman

Nullarbor Plain

Wh

Perth

Esperance

Great Australian Bight

5632 ▾

Port Lincoln

Bunbury

Kanga

C. Leeuwin
Augusta

Albany

I N D I A

O C E

Scale (left side):

ft	m
6000	2000
4000	1500
3000	1000
1200	400
600	200
0	0
200	600
2000	6000
4000	12 000
6000	18 000

m ft

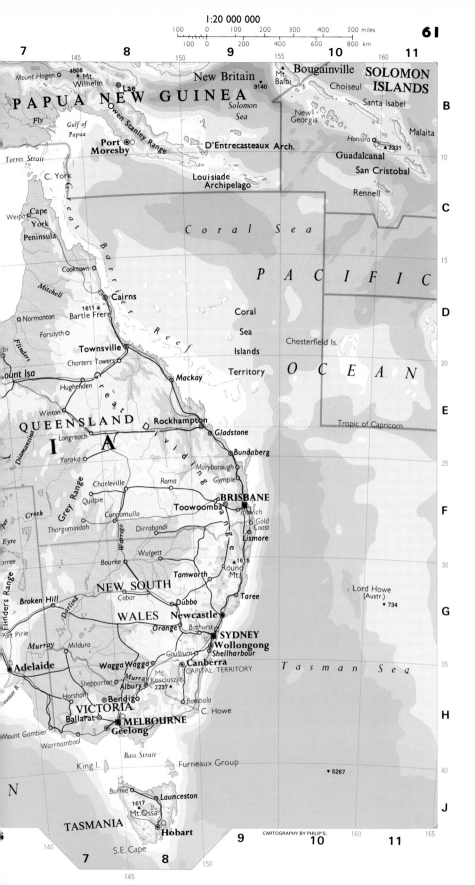

1:20 000 000

100 0 100 200 300 400 500 miles
100 0 200 400 600 800 km

7   8   9   10   11

PAPUA NEW GUINEA

Mount Hagen   4508 Mt.
                Wilhelm   Lae
                           9140
Fly   Owen Stanley Range
Gulf of
Papua
Port
Moresby

New Britain
Solomon
Sea

Mt.
Balbi   **Bougainville**   **SOLOMON**
         Choiseul   **ISLANDS**
         Santa Isabel

D'Entrecasteaux Arch.

New
Georgia

Malaita

B

Honiara   2331
Guadalcanal
San Cristobal

Louisiade
Archipelago

Torres Strait
C. York

Weipa   Cape
         York
         Peninsula

Cooktown

Mitchell

Cairns
1611   Bartle Frere

Normanton
Forsayth

Flinders

ount Isa   Townsville
Charters Towers

Hughenden

Winton   **QUEENSLAND**

Longreach

Diamantina

Yaraka

Grey Range

Charleville
Quilpie

Cunnamulla
Thargomindah

Creek

Eyre

arree

Flinders Range

Port Pirie

Broken Hill

Murray   Mildura

Adelaide

Mount Gambier

Warrnambool

N

140

7   8   9

150

Coral   Sea

PACIFIC

Coral
Sea
Islands
Territory

Chesterfield Is.

Rennell

C

15

D

20

OCEAN

E

Mackay

Rockhampton
Gladstone
Bundaberg
Maryborough
Gympie

Roma

Dirranbandi

Walgett

Cobar

Round
Mt.
1615

Tamworth

NEW SOUTH
WALES   **Newcastle**

Orange   Bathurst

Goulburn   **SYDNEY**
Wollongong
Shellharbour

Canberra
CAPITAL TERRITORY

BRISBANE
Ipswich
Gold
Coast
Lismore

Toowoomba

Bourke

Dubbo

Taree

Lord Howe
(Austr.)
734

Tropic of Capricorn

25

F

30

G

35

Tasman   Sea

Wagga Wagga
Shepparton   Albury   Mt.
                        Kosciuszko
                        2237

Horsham   **Bendigo**
VICTORIA
Ballarat   **MELBOURNE**
Geelong

Bombala
C. Howe

H

5267

Bass Strait

King I.   Furneaux Group

40

Burnie   Launceston
1617
Mt. Ossa
TASMANIA

Hobart

S.E. Cape

7   8

150

J

CARTOGRAPHY BY PHILIP'S.   9   10   11

160   165

145

Mount Wilhelm area labels: Fly, Torres Strait, C. York

Barrier Reef, Great Barrier Reef

Great Dividing Range

Warrego, Darling, Murray

Thargomindah

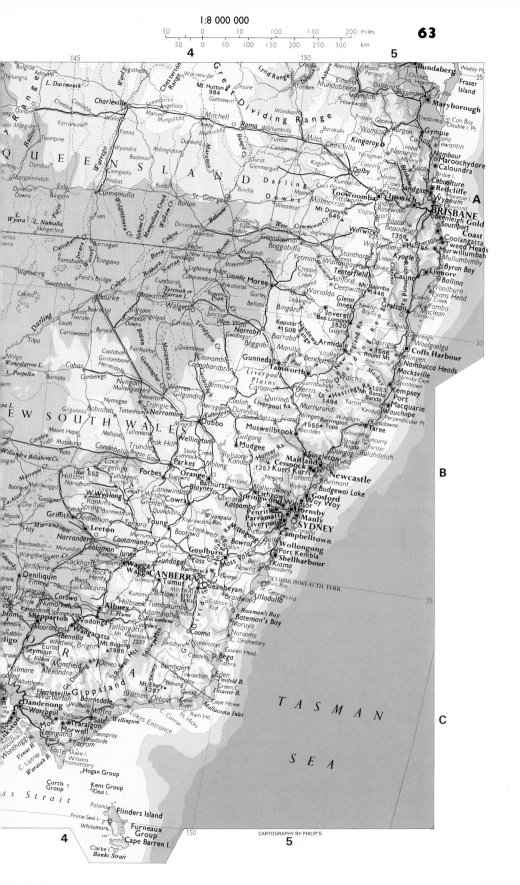

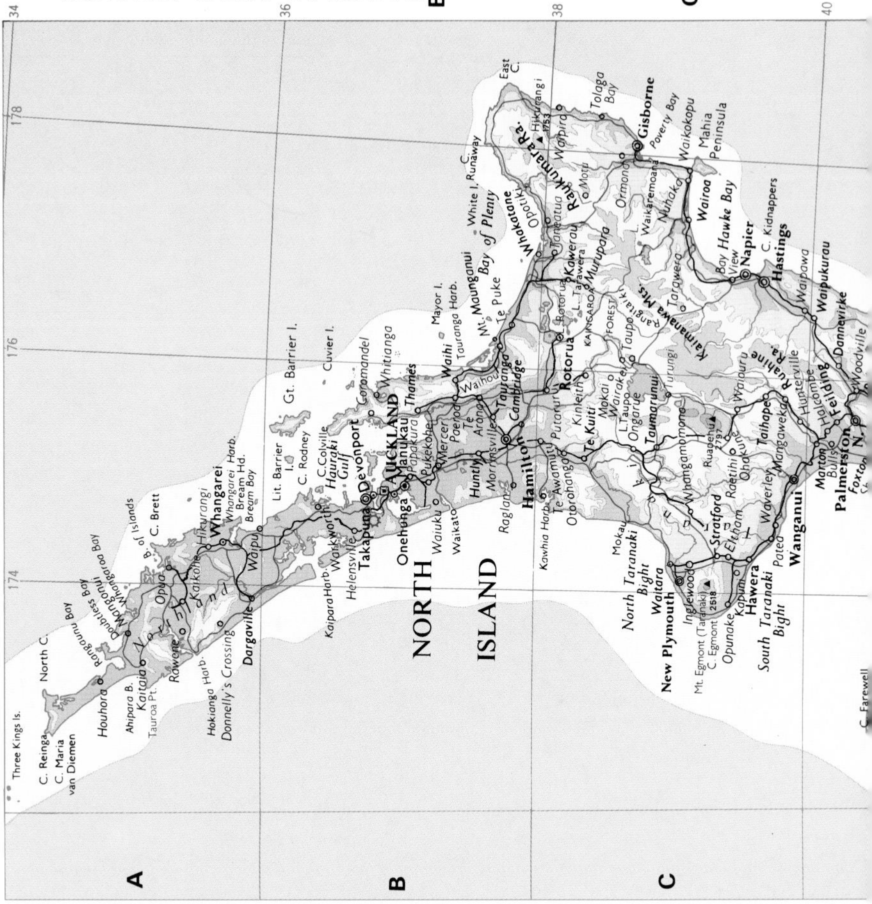

Map 1 — North Island, New Zealand

Three Kings Is.
C. Reinga
C. Maria van Diemen
North C.
Houhora B.
Ahipara B.
Kaitaia
Tauroa Pt.
Reef Point
Bay of Islands
C. Brett
Whangarei
Hikurangi
Bream Hd.
Bream Bay
Hokianga Harb.
Donnelly's Crossing
Dargaville
Kaipara Harb.
Helensville
Waiuku
Waikato
Waiuku
Onehunga
Manukau
Takapuna
Devonport
AUCKLAND
Papakura
Pukekohe
Mercer
Huntly
Hamilton
Cambridge
Te Awamutu
Otorohanga
Te Kuiti
Mokau
North Taranaki Bight
New Plymouth
Inglewood
Mt. Egmont (Taranaki)
Egmont 2518
Opunake
Kaponga
Hawera
South Taranaki Bight
Stratford
Eltham
Waverley
Patea
Wanganui
Waitara
Waikawa
Lit. Barrier I.
Gt. Barrier I.
Cuvier I.
C. Colville
Coromandel
Thames
Paeroa
Te Aroha
Morrinsville
Matamata
Tauranga
Mt. Maunganui
Mayor I.
Bay of Plenty
Te Puke
Whakatane
Opotiki
Te Kaha
East C.
Hikurangi 1753
Tokomaru
Tolaga Bay
Poverty Bay
Gisborne
Waikokopu
Mahia Peninsula
Wairoa
Hawke Bay
Bay View
Napier
Hastings
C. Kidnappers
Waipawa
Waipukurau
Dannevirke
Woodville
Palmerston North
Feilding
Marton
Bulls
Foxton
Ruapehu
Rotorua
Taupo
Lake Taupo
Taumarunui
NORTH ISLAND
C. Farewell

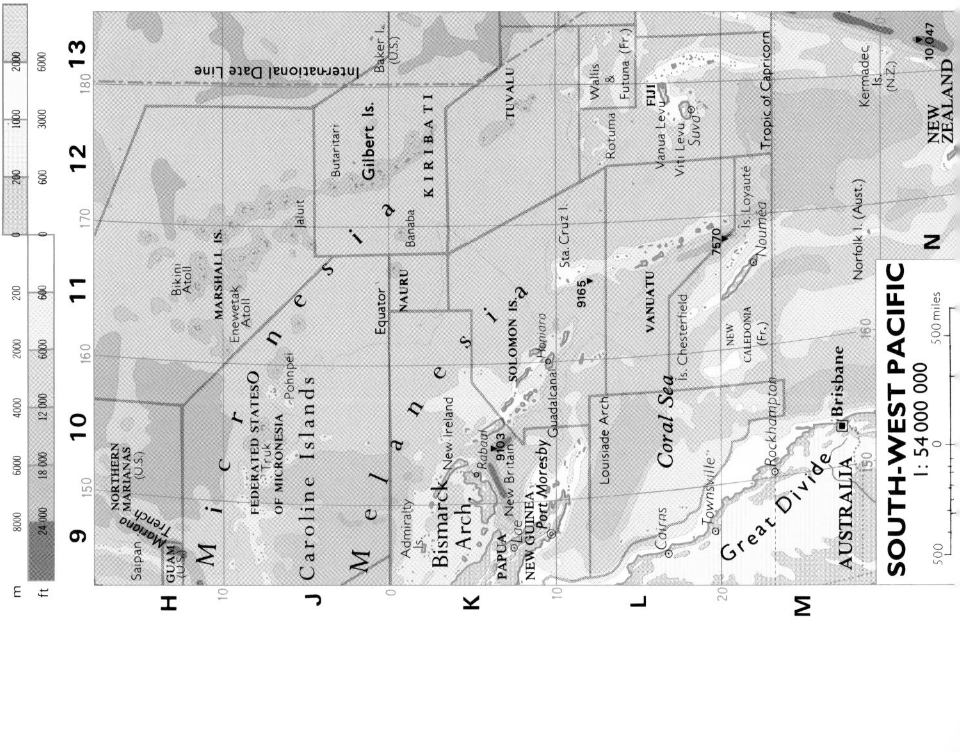

Map 2 — South-West Pacific

NORTHERN MARIANAS (U.S.)
Saipan
GUAM (U.S.)
Mariana Trench
Micronesia
Caroline Islands
FEDERATED STATES OF MICRONESIA
Truk
Pohnpei
MARSHALL IS.
Bikini Atoll
Enewetak Atoll
Jaluit
Butaritari
Banaba
Baker I. (U.S.)
Gilbert Is.
KIRIBATI
NAURU
Equator
TUVALU
Rotuma
Wallis & Futuna (Fr.)
International Date Line
Melanesia
Admiralty Is.
Bismarck Arch.
New Ireland
Rabaul
New Britain
9103
PAPUA NEW GUINEA
Port Moresby
Louisiade Arch.
Coral Sea
SOLOMON IS.
Guadalcanal
Honiara
Sta. Cruz I.
9165
VANUATU
NEW CALEDONIA (Fr.)
7570
Nouméa
Is. Chesterfield
Is. Loyauté
Norfolk I. (Aust.)
FIJI
Vanua Levu
Viti Levu
Suva
Tropic of Capricorn
Kermadec Is. (N.Z.)
10 047
NEW ZEALAND
AUSTRALIA
Brisbane
Rockhampton
Townsville
Cairns
Great Divide
Port Moresby

m | ft
8000 | 24 000
6000 | 18 000
4000 | 12 000
2000 | 6000
200 | 600
0 | 0
200 | 600
1000 | 3000
2000 | 6000

0 | 500 miles
0 | 500

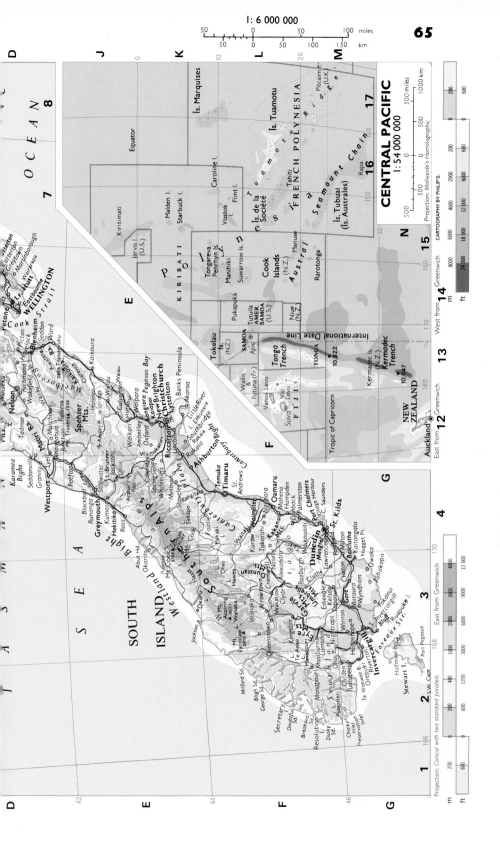

1: 35 000 000

200   0   200   400   600   800 miles
400   0   400   800   1200 km

CARTOGRAPHY BY PHILIP'S.

PACIFIC OCEAN

NORTH ATLANTIC OCEAN

UNITED STATES

OREGON
IDAHO
NEVADA
CALIFORNIA
UTAH
ARIZONA
WYOMING
COLORADO
NEW MEXICO
SOUTH DAKOTA
NEBRASKA
KANSAS
OKLAHOMA
TEXAS
MINNESOTA
IOWA
MISSOURI
ARKANSAS
LOUISIANA
WISCONSIN
ILLINOIS
MICHIGAN
INDIANA
OHIO
KENTUCKY
TENNESSEE
MISSISSIPPI
ALABAMA
GEORGIA
FLORIDA
SOUTH CAROLINA
NORTH CAROLINA
VIRGINIA
W.V.
PENNSYLVANIA
NEW YORK

Seattle
Boise
Carson City
Sacramento
San Francisco
San Jose
LOS ANGELES
San Diego
Salt Lake City
Las Vegas
Phoenix
Tucson
Cheyenne
Denver
Santa Fe
Albuquerque
El Paso
Minneapolis
Lincoln
Topeka
Kansas City
Oklahoma City
Dallas
Austin
Houston
Little Rock
Baton Rouge
New Orleans
Madison
Milwaukee
CHICAGO
Springfield
St. Louis
Memphis
Jackson
Nashville
Birmingham
Montgomery
Tallahassee
Jacksonville
Atlanta
Columbia
Charleston
Charlotte
Raleigh
Richmond
Washington D.C.
Baltimore
Columbus
Cincinnati
Indianapolis
Pittsburgh
Cleveland
Detroit
Lansing
Toledo
Buffalo
Toronto
Hartford
PHILADELPHIA
NEW YORK CITY
Bermuda (U.K.)

L. Michigan
L. Huron
MISS. R.
Mississippi

Gulf of Mexico

Tropic of Cancer

MEXICO

Mexicali
Hermosillo
Colima
Culiacan
Guadalajara
Monterrey
Rio Grande
Acapulco
Puebla
MEXICO
Mérida
Revilla Gigedo Is. (Mex.)
Guadalupe (Mex.)

West from Greenwich

CUBA
Havana
BAHAMAS
Nassau
Miami
Tampa
Florida Str.
Turks & Caicos Is. (U.K.)
Cayman Is. (U.K.)
JAMAICA
Kingston

Caribbean Sea

HAITI
Port-au-Prince
DOMINICAN REP.
Santo Domingo
PUERTO RICO (U.S.A.)
San Juan

BELIZE
Belmopan
GUATEMALA
Guatemala
HONDURAS
Tegucigalpa
EL SALVADOR
San Salvador
NICARAGUA
Managua
L. Nicaragua
COSTA RICA
San José
PANAMA
Panamá

South America
VENEZUELA
Maracaibo
Barranquilla
COLOMBIA
Medellín

Projection: Bonne

7   ■ MÉXICO   Capital Cities   8   9   10   11   12

F   G   H   J

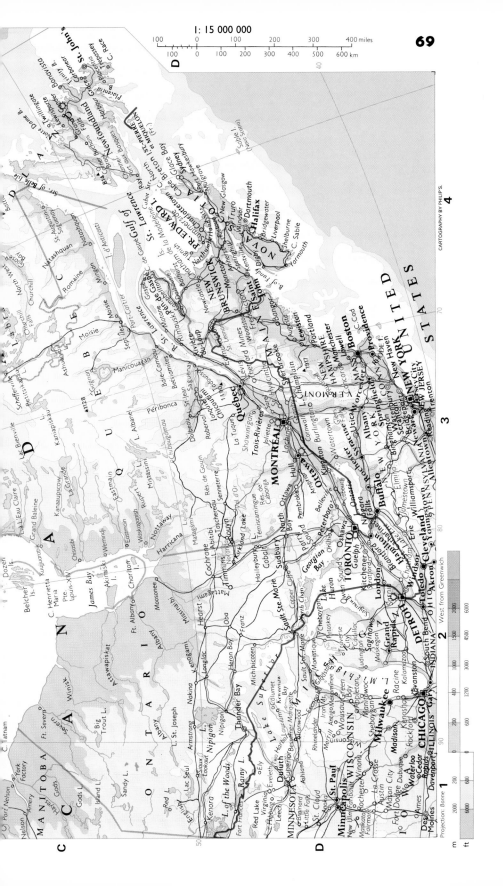

1: 15 000 000

100   0   100   200   300   400 miles

100   0   100   200   300   400   500   600 km

CARTOGRAPHY BY PHILIP'S.

Projection: Bonne

m   ft
2000   6000
1500   4500
1000   3000
600   1200
400   600
200   200

West from Greenwich

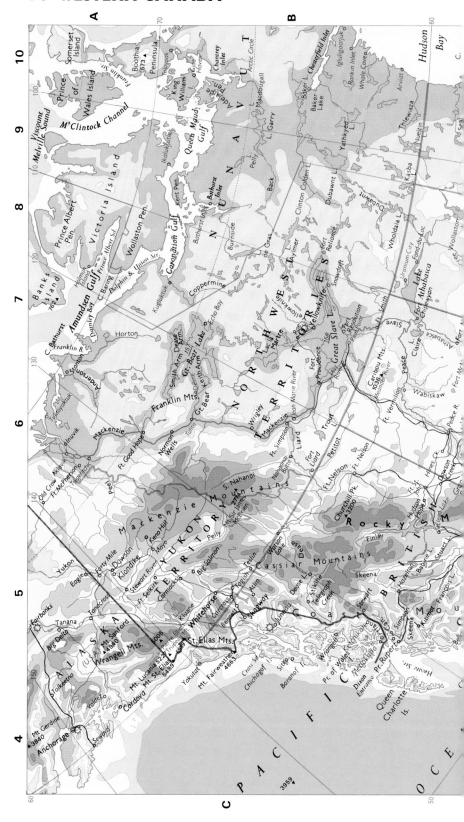

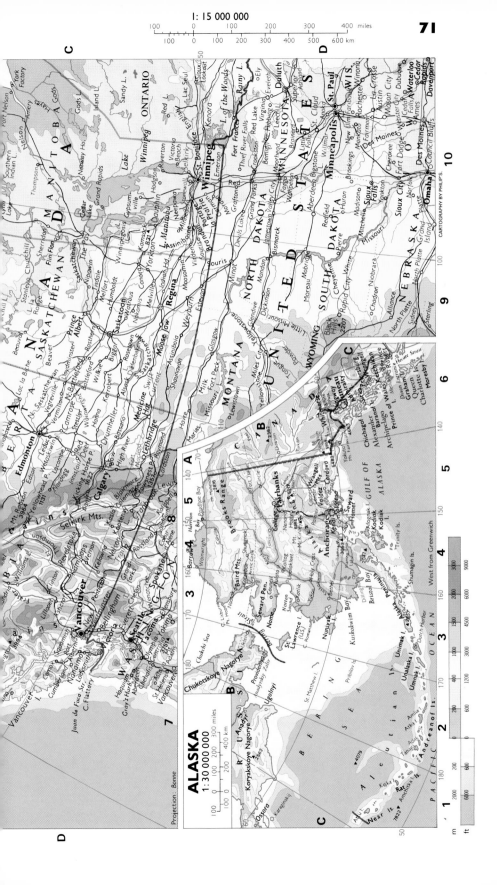

1: 15 000 000

100   200   300   400 miles

100   0   100   200   300   400   500   600 km

CARTOGRAPHY BY PHILIP'S.

ALASKA
1:30 000 000

Projection: Bonne

West from Greenwich

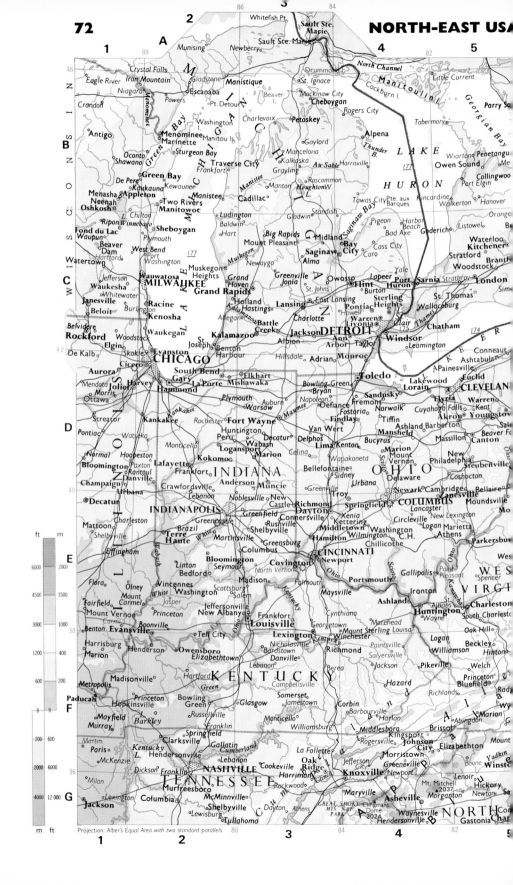

Projection: Alber's Equal Area with two standard parallels

50   0   50   100 miles
50   0   50   100 150 km

6   7   8   9   10

CANADA

Pembroke • Fort Coulonge • Hawkesbury • Ottawa • **MONTREAL** Lachine • Granby • Sherbrooke • Magog • Coaticook • Richardson Lakes

Huntsville • Barry's Bay • Eganville • Renfrew • Arnprior • **Ottawa** • Hull • Buckingham • St. Jean • Beauharnois • Cowansville • Colebrook • B

Bracebridge • Gravenhurst • Bancroft • Smiths Falls • Perth • Carleton Place • Cornwall • Malone • St. Albans • Newport • Island Pond

Lindsay • Peterborough • Belleville • Trenton • Picton • Kingston • Gananoque • Brockville • Prescott • Ogdensburg • Potsdam • Canton • Plattsburg • Winooski • Johnsbury • Berlin • Mt. Washington 1917 • Conway

TORONTO • Cobourg • Watertown • Lowville • Saranac Lakes • Gouverneur • Adirondack Mts 1629 • Ticonderoga • L. George • Middlebury • Barre • Laconia • Franklin • Dover • Portsmouth • C

LAKE ONTARIO • Oswego • Fulton • Rome • Utica • Gloversville • Amsterdam • Saratoga Springs • Glens Falls • Granville • Springfield • Claremont • Concord • Rochester • Newburyport • C. Ann

Niagara Falls • Rochester • Newark • Syracuse • Oneida • Schenectady • Troy • Albany • Keene • Manchester • Haverhill • Lawrence • Salem

Buffalo • West Seneca • Batavia • Canandaigua • Geneva • Auburn • **NEW YORK** • Cortland • Norwich • Oneonta • Catskill • Pittsfield • Northampton • Worcester • **BOSTON** • Quincy • Cape Cod • Brockton

Dunkirk • Penn Yan • Ithaca • Binghamton Mts 1281 • Kingston • New Britain • Providence • Warwick • Fall River • New Bedford

Jamestown • Bradford • Hornell • Bath • Corning • Elmira • Sayre • Towanda • Delaware • Carbondale • Poughkeepsie • Newburgh • Beacon • New Haven • Meriden • New London • Martha's Vineyard • D

PENNSYLVANIA • Scranton • Nanticoke • Wilkes Barre • Hazleton • Paterson • Yonkers • Mount Vernon • Long Island • Riverhead

PITTSBURGH • Altoona • Harrisburg • Allentown • Reading • Trenton • **NEW YORK** • NEW JERSEY • E

PHILADELPHIA • Lancaster • Camden • Chester • Wilmington

Cumberland • Hagerstown • Westminster • Bridgeton • Atlantic City • Ocean City

BALTIMORE • Towson • Columbia • **MARYLAND** • Dover • Cape May

WASHINGTON D.C. • Arlington • Alexandria • Annapolis • **DELAWARE** • Cambridge • Salisbury

VIRGINIA • **Richmond** • Williamsburg • Hampton • Newport News • Norfolk

Roanoke • Lynchburg • Petersburg • Portsmouth • Chesapeake

Raleigh • Durham • Rocky Mount • Wilson • Greenville • G

AROLINA • Goldsboro • Kinston • New Bern

80   West from Greenwich 76

6   7

CARTOGRAPHY BY PHILIP'S.

MAINE inset:

CANADA • Edmundston • Fort Kent • Van Buren • Grand Falls • A

Eagle Lake • Caribou • Presque Isle

Eagle L. • Chamberlain • Houlton • B

Chesuncook • Mt. Katahdin 1605 • Patten • Chiputneticook Lakes • Millinocket

Moosehead L. • Greenville • Mattawamkeag • Lincoln

MAINE • Bangor • Old Town • Brewer • Machias

Rangeley • Farmington • Dover Foxcroft • Galo

NEW HAMPSHIRE • Berlin • Rumford • Waterville • Belfast • Ellsworth • Mt. Desert • Bar Harbor

Mt. Washington 1917 • Auburn • Lewiston • Rockland

Westbrook • Brunswick • Bath • 44

Laconia • Saco • **Portland** • C

Rochester • Biddeford • Dover • Portsmouth • Haverhill

10   11

Continuation Eastwards On same scale

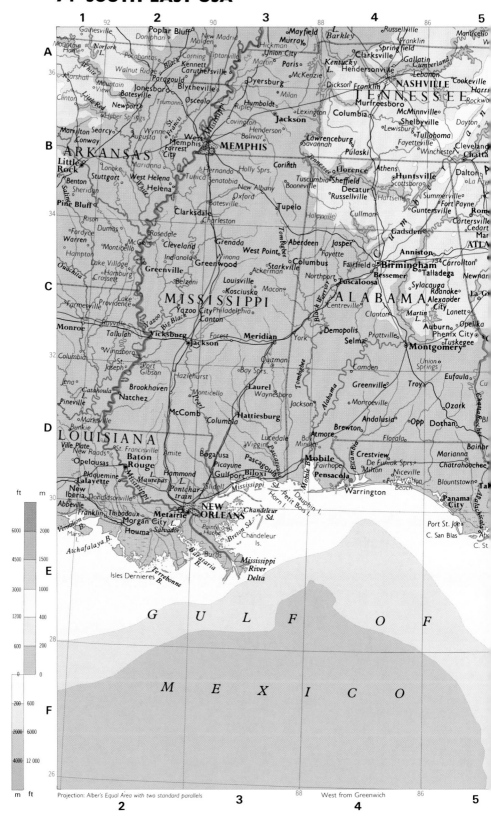

1: 6 000 000

50   0   50   100 miles

50   0   50   100   150   km

CARTOGRAPHY BY PHILIP'S.

1   **2**   104   **3**   102   **4**   100   **5**   98

A

Scobey   Plentywood   Crosby   Bowbells   Mohall   Bottineau   Rolla   Cavalier
Kenmare   Souris   Langdon   Cando   Grafton
48   Wolf Point   Missouri   Williston   Stanley   Minot   Towner   Rugby   Park River
Fairview   New Town   Velva   Devils Lake   Lakota   Larimore   Grand Forks
Fort Peck L.   Sidney   L. Sakakawea   Watford City   Harvey   Fessenden   New Rockford   Sheyenne   Northwood

B

Circle   Glendive   Manning   Garrison   McClusky   Carrington   Cooperstown   Hillsboro
N O R T H   D A K O T A
Terry   Wibaux   Beach   Dickinson   Stanton   Washburn   Center   Jamestown   Valley City
Yellowstone   Miles City   Powder   Little Missouri   Hebron   Mandan   Steele   Fa
Bismarck   Fa
Baker   Heart   Napoleon   Lisbon   La Moure   Wa
46   Tongue   Ekalaka   White Butte 1069   Mott   Carson   Cannonball   Linton   Ashley   Ellendale   Forman
Bowman   Hettinger   Lemmon   Fort Yates   Selfridge   Lake   Mound City   Eureka   Leola   Britton   Sisseton

C

Broadus   Buffalo   McIntosh   Webster
M O N T A N A   Bison   Grand   Oahe   Mound City   Ipswich   Aberdeen
Missouri   Moreau   Timber Lake   Mobridge   Selby
Little   Dupree   Eagle Butte   S O U T H   D A K O T A   Coteau
W Y O M I N G   Belle Fourche   Gettysburg   Faulkton   Redfield   Clark
Sundance   Spearfish   Cheyenne   Onida   Highmore   Miller   De Smet
44   Gillette   Belle Fourche   Sturgis   Deadwood   Oahe Dam   Pierre   Wessington Sprs.   Huron
Lead   Fort Pierre   Woonsocket
Newcastle   Black Hills 2207   Rapid City   Philip   Bad   Kennebec   Madison
Custer   Harney Pk.   Kadoka   Murdo   Chamberlain   Mitchell   Salem

D

Hot Springs   Edgemont   B a d l a n d s   White   White River   L. Francis Case   Alexandria   Parke
White   Martin   Little White   Winner   Missouri   Armour   Lake Andes
Douglas   Pine Ridge   Butte   Yankton
Lusk   Harrison   Chadron   Niobrara   South
N. Platte   Crawford   Rushville   Valentine   Bassett   Atkinson   Plainview   Way

E

42   Laramie Mountains 3131   Torrington   Hemingford   North Loup 1036   Ainsworth   O'Neill   Elkhorn   Neligh   No
Wheatland   Alliance   Mullen   Madison   We
Platte   Scottsbluff   S a n d   H i l l s   Hyannis   Thedford   Taylor   Burwell   Albion   Greeley
Gering   Middle   N E B R A S K A   Fullerton   Co
Laramie   Bridgeport   Loup   Loup City   St. Paul   Central   David City
Harrisburg   Oshkosh   Stapleton   Broken Bow   York   Sewar
Lodgepole Cr.   Kimball   L. McConaughy   South Loup   Platte   Aurora
Cheyenne   Sidney   Ogallala   North Platte   Gothenburg   Cozad   Grand Island   Hastings   Geneva

F

Fort Collins   Sterling   South Platte   Julesburg   Grant   Lexington   Kearney
Loveland   Evans   Greeley   Holyoke   Imperial   Curtis   Elwood   Holdrege
Frenchman Cr.   Boulder   Longmont   Fort Morgan   Akron   Trenton   McCook   Red Cloud   Hebron   Fairbury
Lafayette   Brighton   Wray   Benkelman   Republican   Beaver City   Alma   Franklin
Golden   DENVER   Byers   Atwood   Oberlin   Norton   Smith Center   Mankato   Bellevil
Lakewood   Aurora   Englewood   St. Francis   Phillipsburg   Solomon   Concordia   Republic
Castle Rock   Limon   Colby   N. Fork   Stockton   Osborne   Beloit
Pikes Pk. 4300   Hugo   Burlington   Goodland   Oakley   S. Fork   Solomon   Hill City   Smoky Hills   Minneapolis   Lincoln   Ju
C O L O R A D O   Cheyenne Wells   Saline   Russell   Salina
Colorado Springs   Big Sandy Cr.   Sharon Springs   Smoky Hill   Hays   Ellsworth
Fountain   Eads   Leoti   Scott City   La Crosse   K A N S A S
Canon City   Tribune   Dighton   Great Bend   Lyons   McPhers
Pueblo   Ordway   Las Animas   Lamar   Larned

38   Projection: Alber's Equal Area with two standard parallels   **2**   102   **3**   **4**   100   West from Greenwich   **5**   98

ft   m
12 000   4000
9000   3000
6000   2000
4500   1500
3000   1000
1200   400
600   200
0
200   600
m   ft

1: 6 000 000

50   0   50   100 miles

50   0   50   100   150 km

CANADA

Lake of the Woods

Warroad
Boudette
Rainy River
Rainy Lake
Atikokan
Rainy
International Falls
Fort Frances
Thunder Bay

Isle Royale

183

A

48

Thief River Falls
Upper Red L.
ston
Lower Red L.
Red Lake Falls

Vermilion L.
Lac la Croix

Grand Marais

LAKE SUPERIOR

Copper Harbor
Keweenaw Pt.
Keweenaw Pen.

Bagley
Bemidji
Mahnomen
Winnibigoshish
Cass Lake
Hibbing
Virginia
Eveleth

St. Louis
Two Harbors
Apostle Is.
Ontonagon
Hancock
Houghton
Keweenaw B.

B

604
L'Anse
Ishpeming Marquette
Negaunee

lowley
Detroit Lakes
Park Rapids
Perham
Leech L.
Walker
Grand Rapids

Duluth
Superior
Cloquet
Washburn
Ashland
Hurley Ironwood
Bessemer

MICHIGAN

Crystal Falls

sville
MINNESOTA
Wadena
Staples
Brainerd
Mille Lacs
Aitkin
Moose Lake

Hayward
Park Falls
Eagle River
Iron Mountain
Niagara
Powers

Fergus Falls
Alexandria
eaton
Morris
Glenwood
Little Falls
Mora
Milaca
Pine City
Sauk Rapids
Grantsburg
Spooner
Phillips
Rhinelander
Crandon
Menominee
Green Bay
Marinette

C

Litchfield
St. Cloud
Paynesville
Mississippi
Cumberland
Rice Lake
Ladysmith
Medford
Merrill
Tomahawk
Antigo
Oconto
Shawano
Sturgeon Bay

Willmar
Montevideo
Granite Falls
Canby
Redwood Falls
Marshall New Ulm
Hutchinson
Glencoe
MINNEAPOLIS
St. Paul
Bloomington
Hastings
Red Wing
Stillwater
Hudson
Lake City
St. Croix
Menomonie
Eau Claire
Chippewa Falls
Marshfield
Cornell
WISCONSIN
Stevens Point
De Pere
Green Bay
Kewaunee
Appleton
Two Rivers
Manitowoc

Northfield
St. Peter
Faribault
Mankato
Owatonna
Waseca
Winona
Rochester
Alma
Whitehall
Wisconsin Rapids
Black
Waupaca
Menasha
Neenah
Oshkosh
L. Chilton
Sheboygan
Plymouth

dreau
Pipestone
Windom
St. James
La Crosse
Sparta
Onalaska
Tomah
Montello
Mauston
Fond du Lac
Waupun
Ripon
Winnebago
LAKE

Worthington
Jackson
Fairmont
Albert Lea
Austin
Preston
Viroqua
Reedsburg
Richland Center
Baraboo
Portage
Beaver Dam
Hartford
West Bend
Port Washington
MICHIGAN

Sibley
Estherville
Northwood
Decorah
Waukon
Prairie du Chien
Madison
Jefferson
Watertown
Wauwatosa
MILWAUKEE

D

ls
ton
Spencer
Forest City
Mason City
Charles City
New Hampton
Osage
Dodgeville
Lancaster
Darlington
Waukesha
Whitewater
Janesville
Burlington
Racine
Kenosha

Sheldon
Emmetsburg
Algona
Garner
Clarion
Hampton
Waverly
Oelwein
Independence
Monroe
Beloit
Woodstock
Waukegan

Sioux City
Le Mars
Cherokee
Storm Lake
Sac City
Pocahontas
Fort Dodge
Webster
Iowa Falls
Cedar Falls
Waterloo
Dubuque
Freeport
Rockford
Belvidere
Elgin Skokie
Evanston
CHICAGO

Ida Grove
Denison
Carroll
Jefferson
Boone
IOWA
Ames
Marshalltown
Vinton
Marion
Cedar Rapids
Maquoketa
Clinton
Sterling
Dixon
De Kalb
Aurora
Cicero
Harvey

Little Sioux
Audubon
Perry
Newton
Grinnell
Marengo
Iowa City
Davenport
Moline
Mendota
Princeton
Joliet
Morris
Ottawa

naha
Council Bluffs
Greenfield
W. Des Moines
Des Moines
L. Red Rock
Montezuma
Washington
Muscatine
Rock Island
Kewanee
Peru
Streator
Pontiac
Kankakee

E

smouth
Atlantic
Winterset
Indianola
Pella
Oskaloosa
Ottumwa
Fairfield
Mt. Pleasant
Aledo
Galesburg
Monmouth
Chillicothe
Peoria
Normal
Paxton

Glenwood Red
Creston
Osceola
Albia
Burlington
Fort Madison
Canton
Pekin
Bloomington
Rantoul

coln
ebraska City
ice
Shenandoah
Clarinda
Bedford
Centerville
Bloomfield
Keokuk
Macomb
Lincoln
Champaign

City
Falls City
Auburn
Rockport
Grant City
Bethany
Princeton
Unionville
Kahoka
Rushville
Beardstown
Virginia
Decatur

Hiawatha
ysville
Troy
Savannah
Trenton
Milan
Edina
Kirksville
ILLINOIS
Springfield
Jacksonville
Taylorville
Pana
Shelbyville
Mattoon

Holton
Atchison
St. Joseph
Excelsior Spr.
Chillicothe
Brookfield
Palmyra
Hannibal
Quincy
Macon
Carrollton
Carlinville
Litchfield
Effingham

nsas
Topeka
Leavenworth
Lawrence
Olathe
KANSAS CITY
Independence
KANSAS CITY
Lexington
Marshall
Richmond
Fayette
Mexico
Moberly
Columbia
Fulton
Jerseyville
Troy
St. Charles
Alton
Granite City
E. St. Louis
Belleville
Flora
Fairfield
Centralia

F

Council Grove
Emporia
Garnett
Ottawa
Paola
Warrensburg
Sedalia
Harrisonville
Jefferson City
Boonville
MISSOURI
Missouri
Hermann
Union
ST. LOUIS
Waterloo
Mount Vernon
Benton

Burlington
Clinton
Butler
Lake of the Ozarks
Osage
Sullivan
De Soto
Ste. Genevieve
Pinckneyville
Du Quoin

96   94   92
7   8   9   10

CARTOGRAPHY BY PHILIP'S.

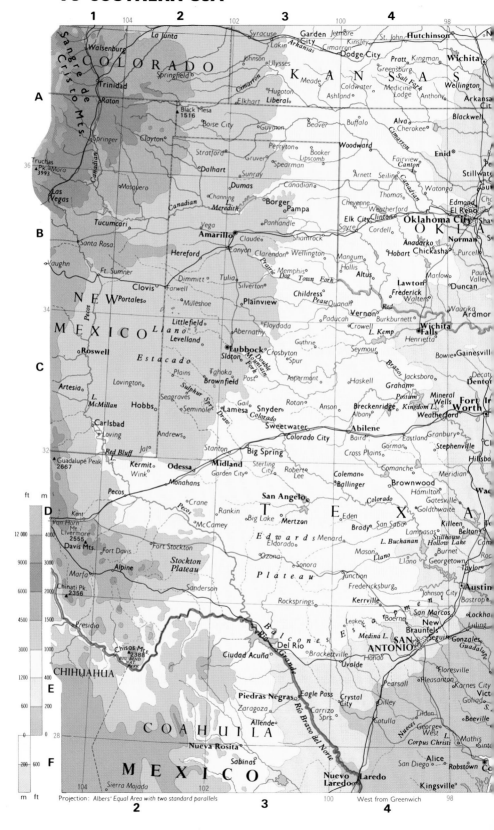

1 : 6 000 000

50   0   50   100 miles
50 0 50 100 150 km

MAP LABELS — top grid numbers: 6   7   8   9

96   94   92   90

MISSOURI

Yates Center, Iola, Nevada, Camdenton, Rolla, Steelville, Salem, Ironton, Murphysboro, Perryville, Fredericktown, Jackson, Marion, Carbondale, Anna, Chanute, Fort Scott, Buffalo, Bolivar, Lebanon, Houston, Cape Girardeau, Metropolis, Paducah, Fredonia, Howard, Girard, Pittsburg, Stockton, Marshfield, Charleston, Cairo, Paducah

Parsons, Carthage, Springfield, Ozark, Cabool, Van Buren, Poplar Bluff, Dexter, New Madrid, Sikeston, Mayfield, Coffeyville, Independence, Joplin, Aurora, West Plains, Doniphan, Malden, Hickman, Union City, Tiptonville

Sedan, Miami, Neosho, Monett, Cassville, Norfolk L., Pocahontas, Black, Corning, Kennett, Caruthersville, McKenzie, Dyersburg, Vinita, Lake O' The Cherokees, Jay, Rogers, White, Berryville, Mountain Home, Walnut Ridge, Paragould, Blytheville, Ripley, Humboldt, Jackson

TENNESSEE

Bartlesville, Claremore, Pryor, Siloam Springs, Springdale, Harrison, Mountain View, Batesville, Jonesboro, Trumann, Osceola, Covington, Henderson, Bolivar

Tulsa, Wagoner, Haskell, Muskogee, Okmulgee, Stilwell, Fayetteville, Marshall, Little Red, Heber Springs, Newport, Wynne, Augusta, Forrest City, Memphis, MEMPHIS, Holly Sprs.

Ozark, Clarksville, Clinton, Searcy, Hernando, Oxford, New Albany

Eufaula, Stigler, Sallisaw, Van Buren, Ft. Smith, Arkansas, Russellville, Morrilton, Conway, Marianna, Tunica, Senatobia, Batesville, Tupelo

Holdenville, Eufaula L., Poteau, Booneville, Lonoke, West Helena, Helena, Clarksdale

McAlester, Wilburton, Heavener, Waldron, Ouachita Mts., ARKANSAS, Little Rock, Benton, Stuttgart, Charleston

Coalgate, Atoka, Antlers, Mena, Ouachita L., Hot Springs, Malvern, Sheridan, Risan, Rosedale, Grenada, Aberdeen, West Point, Columbus, Starkville, Ackerman

Durant, Broken Bow Lake, De Queen, Nashville, Millwood L., Arkadelphia, Pine Bluff, Dumas, McGehee, Cleveland, Winona, Indianola, Greenwood, Louisville, Kosciusko, Macon, Philadelphia

Red, Idabel, Prescott, Hope, Camden, Warren, Monticello, Greenville, Belzoni, Canton

Paris, Bonham, Clarksville, Texarkana, Texarkana, Magnolia, Ouachita, Hampton, Lake Village, Hamburg, Crossett, MISSISSIPPI, Yazoo City, Forest

Kinney, Commerce, Sulphur Springs, Mount Pleasant, Pittsburg, Atlanta, Linden, Haynesville, Homer, Farmerville, Lake Providence, Yazoo, Big Black, Meridian, Quitman

Terrell, Gilmer, Jefferson, Minden, Rayville, Tallulah, Vicksburg, Jackson, Bay Sprs.

Cedar Creek Res., Longview, Marshall, Shreveport, Bossier City, Ruston, Monroe, Winnsboro, St. Joseph, Port Gibson, Hazlehurst, Laurel, Waynesboro

Athens, Kilgore, Tyler, Henderson, Carthage, Jonesboro, Columbia, Coushatta, Mansfield, Winnfield, Natchitoches, Tenaha, Jena, Colfax, Catahoula L., Pineville, Brookhaven, Monticello, Hattiesburg

Jacksonville, Palestine, Fairfield, Center, Toledo Bend Reservoir, San Augustine, Many, Natchez, McComb, Columbia, Lucedale

Crockett, Nacogdoches, Lufkin, Sam Rayburn Res., Alexandria, Leesville, Marksville, Wiggins

Centerville, Groveton, Jasper, Newton, Oakdale, Bunkie, LOUISIANA, St. Francisville, Amite, Bogalusa, Picayune, Biloxi

Madisonville, Livingston, Woodville, De Ridder, Ville Platte, New Roads, Baton Rouge, Hammond, Slidell, Gulfport, Mississippi Sd.

Bryan, Navasota, Huntsville, Livingston, Eunice, Opelousas, Plaquemine, Maurepas, Pontchartrain, NEW ORLEANS, Chandeleur Sd.

Brenham, Hempstead, Kountze, Silsbee, Sulphur, Lake Charles, Crowley, Lafayette, Donaldsonville, Metairie, Pointe à la Hache, Chandeleur Is.

HOUSTON, Pasadena, Conroe, Cleveland, Beaumont, Orange, Calcasieu L., New Iberia, Abbeville, Franklin, Thibodaux, Morgan City, Houma, Salvador, Breton Sd., Barataria

Richmond, Baytown, Liberty, Port Arthur, Sabine L., Cameron, Vermilion B., White L., Marsh I., Atchafalaya B., Terrebonne B., Burās, Mississippi River Delta

Rosenberg, Wharton, Galveston, Texas City, Angleton, Galveston, Freeport, Bay City

Matagorda I., GULF OF MEXICO

Inset map (bottom right):

92   8   Isles Dernieres B.   90   9

Kingsville, Hebbronville, Falfurrias, Sarita, Padre I., MEXICO, Salado, Zapata, Falcon L., Laguna Madre, Rio Grande City, Raymondville, Edinburg, McAllen, Harlingen, San Benito, Brownsville

Continuation Southwards on same scale

28, 26

96   94   7   4   5

CARTOGRAPHY BY PHILIP'S.

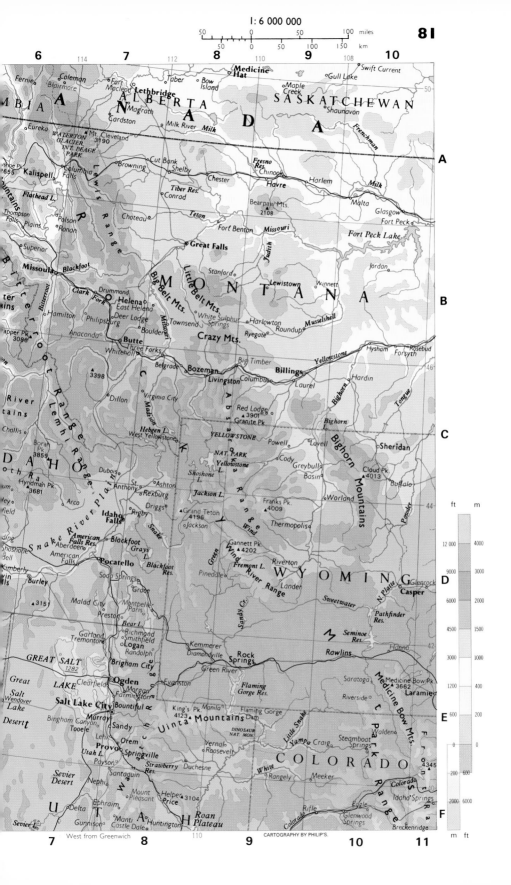

1 : 6 000 000

50   0   50   100   miles
50   0   50   100   150   km

6   114   7   112   8   110   9   108   10

Medicine Hat

Swift Current

Fernie Coleman Blairmore   Fort Macleod **Lethbridge** Taber Bow Island   Maple Creek   Gull Lake

A L B E R **T** A   C A N A D A   S A S K A T C H E W A N   50

Eureka   Magrath Cardston   Milk River **Milk**   Shaunavon

B I A   **N**

MBIA   WATERTON GLACIER INT. PEACE PARK Mt. Cleveland 3190   Frenchman

shoe Pk **Kalispell**   Columbia Falls   Browning Cut Bank Shelby   Fresno Res. Chester Chinook   Harlem Malta   **Milk**   **A**

655   Flathead L.   Tiber Res. Conrad   Havre   Fort Peck   Glasgow

Thompson Falls Polson Plains Ronan   Choteau   Teton   Fort Benton **Missouri**   Fort Peck Lake

Superior   **Great Falls**   Judith   Jordan

Missoula Blackfoot   Stanford   Lewistown Winnett   **B**

Clark Drummond **Helena** East Helena   M O N T A N A

Hamilton Philipsburg Deer Lodge   Big Belt Mts. Little Belt Mts.   White Sulphur Springs Harlowton Musselshell

apper Pk 3098   Anaconda   Boulder Townsend   Ryegate Roundup

Butte   Crazy Mts.   Hysham Rosebud Forsyth

Whitehall Three Forks   Big Timber   **Billings**   Hardin

3398   Belgrade **Bozeman** Livingston Columbus   **Yellowstone**   46

River tains   Dillon Virginia City   Laurel   Bighorn   Tongue

Challis   Hebgen L. West Yellowstone   Red Lodge 3901 Granite Pk   Bighorn

D A H O   Dubois   YELLOWSTONE NAT. PARK Yellowstone L.   Powell Lavell   **Sheridan** **C**

Borah Pk 3859   St. Anthony Ashton   Shoshone L.   Cody Greybull Basin   Cloud Pk 4013 Buffalo

o t h Ra Hyndman Pk 3681   Rexburg Driggs   Jackson L.   Franks Pk 4009   **Worland**

um.   Arco   **Idaho Falls** Rigby   Grand Teton 4196   Thermopolis

ley   Blackfoot Grays L.   Jackson   Wind   Riverton   W Y O M I N G

field   American Falls Res. Aberdeen   Gannett Pk 4202 Fremont L. River Range   Lander   **Casper** **D**

Shoshone lell   Pocatello   Blackfoot Res.   Pinedale Sandy Cr.   Sweetwater   N. Platte Glenrock

Kimberly vin ls   American Falls   Soda Springs Grace   Seminoe Res.   Hanna 42

Burley   Malad City Montpelier Paris   Kemmerer   Rawlins

3151   Preston   Diamondville Rock Springs

GREAT SALT   Bear L. Richmond Smithfield   Green River   Saratoga Medicine Bow Pk 3662 Laramie

Great Salt Lake   Garland Tremonton **Brigham City** Randolph   Flaming Gorge Res.   Riverside Medicine Bow Mts.

Wendover   **LAKE** 1282 Clearfield **Ogden** Morgan Evanston   Riverside   **E**

Desert   Farmington **Salt Lake City** Bountiful   King's Pk Manila   Flaming Gorge   4345

Bingham Canyon **Murray** Sandy   Uinta Mountains   DINOSAUR NAT. MON.   Walden   Park

Tooele   Lehi **Provo** Orem Springville   Vernal Roosevelt   **C** O L O R A D O

Sevier Desert   Payson Santaquin Strawberry Res. Duchesne   White Rangely Meeker   Steamboat Springs Craig   Idaho Springs

Nephi   Colorado

U Delta T A Mount Pleasant Helper Price 3104 H   Rifle Glenwood Springs Eagle Breckenridge **F**

Sevier Lm   Gunnison Manti Castle Dale Roan Plateau   Colorado

West from Greenwich   CARTOGRAPHY BY PHILIP'S.

7   8   110   9   10   11

ft   m

12 000   4000

9000   3000

6000   2000

4500   1500

3000   1000

1200   400

600   200

0   0

200   600

2000   6000

m   ft

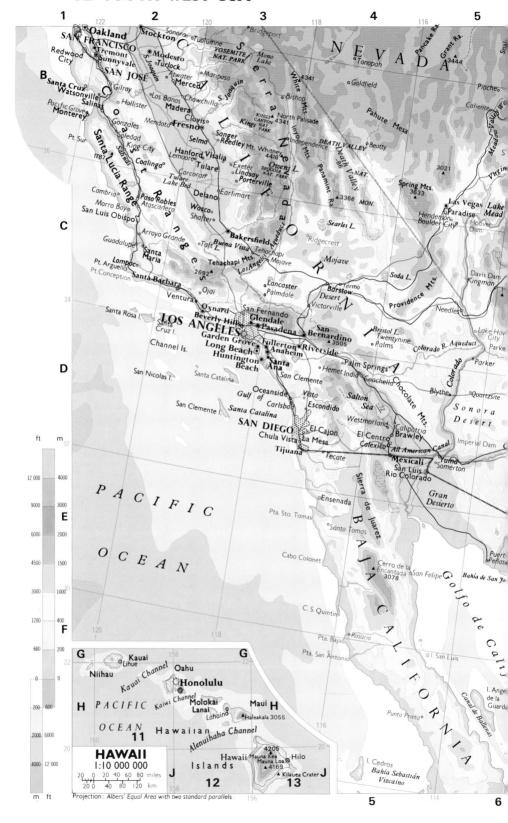

1 122 **2** 120 **3** 118 **4** 116 **5**

N E V A D A

C A L I F O R N I A

Oakland
SAN FRANCISCO
Stockton
Redwood City
Sunnyvale
Fremont
Modesto
Turlock
Sonora
Tuolumne
Bridgeport
Pancake Ra.
Grant Ra.
3444
Tonopah
Pioche
B Santa Cruz
Watsonville
SAN JOSE
Gilroy
Mariposa
YOSEMITE NAT. PARK
Mono Lake
Goldfield
Caliente
Pacific Grove
Monterey
Salinas
Hollister
Los Banos
Chowchilla
Madera
Clovis
Bishop
North Mts.
4341
Inyo Mts.
Pahute Mesa
Meadow Valley
Pt. Sur
Gonzales
Soledad
Mendota
Fresno
Selma
Sanger
Reedley
Mt. Whitney 4418
Kings Canyon 4341
KINGS CANYON NAT. PARK
White Mts.
4341
Independence
DEATH VALLEY
Beatty
3021
Virgin
King City
Coalinga
Hanford
Visalia
Lemoore
Exeter
Lindsay
SEQUOIA NAT. PARK
Owens L.
Panamint Ra.
Spring Mts. 3633
Las Vegas
Lake Mead
Santa Lucia Range
Cambria
Paso Robles
Atascadero
Tulare
Corcoran
Tulare Lake Bed
Porterville
Earlimart
3366 MON.
DEATH VALLEY NAT.
Henderson
Boulder City
Hoover Dam
Morro Bay
San Luis Obispo
Delano
Wasco
Shafter
Mojave
Paradise
Davis Dam
Kingman
C Guadalupe
Santa Maria
Arroyo Grande
Bakersfield
Buena Vista
Taft
Tehachapi Mts.
2692
Tehachapi
Mojave
Searles L.
Ridgecrest
Soda L.
Providence Mts.
Lompoc
Pt. Arguello
Pt. Conception
Santa Barbara
Ventura
Ojai
Los Angeles Aqueduct
Lancaster
Palmdale
Barstow
Termo
Victorville
Needles
Santa Rosa I.
Oxnard
Beverly Hills
San Fernando
Glendale
Pasadena
LOS ANGELES
Garden Grove
Long Beach
Anaheim
Fullerton
San Bernardino
3505
Riverside
Twentynine Palms
Bristol L.
Colorado R. Aqueduct
Lake Hav. City
Parker
D Santa Cruz I.
Channel Is.
Huntington Beach
Santa Ana
San Clemente
Palm Springs
Indio
Coachella
Colorado
Parker
San Nicolas I.
Oceanside
Gulf of Carlsbad
Vista
Escondido
Salton Sea
Westmorland
Blythe
Quartzsite
Santa Catalina
San Clemente I.
SAN DIEGO
Chula Vista
El Cajon
La Mesa
El Centro
Calipatria
Brawley
Sonora Desert
Imperial Dam
Tijuana
Tecate
Calexico
Mexicali
San Luis Rio Colorado
Yuma
Somerton
E P A C I F I C
O C E A N
Ensenada
PTA. Sto. Tomas
Santo Tomas
Sierra de Juarez
B A J A
Gran Desierto
Cabo Colonet
Cerro de la Encantada 3078
San Felipe
Bahía de San Jo
F C. S. Quintin
Pta. Baja
Rosario
Pta. San Antonio
C A L I F O R N I A
Golfo de Cali
Punta Prieta
I. Ange de la Guard

120 118 116 114

G Kauai
Lihue
Oahu
G
Niihau
Kauai Channel
Honolulu
H P A C I F I C
Kaiwi Channel
Molokai
Lanai
Maui **H**
Lahaina
Haleakala 3055
O C E A N Hawaiian
11
Alenuihaha Channel
Hawaii 4205
Mauna Kea
Mauna Loa
4169
Hilo
HAWAII
1:10 000 000
Hawaii Islands
Kilauea Crater **J**
J **12** **13**

Projection: Albers' Equal Area with two standard parallels.

5 **6**

ft m
12 000 4000
9000 3000
6000 2000
4500 1500
3000 1000
1200 400
600 200
0 0
200 600
2000 6000
4000 12 000
m ft

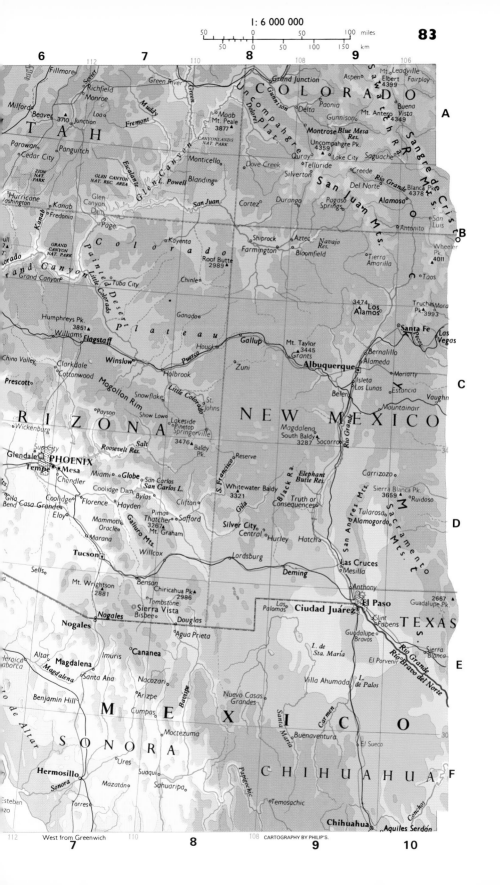

1: 6 000 000

50   0   50   100   miles
50   0   50   100   150   km

COLORADO

Fillmore
Richfield
Monroe
Milford
Beaves
Loa   Junction 3710
Parowan
Cedar City   Panguitch
Zion Washington
Nat. Hurricane
Park
Kanab Fredonia

UTAH

Green River
Muddy
Fremont
Moab Mt. Peale 3877
CANYONLANDS NAT. PARK
Monticello
Blanding
San Juan

Grand Junction
Delta
Paonia
Gunnison
Montrose Blue Mesa Res.
Uncompahgre Pk. 4359
Ouray
Telluride
Silverton
Durango

Aspen Leadville
Elbert Fairplay
4399
Buena Vista
Mt. Antero 4349
Blue Mesa

Lake City Saguache
Creede
Del Norte Rio Grande
Pagosa Springs

Blanca Pk 4378
Alamosa
Antonito
San Luis

A

B

Glen Canyon
Glen Canyon Dam
Page

GLEN CANYON NAT. REC. AREA
L. Powell
Dove Creek
Cortez

San Juan Mts.

C

D

E

F

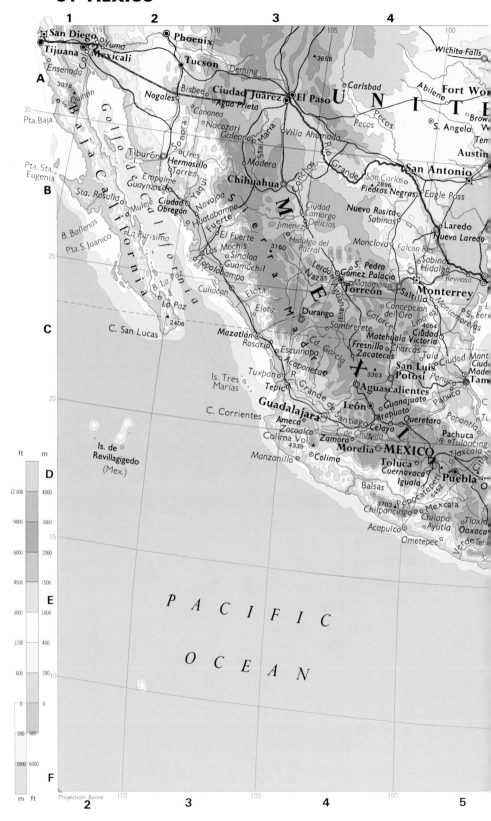

San Diego
Tijuana
Mexicali
Yuma
Phoenix
Ensenada
Tucson
S. Quintin
Deming
Nogales
Bisbee
Ciudad Juarez
El Paso
Agua Prieta
Cananea
Nacozari
Galeana
Villa Ahumada
Sonora
Sta. Maria
Pecos
Tiburón I.
Ures
Hermosillo
Torres
Madera
Chihuahua
Concho
Empalme
Guaymas
Yaqui
Navojoa
Ciudad Obregón
Huatabampo
Fuerte
El Fuerte
Los Mochis
Sinaloa
Guamúchil
Topolobampo
Culiacan
Elota
La Paz
Elota
Mazatlán
Rosario
Escuinapa
Acaponeta R.
Tepic
Durango
Sombrerete
Fresnillo
Zacatecas
Aguascalientes
León
Guadalajara
Zacoalco
Colima Vol.
Manzanillo
Colima
Morelia
Toluca
Cuernavaca
Iguala
Chilpancingo
Acapulco
Ayutla

Carlsbad
Abilene
Fort Wor
UNITE
Brow
S. Angelo
Tem
Austin
San Antonio
Piedras Negras
Eagle Pass
Nueva Rosita
Sabinas
Monclova
Laredo
Nuevo Laredo
S. Pedro
Lerdo
Gómez Palacio
Torreón
Saltillo
Monterrey
Concepcion del Oro
Catorce
Matehuala
Charcas
San Luis Potosi
Ciudad Victoria
Guanajuato
Irapuato
Celaya
Queretaro
Pachuca
Mexico
Tlaxcala
Puebla
Popocatepetl
Mexcala
Chilapa
Oaxaca

Pta. Baja
Pta. Sta. Eugenia
Sta. Rosalia
B. Ballenas
La Purisima
Pta. S. Juanico
B. La Paz
C. San Lucas
Is. Tres Marias
Is. de Revillagigedo (Mex.)
C. Corrientes
Balsas

Golfo de California
Baja California
Sierra Madre

PACIFIC
OCEAN

A
B
C
D
E
F

Projection: Bonne

1: 15 000 000

100   0   100   200   300   400 miles
100   0   100 200 300 400 600 km

6   7   8   9

Dallas
esville
Tyler   Marshall
Shreveport   Birmingham   Columbia   Columbia
        Monroe   Vicksburg Jackson   Atlanta
n   Natchez   S T A T E S   Augusta   C. Royal
        Alexandria   Meridian Montgomery Macon   Charleston
Beaumont Lake Charles Hattiesburg   Columbus Savannah
Port Arthur Lafayette Baton Rouge Mobile Pensacola Dothan Albany   Jacksonville
Galveston   Atchafalaya B.   Tallahassee   Daytona Beach
agorda I.   New Orleans   C. San   Apalachee B.
Christi   Mississippi   Blas   Orlando   C. Canaveral
                Delta   Tampa Lakeland W. Palm Beach
                              St. Petersburg   Grand
G U L F   O F   M E X I C O   Sarasota L. Okeechobee Bahama I.
nde del Norte   Miami Fort Lauderdale
re   C. Sable
                                            Key West   Andros I.
Tropic of Cancer   Florida Str.
                                                    Matanzas
                        Canal de Yucatan   La Habana Cárdenas Sagua la Grande
                                            (Havana)   Colón Caibarién
                    C. Catoche   Marianao   Sta. Clara
                        El Cuyo   Pinar del Rio Batabanó C U B A
cruz Golfo de   Progreso Temax El Diaz   San   Sancti Spiritus
quez   Puerto   Antonio G. de Cienfuegos Trinidad Ciego de Avila
        Campeche Mérida Valladolid Morelos Batabanó
cruz   I. de   I. de Juventud   Jucaro
ado Campeche   Peto   Cozumel
arado Ciudad del Carmen   Vigia Chico   Grand Cayman
actotalpan   Laguna Y u c a t a n   (U.K.)
Coatzacoalcos de Terminos Felipe Carillo Puerto
de Villahermosa   Corozal   Ciudad Chetumal
uantepec Tuxtla Gutierrez Usumacinta Ambergris Cay
uchitan Chiapa   O San Cristobal Belize Turneffe Is.
Tonala Chiapa   Middlesex BELIZE Golfo de Honduras
de Huixtla GUATEMALA Belmopan Pto. Barrios Golfo de Cortés Trujillo Iriona
uantepec   Zacapa Pto. Cortés Tela   L. Caratasca
        Guatemala Sta. Rosa Pedro Sula La Ceiba
San José Sta. Ana HONDURAS Comayagua   Wanks or Coco C. Gracias á Dios
Sonsonate San Vincente Tegucigalpa Jinotega   Puerto Cabezas
San Salvador S. Miguel Nacaome Matagalpa
EL SALVADOR G. de Fonseca Choluteca El Gallo
    Chinandega NICARAGUA   Providencia (Col.)
        Leon Managua Granada   Bluefields   San Andrés (Col.)
            Masaya L. Nicaragua
                San Juan
            COSTA Vol. Irazú
Pen. de Nicoya   RICA Limón   Colón
    Puntarenas Alajuela San José Cartago 3374 P A N A M A Panama
            David   P A N A M A   La Palma
                    Pen. de   Chitré Arch. de las Perlas El Real
West from Greenwich 90 Coiba Azuero G. de Panama

6

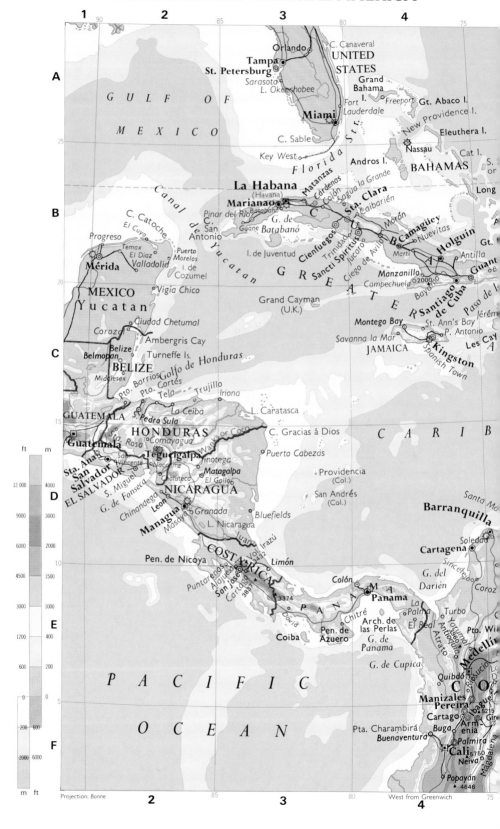

1   2   3   4

90   85   80   75

A

United States

C. Canaveral
Orlando
Tampa
St. Petersburg
Sarasota
L. Okeeshobee
Grand Bahama
Miami
Fort Lauderdale
I.
Freeport
Gt. Abaco I.
New Providence I.
Eleuthera I.

C. Sable

25

GULF OF MEXICO

Key West

Florida Str.
Nassau
Cat I.
BAHAMAS
Andros I.

B

Canal de Yucatan

La Habana
(Havana)
Matanzas
Cárdenas
Colón
Sagua la Grande
Marianao
Batabanó
Sta. Clara
Caibarién
Morón
C. Catoche
El Cuyo
Pinar del Río
C. San Antonio
Guane
Batabanó
G. de
Batabanó
Cienfuegos
Sancti Spíritus
Ciego de Avila
Júcaro
Martí
Camagüey
Nuevitas
Holguin
Antilla
Gt.
Progreso
Temax
El Díaz
Puerto Morelos
Valladolid
I. de Cozumel
Trinidad
GREATER
Manzanillo
2000
Bayamo
Campechuela
Santiago de Cuba
Guant
Long
Mérida

20

MEXICO
Yucatan
Vigía Chico
Grand Cayman
(U.K.)
Jérém
Paso de
Les Cay

Ciudad Chetumal
Montego Bay
St. Ann's Bay
P. Antonio
Corozal
Ambergris Cay
Savanna la Mar
Kingston
Spanish Town
C
Belize
Turneffe Is.
JAMAICA
Belmopan
BELIZE
Golfo de Honduras
Middlesex
Pto. Barrios
Pto. Cortés
Tela
Trujillo
Iriona
GUATEMALA
S. Pedro Sula
La Ceiba
L. Caratasca
CARIB

15

Guatemala
Sta. Rosa
HONDURAS
Comayagua
Wanks or Coco
C. Gracias á Dios
San Salvador
Sta. Ana
San Vincente
Tegucigalpa
Nacaome
Jinotega
Puerto Cabezas
EL SALVADOR
S. Miguel
Jinotega
Nacaome
Matagalpa
El Gallo
Providencia
(Col.)
D
Choluteca
NICARAGUA
Chinandega
León
San Andrés
(Col.)
Barranquilla
G. de Fonseca
Managua
Masaya
Granada
Bluefields
Santa Ma
Juan
L. Nicaragua

10

Cartagena
Soledad
Pen. de Nicoya
Vol. Irazú
3442
Limón
G. del Darién
Coroz
COSTA RICA
Puntarenas
Alajuela
Colón
P A N A
Turbo
San José
Panama
La Palma
Pto. Wi
Cartago
3837
3374
Chitré
El Real
Yolumb
Antioco
Atrato
E
David
Arch. de las Perlas
Medellín
Coiba
Pen. de Azuero
G. de Panama
Quibdó
CO
G. de Cupica

5

PACIFIC
Manizales
Pereira
Cartago
Ibague
5215
Girl
Pta. Charambirá
Buga
Arm enia
Buenaventura
Cali
5750
Palmira
Neiva

F

OCEAN
Popayán
4646

ft   m

12 000   4000
9000   3000
6000   2000
4500   1500
3000   1000
1200   400
600   200
0   0
200   600
2000   6000
m   ft

1: 15 000 000

100   100   200   300   400 miles

100   0   100   200   300   400   500   600 km

A T L A N T I C

O C E A N

Tropic of Cancer

aguana

Caicos I. (U.K.)

Turks Is. (U.K.)

de Paix

Cap Haitien

Monte Cristi

Valverde Pto. Plata

Santiago

S. Francisco de Macoris

Sanchez

Vega

DOMINICAN
REP.

3175

La Romana

1338

Santo Domingo

S. Pedro de Macoris

Hispaniola

TILLES

Prince

2680

Duverge

Azua

Bahani

Barahona

PUERTO RICO (U.S.A.)

Aguadilla

Arecibo

San Juan

Caguas

Guayama

Ponce

Mayagüez

Canal de la Mona

St. Thomas (U.S.A.)

Charlotte Amalie

Virgin Is. (U.K.)

Sombrero (U.K.)

Anguilla (U.K.)

St. Martin (Fr. & Neth.)

St. Croix
(U.S.A.)

Basseterre

Christiansted

Charlestown

ST. KITTS-NEVIS

ANTIGUA &
BARBUDA

St. John's

Plymouth

Montserrat (U.K.)

Guadeloupe (Fr.)

Pointe à Pitre

Leeward
Islands

LESSER

DOMINICA

Roseau

Martinique (Fr.)

Fort de France

Castries

A N S E A

A N T I L L E S

Windward

ST. VINCENT

& Kingstown

THE GRENADINES

ST. LUCIA

BARBADOS

Bridgetown

GRENADA

Islands

La Blanquilla
(Ven.)

St. George's

de Venezuela

Aruba (Neth.)

Curacao

Willemstad

Bonaire

NETH.

ANTILLES

Gallinas

de la
ajira

Golfo de Venezuela

Margarita

La Asunción

Carúpano

La Tortuga
(Ven.)

Cumaná

Tobago

Port of Spain

San Fernando

TRINIDAD & TOBAGO

G. de
Paria

Maiquetía

Caracas

Coro

Dabajuro

Pto. Cabello

Nevada
Marta

Maracaibo

L. de
Maracaibo

Cabimas

Trujillo

Valera

Maracay

Valencia

San Felipe

Barquisimeto

Calabozo

Portuguesa

Cord. de Mérida

Guanare

Apure

San Fernando
de Apure

Barcelona

2596

Caripito

El Tigre

Maturín

Tucupita

Orinoco

Ciudad
Guayana

Ciudad Bolívar

Las Mercedes

Caicara

Tumeremo

El Callao

Georgetown

GUYANA

New
Amsterdam

Wismare

Bartico

Cuyuni

SURINAM

5007

Cord. de Mérida

ta

Rubio

San Cristóbal

Pamplona

Bucaramanga

Arauca

Arauca

V E N E Z U E L A

Pto. Páez

Pto. Carreño

Meta

2285

Pto. Ayacucho

Caura

2560

Roraima

2810

Caroni

Essequibo

Corentyne

1280

cabermeja

unja

OMBIA

otá

quirá

Guaviare

Casiquiare

Sa. Parima

Sierra Pacaraima

B R A Z I L

Guajira

CARTOGRAPHY BY PHILIP'S.

5   70   6   65   7   8

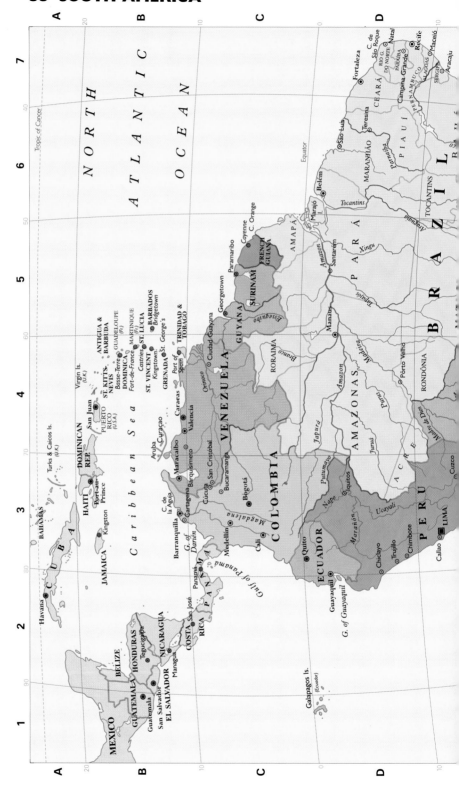

A B C D

7 6 5 4 3 2 1

Tropic of Cancer

N O R T H

A T L A N T I C

O C E A N

Equator

Havana

C U B A

BAHAMAS

Turks & Caicos Is. (U.K.)

JAMAICA
Kingston

HAITI
Port-au-Prince

DOMINICAN
REP.

San Juan
PUERTO
RICO
(U.S.A.)

Virgin Is.
(U.K.)

ST. KITTS-
NEVIS

ANTIGUA &
BARBUDA

GUADELOUPE
(Fr.)
Basse-Terre
DOMINICA

MARTINIQUE
(Fr.)
Fort-de-France
ST. LUCIA
Castries
ST. VINCENT
Kingstown
GRENADA
St. George's

BARBADOS
Bridgetown

TRINIDAD &
TOBAGO
Port of
Spain

C a r i b b e a n   S e a

Aruba
Curaçao

Maracaibo

Barranquilla
C. de
la Aguja
G. of
Cartagena Darién

PANAMA

Panamá
Gulf of Panama

COSTA
RICA San José

NICARAGUA
Managua

HONDURAS
Tegucigalpa

EL SALVADOR
San Salvador

GUATEMALA
Guatemala

BELIZE

MEXICO

Valencia
Caracas
Barquisimeto
San Cristóbal

VENEZUELA

Orinoco

Cúcuta
Bucaramanga
Medellín

Magdalena

Bogotá

Cali

C O L O M B I A

ECUADOR
Quito
Guayaquil
G. of Guayaquil

Galápagos Is.
(Ecuador)

Ciudad Guayana
Orinoco
Georgetown

Essequibo

GUYANA

SURINAM
Paramaribo

FRENCH
GUIANA
Cayenne
C. Orange

Putumayo
Napo
Quitos
Marañón
Ucayali

Chiclayo
Trujillo
Chimbote
Callao LIMA

P E R U

Cuzco
Madre de Dios

A C R E

A M A Z O N A S

Japurá
Furuá
Juruá
Purús
Madeira

Amazon
Manaus
Branco
RORAIMA

Negro

Amazon

Santarém

Xingu

Tapajós

P A R Á

Marajó
I.

Belém

Tocantins

MARANHÃO
São Luís
Teresina
Parnaíba

PIAUÍ

CEARÁ
Fortaleza
C. de
São Roque
Natal
RIO G. DO NORTE
PARAÍBA
Campina Grande
PERNAMBUCO
Recife
Maceió
ALAGOAS
SERGIPE
Aracaju

B R A Z I L

AMAPÁ

RONDÔNIA
Pôrto Velho

TOCANTINS

Araguaia

Tocantins

Cali

A B C D

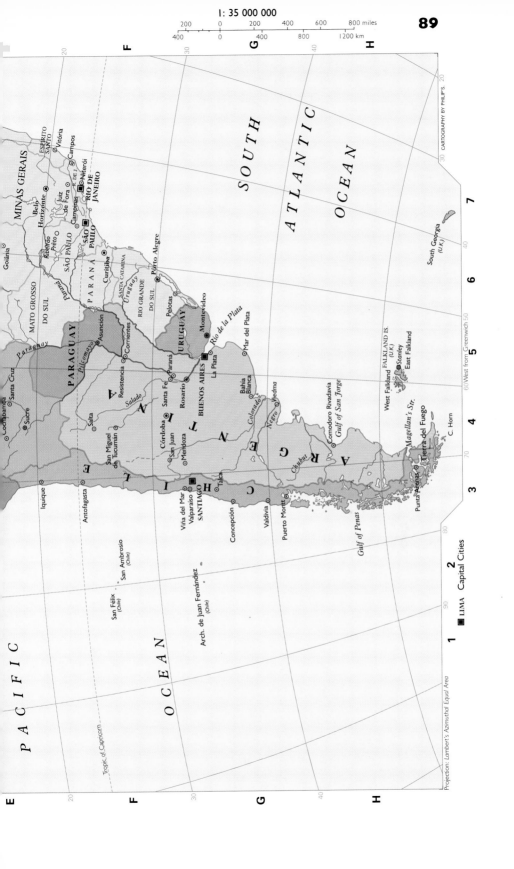

I: 35 000 000

200   0   200   400   600   800 miles
400   0   400   800   1200 km

89

CARTOGRAPHY BY PHILIP'S.

PACIFIC

OCEAN

Tropic of Capricorn

San Félix
(Chile)

San Ambrosio
(Chile)

Arch. de Juan Fernández
(Chile)

■ LIMA   Capital Cities

SOUTH

ATLANTIC

OCEAN

South Georgia
(U.K.)

MINAS GERAIS

ESPÍRITO
SANTO

Vitória

Campos

Belo
Horizonte

Juiz
de Fora

Campinas

Niterói

R. DE J.

RIO DE
JANEIRO

Ribeirão
Prêto

SÃO PAULO

SÃO
PAULO

Goiânia

MATO GROSSO
DO SUL

Paraná

PARANÁ

Curitiba

SANTA CATARINA

Uruguay

RIO GRANDE
DO SUL

Pôrto Alegre

Pelotas

Cochabamba

Santa Cruz

Sucre

Paraguay

Pilcomayo

PARAGUAY

Asunción

Corrientes

Resistencia

Salta

San Miguel
de Tucumán

Salado

Santa Fe

Paraná

Rosario

Córdoba

San Juan

Mendoza

URUGUAY

Montevideo

Río de la Plata

La Plata

BUENOS AIRES

Mar del Plata

Bahía
Blanca

Iquique

Antofagasta

Viña del Mar

Valparaíso

SANTIAGO

Talca

Concepción

Valdivia

Puerto Montt

Gulf of Peñas

Colorado

Negro

Chubut

Río
Negro

A R G E N T I N A

C H I L E

Comodoro Rivadavia

Gulf of San Jorge

West Falkland

FALKLAND IS.
(U.K.)

Stanley

East Falkland

Magellan's Str.

Tierra del Fuego

Punta Arenas

C. Horn

60 West from Greenwich 50

40

20

Projection: Lambert's Azimuthal Equal Area

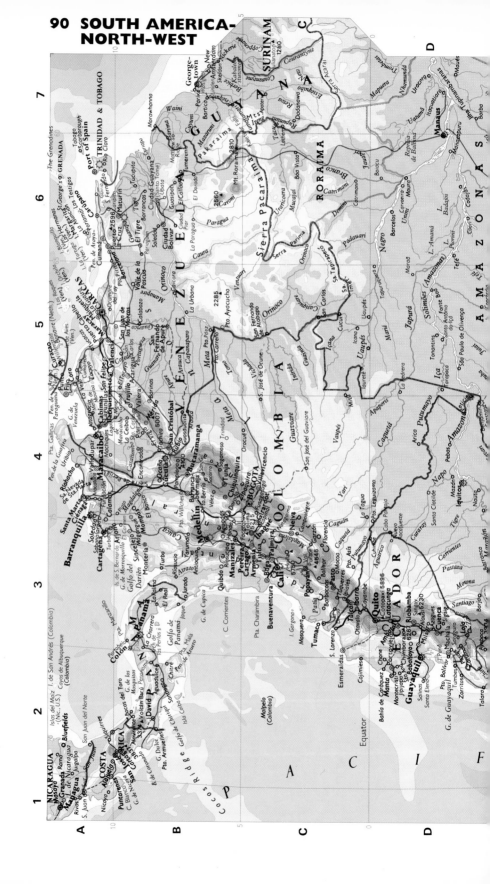

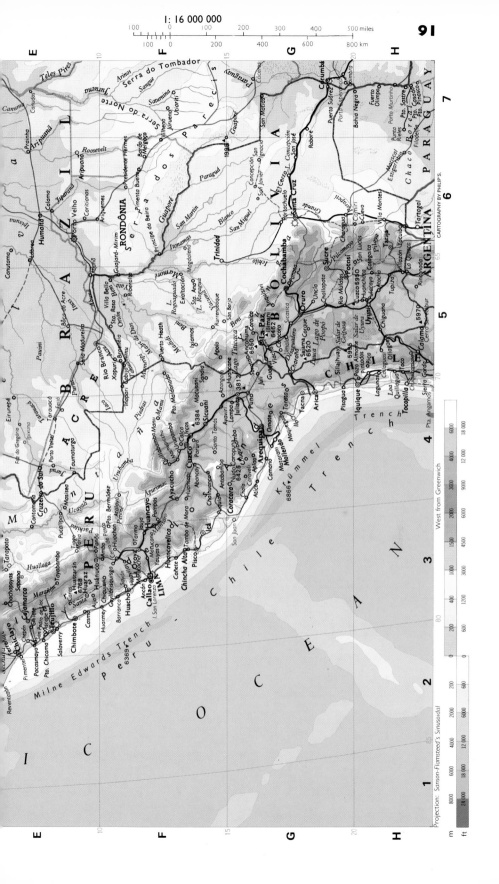

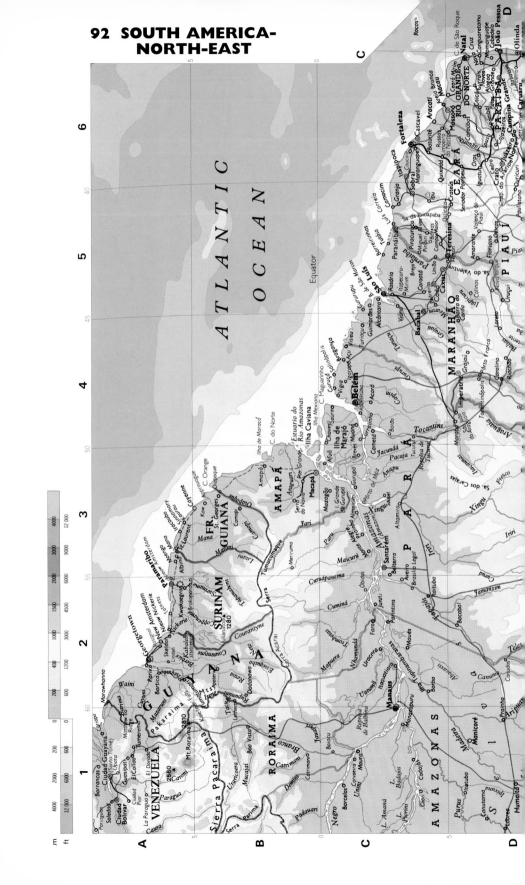

1 : 16 000 000

100   0   100   200   300   400   500 miles

100   0   200   400   600   800 km

CARTOGRAPHY BY PHILIP'S

Tropic of Capricorn

West from Greenwich

Projection: Sanson-Flamsteed's Sinusoidal

1: 16 000 000

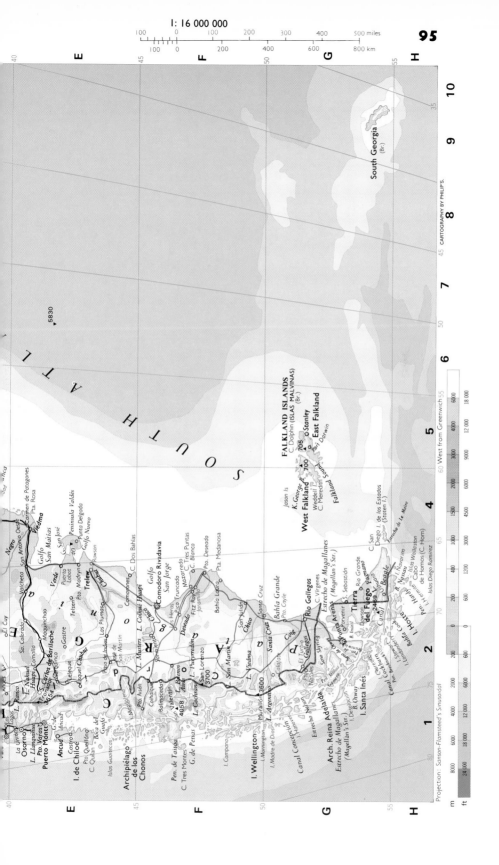

CARTOGRAPHY BY PHILIP'S.

Projection: Sanson-Flamsteed's Sinusoidal

FALKLAND ISLANDS (ISLAS MALVINAS) (Br.)

C. Dolphin

West Falkland
East Falkland
Stanley
Port Darwin
K. George I.
Weddell I.
Jason Is.
C. Meredith
Falkland Sound
705
700

South Georgia (Br.)

SOUTH ATLI

Tierra del Fuego
Estrecho de Magallanes (Magellan's Str.)
I. de los Estados (Staten I.)
C. San Diego Ramírez
Islas Wollaston (C. Horn)
Cabo de Hornos (C. Horn)
Beagle
Canal Beagle
I. Hoste
I. Navarino
Bahía Cook
I. Santa Inés

Archipiélago de los Chonos
I. Wellington
I. Madre de Dios
I. Campana
Pen. de Taitao
C. Tres Montes
G. de Penas
Arch. Reina Adelaida
Estrecho de Magallanes (Magellan's Str.)
Canal Concepción
Pto. Aisén
Coihaique
Balmaceda
Murallón 3600
L. Buenos Aires
L. Cochrane
M. San Lorenzo 3700
L. Pueyrredón
L. San Martín
L. Viedma
L. Argentino
El Turbío
Puerto Natales
Punta Arenas
Porvenir
Río Grande
Río Gallegos
C. Vírgenes
Puerto Deseado
C. Blanco
C. Tres Puntas
Pto. Deseado
Mazar edo
Santa Cruz
Pto. Santa Cruz
Bahía Grande
Pta. Coyle
San Julián
Fitz Roy
Jaramillo
Las Heras
Sarmiento
Comodoro Rivadavia
C. Dos Bahías
Camarones
Golfo San Jorge
Trelew
Rawson
Chubut
Puerto Madryn
Golfo Nuevo
Península Valdés
Punta Delgada
San José
Golfo San Matías
Pto. Lobos
San Antonio Oeste
Carmen de Patagones
Pta. Rosa
Viedma
Negro
Valcheta
Maquinchao
Telsen
Gastre
Esquel
Tecka
Río Senguerr
Gobernador Costa
Los Plumas
L. Colhué Huapi
L. Musters
José de San Martín
Paso de Indios
L. La Plata
Futaleufú
S. Carlos de Bariloche
L. Nahuel Huapi
Osorno
Pto. Varas
Puerto Montt
L. Llanquihue
Ancud
I. de Chiloé
C. Quilán
Pto. Quellón
Castro
Islas Guaitecas
B. Inútil
B. Owen
Seno Skyring
Seno Otway
C. San Sebastián
Estrecho de Le Maire

5830

35
45
45
60 West from Greenwich 55
55

m   ft
8000 24 000
6000 18 000
4000 12 000
2000 6000
1000 3000
400   1200
200   600
0   0
200   600
2000 6000
4000 12 000
6000 18 000

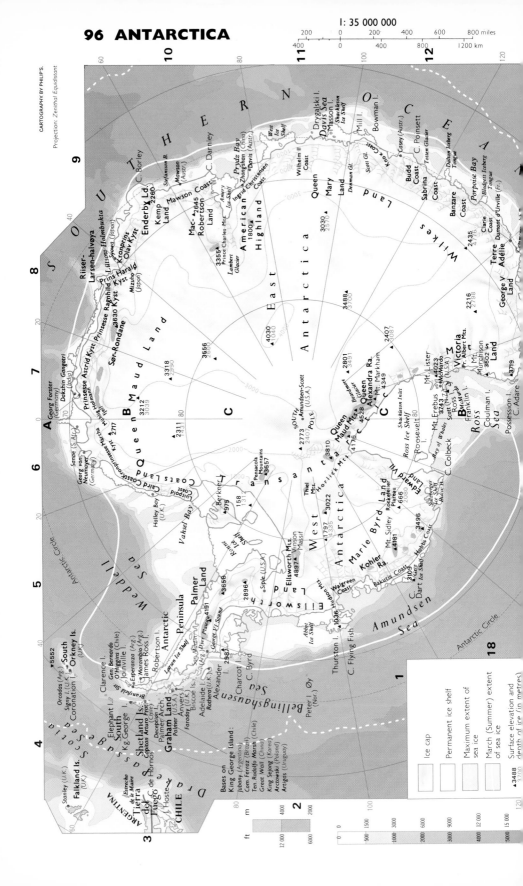

1: 35 000 000

CARTOGRAPHY BY PHILIPS.

Projection: Zenithal Equidistant

Index to Map Pages

The index contains the names of all principal places and features shown on the maps. Physical features composed of a proper name (Erie) and a description (Lake) are positioned alphabetically by the proper name. The description is positioned after the proper name and is usually abbreviated:

Erie, L. **72** **C5**

Where a description forms part of a settlement or administrative name however, it is always written in full and put in its true alphabetical position:

Lake Charles **79** **D7**

Names beginning St. are alphabetized under Saint, but Sankt, Sint, Sant, Santa and San are all spelt in full and are alphabetized accordingly.

The number in bold type which follows each name in the index refers to the number of the map page where that feature or place will be found. This is usually the largest scale at which the place or feature appears.

The letter and figure which are in bold type immediately after the page number give the grid square on the map page, within which the feature is situated.

Rivers carry the symbol ↝ after their names. A solid square ■ follows the name of a country while an open square □ refers to a first order administrative area.

A

A Coruña = La
  Coruña 18 A1
Aachen 14 C4
Aalborg =
  Ålborg 9 G9
Aalen 14 D6
Aarau 13 C8
Aare ↝ 13 C8
Aarhus = Århus 9 G10
Aba 55 G6
Ābādān 47 E7
Ābādeh 44 D3
Abadla 54 B4
Abaetetuba . . . 92 C4
Abakan 30 D7
Abancay 91 F4
Abarqū 44 D3
Abashiri 32 F12
Abay ↝ 29 E8
Abaya, L. 53 G6
Abbay = Nîl el
  Azraq ↝ . . . 53 E5
Abbeville 12 A4
Abbieglassie . . 63 A4
Abbot Ice Shelf 96 B2
Abbottabad . . 42 B8
Abd al Kūrī . . . 49 E5
Abéché 53 F3
Abeokuta 55 G5
Abercorn =
  Mbala 57 F6
Abercorn 63 A5
Aberdeen,
  Australia 63 B5
Aberdeen, U.K. 10 C5
Aberdeen,
  S. Dak., U.S.A. 76 C5

Aberdeen,
  Wash., U.S.A. 80 B2
Aberystwyth . . 11 E4
Abidjan 55 G4
Abilene 78 C4
Abitibi L. 69 D3
Abkhaz
  Republic □ =
  Abkhazia □ . 25 E5
Abkhazia □ . . . 25 E5
Abminga 62 A1
Åbo = Turku . . 9 F12
Abohar 42 D9
Aboméy 55 G5
Abong-Mbang . 56 D2
Abou-Deïa 53 F2
Abri 52 D5
Abrolhos, Banka 93 F6
Abrud 17 E6
Absaroka Range 81 C9
Abū al Khaşīb . 47 E6
Abū 'Alī 47 F7
Abu 'Arīsh 49 D3
Abu Dhabi =
  Abū Ẓāby . . . 44 E3
Abū Dīs 53 E5
Abu Hamed . . . 53 E5
Abū Kamāl 46 D5
Abū Madd, Ra's 47 F4
Abu Matariq . . . 53 F4
Abu Rudeis . . . 47 E3
Abu Tig 52 C5
Abû Zabad 53 F4
Abū Ẓāby 44 E3
Abuja 55 G6
Abukuma-
  Gawa ↝ . . . 33 G12
Abunã 91 E5
Abunã ↝ 91 E5

Abut Hd. 65 E4
Abwong 53 G5
Acaponeta 84 C3
Acapulco 84 D5
Acarigua 90 B5
Accra 55 G4
Aceh □ 36 D1
Achalpur 43 J10
Achill I. 11 E1
Achinsk 30 D7
Acireale 21 F5
Acklins I. 86 B5
Aconcagua,
  Cerro 94 C3
Aconquija, Mt. . 94 B3
Açores, Is. dos
  = Azores . . . 50 C1
Acraman, L. . . . 62 B2
Acre = 'Akko . . 46 D3
Acre □ 91 E4
Acre ↝ 91 E5
Ad Dahnā 47 F7
Ad Dammām . . 47 F7
Ad Dawhah . . . 44 E2
Ad Dilam 47 G6
Ad Dīwānīyah . 47 E6
Ada 79 B5
Adaja ↝ 18 B3
Adam 44 F4
Adamaoua,
  Massif de l' . 53 G1
Adamawa
  Highlands =
  Adamaoua,
  Massif de l' . 53 G1
Adamello, Mte. 20 A3
Adaminaby . . . 63 C4
Adam's Bridge 43 Q11
Adams Mt. 80 B3

Adana 46 C3
Adapazarı 46 B2
Adarama 53 E5
Adare, C. 96 B15
Adaut 39 F4
Adavale 63 A3
Adda ↝ 20 B2
Addis Ababa =
  Addis Abeba 53 G6
Addis Abeba . . 53 G6
Addis Alem . . . 53 G6
Adelaide 62 B2
Adelaide I. 96 A3
Adelaide Pen. . 70 B10
Adélie, Terre . . 96 A14
Adélie Land =
  Adélie, Terre 96 A14
Aden = Al
  'Adan 49 E4
Aden, G. of . . . 49 E4
Adi 39 E4
Adi Ugri 53 F6
Adige ↝ 20 B4
Adilabad 43 K11
Adirondack Mts. 73 C8
Admer 54 D6
Admiralty I. . . . 71 C6
Admiralty Is. . . 64 K9
Ado-Ekiti 55 G6
Adonara 39 F2
Adoni 43 M10
Adour ↝ 12 E3
Adra 18 D4
Adrano 21 F5
Adrar 54 C4
Adré 53 F3
Adri 52 C1
Adriatic Sea . . . 20 C5
Adua 39 E3

97

Adwa

Adwa	53	F6	
Adzhar			
Republic □ =			
Ajaria □	25	E5	
Ægean Sea	23	E5	
Aerhtai Shan	34	B4	
Afghanistan ■	45	C6	
Afgoi	49	G3	
'Afif	47	G5	
Afognak I.	71	C4	
Afuá →	92	C3	
Afyonkarahisar	46	C2	
Agadès =			
Agadez	55	E6	
Agadez	55	E6	
Agadir	54	B3	
Agapa	30	B6	
Agartala	41	F8	
Agats	39	F5	
Agboville	55	G4	
Agde	13	E5	
Agen	12	D4	
Agra	42	F10	
Agri →	21	D6	
Ağrı Dağı	46	C6	
Ağrı Karakose	46	C5	
Agrigento	21	F4	
Agrinion	23	E3	
Água Clara	93	G3	
Agua Prieta	84	A3	
Aguadas	90	B3	
Aguadilla	87	C6	
Aguarico →	90	D3	
Aguas Blancas	94	A3	
Aguascalientes	84	C4	
Aguilas	19	D5	
Agulhas, C.	58	E4	
Agung	37	F5	
Agusan →	38	C3	
Ahaggar	54	D6	
Ahar	46	C6	
Ahipara B.	64	A5	
Ahiri	43	K12	
Ahmadabad	43	H8	
Ahmadnagar	43	K9	
Ahmadpur	42	E7	
Ahmedabad =			
Ahmadabad	43	H8	
Ahmednagar =			
Ahmadnagar	43	K9	
Ahvāz	47	E7	
Ahvenanmaa =			
Åland	9	F11	
Ahwar	49	E4	
Aigues-Mortes	13	E6	
Aihui	35	A7	
Aija	91	E3	
Aiken	75	C7	
Aimere	39	F2	
Aimorés	93	F5	
Ain Banaiyan	44	F2	
Aïn Beïda	54	A6	
Aïn Ben Tili	54	C3	
Aïn-Sefra	54	B4	
Ainabo	49	F4	
Aïr	55	E6	
Aisne →	13	B5	
Aiud	17	E6	
Aix-en-Provence	13	E6	
Aix-la-Chapelle			
= Aachen	14	C4	
Aix-les-Bains	13	D6	
Aiyion	23	E4	
Aizawl	41	F9	
Ajaccio	13	F8	
Ajanta Ra.	43	J9	
Ajari Rep. =			
Ajaria □	25	E5	
Ajaria □	25	E5	
Ajdâbiyah	52	B3	
Ajka	16	E3	
'Ajmān	44	E3	
Ajmer	42	F9	
Ajo, C. de	18	A4	
Akaroa	65	E5	
Akashi	32	B4	
Akelamo	39	D3	
Aketi	56	D4	
Akharnaí	23	E4	
Akhelóös →	23	E3	
Akhisar	23	E6	
Akhmîm	52	C5	
Akimiski I.	69	C2	
Akita	33	G12	
Akjoujt	55	E2	
'Akko	46	D3	
Akkol	29	E8	
Aklavik	70	B6	
Akmolinsk =			
Astana	29	D8	
Akobo →	53	G5	
Akola	43	J10	
Akordat	53	E6	
Akpatok I.	68	B4	
Akreïjit	55	E3	
Akron	72	D5	
Aksai Chin	42	B11	
Aksaray	46	C3	
Aksarka	28	C7	
Akşehir	46	C2	
Aksu	34	B3	
Aksum	53	F6	
Aktogay	29	E8	
Aktsyabrski	17	B9	
Aktyubinsk =			
Aqtöbe	29	D6	
Aku	55	G6	
Akure	55	G6	
Akyab = Sittwe	41	G9	
Al 'Adan	49	E4	
Al Ahsā	47	F7	
Al Amādīyah	46	C5	
Al Amārah	47	E6	
Al 'Aqabah	47	E3	
Al 'Aramah	47	F6	
Al Ashkhara	45	F4	
Al Badi'	47	G6	
Al Başrah	47	E6	
Al Bayḍā	52	B3	
Al Bu'ayrāt al			
Hasūn	52	B2	
Al Fallūjah	46	D5	
Al Fāw	47	E7	
Al Fujayrah	44	E4	
Al Hābah	47	F6	
Al Haddār	47	G6	
Al Hāmad	47	E4	
Al Hamar	47	G6	
Al Hamrā'	47	F4	
Al Hariq	47	G6	
Al Hasakah	46	C5	
Al Hawrah	49	E4	
Al Hayy	47	D6	
Al Hijāz	47	F4	
Al Hillah, Iraq	47	D6	
Al Hillah,			
Si. Arabia	47	G6	
Al Hindīyah	47	D6	
Al Hoceïma	54	A4	
Al Hudaydah	49	E3	
Al Hufūf	47	F7	
Al Hulwah	47	G6	
Al Ittihad =			
Madīnat ash			
Sha'b	49	E3	
Al Jāfūrah	47	F7	
Al Jaghbūb	52	C3	
Al Jahrah	47	E6	
Al Jalāmīd	47	E4	
Al Jawf, Libya	52	D3	
Al Jawf,			
Si. Arabia	47	E4	
Al Jazirah, Iraq	46	D5	
Al Jazirah, Libya	52	C3	
Al Jubayl	47	F7	
Al Jubaylah	47	F6	
Al Junaynah	53	F3	
Al Khābūra	44	F4	
Al Khalīl	47	E3	
Al Kharfah	47	G6	
Al Kharj	47	F6	
Al Khasab	44	E4	
Al Kufrah	52	D3	
Al Kūt	47	D6	
Al Kuwayt	47	E7	
Al Lādhiqīyah	46	D3	
Al Luhayyah	49	D3	
Al Madīnah	47	F4	
Al Majma'ah	47	F6	
Al Manāmah	44	E2	
Al Marj	52	B3	
Al Mawşil	46	C5	
Al Midhnab	47	F6	
Al Mish'āb	47	E7	
Al Mubarraz	47	F7	
Al Muharraq	44	E2	
Al Mukallā	49	E4	
Al Mukhā	49	E3	
Al Musayyib	47	D6	
Al Muwayliḥ	47	F3	
Al Qadīmah	47	G4	
Al Qā'iyah	47	F5	
Al Qāmishli	46	C5	
Al Qaşabát	52	B1	
Al Qaşīm	47	F5	
Al Qaţif	47	F7	
Al Qaţrūn	52	D2	
Al Qayşūmah	47	E6	
Al Quaisūmah	47	E6	
Al Quds =			
Jerusalem	47	E3	
Al Qurayyāt	45	F4	
Al Qurnah	47	E6	
Al 'Ulā	47	F4	
Al Uqaylah ash			
Sharqīgah	52	B2	
Al Uqayr	47	F7	
Al 'Uthmānīyah	47	F7	
Al 'Uwaynid	47	F6	
Al 'Uwayqilah	47	E5	
Al 'Uyūn	47	F5	
Al Wakrah	44	E2	
Al Wari'āh	47	F6	
Al Yamāmah	47	F6	
Alabama □	74	C4	
Alabama →	74	D4	
Alaçam Dağları	23	E7	
Alagoa Grande	92	D6	
Alagoas □	93	D6	
Alagoinhas	93	E6	
Alajuela	86	D3	
Alamosa	83	B10	
Åland	9	F11	
Alania = North			
Ossetia □	25	E5	
Alanya	46	C2	
Alapayevsk	29	D7	
Alaşehir	23	E7	
Alaska □	71	B4	
Alaska, G. of	71	C5	
Alaska Peninsula	71	C4	
Alaska Range	71	B4	
Alataw Shankou	34	B3	
Alatyr	24	C6	
Alausi	90	D3	
Alawoona	62	B3	
Alba	20	B2	
Alba-Iulia	17	E6	
Albacete	19	C5	
Albacutya, L.	62	C3	
Albania ■	23	D3	
Albany,			
Australia	60	H2	
Albany, Ga.,			
U.S.A.	75	D5	
Albany, N.Y.,			
U.S.A.	73	C9	
Albany, Oreg.,			
U.S.A.	80	C2	
Albany →	69	C2	
Albardón	94	C3	
Albemarle	75	B7	
Alberche →	18	C3	
Albert, L.	62	C2	
Albert L.	57	D6	
Albert Nile →	57	D6	
Albertville	13	D7	
Albi	12	E5	
Albina	92	A3	
Alborán	18	E4	
Ålborg	9	G9	
Alborz, Reshteh-			
ye Kūhhā-ye	44	B3	
Albuquerque	83	C9	
Albury	63	C4	
Alcalá de			
Henares	18	B4	
Alcalá la Real	18	D4	
Alcamo	21	F4	
Alcaníz	19	B5	
Alcântara	92	C5	
Alcántara,			
Embalse de	18	C2	
Alcantarilla	19	D5	
Alcaraz, Sierra			
de	19	C4	
Alcaudete	18	D3	
Alcázar de San			
Juan	18	C4	
Alchevsk	25	D4	
Alcira	19	C5	
Alcoy	19	C5	
Aldabra Is.	51	G8	
Aldan →	31	C10	
Alderney	11	G5	
Aleg	55	E2	
Alegrete	94	B6	
Aleisk	29	D9	
Aleksandriya =			
Oleksandriya	17	C8	
Aleksandrovskoye			
	29	C8	
Alemania	94	B3	
Alençon	12	B4	
Aleppo = Halab	46	C4	
Alès	13	D6	
Alessándria	20	B2	
Ålesund	8	F9	
Aleutian Is.	71	C2	
Alexander Arch.	71	C6	
Alexander I.	96	A3	
Alexandra,			
Australia	63	C4	
Alexandra, N.Z.	65	F3	
Alexandria = El			
Iskandarîya	52	B4	
Alexandria,			
Canada	71	C7	
Alexandria,			
Romania	22	C5	
Alexandria,			
S. Africa	59	E5	
Alexandria, La.,			
U.S.A.	79	D7	
Alexandria, Va.,			
U.S.A.	73	E7	

Alexandrina, L. 62 C2
Alexandroúpolis 22 D5
Alga 29 E6
Algarve 18 D1
Algeciras 18 D3
Algemesí 19 C5
Alger 54 A5
Algeria ■ 54 C5
Alghero 21 D2
Algiers = Alger 54 A5
Algoa B. 59 E5
Alhucemas = Al
   Hoceïma 54 A4
'Alī al Gharbī .. 47 D6
'Alī Khēl 42 C6
Aliağa 23 E6
Alibo 53 G6
Alicante 19 C5
Alice Springs .. 60 E5
Aligarh 42 F11
Aligūdarz 46 D7
Alipur 42 E7
Alipur Duar ... 41 D7
Aliwal North .. 59 E5
Aljustrel 18 D1
Alkmaar 14 B3
All American
   Canal 82 D5
Allahabad 40 E3
Allanmyo 41 H10
Allegheny → . 73 D5
Allegheny
   Plateau 73 F5
Allentown 73 D8
Alleppey 43 Q10
Aller → 14 B5
Allier → 13 C5
Allora 63 A5
Alma Ata =
   Almaty 29 E8
Almada 18 C1
Almadén 18 C3
Almansa 19 C5
Almanzor, Pico
   del Moro .. 18 B3
Almanzora → . 19 D5
Almaty 29 E8
Almazán 19 B4
Almeirim 92 C3
Almelo 14 B4
Almendralejo .. 18 C2
Almería 19 D4
Almora 42 E11
Alnwick 10 D6
Alon 41 F10
Alor 39 F2
Alor Setar ... 36 C2
Alps 14 E5
Alsace 13 B7
Alsask 71 C9
Alsásua 19 A4
Alta Gracia 94 C4
Altagracia ... 90 A4
Altai = Aerhtai
   Shan 34 B4
Altamira 92 C3
Altamura 21 D6
Altanbulag 35 A5
Altay 34 B3
Altea 19 C5
Alto Araguaia . 93 F3
Alto Molocue . 59 B7
Alton 77 F9
Alton Downs .. 62 A2
Altoona 73 D6
Altun Shan ... 34 C3
Alùla 49 E5
Alusi 39 F4
Alvarado 85 D5

Alvear 94 B5
Alvie 62 C3
Alwar 42 F10
Alxa Zuoqi 35 C5
Am Dam 53 F3
Am-Timan ... 53 F3
Amâdi, Sudan . 53 G5
Amadi,
   Dem. Rep. of the Congo
   .... 57 D5
Amadjuak 68 B3
Amadjuak L. .. 68 B3
Amagasaki 32 B4
Amakusa-Shotō 32 C2
Amaliás 23 F3
Amalner 43 J9
Amambay,
   Cordillera de 94 A5
Amangeldy ... 29 D7
Amapá 92 B3
Amapá □ 92 B3
Amarante 92 D5
Amargosa 93 E6
Amarillo 78 B3
Amaro, Mte. .. 20 C5
Amasra 46 B3
Amasya 46 B3
Amazon =
   Amazonas → 92 C3
Amazonas □ .. 90 D6
Amazonas → . 92 C3
Ambala 42 D10
Ambalavao ... 59 J9
Ambam 56 D2
Ambanja 59 G9
Ambartsevo ... 29 D9
Ambato 90 D3
Ambatolampy . 59 H9
Ambatondrazaka 59 H9
Amberg 15 D6
Ambergris Cay 85 D7
Amberley 65 E5
Ambikapur ... 40 F4
Ambilobé 59 G9
Ambo 91 F3
Amboise 12 C4
Ambon 39 E3
Ambositra 59 J9
Amboyna I. ... 36 C4
Ambriz 56 F2
Amby 63 A4
Amchitka I. ... 71 C1
Amderma 28 C7
Ameca 84 C4
Ameland 14 B3
American
   Highland 96 B10
American
   Samoa ■ .. 65 L13
Americus 75 C5
Amery 71 C10
Amery Ice Shelf 96 A10
Ames 77 D8
Amherst, Burma 41 J11
Amherst,
   Canada 69 D4
Amiata, Mte. .. 20 C3
Amiens 12 B5
Amirante Is. .. 26 K9
'Ammān 47 E3
Amorgós 23 F5
Amoy = Xiamen 35 D6
Ampanihy ... 59 J8
Ampenan 37 F5
Amper → 15 D6
Amravati 43 J10
Amreli 43 J7
Amritsar 42 D9
Amroha 42 E11

Amsterdam ... 14 B3
Amstetten 15 D8
Amudarya → . 29 E6
Amundsen Gulf 70 A7
Amundsen Sea 96 B1
Amuntai 37 E5
Amur → 31 D12
Amurang 39 D2
Amuri Pass ... 65 E5
Amyderya =
   Amudarya → 29 E6
An Nafūd 47 E5
An Najaf 47 D6
An Nhon 36 B3
An Nu'ayrīyah . 47 F7
Anabar → 30 B9
Anaconda 81 B7
Anadolu 46 C2
'Ānah 46 D5
Anaheim 82 D4
Anakapalle ... 40 J4
Analalava 59 G9
Anambas,
   Kepulauan . 37 D3
Anambas Is. =
   Anambas,
   Kepulauan .. 37 D3
Anamur 46 C3
Anan 32 C4
Anantnag 42 C9
Ananyiv 17 E9
Anápolis 93 F4
Anār 44 D3
Anārak 44 C3
Anatolia =
   Anadolu 46 C2
Añatuya 94 B4
Anaye 53 E1
Anchorage 71 B5
Ancohuma,
   Nevada ... 91 G5
Ancón 91 F3
Ancona 20 C4
Ancud 95 E2
Ancud, G. de .. 95 E2
Andalgalá ... 94 B3
Andalucía □ .. 18 D3
Andalusia 74 D4
Andalusia □ =
   Andalucía □ .. 18 D3
Andaman Is. .. 27 H13
Andaman Sea . 36 B1
Andara 58 B4
Anderson 72 D3
Anderson → .. 70 B7
Andes = Andes,
   Cord. de los . 91 G4
Andes, Cord. de
   los 91 G4
Andhra
   Pradesh □ .. 43 L11
Andijon 29 E8
Andikíthira ... 23 G4
Andizhan =
   Andijon 29 E8
Andkhvoy 45 B6
Andoany 59 G9
Andorra ■ 19 A6
Andorra La Vella 19 A6
Andreanof Is. .. 71 C2
Andrewilla ... 62 A2
Ándria 20 D6
Andriba 59 H9
Andropov =
   Rybinsk ... 24 B4
Ándros 23 F5
Andros I. 86 B4
Andújar 18 C3
Andulo 56 G3

Aného 55 G5
Aneto, Pico de . 19 A6
Angamos, Punta 94 A2
Ang'angxi 35 B7
Angara → 30 D7
Angarsk 30 D8
Angaston 62 B2
Ånge 8 F11
Angeles 38 A2
Angellala 63 A4
Ångermanälven →
   .... 8 F11
Angers 12 C3
Anglesey 11 E4
Ango 57 D5
Angola ■ 58 A3
Angoulême ... 12 D4
Angoumois ... 12 D4
Angra dos Reis 94 A8
Angren 29 E8
Anguilla ■ ... 87 C7
Anhui □ 35 C6
Anhwei □ =
   Anhui □ ... 35 C6
Anjidiv I. 43 M9
Anjou 12 C3
Anjozorobe ... 59 H9
Anju 35 C7
Anka 55 F6
Ankang 35 C5
Ankara 46 C3
Ankazoabo ... 59 J8
Ankazobe 59 H9
Ankoro 57 F5
Ann Arbor 72 C4
Annaba 54 A6
Annan 11 D5
Annapolis 73 E7
Annecy 13 D7
Anning 34 D5
Anniston 74 C5
Annobón ... 51 G4
Annuello 62 B3
Anqing 35 C6
Ansbach 14 D6
Anshan 35 B7
Anshun 35 D5
Ansirabe ... 59 H9
Ansongo 55 E5
Ansudu 39 E5
Antabamba ... 91 F4
Antakya 46 C4
Antalaha ... 59 G10
Antalya 46 C2
Antalya Körfezi 46 C2
Antananarivo .. 59 H9
Antarctic Pen. . 96 A4
Antarctica ... 96 C
Antequera ... 18 D3
Anti Atlas 54 C3
Antibes 13 E7
Anticosti, I. d' . 69 D4
Antigua &
   Barbuda ■ .. 87 C7
Antilla 86 B4
Antioquia 90 B3
Antofagasta .. 94 A2
Antofagasta de
   la Sierra ... 94 B3
Antongila,
   Helodrano . 59 H9
Antonina 94 B7
Antrim 11 D3
Antsalova ... 59 H8
Antsiranana .. 59 G9
Antsohihy ... 59 G9
Antwerp =
   Antwerpen .. 14 C3
Antwerpen 14 C3

Anupgarh

Asturias □ 18 A3
Asunción 94 B5
Aswân 52 D5
Aswân High
Dam = Sadd
el Aali 52 D5
Asyût 52 C5
At Ţafilah 47 E3
At Ţā'if 48 C3
Atacama,
Desierto de . 94 A3
Atacama, Salar
de 94 A3
Atakpamé 55 G5
Atalaya 91 F4
Atami 32 B6
Atapupu 39 F2
Atâr 54 D2
Atasu 29 E8
Atauro 39 F3
Atbara 53 E5
'Atbara → 53 E5
Atbasar 29 D7
Athabasca ... 71 C8
Athabasca → . 70 C8
Athabasca, L. .. 70 C8
Athens =
Athínai 23 F4
Athens, Ala.,
U.S.A. 74 B4
Athens, Ga.,
U.S.A. 75 C6
Athínai 23 F4
Athlone 11 E3
Áthos 23 D5
Athy 11 E3
Ati 53 F2
Atico 91 G4
Atlanta 75 C5
Atlantic City .. 73 E8
Atlas Mts. =
Haut Atlas .. 54 B3
Atrak =
Atrek → 44 B3
Atrek → 44 B3
Attawapiskat → 69 C2
Attock 42 C8
Attopeu 36 B3
Attur 43 P11
Atuel → 94 D3
Atyraū 29 E6
Aubagne 13 E6
Aube → 13 B5
Auburn 74 C5
Auburn Ra. ... 63 A5
Aubusson 12 D5
Auch 12 E4
Auckland 64 B6
Aude → 13 E5
Augathella ... 63 A4
Augsburg 14 D6
Augusta, Italy . 21 F5
Augusta, Ga.,
U.S.A. 75 C7
Augusta, Maine,
U.S.A. 73 B11
Aunis 12 C3
Auponhia 39 E3
Aurangabad,
Bihar, India . 40 E5
Aurangabad,
Maharashtra,
India 43 K9
Aurich 14 B4
Aurillac 12 D5
Aurora, Colo.,
U.S.A. 76 F2
Aurora, Ill.,
U.S.A. 72 D1

Aus 58 D3
Auschwitz =
Oświęcim ... 16 C4
Austin, Minn.,
U.S.A. 77 D8
Austin, Tex.,
U.S.A. 78 D5
Austral Is. =
Tubuai Is. ... 65 M16
Austral
Seamount
Chain 65 M16
Australia ■ ... 60 E6
Australian
Capital
Territory □ .. 63 C4
Austria ■ 15 E8
Autun 13 C6
Auvergne 13 D5
Auvergne, Mts.
d' 13 D5
Auxerre 13 C5
Avallon 13 C5
Aveiro, Brazil . 92 C2
Aveiro, Portugal 18 B1
Ávej 46 D7
Avellaneda ... 94 C5
Avellino 21 D5
Aversa 21 D5
Avezzano 20 C4
Aviá Terai ... 94 B4
Aviemore 10 C5
Avignon 13 E6
Ávila 18 B3
Avilés 18 A3
Avoca → 62 C3
Avola 21 F5
Avranches 12 B3
'Awālī 44 E2
Awash 49 F3
Awatere → ... 65 D6
Awbārī 52 C1
Awjilah 52 C3
Axim 55 H4
Axiós → 23 D4
Ayabaca 90 D3
Ayabe 32 B4
Ayacucho,
Argentina ... 94 D5
Ayacucho,
Peru 91 F4
Ayaguz 29 E9
Ayamonte 18 D2
Ayaviri 91 F4
Āybak 45 B7
Aydın 23 F6
Ayers Rock ... 60 F5
Áyios Evstrátios 23 E5
Aylmer, L. ... 70 B8
Ayn Dār 47 F7
Ayn Zālah ... 46 C5
Ayr 10 D4
Aytos 22 C6
Ayu, Kepulauan 39 D4
Ayutla 84 D5
Ayvacık 23 E6
Ayvalık 23 E6
Aẕ Ẕahrān .. 47 F7
Az Zarqā 46 D4
Az-Zilfī 47 F6
Az Zubayr ... 47 E6
Az Zuwaytīnah 52 B3
Azamgarh ... 40 D4
Azärbayjan =
Azerbaijan ■ 25 E6
Āzarbāyjān-e
Gharbī □ ... 46 C6
Āzarbāyjān-e
Sharqī □ 46 C6

Azare 55 F7
Azbine = Aïr .. 55 E6
Azerbaijan ■ .. 25 E6
Azerbaijchan =
Azerbaijan ■ 25 E6
Azogues 90 D3
Azores 50 C1
Azov 25 D4
Azov, Sea of .. 25 D4
Azovskoye More
= Azov, Sea
of 25 D4
Azovy 28 C7
Azúa 87 C5
Azuaga 18 C3
Azuero, Pen. de 86 E3
Azul 94 D5

B
Ba Don 36 A3
Ba Ria 36 B3
Bab el Mandeb 49 E3
Baba Burnu ... 23 E6
Babadag 22 B7
Babadayhan .. 29 F7
Babaeski 22 D6
Babahoyo 90 D3
Babana 55 F5
Babar 39 F3
Babo 39 E4
Bābol 44 B3
Bābol Sar 44 B3
Baboua 56 C2
Babruysk 17 B9
Babura 55 F6
Babuyan Chan. 38 A2
Babylon 47 D6
Bacabal 92 C5
Bacan,
Kepulauan .. 39 E3
Bacan, Pulau .. 39 E3
Bacarra 38 A2
Bacău 17 E8
Bachelina 29 D7
Back → 70 B9
Backstairs
Passage ... 62 C2
Bacolod 38 B2
Bad Ischl 15 E7
Bad Kissingen . 14 C6
Bad Lands ... 76 D3
Badagara 43 P9
Badajoz 18 C2
Badalona 19 B7
Badalzai 42 E4
Badampahar .. 40 F6
Badanah 47 E5
Badarinath ... 42 D11
Badas 36 D4
Badas,
Kepulauan .. 37 D3
Baddo → 42 E4
Bade 39 F5
Baden 15 D9
Baden-Baden .. 14 D5
Baden-
Württemberg □
.... 14 D5
Badgastein ... 15 E7
Bādghīsāt □ .. 42 B3
Badin 43 G6
Baduen 49 F4
Baena 18 D3
Baeza 18 D4
Bafatá 55 F2

Baffin B. 68 A4
Baffin I. 68 B3
Bafia 56 D2
Bafing → 55 F2
Bafoulabé 55 F2
Bāfq 44 D3
Bafra 46 B3
Bāft 44 D4
Bafwasende ... 57 D5
Bagamoyo 57 F7
Baganga 38 C3
Bagansiapiapi . 37 D2
Bagdarin 30 D9
Bagé 94 C6
Baghdād 46 D6
Bagheria 21 E4
Baghlān 42 A6
Baghlān □ ... 45 C7
Baguio 38 A2
Bahamas ■ .. 86 A4
Baharampur .. 40 E7
Bahawalpur ... 42 E7
Bahía =
Salvador 93 E6
Bahía □ 93 E5
Bahía Blanca . 94 D4
Bahía de
Caráquez ... 90 D2
Bahía Laura ... 95 F3
Bahía Negra .. 91 H7
Bahr Aouk → . 56 C3
Bahr
Salamat → . 53 G2
Bahraich 40 D3
Bahrain ■ 44 E2
Baia Mare ... 17 E6
Baïbokoum ... 53 G2
Baidoa 49 G3
Baie Comeau . 69 D4
Ba'ijī 46 D5
Baikal, L. =
Baykal, Oz. .. 30 D8
Baile Atha Cliath
= Dublin ... 11 E3
Băilești 22 B4
Bailundo 58 A3
Bā'ir 47 E4
Baird Mts. 71 B3
Bairnsdale ... 63 C4
Baitadi 40 C3
Baiyin 35 C5
Baja 16 E4
Baja, Pta. 84 B1
Baja California . 84 A1
Bajimba, Mt. .. 63 A5
Bakala 56 C4
Bakchar 29 D9
Bakel 55 F2
Baker, L. 70 B10
Baker I. 64 J13
Baker Lake ... 70 B10
Baker Mt. 80 A3
Baker's Dozen
Is. 69 C3
Bakersfield ... 82 C3
Bākhtarān ... 46 D6
Bakı 25 E6
Bakony Forest =
Bakony
Hegyseg 16 E3
Bakony Hegyseg 16 E3
Bakouma 56 C4
Baku = Bakı .. 25 E6
Bakutis Coast . 96 B1
Baky = Bakı .. 25 E6
Balabac I. 36 C5
Balabac Str. ... 36 C5
Balabalangan,
Kepulauan .. 37 E5

Balaghat Ra. . . 43 K10
Balaguer 19 B6
Balaklava,
  Australia 62 B2
Balaklava,
  Ukraine 25 E3
Balakovo 24 C6
Balashov 24 C5
Balasore =
  Baleshwar . . 40 G6
Balaton 16 E3
Balbina, Reprêsa
  de 90 D7
Balchik 22 C7
Balclutha 65 G3
Baleares, Is. . . . 19 C7
Balearic Is. =
  Baleares, Is. . 19 C7
Baler 38 A2
Baleshwar . . . 40 G6
Bali, *Cameroon* 55 G7
Bali, *Indonesia* 37 F5
Bali □ 37 F5
Balikeşir 23 E6
Balikpapan . . . 37 E5
Balimbing 38 C1
Balipara 41 D9
Baliza 93 F3
Balkan Mts. =
  Stara Planina 22 C4
Balkh 45 B6
Balkhash =
  Balqash 29 E8
Balkhash, Ozero
  = Balqash Köl 29 E8
Balla 41 E8
Ballarat 62 C3
Ballater 10 C5
Ballina, *Australia* 63 A5
Ballina, *Ireland* 11 D2
Ballinasloe 11 E2
Ballymena 11 D3
Balmaceda . . . 95 F2
Balmoral 62 C3
Balonne ─► . . . 63 A4
Balqash 29 E8
Balqash Köl . . . 29 E8
Balrampur 40 D4
Balranald 62 B3
Balsas ─► 84 D4
Balta 17 D9
Bălţi 17 E8
Baltic Sea . . . 9 G11
Baltimore 73 E7
Baluchistan □ . 42 F4
Balya 23 E6
Bam 44 D4
Bama 53 F1
Bamako 55 F3
Bamba 55 E4
Bambari 56 C4
Bamberg 14 D6
Bambili 57 D5
Bamenda 55 G7
Bāmīān □ 42 B5
Bampūr 45 E5
Ban Don =
  Surat Thani . 36 C1
Ban Mê Thuôt =
  Buon Me
  Thuot 36 B3
Banaba 64 K11
Banalia 57 D5
Banam 36 B3
Banamba 55 F3
Bananal, I. do . 93 E3
Banaras =
  Varanasi 40 E4
Band-e
  Torkestān . . . 45 C6

Banda,
  Kepulauan . . 39 E3
Banda Aceh . . . 36 C1
Banda Banda,
  Mt. 63 B5
Banda Elat 39 F4
Banda Is. =
  Banda,
  Kepulauan . . 39 E3
Banda Sea 39 F3
Bandanaira . . . 39 E3
Bandar =
  Machilipatnam 40 J3
Bandār 'Abbās . 44 E4
Bandar-e Anzalī 46 C7
Bandar-e
  Bushehr =
  Büshehr 44 D2
Bandar-e Chārak 44 E3
Bandar-e
  Deylam 47 E7
Bandar-e
  Khomeynı . . . 47 E7
Bandar-e
  Lengeh 44 E3
Bandar-e
  Ma'shur 47 E7
Bandar-e
  Nakhīlū 44 E3
Bandar-e Rīg . . 44 D2
Bandar-e
  Torkeman . . . 44 B3
Bandar
  Maharani =
  Muar 37 D2
Bandar
  Penggaram =
  Batu Pahat . 37 D2
Bandar Seri
  Begawan . . . 36 D5
Bandawe 59 A6
Bandeira, Pico
  da 93 G5
Bandera 94 B4
Bandiagara . . . 55 F4
Bandırma 23 D7
Bandon 11 F2
Bandundu 56 E3
Bandung 37 F3
Banff, *Canada* . 71 C8
Banff, *U.K.* 10 C5
Banfora 55 F4
Bang Saphan . . 36 B1
Bangalore 43 N10
Bangassou 56 D4
Banggai,
  Kepulauan . . 39 E2
Banggi, P. 36 C5
Banghāzī 52 B3
Bangka, P.,
  Sulawesi,
  Indonesia . . . 39 D3
Bangka, P.,
  Sumatera,
  Indonesia . . . 37 E3
Bangka, Selat . 37 E3
Bangkinang . . . 37 D2
Bangko 37 E2
Bangkok 36 B2
Bangladesh ■ . 41 E7
Bangong Co . . 42 B11
Bangor, *Down,*
  U.K. 11 D4
Bangor,
  Gwynedd,
  U.K. 11 E4
Bangor, *U.S.A.* . 73 B11
Bangued 38 A2
Bangui 56 D3

Bangweulu, L. . 57 G6
Bani 87 C5
Banī Walīd 52 B1
Banīnah 52 B3
Bāniyās 46 D3
Banja Luka . . . 20 B6
Banjarmasin . . 37 E4
Banjul 55 F1
Bankipore 40 E5
Banks I. 70 A7
Banks Pen. . . . 65 E5
Banks Str. 62 D4
Bankura 40 F6
Banningville =
  Bandundu . . 56 E3
Bannu 42 C7
Banská Bystrica 16 D4
Banswara 43 H9
Bantry 11 F2
Banu 42 B6
Banyak,
  Kepulauan . . 37 D1
Banyo 55 G7
Banzare Coast . 96 A13
Banzyville =
  Mobayi 56 D4
Baoding 35 C6
Baoji 35 C5
Baoshan 34 D4
Baotou 35 B6
Bapatla 40 K3
Ba'qūbah 46 D6
Bar,
  Montenegro, Yug.
  . . . . 22 C2
Bar, *Ukraine* . . 17 D8
Bar-le-Duc . . . 13 B6
Barabai 37 E5
Barabinsk 29 D8
Baracaldo 19 A4
Baracoa 86 B5
Barahona 87 C5
Barail Range . . 41 E9
Barakhola 41 E9
Barakpur 41 F7
Barakula 63 A5
Baramula 42 B9
Baran 43 G10
Baranavichy . . 17 B8
Baranof I. 71 C6
Barão de
  Melgaço 91 F6
Barapasi 39 E5
Barat Daya,
  Kepulauan . . 39 F3
Barbacena . . . 93 G5
Barbacoas . . . 90 C3
Barbados ■ . . . 87 D8
Barbastro 19 A6
Barberton 59 D6
Barcellona Pozzo
  di Gotto 21 E5
Barcelona, *Spain* 19 B7
Barcelona,
  Venezuela . . . 90 A6
Barcelos 90 D6
Bardai 52 D2
Barddhaman . . 40 F6
Bardejov 16 D5
Bardera 49 G3
Bardi, Ra's 47 F4
Bardīyah 52 B4
Bareilly 42 E11
Barentu 53 E6
Barfleur, Pte. de 12 B3
Barga 34 C3
Bargal 49 E5
Barhi 40 E5
Bari 20 D6

Bari Doab 42 D8
Barīm 49 E3
Barinas 90 B4
Baring, C. 70 B8
Bârîs 52 D5
Barisal 41 F8
Barisan, Bukit . 37 E2
Barito ─► 37 E4
Barkly Tableland 60 D6
Barlee, L. 60 F2
Barletta 20 D6
Barmedman . . . 63 B4
Barmer 42 G7
Barmera 62 B3
Barnato 63 B4
Barnaul 29 D9
Barnsley 11 E6
Barnstaple 11 F4
Baro ─► 55 G6
Baroda =
  Vadodara . . . 43 H8
Barpeta 41 D8
Barquísimeto . . 90 A5
Barra, *Brazil* . . 93 E5
Barra, *U.K.* 10 C3
Barra do Corda 92 D4
Barra do Piraí . 93 G5
Barra Falsa, Pta.
  da 59 C7
Barraba 63 B5
Barrackpur =
  Barakpur 41 F7
Barraigh =
  Barra 10 C3
Barranca, *Lima,*
  Peru 91 F3
Barranca,
  Loreto, Peru . 90 D3
Barrancabermeja
  . . . . 90 B4
Barrancas 90 B6
Barrancos 18 C2
Barranqueras . . 94 B5
Barranquilla . . 90 A4
Barras 92 C5
Barreiras 93 E5
Barreirinhas . . 92 C5
Barreiro 18 C1
Barreiros 92 D6
Barretos 93 G4
Barrier Ra. 62 B3
Barrington Tops 63 B5
Barringun 63 A4
Barrow 71 A4
Barrow-in-
  Furness 11 D5
Barry 11 F5
Barsi 43 K9
Barsoi 40 E6
Barstow 82 C4
Bartica 90 B7
Bartın 46 B3
Bartle Frere . . . 61 D8
Bartlesville . . . 79 A6
Barysaw 17 A9
Bāsa'idū 44 E3
Basankusu . . . 56 D3
Basarabeasca . 17 E9
Basel 13 C7
Bashi Channel . 35 D7
Bashkir Republic
  =
  Bashkortostan □
  . . . . 29 D6
Bashkortostan □ 29 D6
Basilan 38 C2
Basilan Str. . . . 38 C2
Basildon 11 F7
Basim =
  Washim 43 J10

Basingstoke ...	11	F6
Basle = Basel .	13	C7
Basoka	56	D4
Basongo	56	E4
Basque		
Provinces =		
País Vasco □	19	A4
Basra = Al		
Başrah	47	E6
Bass Str.	61	H8
Bassano	71	C8
Bassano del		
Grappa	20	B3
Bassas da India	59	C7
Bassein	41	J10
Basseterre	87	C7
Bassikounou ..	55	E3
Bastak	44	E3
Bastar	40	H3
Basti	40	D4
Bastia	13	E8
Bastogne	14	C3
Bata	56	D1
Bataan	38	B2
Batabanó	86	B3
Batabanó, G. de	86	B3
Batac	38	A2
Batagoy	31	C11
Batamay	31	C10
Batang	34	C4
Batangafo	56	C3
Batangas	38	B2
Batanta	39	E4
Bateman's B. .	63	C5
Batemans Bay .	63	C5
Bath	11	F5
Bathurst,		
Australia	63	B4
Bathurst,		
Canada	69	D4
Bathurst, C. ..	70	A7
Bathurst Harb. .	62	D4
Bathurst Inlet .	70	B9
Batinah	44	F4
Batlow	63	C4
Batman	46	C5
Batna	54	A6
Baton Rouge ..	79	D8
Batouri	56	D2
Battambang ...	36	B2
Battipáglia	21	D5
Battle Creek ...	72	C3
Battle Harbour .	69	C5
Battleford	71	C9
Batu	49	F2
Batu, Kepulauan	37	E1
Batu Is. = Batu,		
Kepulauan ..	37	E1
Batu Pahat	37	D2
Batuata	39	F2
Batumi	25	E5
Baturaja	37	E2
Baturité	92	C6
Bau	37	D4
Baubau	39	F2
Bauchi	55	F6
Bauer, C.	62	B1
Baukau	39	F3
Bauru	93	G4
Baús	93	F3
Bautzen	15	C8
Bavaria =		
Bayern □ ...	15	D6
Bawdwin	41	F11
Bawean	37	F4
Bawku	55	F4
Bawlake	41	H11
Bay, L. de	38	B2
Bay City	72	C4
Bay View	64	C7
Bayamo	86	B4
Bayan Har Shan	34	C4
Bayan Hot =		
Alxa Zuoqi ..	35	C5
Bayanaüyl	29	D8
Bayanhongor ..	35	B5
Bayázeh	44	C3
Baybay	38	B2
Bayburt	46	B5
Bayern □	15	D6
Bayeux	12	B3
Bayındır	23	E6
Baykal, Oz.	30	D8
Baykit	30	C7
Baykonur =		
Bayqongyr ..	29	E7
Bayombong ...	38	A2
Bayonne	12	E3
Bayovar	91	E2
Bayqongyr	29	E7
Bayram-Ali =		
Bayramaly ..	29	F7
Bayramaly	29	F7
Bayramiç	23	E6
Bayreuth	15	D6
Bayrūt	46	D3
Baytown	79	E6
Baza	19	D4
Bazaruto, I. do .	59	C7
Beachport	62	C2
Beagle, Canal .	95	G3
Beardmore		
Glacier	96	C14
Béarn	12	E3
Beauce, Plaine		
de la	12	B4
Beaudesert ...	63	A5
Beaufort	36	C5
Beaufort Sea ..	66	B6
Beaufort West .	58	E4
Beaumont	79	D6
Beaune	13	C6
Beauvais	12	B5
Beauval	71	C9
Beaver	71	B5
Beaver →	71	C9
Beawar	42	F9
Bečej	22	B3
Béchar	54	B4
Bedford	11	E6
Beenleigh	63	A5
Be'er Sheva ..	47	E3
Beersheba =		
Be'er Sheva .	47	E3
Befale	56	D4
Bega	63	C4
Behbehän	47	E7
Behshahr	44	B3
Bei Jiang → ..	35	D6
Bei'an	35	B7
Beibei	35	D5
Beihai	35	D5
Beijing	35	C6
Beilpajah	63	B3
Beinn na		
Faoghla =		
Benbecula ..	10	C3
Beira	59	B6
Beirut = Bayrūt	46	D3
Beitbridge	59	C6
Beja, Portugal .	18	C2
Béja, Tunisia ..	54	A6
Bejaia	54	A6
Béjar	18	B3
Bejestän	44	C4
Békéscsaba ..	16	E5
Bela, India ...	40	E4
Bela, Pakistan .	42	F5
Bela Crkva	22	B3
Bela Vista	94	A5
Belarus ■	24	C2
Belau = Palau ■	38	C4
Belawan	37	D1
Belaya Tserkov		
= Bila Tserkva	17	D10
Belcher Is.	69	C3
Belém	92	C4
Belén	94	A5
Belet Uen	49	G4
Belev	24	C4
Belfast	11	D4
Belfort	13	C7
Belgaum	43	M9
Belgium ■	14	C3
Belgorod	24	C4
Belgorod-		
Dnestrovskiy		
= Bilhorod-		
Dnistrovskyy	25	D3
Belgrade =		
Beograd	22	B3
Beli Drim → ..	22	C3
Belinga	56	D2
Belinyu	37	E3
Beliton Is. =		
Belitung	37	E3
Belitung	37	E3
Belize ■	85	D7
Belize City	85	D7
Belkovskiy,		
Ostrov	30	B11
Bell Bay	62	D4
Bell Peninsula .	68	B2
Bell Ville	94	C4
Bella Unión ...	94	C5
Bella Vista	94	B5
Bellary	43	M10
Bellata	63	A4
Belle-Ile	12	C2
Belle Isle	69	C5
Belle Isle, Str. of	69	C5
Belleville,		
Canada, ...	69	D3
Belleville, U.S.A.	77	F10
Bellin =		
Kangirsuk ...	68	C4
Bellingen	63	B5
Bellingham	80	A2
Bellingshausen		
Sea	96	A2
Bellinzona ...	13	C8
Belluno	20	A4
Belmont	63	B5
Belmonte	93	F6
Belmopan	85	D7
Belo Horizonte .	93	F5
Belo-Tsiribihina	59	H8
Beloit	77	D10
Belokorovichi .	17	C9
Belomorsk	28	C4
Belonia	41	F8
Belorussia ■ =		
Belarus ■ ...	24	C2
Belovo	29	D9
Beloye, Ozero .	24	A4
Beloye More ..	28	C4
Belozersk	24	A4
Beltana	62	B2
Belterra	92	C3
Beltsy = Bălți .	17	E8
Belukha	29	E9
Beluran	36	C5
Belyy, Ostrov .	28	B8
Belyy Yar	29	D9
Bembéréke ..	55	F5
Bemidji	77	B7
Ben Gardane ..	52	B1
Ben Lomond,		
N.S.W.,		
Australia	63	B5
Ben Lomond,		
Tas., Australia	62	D4
Ben Nevis	10	C4
Bena	55	F6
Bena Dibele ..	56	E4
Benagerie	62	B3
Benalla	63	C4
Benambra, Mt. .	63	C4
Benares =		
Varanasi	40	E4
Benavente ...	18	A3
Benbecula ...	10	C3
Benbonyathe ..	62	B2
Bend	80	C3
Bender Beila .	49	F5
Bendery =		
Tighina	17	E9
Bendigo	63	C3
Benevento	20	D5
Bengal, Bay of .	41	J7
Bengbu	35	C6
Benghazi =		
Banghāzī ...	52	B3
Bengkalis	37	D2
Bengkulu	37	E2
Bengkulu □ ...	37	E2
Benguela	58	A2
Beni	57	D5
Beni →	91	F5
Beni Abbès ...	54	B4
Beni Mazâr ...	52	C5
Beni Mellal ...	54	B3
Beni Ounif ...	54	B4
Beni Suef	52	C5
Benidorm	19	C5
Benin ■	55	G5
Benin, Bight of	55	H5
Benin City	55	G6
Benjamin		
Constant	90	D4
Benoni	59	D5
Bent	44	E4
Benteng	39	F2
Benton Harbor	72	C2
Benue →	55	G6
Benxi	35	B7
Beo	38	D3
Beograd	22	B3
Beppu	32	C2
Berati	23	D2
Berau, Teluk ..	39	E4
Berber	53	E5
Berbera	49	E4
Berbérati	56	D3
Berbice → ...	90	B7
Berdichev =		
Berdychiv ...	17	D9
Berdsk	29	D9
Berdyansk ...	25	D4
Berdychiv	17	D9
Berebere	39	D3
Bereda	49	E5
Berehove	17	D6
Berekum	55	G4
Berestechko ...	17	C7
Bereza	17	B7
Berezhany ...	17	D7
Berezina =		
Byarezina →	17	B10
Berezniki	28	D6
Berezovo	28	C7
Berga	19	A6
Bergama	23	E6
Bérgamo	20	B2
Bergen	8	F9
Bergerac	12	D4

Berhala, Selat . 37 E2
Berhampore =
Baharampur . 40 E7
Berhampur =
Brahamapur . 40 H5
Bering Sea 71 C1
Bering Strait .. 71 B3
Berja 19 D4
Berkeley 80 G2
Berkner I. 96 B4
Berlin 15 B7
Bermejo →,
Formosa,
Argentina .. 94 B5
Bermejo →,
San Juan,
Argentina .. 94 C3
Bermuda ■ ... 67 F13
Bern 13 C7
Bernardo de
Irigoyen 94 B6
Bernburg 15 C6
Berne = Bern . 13 C7
Bernina, Piz .. 13 C8
Beroroha 59 J9
Beroun 16 D2
Berrechid 54 B3
Berri 62 B3
Berry, Australia 63 B5
Berry, France .. 12 C5
Bershad 17 D9
Bertoua 56 D2
Berwick-upon-
Tweed 10 D6
Besalampy 59 H8
Besançon 13 C7
Besar 37 E5
Besni 46 C4
Bessarabiya = 17 E9
Bessarabka =
Basarabeasca 17 E9
Bessemer 74 C4
Betanzos 18 A1
Bétaré Oya ... 56 C2
Bethanien 58 D3
Bethel 71 B3
Bethlehem,
S. Africa 59 D5
Bethlehem,
U.S.A. 73 D8
Béthune 13 A5
Bethungra ... 63 B4
Betioky 59 J8
Betroka 59 J9
Betsiamites ... 69 D4
Bettiah 40 D5
Betul 43 J10
Betung 37 D4
Beverley 11 E6
Beverly Hills . 82 C3
Beyla 55 G3
Beyneu 29 E6
Beypazarı 46 B2
Beyşehir Gölü . 46 C2
Bezhitsa 24 C3
Béziers 13 E5
Bezwada =
Vijayawada . 40 J3
Bhachau 43 H7
Bhadrakh 40 G6
Bhadravati ... 43 N9
Bhagalpur ... 40 E6
Bhakra Dam .. 42 D10
Bhamo 41 E11
Bhandara 43 J11
Bhanrer Ra. .. 43 H11
Bharat =
India ■ 43 J10
Bharatpur 42 F10

Bhatpara 41 F7
Bhaunagar =
Bhavnagar .. 43 J8
Bhavnagar 43 J8
Bhawanipatna . 40 H3
Bhilsa = Vidisha 43 H10
Bhilwara 43 G9
Bhima → 43 L10
Bhimavaram .. 40 J3
Bhind 42 F11
Bhiwandi 43 K8
Bhiwani 42 E10
Bhola 41 F8
Bhopal 43 H10
Bhubaneshwar 40 G5
Bhuj 43 H6
Bhumiphol Dam
= Phumiphon,
Khuan 36 A1
Bhusaval 43 J9
Bhutan ■ 41 D8
Biafra, B. of =
Bonny, Bight
of 56 D1
Biak 39 E5
Biała Podlaska . 17 B6
Białogard 16 A2
Białystok 17 B6
Biaro 39 D3
Biarritz 12 E3
Bibala 58 A2
Biberach 14 D5
Bibiani 55 G4
Bida 55 G6
Bidar 43 L10
Biddeford 73 C10
Bidon 5 = Poste
Maurice
Cortier 54 D5
Bié, Planalto de 58 A3
Biel 13 C7
Bielefeld 14 B5
Biella 20 B2
Bielsk Podlaski 17 B6
Bielsko-Biała .. 16 D4
Bien Hoa 36 B3
Bienne = Biel . 13 C7
Bienville, L. ... 69 C3
Big Horn Mts. =
Bighorn Mts. . 81 C10
Big Spring 78 C3
Big Trout L. ... 69 C2
Biğa 23 D6
Bigadiç 23 E7
Biggar 71 C9
Biggenden ... 63 A5
Bighorn → ... 81 B10
Bighorn Mts. .. 81 C10
Bihać 20 B5
Bihar 40 E5
Bihar □ 40 E5
Bihor, Munții .. 17 E6
Bijagós,
Arquipélago
dos 55 F1
Bijapur,
Karnataka,
India 43 L9
Bijapur, Mad. P.,
India 40 H3
Bijār 46 D6
Bijeljina 20 B7
Bijnor 42 E11
Bikaner 42 E8
Bikini Atoll ... 64 H11
Bila Tserkva .. 17 D10
Bilara 42 F8
Bilaspur 40 F4
Bilauk Taungdan 36 B1

Bilbao 19 A4
Bilbo = Bilbao . 19 A4
Bilecik 46 B2
Bilhorod-
Dnistrovskyy 25 D3
Bilir 31 C11
Billings 81 C9
Billiton Is. =
Belitung 37 E3
Bilma 53 E1
Biloxi 79 D9
Biltine 53 F3
Bima 39 F1
Bimbo 56 D3
Bina-Etawah .. 43 G11
Binalbagan ... 38 B2
Binalong 63 B4
Bīnālūd, Kūh-e 44 B4
Binatang 37 D4
Binda 63 A4
Bindle 63 A4
Bindura 59 B6
Bingara, N.S.W.,
Australia 63 A5
Bingara,
Queens.,
Australia 63 A3
Bingham
Canyon 81 E7
Binghamton ... 73 C8
Bingöl 46 C5
Binh Dinh = An
Nhon 36 B3
Binh Son 36 A3
Binjai 37 D1
Binnaway 63 B4
Binongko 39 F2
Bintan 37 D2
Bintulu 37 D4
Bintuni 39 E4
Binzert = Bizerte 54 A6
Bioko 56 D1
Bir 43 K9
Bir Autrun ... 53 E4
Bir Mogrein ... 54 C2
Bîr Ungât 52 D5
Bira 39 E4
Birao 53 F3
Birchip 62 C3
Birecik 46 C4
Bireuen 36 C1
Bîrlad 17 E8
Bîrlad → 17 F8
Birmingham,
U.K. 11 E6
Birmingham,
U.S.A. 74 C4
Birmitrapur ... 40 F5
Birni Nkonni .. 55 F6
Birnin Kebbi .. 55 F5
Birr 11 E3
Birrie → 63 A4
Birsk 29 D6
Birur 43 N9
Bisa 39 E3
Biscay, B. of .. 12 D2
Biscoe Bay 96 B17
Biscoe Is. 96 A3
Bishkek 29 E8
Biskra 54 B6
Bislig 38 C3
Bismarck 76 B4
Bismarck Arch. 64 K9
Bissagos =
Bijagós,
Arquipélago
dos 55 F1
Bissau 55 F1
Bistrița 17 E7

Bistrița → 17 E8
Bitam 56 D2
Bitkine 53 F2
Bitlis 46 C5
Bitola 22 D3
Bitolj = Bitola . 22 D3
Bitter L. =
Buheirat-
Murrat-el-
Kubra 52 B5
Bitterfontein . 58 E3
Bitterroot Range 81 B6
Biu 53 F1
Biwa-Ko 32 B5
Biysk 29 D9
Bizerte 54 A6
Bjelovar 20 B6
Black Forest =
Schwarzwald 14 D5
Black Hills 76 D3
Black Sea 25 E3
Black Volta → 55 G4
Blackball 65 E4
Blackburn 11 E5
Blackpool 11 E5
Blackwater → . 11 E2
Blagodarnoye =
Blagodarnyy 25 D5
Blagodarnyy .. 25 D5
Blagoevgrad .. 22 C4
Blagoveshchensk
.... 31 D10
Blairmore 71 D8
Blanc, Mont ... 13 D7
Blanca, B. ... 95 D4
Blanca Peak .. 83 B10
Blanche, C. .. 62 B1
Blanche, L. ... 62 A2
Blanes 19 B7
Blantyre 59 B6
Blayney 63 B4
Blednaya, Gora 28 B7
Blenheim 65 D5
Blida 54 A5
Bligh Sound .. 65 F2
Blitta 55 G5
Blodgett Iceberg
Tongue 96 A13
Bloemfontein . 59 D5
Bloemhof 59 D5
Blois 12 C4
Bloomington,
Ill., U.S.A. .. 77 E10
Bloomington,
Ind., U.S.A. .. 72 E2
Blue Mts., Oreg.,
U.S.A. 80 C4
Blue Mts., Pa.,
U.S.A. 73 D7
Blue Nile = Nîl
el Azraq → . 53 E5
Blue Ridge Mts. 75 A7
Bluefields 86 D3
Bluff 65 G3
Blumenau 94 B7
Bo 55 G2
Bo Duc 36 B3
Bo Hai 35 C6
Boa Vista 90 C6
Boatman 63 A4
Bobadah 63 B4
Bobbili 40 H4
Bobo-Dioulasso 55 F4
Bóbr → 16 B2
Bobraomby,
Tanjon' i 59 G9
Bobruysk =
Babruysk ... 17 B9
Bôca do Acre . 91 E5

Boca Raton ...	75	F7
Bocaiúva	93	F5
Bocanda	55	G4
Bocaranga	56	C3
Bochnia	16	D5
Bochum	14	C4
Boda	56	D3
Bodaybo	30	D9
Boden	8	E12
Bodensee	13	C8
Bodhan	43	K10
Bodø	8	E10
Bodrog →	16	D5
Bodrum	23	F6
Boende	56	E4
Boffa	55	F2
Bogalusa	79	D9
Bogan Gate ..	63	B4
Boggabilla	63	A5
Boggabri	63	B5
Bogo	38	B2
Bogong, Mt. ..	63	C4
Bogotá	90	C4
Bogotol	29	D9
Bogra	41	E7
Bogué	55	E2
Bohemian		
Forest =		
Böhmerwald	15	D7
Bohena Cr. →	63	B4
Böhmerwald ..	15	D7
Bohol	38	C2
Bohol Sea ...	38	C2
Bohotleh	49	F4
Boise	80	D5
Boise City ...	78	A2
Bojador C. ...	54	C2
Bojana →	22	D2
Bojnūrd	44	B4
Boké	55	F2
Bokhara → ...	63	A4
Bokoro	53	F2
Bokote	56	E4
Bokungu	56	E4
Bol	53	F1
Bolama	55	F1
Bolan Pass ...	42	E5
Bolbec	12	B4
Bole	34	B3
Bolekhiv	17	D6
Bolekhov =		
Bolekhiv	17	D6
Bolesławiec ...	16	C2
Bolgrad =		
Bolhrad	17	F9
Bolhrad	17	F9
Bolinao C.	38	A1
Bolívar,		
Argentina ...	94	D4
Bolívar,		
Colombia ...	90	C3
Bolivia ■	91	G6
Bollon	63	A4
Bolobo	56	E3
Bologna	20	B3
Bologoye	24	B3
Bolomba	56	D3
Bolong	38	C2
Bolsena, L. di .	20	C3
Bolshereche ...	29	D8
Bolshevik,		
Ostrov	30	B8
Bolshoi Kavkas		
= Caucasus		
Mountains ..	25	E5
Bolshoy Atlym	28	C7
Bolshoy		
Begichev,		
Ostrov	30	B9

Bolshoy		
Lyakhovskiy,		
Ostrov	31	B12
Bolton	11	E5
Bolu	46	B2
Bolvadin	46	C2
Bolzano	20	A3
Bom Despacho	93	F4
Bom Jesus da		
Lapa	93	E5
Boma	56	F2
Bomaderry ...	63	B5
Bombala	63	C4
Bombay	43	K8
Bomboma	56	D3
Bomili	57	D5
Bomongo	56	D3
Bomu →	56	D4
Bon, C.	52	A1
Bonaire	87	D6
Bonang	63	C4
Bonavista	69	D5
Bondo	56	D4
Bondoukou ...	55	G4
Bone, Teluk ..	39	E2
Bonerate	39	F2
Bonerate,		
Kepulauan ..	39	F2
Bong Son =		
Hoai Nhon ..	36	B3
Bongandanga .	56	D4
Bongor	53	F2
Bonifacio	13	F8
Bonn	14	C4
Bonney, L. ...	62	C3
Bonny, Bight of	56	D1
Bonoi	39	E5
Bontang	37	D5
Bonthain	39	F1
Bonthe	55	G2
Bontoc	38	A2
Boolaboolka L.	62	B3
Booligal	63	B3
Boonah	63	A5
Boorindal	63	B4
Boorowa	63	B4
Boothia, Gulf of	68	A2
Boothia Pen. ..	70	A10
Booué	56	E2
Bor,		
Serbia, Yug. .	22	B4
Bôr, Sudan ...	53	G5
Borama	49	F3
Borås	9	G10
Borāzjān	44	D2
Borba	90	D7
Borda, C.	62	C2
Bordeaux	12	D3
Bordertown ...	62	C3
Bordj Fly Ste.		
Marie	54	C4
Bordj-in-Eker ..	54	D6
Bordj Omar		
Driss	54	C6
Bordj-Tarat ...	54	C6
Borger	78	B3
Borisoglebsk ..	24	C5
Borisov =		
Barysaw	17	A9
Borja	90	D3
Borkou	53	E2
Borkum	14	B4
Borley, C.	96	A9
Borneo	37	D4
Bornholm	9	G11
Boromo	55	F4
Borongan	38	B3
Borovichi	24	B3
Borşa	17	E7

Borūjerd	46	D7
Boryslav	17	D6
Bosa	21	D2
Bosanska		
Gradiška ...	20	B6
Bosaso	49	E4
Boshan	35	C6
Boshrūyeh	44	C4
Bosna →	20	B7
Bosna i		
Hercegovina		
= Bosnia-		
Herzegovina ■	20	B6
Bosnia-		
Herzegovina ■	20	B6
Bosnik	39	E5
Bosobolo	56	D3
Bosporus =		
Karadeniz		
Boğazı	22	D7
Bossangoa ...	56	C3
Bossembélé ...	53	G2
Bosso	53	F1
Bosten Hu ...	34	B3
Boston, U.K. ..	11	E6
Boston, U.S.A. .	73	C10
Botany B.	63	B5
Bothnia, G. of .	8	F12
Bothwell	62	D4
Botletle → ...	58	C4
Botoşani	17	E8
Botswana ■ ...	58	C4
Botucatu	94	A7
Bou Djébéha ..	55	E4
Bou Izakarn ...	54	C3
Bouaké	55	G3
Bouar	56	C3
Bouârfa	54	B4
Bouca	56	C3
Bougie = Bejaia	54	A6
Bougouni	55	F3
Boulder	76	E2
Boulder Dam =		
Hoover Dam	82	B5
Boulogne-sur-		
Mer	12	A4
Boultoum	55	F7
Bouna	55	G4
Boundiali	55	G3
Bourbonnais ..	13	C5
Bourem	55	E4
Bourg-en-Bresse	13	C6
Bourg-St.-		
Maurice	13	D7
Bourges	12	C5
Bourgogne ...	13	C6
Bourke	63	B4
Bournemouth .	11	F6
Bousso	53	F2
Boutilimit	55	E2
Bowen Mts. ...	63	C4
Bowman I.	96	A12
Bowmans	62	B2
Bowral	63	B5
Bowraville ...	63	B5
Boyne →	11	E3
Boyni Qara ...	45	B6
Boz Dağları ..	23	E7
Bozburun	23	F7
Bozcaada	23	E6
Bozdoğan	23	F7
Bozeman	81	C8
Bozen =		
Bolzano	20	A3
Bozoum	56	C3
Bra	20	B1
Brač	20	C6
Bracciano, L. di	20	C4
Brach	52	C1

Bräcke	8	F11
Brad	17	E6
Bradenton ...	75	F6
Bradford	11	E6
Bræmar	62	B2
Braga	18	B1
Bragança, Brazil	92	C4
Bragança,		
Portugal, ...	18	B2
Brahamapur ..	40	H5
Brahmanbaria .	41	F8
Brahmani → ..	40	G6
Brahmaputra →	41	F7
Braidwood ...	63	C4
Brăila	17	F8
Branco →	90	D6
Brandenburg =		
Neubrandenburg		
....	15	B7
Brandenburg ..	15	B7
Brandenburg □	15	B7
Brandon	71	D10
Brandvlei	58	E4
Braniewo	16	A4
Bransfield Str. .	96	A4
Brantford	69	D2
Branxholme ..	62	C3
Brasiléia	91	F5
Brasília	93	F4
Braşov	17	F7
Brassey,		
Banjaran	36	D5
Bratislava	16	D3
Bratsk	30	D8
Braunau	15	D7
Braunschweig .	14	B6
Brava	49	G3
Bravo del Norte,		
R. → =		
Grande,		
Rio → ...	79	F5
Brawley	82	D5
Bray	11	E3
Bray, Pays de .	12	B4
Brazil ■	93	E4
Brazos →	79	E6
Brazzaville ...	56	E3
Brčko	20	B7
Breaksea Sd. ..	65	F2
Bream B.	64	A6
Bream Hd.	64	A6
Brecon	11	F5
Breda	14	C3
Bredasdorp ...	58	E4
Bredbo	63	C4
Bregenz	14	E5
Brejo	92	C5
Bremen	14	B5
Bremerhaven ..	14	B5
Bremerton ...	80	B2
Brenner P. ...	15	E6
Bréscia	20	B3
Breslau =		
Wrocław	16	C3
Bressanone ...	20	A3
Brest, Belarus .	17	B6
Brest, France ..	12	B1
Brest-Litovsk =		
Brest	17	B6
Bretagne	12	B2
Brett, C.	64	A6
Brewarrina ...	63	A4
Brezhnev =		
Naberezhnyye		
Chelny	29	D6
Bria	56	C4
Briançon	13	D7
Bribie I.	63	A5
Bridgeport ...	73	D9

Bridgetown

Bridgetown ... 87 D8
Bridgewater ... 69 D4
Bridgewater, C. 62 C3
Bridlington 11 D6
Bridport 62 D4
Brig 13 C7
Brigham City .. 81 E7
Bright 63 C4
Brighton,
  Australia 62 C2
Brighton, U.K. .. 11 F6
Bríndisi 21 D6
Brinkworth 62 B2
Brisbane 63 A5
Brisbane → .. 63 A5
Bristol,
  U.K. 11 F5
Bristol,
  U.S.A. 75 A6
Bristol B. 71 C3
Bristol Channel 11 F4
Britstown 58 E4
Brittany =
  Bretagne 12 B2
Brive-la-
  Gaillarde 12 D4
Brixen =
  Bressanone . 20 A3
Brlik 29 E8
Brno 16 D3
Brocken 14 C6
Brodeur Pen. .. 68 A2
Brodnica 16 B4
Brody 17 C7
Broken Hill =
  Kabwe 59 A5
Broken Hill ... 62 B3
Bronte Park .. 62 D4
Brooks Ra. 71 B5
Brooloo 63 A5
Broome 60 D3
Brown, Pt. 62 B1
Brownsville ... 78 G5
Brownwood ... 78 D4
Bruay-en-Artois 13 A5
Bruce, Mt. 60 E2
Bruck an der
  Mur 15 E8
Bruges =
  Brugge 14 C2
Brugge 14 C2
Brumado 93 E5
Brunei = Bandar
  Seri Begawan 36 D5
Brunei ■ 36 D4
Brunner, L. ... 65 E4
Brunswick =
  Braunschweig 14 B6
Brunswick ... 75 D7
Brunswick, Pen.
  de 95 G2
Brusque 94 B7
Brussel 14 C3
Brussels =
  Brussel 14 C3
Bruthen 63 C4
Bruxelles =
  Brussel 14 C3
Bryan 79 D5
Bryan, Mt. ... 62 B2
Bryansk 24 C3
Bu Craa 54 C2
Buapinang 39 E2
Buayan 38 C3
Bucak 46 C2
Bucaramanga . 90 B4
Buchach 17 D7
Buchanan 55 G2
Buchans 69 D5

Bucharest =
  București ... 22 B6
Buckie 10 C5
Buckleboo 62 B2
București 22 B6
Budalin 41 F10
Budapest 16 E4
Budd Coast .. 96 A12
Bude 11 F4
Budennovsk ... 25 E5
Budgewoi 63 B5
Budjala 56 D3
Buenaventura . 90 C3
Buenos Aires .. 94 C5
Buenos Aires, L. 95 F2
Buffalo 73 C6
Bug → =
  Buh → 25 D3
Bug → 16 B5
Buga 90 C3
Bugel, Tanjung 37 F4
Bugsuk 36 C5
Bugun Shara .. 35 B5
Buguruslan ... 29 D6
Buh → 25 D3
Buheirat-Murrat-
  el-Kubra 52 B5
Buir Nur 35 B6
Bujumbura ... 57 E5
Bukama 57 F5
Bukavu 57 E5
Bukene 57 E6
Bukhara =
  Bukhoro 29 F7
Bukhoro 29 F7
Bukittinggi ... 37 E2
Bukoba 57 E6
Bula 39 E4
Bulahdelah ... 63 B5
Bulan 38 B2
Bulandshahr .. 42 E10
Bulawayo 59 C5
Buldan 23 E7
Bulgan 35 B5
Bulgaria ■ ... 22 C5
Bulgroo 63 A3
Bulgunnia 62 B1
Bulhar 49 E3
Buli, Teluk 39 D3
Buliluyan, C. .. 36 C5
Bulli 63 B5
Bulloo → 63 A3
Bulloo Downs . 62 A3
Bulloo L. 62 A3
Bulls 64 D6
Bulo Burti 49 G4
Bulsar = Valsad 43 J8
Bulukumba ... 39 F2
Bulun 30 B10
Bumba 56 D4
Bumhpa Bum . 41 D11
Buna 57 D7
Bunbah, Khalīj . 52 B3
Bunbury 60 G2
Buncrana 11 D3
Bundaberg ... 63
Bundi 43 G9
Bundoran 11 D2
Bungo-Suidō .. 32 C3
Bunia 57 D6
Bunji 42 B9
Buntok 37 E4
Bunyu 37 D5
Buol 39 D2
Buon Me Thuot 36 B3
Buorkhaya, Mys 31 B11
Buqayq 47 F7
Bur Acaba 49 G3
Bûr Safâga ... 52 C5

Bûr Sa'îd 52 B5
Bûr Sûdân 53 E6
Burao 49 F4
Buraydah 47 F6
Buraymī, Al
  Wāhāt al ... 44 E3
Burcher 63 B4
Burdur 46 C2
Burdwan =
  Barddhaman 40 F6
Burgas 22 C6
Burgersdorp . 59 E5
Burgos 18 A4
Burgundy =
  Bourgogne .. 13 C6
Burhaniye 23 E6
Burhanpur 43 J10
Burias 38 B2
Buriram 36 A2
Burji 53 G6
Burkina Faso ■ 55 F4
Burlington,
  Iowa, U.S.A. . 77 E9
Burlington, N.C.,
  U.S.A. 75 A8
Burlington, Vt.,
  U.S.A. 73 B9
Burlyu-Tyube .. 29 E8
Burma ■ 41 G11
Burnie 62 D4
Burnley 11 E5
Burnside → .. 70 B9
Burqān 47 E6
Burqin 34 B3
Burra 62 B2
Burren Junction 63 B4
Burrendong
  Dam 63 B4
Burrinjuck Res. 63 C4
Burruyacú 94 B4
Bursa 23 D7
Burtundy 62 B3
Buru 39 E3
Burundi ■ ... 57 E6
Burutu 55 G6
Bury St.
  Edmunds ... 11 E7
Buşayyah ... 47 E6
Būshehr 44 D2
Būshehr □ 44 D2
Bushire =
  Būshehr 44 D2
Businga 56 D4
Busra ash Shām 46 D4
Busto Arsízio .. 20 B2
Busu-Djanoa .. 56 D4
Busuanga 38 B1
Buta 57 D4
Butare 57 E5
Butaritari 64 J12
Butembo 57 D5
Butha Qi 35 B7
Buton 39 E2
Butte 81 B7
Butterworth ... 36 C2
Butuan 38 C3
Butung = Buton 39 E2
Buturlinovka .. 24 C5
Buxtehude 14 B5
Buy 24 B5
Büyük
  Menderes → 23 F6
Büyükçekmece 22 D7
Buzău 17 F8
Buzău → 17 F8
Buzen 32 C2
Buzi → 59 B6
Buzuluk 29 D6
Byarezina → .. 17 B10

Bydgoszcz 16 B3
Byelarus =
  Belarus ■ ... 24 C2
Byelorussia =
  Belarus ■ ... 24 C2
Bykhaw 17 B10
Bykhov =
  Bykhaw 17 B10
Bylot I. 68 A3
Byrd, C. 96 A3
Byrock 63 B4
Byron Bay 63 A5
Byrranga, Gory 30 B8
Byrranga Mts. =
  Byrranga,
  Gory 30 B8
Bytom 16 C4
Bytów 16 A3

C

Ca Mau = Quan
  Long 36 C3
Caála 58 A3
Cabanatuan ... 38 A2
Cabedelo 92 D7
Cabimas 90 A4
Cabinda 56 F2
Cabinda □ 56 F2
Cabinet Mts. .. 81 B6
Cabo Blanco .. 95 F3
Cabo Frio 93 G5
Cabo Pantoja .. 90 D3
Cabonga,
  Réservoir ... 69 D3
Caboolture 63 A5
Cabora Bassa
  Dam =
  Cahora Bassa
  Dam 59 B6
Cabot Str. 69 D5
Cabra 18 D3
Cabrera 19 C7
Cabriel → ... 19 C5
Čačak 22 C3
Cáceres, Brazil . 91 G7
Cáceres, Spain 18 C2
Cachimbo, Serra
  do 93 D2
Cachoeira 93 E6
Cachoeira de
  Itapemirim .. 93 G5
Cachoeira do
  Sul 94 C6
Cacólo 56 G3
Caconda 58 A3
Cacongo 56 F2
Cadibarrawirracanna,
  L. 62 A2
Cadiz, Phil. ... 38 B2
Cádiz, Spain .. 18 D2
Cádiz, G. de .. 18 D2
Cadney Park .. 62 A1
Caen 12 B3
Caeté 93 F5
Caetité 93 E5
Cagayan → . 38 A2
Cagayan de Oro 38 C2
Cágliari 21 E2
Cágliari, G. di . 21 E2
Caguas 87 C6
Cahora Bassa
  Dam 59 B6
Cahors 12 D4
Cahuapanas ... 91 E3
Cahul 17 F9

Caia 59 B7
Caibarién 86 B4
Caicara 90 B5
Caicó 92 D6
Caicos Is. 87 B5
Caird Coast .. 96 B5
Cairns 61 D8
Cairo = El
Qâhira 52 B5
Cairo 79 A9
Caiundo 58 B3
Caiza 91 H5
Cajamarca 91 E3
Cajàzeiras ... 92 D6
Calabar 55 H6
Calábria □ 21 E6
Calafate 95 G2
Calahorra 19 A5
Calais 12 A4
Calama, *Brazil* . 91 E6
Calama, *Chile* . 94 A3
Calamar,
Bolívar,
Colombia ... 90 A4
Calamar,
Vaupés,
Colombia ... 90 C4
Calamian Group 38 B1
Calamocha 19 B5
Calang 36 D1
Calapan 38 B2
Cǎlǎraşi 22 B6
Calatayud 19 B5
Calauag 38 B2
Calavite, C. ... 38 B2
Calbayog 38 B2
Calca 91 F4
Calcutta 41 F7
Caldas da
Rainha 18 C1
Caldera 94 B2
Caldwell 80 D5
Caledon 58 E3
Caledon → .. 59 E5
Calgary 71 C8
Cali 90 C3
Calicut 43 P9
California □ ... 82 B3
California, G. de 84 B2
Calingasta ... 94 C3
Callabonna, L. . 62 A3
Callao 91 F3
Caloundra 63 A5
Caltagirone .. 21 F5
Caltanissetta .. 21 F5
Calulo 56 G2
Calunda 58 A4
Calvi 13 E8
Calviá 19 C7
Calvinia 58 E3
Camabatela ... 56 F3
Camacupa 58 A3
Camagüey 86 B4
Camaná 91 G4
Camargo · 91 H5
Camargue 13 E6
Camarones ... 95 E3
Cambay =
Khambhat .. 43 H8
Cambay, G. of =
Khambat, G.
of 43 J8
Cambodia ■ .. 36 B3
Cambrai 13 A5
Cambrian Mts. 11 E5
Cambridge, *N.Z.* 64 B6
Cambridge, *U.K.* 11 E7
Cambridge,
U.S.A. 73 C10

Cambridge Bay
= Ikaluktutiak 70 B9
Cambridge G. . 60 C4
Cambundi-
Catembo 56 G3
Camden, *Ark.,*
U.S.A. 79 C7
Camden, *N.J.,*
U.S.A. 73 E8
Cameroon ■ .. 56 C2
Cameroun, Mt. 56 D1
Cametá 92 C4
Caminha 18 B1
Camira Creek .. 63 A5
Camissombo .. 56 F4
Camocim 92 C5
Camopi → ... 92 B3
Campana, I. .. 95 F1
Campánia □ .. 21 D5
Campbell Town 62 D4
Campbellton .. 69 D4
Campbelltown . 63 B5
Campbeltown . 10 D4
Campeche 85 D6
Campeche, B. de 85 D6
Camperdown .. 62 C3
Campina Grande 92 D6
Campinas 94 A7
Campo 56 D1
Campo Belo ... 93 G4
Campo Formoso 93 E5
Campo Grande 93 G3
Campo Maíor . 92 C5
Campo Mourão 93 G3
Campoalegre .. 90 C3
Campobasso .. 20 D5
Campos 93 G5
Campos Belos . 93 E4
Campuya → .. 90 D4
Camrose 71 C8
Çan 23 D6
Can Tho 36 B3
Canada ■ 70 C8
Cañada de
Gómez 94 C4
Çanakkale 23 D6
Çanakkale
Boğazı 23 D6
Cananeạ 84 A2
Canarias, Is. ... 54 C1
Canary Is. =
Canarias, Is. . 54 C1
Canavieiras ... 93 F6
Canbelego 63 B4
Canberra 63 C4
Candala 49 E4
Candelo 63 C4
Candia =
Iráklion 23 G5
Canea = Khaniá 23 G5
Canelones 94 C5
Cañete, *Chile* . 94 D2
Cañete, *Peru* . 91 F3
Cangas de
Narcea 18 A2
Canguaretama . 92 D6
Canguçu 94 C6
Canicattì 21 F4
Canigou, Mt. .. 12 E5
Canipaan 36 C5
Çankırı 46 B3
Cann River 63 C4
Cannanore 43 P9
Cannes 13 E7
Canoas 94 B6
Canora 71 C9
Canowindra ... 63 B4
Cantabria □ ... 18 A4

Cantabrian Mts.
= Cantábrica,
Cordillera ... 18 A3
Cantábrica,
Cordillera ... 18 A3
Cantal, Plomb
du 13 D5
Canterbury 11 F7
Canterbury □ . 65 E4
Canterbury
Bight 65 F4
Canterbury
Plains 65 E4
Canton =
Guangzhou . 35 D6
Canton 72 D5
Canudos 91 E7
Canutama 91 E6
Cap-Haïtien ... 87 C5
Cap St.-Jacques
= Vung Tau . 36 B3
Capaia 56 F4
Capanaparo → 90 B5
Cape Barren I. . 62 D4
Cape Breton I. . 69 D4
Cape Coast ... 55 G4
Cape Dorset .. 68 B3
Cape Girardeau 79 A9
Cape Jervis .. 62 C2
Cape Town ... 58 E3
Cape Verde
Is. ■ 50 E1
Cape York
Peninsula ... 61 C7
Capela 93 E6
Capim → ... 92 C4
Capraia 20 C2
Capri 21 D5
Caprivi Strip .. 58 B4
Captain's Flat . 63 C4
Caquetá → ... 90 D5
Caracal 22 B5
Caracas 90 A5
Caracol 93 D5
Caradoc 62 B3
Carajás, Serra
dos 92 D3
Carangola 93 G5
Caransebeş ... 17 F6
Caratasca, L. .. 86 C3
Caratinga 93 F5
Caraúbas 92 D6
Caravaca 19 C5
Caravelas 93 F6
Caraveli 91 G4
Carballo 18 A1
Carbonara, C. . 21 E2
Carbondale ... 79 A9
Carbonear 69 D5
Carbonia 21 E2
Carcassonne .. 12 E5
Carcross 70 B6
Cardamon Hills 43 Q10
Cárdenas 86 B3
Cardiff 11 F5
Cardigan B. .. 11 E4
Cardston 71 D8
Carei 17 E6
Careysburg ... 55 G2
Carhué 94 D4
Caria 23 F7
Cariacica 93 G5
Caribbean Sea . 86 D5
Cariboo Mts. .. 71 C7
Carinda 63 B4
Carinhanha ... 93 E5
Carinthia □ =
Kärnten □ .. 15 E7
Caripito 90 A6

Caritianas 91 E6
Carlisle 11 D5
Carlow 11 E3
Carlsbad 78 C1
Carmacks 70 B6
Carman 71 D10
Carmarthen ... 11 F4
Carmaux 12 D5
Carmelo 94 C5
Carmen 90 B3
Carmen de
Patagones .. 95 E4
Carmona 18 D3
Carnac 12 C2
Carnarvon,
Australia 60 E1
Carnarvon,
S. Africa 58 E4
Carnegie, L. ... 60 F3
Carnic Alps =
Karnische
Alpen 20 A4
Carniche Alpi =
Karnische
Alpen 20 A4
Carnot 56 D3
Carnot, C. 62 B2
Carolina 92 D4
Caroline I. 65 K15
Caroline Is. ... 64 J10
Caroni → 90 B6
Caroníe =
Nébrodi,
Monti 21 F5
Caroona 63 B5
Carpathians ... 16 D5
Carpaţii
Meridionali .. 17 F7
Carpentaria, G.
of 60 C6
Carpentras 13 D6
Carpi 20 B3
Carpolac =
Morea 62 C3
Carrara 20 B3
Carrauntoohill . 11 E2
Carrick-on-Suir 11 E3
Carrieton 62 B2
Carrizal Bajo .. 94 B2
Çarşamba 46 B4
Carson City ... 80 F4
Cartagena,
Colombia ... 90 A3
Cartagena,
Spain 19 D5
Cartago,
Colombia ... 90 C3
Cartago,
Costa Rica .. 86 E3
Carterton 65 D6
Carthage 79 A6
Cartwright ... 68 C5
Caruaru 92 D6
Carúpano 90 A6
Carvoeiro 90 D6
Carvoeiro, C. .. 18 C1
Casablanca ... 54 B3
Cascade Ra. .. 80 B3
Cascais 18 C1
Cascavel 94 A6
Cáscina 20 C3
Caserta 20 D5
Casiguran 38 A2
Casilda 94 C4
Casino 63 A5
Casiquiare → . 90 C5
Casma 91 E3
Caspe 19 B5
Casper 81 D10

Caspian Sea .. 29 E6
Cassinga 58 B3
Castellammare
di Stábia 21 D5
Castellón de la
Plana 19 C5
Castelo Branco 18 C2
Castelsarrasin . 12 D4
Castelvetrano . 21 F4
Casterton 62 C3
Castilla La
Mancha □ . 18 C4
Castilla y
Leon □ 18 A3
Castlebar 11 E2
Castleblaney .. 11 D3
Castlemaine ... 63 C3
Castlereagh → 63 B4
Castres 12 E5
Castries 87 D7
Castro 95 E2
Castro Alves .. 93 E6
Castuera 18 C3
Cat I. 86 B4
Catacáos 91 E2
Catalão 93 F4
Çatalca 22 D7
Catalonia =
Cataluña □ .. 19 B6
Cataluña □ ... 19 B6
Catamarca 94 B3
Catanduanes .. 38 B2
Catanduva 93 G4
Catánia 21 F5
Catanzaro 21 E6
Catarman 38 B2
Cateel 38 C3
Catoche, C. ... 85 C7
Catrimani 90 C6
Catskill Mts. ... 73 C8
Cauca → 90 B4
Caucaia 92 C6
Caucasus
Mountains .. 25 E5
Caúngula 56 F3
Cauquenes 94 D2
Caura → 90 B6
Cauvery → ... 43 P11
Caux, Pays de . 12 B4
Cavan 11 D3
Cavendish 62 C3
Caviana, I. 92 B3
Cavite 38 B2
Cawndilla L. ... 62 B3
Cawnpore =
Kanpur ... 40 D3
Caxias 92 C5
Caxias do Sul . 94 B6
Caxito 56 F2
Cayambe 90 C3
Cayenne 92 A3
Cayman Is. ■ .. 67 H11
Cazombo 58 A4
Ceadâr-Lunga . 17 E9
Ceanannus Mor 11 E3
Ceará =
Fortaleza 92 C6
Ceará □ . 92 D6
Ceará Mirim .. 92 D6
Cebollar 94 B3
Cebu 38 B2
Cecil Plains .. 63 A5
Cedar L. 71 C10
Cedar Rapids .. 77 E9
Cedro 92 D6
Ceduna 62 B1
Cefalù 21 E5
Cegléd 16 E4
Celaya 84 C4

Celebes =
Sulawesi □ . 39 E2
Celebes Sea ... 39 D2
Celje 20 A5
Celle 14 B6
Celtic Sea 11 F2
Central,
Cordillera ... 90 C3
Central African
Rep. ■ 56 C4
Central Makran
Range 42 F4
Cephalonia =
Kefallinía ... 23 E3
Ceram = Seram 39 E3
Ceram Sea =
Seram Sea .. 39 E3
Ceres, Argentina 94 B4
Ceres, S. Africa 58 E3
Cerignola 20 D5
Cerigo = Kíthira 23 F4
Çerkeş 46 B3
Çerkeşköy 22 D6
Cervera 19 B6
Cesena 20 B4
Česka Republika
= Czech
Rep. ■ 16 D2
České
Budějovice .. 16 D2
Ceskomoravská
Vrchovina ... 16 D2
Çeşme 23 E6
Cessnock 63 B5
Cetinje 22 C2
Cetraro 21 E5
Ceuta 18 E3
Cévennes 13 D5
Ceyhan 46 C3
Ceylon = Sri
Lanka ■ 43 R12
Chachapoyas .. 91 E3
Chachran 42 E7
Chad ■ 53 E2
Chad, L. =
Tchad, L. ... 53 F1
Chadileuvú → 94 D3
Chadyr-Lunga =
Ceadâr-Lunga 17 E9
Chagai Hills ... 42 E3
Chagos Arch. .. 27 K11
Chāh Bahār ... 45 E5
Chāh Gay Hills 45 D6
Chahar Burjak . 42 D3
Chaibasa 40 F5
Chakhānsūr ... 42 D3
Chakradharpur 40 F5
Chakwal 42 C8
Chala 91 G4
Chalcis =
Khalkís 23 E4
Chalhuanca ... 91 F4
Chalisgaon ... 43 J9
Challapata 91 G5
Chalon-sur-
Saône 13 C6
Châlons-en-
Champagne . 13 B6
Chaman 42 D5
Chamba, India . 42 C10
Chamba,
Tanzania 59 A7
Chambal → .. 42 F11
Chambéry 13 D6
Chamical 94 C3
Chamonix-Mont
Blanc 13 D7
Champagne ... 13 B6

Champaign ... 72 D1
Champlain, L. . 73 B9
Chañaral 94 B2
Chandigarh ... 42 D10
Chandler 62 A1
Chandmani ... 34 B4
Chandpur 41 F8
Chandrapur ... 43 K11
Chang Jiang → 35 C7
Changanacheri 43 Q10
Changane → . 59 C6
Changchiak'ou
= Zhangjiakou 35 B6
Changzhou .. 35 C6
Changchun ... 35 B7
Changde 35 D6
Changhai =
Shanghai ... 35 C7
Changjiang ... 35 E5
Changsha 35 D6
Changting 35 D6
Changzhi 35 C6
Changzhou ... 35 C6
Channapatna .. 43 N10
Channel Is. 11 G5
Chantada 18 A2
Chanthaburi .. 36 B2
Chantrey Inlet . 70 B10
Chanute 79 A6
Chao Phraya → 36 B2
Chao'an 35 D6
Chaoyang 35 D6
Chapala, L. de . 84 C4
Chapayevsk ... 24 C6
Chapra =
Chhapra 40 E5
Châr 54 D2
Chara 31 D9
Charadai 94 B5
Charagua 91 G6
Charaña 91 G5
Chardara 29 E7
Chardzhou =
Chärjew ... 29 F7
Charente → .. 12 D3
Chari → 53 F1
Chārīkār 42 B6
Chärjew 29 F7
Charleroi 14 C3
Charles, C. ... 73 F8
Charleston, S.C.,
U.S.A. 75 C8
Charleston,
W. Va., U.S.A. 72 E5
Charlesville ... 56 F4
Charleville 63 A4
Charleville-
Mézières 13 B6
Charlotte 75 B7
Charlotte Amalie 87 C7
Charlottesville . 73 E6
Charlottetown . 69 D4
Charlton 62 C3
Charolles 13 C6
Charouine 54 C4
Charters Towers 61 E8
Chartres 12 B4
Chascomús ... 94 D5
Châteaubriant . 12 C3
Châteaulin 12 B1
Châteauroux .. 12 C4
Châtellerault .. 12 C4
Chatham, N.B.,
Canada ... 69 D4
Chatham, Ont.,
Canada 69 D2
Chatham, U.K. . 11 F7
Chatrapur 40 H5

Chattahoochee →
.... 74 D5
Chattanooga .. 74 B5
Chauk 41 G10
Chaukan La ... 41 D11
Chaumont 13 B6
Chaves, Brazil . 92 C4
Chaves, Portugal 18 B2
Chavuma 58 A4
Cheb 16 C1
Cheboksary ... 24 B6
Chech, Erg ... 54 D4
Chechenia □ .. 25 E6
Checheno-
Ingush
Republic =
Chechenia □ 25 E6
Chechnya =
Chechenia □ 25 E6
Cheduba I. 41 H9
Cheepie 63 A4
Chegga 54 C3
Chegutu 59 B6
Chehalis 80 B2
Cheju Do 35 C7
Chekiang =
Zhejiang □ .. 35 D7
Cheleken 29 F6
Chelforó 95 D3
Chelkar =
Shalqar 29 E6
Chelkar Tengiz,
Solonchak .. 29 E7
Chełm 17 C6
Chełmno 16 B4
Chelmsford ... 11 F7
Cheltenham ... 11 F5
Chelyabinsk ... 29 D7
Chemnitz 15 C7
Chen Xian 35 D6
Chenab → ... 42 D7
Chencha 53 G6
Chenchiang =
Zhenjiang .. 35 C6
Chengde 35 B6
Chengdu 35 C5
Chengjiang ... 34 D5
Ch'engtu =
Chengdu 35 C5
Chennai =
Madras 43 N12
Cheo Reo 36 B3
Cheom Ksan .. 36 B2
Chepén 91 E3
Chepes 94 C3
Cher → 12 C4
Cherbourg ... 12 B3
Cherchell 54 A5
Cherdyn 28 C6
Cherepanovo .. 29 D9
Cherepovets .. 24 B4
Chergui, Chott
ech 54 B5
Cherikov =
Cherykaw ... 17 B10
Cherkasy 24 D3
Cherlak 29 D8
Chernaya 30 B6
Chernigov =
Chernihiv ... 24 C3
Chernihiv 24 C3
Chernivtsi 17 D7
Chernobyl =
Chornobyl .. 17 C10
Chernovtsy =
Chernivtsi ... 17 D7
Chernyakhovsk 28 D3
Cherquenco ... 94 D2
Cherrapunji ... 41 E8

Cherven 17 B9
Chervonohrad . 17 C7
Cherykaw 17 B10
Chesapeake ... 73 F7
Chesapeake B. . 73 E7
Cheshskaya
  Guba 28 C5
Chester, U.K. .. 11 E5
Chester, U.S.A. 73 E8
Chesterfield .. 11 E6
Chesterfield, Is. 64 L10
Chesterfield Inlet 70 B10
Chesterton Ra. 63 A4
Cheviot Hills .. 10 D5
Chew Bahir .. 53 H6
Cheyenne 76 E2
Cheyenne ➝ . 76 C4
Chhapra 40 E5
Chhatarpur ... 43 G11
Chhattisgarh
  □ 40 G3
Chhindwara .. 43 H11
Chhlong 36 B3
Chi ➝ 36 A2
Chiamussu =
  Jiamusi 35 B8
Chiange 58 B2
Chiapa ➝ 85 D6
Chiávari 20 B2
Chiavenna 20 A2
Chiba 32 B7
Chibemba 58 B2
Chibia 58 B2
Chibougamau . 69 D3
Chibuk 53 F1
Chicacole =
  Srikakulam .. 40 H4
Chicago 72 D2
Chichagof I. ... 71 C6
Chichibu 32 A6
Chickasha 78 B5
Chiclana de la
  Frontera 18 D2
Chiclayo 91 E3
Chico 80 F3
Chico ➝,
  Chubut,
  Argentina ... 95 E3
Chico ➝,
  Santa Cruz,
  Argentina ... 95 F3
Chicoutimi 69 D3
Chidambaram . 43 P11
Chidley, C. ... 68 B4
Chiemsee 15 E7
Chiengi 57 F5
Chiese ➝ 20 B3
Chieti 20 C5
Chiguana 91 H5
Chihli, G. of =
  Bo Hai 35 C6
Chihuahua 84 B3
Chiili 29 E7
Chik Bollapur . 43 N10
Chikmagalur .. 43 N9
Chilapa 84 D5
Chilas 42 B9
Chilaw 43 R11
Childers 63 A5
Chile ■ 94 D2
Chilete 91 E3
Chililabombwe 59 A5
Chilin = Jilin . 35 B7
Chilka L. 40 H5
Chillán 94 D2
Chiloé, I. de .. 95 E2
Chilpancingo . 84 D5
Chiluage 56 F4
Chilwa, L. 59 B7

Chimbay 29 E6
Chimborazo ... 90 D3
Chimbote 91 E3
Chimkent =
  Shymkent ... 29 E7
Chimoio 59 B6
Chin □ 41 F9
China ■ 35 C5
Chinan = Jinan 35 C6
Chinandega .. 85 E7
Chincha Alta . 91 F3
Chinchilla 63 A5
Chinchou =
  Jinzhou 35 B7
Chinde 59 B7
Chindwin ➝ .. 41 G10
Chingola 59 A5
Ch'ingtao =
  Qingdao ... 35 C7
Chinguetti 54 D2
Chinhoyi 59 B6
Chiniot 42 D8
Chinju 35 C7
Chinnampo ... 35 C7
Chinon 12 C4
Chinsali 57 G6
Chióggia 20 B4
Chíos = Khíos . 23 E6
Chipata 59 A6
Chiquián 91 F3
Chiquinquira . 90 B4
Chirchiq 29 E7
Chirmiri 40 F4
Chiromo 59 B7
Chisamba 59 A5
Chisapani Garhi 40 D5
Chișinău 17 E9
Chistopol 24 B7
Chita 30 D9
Chitado 58 B2
Chitembo 58 A3
Chitral 42 B7
Chitré 86 E3
Chittagong ... 41 F8
Chittagong □ . 41 E8
Chittaurgarh .. 43 G9
Chittoor 43 N11
Chiusi 20 C3
Chivasso 20 B1
Chivilcoy 94 B4
Chkalov =
  Orenburg ... 29 D6
Choele Choel .. 95 D3
Chojnice 16 B3
Cholet 12 C3
Choluteca 85 E7
Choma 59 B5
Chomutov 16 C1
Chon Buri ... 36 B2
Chone 90 D3
Chŏngjin 35 B7
Chŏngju 35 C7
Chongqing ... 35 D5
Chŏnju 35 C7
Chonos, Arch.
  de los 95 F2
Chop 17 D6
Chornobyl ... 17 C10
Chortkiv 17 D7
Chorzów 16 C4
Chos-Malal .. 94 D2
Chōshi 32 B7
Choszczno ... 16 B2
Chotila 43 H7
Choybalsan ... 35 B6
Christchurch .. 65 E5
Christiana 59 D5
Christmas I. =
  Kiritimati ... 65 J15

Chu = Shu 29 E8
Ch'uanchou =
  Quanzhou ... 35 D6
Chubut ➝ 95 E3
Chudskoye, Oz. 24 B2
Chūgoku-Sanchi 32 B3
Chula Vista ... 82 D4
Chulucanas ... 90 E2
Chulym ➝ ... 29 D9
Chumbicha ... 94 B3
Chumphon 36 B1
Chuna ➝ 30 D7
Chunchŏn 35 C7
Chungking =
  Chongqing .. 35 D5
Chunya 57 F6
Chuquibamba . 91 G4
Chuquicamata . 94 A3
Chur 13 C8
Churachandpur 41 E9
Churchill 70 C10
Churchill ➝,
  Man., Canada 70 C10
Churchill ➝,
  Nfld., Canada 69 C4
Churchill, C. ... 70 C10
Churchill Falls . 69 C4
Churchill L. ... 71 C9
Churu 42 E9
Chushal 42 C11
Chusovoy 28 D6
Chuvash
  Republic □ =
  Chuvashia □ 24 B6
Chuvashia □ . 24 B6
Cicero 72 D2
Ciechanów ... 16 B5
Ciego de Avila . 86 B4
Ciénaga 90 A4
Cienfuegos ... 86 B3
Cieszyn 16 D4
Cieza 19 C5
Cijara, Pantano
  de 18 C3
Cilacap 37 F3
Cilician Gates P. 46 C3
Cill Chainnigh =
  Kilkenny 11 E3
Cimișlia 17 E9
Cimone, Mte. .. 20 B3
Cîmpina 17 F7
Cîmpulung ... 17 F7
Cinca ➝ 19 B6
Cincar 20 C6
Cincinnati 72 E3
Çine 23 F7
Cinto, Mte. ... 13 E8
Circle 71 B5
Cirebon 37 F3
Citlaltépetl ... 84 D5
Città di Castello 20 C4
Ciudad Bolívar 90 B6
Ciudad
  Chetumal ... 85 D7
Ciudad del
  Carmen ... 85 D6
Ciudad Delicias
  = Delicias .. 84 B3
Ciudad Guayana 90 B6
Ciudad Juárez . 84 A3
Ciudad Madero 84 C5
Ciudad Mante . 84 C5
Ciudad Obregón 84 B3
Ciudad Real .. 18 C4
Ciudad Rodrigo 18 B2
Ciudad Trujillo
  = Santo
  Domingo ... 87 C6
Ciudad Victoria 84 C5
Civitanova
  Marche 20 C4

Civitavécchia .. 20 C3
Cizre 46 C5
Clanwilliam .. 58 E3
Clare 62 B2
Clarence ➝,
  Australia 63 A5
Clarence ➝,
  N.Z. 65 E5
Clarence, I. ... 95 G2
Clarence I. ... 96 A4
Clarie Coast ... 96 A13
Clarke I. 62 D4
Clarksdale ... 79 B8
Clarksville 74 A4
Claveria 38 A2
Clear, C. 11 F2
Clearwater ... 75 F6
Clearwater Mts. 81 B6
Clermont-
  Ferrand 13 D5
Cleveland,
  Australia 63 A5
Cleveland,
  U.S.A. 72 D5
Clifden 65 G2
Clifton 63 A5
Clifton Hills .. 62 A2
Clinton, Canada 71 C7
Clinton, N.Z. .. 65 G3
Clinton, U.S.A. 77 E9
Clinton Colden
  L. 70 B9
Clones 11 D3
Clonmel 11 E3
Clovis 78 B2
Cluj-Napoca .. 17 E6
Clunes 62 C3
Clutha ➝ 65 G3
Clyde 65 F3
Clyde ➝ 10 D4
Clyde, Firth of . 10 D4
Clyde River .. 68 A4
Coari 90 D6
Coast Mts. ... 70 C7
Coast Ranges . 80 F2
Coats I. 68 B2
Coats Land ... 96 B5
Coatzacoalcos . 85 D6
Cobalt 69 D3
Cobar 63 B4
Cóbh 11 F2
Cobham 62 B3
Cobija 91 F5
Cobourg 69 D3
Cobram 63 C4
Cóbué 59 A6
Coburg 15 C6
Cocanada =
  Kakinada ... 40 J4
Cochabamba . 91 G5
Cochin 43 Q10
Cochin China =
  Nam-Phan . 36 B3
Cochrane 69 D2
Cochrane, L. .. 95 F2
Cockburn 62 B3
Cockburn, Canal 95 G2
Coco ➝ 86 D3
Cocobeach ... 56 D1
Cod, C. 73 C10
Codajás 90 D6
Codó 92 C5
Cœur d'Alene . 80 B5
Coffeyville ... 79 A6
Coffin B. 62 B2
Coffin Bay
  Peninsula .. 62 B2
Coffs Harbour . 63 B5
Cognac 12 D3

Cohuna 63 C3
Coiba, I. 86 E3
Coig → 95 G3
Coihaique ... 95 F2
Coimbatore ... 43 P10
Coimbra, *Brazil* 91 G7
Coimbra,
  Portugal 18 B1
Coín 18 D3
Cojimies 90 C3
Colac 62 C3
Colatina 93 F5
Colbeck, C. 96 B17
Colbinabbin .. 63 C3
Colchester 11 F7
Colebrook 62 D4
Coleman 71 D8
Coleraine,
  Australia 62 C3
Coleraine, *U.K.* 11 D3
Coleridge, L. .. 65 E4
Colesberg 59 E5
Colhué Huapi, L. 95 F3
Colima 84 D4
Colinas 92 D5
Coll 10 C3
Collaguasi 91 H5
Collarenebri ... 63 A4
Collingwood .. 64 D5
Colmar 13 B7
Colo → 63 B5
Cologne = Köln 14 C4
Colomb-Béchar
  = Béchar ... 54 B4
Colômbia 93 G4
Colombia ■ ... 90 C4
Colombo 43 R11
Colón, *Cuba* .. 86 B3
Colón, *Panama* 85 F9
Colonia 94 C5
Colonia Dora .. 94 B4
Colonsay 10 C3
Colorado □ ... 83 A10
Colorado →,
  Argentina ... 95 D4
Colorado →,
  N. Amer. 82 E5
Colorado
  Plateau 83 B7
Colorado
  Springs 76 F2
Columbia, *Mo.,*
  U.S.A. 77 F8
Columbia, *S.C.,*
  U.S.A. 75 B7
Columbia,
  Tenn., U.S.A. 74 B4
Columbia → .. 80 B1
Columbia,
  District of □ . 73 E7
Columbia Basin 80 B4
Columbretes, Is. 19 C6
Columbus, *Ga.,*
  U.S.A. 74 C5
Columbus,
  Miss., U.S.A. 74 C3
Columbus, *Ohio,*
  U.S.A. 72 E4
Colville → 71 A4
Colville, C. 64 B6
Colwyn Bay ... 11 E5
Comácchio 20 B4
Comallo 95 E2
Comilla 41 F8
Comino, C. ... 21 D2
Committee B. . 68 B2
Commonwealth
  B. 96 A14
Commoron
  Cr. → 63 A5

Communism Pk.
  =
  Kommunizma,
  Pik 29 F8
Como 20 B2
Como, L. di ... 20 B2
Comodoro
  Rivadavia ... 95 F3
Comorin, C. ... 43 Q10
Comoro Is. =
  Comoros ■ . 51 H8
Comoros ■ ... 51 H8
Comox 71 D7
Compiègne ... 13 B5
Compton Downs 63 B4
Comrat 17 E9
Conakry 55 G2
Conara Junction 62 D4
Concarneau ... 12 C2
Conceição da
  Barra 93 F6
Concepción,
  Bolivia 91 G6
Concepción,
  Chile 94 D2
Concepción,
  Paraguay ... 94 A5
Concepción, L. 91 G6
Concepción del
  Oro 84 C4
Concepción del
  Uruguay 94 C5
Conchos → .. 84 B3
Concord, *N.C.,*
  U.S.A. 75 B7
Concord, *N.H.,*
  U.S.A. 73 C10
Concordia,
  Argentina ... 94 C5
Concórdia, *Brazil* 90 D5
Condamine ... 63 A5
Condeúba 93 E5
Condobolin ... 63 B4
Conegliano ... 20 B4
Confuso → ... 94 B5
Congo ■ 56 E3
Congo → 56 F2
Congo, Dem.
  Rep. of the ■ 56 E4
Conjeeveram =
  Kanchipuram 43 N11
Conlea 63 B3
Conn, L. 11 D2
Connacht □ ... 11 E2
Connecticut □ . 73 D9
Connecticut → 73 D9
Connemara ... 11 E2
Conoble 63 B3
Cononaco → . 90 D3
Conran, C. 63 C4
Conselheiro
  Lafaiete 93 G5
Constance =
  Konstanz .. 14 E5
Constance, L. =
  Bodensee ... 13 C8
Constanţa 22 B7
Constantine .. 54 A6
Constitución .. 94 D2
Contai 40 G6
Contamana .. 91 E4
Contas → 93 E6
Conway, L. ... 62 A2
Coober Pedy . 62 A1
Cooch Behar =
  Koch Bihar .. 41 D7
Cook, B. 95 H2
Cook, Aoraki Mt. 65 E4
Cook Inlet 71 C4

Cook Is. 65 L14
Cook Strait 65 D6
Cooktown 61 D8
Coolabah 63 B4
Cooladdi 63 A4
Coolah 63 B4
Coolamon 63 B4
Coolangatta ... 63 A5
Cooma 63 C4
Coonabarabran 63 B4
Coonamble ... 63 B4
Coondapoor . 43 N9
Coongie 62 A3
Coongoola ... 63 A4
Cooninie, L. ... 62 A2
Cooper Cr. →,
  N. Terr.,
  Australia 60 C5
Cooper Cr. →,
  S. Austral.,
  Australia 62 A2
Cooroy 63 A5
Cootamundra . 63 B4
Cooyar 63 A5
Copenhagen =
  København .. 9 G10
Copiapó 94 B2
Copiapó → .. 94 B2
Copley 62 B2
Copper Center . 71 B5
Copper Cliff ... 69 D2
Coppermine =
  Kugluktuk ... 70 B8
Coppermine → 70 B8
Coquimbo 94 C2
Corabia 22 C5
Coracora 91 G4
Coral Harbour =
  Salliq 68 B2
Coral Sea 64 L10
Corato 21 D6
Corby 11 E6
Corcaigh = Cork 11 F2
Corcubión 18 A1
Córdoba,
  Argentina ... 94 C4
Córdoba, *Spain* 18 D3
Córdoba, Sierra
  de 94 C4
Cordon 38 A2
Córdova 71 B5
Corfu = Kérkira 23 E2
Coria 18 C2
Corigliano
  Cálabro ... 21 E6
Corinna 62 D4
Corinth =
  Kórinthos ... 23 F4
Corinth, G. of =
  Korinthiakós
  Kólpos 23 E4
Corinto 93 F5
Cork 11 F2
Çorlu 22 D6
Corner Brook .. 69 D5
Cornești 17 E9
Cornwall 69 D3
Corny Pt. 62 B2
Coro 90 A5
Coroatá 92 C5
Corocoro 91 G5
Coroico 91 G5
Coromandel .. 64 B6
Corona 62 B3
Coronation Gulf 70 B8
Coronation I. .. 96 A4
Coronel 94 D2
Coronel Dorrego 94 D4
Coronel Suárez 94 D4

Corowa 63 C4
Corpus Christi . 78 F5
Corque 91 G5
Corrib, L. 11 E2
Corrientes 94 B5
Corrientes → . 90 D4
Corrientes, C.,
  Colombia .. 90 B3
Corrientes, C.,
  Mexico 84 C3
Corse 13 E8
Corse, C. 13 E8
Corsica = Corse 13 E8
Corsicana 79 C5
Corte 13 E8
Çorum 46 B3
Corumbá 91 G7
Corumbá de
  Goiás 93 F4
Corunna = La
  Coruña 18 A1
Corvallis 80 C2
Cosenza 21 E6
Costa Blanca . 19 C5
Costa Brava .. 19 B7
Costa del Sol . 18 D3
Costa Dorada . 19 B6
Costa Rica ■ . 86 E3
Cotabato 38 C2
Cotagaita 91 H5
Côte d'Azur . 13 E7
Côte-d'Ivoire ■
  = Ivory
  Coast ■ 55 G3
Cotentin 12 B3
Cotonou 55 G5
Cotopaxi 90 D3
Cotswold Hills . 11 F5
Cottbus 15 C8
Couedic, C. du . 62 C2
Coulman I. ... 96 B15
Council 71 B3
Council Bluffs . 77 E7
Courantyne → 90 B7
Courtrai =
  Kortrijk 14 C2
Coventry 11 E6
Covilhã 18 B2
Covington 72 E3
Cowal, L. 63 B4
Cowangie 62 C3
Cowarie 62 A2
Cowell 62 B2
Cowra 63 B4
Coxim 93 F3
Cox's Bazar .. 41 G8
Cozumel, I. de . 85 C7
Craboon 63 B4
Cracow =
  Kraków 16 C4
Cracow 63 A5
Cradock 59 E5
Craigavon 11 D3
Crailsheim ... 14 D6
Craiova 22 B4
Cranbrook,
  Australia ... 62 C2
Cranbrook,
  Canada 71 D8
Crateús 92 D5
Crato 92 D6
Crawley 11 F6
Crazy Mts. ... 81 B8
Crema 20 B2
Cremona 20 B3
Cres 20 B5
Cressy 62 C3
Crete = Kríti .. 23 G5
Créteil 12 B5

Creus, C. de ... 19 A7
Creuse → ... 12 C4
Crewe 11 E5
Criciúma 94 B7
Crimean Pen. =
  Krymskyy
  Pivostriv ... 25 D3
Crişul Alb → . 16 E5
Crişul Negru → 16 E5
Crna Gora =
  Montenegro □ 22 C2
Crna Gora .. 22 C3
Crna Reka → . 22 D3
Croatia ■ 20 B6
Crocker,
  Banjaran 36 C5
Croker, C. 60 C5
Cromer 11 E7
Cromwell 65 F3
Cronulla 63 B5
Crookwell 63 B4
Cross Sound . 71 C6
Crotone 21 E6
Crows Nest ... 63 A5
Crowsnest Pass 71 D8
Cruz Alta 94 B6
Cruz del Eje .. 94 C4
Cruzeiro 93 G5
Cruzeiro do Sul 91 E4
Crystal Brook .. 62 B2
Csongrád 16 E5
Cuamba 59 A7
Cuando → ... 58 B4
Cuarto → ... 94 C4
Cuba ■ 86 B4
Cubango → .. 58 B4
Cuchi 58 A3
Cúcuta 90 B4
Cuddalore 43 P11
Cuddapah ... 43 M11
Cudgewa 63 C4
Cuenca, Ecuador 90 D3
Cuenca, Spain . 19 B4
Cuenca,
  Serranía de . 19 C5
Cuernavaca .. 84 D5
Cuevas del
  Almanzora .. 19 D5
Cuevo 91 H6
Cuiabá 93 F2
Cuiabá → .. 93 F2
Cuima 58 A3
Cuito → ... 58 B4
Cukai 36 D2
Culcairn 63 C4
Culgoa → ... 63 A4
Culiacán 84 C3
Culion 38 B2
Cullarin Ra. ... 63 B4
Cullera 19 C5
Culuene → ... 93 E3
Culverden 65 E5
Cumaná 90 A6
Cumberland,
  Canada 71 D7
Cumberland,
  U.S.A. 73 E6
Cumberland
  Pen. 68 B4
Cumberland
  Plateau 72 F3
Cumberland Sd. 68 B4
Cumborah ... 63 A4
Cumbum 43 M11
Cummins 62 B2
Cumnock 63 B4
Cunene → ... 58 B2
Cúneo 20 B1
Cunnamulla ... 63 A4

Cupica, G. de .. 90 B3
Curaçao 87 D6
Curaray → ... 90 D4
Curiapo 90 B6
Curicó 94 C2
Curitiba 94 B7
Currabubula .. 63 B5
Currais Novos . 92 D6
Curralinho ... 92 C4
Curraweena ... 63 B4
Currie 62 C3
Curtea de Argeş 17 F7
Curtis Group .. 62 C4
Curuápanema →
  .... 92 C2
Curuçá 92 C4
Curup 37 E2
Cururupu 92 C5
Curuzú Cuatiá . 94 B5
Cuttaburra → . 63 A3
Cuttack 40 G5
Cuvier I. 64 B6
Cuxhaven 14 B5
Cuyo 38 B2
Cuzco, Bolivia . 91 H5
Cuzco, Peru ... 91 F4
Cwmbran 11 F5
Cyclades =
  Kikládhes .. 23 F5
Cygnet 62 D4
Cyprus ■ 46 D3
Cyrenaica 52 C3
Cyrene =
  Shahhât ... 52 B3
Czech Rep. ■ .. 16 D2
Częstochowa .. 16 C4

D

Da Hinggan Ling 35 B7
Da Lat 36 B3
Da Nang 36 A3
Da Qaidam ... 34 C4
Da Yunhe → . 35 C7
Daba Shan ... 35 C5
Dabakala 55 G4
Dabo 37 E2
Dabola 55 F2
Daboya 55 G4
Dacca = Dhaka 41 F8
Dacca =
  Dhaka □ .. 41 E8
Dachau 15 D6
Dadanawa 90 C7
Dadra and
  Nagar
  Haveli □ 43 J8
Dadu 42 F5
Daet 38 B2
Dagana 55 E1
Dagestan □ ... 25 E6
Daghestan
  Republic =
  Dagestan □ . 25 E6
Dagö = Hiiumaa 24 B1
Dagupan 38 A2
Dahlak Kebir .. 49 D3
Dahod 43 H9
Dahomey =
  Benin ■ 55 G5
Dahra 55 E1
Daiõ-Misaki ... 32 B5
Dairût 52 C5
Dakar 55 F1
Dakhla 54 D1

Dakhla, El
  Wâhât el- ... 52 C4
Dakhovskaya .. 25 E5
Đakovica 22 C3
Dalaman → .. 23 F7
Dalandzadgad . 35 B5
Dālbandīn 42 E4
Dalby 63 A5
Dalhousie 69 D4
Dali 34 D5
Dalian 35 C7
Daliang Shan .. 34 D5
Dallarnil 63 A5
Dallas 79 C5
Dalmacija 20 C6
Dalmatia =
  Dalmacija .. 20 C6
Daloa 55 G3
Dalton 74 B5
Dalton Iceberg
  Tongue 96 A13
Daly Waters ... 60 D5
Daman 43 J8
Damanhûr 52 B5
Damar 39 F3
Damaraland ... 58 C3
Damascus =
  Dimashq 46 D4
Damāvand 44 C3
Damāvand,
  Qolleh-ye ... 44 C3
Damba 56 F3
Dāmghān 44 B3
Damiel 18 C4
Damietta =
  Dumyât 52 B5
Dammam = Ad
  Dammām ... 47 F7
Damoh 43 H11
Dampier 60 E2
Dampier, Selat . 39 E4
Danbury 73 D9
Dandeldhura .. 40 C3
Dandeli 43 M9
Dandenong ... 63 C4
Dandong 35 B7
Danger Is. =
  Pukapuka ... 65 L14
Danger Pt. 58 E3
Dangora 55 F6
Danilov 24 B5
Dankhar Gompa 42 C11
Dannemora ... 9 F11
Dannevirke ... 64 D7
Dante 49 E5
Danube =
  Dunărea → . 17 F9
Danville 75 A8
Danzig =
  Gdańsk 16 A4
Dao 38 B2
Daoud = Aïn
  Beïda 54 A6
Dar el Beida =
  Casablanca . 54 B3
Dar es Salaam . 57 F7
Dārāb 44 D3
Daraj 54 B7
Darband 42 B8
Darbhanga ... 40 D5
Dardanelles =
  Çanakkale
  Boğazı 23 D6
Dârfûr 53 F3
Dargai 42 B7
Dargan Ata ... 29 E7
Dargaville 64 A5
Darıca 22 D7
Darién, G. del . 90 B3

Darjeeling =
  Darjiling 40 D7
Darjiling 40 D7
Darling → ... 62 B3
Darling Downs . 63 A5
Darling Ra. ... 60 G2
Darlington ... 11 D6
Darłowo 16 A3
Darmstadt ... 14 D5
Darnah 52 B3
Darnley, C. ... 96 A10
Darnley B. 70 B7
Dart, C. 96 B18
Dartmoor 11 F5
Dartmouth ... 69 D4
Dartmouth, L. . 63 A4
Darvaza 29 E6
Darvel, Teluk . 38 D1
Darwha 43 J10
Darwin 60 C5
Daryoi Amu =
  Amudarya → 29 E6
Dās 44 E3
Dashhowuz ... 29 E6
Dasht → 42 G2
Dasht-e Kavīr .. 44 C3
Dasht-e Mārgow 42 D3
Datça 23 F6
Datia 43 G11
Datong 35 B6
Datu, Tanjung . 37 D3
Datu Piang ... 38 C2
Daugava → .. 24 B1
Daugavpils ... 24 B2
Daulpur 42 F10
Dauphin 71 C9
Dauphiné ... 13 D6
Davangere ... 43 M9
Davao 38 C3
Davao, G. of .. 38 C3
Dāvar Panāh .. 45 E5
Davenport ... 77 E9
David 86 E3
David Gorodok
  = Davyd
  Haradok ... 17 B8
Davis Sea ... 96 A11
Davis Str. 68 B5
Davos 13 C8
Davyd Haradok 17 B8
Dawson 70 B6
Dawson, I. ... 95 G2
Dax 12 E3
Daxian 35 C5
Daxue Shan ... 34 C5
Daylesford ... 62 C3
Dayr az Zawr .. 46 D5
Dayton 72 E3
Daytona Beach 75 E7
Dead Sea 47 E3
Deakin 60 G4
Deal I. 62 C4
Deán Funes .. 94 C4
Death Valley . 82 B4
Deba Habe ... 55 F7
Debar 22 D3
Dębica 16 C5
Debre Markos . 53 F6
Debre Tabor . 53 F6
Debrecen 16 E5
Decatur, Ala.,
  U.S.A. 74 B4
Decatur, Ill.,
  U.S.A. 77 F10
Deccan 43 L11
Děčín 16 C2
Dedéagach =
  Alexandroúpolis
  .... 22 D5

Dédougou

Dédougou 55 F4
Dee → 10 C5
Deepwater 63 A5
Degeh Bur 49 F3
Deggendorf .. 15 D7
Deh Bid 44 D3
Dehi Titan 42 C3
Dehibat 54 B7
Dehkareqan .. 46 C6
Dehra Dun 42 D11
Dej 17 E6
Dekese 56 E4
Delano 82 C3
Delaware □ .. 73 E8
Delaware → .. 73 E8
Delegate 63 C4
Delgado, C. ... 57 G8
Delgo 53 D5
Delhi 42 E10
Delice → 46 C3
Delicias 84 B3
Déline........ 70 B7
Delmenhorst .. 14 B5
Delmiro Gouveia 93 D6
Deloraine 62 D4
Delungra 63 A5
Delvinë 23 E3
Demanda, Sierra
  de la 18 A4
Demavand =
  Damāvand .. 44 C3
Demba 56 F4
Dembecha 53 F6
Dembidolo 53 G5
Demini → 90 D6
Demirci 23 E7
Demirköy 22 D6
Dempo 37 E2
Den Haag = 's-
  Gravenhage . 14 B3
Den Helder ... 14 B3
Denau 29 F7
Dendang 37 E3
Denia 19 C6
Denial B. 62 B1
Deniliquin 63 C3
Denman Glacier 96 A11
Denmark ■ .. 9 G9
Denmark Str. .. 66 C17
Denpasar 37 F5
Denton 78 C5
D'Entrecasteaux
  Is. 61 B9
Denver 76 F2
Deoghar 40 E6
Deolali 43 K8
Deoria 40 D4
Deosai Mts. ... 42 B9
Dêqên 34 D4
Dera Ghazi Khan 42 D7
Dera Ismail
  Khan 42 D7
Derbent 25 E6
Derby, Australia 60 D3
Derby, U.K. ... 11 E6
Derg, L. 11 E2
Dergaon 41 D9
Derry =
  Londonderry 11 D3
Derudub 53 E6
Des Moines ... 77 E8
Des Moines → 77 E9
Desaguadero → 91 G5
Dese 49 E2
Desna → 17 C10
Desolación, I. .. 95 G2
Despeñaperros,
  Paso 18 C4
Dessau 15 C7

D'Estrees B. ... 62 C2
Detmold 14 C5
Detroit 72 C4
Deutsche Bucht 14 A5
Deva 17 F6
Devakottai ... 43 Q11
Deventer 14 B4
Devonport,
  Australia 62 D4
Devonport, N.Z. 64 B6
Dewas 43 H10
Deyhūk 44 C4
Deyyer 44 E2
Dezfūl 47 D7
Dezhneva, Mys 31 C16
Dhafra 44 F3
Dhahira 44 F4
Dhahran = Az
  Zahrān 47 F7
Dhaka 41 F8
Dhaka □ 41 E8
Dhamar 49 E3
Dhamtari 40 G3
Dhanbad 40 F6
Dhangarhi 40 C3
Dhankuta 40 D6
Dhar 43 H9
Dharmapuri ... 43 N11
Dharwad 43 M9
Dhaulagiri 40 C4
Dhenkanal 40 G5
Dhíkti Óros ... 23 G5
Dhírfis 23 E4
Dhodhekánisos 23 F6
Dhrol 43 H7
Dhubaibah ... 44 F3
Dhuburi 41 D7
Dhule 43 J9
Dhut → 49 E5
Diafarabé 55 F4
Diamantina .. 93 F5
Diamantina → 62 A2
Diamantino → 93 E2
Diamond
  Harbour ... 40 F7
Diapaga 55 F5
Dībā 44 E4
Dibaya 56 F4
Dibaya-Lubue . 56 E3
Dibbi 49 G3
Dibrugarh 41 D10
Dickson 28 B9
Didiéni 55 F3
Diébougou 55 F4
Diefenbaker L. . 71 C9
Dieppe 12 B4
Digby 69 D4
Digges Is. 68 B3
Dighinala 41 F9
Digne-les-Bains 13 D7
Digos 38 C3
Digul → 39 F5
Dihang → 41 D10
Dijlah, Nahr → 47 E6
Dijon 13 C6
Dikimdya 31 D10
Dikson =
  Dickson ... 28 B9
Dikwa 53 F1
Dili 39 F3
Dilling 53 F4
Dillingham ... 71 C4
Dilolo 56 G4
Dilston 62 D4
Dimashq 46 D4
Dimbokro 55 G4
Dimboola 62 C3
Dimbovița → .. 22 B6
Dimitrovgrad,
  Bulgaria 22 C5

Dimitrovgrad,
  Russia 24 C6
Dimitrovo =
  Pernik 22 C4
Dinagat 38 B3
Dinajpur 41 E7
Dinan 12 B2
Dinant 14 C3
Dinar 46 C2
Dīnār, Kūh-e .. 44 D2
Dinara Planina . 20 B6
Dinard 12 B2
Dinaric Alps =
  Dinara Planina 20 B6
Dindigul 43 P11
Dingle 11 E1
Dinguiraye ... 55 F2
Dingwall 10 C4
Dinosaur
  National
  Monument .. 81 E9
Diourbel 55 F1
Dipolog 38 C2
Dir 42 B7
Diré 55 E4
Dire Dawa 49 F3
Dirico 58 B4
Dirranbandi ... 63 A4
Disa 43 G8
Disappointment,
  L. 60 E3
Disaster B. 63 C4
Discovery B. .. 62 C3
Disteghil Sar .. 42 A9
Distrito
  Federal □ ... 93 F4
Diu 43 J7
Divinópolis ... 93 G5
Divnoye 25 D5
Dīwāl Kol 42 B5
Diyarbakır ... 46 C5
Diz Chah 44 C3
Djado 52 D1
Djakarta =
  Jakarta 37 F3
Djambala 56 E2
Djanet 54 D6
Djawa = Jawa . 37 F3
Djelfa 54 B5
Djema 57 C5
Djenné 55 F4
Djerba, I. de .. 52 B1
Djerid, Chott .. 54 B6
Djibo 55 F4
Djibouti 49 E3
Djibouti ■ ... 49 E3
Djolu 56 D4
Djougou 55 G5
Djoum 56 D2
Djourab 53 E2
Djugu 57 D6
Dmitriya
  Lapteva, Proliv 31 B12
Dnepr → =
  Dnipro → .. 25 D3
Dneprodzerzhinsk
  =
  Dniprodzerzhynsk
  ...... 25 D3
Dnepropetrovsk
  =
  Dnipropetrovsk
  ...... 25 D4
Dnestr → =
  Dnister → .. 17 E10
Dnestrovski =
  Belgorod ... 24 C4
Dnieper =
  Dnipro → .. 25 D3

Dniester =
  Dnister → .. 17 E10
Dnipro → 25 D3
Dniprodzerzhynsk
  .... 25 D3
Dnipro
  petrovsk..... 25 D4
Dnister → .. 17 E10
Dnistrovskyy
  Lyman 17 E10
Dnyapro =
  Dnipro → .. 25 D3
Doba 53 G2
Doberai,
  Jazirah 39 E4
Doblas 94 D4
Dobo 39 F4
Doboj 20 B7
Dobrich 22 C6
Dobruja 22 B7
Dobrush 17 B10
Dodecanese =
  Dhodhekánisos
  .... 23 F6
Dodge City 78 A3
Dodoma 57 F7
Dogi 42 C3
Doha = Ad
  Dawhah ... 44 E2
Dohazari 41 F9
Doi 39 D3
Dois Irmãos, Sa. 93 D5
Dolbeau 69 D3
Dole 13 C6
Dolomites =
  Dolomiti 20 A3
Dolomiti 20 A3
Dolores 94 D5
Dolphin, C. ... 95 G5
Dolphin and
  Union Str. ... 70 B8
Dombarovskiy . 29 D6
Dominica ■ .. 87 C7
Dominican
  Rep. ■ 87 C5
Domo 49 F4
Domodóssola . 20 A2
Domville, Mt. .. 63 A5
Don →, Russia 25 D4
Don →, U.K. .. 10 C5
Don Benito ... 18 C3
Donald 62 C3
Donau =
  Dunărea → . 17 F9
Donauwörth .. 14 D6
Doncaster ... 11 E6
Dondo, Angola 56 F2
Dondo, Mozam. 59 B6
Dondo, Teluk .. 39 D2
Donegal 11 D2
Donets → 25 D5
Donetsk 25 D4
Donggala 39 E1
Dongola 53 E5
Dongou 56 D3
Dongting Hu .. 35 D6
Dongxing 35 D5
Donington, C. . 62 B2
Donnelly's
  Crossing ... 64 A5
Donostia = San
  Sebastián ... 19 A5
Dora Báltea → 20 B2
Dorchester, C. . 68 B3
Dordogne → .. 12 D3
Dordrecht ... 14 C3
Dori 55 F4
Dornbirn 14 E5
Dorohoi 17 E8

Döröö Nuur ...	34	B4
Dorrigo	63	B5
Dortmund	14	C4
Doruma	57	D5
Dos Bahías, C. .	95	E3
Dos Hermanas	18	D3
Dosso	55	F5
Dothan	74	D5
Douai	13	A5
Douala	56	D1
Douarnenez ...	12	B1
Double Island Pt.	63	A5
Doubs ➤	13	C6
Doubtful Sd. .	65	F2
Doubtless B. .	64	A5
Douentza	55	F4
Douglas, *U.K.* .	11	D4
Douglas, *U.S.A.*	83	E8
Doumé	56	D2
Dourados	94	A6
Douro ➤	18	B1
Dover, *Australia*	62	D4
Dover, *U.K.* ..	11	F7
Dover, Str. of . .	11	F7
Dovrefjell	8	F9
Dowlat Yār ...	45	C6
Dowlatābād ..	44	D4
Dowshī	45	C7
Draa, Oued ➤	54	C2
Drăgăşani ...	22	B5
Dragichyn	17	B7
Dragoman, Prokhod ...	22	C4
Draguignan ...	13	E7
Drake	63	A5
Drakensberg .	59	E5
Dráma	22	D5
Drammen	9	G10
Drau = Drava ➤ ...	20	B7
Drava ➤	20	B7
Dresden	15	C7
Dreux	12	B4
Drina ➤	20	B7
Drini ➤	22	C2
Drobeta-Turnu-Severin	22	B4
Drochia	17	D8
Drogheda	11	E3
Drogobych = Drohobych ..	17	D6
Drohobych ...	17	D6
Droichead Atha = Drogheda .	11	E3
Dromedary, C. .	63	C5
Drumheller ...	71	C8
Drummond Pt.	62	B2
Drut ➤	17	B10
Drygalski I. ...	96	A11
Dschang	55	G7
Dubā	47	F3
Dubai = Dubayy	44	E3
Dubăsari	17	E9
Dubăsari Vdkhr.	17	E9
Dubawnt ➤ ..	70	B9
Dubawnt, L. ..	70	B9
Dubayy	44	E3
Dubbo	63	B4
Dublin, *Ireland*	11	E3
Dublin, *U.S.A.* .	75	C6
Dubno	17	C7
Dubossary = Dubăsari	17	E9
Dubossary Vdkhr. = Dubăsari Vdkhr.	17	E9
Dubovka	24	D5
Dubréka	55	G2
Dubrovitsa = Dubrovytsya	17	C8
Dubrovnik	20	C7
Dubrovytsya ..	17	C8
Dudhi	40	E4
Dudinka	30	C6
Duero = Douro ➤ ...	18	B1
Dugi Otok	20	B5
Duisburg	14	C4
Dukelský Průsmyk	16	D5
Dukhān	44	E2
Duki	42	D6
Duku	55	F7
Dulce ➤	94	C4
Dulit, Banjaran	37	D4
Duluth	77	B8
Dum Duma ...	41	D10
Dum Hadjer ..	53	F2
Dumaguete ...	38	C2
Dumai	37	D2
Dumaran	38	B1
Dumfries	11	D5
Dumyât	52	B5
Dún Dealgan = Dundalk ...	11	D3
Dun Laoghaire	11	E3
Duna = Dunărea ➤ .	17	F9
Dunaj = Dunărea ➤ .	17	F9
Dunakeszi	16	E4
Dunărea ➤ ...	17	F9
Dunaújváros ..	16	E4
Dunav = Dunărea ➤ .	17	F9
Dunback	65	F4
Dunbar	10	D5
Duncan	78	B5
Dundalk	11	D3
Dundee, *S. Africa* ...	59	D6
Dundee, *U.K.* ..	10	C5
Dundoo	63	A3
Dunedin	65	F4
Dunfermline ..	10	C5
Dungarvan	11	E3
Dungog	63	B5
Dungu	57	D5
Dunhuang ...	34	B4
Dunkerque ...	12	A5
Dunkirk = Dunkerque ..	12	A5
Dunkwa	55	G4
Dúnleary = Dun Laoghaire ...	11	E3
Dunolly	62	C3
Dunqul	52	D5
Dunstan Mts. ..	65	F3
Durance ➤ ...	13	E6
Durango, *Mexico*	84	C4
Durango, *Spain*	19	A4
Durazno	94	C5
Durazzo = Durrësi	22	D2
Durban	59	D6
Düren	14	C4
Durg	40	G3
Durgapur	40	F6
Durham, *U.K.* .	11	D6
Durham, *U.S.A.*	75	B8
Durham Downs	63	A4
Durmitor	22	C2
Durrësi	22	D2
Dursunbey	23	E7
D'Urville, Tanjung	39	E5
D'Urville I.	65	D5
Dusa Mareb ...	49	F4
Dushak	29	F7
Dushanbe	29	F7
Dusky Sd.	65	F2
Düsseldorf ...	14	C4
Dutch Harbor ..	71	C3
Duwādimi ...	47	F6
Duyun	35	D5
Düzce	46	B2
Duzdab = Zāhedān	45	D5
Dvina, Severnaya ➤	28	C5
Dvinsk = Daugavpils ..	24	B2
Dwarka	43	H6
Dyatlovo = Dzyatlava ...	17	B7
Dyer, C.	68	B4
Dyer Plateau ..	96	B3
Dyersburg ...	79	A9
Dymer	17	C10
Dynevor Downs	63	A3
Dzamin Üüd ..	35	B6
Dzerzhinsk ...	24	B5
Dzhambul = Taraz........	29	E8
Dzhankoy	25	D3
Dzhardzhan ...	30	C10
Dzhezkazgan = Zhezqazghan	29	E7
Dzhizak = Jizzakh	29	E7
Działdowa ...	16	B5
Dzierzoniów ...	16	C3
Dzungaria = Junggar Pendi	34	B3
Dzungarian Gate = Alataw Shankou	34	B3
Dzuumod	35	B5
Dzyarzhynsk ..	17	B8
Dzyatlava	17	B7

E

Earnslaw, Mt. .	65	F3
East Bengal ...	41	E7
East Beskids = Vychodné Beskydy	17	D5
East C.	64	B8
East China Sea	35	C7
East Falkland ..	95	G5
East Kilbride ..	10	D4
East London ..	59	E5
East Orange ..	73	D8
East St. Louis .	77	F9
East Sea = Japan, Sea of	31	G11
East Timor ...	39	F3
East Toorale ..	63	B4
Eastbourne, *N.Z.*	65	D6
Eastbourne, *U.K.*	11	F7
Eastern Ghats .	43	N11
Eastmain	69	C3
Eastmain ➤ ..	69	C3
Eau Claire ...	77	C9
Eberswalde-Finow	15	B7
Ebolowa	56	D2
Ebro ➤	19	B6
Eceabat	23	D6
Ech Cheliff	54	A5
Echo Bay	70	B8
Echuca	63	C3
Ecija	18	D3
Ecuador ■	90	D3
Ed Dâmer	53	E5
Ed Debba	53	E5
Ed Dueim	53	F5
Edd	49	E3
Eddystone Pt. .	62	D4
Édea	56	D2
Eden	63	C4
Eder ➤	14	C5
Édhessa	23	D4
Edievale	65	F3
Edinburg	78	F4
Edinburgh ...	10	D5
Edinița	17	D8
Edirne	22	D6
Edithburgh ...	62	C2
Edmonton ...	71	C8
Edmundston ..	69	D4
Edremit	23	E6
Edremit Körfezi	23	E6
Edson	71	C8
Edward ➤ ...	62	C3
Edward, L. ...	57	E5
Edward VII Land	96	C17
Edwards Plateau	78	D3
Égadi, Ísole ...	21	F4
Eger = Cheb ..	16	C1
Eger	16	E5
Egersund	9	G9
Egmont, C. ...	64	C5
Egmont, Mt. ..	64	C6
Eğridir	46	C2
Eğridir Gölü ..	46	C2
Egypt ■	52	C5
Eibar	19	A4
Eidsvold	63	A5
Eifel	14	C4
Eigg	10	C3
Eil	49	F4
Eildon, L.	63	C4
Eindhoven	14	C3
Eire = Ireland ■	11	E3
Eirunepé	91	E5
Eisenach	14	C6
Eisenerz	15	E8
Eivissa = Ibiza .	19	C6
Eketahuna ...	64	D6
Ekibastuz	29	D8
El Aaiún	54	C2
El Alamein ...	52	B4
El Aricha	54	B4
El 'Arîsh	52	B5
El Asnam = Ech Cheliff	54	A5
El Bawiti	52	C4
El Bayadh ...	54	B5
El Callao	90	B6
El Centro	82	D5
El Cerro	91	G6
El Cuy	95	D3
El Cuyo	85	C7
El Dere	49	G4
El Diviso	90	C3
El Djouf	55	D3
El Dorado, *Ark., U.S.A.*	79	C7
El Dorado, *Kans., U.S.A.*	78	A5
El Dorado, *Venezuela* ...	90	B6
El Escorial ...	18	B3
El Faiyûm ...	52	C5
El Fâsher	53	F4
El Ferrol	18	A1
El Fuerte	84	B3
El Gal	49	E5

El Geneina = Al
Junaynah ... 53 F3
El Geteina 53 F5
El Gîza 52 C5
El Iskandarîya . 52 B4
El Jadida 54 B3
El Jebelein 53 F5
El Kab 53 E5
El Kala 54 A6
El Kamlin 53 E5
El Kef 54 A6
El Khandaq ... 53 E5
El Khârga 52 C5
El Khartûm ... 53 E5
El Khartûm
Bahrî 53 E5
El Laqâwa 53 F4
El Mafâza 53 F5
El Mahalla el
Kubra 52 B5
El Mansûra ... 52 B5
El Minyâ 52 C5
El Obeid 53 F5
El Odaiya 53 F4
El Oued 54 B6
El Paso 83 E9
El Prat de
Llobregat ... 19 B7
El Puerto de
Santa María . 18 D2
El Qâhira 52 B5
El Qantara 52 B5
El Qasr 52 C4
El Reno 78 B5
El Salvador ■ . 85 E7
El Shallal 52 D5
El Suweis 52 C5
El Tigre 90 B6
El Tocuyo 90 B5
El Turbio 95 G2
El Uqsur 52 C5
El Vigía 90 B4
El Wak 57 D8
El Wuz 53 E5
Elat 47 E3
Elâzığ 46 C4
Elba 20 C3
Elbasani 22 D3
Elbe → 14 B5
Elbert, Mt. 83 A9
Elbeuf 12 B4
Elbidtan 46 C4
Elbing = Elbląg 16 A4
Elbląg 16 A4
Elbrus 25 E5
Elburz Mts. =
Alborz,
Reshteh-ye
Kühhā-ye ... 44 B3
Elche 19 C5
Elda 19 C5
Elde → 15 B6
Eldoret 57 D7
Elektrostal 24 B4
Elephant I. 96 A4
Eleuthera 86 A4
Elgin, U.K. 10 C5
Elgin, U.S.A. .. 72 C1
Elgon, Mt. 57 D6
Eliase 39 F4
Elisabethville =
Lubumbashi . 59 A5
Elista 25 D5
Elizabeth,
Australia .. 62 B2
Elizabeth, U.S.A. 73 D8
Elizabeth City . 75 A9
Elizabethton ... 75 A6
Ełk 16 B6

Elkhart 72 D3
Elkhovo 22 C6
Elko 80 E6
Ellery, Mt. 63 C4
Ellesmere, L. .. 65 G5
Ellice Is. =
Tuvalu ■ ... 64 K12
Elliston 62 B1
Ellore = Eluru . 40 J3
Ellsworth Land 96 B2
Ellsworth Mts. . 96 B2
Elmore 63 C3
Elmshorn 14 B5
Eltham 64 C6
Eluru 40 J3
Elvas 18 C2
Elx = Elche ... 19 C5
Ely 11 E7
Emāmrūd 44 B3
Emba = Embi . 29 E6
Emba → =
Embi → 29 E6
Embarcación .. 94 A4
Embi 29 E6
Embi → 29 E6
Embrun 13 D7
Embu 57 E7
Emden 14 B4
Emerson 71 D10
Emet 23 E7
Emi Koussi ... 53 E2
Emine, Nos ... 22 C6
Emmen 14 B4
Empalme 84 B2
Empangeni ... 59 D6
Empedrado ... 94 B5
Empty Quarter
= Rub' al
Khali 48 D4
Ems → 14 B4
En Nahud 53 F4
Enaratoli 39 E5
Enare =
Inarijärvi 8 E13
Encanto, C. ... 38 A2
Encarnación ... 94 B5
Encounter B. .. 62 C2
Ende 39 F2
Enderby Land . 96 A9
Enewetak Atoll 64 H11
Enez 23 D6
Engadin 13 C9
Engaño, C. 38 A2
Engels 24 C6
Enggano 37 F2
Engkilili 37 D4
England □ 11 E6
Englewood ... 76 F2
English Bazar =
Ingraj Bazar . 40 E7
English Channel 11 F5
Enid 78 A5
Enna 21 F5
Ennedi 53 E3
Enngonia 63 A4
Ennis 11 E2
Enniskillen 11 D3
Enns → 15 D8
Enschede 14 B4
Ensenada 84 A1
Entebbe 57 D6
Entroncamento 18 C1
Enugu 55 G6
Enugu Ezike ... 55 G6
Eólie, Ís. 21 E5
Épernay 13 B5
Ephesus 23 F6
Épinal 13 B7
Epukiro 58 C3

Equatorial
Guinea ■ ... 56 D1
Er Rahad 53 F5
Er Rif 54 A4
Er Roseires ... 53 F5
Erāwadī Myit =
Irrawaddy → 41 K10
Erbil = Arbīl .. 46 C6
Erciyaş Dağı ... 46 C3
Érd 16 E4
Erdek 23 D6
Erebus, Mt. ... 96 B15
Erechim 94 B6
Ereğli, Konya,
Turkey 46 C3
Ereğli,
Zonguldak,
Turkey 46 B2
Eresma → ... 18 B3
Erewadi
Myitwanya . 41 K10
Erfurt 15 C6
Ergani 46 C4
Érice 21 E4
Erie 73 C5
Erie, L. 72 C5
Erigavo 49 E4
Erímanthos ... 23 F3
Erimo-misaki .. 32 F12
Eritrea ■ 49 E2
Erlangen 15 D6
Ermenak 46 C3
Ermoúpolis =
Síros 23 F5
Ernakulam =
Cochin 43 Q10
Erne, Lower L. . 11 D3
Erode 43 P10
Eromanga 63 A3
Erramala Hills . 43 M11
Ertis → =
Irtysh → ... 28 C7
Erzgebirge 15 C7
Erzincan 46 C4
Erzurum 46 C5
Es Sahrâ' Esh
Sharqîya ... 52 C5
Es Sînâ' 52 C5
Esbjerg 9 G9
Esch-sur-Alzette 13 B6
Escuinapa 84 C3
Eşfahān 44 C2
Esh Sham =
Dimashq 46 D4
Esil → =
Ishim → ... 29 D8
Eskilstuna 9 G11
Eskimo Pt. =
Arviat 70 B10
Eskişehir 46 C2
Esla → 18 B2
Eslāmābād-e
Gharb 46 D6
Eşme 23 E7
Esmeraldas ... 90 C3
Esperance 60 G3
Esperanza 94 C4
Espichel, C. ... 18 C1
Espinal 90 C4
Espinazo, Sierra
del = ...
Espinhaço,
Serra do 93 F5
Espinhaço, Serra
do 93 F5
Espírito Santo □ 93 G5
Esquel 95 E2
Esquina 94 C5
Essaouira 54 B3

Essen 14 C4
Essequibo → . 90 B7
Esslingen 14 D5
Estados, I. de
Los 95 G4
Estância 93 E6
Estevan 71 D9
Estonia ■ 24 B2
Estrêla, Serra da 18 B2
Estremoz 18 C2
Estrondo, Serra
do 92 D4
Esztergom 16 E4
Etadunna 62 A2
Étampes 12 B5
Etawah 42 F11
Ethiopia ■ ... 49 F2
Etna 21 F5
Etosha Pan ... 58 B3
Euboea =
Évvoia 23 E5
Eucumbene, L. 63 C4
Eufaula 74 D5
Eugene 80 C2
Eugowra 63 B4
Eulo 63 A4
Euphrates =
Furāt, Nahr
al → 47 E6
Eureka 80 E1
Euroa 63 C4
Europa, I. 59 J8
Europa, Picos de 18 A3
Europa, Pta. de 18 D3
Europa Pt. =
Europa, Pta.
de 18 D3
Evans Head ... 63 A5
Evanston 72 C2
Evansville 72 F2
Everard, L. 62 B1
Everest, Mt. ... 40 C6
Everett 80 B2
Everglades
National Park 75 G7
Evinayong 56 D2
Évora 18 C2
Évreux 12 B4
Évry 12 B5
Évvoia 23 E5
Ewo 56 E2
Exaltación 91 F5
Exeter 11 F5
Exmoor 11 F5
Exmouth 11 F5
Extremadura □ 18 C2
Eyasi, L. 57 E6
Eyre (North), L. 62 A2
Eyre (South), L. 62 A2
Eyre, L. 60 F6
Eyre Cr. → ... 62 A2
Eyre Mts. 65 F3
Eyre Pen. 62 B2
Ezine 23 E6

F

F.Y.R.O.M. =
Macedonia ■ 22 D3
Fabriano 20 C4
Facatativá 90 C4
Fachi 55 E7
Fada 53 E3
Fada-n-Gourma 55 F5
Faddeyevskiy,
Ostrov 31 B12

Fāḍilī	47	F7	
Faenza	20	B3	
Færoe Is. =			
Føroyar	6	C4	
Fāgăras	17	F7	
Fagnano, L.	95	G3	
Fahraj	45	D4	
Fahūd	44	F4	
Fair Isle	10	B6	
Fairbanks	71	B5	
Fairfield, *Ala.,*			
U.S.A.	74	C4	
Fairfield, *Calif.,*			
U.S.A.	80	F2	
Fairlie	65	F4	
Fairweather, Mt.	71	C6	
Faisalabad	42	D8	
Faizabad	40	D4	
Fakfak	39	E4	
Falaise	12	B3	
Falam	41	F9	
Falconara			
Maríttima	20	C4	
Falcone, C.	20	D2	
Faleshty =			
Fălești	17	E8	
Fălești	17	E8	
Falkland Is. □	95	G5	
Falkland Sd.	95	G5	
Fall River	73	D10	
Falmouth	11	F4	
False B.	58	E3	
Fălticeni	17	E8	
Falun	9	F11	
Famagusta	46	D3	
Fandriana	59	J9	
Fano	20	C4	
Fao = Al Fāw	47	E7	
Faradje	57	D5	
Farafangana	59	J9	
Farāh	42	C3	
Farāh □	42	C3	
Faranah	55	F2	
Farasān, Jazā'ir	49	D3	
Farasan Is. =			
Farasān,			
Jazā'ir	49	D3	
Fareham	11	F6	
Farewell, C.	64	D5	
Farewell C. =			
Farvel, Kap	68	C6	
Farghona	29	E8	
Fargo	76	B6	
Farim	55	F1	
Farīmān	45	C4	
Farina	62	B2	
Faro, *Brazil*	92	C2	
Faro, *Portugal*	18	D2	
Farrāshband	44	D3	
Farrell Flat	62	B2	
Farrukhabad-			
cum-			
Fatehgarh	42	F11	
Fārs □	44	D3	
Fársala	23	E4	
Fartak, Rās	47	E3	
Farvel, Kap	68	C6	
Fāryāb □	45	B6	
Fasā	44	D3	
Fasano	21	D6	
Fastiv	17	C9	
Fastov = Fastiv	17	C9	
Fatagar, Tanjung	39	E4	
Fatehgarh	42	F11	
Fatehpur, *Raj.,*			
India	42	F9	
Fatehpur, *Ut. P.,*			
India	40	E3	
Favara	21	F4	
Favignana	21	F4	
Faya-Largeau	53	E2	
Fayd	47	F5	
Fayetteville,			
Ark., U.S.A.	79	A6	
Fayetteville,			
N.C., U.S.A.	75	B8	
Fazilka	42	D9	
Fdérik	54	D2	
Feather →	80	F3	
Featherston	65	D6	
Fécamp	12	B4	
Fehmarn	15	A6	
Feilding	64	D6	
Feira de Santana	93	E6	
Feldkirch	14	E5	
Felipe Carrillo			
Puerto	85	D7	
Felixstowe	11	F7	
Fengjie	35	C5	
Fenyang	35	C6	
Feodosiya	25	D4	
Ferdows	44	C4	
Ferfer	49	F4	
Fergana =			
Farghona	29	E8	
Fermo	20	C4	
Fernando de			
Noronha	92	C7	
Fernando Póo =			
Bioko	56	D1	
Ferozepore =			
Firozpur	42	D9	
Ferrara	20	B3	
Ferreñafe	91	E3	
Ferret, C.	12	D3	
Ferrol = El			
Ferrol	18	A1	
Fès	54	B4	
Feshi	56	F3	
Feteşti	22	B6	
Fetlar	10	A6	
Feuilles →	68	C3	
Fezzan	52	C2	
Fianarantsoa	59	J9	
Fianga	53	G2	
Ficksburg	59	D5	
Fieri	23	D2	
Figeac	12	D5	
Figueira da Foz	18	B1	
Figueras	19	A7	
Figuig	54	B4	
Fiji ■	64	L12	
Filiatrá	23	F3	
Filyos →	46	B3	
Fíngöe	59	A6	
Finike	46	C2	
Finisterre, C.	18	A1	
Finke →	62	A2	
Finland ■	8	F13	
Finland, G. of	9	G13	
Finlay →	70	C7	
Finley	63	C4	
Finniss, C.	62	B1	
Fiora →	20	C3	
Firat = Furāt,			
Nahr al →	47	E6	
Firenze	20	C3	
Firozabad	42	F11	
Firozpur	42	D9	
Firūzābād	44	D3	
Firūzkūh	44	C3	
Fish →	58	D3	
Fishguard	11	E4	
Fitri, L.	53	F2	
Fitz Roy	95	F3	
Fiume = Rijeka	20	B5	
Fizi	57	E5	
Flagstaff	83	C7	
Flaming Gorge			
Reservoir	81	E9	
Flamingo, Teluk	39	F5	
Flandre	14	C2	
Flathead L.	81	B6	
Flattery, C.	80	A1	
Flensburg	14	A5	
Flers	12	B3	
Flesko, Tanjung	39	D2	
Flin Flon	71	C9	
Flinders →	61	D7	
Flinders I.	62	C4	
Flinders Ras.	62	B2	
Flint	72	C4	
Flint I.	65	L15	
Flinton	63	A4	
Florence =			
Firenze	20	C3	
Florence, *Ala.,*			
U.S.A.	74	B4	
Florence, *S.C.,*			
U.S.A.	75	B8	
Florence, L.	62	A2	
Flores	39	F2	
Flores Sea	39	F2	
Floreşti	17	E9	
Floriano	92	D5	
Florianópolis	94	B7	
Florida	94	C5	
Florida □	75	F6	
Florida, Straits			
of	86	B3	
Flórina	23	D3	
Florø	8	F9	
Fluk	39	E3	
Flushing =			
Vlissingen	14	C2	
Fly →	61	B7	
Flying Fish, C.	96	B1	
Foça	23	E6	
Focşani	17	F8	
Fóggia	20	D5	
Föhr	14	A5	
Foix	12	E4	
Foligno	20	C4	
Folkestone	11	F7	
Fond du Lac	77	D10	
Fondi	20	D4	
Fonsagrada	18	A2	
Fonseca, G. de	85	E7	
Fontainebleau	13	B5	
Fonte Boa	90	D5	
Fontenay-le-			
Comte	12	C3	
Foochow =			
Fuzhou	35	D6	
Forbes	63	B4	
Ford's Bridge	63	A4	
Forécariah	55	G2	
Forestier Pen.	62	D4	
Forfar	10	C5	
Forlì	20	B4	
Formentera	19	C6	
Formentor, C. de	19	C7	
Former			
Yugoslav			
Republic of			
Macedonia =			
Macedonia ■	22	D3	
Fórmia	20	D4	
Formosa =			
Taiwan ■	35	D7	
Formosa	94	B5	
Formosa, Serra	93	E3	
Formosa Bay	57	E8	
Føroyar =			
Føroyar	6	C4	
Føroyar	6	C4	
Forrest	62	C3	
Forsayth	61	D7	
Forst	15	C8	
Forster	63	B5	
Fort Albany	69	C2	
Fort Collins	76	E2	
Fort-de-France	87	D7	
Fort de Possel =			
Possel	56	C3	
Fort Dodge	77	D7	
Fort			
Good-Hope	70	B7	
Fort Hertz =			
Putao	41	D11	
Fort Lauderdale	75	F7	
Fort Liard	70	B7	
Fort Macleod	71	D8	
Fort MacMahon	54	C5	
Fort McPherson	70	B6	
Fort Miribel	54	C5	
Fort Myers	75	F7	
Fort Peck L.	81	B10	
Fort Pierce	75	F7	
Fort Portal	57	D6	
Fort Providence	70	B8	
Fort Resolution	70	B8	
Fort Rosebery =			
Mansa	57	G5	
Fort Rupert =			
Waskaganish	69	C3	
Fort Sandeman	42	D6	
Fort Scott	79	A6	
Fort Severn	69	C2	
Fort			
Shevchenko	29	E6	
Fort Simpson	70	B7	
Fort Smith,			
Canada	70	B8	
Fort Smith,			
U.S.A.	79	B6	
Fort Trinquet =			
Bir Mogrein	54	C2	
Fort Walton			
Beach	74	D4	
Fort Wayne	72	D3	
Fort William	10	C4	
Fort Worth	78	C5	
Fort Yukon	71	B5	
Fortaleza	92	C6	
Forūr	44	E3	
Foshan	35	D6	
Fossano	20	B1	
Fouçamou	56	E2	
Fougères	12	B3	
Foula	10	A5	
Foumban	55	G7	
Foúrnoi	23	F6	
Fouta Djalon	55	F2	
Foveaux Str.	65	G3	
Foxe Basin	68	B3	
Foxe Chan.	68	B2	
Foxe Pen.	68	B3	
Foxton	64	D6	
Foz do Gregório	91	E4	
Foz do Iguaçu	94	B6	
Franca	93	G4	
Francavilla			
Fontana	21	D6	
France ■	13	C5	
Frances	62	C3	
Franceville	56	E2	
Franche-Comté	13	C6	
Francistown	59	C5	
Frankfurt,			
Brandenburg,			
Germany	15	B8	
Frankfurt,			
Hessen,			
Germany	14	C5	
Fränkische Alb	15	D6	

Franklin B. 70 B7
Franklin I. 96 B15
Franklin Mts. ... 70 B7
Franklin Str. ... 70 A10
Frankston 63 C4
Frantsa Iosifa,
  Zemlya 28 A6
Franz 69 D2
Franz Josef
  Land =
  Frantsa Iosifa,
  Zemlya 28 A6
Fraser → ... 71 D7
Fraser I. 63 A5
Fraserburgh ... 10 C5
Fray Bentos ... 94 C5
Fredericksburg 73 E7
Fredericton .. 69 D4
Fredrikstad 9 G10
Freeport,
  Bahamas ... 86 A4
Freeport, U.S.A. 77 D10
Freetown 55 G2
Fregenal de la
  Sierra 18 C2
Freibourg =
  Fribourg 13 C7
Freiburg 14 E4
Freire 95 D2
Freising 15 D6
Freistadt 15 D8
Fréjus 13 E7
Fremont 82 B2
French
  Guiana ■ ... 92 B3
French
  Polynesia ■ . 65 M16
Fresco → 92 D3
Freshfield, C. .. 96 A14
Fresnillo 84 C4
Fresno 82 B3
Freycinet Pen. . 62 D4
Fria, C. 58 B2
Frías 94 B3
Fribourg 13 C7
Friedrichshafen 14 E5
Friendly Is. =
  Tonga ■ 65 L13
Frobisher B. .. 68 B4
Frobisher Bay =
  Iqaluit 68 B4
Frome, L. 62 B2
Frome Downs . 62 B2
Front Range ... 81 E11
Frosinone 20 D4
Frunze =
  Bishkek 29 E8
Frutal 93 F4
Frýdek-Místek . 16 D4
Fuchou =
  Fuzhou 35 D6
Fuengirola 18 D3
Fuentes de
  Oñoro 18 B2
Fuerte → 84 B3
Fuerte Olimpo . 91 H7
Fuerteventura . 54 C2
Fuhai 34 B3
Fuji-San 32 B6
Fujian □ 35 D6
Fujinomiya ... 32 B6
Fujisawa 32 B6
Fukien =
  Fujian □ ... 35 D6
Fukuchiyama . 32 B4
Fukui 32 A5
Fukuoka 32 C2
Fukushima .. 33 G12
Fukuyama 32 B3

Fulda 14 C5
Fulda → 14 C5
Fullerton 82 D4
Funabashi 32 B7
Funchal 54 B1
Fundación 90 A4
Fundão 18 B2
Fundy, B. of ... 69 D4
Funtua 55 F6
Furāt, Nahr
  al → 47 E6
Furneaux Group 62 D4
Fürstenwalde .. 15 B8
Fürth 14 D6
Fury and Hecla
  Str. 68 B2
Fusagasuga ... 90 C4
Fushun 35 B7
Futuna 64 L12
Fuxin 35 B7
Fuyuan 35 B8
Fuzhou 35 D6
Fyn 9 G10

G

Gabela 56 G2
Gabès 54 B7
Gabès, G. de .. 52 B1
Gabon ■ 56 E2
Gaborone 59 C5
Gabrovo 22 C5
Gachsārān 44 D2
Gadag 43 M9
Gadarwara 43 H11
Gadhada 43 J7
Gadsden 74 B4
Gadwal 43 L10
Gafsa 54 B6
Gagnoa 55 G3
Gagnon 69 C4
Gaillimh =
  Galway 11 E2
Gainesville, Fla.,
  U.S.A. 75 E6
Gainesville, Ga.,
  U.S.A. 75 B6
Gainesville,
  Tex., U.S.A. . 78 C5
Gairdner, L. ... 62 B2
Galangue 58 A3
Galashiels 10 D5
Galaţi 17 F9
Galatina 21 D7
Galcaio 49 F4
Galdhøpiggen . 8 F9
Galela 39 D3
Galesburg 77 E9
Galich 24 B5
Galicia □ 18 A2
Galilee, Sea of
  = Yam
  Kinneret 46 D3
Gallabat 53 F6
Gállego → ... 19 B5
Gallegos → ... 95 G3
Gallinas, Pta. .. 90 A4
Gallipoli =
  Gelibolu 23 D6
Gallípoli 21 D6
Gällivare 8 E12
Galloway, Mull
  of 11 D4
Galong 63 B4
Galveston 79 E6
Gálvez 94 C4

Galway 11 E2
Galway B. ... 11 E2
Gambaga 55 F4
Gambela 53 G5
Gambia ■ 55 F1
Gambia → ... 55 F1
Gambier Is. ... 62 C2
Gamboma ... 56 E3
Gan Jiang → . 35 D6
Ganāveh 44 D2
Gäncä 25 E6
Gand = Gent .. 14 C2
Ganda 58 A2
Gandak → ... 40 E5
Gandava 42 E5
Gander 69 D5
Gandhi Sagar . 43 G9
Gandi 55 F6
Gandía 19 C5
Ganedidalem =
  Gani 39 E3
Ganga → 41 F8
Ganganagar .. 42 E8
Gangara 55 F6
Gangaw 41 F10
Gangdisê Shan 40 B3
Ganges =
  Ganga → .. 41 F8
Gangtok 41 D7
Gani 39 E3
Gansu □ 34 C5
Ganta 55 G3
Gantheaume, C. 62 C2
Gantsevichi =
  Hantsavichy . 17 B8
Ganyem 39 E6
Ganzhou 35 D6
Gaoua 55 F4
Gaoual 55 F2
Gaoxiong 35 D7
Gap 13 D7
Gar 34 C2
Garabogazköl
  Aylagy 29 E6
Garanhuns 92 D6
Garawe 55 H3
Gard 49 F4
Garda, L. di ... 20 B3
Garden City ... 78 A3
Garden Grove . 82 D4
Gardēz 42 C6
Gargano, Mte. . 20 D5
Garigliano → . 20 D4
Garland 81 E7
Garm 29 F8
Garmisch-
  Partenkirchen 14 E6
Garmsār 44 C3
Garoe 49 F4
Garonne → .. 12 D3
Garoua 53 G1
Garrison Res. =
  Sakakawea, L. 76 B4
Garry, L. 70 B9
Garsen 57 E8
Garvie Mts. ... 65 F3
Garwa =
  Garoua 53 G1
Gary 72 D2
Garzê 34 C5
Garzón 90 C3
Gasan Kuli =
  Hasan Kuli .. 29 F6
Gascogne 12 E4
Gascogne, G. de 12 D2
Gascony =
  Gascogne ... 12 E4
Gashaka 55 G7
Gaspé 69 D4

Gaspé, C. de .. 69 D4
Gaspé, Pén. de 69 D4
Gasteiz = Vitoria 19 A4
Gastonia 75 B7
Gastre 95 E3
Gata, C. de 19 D4
Gata, Sierra de 18 B2
Gateshead 11 D6
Gauhati 41 D8
Gaväter 45 E5
Gávdhos 23 G5
Gävle 8 F11
Gawilgarh Hills 43 J10
Gawler 62 B2
Gaxun Nur ... 34 B5
Gaya, India ... 40 E5
Gaya, Niger ... 55 F5
Gayndah 63 A5
Gaysin =
  Haysyn 17 D9
Gayvoron =
  Hayvoron ... 17 D9
Gaza 47 E3
Gaziantep 46 C4
Gazli 29 E7
Gdańsk 16 A4
Gdańska, Zatoka 16 A4
Gdov 24 B2
Gdynia 16 A4
Gebe 39 D3
Gebeit Mine ... 52 D6
Gebze 22 D7
Gedaref 53 F6
Gede, Tanjung 37 F3
Gediz → 23 E6
Gedser 9 H10
Geelong 63 C3
Geesthacht ... 14 B6
Geidam 53 F1
Geili 53 E5
Geita 57 E6
Gejiu 34 D5
Gela 21 F5
Geladi 49 F4
Gelehun 55 G2
Gelibolu 23 D6
Gelsenkirchen . 14 C4
Gemas 37 D2
Gemena 56 D3
Gemerek 46 C4
Gemlik 23 D7
General Acha . 94 D4
General Alvear,
  Buenos Aires,
  Argentina ... 94 D5
General Alvear,
  Mendoza,
  Argentina ... 94 D3
General Artigas 94 B5
General
  Belgrano 94 D5
General Guido . 94 D5
General Juan
  Madariaga .. 94 D5
General La
  Madrid 94 D4
General
  MacArthur . 38 B3
General Martin
  Miguel de
  Güemes 94 A4
General Paz ... 94 B5
General Pico .. 94 D4
General Pinedo 94 B3
General Santos 38 C3
General Villegas 94 D4
Geneva =
  Genève 13 C7

Geneva, L. =
Léman, L. . . . 13 C7
Genève 13 C7
Genil → 18 D3
Gennargentu,
Mti. del 21 D2
Genoa =
Génova 20 B2
Genoa 63 C4
Génova 20 B2
Génova, G. di . 20 C2
Gent 14 C2
Georga, Zemlya 28 A5
George 58 E4
George → 68 C4
George, L.,
N.S.W.,
Australia 63 C4
George, L.,
S. Austral.,
Australia 62 C3
George, L.,
Uganda 57 D6
George River =
Kangiqsualujjuaq
. . . . 68 C4
George Sound . 65 F2
George Town . 36 C2
George V Land 96 A14
George VI
Sound 96 B3
Georgetown,
Gambia 55 F2
Georgetown,
Guyana 90 B7
Georgia □ 75 C6
Georgia ■ 25 E5
Georgian B. . . . 69 D2
Georgiu-Dezh =
Liski 24 C4
Georgiyevsk . . 25 E5
Gera 15 C7
Geral de Goiás,
Serra 93 E4
Geraldton 60 F1
Gerede 46 B3
Gereshk 42 D4
Gerlogubi 49 F4
Germany ■ . . 14 C6
Germiston 59 D5
Gerona 19 B7
Geser 39 E4
Getafe 18 B4
Gettysburg . . . 73 E7
Getz Ice Shelf . 96 B18
Ghaghara → . 40 E5
Ghana ■ 55 G4
Ghanzi 58 C4
Ghardaïa 54 B5
Gharyān 52 B3
Ghat 54 D7
Ghawdex =
Gozo 21 F5
Ghayl 47 G6
Ghazal, Bahr
el →, Chad . 53 F2
Ghazâl, Bahr
el →, Sudan 57 C6
Ghazaouet 54 A4
Ghaziabad . . . 42 E10
Ghazipur 40 E4
Ghaznī 42 C6
Ghaznī □ 42 C6
Ghèlinsor 49 F4
Ghent = Gent . 14 C2
Ghizao 42 C4
Ghowr □ 42 C4
Ghugus 43 K11
Ghūriān 42 B2

Gia Lai = Pleiku 36 B3
Gian 38 C3
Giarabub = Al
Jaghbūb 52 C3
Giarre 21 F5
Gibraltar ■ . . . 18 D3
Gibraltar, Str. of 18 E3
Gibson Desert . 60 E4
Gidole 53 G6
Giessen 14 C5
Gifu 32 B5
Giglio 20 C3
Gijón 18 A3
Gila → 82 D5
Gīlān □ 46 C7
Gilbert Is. 64 J12
Gilgandra 63 B4
Gilgit 42 B9
Gilles, L. 62 B2
Gilmore 63 C4
Gimbi 53 G6
Gin Gin 63 A5
Ginir 49 F3
Giohar 49 G4
Gióna, Óros . . 23 E4
Girardot 90 C4
Giresun 46 B4
Girga 52 C5
Giridih 40 E6
Girilambone . . 63 B4
Girne = Kyrenia 46 D3
Girona =
Gerona 19 B7
Gironde → . . 12 D3
Girvan 10 D4
Gisborne 64 C8
Gisenyi 57 E5
Gitega 57 E5
Giuba → 49 G3
Giurgiu 22 C5
Giza = El Gîza . 52 C5
Giżycko 16 A5
Gjirokastra . . . 23 D3
Gjoa Haven . . 70 B10
Glace Bay 69 D5
Gladstone,
Queens.,
Australia 61 E9
Gladstone,
S. Austral.,
Australia 62 B2
Glåma =
Glomma → . 9 G10
Glasgow 10 D4
Glazov 28 D6
Gleiwitz =
Gliwice 16 C4
Glen Canyon
National
Recreation
Area 83 B7
Glen Innes . . . 63 A5
Glendale 82 C3
Glenelg 62 B2
Glenelg → . . . 62 C3
Glenmorgan . . 63 A4
Glenorchy 62 D4
Glenreagh 63 B5
Glenrothes . . . 10 C5
Glens Falls . . . 73 C9
Gliwice 16 C4
Głogów 16 C3
Glomma → . . 9 G10
Glorieuses, Is. . 59 G9
Gloucester,
Australia 63 B5
Gloucester, U.K. 11 F5
Glusk 17 B9
Gmünd 15 D8

Gmunden 15 E7
Gniezno 16 B3
Go Cong 36 B3
Goa 43 M8
Goa □ 43 M8
Goalen Hd. . . . 63 C5
Goalpara 41 D8
Goba, Ethiopia 49 F2
Goba, Mozam. . 59 D6
Gobabis 58 C3
Gobi 35 B6
Gochas 58 C3
Godavari → . . 40 J4
Godavari Point 40 J4
Godhra 43 H8
Gods → 71 C10
Gods L. 71 C10
Godthåb =Nuuk . 68 B5
Godwin Austen
= K2 . . . . 42 B10
Goeie Hoop,
Kaap die =
Good Hope, C.
of 58 E3
Gogra =
Ghaghara → 40 E5
Goiânia 93 F4
Goiás 93 F3
Goiás □ 93 E4
Goio-Ere 94 A6
Gojra 42 D8
Gökçeada 23 D5
Gokteik 41 F11
Gold Coast . . . 63 A5
Golden Gate . . 80 G2
Goldsboro 75 B9
Goleniów 16 B2
Golfo Aranci . . 20 D2
Golspie 10 C5
Goma 57 E5
Gomel =
Homyel 17 B10
Gomera 54 C1
Gómez Palacio 84 B4
Gomogomo . . . 39 F4
Gomoh 40 F6
Gompa = Ganta 55 G3
Gonābād 44 C4
Gonaïves 87 C5
Gonbad-e Kāvūs 44 B3
Gonda 40 D3
Gonder 53 F6
Gönen 23 D6
Gonghe 34 C5
Gongolgon . . . 63 B4
Goniri 53 F1
Good Hope, C.
of 58 E3
Goodooga 63 A4
Goolgowi 63 B4
Goombalie . . . 63 A4
Goondiwindi . . 63 A5
Gooray 63 A5
Gop 43 H6
Göppingen . . . 14 D5
Gorakhpur 40 D4
Goražde 20 C7
Gordon → . . . 62 D4
Gore, Australia 63 A5
Goré, Chad . . . 53 G2
Gore, Ethiopia 53 G6
Gore, N.Z. 65 G3
Gorgān 44 B3
Gorgona, I. . . . 90 C3
Gorízia 20 B4
Gorki = Nizhniy
Novgorod . . . 24 B5
Gorkiy =
Nizhniy
Novgorod . . . 24 B5

Gorkovskoye
Vdkhr. 24 B5
Görlitz 15 C8
Gorlovka =
Horlivka 25 D4
Gorna
Dzhumayo =
Blagoevgrad 22 C4
Gorna
Oryakhovitsa 22 C5
Gorno-Altay □ . 29 D9
Gorno-Altaysk . 29 D9
Gorno Slinkino
=
Gornopravdinsk
. . . . 29 C8
Gornopravdinsk 29 C8
Gorodenka =
Horodenka . . 17 D7
Gorodok =
Horodok 17 D6
Gorokhov =
Horokhiv 17 C7
Gorontalo 39 D2
Gorzów
Wielkopolski 16 B2
Gosford 63 B5
Goslar 14 C6
Gospič 20 B5
Göta kanal 9 G11
Göteborg 9 G10
Gotha 14 C6
Gothenburg =
Göteborg . . . 9 G10
Gotland 9 G11
Göttingen 14 C5
Gottwaldov =
Zlin 16 D3
Gouda 14 B3
Gouin, Rés. . . . 69 D3
Goulburn 63 B4
Gounou-Gaya . 53 G2
Gourock Ra. . . 63 C4
Gourma
Rharous 55 E4
Gourock Ra. . . 63 C4
Governador
Valadares . . . 93 F5
Gowd-e Zirreh . 42 E3
Goya 94 B5
Goyder Lagoon 62 A2
Goyllarisquisga 91 F3
Goz Beïda 53 F3
Gozo 21 F5
Graaff-Reinet . . 58 E4
Gračac 20 B5
Gracias a Dios,
C. 86 D3
Grado 18 A2
Gradule 63 A4
Grafton 63 A5
Graham Bell,
Os. 28 A7
Graham Land . 96 A3
Grahamstown . 59 E5
Grajaú 92 D4
Grajaú → 92 C5
Grampian
Highlands =
Grampian
Mts. 10 C4
Grampian Mts. 10 C4
Gran Canaria . . 54 C1
Gran Chaco . . . 94 B4
Gran Paradiso . 20 B1
Gran Sasso
d'Italia 20 C4
Granada, Nic. . 85 E7
Granada, Spain 18 D4

Granby

Granby	69	D3	
Grand Bahama	86	A4	
Grand Bassam	55	G4	
Grand Canyon	83	B6	
Grand Cayman	86	C3	
Grand Coulee Dam	80	B4	
Grand Forks, Canada	71	D8	
Grand Forks, U.S.A.	76	B6	
Grand Island	76	E5	
Grand Lahou	55	G3	
Grand Rapids, Canada	71	C10	
Grand Rapids, U.S.A.	72	C3	
Grand St.-Bernard, Col du	13	D7	
Grand Teton	81	D8	
Grande →, Argentina	94	A3	
Grande →, Bolivia	91	G6	
Grande →, Bahia, Brazil	93	E5	
Grande →, Minas Gerais, Brazil	93	G3	
Grande, B.	95	G3	
Grande, Rio →	79	F5	
Grande Baleine, R. de la →	69	C3	
Grande de Santiago →	84	C3	
Granite City	77	F9	
Granity	65	D4	
Granja	92	C5	
Granollers	19	B7	
Grantham	11	E6	
Granville	12	B3	
Gras, L. de	70	B8	
Grasse	13	E7	
Grassmere	62	B3	
Graulhet	12	E4	
's-Gravenhage	14	B3	
Gravesend	63	A5	
Graz	15	E8	
Great Abaco I.	86	A4	
Great Australian Bight	60	G4	
Great Barrier I.	64	B6	
Great Barrier Reef	61	D8	
Great Basin	80	F5	
Great Bear →	70	B7	
Great Bear L.	70	B7	
Great Belt = Store Bælt	9	G10	
Great Dividing Ra.	61	E8	
Great Falls	81	B8	
Great Inagua I.	86	B5	
Great Indian Desert = Thar Desert	42	F7	
Great Karoo	58	E4	
Great Lake	62	D4	
Great Ouse →	11	E7	
Great Ruaha →	57	F7	
Great Saint Bernard P. = Grand St.-Bernard, Col du	13	D7	
Great Salt L.	81	E7	
Great Salt Lake Desert	81	E7	
Great Sandy Desert	60	E3	
Great Sangi = Sangihe, P.	39	D3	
Great Slave L.	70	B8	
Great Smoky Mts. Nat. Pk.	75	B6	
Great Victoria Desert	60	F4	
Great Wall	35	C5	
Great Yarmouth	11	E7	
Greater Antilles	86	C5	
Greater Sunda Is.	37	F4	
Gredos, Sierra de	18	B3	
Greece ■	23	E4	
Greeley	76	E2	
Green →	83	A8	
Green Bay	72	B2	
Green C.	63	C5	
Greenland ■	66	C9	
Greenock	10	D4	
Greensboro	75	A8	
Greenville, Liberia	55	G3	
Greenville, Ala., U.S.A.	74	D4	
Greenville, Miss., U.S.A.	79	C8	
Greenville, N.C., U.S.A.	75	B9	
Greenville, S.C., U.S.A.	75	B6	
Greenwood, Miss., U.S.A.	79	C8	
Greenwood, S.C., U.S.A.	75	B6	
Gregory, L.	62	A2	
Greifswald	15	A7	
Greiz	15	C7	
Gremikha	28	C4	
Grenada ■	87	D7	
Grenfell	63	B4	
Grenoble	13	D6	
Grey →	65	E4	
Grey Ra.	63	A3	
Greymouth	65	E4	
Greytown, N.Z.	65	D6	
Greytown, S. Africa	59	D6	
Griffin	75	C5	
Griffith	63	B4	
Grimari	56	C4	
Grimaylov = Hrymayliv	17	D8	
Grimsby	11	E6	
Gris-Nez, C.	12	A4	
Grodno = Hrodna	17	B6	
Grodzyanka = Hrodzyanka	17	B9	
Grójec	16	C5	
Groningen	14	B4	
Grootfontein	58	B3	
Gross Glockner	15	E7	
Grosser Arber	15	D7	
Grosseto	20	C3	
Groznyy	25	E6	
Grudziądz	16	B4	
Gryazi	24	C4	
Gryazovets	28	D5	
Gua	40	F5	
Guadalajara, Mexico	84	C4	
Guadalajara, Spain	18	B4	
Guadalcanal	64	K11	
Guadalete →	18	D2	
Guadalquivir →	18	D2	
Guadalupe = Guadeloupe ■	87	C7	
Guadalupe, Sierra de	18	C3	
Guadarrama, Sierra de	18	B4	
Guadeloupe ■	87	C7	
Guadiana →	18	D2	
Guadix	18	D4	
Guafo, Boca del	95	E2	
Guaíra	94	A6	
Guaitecas, Is.	95	E2	
Guajará-Mirim	91	F5	
Guajira, Pen. de la	90	A4	
Gualeguay	94	C5	
Gualeguaychú	94	C5	
Guam ■	64	H9	
Guamúchil	84	B3	
Guan Xian	34	C5	
Guanahani = San Salvador	86	B5	
Guanajuato	84	C4	
Guandacol	94	B3	
Guane	86	B3	
Guangdong □	35	D6	
Guanghua	35	C6	
Guangxi Zhuangzu Zizhiqu □	35	D5	
Guangzhou	35	D6	
Guanipa →	90	B6	
Guantánamo	86	B4	
Guaporé →	91	F5	
Guaqui	91	G5	
Guarapuava	94	B6	
Guarda	18	B2	
Guardafui, C. = Asir, Ras	49	E5	
Guasdualito	90	B4	
Guasipati	90	B6	
Guatemala	85	E6	
Guatemala ■	85	D6	
Guatire	90	A5	
Guaviare □	90	C4	
Guaviare →	90	C5	
Guaxupé	93	G4	
Guayama	87	C6	
Guayaquil	90	D3	
Guayaquil, G. de	90	D2	
Guaymas	84	B2	
Guddu Barrage	42	E6	
Gudivada	40	J3	
Gudur	43	M11	
Guecho	19	A4	
Guékédou	55	G2	
Guelma	54	A6	
Guelph	69	D2	
Guéréda	53	F3	
Guéret	12	C4	
Guernica	19	A4	
Guernsey	11	G5	
Guidónia-Montecélio	20	C4	
Guiglo	55	G3	
Guildford	11	F6	
Guilin	35	D6	
Guimarães, Brazil	92	C5	
Guimarães, Portugal	18	B1	
Guimaras	38	B2	
Guinea ■	55	F2	
Guinea, Gulf of	51	F3	
Guinea-Bissau ■	55	F1	
Guingamp	12	B2	
Guiping	35	D6	
Güiria	90	A6	
Guiuan	38	B3	
Guiyang	35	D5	
Guizhou □	35	D5	
Gujarat □	43	H7	
Gujranwala	42	C9	
Gujrat	42	C9	
Gulbarga	43	L10	
Gulf, The	44	E2	
Gulgong	63	B4	
Güllük	23	F6	
Gulshad	29	E8	
Gulu	57	D6	
Gum Lake	62	B3	
Gummi	55	F6	
Gunnedah	63	B5	
Gunningbar Cr. →	63	B4	
Guntakal	43	M10	
Guntur	40	J3	
Gunungapi	39	F3	
Gunungsitoli	37	D1	
Gunza	56	G2	
Gupis	42	A8	
Gürchān	46	D7	
Gurdaspur	42	C9	
Gurgaon	42	E10	
Gurkha	40	C5	
Gurley	63	A4	
Gurupá	92	C3	
Gurupá, I. Grande de	92	C3	
Gurupi	92	C4	
Guryev = Atyraū	29	E6	
Gusau	55	F6	
Güstrow	15	B7	
Gütersloh	14	C5	
Guthrie	78	B5	
Guyana ■	90	B7	
Guyane française ■ = French Guiana ■	92	B3	
Guyenne	12	D4	
Guyra	63	B5	
Gwa	41	J10	
Gwaai	59	B5	
Gwabegar	63	B4	
Gwädar	42	G3	
Gwalior	42	F11	
Gwanda	59	C5	
Gweru	59	B5	
Gwydir →	63	A4	
Gyandzha = Gäncä	25	E6	
Gyaring Hu	34	C4	
Gydanskiy P-ov.	28	B8	
Gympie	63	D5	
Gyöngyös	16	E4	
Győr	16	E3	
Gypsumville	71	C10	
Gyula	16	E5	
Gyumri	25	E5	
Gyzylarbat	29	F6	

H

Ha 'Arava →	47	E3	
Haarlem	14	B3	
Haast →	65	E3	
Habaswein	57	D7	
Hachinohe	33	F12	
Hadarba, Ras	52	D6	

Hadd, R'as al .. 45 F4
Hadejia 55 F7
Haden 63 A5
Hadera 46 D3
Hadhramaut =
  Haḍramawt . 49 D4
Haḍramawt ... 49 D4
Haeju 35 C7
Haerhpin =
  Harbin 35 B7
Hafar al Bāṭin . 47 E6
Hafizabad 42 C8
Haflong 41 E9
Haft Gel 47 E7
Hafun, Ras ... 49 E5
Hagen 14 C4
Hagerstown ... 73 E7
Hagi 32 B2
Hagondange-
  Briey 13 B7
Hague, C. de la 12 B3
Hague, The = 's-
  Gravenhage . 14 B3
Haguenau ... 13 B7
Hai'an 35 C7
Haifa = Ḥefa . 46 D3
Haikou 35 D6
Ḥā'il 47 F5
Hailar 35 B6
Haileybury 69 D3
Hailun 35 B7
Hainan □ 35 E5
Haiphong 35 D5
Haiti ■ 87 C5
Haiya Junction 53 E6
Hajar Bangar .. 53 F3
Hajdúböszörmény
  .... 16 E5
Hajnówka 17 B6
Hakken-Zan .. 32 B4
Hakodate 32 F12
Hala 42 G6
Ḥalab 46 C4
Ḥalabjah 46 D6
Halaib 52 D6
Halberstadt ... 15 C6
Halcombe 64 D6
Halcon, Mt. .. 38 B2
Halden 9 G10
Haldia 40 F7
Haldwani 42 E11
Halifax, Canada 69 D4
Halifax, U.K. .. 11 E6
Halīl → 44 E4
Hall Beach =
  Sanirajak ... 68 B2
Halle 15 C6
Hallett 62 B2
Halmahera 39 D3
Halmstad 9 G10
Halq el Oued . 52 A1
Hälsingborg =
  Helsingborg . 9 G10
Halul 44 E3
Hamada 32 B3
Hamadān 46 D7
Hamadān □ ... 46 D7
Hamāh 46 D4
Hamamatsu .. 32 B5
Hamar 8 F10
Hamburg 14 B5
Hameln 14 B5
Hamersley Ra. . 60 E2
Hamhung ... 35 C7
Hami 34 B4
Hamilton,
  Australia 62 C3
Hamilton,
  Canada 69 D3

Hamilton, N.Z. . 64 B6
Hamilton, U.K. . 10 D4
Hamley Bridge 62 B2
Hamlin =
  Hameln 14 B5
Hamm 14 C4
Hammerfest .. 8 D12
Hammond 72 D2
Hampden 65 F4
Hampton 73 F7
Hamrat esh
  Sheykh 53 F4
Han Pijesak ... 20 B7
Hanamaki 33 G12
Hanau 14 C5
Hancock 77 C7
Handa 49 E5
Handan 35 C6
Handeni 57 F7
Hangayn Nuruu 34 B4
Hangchou =
  Hangzhou ... 35 C7
Hangu 35 C6
Hangzhou ... 35 C7
Hangzhou Wan 35 C7
Ḥanīsh 49 E3
Hanle 42 C11
Hanmer Springs 65 E5
Hanna 71 C8
Hannibal 77 F9
Hannover 14 B5
Hanoi 35 D5
Hanover =
  Hannover ... 14 B5
Hanover, I. 95 G2
Hansi 42 E9
Hanson, L. 62 B2
Hantsavichy ... 17 B8
Hanzhong ... 35 C5
Haora 40 F7
Haparanda ... 8 E12
Happy Valley-
  Goose Bay .. 69 C4
Hapur 42 E10
Ḥaql 47 E3
Har 39 F4
Har Hu 34 C4
Har Us Nuur .. 34 B4
Ḥaraḍ 47 F7
Haraisan Plateau
  = Huraysān . 47 G6
Harardera 49 G4
Harare 59 B6
Harazé 53 F2
Harbin 35 B7
Harbour Grace 69 D5
Hardangerfjorden
  .... 8 F9
Hardap Dam .. 58 C3
Hardwar =
  Haridwar .. 42 E11
Hardy, Pen. ... 95 H3
Harer 49 F3
Hargeisa 49 F3
Hari → 37 E2
Haridwar 42 E11
Haringhata → . 41 G7
Harīrūd → ... 45 C5
Harīrūd → ... 42 A2
Harlingen 78 F5
Harlow 11 F7
Harney Basin .. 80 D4
Härnösand ... 8 F11
Ḥarrat al Kishb 47 G5
Harrat al
  'Uwairidh .. 47 F4
Harris 10 C3
Harris L. 62 B2
Harrisburg 73 D7

Harrison, C. ... 68 C5
Harrison Bay .. 71 A4
Harrogate ... 11 D6
Hart, L. 62 B2
Hartford 73 D9
Hartlepool ... 11 D6
Harvey 72 D2
Harwich 11 F7
Haryana □ ... 42 E10
Haryn → 17 B8
Harz 14 C6
Ḥasa 47 F7
Hasan Kuli .. 29 F6
Hassi Inifel ... 54 C5
Hassi Messaoud 54 B6
Hastings, N.Z. . 64 C7
Hastings, U.K. . 11 F7
Hastings, U.S.A. 76 E5
Hastings Ra. .. 63 B5
Hatay = Antalya 46 C2
Hatfield P.O. .. 62 B3
Hatgal 34 A5
Hathras 42 F11
Hatia 41 F8
Hattah 62 B3
Hatteras, C. .. 75 B10
Hattiesburg ... 79 D9
Hatvan 16 E4
Hau Bon = Cheo
  Reo 36 B3
Haugesund ... 9 G9
Hauraki G. ... 64 B6
Haut Atlas ... 54 B3
Hautah, Wahāt
  al 47 G6
Hauts Plateaux 54 B4
Havana = La
  Habana 86 B3
Havant 11 F6
Havel → 15 B7
Havelock ... 65 D5
Haverfordwest . 11 F4
Havre 81 A9
Havza 46 B3
Hawaii □ 82 J12
Hawaiian Is. ... 82 H12
Hawea, L. 65 F3
Hawera 64 C6
Hawick 10 D5
Hawke B. 64 C7
Hawker 62 B2
Hawkwood ... 63 A5
Hay 63 B3
Hay River ... 70 B8
Haya 39 E3
Hayes → 71 C10
Hayrabolu ... 22 D6
Haysyn 17 D9
Hayvoron ... 17 D9
Hazaribag ... 40 F5
Healesville ... 63 C4
Hearst 69 D2
Hebei □ 35 C6
Hebel 63 A4
Hebron = Al
  Khalīl 47 E3
Hebron 68 C4
Hechi 35 D5
Hechuan 35 C5
Heerlen 13 A6
Ḥefa 46 D3
Hefei 35 C6
Hegang 35 B8
Heidelberg ... 14 D5
Heilbron 59 D5
Heilbronn 14 D5
Heilongjiang □ 35 B7

Heilunkiang =
  Heilongjiang □
  .... 35 B7
Heinze Is. 41 K11
Hejaz = Al Ḥijāz 47 F4
Hekimhan 46 C4
Hekou 34 D5
Helena, Ark.,
  U.S.A. 79 B8
Helena, Mont.,
  U.S.A. 81 B7
Helensville ... 64 B6
Helgoland ... 14 A4
Heligoland =
  Helgoland .. 14 A4
Heligoland B. =
  Deutsche
  Bucht 14 A5
Hellín 19 C5
Helmand □ ... 42 D3
Helmand → . 42 D2
Helmand,
  Hamun 45 D5
Helmsdale ... 10 B5
Helsingborg . 9 G10
Helsingfors =
  Helsinki 9 F13
Helsinki 9 F13
Helwân 52 C5
Hemel
  Hempstead .. 11 F6
Henan □ 35 C6
Henares → ... 18 B4
Henderson .. 75 A8
Hendon 63 A5
Hengyang ... 35 D6
Henrietta Maria,
  C. 69 C2
Hentiyn Nuruu 35 B5
Henty 63 C4
Henzada 41 J10
Herāt 42 B3
Herāt □ 42 B3
Hercegnovi ... 22 C2
Hereford 11 E5
Herford 14 B5
Hermidale ... 63 B4
Hermitage ... 65 E4
Hermite, I. 95 H3
Hermon, Mt. =
  Ash Shaykh,
  J. 46 D3
Hermosillo .. 84 B2
Hernád → ... 16 E5
Hernandarias . 94 B6
Heroica Nogales
  = Nogales .. 84 A2
Heron Bay ... 69 D2
Herrick 62 D4
's-
  Hertogenbosch
  .... 14 C3
Hesse =
  Hessen □ ... 14 C5
Hessen □ 14 C5
Hewett, C. ... 68 A4
Hexham 11 D5
Heyfield 63 C4
Heywood ... 62 C3
Hibbing 77 B8
Hibbs B. 62 D4
Hickory 75 B7
Hicks, Pt. ... 63 C4
Hida-Sammyaku 32 A5
Hidalgo del
  Parral 84 B3
Higashiōsaka . 32 B4
High Atlas =
  Haut Atlas .. 54 B3

High Point

High Point 75 B8
High River 71 C8
High Tatra =
Tatry 16 D4
High Wycombe 11 F6
Hiiumaa 24 B1
Ḥijārah, Ṣaḥrā'
al 47 E6
Ḥijāz □ 48 C2
Hijo = Tagum . 38 C3
Hikone 32 B5
Hikurangi 64 A6
Hikurangi, Mt. . 64 C7
Hildesheim ... 14 B5
Hillston 63 B4
Hilo 82 J13
Hilversum 14 B3
Himachal
Pradesh □ .. 42 D10
Himalaya 40 C5
Himatnagar ... 43 H8
Himeji 32 B4
Himi 32 A5
Ḥimṣ 46 D4
Hindmarsh, L. . 62 C3
Hindu Kush .. 42 B7
Hindubagh ... 42 D5
Hindupur 43 N10
Hinganghat ... 43 J11
Hingoli 43 K10
Hinna = Imi .. 49 F3
Hinojosa del
Duque 18 C3
Hirakud Dam . 40 G4
Hiratsuka 32 B6
Hirosaki 33 F12
Hiroshima 32 B3
Hisar 42 E9
Hispaniola ... 87 C5
Hita 32 C2
Hitachi 32 A7
Hjälmaren ... 9 G11
Hlyboka 17 D7
Ho 55 G5
Ho Chi Minh
City = Phanh
Bho Ho Chi
Minh 36 B3
Hoai Nhon 36 B3
Hoare B. 68 B4
Hobart 62 D4
Hobbs Coast .. 96 B18
Hodgson 71 C10
Hódmezövásárhely
.... 16 E5
Hodna, Chott el 54 A5
Hodonín 16 D3
Hoek van
Holland 14 B3
Hof 15 C6
Hōfu 32 B2
Hogan Group . 62 C4
Hoggar =
Ahaggar 54 D6
Hoh Xil Shan .. 34 C3
Hohe Rhön ... 14 C5
Hohhot 35 B6
Hoi An 36 A3
Hokianga
Harbour ... 64 A5
Hokitika 65 E4
Hokkaidō □ ... 32 F12
Holbrook 63 C4
Holguín 86 B4
Hollandia =
Jayapura ... 39 E6
Holman Island . 70 A8
Holy Cross ... 71 B4
Holyhead 11 E4

Homalin 41 E10
Hombori 55 E4
Home B. 68 B4
Homer 71 C4
Homs = Ḥimṣ . 46 D4
Homyel 17 B10
Hon Chong ... 36 B2
Honan =
Henan □ 35 C6
Honda 90 B4
Hondeklipbaai . 58 E3
Honduras ■ ... 85 E7
Honduras, G. de 85 D7
Honfleur 12 B4
Hong Kong ... 35 D6
Hongjiang 35 D5
Hongshui He → 35 D5
Hongze Hu ... 35 C6
Honiara 64 K10
Honolulu 82 H12
Honshū 32 G11
Hood, Mt. 80 C3
Hooghly → =
Hughli → .. 40 G7
Hook of Holland
= Hoek van
Holland 14 B3
Hoorn 14 B3
Hoover Dam . 82 B5
Hope, L. 62 A2
Hope, Pt. 71 B3
Hopedale 68 C4
Hopei =
Hebei □ 35 C6
Hopetoun 62 C3
Hopetown 58 D4
Hoquiam 80 B2
Horlick Mts. ... 96 C1
Horlivka 25 D4
Hormoz 44 E3
Hormoz, Jaz. ye 44 E4
Hormozgān □ . 44 E3
Hormuz, Str. of 44 E4
Horn 15 D8
Horn, Cape =
Hornos, C. de 95 H3
Hornavan 8 E11
Hornos, C. de . 95 H3
Hornsby 63 B5
Horodenka ... 17 D7
Horodok,
Khmelnytskyy,
Ukraine ... 17 D8
Horodok, Lviv,
Ukraine ... 17 D6
Horokhiv 17 C7
Horqin Youyi
Qianqi 35 B7
Horqueta 94 A5
Horsham 62 C3
Horton → 70 B7
Hose, Gunung-
Gunung ... 37 D4
Hoshangabad . 43 H10
Hoshiarpur ... 42 D9
Hospet 43 M10
Hospitalet de
Llobregat ... 19 B7
Hoste, I. 95 H3
Hot Springs ... 79 B7
Hotan 34 C2
Houhora Heads 64 A5
Houlton 73 A12
Houma 79 E8
Houston 79 E6
Hovd 34 B4
Hövsgöl Nuur . 34 A5
Howard 63 A5
Howe, C. 63 C5

Howitt, L. 62 A2
Howrah = Haora 40 F7
Höxter 14 C5
Hoy 10 B5
Høyanger 8 F9
Hoyerswerda . 15 C8
Hpungan Pass . 41 D11
Hradec Králové 16 C2
Hrodna 17 B6
Hrodzyanka ... 17 B9
Hron → 16 E4
Hrvatska =
Croatia ■ .. 20 B6
Hrymayliv 17 D8
Hsenwi 41 F11
Hsiamen =
Xiamen 35 D6
Hsian = Xi'an . 35 C5
Hsinhailien =
Lianyungang 35 C6
Hsisha Chuntao 36 A4
Hsüchou =
Xuzhou 35 C6
Hua Hin 36 B1
Huacho 91 F3
Huachón 91 F3
Huai He → ... 35 C6
Huainan 35 C6
Huallaga → . 90 E3
Huambo 58 A3
Huancabamba . 91 E3
Huancane 91 G5
Huancapi 91 F4
Huancavelica . 91 F3
Huancayo 91 F3
Huang Hai =
Yellow Sea . 35 C7
Huang He → .. 35 C6
Huangliu 35 E5
Huangshi 35 C6
Huánuco 91 E3
Huaraz 91 E3
Huarmey 91 F3
Huascarán ... 91 E3
Huasco 94 B2
Huatabampo .. 84 B3
Huayllay 91 F3
Hubei □ 35 C6
Hubli-Dharwad
= Dharwad . 43 M9
Huddersfield . 11 E6
Hudiksvall 8 F11
Hudson → ... 73 D8
Hudson Bay .. 68 B2
Hudson Mts. .. 96 B2
Hudson Str. .. 68 B4
Hue 36 A3
Huelva 18 D2
Huesca 19 A5
Hughenden ... 61 E7
Hughli → 40 G7
Huila, Nevado
del 90 C3
Huinca Renancó 94 C4
Huize 34 D5
Hukawng Valley 41 D11
Hulan 35 B7
Ḥulayfā' 47 F5
Huld 35 B5
Hull = Kingston
upon Hull .. 11 E6
Hull 69 D3
Hulun Nur ... 35 B6
Humahuaca .. 94 A3
Humaitá, Brazil 91 E6
Humaitá,
Paraguay ... 94 B5
Humber → ... 11 E6
Humboldt 71 C9

Humboldt → . 80 F4
Hume, L. 63 C4
Humenné 16 D5
Hūn 52 C2
Hunan □ 35 D6
Hunedoara ... 17 F6
Hungary ■ ... 16 E4
Hungerford ... 63 A3
Hŭngnam 35 C7
Hunsrück 14 D4
Hunter I. 62 D3
Hunter Ra. ... 63 B5
Hunterville ... 64 C6
Huntington .. 72 E4
Huntington
Beach 82 D3
Huntly, N.Z. ... 64 B6
Huntly, U.K. ... 10 C5
Huntsville 74 B4
Huonville 62 D4
Hupeh =
Hubei □ ... 35 C6
Huraysān 47 G6
Huron, L. 72 B4
Hurunui 65 E5
Huşi 17 E9
Hutchinson .. 78
Hutton, Mt. .. 63 A4
Hvar 20 C6
Hwang Ho =
Huang He → 35 C6
Hwange 59 B5
Hyargas Nuur . 34 B4
Hyderabad,
India 43 L11
Hyderabad,
Pakistan ... 42 G6
Hyères 13 E7
Hyères, Is. d' .. 13 E7

I

I-n-Gall 55 E6
Iaco → 91 E5
Ialomiţa → ... 22 B6
Iaşi 17 E8
Iba 38 A2
Ibadan 55 G5
Ibagué 90 C3
Ibar → 22 C3
Ibarra 90 C3
Ibi 55 G6
Ibiá 93 F4
Ibicuy 94 C5
Ibioapaba, Sa.
da 92 C5
Ibiza 19 C6
Ibonma 39 E4
Ibotirama 93 E5
Ibu 39 D3
Icá 91 F3
Içá → 90 D5
Içana 90 C5
İçel = Mersin . 46 C3
Iceland ■ 8 B4
Ich'ang =
Yichang ... 35 C6
Ichchapuram .. 40 H5
Ichihara 32 B7
Ichikawa 32 B6
Ichilo → 91 G6
Ichinomiya ... 32 B5
Idaho □ 81 C6
Idaho Falls ... 81 D7
Idar-Oberstein . 14 D4
Idd el Ghanam 53 F3

Iddan	49	F4
Idehan	52	C1
Idehan Marzūq	52	D1
Idelès	54	D6
Idfû	52	D5
Ídhi Óros	23	G5
Ídhra	23	F4
Idi	36	C1
Idiofa	56	E3
Idlip	46	D4
Ierápetra	23	G5
Iesi	20	C4
Ifanadiana	59	J9
Ife	55	G5
Ifni	54	C2
Iforas, Adrar des	54	
Igarapava	93	G4
Igarapé Açu	92	C4
Igarka	28	C9
Igbetti	55	G5
Iglésias	21	E2
Igli	54	B4
Igloolik	68	B2
Igluligaarjuk	68	B1
Iğneada Burnu	22	D7
Igoumenítsa	23	E3
Iguaçu →	94	B6
Iguaçu, Cat. del	94	B6
Iguaçu Falls = Iguaçu, Cat. del	94	B6
Iguala	84	D5
Igualada	19	B6
Iguassu = Iguaçu →	94	B6
Iguatu	92	D6
Iguéla	56	E1
Ihosy	59	J9
Iida	32	B5
Iisalmi	8	F13
Iizuka	32	C2
Ijebu-Ode	55	G5
IJsselmeer	14	B3
Ikalukutiak	70	B9
Ikaría	23	F6
Ikela	56	E4
Iki	32	C1
Ilagan	38	A2
Īlām	46	D6
Ilawa	16	B4
Île-de-France	12	B5
Ilebo	56	E4
Ilhéus	93	E6
Ili →	29	E8
Ilich	29	E7
Iligan	38	C2
Illampu = Ancohuma, Nevada	91	G5
Illana B.	38	C2
Illapel	94	C2
Iller →	14	D5
Illimani	91	G5
Illium = Troy	23	E6
Ilmen, Ozero	24	B3
Ilo	91	G4
Iloilo	38	B2
Ilorin	55	G5
Ilwaki	39	F3
Imabari	32	B3
Imandra, Ozero	28	C4
Imari	32	C1
imeni 26 Bakinskikh Komissarov = Neftçala	46	C7
Imeri, Serra	90	C5
Imi	49	F3
Imola	20	B3
Imperatriz	92	D4
Impéria	20	C2
Imperial Dam	82	D5
Impfondo	56	D3
Imphal	41	E9
İmroz = Gökçeada	23	D5
Imuruan B.	38	B1
In Belbel	54	C5
In Salah	54	C5
Ina	32	B5
Inangahua Junction	65	D4
Inanwatan	39	E4
Iñapari	91	F5
Inarijärvi	8	E13
Inca	19	C7
İnce-Burnu	46	B3
Inchon	35	C7
İncirliova	23	F6
Incomáti →	59	D6
Indalsälven →	8	F11
Indaw	41	E11
Independence, Kans., U.S.A.	79	A6
Independence, Mo., U.S.A.	77	F7
India ■	43	J10
Indian →	75	F7
Indian Harbour	68	C5
Indian Head	71	C9
Indiana □	72	D3
Indianapolis	72	E2
Indiga	28	C5
Indigirka →	31	B12
Indonesia ■	37	E4
Indore	43	H9
Indravati →	40	H3
Indre →	12	C4
Indus →	43	G5
İnebolu	46	B3
Ingende	56	E3
Inglewood, Queens., Australia	63	A5
Inglewood, Vic., Australia	62	C3
Inglewood, N.Z.	64	C6
Ingolstadt	15	D6
Ingraj Bazar	40	E7
Ingrid Christensen Coast	96	A10
Ingulec = Inhulec	25	D3
Inhambane	59	C7
Inhaminga	59	B7
Inharrime	59	C7
Inhulec	25	D3
Ining = Yining	34	B3
Inírida →	90	C5
Injune	63	A4
Inle L.	41	G11
Inn →	15	D7
Innamincka	62	A3
Inner Hebrides	10	C3
Inner Mongolia = Nei Monggol Zizhiqu □	35	B6
Innisfail	71	C8
Innsbruck	15	E6
Inongo	56	E3
Inoucdjouac = Inukjuak	68	C3
Inowrocław	16	B4
Inquisivi	91	G5
Insein	41	J11
Interlaken	13	C7
International Falls	77	A8
Intiyaco	94	B4
Inukjuak	68	C3
Inútil, B.	95	G2
Inuvik	70	B6
Invercargill	65	G3
Inverell	63	A5
Invergordon	10	C4
Inverness	10	C4
Inverurie	10	C5
Investigator Group	62	B1
Investigator Str.	62	C2
Inya	29	D9
Inza	24	C6
Ioánnina	23	E3
Ionian Is. = Iónioi Nísoi	23	E3
Ionian Sea	21	F6
Iónioi Nísoi	23	E3
Íos	23	F5
Iowa □	77	D8
Iowa City	77	E9
Ipameri	93	F4
Ipatinga	93	F5
Ipiales	90	C3
Ipin = Yibin	35	D5
Ipixuna	91	E4
Ipoh	36	D2
Ippy	56	C4
İpsala	22	D6
Ipswich, Australia	63	A5
Ipswich, U.K.	11	E7
Ipu	92	C5
Iqaluit	68	B4
Iquique	91	H4
Iquitos	90	D4
Iracoubo	92	A3
Iráklion	23	G5
Iran ■	44	C3
Iran, Gunung-Gunung	37	D4
Iran Ra. = Iran, Gunung-Gunung	37	D4
Īrānshahr	45	E5
Irapuato	84	C4
Iraq ■	46	D5
Irbid	46	D3
Irebu	56	E3
Ireland ■	11	E3
Irian Jaya □	39	E5
Iringa	57	F7
Iriri →	92	C3
Irish Sea	11	E4
Irkineyeva	30	D7
Irkutsk	30	D8
Iron Baron	62	B2
Iron Gate = Portile de Fier	22	B4
Iron Knob	62	B2
Ironwood	77	B9
Irpin	17	C10
Irrara Cr. →	63	A4
Irrawaddy □	41	J10
Irrawaddy →	41	K10
Irtysh →	28	C7
Irumu	57	D5
Irún	19	A5
Irunea = Pamplona	19	A5
Irvine	10	D4
Irymple	62	B3
Isabella	38	C2
Isangi	56	D4
Isar →	15	D7
Íschia	21	D4
Ise	32	B5
Ise-Wan	32	B5
Isère →	13	D6
Isérnia	20	D5
Ishikari-Wan	32	F12
Ishim →	29	D8
Ishinomaki	33	G12
Ishkuman	42	A8
Isil Kul	29	D8
Isiolo	57	D7
Isiro	57	D5
İskenderun	46	C4
İskŭr →	22	C5
Islamabad	42	C8
Island L.	71	C10
Island Lagoon	62	B2
Islay	10	D3
Isle →	12	D3
Isle of Wight □	11	F6
Ismail = Izmayil	17	F9
Ismâ'ilîya	47	E3
Isna	52	C5
İsparta	46	C2
İspica	21	F5
Israel ■	46	E3
Issoire	13	D5
Issyk-Kul, Ozero = Ysyk-Köl, Ozero	29	E8
İstanbul	22	D7
Istiaía	23	E4
Istra	20	B4
İstranca Dağları	22	D6
Istres	13	E6
Istria = Istra	20	B4
Itabaiana	92	D6
Itaberaba	93	E5
Itabira	93	F5
Itabuna	93	E6
Itaipú, Reprêsa de	94	B6
Itaituba	92	C2
Itajaí	94	B7
Italy ■	20	C4
Itapecuru-Mirim	92	C5
Itaperuna	93	G5
Itapicuru →, Bahia, Brazil	93	E6
Itapicuru →, Maranhão, Brazil	92	C5
Itapipoca	92	C6
Itaquatiara	90	D7
Itaquí	94	B5
Itatuba	91	E6
Ithaca = Itháki	23	E3
Itháki	23	E3
Ito	32	B6
Itonamas →	91	F6
Ituaçu	93	E5
Ituiutaba	93	F4
Itumbiara	93	F4
Iturbe	94	A3
Itzehoe	14	B5
Ivanava	17	B7
Ivanhoe	63	B3
Ivano-Frankivsk	17	D7
Ivano-Frankovsk = Ivano-Frankivsk	17	D7
Ivanovo = Ivanava	17	B7
Ivanovo	24	B5
Ivatsevichy	17	B7
Ivory Coast ■	55	G3
Ivrea	20	B1
Ivujivik	68	B3
Iwahig	36	C5
Iwaki	33	G12

Iwakuni	32	B3
Iwata	33	H11
Iwate-San	33	G12
Iwo	55	G5
Ixiamas	91	F5
Izhevsk	28	D6
Izmayil	17	F9
İzmir	23	E6
İzmit	25	E2
İznik Gölü	23	D7
Izumi-sano	32	B4
Izumo	32	B3
Izyaslav	17	C8

J

Jabalpur	43	H11
Jablah	46	D4
Jablanica	22	D3
Jablonec	16	C2
Jaboatão	92	D6
Jaca	19	A5
Jacareí	94	A7
Jacarèzinho	94	A7
Jackson, Australia	63	A4
Jackson, Mich., U.S.A.	72	C3
Jackson, Miss., U.S.A.	79	C8
Jackson, Tenn., U.S.A.	74	B3
Jackson B.	65	E3
Jacksons	65	E4
Jacksonville, Fla., U.S.A.	75	D7
Jacksonville, Ill., U.S.A.	77	F9
Jacksonville, N.C., U.S.A.	75	B9
Jacmel	87	C5
Jacobabad	42	E6
Jacobina	93	E5
Jacundá	92	C3
Jadotville = Likasi	57	G5
Jādū	52	B1
Jaén, Peru	91	E3
Jaén, Spain	18	D4
Jaffa = Tel Aviv-Yafo	46	D3
Jaffa, C.	62	C2
Jaffna	43	Q12
Jagadhri	42	D10
Jagdalpur	40	H3
Jagraon	42	D9
Jagtial	43	K11
Jaguariaíva	94	A7
Jaguaribe →	92	C6
Jahrom	44	D3
Jailolo	39	D3
Jailolo, Selat	39	D3
Jaipur	42	F9
Jakarta	37	F3
Jalalabad	42	B7
Jalapa Enríquez	84	D5
Jalas, Jabal al	47	F4
Jalgaon, Maharashtra, India	43	J10
Jalgaon, Maharashtra, India	43	J9
Jalna	43	K9
Jalón →	19	B5
Jalpaiguri	41	D7

Jalq	45	E5
Jaluit I.	64	J11
Jamaica ■	86	C4
Jamalpur, Bangla.	41	E7
Jamalpur, India	40	E6
Jamanxim →	92	C2
Jambe	39	E4
Jambi	37	E2
Jambi □	37	E2
James →	76	D6
James B.	69	C2
James Ross I.	96	A4
Jamestown, Australia	62	B2
Jamestown, N. Dak., U.S.A.	76	B5
Jamestown, N.Y., U.S.A.	73	C6
Jamkhandi	43	L9
Jammu	42	C9
Jammu & Kashmir □	42	B10
Jamnagar	43	H7
Jamrud	42	C7
Jamshedpur	40	F6
Jand	42	C8
Jandaq	44	C3
Jandowae	63	A5
Janesville	77	D10
Januária	93	F5
Jaora	43	H9
Japan ■	33	G11
Japan, Sea of	33	G11
Japen = Yapen	39	E5
Japurá →	90	D5
Jaque	90	B3
Jarama →	18	B4
Jargalant = Hovd	34	B4
Jarosław	17	C6
Jarso	53	G6
Jarvis I.	65	K15
Jarwa	40	D4
Jāsk	44	E4
Jasło	16	D5
Jasper	74	C4
Jászberény	16	E4
Jataí	93	F3
Játiva	19	C5
Jaú	93	G4
Jauja	91	F3
Jaunpur	40	E4
Java = Jawa	37	F3
Java Sea	37	E3
Javhlant = Ulyasutay	34	B4
Jawa	37	F3
Jaya, Puncak	39	E5
Jayanti	41	D7
Jayapura	39	E6
Jayawijaya, Pegunungan	39	E5
Jaynagar	40	D6
Jean Marie River	70	B7
Jebba	55	G5
Jebel, Bahr el →	53	G5
Jedburgh	10	D5
Jedda = Jiddah	47	G4
Jędrzejów	16	C5
Jefferson City	77	F8
Jega	55	F5
Jelenia Góra	16	C2
Jelgava	24	B1
Jemaja	37	D3
Jembongan	36	C5
Jena	15	C6

Jeparit	62	C3
Jequié	93	E5
Jequitinhonha	93	F5
Jequitinhonha →	93	F6
Jerada	54	B4
Jerantut	37	D2
Jérémie	86	C5
Jerez de la Frontera	18	D2
Jerez de los Caballeros	18	C2
Jerilderie	63	C4
Jersey	11	G5
Jersey City	73	D8
Jerusalem	47	E3
Jervis B.	63	C5
Jesselton = Kota Kinabalu	36	C5
Jessore	41	F7
Jeypore	40	H4
Jhal Jhao	42	F4
Jhalawar	43	G10
Jhang Maghiana	42	D8
Jhansi	43	G11
Jharkand □	40	F5
Jharsaguda	40	G5
Jhelum	42	C8
Jhelum →	42	D8
Jhunjhunu	42	E9
Jiamusi	35	B8
Ji'an	35	D6
Jianchuan	34	D4
Jiangling	35	C6
Jiangmen	35	D6
Jiangsu □	35	C6
Jiangxi □	35	D6
Jian'ou	35	D6
Jianshui	34	D5
Jiao Xian	35	C7
Jiaozuo	35	C6
Jiaxing	35	C7
Jiayi	35	D7
Jibuti = Djibouti ■	49	E3
Jiddah	47	G4
Jido	41	C10
Jihlava	16	D2
Jihlava →	16	D3
Jijel	54	A6
Jijiga	49	F3
Jilin	35	B7
Jilong	35	D7
Jima	53	G6
Jiménez	84	B4
Jinan	35	C6
Jindabyne	63	C4
Jindrichuv Hradeç	16	D2
Jingdezhen	35	D6
Jinggu	34	D5
Jingxi	35	D5
Jinhua	35	D6
Jining, Nei Mongol Zizhiqu, China	35	B6
Jining, Shandong, China	35	C6
Jinja	57	D6
Jinnah Barrage	42	C7
Jinotega	85	E7
Jinshi	35	D6
Jinzhou	35	B7
Jiparaná →	91	E6
Jipijapa	90	D2
Jisr ash Shughūr	46	D4
Jiu →	22	C4
Jiujiang	35	D6

Jiuquan	34	C4
Jixi	35	B8
Jizzakh	29	E7
Joaçaba	94	B6
João Pessoa	92	D7
Joaquín V. González	94	B4
Jodhpur	42	F8
Jofane	59	C6
Jogjakarta = Yogyakarta	37	F4
Johannesburg	59	D5
Johnson City	75	A6
Johnston Falls = Mambilima Falls	57	G5
Johnstown	73	D6
Johor Baharu	37	D2
Joinvile	94	B7
Joinville I.	96	A4
Joliet	72	D1
Joliette	69	D3
Jolo	38	C2
Jome	39	E3
Jonesboro	79	B8
Jönköping	9	G10
Jonquière	69	D3
Joplin	79	A6
Jordan ■	47	E4
Jorhat	41	D10
Jorong	37	E4
Jos	55	G6
Jowzjān □	45	B6
Juan de Fuca Str.	80	A1
Juan de Nova	59	H8
Juan Fernández, Arch. de	89	G3
Juárez	94	D5
Juàzeiro	93	D5
Juàzeiro do Norte	92	D6
Jubbulpore = Jabalpur	43	H11
Juby, C.	54	C2
Júcar →	19	C5
Juchitán	85	D5
Jugoslavia = Yugoslavia ■	22	B3
Juiz de Fora	93	G5
Juli	91	G5
Juliaca	91	G4
Jullundur	42	D9
Jumilla	19	C5
Jumla	40	C4
Jumna = Yamuna →	40	E3
Junagadh	43	J7
Jundiaí	94	A7
Juneau	71	C6
Junee	63	B4
Jungfrau	13	C7
Junggar Pendi	34	B3
Junín	94	C4
Junín de los Andes	95	D2
Jūniyah	46	D3
Jur, Nahr el →	53	G4
Jura = Jura, Mts. du	13	C7
Jura = Schwäbische Alb	14	D5
Jura	10	D4
Jura, Mts. du	13	C7
Jurado	90	B3
Juruá →	90	D5
Juruena →	91	E7
Juruti	92	C2

Justo Daract	94	C3
Jutland =		
Jylland	9	G9
Juventud, I. de		
la	86	B3
Juwain	42	D2
Jylland	9	G9
Jyväskylä	8	F13

K

K2	42	B10
Kaapkruis	58	C2
Kaapstad =		
Cape Town	58	E3
Kabaena	39	F2
Kabala	55	G2
Kabale	57	E6
Kabalo	57	F5
Kabambare	57	E5
Kabanjahe	37	D1
Kabara	55	E4
Kabardino-		
Balkar		
Republic =		
Kabardino		
Balkaria □	25	E5
Kabardino		
Balkaria □	25	E5
Kabare	39	E4
Kabarega Falls	57	D6
Kabasalan	38	C2
Kabba	55	G6
Kabīr, Zab al →	46	C5
Kabīr Kūh	47	D6
Kabkabīyah	53	F3
Kabompo →	58	A4
Kabongo	57	F5
Kabūd Gonbad	44	B4
Kābul	42	B6
Kābul □	42	B6
Kabul →	42	C8
Kaburuang	39	D3
Kabwe	59	A5
Kachchh, Gulf of	43	H6
Kachchh, Rann		
of	43	G6
Kachin □	41	D11
Kachiry	29	D8
Kaçkar	46	B5
Kadan Kyun	36	B1
Kadina	62	B2
Kadirli	46	C4
Kadiyevka =		
Stakhanov	25	D4
Kadoma	59	B5
Kâdugli	53	F4
Kaduna	55	F6
Kaédi	55	E2
Kaélé	53	F1
Kaesŏng	35	C7
Kāf	47	E4
Kafakumba	56	F4
Kafan = Kapan	25	F6
Kafanchan	55	G6
Kaffrine	55	F1
Kafia Kingi	53	G3
Kafirévs, Ákra	23	E5
Kafue →	59	B5
Kafulwe	57	F5
Kaga Bandoro	56	C3
Kagan	29	F7
Kağizman	46	B5
Kagoshima	33	D2
Kagoshima-Wan	33	D2
Kagul = Cahul	17	F9

Kahama	57	E6
Kahayan →	37	E4
Kahemba	56	F3
Kahnūj	44	E4
Kahoolawe	82	H12
Kahramanmaraş	46	C4
Kai, Kepulauan	39	F4
Kai Besar	39	F4
Kai Is. = Kai,		
Kepulauan	39	F4
Kai Kecil	39	F4
Kaiama	55	G5
Kaiapoi	65	E5
Kaieteur Falls	90	B7
Kaifeng	35	C6
Kaikohe	64	A5
Kaikoura	65	E5
Kaikoura Ra.	65	D5
Kaimana	39	E4
Kaimanawa Mts.	64	C6
Kaingaroa		
Forest	64	C7
Kainji Res.	55	F5
Kaipara Harbour	64	B6
Kaironi	39	E4
Kairouan	54	A7
Kaiserslautern	14	D4
Kaitaia	64	A5
Kaitangata	65	G3
Kajaani	8	F13
Kajabbi	61	D6
Kajana =		
Kajaani	8	F13
Kajo Kaji	53	H5
Kaka	53	F5
Kakamas	58	D4
Kakamega	57	D6
Kakanui Mts.	65	F4
Kakhovka	25	D3
Kakhovske		
Vdskh.	25	D3
Kakinada	40	J4
Kalaallit Nunaat		
=		
Greenland ■	66	C9
Kalabagh	42	C7
Kalabahi	39	F2
Kalabo	58	A4
Kalach	24	C5
Kaladan →	41	G9
Kalahari	58	C4
Kalakan	31	D9
Kalámai	23	F4
Kalamata =		
Kalámai	23	F4
Kalamazoo	72	C3
Kalan	46	C4
Kalao	39	F2
Kalaotoa	39	F2
Kalat	42	E5
Kalce	20	B5
Kale	23	F7
Kalegauk Kyun	41	K11
Kalemie	57	F5
Kalewa	41	F10
Kalgan =		
Zhangjiakou	35	B6
Kalgoorlie-		
Boulder	60	G3
Kaliakra, Nos	22	C7
Kalianda	37	F3
Kalibo	38	B2
Kalima	57	E5
Kalimantan	37	E4
Kalimantan		
Barat □	37	D4
Kalimantan		
Selatan □	37	E5

Kalimantan		
Tengah □	37	E4
Kalimantan		
Timur □	37	D5
Kálimnos	23	F6
Kalinin = Tver	24	B4
Kaliningrad,		
Kaliningd.,		
Russia	24	C1
Kaliningrad,		
Moskva,		
Russia	24	B4
Kalinkavichy	17	B9
Kalinkovichi =		
Kalinkavichy	17	B9
Kalispell	81	A6
Kalisz	16	C4
Kaliua	57	F6
Kalkrand	58	C3
Kalmar	9	G11
Kalmyk Republic		
= Kalmykia □	25	D6
Kalmykia □	25	D6
Kalocsa	16	E4
Kalomo	59	B5
Kaluga	24	C4
Kalush	17	D7
Kalutara	43	R11
Kama →	29	D6
Kamaishi	33	G12
Kamaran	49	D3
Kamchatka, P-		
ov.	31	D13
Kamchatka Pen.		
= Kamchatka,		
P-ov.	31	D13
Kamchiya →	22	C6
Kamen	29	D9
Kamenjak, Rt.	20	B4
Kamenka		
Bugskaya =		
Kamyanka-		
Buzka	17	C7
Kamensk		
Uralskiy	29	D7
Kamin-		
Kashyrskyy	17	C7
Kamina	57	F5
Kamloops	71	C7
Kampala	57	D6
Kampar →	37	D2
Kampen	14	B3
Kampot	36	B2
Kampuchea =		
Cambodia ■	36	B3
Kampung →	39	F5
Kampungbaru =		
Tolitoli	39	D2
Kamrau, Teluk	39	E4
Kamsack	71	C9
Kamyanets-		
Podilskyy	17	D8
Kamyanka-Buzka	17	C7
Kamyshin	24	C6
Kanaaupscow	69	C3
Kananga	56	F4
Kanash	24	B6
Kanastraíon,		
Ákra =		
Palioúrion,		
Ákra	23	E4
Kanazawa	32	A5
Kanchanaburi	36	B1
Kanchenjunga	40	D7
Kanchipuram	43	N11
Kanda Kanda	56	F4
Kandahar =		
Qandahār	42	D4
Kandalaksha	28	C4

Kandalu	42	E3
Kandangan	37	E5
Kandi	55	F5
Kandla	43	H7
Kandos	63	B4
Kandy	43	R12
Kangaroo I.	62	C2
Kangāvar	46	D7
Kangean,		
Kepulauan	37	F5
Kangean Is. =		
Kangean,		
Kepulauan	37	F5
Kangiqsualujjuaq		
	68	C4
Kangiqsujuaq	68	B3
Kangirsuk	68	C4
Kangnŭng	35	C7
Kango	56	D2
Kangto	41	D9
Kaniapiskau →	68	C4
Kaniapiskau L.	69	C4
Kanin,		
Poluostrov	28	C5
Kanin Nos, Mys	28	C5
Kanin Pen. =		
Kanin,		
Poluostrov	28	C5
Kaniva	62	C3
Kankakee	72	D2
Kankan	55	F3
Kankendy =		
Xankändi	25	F6
Kanker	40	G3
Kannapolis	75	B7
Kannauj	42	F11
Kannod	43	H10
Kano	55	F6
Kanowit	37	D4
Kanoya	33	D2
Kanpetlet	41	G9
Kanpur	40	D3
Kansas □	76	F5
Kansas City,		
Kans., U.S.A.	77	F7
Kansas City,		
Mo., U.S.A.	77	F7
Kansk	30	D7
Kansu =		
Gansu □	34	C5
Kantang	36	C1
Kanuma	32	A6
Kanye	59	C5
Kaohsiung =		
Gaoxiong	35	D7
Kaokoveld	58	B2
Kaolack	55	F1
Kapan	25	F6
Kapanga	56	F4
Kapchagai =		
Qapshaghay	29	E8
Kapfenberg	15	E8
Kapiri Mposhi	59	A5
Kāpīsā □	45	C7
Kapit	37	D4
Kapoeta	53	H5
Kaposvár	16	E3
Kapuas →	37	E3
Kapuas Hulu,		
Pegunungan	37	D4
Kapuas Hulu Ra.		
= Kapuas		
Hulu,		
Pegunungan	37	D4
Kapunda	62	B2
Kapuni	64	C6
Kaputar	63	B5
Kara	28	C7

Kara Bogaz Gol, Zaliv

Kara Bogaz Gol,
Zaliv =
Garabogazköl
Aylagy 29 E6
Kara Kalpak
Republic □ =
Karakalpakstan □
.... 29 E6
Kara Kum 29 F6
Kara Sea 28 B8
Karabiğa 23 D6
Karabük 46 B3
Karaburun ... 23 E6
Karabutak =
Qarabutaq .. 29 E7
Karacabey 23 D7
Karacasu 23 F7
Karachi 43 G5
Karad 43 L9
Karadeniz
Boğazı 22 D7
Karaganda =
Qaraghandy . 29 E8
Karagayly 29 E8
Karaikal 43 P11
Karaikkudi 43 P11
Karaj 44 C2
Karakalpakstan □
.... 29 E6
Karakas 29 E9
Karakelong ... 38 D3
Karakitang 39 D3
Karaklis =
Vanadzor ... 25 E5
Karakoram Pass 42 B10
Karakoram Ra. 42 B10
Karalon 30 D9
Karaman 46 C3
Karamay 34 B3
Karambu 37 E5
Karamea Bight 65 D4
Karasburg ... 58 D3
Karasino 28 C9
Karasuk 29 D8
Karatau =
Qarataū 29 E8
Karatau, Khrebet 29 E7
Karawanken ... 20 A5
Karazhal 29 E8
Karbalā 47 D6
Karcag 16 E5
Kardhítsa 23 E3
Karelia □ ... 28 C4
Karelian
Republic □ =
Karelia □ ... 28 C4
Kargānrūd 46 C7
Kargasok 29 D9
Kargat 29 D9
Kargil 42 B10
Kariba, L. 59 B5
Kariba Dam .. 59 B5
Kariba Gorge . 59 B5
Karibib 58 C3
Karimata,
Kepulauan .. 37 E3
Karimata, Selat 37 E3
Karimata Is. =
Karimata,
Kepulauan .. 37 E3
Karimnagar ... 43 K11
Karimunjawa,
Kepulauan .. 37 F4
Karin 49 E4
Karkaralinsk =
Qarqaraly ... 29 E8
Karkinitska
Zatoka 25 D3

Karkinitskiy Zaliv
= Karkinitska
Zatoka 25 D3
Karl-Marx-Stadt
= Chemnitz . 15 C7
Karlovac 20 B5
Karlovo 22 C5
Karlovy Vary .. 16 C1
Karlsbad =
Karlovy Vary 16 C1
Karlskrona ... 9 G11
Karlsruhe 14 D5
Karlstad 9 G10
Karnal 42 E10
Karnali → 40 C3
Karnaphuli Res. 41 F9
Karnataka □ .. 43 N10
Karnische Alpen 20 A4
Kärnten □ ... 15 E7
Karonga 57 F6
Karoonda 62 C2
Karora 53 E6
Kárpathos 23 G6
Kars 46 B5
Karsakpay 29 E7
Karshi = Qarshi 29 F7
Karsun 24 C6
Karufa 39 E4
Karungu 57 E6
Karviná 16 D4
Karwar 43 M9
Kasai → 56 E3
Kasama 57 G6
Kasanga 57 F6
Kasangulu ... 56 E3
Kasaragod 43 N9
Kasba L. 70 B9
Kasempa 59 A5
Kasenga 57 G5
Kāshān 44 C2
Kashi 34 C2
Kashk-e Kohneh 42 B3
Kāshmar 44 C4
Kashun Noerh =
Gaxun Nur .. 34 B5
Kasimov 24 C5
Kasiruta 39 E3
Kasongo 57 E5
Kasongo Lunda 56 F3
Kásos 23 G6
Kassalâ 53 E6
Kassel 14 C5
Kassue 39 F5
Kastamonu ... 46 B3
Kasulu 57 E6
Kasur 42 D9
Katako Kombe . 56 E4
Katamatite ... 63 C4
Katanga =
Shaba □ 57 F4
Katangi 43 J11
Kateríni 23 D4
Katha 41 E11
Kathiawar 43 H7
Katihar 40 E6
Katima Mulilo . 58 B4
Katingan =
Mendawai → 37 E4
Katiola 55 G3
Katmandu 40 D5
Katoomba 63 B5
Katowice 16 C4
Katsina 55 F6
Kattegat 9 G10
Kauai 82 G11
Kaunas 24 C1
Kaura Namoda 55 F6
Kavála 22 D5
Kaw 92 B3

Kawagoe 32 B6
Kawaguchi 32 B6
Kawambwa ... 57 F5
Kawardha 40 G3
Kawasaki 32 B6
Kawerau 64 C7
Kawhia Harbour 64 C6
Kawio,
Kepulauan .. 38 D3
Kawnro 41 F12
Kawthoolei =
Kawthule □ . 41 H11
Kawthule □ .. 41 H11
Kaya 55 F4
Kayah □ 41 H11
Kayan → 37 D5
Kayeli 39 E3
Kayes 55 F2
Kayoa 39 D3
Kayrunnera .. 62 B3
Kayseri 46 C3
Kayuagung ... 37 E2
Kazachye 31 B11
Kazakstan ■ .. 29 E7
Kazan 24 B6
Kazanlŭk 22 C5
Kazatin =
Kozyatyn ... 17 D9
Käzerūn 44 D2
Kazumba 56 F4
Kazym → 28 C7
Ké-Macina ... 55 F3
Kéa 23 F5
Kebnekaise ... 8 E11
Kebri Dehar .. 49 F3
Kecskemét ... 16 E4
Kediri 37 F4
Kédougou ... 55 F2
Keetmanshoop 58 D3
Kefallinía 23 E3
Kefamenanu .. 39 F2
Keffi 55 G6
Keighley 11 E6
Keith 62 C3
Keith Arm 70 B7
Kekri 42 G9
Kël 30 C10
Kelang 37 D2
Kelibia 52 A1
Kellé 56 E2
Kells =
Ceannannus
Mor 11 E3
Kélo 53 G2
Kelowna 71 D8
Kelso 65 F3
Keluang 37 D2
Kem 28 C4
Kema 39 D3
Kemah 46 C4
Kemerovo ... 29 D9
Kemi 8 E12
Kemi älv =
Kemijoki → . 8 E12
Kemijoki → .. 8 E12
Kemp Land .. 96 A9
Kempsey 63 B5
Kempten 14 E6
Kendal 37 F4
Kendall 63 B5
Kendari 39 E2
Kendawangan . 37 E4
Kende 55 F5
Kendrapara .. 40 G6
Kenema 55 G2
Keng Tawng . 41 G12
Keng Tung .. 41 G12
Kenge 56 E3
Kenhardt 58 D4

Kenitra 54 B3
Kennedy
Taungdeik .. 41 F9
Kennewick 80 B4
Kenogami → . 69 C2
Kenosha 72 C2
Kent Group .. 62 C4
Kent Pen. 70 B9
Kentau 29 E7
Kentucky □ .. 72 F3
Kentville 69 D4
Kenya ■ 57 D7
Kenya, Mt. ... 57 E7
Kepi 39 F5
Kerala □ 43 P10
Kerang 62 C3
Kerch 25 D4
Kerchoual ... 55 E5
Keren 53 E6
Kericho 57 E7
Kerinci 37 E2
Kerki 29 F7
Kérkira 23 E2
Kermadec Is. .. 64 M13
Kermadec
Trench 65 N13
Kermān 44 D4
Kermān □ ... 44 D4
Kermānshāh =
Bākhtarān .. 46 D6
Kerme Körfezi . 23 F6
Kerrobert 71 C9
Kerulen → ... 35 B6
Kerzaz 54 C4
Keşan 22 D6
Kestenga 28 C4
Ket → 29 D9
Keta 55 G5
Ketapang ... 37 E4
Ketchikan 71 C6
Ketrzyn 16 A5
Keweenaw B. . 69 D2
Key West 86 B3
Khabarovo .. 28 C7
Khabarovsk .. 31 E11
Khābūr → ... 46 D5
Khairpur 42 F6
Khakassia □ .. 30 D6
Khakhea 58 C4
Khalkhāl 46 C7
Khalkís 23 E4
Khalmer-Sede =
Tazovskiy ... 28 C8
Khalmer Yu ... 28 C7
Khalturin 24 B6
Khalûf 48 C6
Khambat, G. of 43 J8
Khambhat 43 H8
Khamir 49 D3
Khānābād 45 B7
Khānaqīn 46 D6
Khandwa 43 J10
Khanewal 42 D7
Khaniá 23 G5
Khaníon, Kólpos 23 G4
Khankendy =
Xankändi ... 25 F6
Khanty-
Mansiysk ... 29 C7
Khapcheranga . 30 E9
Kharagpur ... 40 F6
Kharan Kalat .. 42 E4
Kharānaq 44 C3
Kharda 43 K9
Khârga, El
Wâhât el ... 52 C5
Khargon 43 J9
Khārk, Jazireh . 47 E7
Kharkiv 24 D4

Name	Map	Grid
Kharkov = Kharkiv	24	D4
Kharovsk	24	B5
Kharsānīya	47	F7
Kharta	22	D7
Khartoum = El Khartûm	53	E5
Khāsh	42	E2
Khashm el Girba	53	F6
Khaskovo	22	D5
Khatanga	30	B8
Khatanga →	30	B8
Khaybar, Harrat	47	F5
Khed Brahma	43	G8
Khemmarat	36	A3
Khenchela	54	A6
Khenifra	54	B3
Kherson	25	D3
Kheta →	30	B8
Khilok	30	D9
Khíos	23	E6
Khiuma = Hiiumaa	24	B1
Khiva	29	E7
Khīyāv	46	C6
Khmelnik	17	D8
Khmelnitskiy = Khmelnytskyy	17	D8
Khmelnytskyy	17	D8
Khmer Rep. = Cambodia ■	36	B3
Khodoriv	17	D7
Khodzent = Khudzhand	29	E7
Khojak P.	42	D5
Kholm, Afghan.	45	B6
Kholm, Russia	24	B3
Khomeyn	44	C2
Khon Kaen	36	A2
Khoper →	29	E5
Khóra Sfakíon	23	G5
Khorat = Nakhon Ratchasima	36	B2
Khorramābād	46	D7
Khorrāmshahr	47	E7
Khotyn	17	D8
Khouribga	54	B3
Khowai	41	E8
Khoyniki	17	C9
Khu Khan	36	B2
Khudzhand	29	E7
Khūgīānī	42	D4
Khulna	41	F7
Khulna □	41	F7
Khūr	44	C4
Khurayş	47	F7
Khūrīyā Mūrīyā, Jazā 'ir	48	D6
Khush	42	C3
Khushab	42	C8
Khust	17	D6
Khuzdar	42	F5
Khvor	44	C3
Khvormūj	44	D2
Khvoy	46	C6
Khyber Pass	42	B7
Kiama	63	B5
Kiamba	38	C2
Kiangsi = Jiangxi □	35	D6
Kiangsu = Jiangsu □	35	C6
Kibangou	56	E2
Kibombo	57	E5
Kibondo	57	E6
Kibwesa	57	F5
Kibwezi	57	E7
Kicking Horse Pass	71	C8
Kidal	55	E5
Kidnappers, C.	64	C7
Kiel	14	A6
Kiel Canal = Nord-Ostsee-Kanal →	14	A5
Kielce	16	C5
Kieler Bucht	14	A6
Kiev = Kyyiv	17	C10
Kiffa	55	E2
Kifrī	46	D6
Kigali	57	E6
Kigoma-Ujiji	57	E5
Kihee	62	A3
Kii-Suidō	32	C4
Kikinda	22	B3
Kikládhes	23	F5
Kikwit	56	E3
Kilcoy	63	A5
Kilimanjaro	57	E7
Kilindini	57	E7
Kilis	46	C4
Kiliya	17	F9
Kilkenny	11	E3
Kilkís	23	D4
Killarney, Australia	63	A5
Killarney, Ireland	11	E2
Killeen	78	D5
Killíni	23	F4
Kilmarnock	10	D4
Kilmore	63	C3
Kilosa	57	F7
Kilrush	11	E2
Kilwa Kivinje	57	F7
Kimaam	39	F5
Kimba	62	B2
Kimberley	58	D4
Kimberley Plateau	60	D4
Kimry	24	B4
Kinabalu, Gunong	36	C5
Kindia	55	G2
Kindu	57	E5
Kineshma	24	B5
King George B.	95	G4
King George I.	96	A4
King George Is.	69	C2
King I. = Kadan Kyun	36	B1
King I.	62	C3
King William I.	70	B10
King William's Town	59	E5
Kingaroy	63	A5
Kingoonya	62	B2
Kings Canyon National Park	82	B3
King's Lynn	11	E7
Kingscote	62	C2
Kingsport	75	A6
Kingston, Canada	69	D3
Kingston, Jamaica	86	C4
Kingston, N.Z.	65	F3
Kingston South East	62	C2
Kingston upon Hull	11	E6
Kingstown	87	D7
Kingsville	78	F5
Kınık	23	E6
Kinkala	56	E2
Kinleith	64	C6
Kinsale	11	F2
Kinshasa	56	E3
Kinston	75	B9
Kintampo	55	G4
Kintap	37	E5
Kiparissía	23	F3
Kiparissiakós Kólpos	23	F3
Kipembawe	57	F6
Kipili	57	F6
Kipushi	59	A5
Kirghizia ■ = Kyrgyzstan ■	29	E8
Kirghizstan = Kyrgyzstan ■	29	E8
Kiri	56	E3
Kiribati ■	64	K12
Kırıkkale	46	C3
Kirillov	24	B4
Kirin = Jilin	35	B7
Kiritimati	65	J15
Kirkcaldy	10	C5
Kirkcudbright	11	D4
Kirkee	43	K8
Kirkenes	8	E14
Kirkland Lake	69	D2
Kırklareli	22	D6
Kirkūk	46	D6
Kirkwall	10	B5
Kirov	28	D5
Kirovabad = Gäncä	25	E6
Kirovakan = Vanadzor	25	E5
Kirovograd = Kirovohrad	25	D3
Kirovohrad	25	D3
Kirovsk = Babadayhan	29	F7
Kirovsk	28	C4
Kirsanov	24	C5
Kırşehir	46	C3
Kirteh	45	C5
Kirthar Range	42	F5
Kiruna	8	E12
Kirundu	57	E5
Kiryū	32	A6
Kisangani	57	D5
Kisar	39	F3
Kiselevsk	29	D9
Kishanganj	40	D7
Kishangarh	42	F7
Kishinev = Chişinău	17	E9
Kishiwada	32	B4
Kishtwar	42	C9
Kisii	57	E6
Kisiju	57	F7
Kiska I.	71	C1
Kiskörös	16	E4
Kiskunfélegyháza	16	E4
Kiskunhalas	16	E4
Kislovodsk	25	E5
Kiso-Sammyaku	32	B5
Kissidougou	55	G2
Kisumu	57	E6
Kita	55	F3
Kitab	29	F7
Kitakami-Gawa →	33	G12
Kitakyūshū	32	C2
Kitale	57	D7
Kitchener	69	D2
Kitega = Gitega	57	E5
Kitgum	57	D6
Kíthira	23	F4
Kíthnos	23	F5
Kittakittaooloo, L.	62	A2
Kitui	57	E7
Kitwe	59	A5
Kivertsi	17	C7
Kivu, L.	57	E5
Kiyev = Kyyiv	17	C10
Kiyevskoye Vdkhr. = Kyyivske Vdskh.	17	C10
Kızıl Irmak →	25	E4
Kizlyar	25	E6
Kizyl-Arvat = Gyzylarbat	29	F6
Kladno	16	C2
Klagenfurt	15	E8
Klaipeda	24	B1
Klamath Falls	80	D3
Klamath Mts.	80	E2
Klarälven →	9	G10
Klatovy	16	D1
Klawer	58	E3
Klerksdorp	59	D5
Kletsk = Klyetsk	17	B8
Klin	28	D4
Kłodzko	16	C3
Klondike	70	B6
Klouto	55	G5
Kluane L.	70	B6
Kluczbork	16	C4
Klyetsk	17	B8
Knossós	23	G5
Knox Coast	96	A12
Knoxville	75	B6
Koartac = Quaqtaq	68	B4
Koba, Aru, Indonesia	39	F4
Koba, Bangka, Indonesia	37	E3
Kobarid	20	A4
Kobdo = Hovd	34	B4
Kōbe	32	B4
København	9	G10
Koblenz	14	C4
Kobroor, Kepulauan	39	F4
Kobryn	17	B7
Kocaeli = İzmit	25	E2
Kočani	22	D4
Koch Bihar	41	D7
Kōchi	32	C3
Kochiu = Gejiu	34	D5
Kodiak	71	C4
Kodiak I.	71	C4
Koes	58	D3
Kofiau	39	E3
Koforidua	55	G4
Kōfu	32	B6
Kogan	63	A5
Koh-i-Bābā	42	B5
Kohat	42	C7
Kohima	41	E10
Kohkīlūyeh va Būyer Aḥmadi □	44	D2
Kohler Ra.	96	B1
Kokand = Qūqon	29	E8
Kokas	39	E4
Kokchetav = Kökshetaū	29	D7
Koko Kyunzu	41	K9
Kokomo	72	D2
Kokonau	39	E5
Kökshetaū	29	D7
Koksoak →	68	C4
Kokstad	59	E5
Kola, Indonesia	39	F4
Kola, Russia	28	C4
Kola Pen. = Kolskiy Poluostrov	28	C4

Kolaka

Kolaka	39	E2
Kolar	43	N11
Kolar Gold Fields	43	N11
Kolayat	42	F8
Kolchugino =		
Leninsk-		
Kuznetskiy	29	D9
Kolda	55	F2
Kole	56	E4
Kolepom = Yos		
Sudarso,		
Pulau	39	F5
Kolguyev,		
Ostrov	28	C5
Kolhapur	43	L9
Kolín	16	C2
Kolkata	41	F7
Köln	14	C4
Koło	16	B4
Kołobrzeg	16	A2
Kolokani	55	F3
Kolomna	24	B4
Kolomyya	17	D7
Kolonodale	39	E2
Kolosib	41	E9
Kolpashevo	29	D9
Kolpino	24	B3
Kolskiy		
Poluostrov	28	C4
Kolwezi	57	G5
Kolyma →	31	C13
Komárno	16	E4
Komatsu	32	A5
Komi □	28	C6
Kommunarsk =		
Alchevsk	25	D4
Kommunizma,		
Pik	29	F8
Komodo	39	F1
Komono	56	E2
Komoran, Pulau	39	F5
Komotini	22	D5
Kompong Cham	36	B3
Kompong		
Chhnang	36	B2
Kompong Som	36	B2
Komrat =		
Comrat	17	E9
Komsomolets,		
Ostrov	30	A7
Konarhá □	42	B7
Konch	42	G11
Kondoa	57	E7
Konduga	53	F1
Köneürgench	29	E6
Kong	55	G4
Kong, Koh	36	B2
Konglu	41	D11
Kongolo	57	F5
Kongor	53	G5
Königsberg =		
Kaliningrad	24	C1
Konin	16	B4
Konjic	20	C6
Konosha	28	C5
Konotop	24	C3
Konqi He →	34	B4
Końskie	16	C5
Konstanz	14	E5
Kontagora	55	F6
Kontum	36	B3
Konya	46	C2
Konya Ovası	46	C3
Konza	57	E7
Kooloonong	62	B3
Koondrook	63	C3
Koonibba	62	B1
Koorawatha	63	B4
Kootenay L.	71	D8
Kopaonik	22	C3
Koper	20	B4
Kopeysk	29	D7
Kopi	62	B2
Koprivnica	20	A6
Kopychyntsi	17	D7
Korab	22	D3
Korça	23	D3
Korce = Korça	23	D3
Korčula	20	C6
Kordestan	46	D5
Kordestān □	46	D6
Kordofân	53	F4
Korea, North ■	35	C7
Korea, South ■	35	C7
Korea Bay	35	C7
Korea Strait	35	C7
Korets	17	C8
Korhogo	55	G3
Korim	39	E5
Korinthiakós		
Kólpos	23	E4
Kórinthos	23	F4
Kōriyama	33	G12
Korneshty =		
Cornești	17	E9
Koro, Ivory C.	55	G3
Koro, Mali	55	F4
Korogwe	57	F7
Koroit	62	C3
Koror	38	C4
Körös →	16	E5
Korosten	17	C9
Korostyshev	17	C9
Korti	53	E5
Kortrijk	14	C2
Kos	23	F6
Kościan	16	B3
Kosciuszko, Mt.	63	C4
Kosha	52	D5
K'oshih = Kashi	34	C2
Košice	16	D5
Kosovo □	22	C3
Kosovska-		
Mitrovica	22	C3
Kôstî	53	F5
Kostopil	17	C8
Kostroma	24	B5
Kostrzyn	16	B2
Koszalin	16	A3
Kota	43	G9
Kota Baharu	36	C2
Kota Belud	36	C5
Kota Kinabalu	36	C5
Kota Tinggi	37	D2
Kotaagung	37	F2
Kotabaru	37	E5
Kotabumi	37	E2
Kotamobagu	39	D2
Kotawaringin	37	E4
Kotelnich	24	B6
Kotelnyy, Ostrov	31	B11
Kotka	9	F13
Kotlas	28	C5
Kotli	42	C8
Kotor	22	C2
Kotovsk	17	E9
Kotri	42	G6
Kottayam	43	Q10
Kotturu	43	M10
Kotuy →	30	B8
Kotzebue	71	B3
Kouango	56	D4
Koudougou	55	F4
Kouilou →	56	E2
Kouki	56	C3
Koula Moutou	56	E2
Koulen	36	B2
Koulikoro	55	F3
Koumra	53	G2
Kounradskiy	29	E8
Kouroussa	55	F3
Kousseri	53	F1
Koutiala	55	F3
Kovel	17	C7
Kovrov	24	B5
Kowloon	35	D6
Köyceğiz	23	F7
Koyuk	71	B3
Koyukuk →	71	B4
Kozan	46	C3
Kozáni	23	D3
Kozhikode =		
Calicut	43	P9
Kozyatyn	17	D9
Kpalimé	55	G5
Kra, Isthmus of		
= Kra, Kho		
Khot	36	B1
Kra, Kho Khot	36	B1
Kragujevac	22	B3
Krajina	20	B6
Krakatau =		
Rakata, Pulau	37	F3
Kraków	16	C4
Kraljevo	22	C3
Kramatorsk	25	D4
Kranj	20	A5
Kraśnik	16	C6
Krasnoarmeysk	29	D5
Krasnodar	25	D4
Krasnoperekopsk		
	25	D3
Krasnoselkupsk	28	C9
Krasnoturinsk	28	D7
Krasnoufimsk	29	D6
Krasnouralsk	29	D7
Krasnovodsk =		
Krasnowodsk	29	E6
Krasnowodsk	29	E6
Krasnoyarsk	30	D7
Krasnyy Luch	25	D4
Krasnyy Yar	25	D6
Kratie	36	B3
Krau	39	E6
Krefeld	14	C4
Kremen	20	B5
Kremenchug =		
Kremenchuk	24	D3
Kremenchuk	24	D3
Kremenchuksk		
Vdskh.	24	D3
Kremenets	17	C7
Krems	15	D8
Kribi	56	D1
Krichev =		
Krychaw	17	B10
Krishna →	40	K3
Krishnanagar	41	F7
Kristiansand	9	G9
Kristiansund	8	F9
Kríti	23	G5
Krivoy Rog =		
Kryvyy Rih	25	D3
Krk	20	B5
Kronprins Olav		
Kyst	96	A9
Kronshtadt	24	B2
Kroonstad	59	D5
Kropotkin,		
Irkutsk, Russia	30	D9
Kropotkin,		
Krasnodar,		
Russia	25	D5
Krosno	16	D5
Krotoszyn	16	C3
Krugersdorp	59	D5
Krung Thep =		
Bangkok	36	B2
Krupki	17	A9
Kruševac	22	C3
Krychaw	17	B10
Krymskiy		
Poluostrov =		
Krymskyy		
Pivostriv	25	D3
Krymskyy		
Pivostriv	25	D3
Kryvyy Rih	25	D3
Ksar el Boukhari	54	A5
Ksar el Kebir	54	B3
Ksar es Souk =		
Ar Rachidiya	54	B4
Kuala	37	D3
Kuala Kubu		
Baharu	37	D2
Kuala Lipis	37	D2
Kuala Lumpur	37	D2
Kuala		
Terengganu	36	C2
Kualajelai	37	E4
Kualakapuas	37	E4
Kualakurun	37	E4
Kualapembuang	37	E4
Kualasimpang	37	D1
Kuandang	39	D2
Kuangchou =		
Guangzhou	35	D6
Kuantan	37	D2
Kuba = Quba	25	E6
Kuban →	25	D4
Kucing	37	D4
Kuda	43	H7
Kudat	36	C5
Kudymkar	28	D6
Kueiyang =		
Guiyang	35	D5
Kufra Oasis = Al		
Kufrah	52	D3
Kufstein	15	E7
Kugluktuk	70	B8
Küh-e 'Alijūq	44	D2
Küh-e-Hazārām	44	D4
Küh-e Sorkh	44	C4
Küh-e Taftān	45	D5
Kühak	42	F3
Kühhā-ye-		
Bashākerd	45	E4
Kühpāyeh	44	C3
Kuito	58	A3
Kujū-San	32	C2
Kukawa	53	F1
Kukësi	22	C3
Kula	23	E7
Kulasekarappattinam		
	43	Q11
Kuldja = Yining	34	B3
Kŭlob	29	F7
Kulsary	29	E6
Kulunda	29	D8
Kulwin	62	C3
Kulyab = Kŭlob	29	F7
Kum Tekei	29	E8
Kuma →	25	E6
Kumagaya	32	A6
Kumai	37	E4
Kumamba,		
Kepulauan	39	E5
Kumamoto	32	C2
Kumanovo	22	C3
Kumara	65	E4
Kumasi	55	G4
Kumayri =		
Gyumri	25	E5
Kumba	56	D1
Kumbakonam	43	P11

126

Kumbarilla 63 A5
Kumo 55 F7
Kumon Bum .. 41 D11
Kunama 63 C4
Kungala 63 A5
Kungrad =
  Qŭnghirot ... 29 E6
Kungur 29 D6
Kunlong 41 F12
Kunlun Shan .. 34 C3
Kunming 34 D5
Kunsan 35 C7
Kunya-Urgench
  =
  Köneürgench 29 E6
Kuopio 8 F13
Kupa → 20 B6
Kupyansk 28 E4
Kuqa 34 B3
Kür → 25 E6
Kura = Kür → 25 E6
Kurashiki 32 B3
Kurayoshi 32 B3
Kŭrdzhali 22 D5
Kure 32 B3
Kurgaldzhinskiy 29 D8
Kurgan 29 D7
Kuria Maria Is.
  = Khŭrīyā
  Mŭrīyā, Jazā
  'ir 48 D6
Kurigram 41 E7
Kuril Is. =
  Kurilskiye
  Ostrova 31 E12
Kurilskiye
  Ostrova 31 E12
Kurmuk 53 F5
Kurnool 43 L11
Kurow 65 F4
Kurrajong 63 B5
Kurri Kurri 63 B5
Kursk 24 C4
Kuruktag 34 B3
Kuruman 58 D4
Kurume 32 C2
Kus Gölü 23 D6
Kuşadası 23 F6
Kushiro 32 F12
Kushtia 41 F7
Kuskokwim → 71 B3
Kuskokwim B. . 71 C3
Kustanay =
  Qostanay ... 29 D7
Kütahya 46 C2
Kutaisi 25 E5
Kutaraja =
  Banda Aceh . 36 C1
Kutch, Gulf of =
  Kachchh, Gulf
  of 43 H6
Kutch, Rann of
  = Kachchh,
  Rann of 43 G6
Kutno 16 B4
Kutu 56 E3
Kutum 53 F3
Kuujjuaq 68 C4
Kuwait = Al
  Kuwayt 47 E7
Kuwait ■ 47 E6
Kuwana 32 B5
Kuybyshev =
  Samara 24 C7
Kuybyshev ... 29 D8
Kuybyshevskoye
  Vdkhr. 24 B6
Kūysanjaq 46 C6
Kuyumba 30 C7

Kuzey Anadolu
  Dağları 46 B3
Kuznetsk 24 C6
Kvarner 20 B5
Kvarnerič 20 B5
Kwakoegron .. 92 A2
Kwamouth 56 E3
Kwando → 58 B4
Kwangju 35 C7
Kwangsi-Chuang
  = Guangxi
  Zhuangzu
  Zizhiqu □ ... 35 D5
Kwangtung =
  Guangdong □ 35 D6
Kwatisore 39 E4
Kweichow =
  Guizhou □ .. 35 D5
Kwekwe 59 B5
Kwidzyn 16 B4
Kwoka 39 E4
Kyabé 53 G2
Kyabra Cr. → . 63 A3
Kyabram 63 C4
Kyancutta 62 B2
Kyangin 41 H10
Kyaukpadaung 41 G10
Kyaukpyu 41 H9
Kyaukse 41 G11
Kyle Dam 59 C6
Kyneton 63 C3
Kyō-ga-Saki .. 32 B4
Kyoga, L. 57 D6
Kyogle 63 A5
Kyongpyaw .. 41 J10
Kyōto 32 B4
Kyrenia 46 D3
Kyrgyzstan ■ .. 29 E8
Kystatyam 30 C10
Kytal Ktakh ... 31 C10
Kyunhla 41 F10
Kyūshū 32 C2
Kyūshū-Sanchi 32 C2
Kyustendil ... 22 C4
Kyusyur 30 B10
Kywong 63 B4
Kyyiv 17 C10
Kyyivske Vdskh. 17 C10
Kyzyl Kum ... 29 E7
Kyzyl-Kyya ... 29 E8
Kzyl-Orda =
  Qyzylorda ... 29 E7

L

La Albufera ... 19 C5
La Alcarria ... 19 B4
La Asunción .. 90 A6
La Banda 94 B4
La Calera 94 C2
La Carlota 94 C4
La Ceiba 85 D7
La Chaux de
  Fonds 13 C7
La Cocha 94 B3
La Coruña ... 18 A1
La Crosse 77 D9
La Dorada 90 B4
La Estrada ... 18 A1
La Grange 74 C5
La Guaira 90 A5
La Güera 54 D1
La Habana ... 86 B3
La Línea de la
  Concepción . 18 D3
La Mancha 19 C4

La Palma,
  Canary Is. ... 54 C1
La Palma,
  Panama 86 E4
La Palma del
  Condado ... 18 D2
La Paragua ... 90 B6
La Paz,
  Entre Ríos,
  Argentina ... 94 C5
La Paz, San Luis,
  Argentina ... 94 C3
La Paz, Bolivia . 91 G5
La Paz, Mexico 84 C2
La Pedrera ... 90 D5
La Plata 94 D5
La Quiaca 94 A3
La Rioja 94 B3
La Rioja □ 19 A4
La Robla 18 A3
La Roche-sur-
  Yon 12 C3
La Rochelle ... 12 C3
La Roda 19 C4
La Romana ... 87 C6
La Serena 94 B2
La Seyne-sur-
  Mer 13 E6
La Spézia 20 B2
La Tortuga 87 D6
La Tuque 69 D3
La Unión 95 E2
La Urbana 90 B5
La Vega 87 C5
Labe = Elbe → 14 B5
Labé 55 F2
Labis 37 D2
Laboulaye 94 C4
Labrador
  □........... 69 C4
Lábrea 91 E6
Labuan........ 36 C5
Labuha 39 E3
Labuhanbajo .. 39 F2
Labuk, Telok . 36 C5
Labyrinth, L. .. 62 B2
Labytnangi ... 28 C7
Lac La Biche .. 71 C8
Lac la Martre .. 70 B8
Lacanau 12 D3
Laccadive Is. =
  Lakshadweep
  Is. 26 H11
Lacepede B. .. 62 C2
Lachine 69 D3
Lachlan → ... 63 B3
Lackawanna .. 73 C6
Lacombe 71 C8
Ladakh Ra. ... 42 B10
Ladíz 45 D5
Ladoga, L. =
  Ladozhskoye
  Ozero 28 C4
Ladozhskoye
  Ozero 28 C4
Ladysmith,
  Canada 71 D7
Ladysmith,
  S. Africa 59 D5
Lae 61 B8
Lafayette 79 D7
Lafia 55 G6
Laghmān □ ... 45 C7
Laghouat 54 B5
Lagonoy Gulf . 38 B2
Lagos, Nigeria . 55 G5
Lagos, Portugal 18 D1
Laguna 94 B7
Lagunas, Chile 91 H5

Lagunas, Peru . 90 E3
Lahad Datu ... 38 C1
Lahat 37 E2
Lahewa 37 D1
Lāhījān 46 C7
Lahn → 14 C4
Lahore 42 D9
Lahti 8 F13
Lahtis = Lahti . 8 F13
Laï 53 G2
Laibin 35 D5
Laidley 63 A5
Laila = Laylá .. 47 G6
Lairg 10 B4
Lajere 55 F7
Lajes 94 B6
Lake Cargelligo 63 B4
Lake Charles . 79 D7
Lake City 75 D6
Lake Worth ... 75 F7
Lakeland 75 E7
Lakes Entrance 63 C4
Lakewood 72 D5
Lakonikós
  Kólpos 23 F4
Lakor 39 F3
Lakota 55 G3
Lakshadweep
  Is. 26 H11
Lala Ghat 41 E9
Lalibela 53 F6
Lalín 18 A1
Lalitapur =
  Patan 40 D5
Lamaing 41 K11
Lamas 91 E3
Lambaréné ... 56 E2
Lambert Glacier 96 B10
Lame 55 F6
Lamego 18 B2
Lameroo 62 C3
Lamía 23 E4
Lamon Bay ... 38 B2
Lampa 91 G4
Lampedusa ... 21 G4
Lampione 21 G4
Lampung □ ... 37 F2
Lamu 57 E8
Lanai I. 82 H12
Lanak La 42 B11
Lanak'o
  Shank'ou =
  Lanak La ... 42 B11
Lanao, L. 38 C2
Lancaster, U.K. 11 D5
Lancaster,
  U.S.A. 73 D7
Lancaster Sd. . 68 A2
Lanchow =
  Lanzhou ... 35 C5
Lanciano 20 C5
Landeck 14 E6
Landes 12 D3
Landi Kotal ... 42 B7
Land's End 11 F4
Landshut 15 D7
La'nga Co 40 B3
Langkawi, P. . 36 C1
Langkon 36 C5
Langres 13 C6
Langres, Plateau
  de 13 C6
Langsa 36 D1
Languedoc ... 13 E5
Langzhong ... 35 C5
Lannion 12 B2
Lansdowne ... 63 B5
Lansing 72 C3
Lanusei 21 E2

Lanzarote

Lanzarote 54 C2
Lanzhou 35 C5
Laoag 38 A2
Laoang 38 B3
Laon 13 B5
Laos ■ 36 A3
Lapa 94 B7
Laparan 38 C1
Lapland =
Lappland ... 8 E12
Lappland 8 E12
Lapseki 23 D6
Laptev Sea 30 B10
L'Áquila 20 C4
Lār 44 E3
Larache 54 A3
Laramie 76 E2
Larantuka 39 F2
Larap 38 B2
Larat 39 F4
Laredo 78 F4
Lariang 39 E1
Lárisa 23 E4
Larnaca 46 D3
Larne 11 D4
Larrimah 60 D5
Larsen Ice Shelf 96 A3
Larvik 9 G9
Laryak 29 C8
Las Anod 49 F4
Las Cruces ... 83 D9
Las Flores 94 D5
Las Khoreh ... 49 E4
Las Lajas 94 D2
Las Lomitas .. 94 A4
Las Palmas ... 54 C1
Las Pipinas .. 94 D5
Las Plumas ... 95 E3
Las Rosas 94 C4
Las Varillas .. 94 C4
Las Vegas 82 B5
Lashio 41 F11
Lassen Pk. ... 80 E3
Lastoursville .. 56 E2
Lastovo 20 C6
Latacunga 90 D3
Latakia = Al
Lādhiqīyah .. 46 D3
Latina 20 D4
Latium =
Lazio □ 20 C4
Latrobe 62 D4
Latvia ■ 24 B1
Lauchhammer . 15 C7
Launceston ... 62 D4
Laurel 79 D9
Lauria 21 D5
Laurium 69 D2
Lausanne 13 C7
Laut 36 D3
Laut Kecil,
Kepulauan .. 37 E5
Laval 12 B3
Lávrion 23 F5
Lawas 36 D5
Lawele 39 F2
Lawng Pit 41 E11
Lawrence, N.Z. 65 F3
Lawrence,
U.S.A. 77 F7
Lawton 78 B4
Laylá 47 G6
Lazio □ 20 C4
Le Creusot 13 C6
Le Havre 12 B4
Le Mans 12 C4
Le Mont-St.-
Michel 12 B3
Le Moule 87 C7

Le Puy-en-Velay 13 D5
Le Touquet-
Paris-Plage .. 12 A4
Le Tréport 12 A4
Le Verdon-sur-
Mer 12 D3
Leamington Spa
= Royal
Leamington
Spa 11 E6
Leandro Norte
Alem 94 B5
Leavenworth .. 77 F7
Lebak 38 C2
Lebanon ■ ... 46 D3
Lębork 16 A3
Lebrija 18 D2
Lebu 94 D2
Lecce 23 D2
Lecco 20 B2
Lech → 14 D6
Łęczyca 16 B4
Leduc 71 C8
Leeds 11 E6
Leer 14 B4
Leeton 63 B4
Leeuwarden .. 14 B3
Leeuwin, C. ... 60 G2
Leeward Is. ... 87 C7
Leganés 18 B4
Legazpi 38 B2
Leghorn =
Livorno 20 C3
Legionowo 16 B5
Legnago 20 B3
Legnica 16 C3
Legume 63 A5
Leh 42 B10
Leicester 11 E6
Leiden 14 B3
Leie → 14 C2
Leine → 14 B5
Leinster □ 11 E3
Leipzig 15 C7
Leiria 18 C1
Leitrim 11 D2
Leizhou Bandao 35 D6
Leksula 39 E3
Lékva Ori 23 G5
Leleque 95 E2
Léman, L. 13 C7
Lemhi Ra. 81 C7
Lena → 30 B10
Leninabad =
Khudzhand .. 29 E7
Leninakan =
Gyumri 25 E5
Leningrad =
Sankt-
Peterburg ... 24 B3
Leninogorsk =
Ridder 29 D9
Leninsk 25 D6
Leninsk-
Kuznetskiy .. 29 D9
Lenmalu 39 E4
Lens 13 A5
Lentini 21 F5
Leoben 15 E8
Leodhas =
Lewis 10 B3
León, Mexico . 84 C4
León, Nic. 85 E7
León, Spain .. 18 A3
León, Montañas
de 18 A2
Leongatha 63 C4
Léopold II, Lac
= Mai-
Ndombe, L. . 56 E3

Léopoldville =
Kinshasa 56 E3
Leova 17 E9
Lepel = Lyepyel 24 C2
Lepikha 31 C10
Léré 53 G1
Lérida 19 B6
Lerwick 10 A6
Les Cayes 86 C5
Les Sables-
d'Olonne .. 12 C3
Lesbos =
Lésvos 23 E6
Leskovac 22 C3
Lesotho ■ ... 59 D5
Lesser Antilles . 87 D7
Lesser Sunda Is. 39 F2
Lésvos 23 E6
Leszno 16 C3
Lethbridge ... 71 D8
Leti, Kepulauan 39 F3
Leti Is. = Leti,
Kepulauan .. 39 F3
Leticia 90 D4
Letpadan 41 J10
Letpan 41 H10
Letterkenny ... 11 D3
Leuser, G. 37 D1
Leuven 14 C3
Levádhia 23 E4
Levice 16 D4
Levin 64 D6
Lévis 69 D3
Levkás 23 E3
Levkôsia =
Nicosia 46 D3
Levskigrad =
Karlovo 22 C5
Lewis 10 B3
Lewisporte ... 69 D5
Lewiston, Idaho,
U.S.A. 80 B5
Lewiston,
Maine, U.S.A. 73 B10
Lexington, Ky.,
U.S.A. 72 E3
Lexington, N.C.,
U.S.A. 75 B7
Leyte 38 B2
Lezha 22 D2
Lhasa 34 D4
Lhazê 34 D3
Lhokkruet 36 D1
Lhokseumawe . 36 C1
Lhuntsi Dzong . 41 D8
Lianga 38 C3
Lianyungang .. 35 C6
Liaoning □ ... 35 B7
Liaoyuan 35 B7
Liard → 70 B7
Libau = Liepāja 24 B1
Libenge 56 D3
Liberal 78 A3
Liberec 16 C2
Liberia ■ 55 G3
Lîbîya, Sahrâ' . 52 C4
Libobo, Tanjung 39 E3
Libonda 58 A4
Libourne 12 D3
Libreville 56 D1
Libya ■ 52 C2
Libyan Desert =
Lîbîya, Sahrâ' 52 C4
Licantén 94 D2
Licata 21 F4
Lichinga 59 A7
Lichtenburg ... 59 D5
Lida 17 B7
Liechtenstein ■ 14 E5

Liège 14 C3
Liegnitz =
Legnica 16 C3
Lienyünchiangshih
=
Lianyungang . 35 C6
Lienz 15 E7
Liepāja 24 B1
Liffey → 11 E3
Lifford 11 D3
Lightning Ridge 63 A4
Liguria □ 20 B2
Ligurian Sea .. 20 C2
Lijiang 34 D5
Likasi 57 G5
Lille 13 A5
Lillehammer .. 8 F10
Lilongwe 59 A6
Liloy 38 C2
Lim → 20 C7
Lima, Indonesia 39 E3
Lima, Peru 91 F3
Lima, U.S.A. .. 72 D3
Limassol 46 D3
Limay Mahuida 94 D3
Limbang 36 D5
Limbe 56 D1
Limbri 63 B5
Limburg 14 C5
Limeira 94 A7
Limerick 11 E2
Limfjorden ... 9 G9
Limia =
Lima → 18 B1
Límnos 23 E5
Limoeiro do
Norte 92 D6
Limoges 12 D4
Limón 86 E3
Limousin 12 D4
Limoux 12 E5
Limpopo → .. 59 D6
Limuru 57 E7
Linares, Chile . 94 D2
Linares, Mexico 84 C5
Linares, Spain . 18 C4
Linchuan 35 D6
Lincoln,
Argentina ... 94 C4
Lincoln, N.Z. . 65 E5
Lincoln, U.K. .. 11 E6
Lincoln, U.S.A. 77 E6
Linden 90 B7
Líndhos 23 F7
Lindi 57 F7
Lingayen 38 A2
Lingayen G. ... 38 A2
Lingen 14 B4
Lingga 37 E2
Lingga,
Kepulauan . 37 E2
Lingga Arch. =
Lingga,
Kepulauan . 37 E2
Linguéré 55 E1
Lingyun 35 D5
Linhai 35 D7
Linhares 93 F5
Linköping 9 G11
Linosa, I. 21 G4
Lins 94 A7
Linville 63 A5
Linxia 34 C5
Linxi 12 D8
Lion, G. du .. 13 E6
Lions, G. of =
Lion, G. du .. 13 E6
Lipa 38 B2

128

Lípari 21 E5
Lípari, Is. =
  Eólie, Ís. 21 E5
Lipcani 17 D8
Lipetsk 24 C4
Lipkany =
  Lipcani 17 D8
Lipovets 17 D9
Lippe → 14 C4
Liptrap C. 63 C4
Lira 57 D6
Liria 19 C5
Lisala 56 D4
Lisboa 18 C1
Lisbon = Lisboa 18 C1
Lisburn 11 D3
Lisburne, C. ... 71 B3
Lishui 35 D6
Lisichansk =
  Lysychansk . 25 D4
Lisieux 12 B4
Liski 24 C4
Lismore 63 A5
Lister, Mt. 96 B15
Liston 63 A5
Listowel 11 E2
Litang 38 C1
Litani → 46 D3
Lithgow 63 B5
Líthinon, Ákra . 23 G5
Lithuania ■ ... 24 B1
Litoměřice 16 C2
Little Barrier I. . 64 B6
Little Laut Is. =
  Laut Kecil,
  Kepulauan .. 37 E5
Little
  Missouri → . 76 B3
Little River ... 65 E5
Little Rock 79 B7
Liukang
  Tenggaja ... 39 F1
Liuwa Plain ... 58 A4
Liuzhou 35 D5
Liverpool,
  Australia 63 B5
Liverpool,
  Canada 69 D4
Liverpool, U.K. 11 E5
Liverpool Plains 63 B5
Liverpool Ra. .. 63 B5
Livingstone ... 59 B5
Livingstonia .. 57 G6
Livny 24 C4
Livorno 20 C3
Livramento ... 94 C5
Liwale 57 F7
Ljubljana 20 A5
Ljungan → .. · 8 F11
Ljusnan → ... 8 F11
Llancanelo,
  Salina 94 D3
Llanelli 11 F4
Llanes 18 A3
Llano Estacado 78 C2
Llanos 90 C4
Lleida = Lérida 19 B6
Llobregat → .. 19 B7
Lloret de Mar . 19 B7
Lluchmayor ... 19 C7
Llullaillaco,
  Volcán 94 A3
Loa → 94 A2
Lobatse 59 D5
Lobería 94 D5
Lobito 58 A2
Locarno 13 C8
Loch Garman =
  Wexford 11 E3

Loches 12 C4
Lock 62 B2
Lodhran 42 E7
Lodi, Italy 20 B2
Lodi, U.S.A. ... 80 F3
Lodja 56 E4
Lodwar 57 D7
Łódź 16 C4
Lofoten 8 E10
Logan 81 E8
Logan, Mt. =
  Pierre Elliott
  Trudeau, Mt. .. 70 B5
Logone → 53 F2
Logroño 19 A4
Lohardaga ... 40 F5
Loi-kaw 41 H11
Loir → 12 C3
Loire → 12 C2
Loja, Ecuador . 90 D3
Loja, Spain ... 18 D3
Loji 39 E3
Lokandu 57 E5
Lokitaung 57 D7
Lokolama 56 E3
Loliondo 57 E7
Lom 22 C4
Lomami → ... 56 D4
Lombardy =
  Lombárdia □ 20 B2
Lomblen 39 F2
Lombok 37 F5
Lomé 55 G5
Lomela 56 E4
Lomela → 56 E4
Lomié 56 D2
Lomond, L. ... 10 C4
Lompobatang . 39 F1
Łomza 16 B6
Loncoche 95 D2
Londa 43 M9
London 11 F6
Londonderry .. 11 D3
Londonderry, C. 60 C4
Londonderry, I. 95 H2
Londrina 94 A6
Long Beach ... 82 D3
Long I.,
  Bahamas ... 86 B4
Long I., U.S.A. . 73 D9
Long Xuyen ... 36 B3
Longford,
  Australia 62 D4
Longford,
  Ireland 11 E3
Longiram 37 E5
Longlac 69 D2
Longnawan ... 37 D4
Longreach 61 E7
Longview, Tex.,
  U.S.A. 79 C6
Longview,
  Wash., U.S.A. 80 B2
Lons-le-Saunier 13 C6
Lop Nor = Lop
  Nur 34 B4
Lopez, C. 56 E1
Lora → 42 D4
Lora, Hamun-i- 42 E4
Lora Cr. → ... 62 A2
Lora del Río ... 18 D3
Lorain 72 D4
Loralai 42 D6
Lorca 19 D5
Lorestān □ ... 46 D6
Loreto 92 D4
Lorient 12 C2
Lorne 62 C3

Lorraine 13 B7
Los Alamos ... 83 C9
Los Andes ... 94 C2
Los Angeles,
  Chile 94 D2
Los Angeles,
  U.S.A. 82 C3
Los Blancos ... 94 A4
Los Hermanos . 90 A6
Los Mochis ... 84 B3
Los Roques ... 90 A5
Los Testigos .. 90 A6
Los Vilos 94 C2
Lošinj 20 B5
Lot → 12 D4
Lota 94 D2
Loubomo 56 E2
Louga 55 E1
Louis Trichardt 59 C5
Louis XIV, Pte. . 69 C3
Louisiade Arch. 61 C9
Louisiana □ ... 79 D8
Louisville 72 E3
Loulé 18 D1
Lourdes 12 E3
Louth, Australia 63 B4
Louth, U.K. ... 11 E6
Louvain =
  Leuven 14 C3
Lovech 22 C5
Low Tatra =
  Nízké Tatry . 16 D4
Lowell 73 C10
Lower California
  = Baja
  California ... 84 A1
Lower Hutt 65 D6
Lower Saxony =
  Niedersachsen □
  .... 14 B5
Lower Tunguska
  = Tunguska,
  Nizhnyaya → 30 C6
Lowestoft 11 E7
Łowicz 16 B4
Lowyar □ 45 C7
Loxton 62 B3
Loyalty Is. =
  Loyauté, Is. . 64 M11
Loyang =
  Luoyang ... 35 C6
Loyauté, Is. ... 64 M11
Loyev = Loyew 17 C10
Loyew 17 C10
Luachimo 56 F4
Luacono 56 G4
Lualaba → ... 57 D5
Luanda 56 F2
Luangwa 59 B6
Luangwa → .. 59 A6
Luanshya 59 A5
Luapula → ... 57 F5
Luarca 18 A2
Luashi 56 G4
Luau 56 G4
Lubalo 56 F3
Lubang Is. 38 B2
Lubbock 78 C3
Lübeck 15 B6
Lubefu 56 E4
Lubero = Luofu 57 E5
Lubin 16 C3
Lublin 17 C6
Lubuagan 38 A2
Lubuk Antu ... 37 D4
Lubuklinggau . 37 E2
Lubuksikaping . 37 D2
Lubumbashi .. 59 A5
Lubutu 57 E5

Lucca 20 C3
·Lucena, Phil. .. 38 B2
Lucena, Spain . 18 D3
Lučenec 16 D4
Lucerne =
  Luzern 13 C8
Lucira 58 A2
Luckenwalde .. 15 B7
Lucknow 40 D3
Lüda = Dalian . 35 C7
Lüderitz 58 D3
Ludhiana 42 D9
Ludwigsburg . 14 D5
Ludwigshafen . 14 D5
Luebo 56 F4
Lufira → 57 F5
Lufkin 79 D6
Luga 24 B2
Lugano 13 C8
Lugansk =
  Luhansk 25 D4
Lugh Ganana . 49 G3
Lugo, Italy 20 B3
Lugo, Spain ... 18 A2
Lugoj 17 F5
Lugovoy 29 E8
Luhansk 25 D4
Luiana 58 B4
Luimneach =
  Limerick 11 E2
Luís Correia ... 92 C5
Luitpold Coast . 96 B5
Luiza 56 F4
Luján 94 C5
Lukanga Swamp 59 A5
Lukenie → ... 56 E3
Lukolela 56 E3
Łuków 17 C6
Lule älv → ... 8 E12
Luleå 8 E12
Lüleburgaz ... 22 D6
Lulonga → ... 56 D3
Lulua → 56 E4
Luluabourg =
  Kananga ... 56 F4
Lumai 58 A4
Lumbala
  N'guimbo ... 58 A4
Lumsden 65 F3
Lumut, Tg. 37 E3
Lundazi 59 A6
Lundu 37 D3
Lüneburg 14 B6
Lüneburg Heath
  = Lüneburger
  Heide 14 B6
Lüneburger
  Heide 14 B6
Lunéville 13 B7
Lunglei 41 F9
Luni 42 G8
Luni → 43 G7
Luninets =
  Luninyets ... 17 B8
Luninyets 17 B8
Luofu 57 E5
Luoyang 35 C6
Luozi 56 E2
Luremo 56 F3
Lurgan 11 D3
Lusaka 59 B5
Lusambo 56 E4
Lushnja 23 D2
Lushoto 57 E7
Luta = Dalian . 35 C7
Luton 11 F6
Lutong 36 D4
Lutsk 17 C7

Lützow
  Holmbukta .. 96 A8
Luwuk 39 E2
Luxembourg .. 13 B7
Luxembourg ■ 14 D4
Luxor = El
  Uqsur 52 C5
Luza 24 A6
Luzern 13 C8
Luzhou 35 D5
Luziânia 93 F4
Luzon 38 A2
Lviv 17 D7
Lvov = Lviv ... 17 D7
Lyakhavichy .. 17 B8
Lyakhovskiye,
  Ostrova 31 B12
Lyallpur =
  Faisalabad .. 42 D8
Lydenburg 59 D6
Lydia 23 E7
Lyell 65 D5
Lyepyel 24 C2
Łyna → 16 A5
Lynchburg ... 73 F6
Lynd Ra. 63 A4
Lyndhurst 62 B2
Lynn Lake 71 C9
Lyon 13 D6
Lyonnais .. 13 D6
Lyons = Lyon . 13 D6
Lys = Leie → . 14 C2
Lysychansk .. 25 D4
Lyttelton 65 E5
Lyubertsy 24 B4
Lyuboml 17 C7

M

Ma'alah 47 F6
Ma'ān 47 E3
Ma'anshan 35 C6
Ma'arrat an
  Nu'mān 46 D4
Maas → 14 C3
Maastricht 13 A6
Mabrouk 55 E4
Macaé 93 G5
McAllen 78 F4
Macao =
  Macau ■ ... 35 D6
Macapá 92 B3
Macau 92 D6
Macau ■ ... 35 D6
M'Clintock Chan. 70 A9
McComb 79 D8
MacDonnell Ras. 60 E5
McDouall Peak 62 A1
Macdougall L. . 70 B10
Macedonia =
  Makedhonía □ 23 D4
Macedonia ■ .. 22 D3
Maceió 93 D6
Macenta 55 G3
Macerata 20 C4
Macfarlane, L. . 62 B2
Macgillycuddy's
  Reeks 11 F2
McGregor Ra. . 62 A3
Mach 42 E5
Machado =
  Jiparaná → . 91 E6
Machakos 57 E7
Machala 90 D3
Machilipatnam 40 J3
Machiques 90 A4

Machupicchu .. 91 F4
Macintyre → . 63 A5
Mackay 61 E8
Mackay, L. 60 E4
Mackenzie → . 70 B6
Mackenzie City
  = Linden ... 90 B7
Mackenzie Mts. 70 B6
McKinley, Mt. . 71 B4
McKinney 79 C5
Macksville 63 B5
Maclean 63 A5
Maclear 59 E5
Macleay → ... 63 B5
McMurdo Sd. . 96 B15
Mâcon, France . 13 C6
Macon, U.S.A. . 75 C6
Macondo 58 A4
McPherson Ra. . 63 A5
Macquarie
  Harbour 62 D4
MacRobertson
  Land 96 B10
Madagali 53 F1
Madagascar ■ . 59 J9
Madā'in Sālih . 47 F4
Madama 52 D1
Madang 61 B8
Madaoua 55 F6
Madaripur 41 F8
Madauk 41 J11
Madaya 41 F11
Maddalena ... 20 D2
Madeira 54 B1
Madeira → ... 90 D7
Madha 43 L9
Madhya
  Pradesh □ .. 43 H10
Madikeri 43 N9
Madimba 56 E3
Madīnat ash
  Sha'b 49 E3
Madingou 56 E2
Madison 77 D10
Madiun 37 F4
Madras = Tamil
  Nadu □ 43 P10
Madras 43 N12
Madre, Laguna 78 F5
Madre, Sierra . 38 A2
Madre de
  Dios → 91 F5
Madre de Dios,
  I. 95 G1
Madre
  Occidental,
  Sierra 84 B3
Madrid 18 B4
Madurai 43 Q11
Madurantakam 43 N11
Mae Sot 36 A1
Maebashi 32 A6
Maestrazgo,
  Mts. del 19 B5
Maevatanana . 59 H9
Mafeking =
  Mafikeng .. 59 D5
Maffra 63 C4
Mafia I. 57 F7
Mafikeng 59 D5
Mafra, Brazil . 94 B7
Mafra, Portugal 18 C1
Magadan 31 D13
Magadi 57 E7
Magallanes,
  Estrecho de . 95 G2
Magangué 90 B4
Magburaka ... 55 G2
Magdalena,
  Argentina .. 94 D5

Magdalena,
  Bolivia 91 F6
Magdalena,
  Malaysia 36 D5
Magdalena → . 90 A4
Magdeburg ... 15 B6
Magelang 37 F4
Magellan's Str.
  = Magallanes,
  Estrecho de . 95 G2
Maggiore, L. .. 20 B2
Magnetic Pole
  (South) =
  South
  Magnetic Pole 96 A13
Magnitogorsk . 29 D6
Magosa =
  Famagusta .. 46 D3
Maguarinho, C. 92 C4
Mağusa =
  Famagusta .. 46 D3
Magwe 41 G10
Mahābād 46 C6
Mahabo 59 J8
Mahagi 57 D6
Mahajanga ... 59 H9
Mahakam → . 37 E5
Mahalapye ... 59 C5
Mahallāt 44 C2
Mahanadi → . 40 G6
Mahanoro 59 H9
Maharashtra □ 43 J9
Mahbubnagar . 43 L10
Mahdia 52 A1
Mahenge 57 F7
Maheno 65 F4
Mahesana 43 H8
Mahia Pen. ... 64 C7
Mahilyow 17 B10
Mahón 19 C8
Mai-Ndombe, L. 56 E3
Maicurú → ... 92 C3
Maidstone ... 11 F7
Maiduguri ... 53 F1
Maijdi 41 F8
Maikala Ra. .. 40 G3
Main → 14 D5
Maine 12 C3
Maingkwan ... 41 D11
Mainit, L. 38 C3
Mainland,
  Orkney, U.K. 10 B5
Mainland, Shet.,
  U.K. 10 A6
Maintirano 59 H8
Mainz 14 C5
Maipú 94 D5
Maiquetía 90 A5
Mairabari 41 D9
Maitland,
  N.S.W.,
  Australia 63 B5
Maitland,
  S. Austral.,
  Australia 62 B2
Maizuru 32 B4
Majene 39 E1
Maji 53 G6
Majorca =
  Mallorca ... 19 C7
Maka 55 F2
Makale 39 E1
Makari 56 B2
Makarikari =
  Makgadikgadi
  Salt Pans ... 59 C5
Makasar =
  Ujung
  Pandang ... 39 F1

Makasar, Selat 39 E1
Makasar, Str. of
  = Makasar,
  Selat 39 E1
Makat 29 E6
Makedhonía □ 23 D4
Makedonija =
  Macedonia ■ 22 D3
Makeni 55 G2
Makeyevka =
  Makiyivka ... 25 D4
Makgadikgadi
  Salt Pans .. 59 C5
Makhachkala . 25 E6
Makian 39 D3
Makindu 57 E7
Makinsk 29 D8
Makiyivka ... 25 D4
Makkah 47 G4
Makó 16 E5
Makokou 56 D2
Makoua 56 E3
Makrai 43 H10
Makran 45 E5
Makran Coast
  Range 42 G4
Maksimkin Yar 29 D9
Mākū 46 C6
Makumbi 56 F4
Makurazaki .. 33 D2
Makurdi 55 G6
Malabang ... 38 C2
Malabar Coast . 43 P9
Malabo = Rey
  Malabo 56 D1
Malacca, Str. of 36 D1
Maladzyechna . 17 A8
Málaga 18 D3
Malakâl 53 G5
Malakand ... 42 B7
Malang 37 F4
Malanje 56 F3
Mälaren 9 G11
Malargüe 94 D3
Malaryta 17 C7
Malatya 46 C4
Malawi ■ 59 A6
Malawi, L. 59 A6
Malaybalay .. 38 C3
Mālāyer 46 D7
Malaysia ■ ... 36 D4
Malazgirt 46 C5
Malbooma ... 62 B1
Malbork 16 A4
Malden I. 65 K15
Maldives ■ ... 26 J11
Maldonado ... 94 C6
Malé Karpaty . 16 D3
Maléa, Ákra .. 23 F4
Malegaon 43 J9
Malema 59 A7
Malha 53 E4
Mali ■ 55 F4
Mali → 41 E11
Malik 39 E2
Malili 39 E2
Malin Hd. 10 D3
Malindi 57 E8
Malines =
  Mechelen ... 14 C3
Malino 39 D2
Malita 38 C3
Malkara 22 D6
Mallacoota .. 63 C4
Mallacoota Inlet 63 C4
Mallaig 10 C4
Mallawi 52 C5
Mallorca 19 C7
Mallow 11 E2

Malmö	9	G10
Malolos	38	B2
Malpelo	90	C2
Malta ■	21	G5
Maltahöhe	58	C3
Maluku	39	E3
Maluku □	39	E3
Maluku Sea =		
Molucca Sea	39	E2
Malvan	43	L8
Malvinas, Is. =		
Falkland Is. □	95	G5
Malyn	17	C9
Malyy Lyakhovskiy,		
Ostrov	31	B12
Mamahatun	46	C5
Mamanguape	92	D6
Mamasa	39	E1
Mamberamo →	39	E5
Mambilima Falls	57	G5
Mamburao	38	B2
Mamfe	55	G6
Mamoré →	91	F5
Mamou	55	F2
Mamuju	39	E1
Man	55	G3
Man, I. of	11	D4
Man Na	41	F11
Mana	92	A3
Manaar, G. of =		
Mannar, G. of	43	Q11
Manacapuru	90	D6
Manacor	19	C7
Manado	39	D2
Managua	85	E7
Manakara	59	J9
Manama = Al		
Manāmah	44	E2
Mananara	59	H9
Mananjary	59	J9
Manaos =		
Manaus	90	D7
Manapouri	65	F2
Manapouri, L.	65	F2
Manas	34	B3
Manas →	41	D8
Manasir	44	E2
Manaung	41	H9
Manaus	90	D7
Manay	38	C3
Manchester, U.K.	11	E5
Manchester, U.S.A.	73	C10
Mand →	44	D3
Manda	57	G6
Mandal	9	G9
Mandalay	41	F11
Mandale =		
Mandalay	41	F11
Mandalī	46	D6
Mandar, Teluk	39	E1
Mandaue	38	B2
Mandi	42	D10
Mandimba	59	A7
Mandioli	39	E3
Mandla	40	F3
Mandritsara	59	H9
Mandsaur	43	G9
Mandvi	43	H6
Mandya	43	N10
Manfalût	52	C5
Manfred	63	B3
Manfredónia	20	D5
Mangalia	22	C7
Mangalore	43	N9
Mangaweka	64	C6
Manggar	37	E3
Manggawitu	39	E4
Mangkalihat,		
Tanjung	39	D1
Mangla Dam	42	C8
Mangnai	34	C4
Mango	55	F5
Mangoche	59	A7
Mangole	39	E3
Mangonui	64	A5
Mangueigne	53	F3
Mangueira, L. da	94	C6
Mangyshlak		
Poluostrov	29	E6
Manhuaçu	93	G5
Manica	59	B6
Manicoré	91	E6
Manicouagan →	69	D4
Manīfah	47	F7
Manihiki	65	L14
Manila	38	B2
Manila B.	38	B2
Manilla	63	B5
Manipur □	41	E9
Manipur →	41	F10
Manisa	23	E6
Manitoba □	71	C10
Manitoba, L.	71	C10
Manitowoc	72	B2
Manizales	90	B3
Manja	59	J8
Manjacaze	59	C6
Manjhand	42	G6
Manjil	46	C7
Manjra →	43	K10
Mankono	55	G3
Manly	63	B5
Manmad	43	J9
Manna	37	E2
Mannahill	62	B3
Mannar	43	Q11
Mannar, G. of	43	Q11
Mannar I.	43	Q11
Mannheim	14	D5
Mannum	62	B2
Mano	55	G2
Manokwari	39	E4
Manombo	59	J8
Manono	57	F5
Manosque	13	E6
Manresa	19	B6
Mansa	57	G5
Mansel I.	68	B2
Mansfield, Australia	63	C4
Mansfield, U.K.	11	E6
Mansfield, U.S.A.	72	D4
Manta	90	D2
Mantalingajan, Mt.	36	C5
Mantes-la-Jolie	12	B4
Manthani	43	K11
Mantiqueira,		
Serra da	93	G5
Mántova	20	B3
Mantua =		
Mántova	20	B3
Manu	91	F4
Manuae	65	L15
Manuel		
Alves →	93	E4
Manui	39	E2
Manyara, L.	57	E7
Manych-Gudilo,		
Ozero	25	D5
Manyoni	57	F6
Manzai	42	C7
Manzanares	18	C4
Manzanillo, Cuba	86	B4
Manzanillo, Mexico	84	D4
Manzhouli	35	B6
Mao	53	F2
Maoke, Pegunungan	39	E5
Maoming	35	D6
Mapam Yumco	40	B3
Mapia, Kepulauan	39	D4
Mapuera →	90	D7
Maputo	59	D6
Maqnā	47	E3
Maquela do Zombo	56	F3
Maquinchao	95	E3
Mar, Serra do	94	B7
Mar Chiquita, L.	94	C4
Mar del Plata	94	D5
Mar Menor	19	D5
Maraã	90	D5
Marabá	92	D4
Maracá, I. de	92	B3
Maracaibo	90	A4
Maracaibo, L. de	90	B4
Maracay	90	A5
Marādah	52	C2
Maradi	55	F6
Marāgheh	46	C6
Marāh	47	F6
Marajó, I. de	92	C4
Maralal	57	D7
Marama	62	C3
Marampa	55	G2
Marand	46	C6
Maranguape	92	C6
Maranhão =		
São Luís	92	C5
Maranhão □	92	D4
Maranoa →	63	A4
Marañón →	90	D4
Marão	59	C6
Maraş =		
Kahramanmaraş	46	C4
Maratua	39	D1
Marbella	18	D3
Marburg	14	C5
Marche	12	C4
Marchena	18	D3
Mardan	42	B8
Mardin	46	C5
Marek = Stanke		
Dimitrov	22	C4
Marek	39	E2
Margarita, I. de	90	A6
Margate	11	F7
Margelan =		
Marghilon	29	E8
Marghilon	29	E8
Mari El □	24	B6
Mari Republic □		
= Mari El □	24	B6
Maria I.	62	D4
Maria van		
Diemen, C.	64	A5
Mariana Trench	64	H9
Marianao	86	B3
Ma'rib	49	D4
Maribor	20	A5
Marīdī	53	H4
Marie Byrd Land	96	B18
Marie-Galante	87	C7
Mariecourt =		
Kangiqsujuaq	68	B3
Mariental	58	C3
Mariinsk	29	D9
Marília	93	G3
Marín	18	A1
Marinduque	38	B2
Maringá	94	A6
Marion	79	A9
Mariscal		
Estigarribia	91	H6
Maritime Alps =		
Maritimes, Alpes	13	D7
Maritimes, Alpes	13	D7
Maritsa =		
Évros →	22	D6
Mariupol	25	D4
Marīvān	46	D6
Markazi □	44	C2
Markham, Mt.	96	C15
Marks	24	C6
Marla	62	A1
Marmagao	43	M8
Marmara	23	D6
Marmara, Sea of		
= Marmara Denizi	22	D7
Marmara Denizi	22	D7
Marmaris	23	F7
Marmolada, Mte.	20	A3
Marne →	12	B5
Maroantsetra	59	H9
Marondera	59	B6
Maroni →	92	A3
Maroochydore	63	A5
Maroona	62	C3
Maroua	53	F1
Marovoay	59	H9
Marquesas Is. =		
Marquises, Is.	65	K17
Marquette	69	D2
Marquises, Is.	65	K17
Marrakech	54	B3
Marrawah	62	D3
Marree	62	A2
Marromeu	59	B7
Marrowie Cr. →	63	B4
Marrupa	59	A7
Marsá Matrûh	52	B4
Marsá Susah	52	B3
Marsabit	57	D7
Marsala	21	F4
Marsden	63	B4
Marseille	13	E6
Marseilles =		
Marseille	13	E6
Marshall, Liberia	55	G2
Marshall, U.S.A.	79	C6
Marshall Is. ■	64	J12
Marshalltown	77	D8
Martaban	41	J11
Martaban, G. of	41	J11
Martapura, Kalimantan, Indonesia	37	E4
Martapura, Sumatera, Indonesia	37	E2
Marte	53	F1
Martigny	13	C7
Martigues	13	E6
Martin	16	D4
Martina Franca	21	D6
Martinborough	65	D6
Martinique ■	87	D7
Martinique Passage	87	C7
Martinsville	75	A8
Marton	64	D6
Martos	18	D4
Marudi	37	D4

Ma'ruf

Ma'ruf 42 D5
Marugame 32 B3
Marulan 63 B5
Marwar 42 G8
Mary 29 F7
Maryborough =
  Port Laoise .. 11 E3
Maryborough,
  Queens.,
  Australia 63 A5
Maryborough,
  Vic., Australia 62 C3
Maryland □ ... 73 E7
Maryvale 63 A5
Marzūq 52 C1
Masaka 57 E6
Masalembo,
  Kepulauan .. 37 F4
Masalima,
  Kepulauan .. 37 F5
Masamba 39 E2
Masan 35 C7
Masandam, Ras 44 E4
Masasi 57 G7
Masaya 85 E7
Masbate 38 B2
Mascara 54 A5
Masela 39 F3
Maseru 59 D5
Mashābih 47 F4
Mashhad 44 B4
Mashike 32 F12
Mashkel,
  Hamun-i- ... 42 E3
Mashki Chāh .. 42 E3
Masi Manimba 56 E3
Masindi 57 D6
Masisea 91 E4
Masjed
  Soleyman ... 47 E7
Mask, L. 11 E2
Masohi 39 E3
Mason City ... 77 D8
Masqat 45 F4
Massa 20 B3
Massachusetts □
  .... 73 C9
Massaguet ... 53 F2
Massakory 53 F2
Massangena .. 59 C6
Massawa =
  Mitsiwa 53 E6
Massena 73 B8
Massénya 53 F2
Massif Central . 13 D5
Massinga 59 C7
Masson I. 96 A11
Mastanli =
  Momchilgrad 22 D5
Masterton 65 D6
Mastuj 42 A8
Mastung 42 E5
Masty 17 B7
Masuda 32 B2
Masvingo 59 C6
Mataboor 39 E5
Matad 35 B6
Matadi 56 F2
Matagalpa 85 E7
Matagami, L. .. 69 D3
Matak, P. 37 D3
Matakana 63 B4
Matam 55 E2
Matamoros,
  Coahuila,
  Mexico 84 B4
Matamoros,
  Tamaulipas,
  Mexico 84 B5

Ma'ṭan as Sarra 52 D3
Matane 69 D4
Matanzas 86 B3
Matapan, C. =
  Taínaron, Ákra 23 F4
Mataram 37 F5
Matarani 91 G4
Mataró 19 B7
Mataura 65 G3
Matehuala 84 C4
Matera 21 D6
Mathura 42 F10
Mati 38 C3
Matiri Ra. 65 D5
Matmata 54 B6
Mato Grosso □ 93 E3
Mato Grosso,
  Planalto do .. 93 F3
Mato Grosso do
  Sul □ 93 F3
Matochkin Shar 28 B6
Matosinhos ... 18 B1
Matrah 45 F4
Matsue 32 B3
Matsumoto ... 32 A6
Matsusaka ... 32 B5
Matsuyama ... 32 C3
Mattagami → . 69 C2
Mattancheri .. 43 Q10
Matterhorn ... 13 D7
Matthew's Ridge 90 B6
Matucana 91 F3
Matun 42 C6
Maturín 90 B6
Mau Ranipur .. 43 G11
Maubeuge ... 13 A5
Maude 63 B3
Maudin Sun ... 41 K10
Maués 90 D7
Mauganj 40 E3
Maui 82 H12
Maulamyaing =
  Moulmein ... 41 J11
Maumere 39 F2
Maun 58 B4
Maungmagan
  Kyunzu 41 K11
Mauritania ■ .. 55 D2
Mauritius ■ ... 51 H9
Mavinga 58 B4
Mawk Mai ... 41 G11
Mawlaik 41 F10
Mawson Coast 96 A10
Maxixe 59 C7
Mayaguana ... 87 B5
Mayagüez 87 C6
Maydena 62 D4
Mayenne → .. 12 C3
Maykop 25 E5
Mayo 70 B6
Mayo L. 70 B6
Mayon Volcano 38 B2
Mayor I. 64 B7
Mayu 39 D3
Mazabuka ... 59 B5
Mazagán = El
  Jadida 54 B3
Mazagão 92 C3
Mazán 90 D4
Māzandarān □ 44 B3
Mazar-e Sharīf . 45 B6
Mazara del Vallo 21 F4
Mazarredo ... 95 F3
Mazarrón 19 D5
Mazaruni → .. 90 B7
Mazatlán 84 C3
Māzhān 44 C4
Mazīnān 44 B4
Mazoe → 59 B6

Mazurian Lakes
  = Mazurski,
  Pojezierze ... 16 B5
Mazurski,
  Pojezierze ... 16 B5
Mazyr 17 C9
Mbabane 59 D6
Mbaïki 56 D3
Mbala 57 F6
Mbale 57 D6
Mbalmayo ... 56 D2
Mbamba Bay .. 57 G6
Mbandaka ... 56 D3
Mbanza Congo 56 F2
Mbanza Ngungu 56 F2
Mbarara 57 E6
Mbeya 57 F6
Mbini □ 56 D2
Mbour 55 F1
Mbout 55 E2
Mbuji-Mayi ... 56 F4
Mbulu 57 E7
Mchinji 59 A6
Mead, L. 82 B5
Mearim → 92 C5
Meaux 13 B5
Mecca =
  Makkah 47 G4
Mechelen 14 C3
Mecheria 54 B4
Mecklenburg .. 15 B6
Mecklenburger
  Bucht 15 A6
Meconta 59 A7
Medan 37 D1
Medanosa, Pta. 95 F3
Medéa 54 A5
Medellín 90 B3
Mederdra 55 E1
Medford 80 D2
Medgidia 22 B7
Mediaş 17 E7
Medicine Bow
  Ra. 81 E10
Medicine Hat .. 71 C8
Medina = Al
  Madīnah ... 47 F4
Medina del
  Campo 18 B3
Medina-Sidonia 18 D3
Medinipur 40 F6
Mediterranean
  Sea 50 C5
Médoc 12 D3
Medveditsa → 24 D5
Medvezhyegorsk 28 C4
Meekatharra .. 60 F2
Meerut 42 E10
Mega 53 H6
Mégara 23 F4
Meghalaya □ .. 41 E8
Mei Xian 35 D6
Meiganga 56 C2
Meiktila 41 G10
Meissen 15 C7
Mejillones ... 94 A2
Mékambo 56 D2
Mekdela 53 F6
Mekhtar 42 D6
Meknès 54 B3
Mekong → ... 36 C3
Mekongga ... 39 E2
Mekvari =
  Kür → 25 E6
Melagiri Hills .. 43 N10
Melaka 37 D2
Melalap 36 C5
Melanesia ... 64 K10
Melbourne,
  Australia 63 C3

Melbourne,
  U.S.A. 75 E7
Mélèzes → ... 68 C3
Melfi 53 F2
Melfort 71 C9
Melilla 19 E4
Melitopol 25 D4
Melk 15 D8
Melo 94 C6
Melolo 39 F2
Melrose 63 B4
Melun 13 B5
Melut 53 F5
Melville 71 C9
Melville I. 60 C5
Melville Pen. .. 68 B2
Memba 59 G8
Memboro 39 F1
Memel =
  Klaìpeda 24 B1
Memmingen .. 14 E6
Mempawah ... 37 D3
Memphis, *Tenn.,*
  U.S.A. 74 B3
Memphis, *Tex.,*
  U.S.A. 78 B3
Ménaka 55 E5
Menan = Chao
  Phraya → . 36 B2
Menate 37 E4
Mendawai → . 37 E4
Mende 13 D5
Mendocino, C. . 80 E1
Mendoza 94 C3
Mene Grande . 90 B4
Menemen ... 23 E6
Menggala ... 37 E3
Mengzi 34 D5
Menindee 62 B3
Menindee L. .. 62 B3
Meningie 62 C2
Menominee .. 72 B2
Menongue ... 58 A3
Menorca 19 C7
Mentawai,
  Kepulauan .. 37 E1
Menton 13 E7
Meppel 14 B4
Merabéllou,
  Kólpos 23 G5
Meran =
  Merano 20 A3
Merano 20 A3
Merauke 39 F6
Merbein 62 B3
Merca 49 G3
Merced 82 B2
Mercedes,
  Buenos Aires,
  Argentina ... 94 C5
Mercedes,
  Corrientes,
  Argentina ... 94 B5
Mercedes,
  San Luis,
  Argentina ... 94 C3
Mercedes,
  Uruguay 94 C5
Merceditas ... 94 B2
Mercer 64 B6
Mercy C. 68 B4
Meredith, C. .. 95 G4
Merga =
  Nukheila ... 53 E4
Mergui Arch. =
  Myeik Kyunzu 36 B1
Mérida, *Mexico* 85 C7
Mérida, *Spain* . 18 C2

Mérida,
   Venezuela . . . 90 B4
Mérida, Cord. de 87 E5
Meridian 74 C3
Meriruma 92 B3
Merowe 53 E5
Merriwa 63 B5
Merriwagga . . . 63 B4
Merrygoen 63 B4
Mersa Fatma . . 49 E3
Merseburg 15 C6
Mersin 46 C3
Mersing 37 D2
Merthyr Tydfil . 11 F5
Mértola 18 D2
Meru 57 D7
Mesa 83 D7
Meshed =
   Mashhad . . . 44 B4
Meshra er Req . 53 G4
Mesolóngion . . 23 E3
Mesopotamia =
   Al Jazirah . . . 46 D5
Messina, *Italy* . 21 E5
Messina,
   S. Africa 59 C6
Messina, Str. di 21 E5
Messíni 23 F4
Messiniakós
   Kólpos 23 F4
Mesta → 22 D5
Meta → 90 B5
Metairie 79 E8
Metán 94 B4
Metangula 59 A6
Metema 53 F6
Methven 65 E4
Metil 59 B7
Metlakatla 71 C6
Mettur Dam . . . 43 P10
Metz 13 B7
Meulaboh 37 D1
Meureudu 36 C1
Meuse → 13 A6
Mexiana, I. 92 C4
Mexicali 84 A1
México 84 D5
México □ 84 D5
Mexico ■ 84 C4
Mexico, G. of . . 85 B7
Meymaneh . . . 42 B4
Mezen 28 C5
Mezen → 28 C5
Mézene 13 D6
Mezőkövesd . . 16 E5
Mezőtúr 16 E5
Mhow 43 H9
Miami 75 G7
Miami Beach . . 75 G7
Miándowāb . . . 46 C6
Miandrivazo . . 59 H9
Miāneh 46 C6
Mianwali 42 C7
Miaoli 35 D7
Miarinarivo . . . 59 H9
Miass 29 D7
Michalovce . . . 17 D5
Michigan □ . . . 72 C3
Michigan, L. . . . 72 C2
Michipicoten . . 69 D2
Michurin 22 C6
Michurinsk 24 C5
Micronesia,
   Federated
   States of ■ . . 64 J10
Middelburg . . . 58 E5
Middlesbrough 11 D6
Midi, Canal
   du → 12 E4

Midland 78 D3
Midyat 46 C5
Midzŏr 22 C4
Międzychód . . . 16 B2
Międzyrzec
   Podlaski 17 C6
Mielec 16 C5
Miercurea Ciuc 17 E7
Mieres 18 A3
Miguel Alves . . 92 C5
Mihara 32 B3
Mikhaylovgrad 22 C4
Míkonos 23 F5
Mikura-Jima . . 32 C6
Milagro 90 D3
Milan = Milano 20 B2
Milang 62 B2
Milano 20 B2
Milâs 23 F6
Milazzo 21 E5
Mildura 62 B3
Miles 63 A5
Miletus 23 F6
Milford Haven . 11 F4
Milford Sd. 65 F2
Milḥ, Baḥr al . . 47 D5
Miliana 54 C5
Mill I. 96 A12
Millau 13 D5
Millicent 62 C3
Millinocket 73 B11
Millmerran 63 A5
Milne Inlet 68 A2
Mílos 23 F5
Milparinka P.O. 62 A3
Milton 65 G3
Milton Keynes . 11 E6
Miltou 53 F2
Milwaukee 72 C2
Min Chiang → . 35 D6
Min Jiang → . . 35 D5
Mina Pirquitas . 94 A3
Mīnā Su'ud . . . 47 E7
Mīnā'al Aḥmadī 47 E7
Mīnāb 44 E4
Minamata 32 C2
Minas 94 C5
Minas Gerais □ 93 F4
Minbu 41 G10
Mindanao 38 C2
Mindanao Sea =
   Bohol Sea . . 38 C2
Mindanao
   Trench 38 B3
Minden 14 B5
Mindiptana . . . 39 F6
Mindoro 38 B2
Mindoro Str. . . 38 B2
Mindouli 56 E2
Mingäçevir Su
   Anbarı 25 E6
Mingan 69 C4
Mingechaurskoye
   Vdkhr. =
   Mingäçevir Su
   Anbarı 25 E6
Mingin 41 F10
Mingt'iehkaitafan
   = Mintaka
   Pass 42 A9
Minho =
   Miño → 18 B1
Minho 18 B1
Minna 55 G6
Minneapolis . . . 77 C8
Minnedosa . . . 71 C10
Minnesota □ . . 77 B7
Minnipa 62 B2
Miño → 18 B1

Minorca =
   Menorca 19 C7
Minore 63 B4
Minot 76 A4
Minsk 24 C2
Mińsk
   Mazowiecki . 16 B5
Mintaka Pass . . 42 A9
Minto 71 B5
Minutang 41 C11
Minvoul 56 D2
Mir 53 F1
Mira 20 B4
Miraj 43 L9
Miram Shah . . . 42 C7
Miranda 93 G2
Miranda de Ebro 19 A4
Miranda do
   Douro 18 B2
Miri 36 D4
Mirim, L. 94 C6
Mirpur Khas . . 42 G6
Mirzapur 40 E4
Mirzapur-cum-
   Vindhyachal =
   Mirzapur . . . 40 E4
Mish'āb, Ra'as
   al 47 E7
Mishan 35 B8
Miskin 44 F4
Miskolc 16 D5
Misool 39 E4
Misrātah 52 B2
Misriç 46 C5
Missinaibi → . . 69 C2
Mississippi □ . 79 C9
Mississippi → . 79 E9
Mississippi River
   Delta 79 E9
Missoula 81 B6
Missouri □ 77 F8
Missouri → . . . 77 F9
Mistassini L. . . 69 C3
Misurata =
   Misrātah 52 B2
Mitchell,
   Australia . . . 63 A4
Mitchell, *U.S.A.* 76 D5
Mitchell → 61 D7
Mitilíni 23 E6
Mito 32 A7
Mitrovica =
   Titova-
   Mitrovica . . . 22 C3
Mitsinjo 59 H9
Mitsiwa 53 E6
Mittagong 63 B5
Mitú 90 C4
Mitumba,
   Chaîne des . . 57 F5
Mitumba Mts. =
   Mitumba,
   Chaîne des . . 57 F5
Mitwaba 57 F5
Mitzic 56 D2
Miyake-Jima . . 32 B6
Miyako 33 G12
Miyakonojō . . . 32 D2
Miyazaki 32 D2
Miyet, Bahr el =
   Dead Sea . . . 47 E3
Mizal 47 G6
Mizdah 52 B1
Mizoram □ . . . 41 F9
Mjøsa 8 F10
Mladá Boleslav 16 C2
Mława 16 B5
Mljet 20 C6
Mmabatho . . . 59 D5

Moa 39 F3
Moabi 56 E2
Moalie Park . . . 62 A3
Moba 57 F5
Mobaye 56 D4
Mobayi 56 D4
Mobile 74 D3
Mobutu Sese
   Seko, L. =
   Albert L. 57 D6
Moçambique . . 59 H8
Moçâmedes =
   Namibe 58 B2
Mochudi 59 C5
Mocimboa da
   Praia 57 G8
Mocoa 90 C3
Mocuba 59 B7
Modane 13 D7
Módena 20 B3
Modesto 82 B2
Módica 21 F5
Moe 63 C4
Moengo 92 A3
Mogadishu =
   Muqdisho . . 49 G4
Mogador =
   Essaouira . . . 54 B3
Mogami → . . . 33 G12
Mogaung 41 E11
Mogi das Cruzes 94 A7
Mogi-Mirim . . . 94 A7
Mogilev =
   Mahilyow . . 17 B10
Mogilev-
   Podolskiy =
   Mohyliv-
   Podilskyy . . . 17 D8
Mogoi 39 E4
Mogok 41 F11
Mohács 16 F4
Moḥammadābād
   . . . . 44 B4
Mohoro 57 F7
Mohyliv-
   Podilskyy . . . 17 D8
Mointy 29 E8
Moisie 69 C4
Moisie → 69 C4
Moïssala 53 G2
Mojave Desert . 82 C4
Mokai 64 C6
Mokokchung . . 41 D10
Mokra Gora . . . 22 C3
Molchanovo . . 29 D9
Moldavia ■ =
   Moldova ■ . . 17 E9
Molde 8 F9
Moldova ■ . . . 17 E9
Moldoveanu, Vf. 17 F7
Molepolole . . . 59 C5
Molfetta 20 D6
Moline 77 E9
Moliro 57 F6
Mollendo 91 G4
Molodechno =
   Maladzyechna 17 A8
Molokai 82 H12
Molong 63 B4
Molopo → 58 D4
Molotov = Perm 29 D6
Moloundou . . . 56 D3
Molu 39 F4
Molucca Sea . . 39 E2
Moluccas =
   Maluku 39 E3
Moma 59 B7
Mombasa 57 E7
Momchilgrad . . 22 D5

Mompós

Mompós	90	B4
Mon →	41	G10
Mona, Canal de		
la	87	C6
Monaco ■	13	E7
Monahans	78	D2
Monastir =		
Bitola	22	D3
Monastir	52	A1
Moncayo, Sierra		
del	19	B5
Mönchengladbach	14	C4
Monchique	18	D1
Monclova	84	B4
Mondego →	18	B1
Mondeodo	39	E2
Mondovì	20	B1
Monforte de		
Lemos	18	A2
Mong Hsu	41	G12
Mong Kung	41	G11
Mong Nai	41	G11
Mong Pawk	41	F12
Mong Ton	41	G12
Mong Wa	41	G13
Mong Yai	41	F12
Mongalla	53	G5
Monghyr =		
Munger	40	E6
Mongibello =		
Etna	21	F5
Mongo	53	F2
Mongolia ■	35	B5
Mongororo	53	F3
Mongu	58	B4
Monkoto	56	E4
Monópoli	21	D6
Monqoumba	56	D3
Monroe, La.,		
U.S.A.	79	C7
Monroe, N.C.,		
U.S.A.	75	B7
Monrovia	55	G2
Mons	14	C2
Monse	39	E2
Mont-de-Marsan	12	E3
Mont-St.-Michel,		
Le = Le Mont-		
St.-Michel	12	B3
Montalbán	19	B5
Montana □	81	B9
Montargis	13	C5
Montauban	12	D4
Montbéliard	13	C7
Montceau-les-		
Mines	13	C6
Monte Alegre	92	C3
Monte Azul	93	F5
Monte-Carlo	20	C1
Monte Caseros	94	C5
Monte Comán	94	C3
Monte Santu, C.		
di	21	D2
Montecristi	90	D2
Montecristo	20	C3
Montego Bay	86	C4
Montélimar	13	D6
Montemorelos	84	B5
Montenegro □	22	C2
Montepuez	59	A7
Monterey	82	B2
Montería	90	B3
Monterrey	84	B4
Montes Claros	93	F5
Montesilvano		
Marina	20	C5
Montevideo	94	C5
Montgomery =		
Sahiwal	42	D8
Montgomery	74	C4
Montijo	18	C2
Montilla	18	D3
Montluçon	13	C5
Montmorillon	12	C4
Montoro	18	C3
Montpellier	13	E5
Montréal	69	D3
Montreux	13	C7
Montrose, U.K.	10	C5
Montrose,		
U.S.A.	83	A9
Montserrat ■	87	C7
Monveda	56	D4
Monywa	41	F10
Monza	20	B2
Monze	59	B5
Monze, C.	43	G5
Monzón	19	B6
Moolawatana	62	A2
Moomin Cr. →	63	A4
Moonie	63	A5
Moonie →	63	A4
Moonta	62	B2
Mooroopna	63	C4
Moose Jaw	71	C9
Moosomin	71	C9
Moosonee	69	C2
Mopeia Velha	59	B7
Mopti	55	F4
Moquegua	91	G4
Mora	8	F10
Moradabad	42	E11
Morafenobe	59	H8
Moramanga	59	H9
Moratuwa	43	R11
Morava →,		
Serbia, Yug.	22	B3
Morava →,		
Slovak Rep.	16	D3
Moravian Hts. =		
Ceskomoravská		
Vrchovina	16	D2
Morawhanna	90	B7
Moray Firth	10	C5
Morden	71	D10
Mordovian		
Republic □ =		
Mordvinia □	24	C5
Mordvinia □	24	C5
Morea	62	C3
Moree	63	A4
Morelia	84	D4
Morella	19	B5
Morena, Sierra	18	C3
Moreton I.	63	A5
Morgan	62	B2
Morgan City	79	E8
Morioka	33	G12
Morlaix	12	B2
Mornington	63	C4
Mornington, I.	95	F1
Moro G.	38	C2
Morocco ■	54	B3
Morococha	91	F3
Morogoro	57	F7
Morombe	59	J8
Morón	86	B4
Mörön →	35	B6
Morón de la		
Frontera	18	D3
Morondava	59	J8
Morotai	39	D3
Moroto	57	D6
Morphou	46	D3
Morrinhos	93	F4
Morrinsville	64	B6
Morristown	75	A6
Morrumbene	59	C7
Morshansk	24	C5
Morteros	94	C4
Mortes, R.		
das →	93	E3
Mortlake	62	C3
Morundah	63	B4
Moruya	63	C5
Morvan	13	C6
Morven	63	A4
Morwell	63	C4
Moscos Is.	41	L11
Moscow =		
Moskva	24	B4
Moscow	80	B5
Mosel →	13	A7
Moselle =		
Mosel →	13	A7
Mosgiel	65	F4
Moshi	57	E7
Moskva	24	B4
Moskva →	24	B4
Moson-		
magyaróvár	16	E3
Mosquera	90	C3
Moss Vale	63	B5
Mossaka	56	E3
Mossburn	65	F3
Mosselbaai	58	E4
Mossendjo	56	E2
Mossgiel	63	B3
Mossoró	92	D6
Mossuril	59	G8
Most	16	C1
Mostaganem	54	A5
Mostar	20	C6
Mostardas	94	C6
Mostiska =		
Mostyska	17	D6
Mosty = Masty	17	B7
Mostyska	17	D6
Mosul = Al		
Mawṣil	46	C5
Motihari	40	D5
Motril	18	D4
Motueka	65	D5
Motueka →	65	D5
Mouanda	56	E2
Moúdhros	23	E5
Moudjeria	55	E2
Mouila	56	E2
Moulamein	63	C3
Moulins	13	C5
Moulmein	41	J11
Moundou	53	G2
Mount Barker	62	C2
Mount Darwin	59	B6
Mount Eba	62	B2
Mount Gambier	62	C3
Mount Hope,		
N.S.W.,		
Australia	63	B4
Mount Hope,		
S. Austral.,		
Australia	62	B2
Mount Howitt	62	A3
Mount Isa	61	E6
Mount Lofty Ra.	62	B2
Mount McKinley		
National Park	71	B4
Mount Margaret	63	A3
Mount		
Maunganui	64	B7
Mount Olympus		
= Uludağ	23	D7
Mount Perry	63	A5
Mount Vernon	73	D9
Mountain View	82	B1
Moura, Brazil	90	D6
Moura, Portugal	18	C2
Mourdi,		
Dépression du	53	E3
Mourdiah	55	F3
Moussoro	53	F2
Moutohara	64	C7
Moutong	39	D2
Moyale	57	D7
Moyamba	55	G2
Moyen Atlas	54	B3
Moyo	37	F5
Moyyero →	30	C8
Mozambique =		
Moçambique	59	H8
Mozambique ■	59	B7
Mozambique		
Chan.	59	H8
Mozdok	25	E5
Mozyr = Mazyr	17	C9
Mpanda	57	F6
Mpika	59	A6
Mpwapwa	57	F7
Msaken	52	A1
Msoro	59	A6
Mu Us Shamo	35	C5
Muaná	92	C4
Muar	37	D2
Muarabungo	37	E2
Muaraenim	37	E2
Muarajuloi	37	E4
Muarakaman	37	E5
Muaratebo	37	E2
Muaratembesi	37	E2
Muaratewe	37	E4
Mubarraz = Al		
Mubarraz	47	F7
Mubende	57	D6
Mubi	53	F1
Muckadilla	63	A4
Muconda	56	G4
Mucuri	93	F6
Mudanjiang	35	B7
Mudanya	23	D7
Mudgee	63	B4
Mufulira	59	A5
Muğla	23	F7
Mugu	40	C4
Muhammad Qol	52	D6
Mühlhausen	14	C6
Mühlig Hofmann		
fjell	96	B7
Mukacheve	17	D6
Mukachevo =		
Mukacheve	17	D6
Mukah	37	D4
Mukden =		
Shenyang	35	B7
Mukomuko	37	E2
Muktsar	42	D9
Mukur	42	C5
Mula	19	C5
Mulchén	94	D2
Mulde →	15	C7
Mulgathing	62	B1
Mulgrave	69	D4
Mulhacén	18	D4
Mulhouse	13	C7
Mull	10	C4
Mullengudgery	63	B4
Muller,		
Pegunungan	37	D4
Mullingar	11	E3
Mullumbimby	63	A5
Multan	42	D7
Mulwala	63	C4
Mumbaï =		
Bombay	43	K8
Mumbwa	59	A5
Muna	39	F2
München	15	D6

Munchen-
Gladbach =
Mönchengladbach
.... 14 C4
Muncie 72 D3
Mundala 39 E6
Münden 14 C5
Mundo Novo .. 93 E5
Mungallala ... 63 A4
Mungallala
Cr. → 63 A4
Mungbere ... 57 D5
Munger 40 E6
Mungindi 63 A4
Munhango ... 58 A3
Munich =
München ... 15 D6
Muñoz Gamero,
Pen. 95 G2
Münster 14 C4
Munster □ ... 11 E2
Muntok 37 E3
Mupa 58 B3
Muqdisho 49 G4
Murallón,
Cuerro ... 95 F2
Murang'a 57 E7
Murashi 24 B6
Muratlı 22 D6
Murchison → . 60 F1
Murchison, Mt. 96 B15
Murchison Falls
= Kabarega
Falls 57 D6
Murcia 19 C5
Murcia □ 19 D5
Mureş → 16 E5
Mureşul =
Mureş → ... 16 E5
Murfreesboro . 74 B4
Murgab =
Murghob ... 29 F8
Murghob 29 F8
Murgon 63 A5
Müritz-see .. 15 B7
Murmansk 28 C4
Murom 24 B5
Muroran 32 F12
Muroto-Misaki . 32 C4
Murray → ... 62 C2
Murray Bridge . 62 C2
Murree 42 C8
Murrumbidgee →
.... 62 B3
Murrumburrah . 63 B4
Murrurundi ... 63 B5
Murtoa 62 C3
Murwara 40 F3
Murwillumbah . 63 A5
Mürzzuschlag . 15 E8
Muş 46 C5
Mûsa, G. 47 E3
Musa Khel ... 42 D6
Mūsá Qal'eh .. 42 C4
Musaffargarh .. 42 D7
Musala, Bulgaria 22 C4
Musala,
Indonesia . 37 D1
Musay'īd 44 E2
Muscat =
Masqat 45 F4
Muscat & Oman
= Oman ■ .. 48 C6
Muscatine ... 77 E9
Musgrave Ras. 60 F5
Mushie 56 E3
Musi → 37 E2
Muskogee 79 B6
Musmar 53 E6

Musoma 57 E6
Mussoorie ... 42 D11
Mustafakemalpaşa
.... 23 D7
Mustang 40 C4
Musters, L. ... 95 F3
Muswellbrook . 63 B5
Mût, Egypt 52 C4
Mut, Turkey .. 46 C3
Mutare 59 B6
Muting 39 F6
Mutoray 30 C8
Muxima 56 F2
Muynak 29 E6
Muzaffarabad . 42 B8
Muzaffarnagar . 42 E10
Muzaffarpur ... 40 D5
Muzhi 28 C7
Muztag 34 C3
Mvuma 59 B6
Mwanza,
Tanzania 57 E6
Mwanza,
Dem. Rep. of the Congo
.... 57 F5
Mweka 56 E4
Mwenezi 59 C6
Mwenga 57 E5
Mweru, L. ... 57 F5
Mwinilunga ... 58 A4
My Tho 36 B3
Myanaung ... 41 H10
Myanmar =
Burma ■ ... 41 G11
Myaungmya ... 41 J10
Mycenæ 23 F4
Myeik Kyunzu . 36 B1
Myingyan ... 41 G10
Myitkyina 41 E11
Mykolayiv ... 25 D3
Mymensingh .. 41 E8
Mysia 23 E6
Mysore =
Karnataka □ . 43 N10
Mysore 43 N10
Myszków 16 C4
Mytishchi 24 B4

N

Na Hearadh =
Harris 10 C3
Naab → 15 D7
Naberezhnyye
Chelny ... 29 D6
Nabeul 52 A1
Nabire 39 E5
Nablus =
Nābulus 46 D3
Nābulus 46 D3
Nachingwea ... 57 G7
Nackara 62 B2
Nacogdoches . 79 D6
Nacozari 84 A3
Nadiad 43 H8
Nadūshan 44 C3
Nadvirna ... 17 D7
Nadvornaya =
Nadvirna ... 17 D7
Nadym 28 C8
Nadym → 28 C8
Nafada 55 F7
Nafūd ad Dahy 47 G6
Nafud Desert =
An Nafūd ... 47 E5
Naga 38 B2

Nagaland □ ... 41 E10
Nagano 32 A6
Nagaoka 33 G11
Nagappattinam 43 P11
Nagar Parkar . 43 G7
Nagasaki 32 C1
Nagaur 42 F8
Nagercoil 43 Q10
Nagīneh 44 C4
Nagoya 32 B5
Nagpur 43 J11
Nagykanizsa .. 16 E3
Nagykörös ... 16 E4
Nahanni Butte . 70 B7
Nahāvand 46 D7
Na'ifah 48 D5
Nain, Canada .. 68 C4
Nā'īn, Iran 44 C3
Nairn 10 C5
Nairobi 57 E7
Naivasha 57 E7
Najafābād 44 C2
Najd 47 F5
Najibabad ... 42 E11
Nakamura 32 C3
Nakfa 53 E6
Nakhichevan =
Naxçıvan .. 25 F6
Nakhichevan
Republic □ =
Naxçıvan □ . 25 F6
Nakhodka ... 31 E11
Nakhon Phanom 36 A2
Nakhon
Ratchasima . 36 B2
Nakhon Sawan 36 A2
Nakhon Si
Thammarat . 36 C2
Nakina 69 C2
Nakuru 57 E7
Nal → 42 G4
Nalchik 25 E5
Nalgonda 43 L11
Nallamalai Hills 43 M11
Nālūt 52 B1
Nam Co 34 C4
Nam-Phan ... 36 B3
Namacurra ... 59 B7
Namak,
Daryācheh-ye 44 C3
Namak, Kavir-e 44 C4
Namaland ... 58 C3
Namangan ... 29 E8
Namapa 59 A7
Namber 39 E4
Nambour ... 63 A5
Nambucca
Heads 63 B5
Nameh 37 D5
Namib Desert =
Namibwoestyn
.... 58 C2
Namibe 58 B2
Namibia ■ ... 58 C3
Namibwoestyn 58 C2
Namlea 39 E3
Namoi → 63 B4
Nampa 80 D5
Nampula 59 B7
Namrole 39 E3
Namse Shankou 40 C4
Namtu 41 F11
Namur 14 C3
Namutoni ... 58 B3
Namwala ... 59 B5
Nanaimo 71 D7
Nanango 63 A5
Nanao 32 A5
Nanchang 35 D6

Nanching =
Nanjing 35 C6
Nanchong 35 C5
Nancy 13 B7
Nanda Devi .. 42 D11
Nanded 43 K10
Nandewar Ra. . 63 B5
Nandurbar ... 43 J9
Nandyal 43 M11
Nanga-Eboko .. 56 D2
Nanga Parbat . 42 B9
Nangapinoh .. 37 E4
Nangarhár □ .. 42 B7
Nangatayap ... 37 E4
Nanjing 35 C6
Nanking =
Nanjing 35 C6
Nanning 35 D5
Nanping 35 D6
Nansei-Shotō =
Ryūkyū-rettō 35 D7
Nantes 12 C3
Nanuque 93 F5
Nanusa,
Kepulauan .. 38 D3
Nanyang 35 C6
Nanyuki 57 D7
Nao, C. de la .. 19 C6
Naoetsu 32 A6
Napa 80 F2
Napier 64 C7
Naples = Nápoli 21 D5
Naples 75 F7
Napo → 90 D4
Nápoli 21 D5
Nappa Merrie . 62 A3
Nara, Japan .. 32 B4
Nara, Mali ... 55 E3
Naracoorte ... 62 C3
Naradhan ... 63 B4
Narasapur ... 40 J3
Narathiwat ... 36 C2
Narayanganj .. 41 F8
Narayanpet ... 43 L10
Narbonne ... 13 E5
Nardò 23 D2
Narew → ... 16 B5
Narin 42 A6
Narmada → .. 43 J8
Narooma ... 63 C5
Narrabri 63 B4
Narran → ... 63 A4
Narrandera .. 63 B4
Narromine ... 63 B4
Narsimhapur .. 43 H11
Narva 24 B2
Narvik 8 E11
Naryan-Mar .. 28 C6
Naryilco 62 A3
Narym 29 D9
Narymskoye .. 29 E9
Naryn 29 E8
Nasarawa ... 55 G6
Naseby 65 F4
Naser, Buheirat
en 52 D5
Nashville 74 A4
Nasik 43 K8
Nasirabad ... 42 F9
Nassau 86 A4
Nassau, B. ... 95 H3
Nasser, L. =
Naser,
Buheirat en . 52 D5
Nat Kyizin 41 K11
Nata 59 C5
Natagaima ... 90 C3
Natal, Brazil ... 92 D6
Natal, Indonesia 37 D1

Naţanz

Naţanz 44 C2
Natashquan ... 69 C4
Natashquan ↝ 69 C4
Natchez 79 D8
Nathalia 63 C4
Nathdwara 43 G8
Natitingou 55 F5
Natron, L. 57 E7
Natuna Besar,
  Kepulauan .. 37 D3
Natuna Is. =
  Natuna Besar,
  Kepulauan .. 37 D3
Natuna Selatan,
  Kepulauan .. 37 D3
Naturaliste, C. . 62 D4
Naumburg 15 C6
Nauru ■ 64 K11
Naushahra =
  Nowshera ... 42 B8
Nauta 90 D4
Nautanwa 40 D4
Navahrudak ... 17 B7
Navalmoral de
  la Mata 18 C3
Navarino, I. ... 95 H3
Navarra □ 19 A5
Năvodari 22 B7
Navoi = Nawoiy 29 E7
Navojoa 84 B3
Návpaktos ... 23 E3
Návplion 23 F4
Navsari 43 J8
Nawabshah ... 42 F6
Nawakot 40 D5
Nawalgarh ... 42 F9
Nawāsif, Harrat 47 G5
Nawoiy 29 E7
Naxçıvan 25 F6
Naxçıvan □ ... 25 F6
Náxos 23 F5
Nãy Band 44 E3
Nazas ↝ 84 B4
Nazilli 23 F7
Nazir Hat 41 F8
Ncheu 59 A6
Ndalatando ... 56 F2
Ndélé 56 C4
Ndendé 56 E2
Ndjamena 53 F1
Ndjolé 56 E2
Ndola 59 A5
Neagh, Lough . 11 D3
Near Is. 71 C1
Neath 11 F5
Nebine Cr. ↝ . 63 A4
Nebitdag 29 F6
Nebraska □ ... 76 E5
Nébrodi, Monti 21 F5
Neckar ↝ 14 D5
Necochea 94 D5
Neemuch =
  Nimach 43 G9
Neepawa 71 C10
Nefta 54 B6
Neftçala 46 C7
Negapatam =
  Nagappattinam
  .... 43 P11
Negele 49 F2
Negombo 43 R11
Negotin 22 B4
Negra Pt. 38 A2
Negrais, C. =
  Maudin Sun . 41 K10
Negro ↝,
  Argentina ... 95 E4
Negro ↝, Brazil 90 D6

Negro ↝,
  Uruguay 94 C5
Negros 38 C2
Nehbandān ... 45 D5
Nei Monggol
  Zizhiqu □ ... 35 B6
Neijiang 35 D5
Neiva 90 C3
Nejd = Najd .. 47 F5
Nekemte 53 G6
Nellore 43 M11
Nelson, Canada 71 D8
Nelson, N.Z. .. 65 D5
Nelson ↝ 71 C10
Nelson, C. 62 C3
Nelson, Estrecho 95 G2
Nelspruit 59 D6
Néma 55 E3
Neman ↝ 24 B1
Nemunas =
  Neman ↝ .. 24 B1
Nemuro 32 F13
Nemuro-Kaikyō 32 F13
Nenagh 11 E2
Nenana 71 B5
Nenjiang 35 B7
Nepal ■ 40 D5
Nepalganj 40 C3
Neretva ↝ ... 20 C6
Ness, L. 10 C4
Nesterov 17 C6
Nesvizh =
  Nyasvizh 17 B8
Netherlands ■ . 14 B3
Netherlands
  Antilles ■ ... 87 D6
Nettilling L. ... 68 B3
Neubrandenburg
  .... 15 B7
Neuchâtel 13 C7
Neuchâtel, Lac
  de 13 C7
Neumünster .. 14 A5
Neunkirchen .. 14 D4
Neuquén 94 D3
Neuruppin 15 B7
Neustrelitz ... 15 B7
Neva ↝ 24 B3
Nevada □ 80 F5
Nevada, Sierra,
  Spain 18 D4
Nevada, Sierra,
  U.S.A. 80 F3
Nevers 13 C5
Nevertire 63 B4
Nevinnomyssk 25 E5
Nevis 87 C7
Nevşehir 46 C3
New Amsterdam 90 B7
New Angledool 63 A4
New Bedford .. 73 D10
New Bern 75 B9
New Brighton . 65 E5
New Britain,
  Papua N. G. . 64 K10
New Britain,
  U.S.A. 73 D9
New
  Brunswick □ 69 D4
New
  Caledonia ■ . 64 M11
New Delhi 42 E10
New England
  Ra. 63 B5
New Glasgow . 69 D4
New Guinea .. 64
New
  Hampshire □ 73 C10
New Haven ... 73 D9

New Hebrides =
  Vanuatu ■ .. 64 L11
New Ireland .. 64 K10
New Jersey □ . 73 E9
New London .. 73 D9
New Mexico □ 83 C9
New Norfolk .. 62 D4
New Orleans .. 79 E8
New Plymouth 64 C6
New Providence 86 A4
New Siberian Is.
  =
  Novosibirskiye
  Ostrova 31 B12
New South
  Wales □ 63 B4
New
  Westminster 71 D7
New York □ .. 73 C8
New York City . 73 D9
New Zealand ■ 64 D7
Newala 57 G7
Newark 73 D8
Newburgh 73 D8
Newbury 11 F6
Newcastle,
  Australia 63 B5
Newcastle,
  S. Africa 59 D5
Newcastle-upon-
  Tyne 11 D6
Newfoundland □
  .... 69 C5
Newman 60 E2
Newport,
  I. of W., U.K. 11 F6
Newport, Newp.,
  U.K. 11 F5
Newport, U.S.A. 73 D10
Newport News 73 F7
Newquay 11 F4
Newry 11 D3
Newton Boyd . 63 A5
Neya 24 B5
Neyrīz 44 D3
Neyshābūr ... 44 B4
Nezhin = Nizhyn 24 C3
Ngabang 37 D3
Ngabordamlu,
  Tanjung 39 F4
Ngami
  Depression .. 58 C4
Nganglong
  Kangri 40 A3
Ngaoundéré .. 56 C2
Ngapara 65 F4
Ngoring Hu ... 34 C4
Ngudu 57 E6
Nguigmi 53 F1
Nguru 55 F7
Nha Trang ... 36 B3
Nhill 62 C3
Niafounké 55 E4
Niagara Falls,
  Canada 69 D3
Niagara Falls,
  U.S.A. 73 C6
Niah 37 D4
Niamey 55 F5
Niangara 57 D5
Nias 37 D1
Nicaragua ■ .. 85 E7
Nicaragua, L. de 85 E7
Nicastro 21 E6
Nice 13 E7
Nichinan 33 D2
Nicobar Is. ... 27 J13
Nicosia 46 D3
Nicoya, Pen. de 85 F7

Niedersachsen □
  .... 14 B5
Niemen =
  Neman ↝ .. 24 B1
Nienburg 14 B5
Nieuw
  Amsterdam . 92 A2
Nieuw Nickerie 92 A2
Niğde 46 C3
Niger ■ 55 E6
Niger ↝ 55 G6
Nigeria ■ 55 G6
Nightcaps ... 65 F3
Nii-Jima 32 B6
Niigata 33 G11
Niihama 32 C3
Niihau 82
Nijmegen 14 C3
Nikiniki 39 F2
Nikki 55 G5
Nikolayev =
  Mykolayiv ... 25 D3
Nikolayevsk ... 24 C6
Nikopol 25 D3
Nīkshahr 45 E5
Nikšić 22 C2
Nîl, Nahr en ↝ 52 B5
Nîl el Abyad ↝ 53 E5
Nîl el Azraq ↝ 53 E5
Nile = Nîl, Nahr
  en ↝ 52 B5
Nimach 43 G9
Nîmes 13 E6
Nimfaíon, Ákra
  = Pínnes,
  Ákra 23 D5
Nimmitabel ... 63 C4
Nimrūz □ 45 D5
Nimule 57 D6
Nīnawá 46 C5
Nindigully ... 63 A4
Nineveh =
  Nīnawá 46 C5
Ningbo 35 D7
Ningde 35 D6
Ningpo =
  Ningbo 35 D7
Ningsia Hui A.R.
  = Ningxia
  Huizu
  Zizhiqu □ ... 35 C5
Ningxia Huizu
  Zizhiqu □ ... 35 C5
Niobrara ↝ .. 76 D5
Nioro du Sahel 55 E3
Niort 12 C3
Nipawin 71 C9
Nipigon, L. ... 69 D2
Niquelândia .. 93 E4
Nirmal 43 K11
Nirmali 40 D6
Niš 22 C3
Nişāb, Si. Arabia 47 E6
Nişāb, Yemen . 49 E4
Nishinomiya .. 32 C3
Nistru =
  Dnister ↝ .. 17 E10
Niţā' 47 F7
Niterói 93 G5
Nitra 16 D4
Nitra ↝ 16 E4
Niue 65 L14
Niut 37 D4
Nivernais 13 C5
Nizamabad ... 43 K11
Nizamghat ... 41 C10
Nizhne-Vartovsk 29 C8
Nizhneyansk . 31 B11
Nizhniy
  Novgorod ... 24 B5

Nizhniy Tagil .. 29 D6
Nizhyn 24 C3
Nizip 46 C4
Nízké Tatry ... 16 D4
Njombe 57 F6
Nkambe 55 G7
Nkawkaw 55 G4
Nkhata Bay .. 57 G6
Nkhota Kota .. 59 A6
Nkongsamba .. 56 D1
Nmai → 41 E11
Noakhali =
  Maijdi 41 F8
Noatak 71 B3
Nobeoka 32 C2
Nocera Inferiore 21 D5
Nockatunga ... 62 A3
Nogales, *Mexico* 84 A2
Nogales, *U.S.A.* 83 E7
Nōgata 32 C2
Noginsk 30 C7
Noire, Mts. ... 12 B2
Noirmoutier, I.
  de 12 C2
Nok Kundi 42 E3
Nokhtuysk 30 C9
Nokomis 71 C9
Nola 56 D3
Nome 71 B3
Nong Khai 36 A2
Noondoo 63 A4
Nóqui 56 F2
Noranda 69 D3
Nord-Ostsee-
  Kanal → ... 14 A5
Nordegg 71 C8
Norderney 14 B4
Norderstedt ... 14 B5
Nordfriesische
  Inseln 14 A5
Nordhausen .. 14 C6
Nordkapp 8 D13
Nordrhein-
  Westfalen □ .. 14 C4
Nordvik 30 B9
Norfolk 73 F7
Norfolk I. 64 M11
Norilsk 30 C6
Norley 63 A3
Norman 78 B5
Norman Wells . 70 B7
Normandie .. 12 B4
Normandy =
  Normandie .. 12 B4
Normanton 61 D7
Norquinco 95 E2
Norrköping ... 9 G11
Norrland 8 F11
Norseman 60 G3
North Battleford 71 C9
North Bay 69 D3
North Bend ... 80 D1
North C. 64 A5
North Cape =
  Nordkapp ... 8 D13
North
  Carolina □ .. 75 B7
North Channel,
  Canada 69 D2
North Channel,
  U.K. 11 D4
North Dakota □ 76 B4
North Frisian Is.
  =
  Nordfriesische
  Inseln 14 A5
North I. 64 B5
North Korea ■ . 35 C7

North
  Lakhimpur .. 41 D10
North Minch .. 10 B4
North Ossetia □ 25 E5
North Pagai, I. =
  Pagai Utara . 37 E2
North Platte ... 76 E4
North Platte → 76 E4
North Rhine
  Westphalia □
  = Nordrhein-
  Westfalen □ . 14 C4
North
  Saskatchewan →
  .... 71 C8
North Sea 10 D8
North Sporades
  = Voríai
  Sporádhes .. 23 E4
North Taranaki
  Bight 64 C6
North
  Thompson → 71 C7
North Uist 10 C3
North West C. . 60 E1
North West
  Frontier □ .. 42 B8
North West
  Highlands .. 10 C4
North West
  River 69 C4
North West
  Territories □ 70 B7
Northampton .. 11 E6
Northern Circars 40 J4
Northern
  Ireland □ ... 11 D3
Northern
  Marianas ■ . 64 H9
Northern
  Territory □ .. 60 D5
Northland □ .. 64 A5
Northumberland,
  C. 62 C3
Northumberland
  Str. 69 D4
Norton Sd. 71 B3
Norway ■ 8 F10
Norway House 71 C10
Norwegian Sea 6 B5
Norwich 11 E7
Nosok 28 B9
Noşratābād ... 45 D4
Nossob → ... 58 D4
Nosy Bé 59 G9
Nosy Boraha .. 59 H9
Nosy Mitsio .. 59 G8
Nosy Varika .. 59 J9
Noteć → 16 B2
Noto-Hanto .. 33 G11
Notre Dame B. 69 D5
Notre Dame de
  Koartac =
  Quaqtaq 68 B4
Notre Dame
  d'Ivugivic =
  Ivujivik 68 B3
Nottaway → .. 69 C3
Nottingham .. 11 E6
Nouâdhibou .. 54 D1
Nouâdhibou,
  Ras 54 D1
Nouakchott .. 55 E1
Nouméa 64 M11
Noupoort 58 E4
Nouveau
  Comptoir =
  Wemindji .. 69 C3

Nouvelle-
  Calédonie =
  New
  Caledonia ■ . 64 M11
Nova Casa Nova 93 D5
Nova Cruz 92 D6
Nova Friburgo . 93 G5
Nova Gaia =
  Cambundi-
  Catembo 56 G3
Nova Iguaçu .. 93 G5
Nova Iorque .. 92 D5
Nova Lima 93 F5
Nova Mambone 59 C7
Nova Scotia □ . 69 D4
Nova Sofala .. 59 C6
Nova Venécia . 93 F5
Nova Zagora .. 22 C5
Novara 20 B2
Novaya Ladoga 24 A3
Novaya Lyalya 29 D7
Novaya Zemlya 28 B6
Nové Zámky .. 16 D4
Novgorod 24 B3
Novgorod-
  Severskiy =
  Novhorod-
  Siverskyy ... 24 C3
Novhorod-
  Siverskyy ... 24 C3
Novi Lígure ... 20 B2
Novi Pazar ... 22 C3
Novi Sad 22 B2
Novo Mesto .. 20 B5
Novo Remanso 93 D5
Novoataysk ... 29 D9
Novocherkassk 25 D5
Novogrudok =
  Navahrudak . 17 B7
Novohrad-
  Volynskyy ... 17 C8
Novokazalinsk =
  Zhangaqazaly 29 E7
Novokuybyshevsk
  .... 24 C6
Novokuznetsk . 29 D9
Novomoskovsk 24 C4
Novorossiysk .. 25 E4
Novorybnoye .. 30 B8
Novoselytsya .. 17 D8
Novoshakhtinsk 25 D4
Novosibirsk ... 29 D9
Novosibirskiye
  Ostrova 31 B12
Novotroitsk ... 29 D6
Novouzensk .. 24 C6
Novovolynsk .. 17 C7
Novska 20 B6
Novyy Port ... 28 C8
Now Shahr ... 44 B2
Nowa Sól 16 C2
Nowgong 41 D9
Nowra 63 B5
Nowshera 42 B8
Nowy Sącz ... 16 D5
Nowy Targ ... 16 D5
Nowy Tomyśl . 16 B3
Noyon 13 B5
Nsanje 59 B7
Nsawam 55 G4
Nsukka 55 G6
Nubian Desert =
  Nûbîya, Es
  Sahrâ En ... 52 D5
Nûbîya, Es
  Sahrâ En ... 52 D5
Nuboai 39 E5
Nueltin L. 70 B10
Nueva Imperial 94 D2

Nueva Rosita .. 84 B4
Nuéve de Julio 94 D4
Nuevitas 86 B4
Nuevo, G. 95 E4
Nuevo Laredo . 84 B5
Nugget Pt. 65 G3
Nuhaka 64 C7
Nukey Bluff .. 62 B2
Nukheila 53 E4
Nukus 29 E6
Nulato 71 B4
Nullarbor Plain 60 G4
Numalla, L. ... 63 A3
Numan 53 G1
Numazu 32 B6
Numfoor 39 E4
Numurkah 63 C4
Nunavut □ 66 C10
Nuneaton 11 E6
Nunivak I. 71 B3
Nunkun 42 C10
Núoro 21 D2
Nuremberg =
  Nürnberg ... 15 D6
Nuriootpa 62 B2
Nürnberg 15 D6
Nurran, L. =
  Terewah, L. . 63 A4
Nusa Tenggara
  Barat □ 37 F5
Nusa Tenggara
  Timur □ 39 F2
Nushki 42 E5
Nutak 68 C4
Nuuk 68 B5
Nuwakot 40 C4
Nuweveldberge 58 E4
Nuyts Arch. ... 62 B1
Nyah West ... 62 C3
Nyahanga 57 E6
Nyahururu ... 57 D7
Nyainqentanglha
  Shan 34 C4
Nyâlâ 53 F3
Nyasa, L. =
  Malawi, L. .. 59 A6
Nyasvizh 17 B8
Nyda 28 C8
Nyeri 57 E7
Nyíregyháza .. 17 E5
Nylstroom ... 59 C5
Nymagee 63 B4
Nyngan 63 B4
Nyoman =
  Neman → .. 24 B1
Nysa 16 C3
Nysa → 16 B2
Nyurbe 30 C9
Nzega 57 E6
N'Zérékoré ... 55 G3
Nzeto 56 F2

O

Ō-Shima 32 B6
Oahe, L. 76 C4
Oahu 82 H12
Oak Ridge ... 75 A5
Oakbank 62 B3
Oakey 63 A5
Oakland 82 B1
Oamaru 65 F4
Oates Land .. 96 A15
Oaxaca 84 D5
Ob → 28 C7

Oba

Oba	69	D2
Oban	10	C4
Obbia	49	F4
Oberhausen	14	C4
Oberon	63	B4
Obi, Kepulauan	39	E3
Obi Is. = Obi, Kepulauan	39	E3
Óbidos	92	C2
Obihiro	32	F12
Obilatu	39	E3
Obo	57	C5
Obozerskaya = Obozerskiy	28	C5
Obozerskiy	28	C5
Obskaya Guba	28	C8
Obuasi	55	G4
Ocala	75	E6
Ocaña	18	C4
Occidental, Cordillera	90	C3
Ocean I. = Banaba	64	K11
Oceanside	82	D4
Ocnița	17	D8
Ocumare del Tuy	90	A5
Odate	33	F12
Odawara	32	B6
Oddur	49	G3
Ödemiş	23	E7
Odense	9	G10
Oder →	15	B8
Odesa	25	D3
Odessa = Odesa	25	D3
Odessa	78	D2
Odienné	55	G3
Odintsovo	24	B4
Odorheiu Secuiesc	17	E7
Odra = Oder →	15	B8
Odra →	16	B2
Oeiras	92	D5
Ofanto →	20	D6
Offa	55	G5
Offenbach	14	C5
Offenburg	14	D4
Oga-Hantō	33	G11
Ōgaki	32	B5
Ogbomosho	55	G5
Ogden	81	E8
Ogdensburg	73	B8
Oglio →	20	B3
Ogooué →	56	E1
Ogowe = Ogooué →	56	E1
Ohai	65	F2
Ohakune	64	C6
Ohanet	54	C6
Ohau, L.	65	F3
Ohio □	72	D4
Ohio →	72	F1
Ohre →	16	C2
Ohrid	22	D3
Ohridsko Jezero	23	D3
Oise →	12	B5
Ōita	32	C2
Oiticica	92	D5
Ojos del Salado, Cerro	94	B3
Oka →	28	D5
Okaba	39	F5
Okahandja	58	C3
Okahukura	64	C6
Okandja	56	E2
Okanogan →	80	A4
Okara	42	D8
Okarito	65	E4
Okaukuejo	58	B3
Okavango Swamps	58	B4
Okaya	32	A6
Okayama	32	B3
Okazaki	32	B5
Okeechobee, L.	75	F7
Okefenokee Swamp	75	D6
Okhotsk, Sea of	31	D12
Oki-Shotō	32	A3
Okiep	58	D3
Okinawa-Jima	35	D7
Oklahoma □	78	B5
Oklahoma City	78	B5
Okmulgee	79	B6
Oknitsa = Ocnița	17	D8
Okrika	55	H6
Oktabrsk = Oktyabrsk	29	E6
Oktyabrsk	29	E6
Oktyabrskiy = Aktsyabrski	17	B9
Oktyabrskoy Revolyutsii, Os.	30	B7
Oktyabrskoye	28	C7
Okuru	65	E3
Okushiri-Tō	32	F11
Öland	9	G11
Olary	62	B3
Olavarría	94	D4
Oława	16	C3
Ólbia	20	D2
Old Crow	70	B6
Oldenburg	14	B5
Oldham	11	E5
Olekma →	31	C10
Olekminsk	31	C10
Oleksandriya	17	C8
Olenek	30	C9
Olenek →	30	B10
Oléron, I. d'	12	D3
Oleśnica	16	C3
Olevsk	17	C8
Olhão	18	D2
Olifants →	59	C6
Olinda	92	D7
Oliveira	93	G5
Olivenza	18	C2
Ollagüe	91	H5
Olomouc	16	D3
Olongapo	38	B2
Olot	19	A7
Olsztyn	16	B5
Olt →	22	C5
Oltenița	22	B6
Oltu	46	B5
Olympia, Greece	23	F3
Olympia, U.S.A.	80	B2
Olympic Mts.	80	B2
Olympus, Mt. = Ólimbos, Óros	23	D4
Om →	29	D8
Omagh	11	D3
Omaha	77	E7
Oman ■	48	C6
Oman, G. of	45	E4
Omaruru	58	C3
Omate	91	G4
Ombai, Selat	39	F2
Omboué	56	E1
Ombrone →	20	C3
Omdurmân	53	E5
Ometepec	84	D5
Ōmiya	32	B6
Omo →	53	G6
Omsk	29	D8
Omul, Vf.	17	F7
Ōmura	32	C1
Omuramba Omatako →	58	B4
Ōmuta	32	C2
Onang	39	E1
Oncócua	58	B2
Onda	19	C5
Ondangua	58	B3
Ondo	55	G5
Öndörhaan	35	B6
Onega	28	C4
Onega →	8	F15
Onega, G. of = Onezhskaya Guba	28	C4
Onega, L. = Onezhskoye Ozero	28	C4
Onehunga	64	B6
Oneşti	17	E8
Onezhskaya Guba	28	C4
Onezhskoye Ozero	28	C4
Ongarue	64	C6
Onilahy →	59	J8
Onitsha	55	G6
Onoda	32	B2
Ontario □	69	D2
Ontario, L.	73	C7
Oodnadatta	62	A2
Oostende	14	C2
Ootacamund	43	P10
Opala	56	E4
Opava	16	D3
Opole	16	C3
Oporto = Porto	18	B1
Opotiki	64	C7
Opua	64	A6
Opunake	64	C5
Oradea	17	E5
Orai	42	G11
Oral = Zhayyq →	29	E6
Oral	24	C7
Oran, Algeria	54	A4
Oran, Argentina	94	A4
Orange, Oranje →	58	D3
Orange, Australia	63	B4
Orange, France	13	D6
Orange, U.S.A.	79	D7
Orange, C.	92	B3
Orangeburg	75	C7
Oranienburg	15	B7
Oranje →	58	D3
Oranjemund	58	D3
Oras	38	B3
Orașul Stalin = Brașov	17	F7
Orbetello	20	C3
Orbost	63	C4
Orchila, I.	90	A5
Ordos = Mu Us Shamo	35	C5
Ordu	46	B4
Ordzhonikidze = Vladikavkaz	25	E5
Ore Mts. = Erzgebirge	15	C7
Örebro	9	G11
Oregon □	80	C3
Orekhovo-Zuyevo	24	B4
Orel	24	C4
Ören	23	F6
Orenburg	29	D6
Orense	18	A2
Orepuki	65	G2
Øresund	9	G10
Orgaz	18	C4
Orgeyev = Orhei	17	E9
Orgün	45	C7
Orhaneli	23	E7
Orhangazi	23	D7
Orhei	17	E9
Orhon Gol →	35	A5
Orient	62	A3
Oriental, Cordillera	90	B4
Orihuela	19	C5
Orinoco →	90	B6
Orissa □	40	G5
Oristano	21	E2
Oristano, G. di	21	E2
Orizaba	84	D5
Orkney Is.	10	B5
Orlando	75	E7
Orléanais	12	C5
Orléans	12	C4
Ormara	42	G4
Ormoc	38	B2
Ormond	64	C7
Örnsköldsvik	8	F11
Orocué	90	C4
Orol Dengizi = Aral Sea	29	E6
Oroquieta	38	C2
Orós	92	D6
Orosháza	16	E5
Orroroo	62	B2
Orsha	24	C3
Orsk	29	D6
Orşova	22	B4
Ortaca	23	F7
Ortegal, C.	18	A2
Orthez	12	E3
Ortigueira	18	A2
Ortles	20	A3
Ortón →	91	F5
Orümīyeh	46	C6
Orümīyeh, Daryācheh-ye	46	C6
Oruro	91	G5
Oruzgān □	42	C5
Orvieto	20	C4
Oryakhovo	22	C4
Ōsaka	32	B4
Ösel = Saaremaa	24	B1
Osh	29	E8
Oshawa	69	D3
Oshkosh	76	E3
Oshmyany = Ashmyany	17	A7
Oshogbo	55	G5
Oshwe	56	E3
Osijek	20	B7
Osipenko = Berdyansk	25	D4
Osipovichi = Asipovichy	17	B9
Oskarshamn	9	G11
Öskemen	29	E9
Oslo	9	G10
Oslob	38	C2
Oslofjorden	9	G10
Osmanabad	43	K10
Osmaniye	46	C4
Osnabrück	14	B5
Osorio	94	B6
Osorno	95	E2
Ossa, Mt.	62	D4
Óssa, Oros	23	E4
Ostend = Oostende	14	C2

Oster	17	C10	
Österdalälven .	8	F10	
Östersund	8	F10	
Ostfriesische Inseln	14	B4	
Ostrava	16	D4	
Ostróda	16	B4	
Ostroh	17	C8	
Ostrołęka	16	B5	
Ostrów Mazowiecka .	16	B5	
Ostrów Wielkopolski	16	C3	
Ostrowiec-Świętokrzyski	16	C5	
Ostuni	21	D6	
Ōsumi-Kaikyō .	33	D2	
Osuna	18	D3	
Oswego	73	C7	
Oświęcim	16	C4	
Otago □	65	F3	
Otago Harbour	65	F4	
Ōtake	32	B3	
Otaki	64	D6	
Otaru	32	F12	
Otaru-Wan = Ishikari-Wan .	32	F12	
Otavalo	90	C3	
Otavi	58	B3	
Otira Gorge ..	65	E4	
Otjiwarongo ..	58	C3	
Otorohanga ...	64	C6	
Otranto	23	D2	
Otranto, C. d' .	23	D2	
Otranto, Str. of	23	D2	
Ōtsu	32	B4	
Ottawa	69	D3	
Ottawa Is. ...	68	C2	
Ottumwa	77	E8	
Oturkpo	55	G6	
Otway, B.	95	G2	
Otway, C.	62	C3	
Otwock	16	B5	
Ouachita Mts. .	79	B6	
Ouadâne	54	D2	
Ouadda	56	C4	
Ouagadougou .	55	F4	
Ouahran = Oran	54	A4	
Ouallene	54	D5	
Ouanda Djallé .	56	C4	
Ouango	56	D4	
Ouargla	54	B6	
Ouarzazate ...	54	B3	
Oubangi → ..	56	E3	
Oudtshoorn ...	58	E4	
Ouessant, I. d' .	12	B1	
Ouesso	56	D3	
Ouezzane	54	B3	
Ouidah	55	G5	
Oujda	54	B4	
Oujeft	55	D2	
Ouled Djellal .	54	B6	
Oulu	8	E13	
Oulujärvi	8	F13	
Oulujoki → ..	8	E13	
Oum Chalouba .	53	E3	
Ounianga-Kébir	53	E3	
Ounianga Sérir	53	E3	
Ourense = Orense	18	A2	
Ouricuri	92	D5	
Ouro Prêto ..	93	G5	
Ouse	62	D4	
Outer Hebrides	10	C3	
Outjo	58	C3	
Ouyen	62	C3	
Ovalle	94	C2	
Ovamboland .	58	B3	
Oviedo	18	A3	
Ovruch	17	C9	
Owaka	65	G3	
Owambo = Ovamboland	58	B3	
Owase	32	B5	
Owbeh	42	B3	
Owen Sound .	69	D2	
Owen Stanley Ra.	61	B8	
Owendo	56	D1	
Owo	55	G6	
Owyhee → ..	80	D5	
Oxford, N.Z. ..	65	E5	
Oxford, U.K. .	11	F6	
Oxley	63	B3	
Oxnard	82	C3	
Oxus = Amudarya →	29	E6	
Oya	37	D4	
Oyama	32	A6	
Oyem	56	D2	
Oyo	55	G5	
Ozamiz	38	C2	
Ozark Plateau .	79	A8	
Ózd	16	D5	

P

Paamiut	68	B6	
Pa-an	41	J11	
Paarl	58	E3	
Pab Hills	42	F5	
Pabianice	16	C4	
Pabna	41	E7	
Pacaja →	92	C3	
Pacaraima, Sierra	90	C6	
Pacasmayo ..	91	E3	
Pachpadra ...	42	G8	
Pachuca	84	C5	
Padaido, Kepulauan .	39	E5	
Padang	37	E2	
Padangpanjang	37	E2	
Padangsidempuan	37	D1	
Paderborn ..	14	C5	
Pádova	20	B3	
Padua = Pádova	20	B3	
Paducah	72	F1	
Paeroa	64	B6	
Pafúri	59	C6	
Pag	20	B5	
Pagadian	38	C2	
Pagai Selatan, P.	37	E2	
Pagai Utara ..	37	E2	
Pagalu = Annobón	51	G4	
Pagastikós Kólpos	23	E4	
Pagatan	37	E5	
Pahiatua	64	D6	
Painan	37	E2	
Paint Hills = Wemindji	69	C3	
Painted Desert .	83	C7	
País Vasco □ .	19	A4	
Paisley	10	D4	
Paita	90	E2	
Pajares, Puerto de	18	A3	
Pakaraima Mts.	90	B6	
Pakistan ■ ..	42	E7	
Pakokku	41	G10	
Pakse □	36	A3	
Paktïā □	42	C6	
Pala	53	G2	
Palagruža ...	20	C6	
Palam	43	K10	
Palampur	42	C10	
Palana	62	C4	
Palanan	38	A2	
Palanan Pt. ..	38	A2	
Palangkaraya .	37	E4	
Palani Hills	43	P10	
Palanpur	43	G8	
Palanro	39	E1	
Palapye	59	C5	
Palau ■	38	C4	
Palawan	36	C5	
Palayankottai .	43	Q10	
Paleleh	39	D2	
Palembang ...	37	E2	
Palencia	18	A3	
Palermo	21	E4	
Palestine	79	D6	
Paletwa	41	G9	
Palghat	43	P10	
Pali	42	G8	
Palioúrion, Ákra	23	E4	
Palitana	43	J7	
Palk Bay	43	Q11	
Palk Strait ...	43	Q11	
Pallanza = Verbánia	20	B2	
Palm Springs .	82	D4	
Palma	57	G8	
Palma → ...	93	E4	
Palma, B. de .	19	C7	
Palma de Mallorca	19	C7	
Palmares	92	D6	
Palmas, C. ..	55	H3	
Pálmas, G. di .	21	E2	
Palmeira dos Índios	93	D6	
Palmeirinhas, Pta. das	56	F2	
Palmer	71	B5	
Palmer Arch. .	96	A3	
Palmer Land .	96	B3	
Palmerston ..	65	F4	
Palmerston North	64	D6	
Palmi	21	E5	
Palmira	90	C3	
Palmyra = Tudmur	46	D4	
Palopo	39	E2	
Palos, C. de ...	19	D5	
Palu, *Indonesia*	39	E1	
Palu, *Turkey* ..	46	C5	
Paluan	38	B2	
Pama	55	F5	
Pamiers	12	E4	
Pamirs	29	F8	
Pamlico Sd. ...	75	B10	
Pampa	78	B3	
Pampa de las Salinas	94	C3	
Pampanua ...	39	E2	
Pampas, *Argentina*	94	D4	
Pampas, *Peru* .	91	F4	
Pamplona, *Colombia*	90	B4	
Pamplona, *Spain*	19	A5	
Panaji	43	M8	
Panamá	85	F9	
Panamá ■ ..	86	E4	
Panamá, G. de	86	E4	
Panama City ..	74	D5	
Panão	91	E3	
Panay	38	B2	
Panay, G.	38	B2	
Pančevo	22	B3	
Pandan	38	B2	
Pandharpur ..	43	L9	
Pando	94	C5	
Pando, L. = Hope, L.	62	A2	
Panevežys ..	24	B1	
Panfilov	29	E8	
Pang-Long ...	41	F12	
Pang-Yang ..	41	F12	
Pangani	57	F7	
Pangfou = Bengbu	35	C6	
Pangkajene ...	39	E1	
Pangkalanbrandan	37	D1	
Pangkalanbuun	37	E4	
Pangkalansusu	37	D1	
Pangkalpinang	37	E3	
Pangkoh	37	E4	
Pangnirtung ...	68	B4	
Pangutaran Group	38	C2	
Panjgur	42	F4	
Panjim = Panaji	43	M8	
Panjinad Barrage	42	E7	
Panorama ...	94	A6	
Pantar	39	F2	
Pante Macassar	39	F2	
Pantelleria ...	21	F3	
Pánuco	84	C5	
Panyam	55	G6	
Paoting = Baoding	35	C6	
Paot'ou = Baotou	35	B6	
Paoua	56	C3	
Pápa	16	E3	
Papakura	64	B6	
Papantla	84	C5	
Papar	36	C5	
Papua New Guinea ■	61	B8	
Papudo	94	C2	
Papun	41	H11	
Pará = Belém .	92	C4	
Pará □	92	C3	
Paracatu	93	F4	
Paracel Is. = Hsisha Chuntao	36	A4	
Parachilna ...	62	B2	
Parachinar ...	42	C7	
Paradip	40	G6	
Parado	39	F1	
Paragua → ..	90	B6	
Paraguaçu → .	93	E6	
Paraguaná, Pen. de	90	A4	
Paraguarí	94	B5	
Paraguay ■ ..	94	A5	
Paraguay → ..	94	B5	
Paraíba = João Pessoa	92	D7	
Paraíba □	92	D6	
Paraíba do Sul →	93	G5	
Parakou	55	G5	
Paramaribo ..	92	A2	
Paraná, *Argentina*	94	C4	
Paranã, *Brazil* .	93	E4	
Paraná □ ...	94	A6	
Paraná → ...	94	C5	
Paranaguá → .	94	B7	
Paranaíba → .	93	G3	

Paranapanema

Paranapanema → 94 A6
Paranapiacaba,
  Serra do 94 A7
Parang, *Jolo,*
  Phil. 38 C2
Parang,
  Mindanao,
  Phil. 38 C2
Paratinga 93 E5
Paratoo 62 B2
Parattah 62 D4
Parbhani 43 K10
Parchim 15 B6
Pardo →,
  Bahia, Brazil . 93 F6
Pardo →,
  Mato Grosso,
  Brazil 93 G3
Pardo →,
  São Paulo,
  Brazil 93 G4
Pardubice 16 C2
Parecis, Serra
  dos 91 F7
Parepare 39 E1
Párga 23 E3
Pariaguán 90 B6
Pariaman 37 E2
Parigi 39 E2
Parika 90 B7
Parima, Serra . 90 C6
Parinari 90 D4
Parîngul Mare . 17 F6
Parintins 92 C2
Pariparit Kyun . 41 K9
Paris, *France* .. 12 B5
Paris, *U.S.A.* .. 79 C6
Park Range ... 81 F10
Parkersburg ... 72 E5
Parkes 63 B4
Parla 18 B4
Parma 20 B3
Parnaguá 93 E5
Parnaíba, *Piauí,*
  Brazil 92 C5
Parnaíba,
  São Paulo,
  Brazil 93 F3
Parnaíba → .. 92 C5
Parnassós 23 E4
Parnu 24 B1
Paroo → 63 B3
Páros 23 F5
Parral 94 D2
Parramatta ... 63 B5
Parry Sound .. 69 D3
Partinico 21 E4
Paru → 92 C3
Paruro 91 F4
Parvän □ .. 42 B6
Parvatipuram .. 40 H4
Pasadena, *Calif.,*
  U.S.A. 82 C3
Pasadena, *Tex.,*
  U.S.A. 79 E6
Pasaje 90 D3
Pascagoula ... 79 D9
Pașcani 17 E8
Pasco 80 B4
Pasco, Cerro de 91 F3
Pashmakli =
  Smolyan 22 D5
Pašman 20 C5
Pasni 42 G3
Paso de Indios . 95 E3
Passau 15 D7
Passero, C. 21 F5
Passo Fundo .. 94 B6

Passos 93 G4
Pastaza → ... 90 D3
Pasto 90 C3
Patagonia 95 F3
Patan, *India* .. 43 H8
Patan, *Nepal* .. 40 D5
Patani 39 D3
Patchewollock . 62 C3
Patea 64 C6
Pategi 55 G6
Paternò 21 F5
Paterson 73 D8
Pathankot 42 C9
Patiala 42 D10
Patkai Bum ... 41 D10
Pátmos 23 F6
Patna 40 E5
Patos, L. dos .. 94 C6
Patos de Minas 93 F4
Patquía 94 C3
Pátrai 23 E3
Pátraikós Kólpos 23 E3
Patras = Pátrai 23 E3
Patrocínio 93 F4
Pattani 36 C2
Patuakhali ... 41 F8
Pau 12 E3
Pauini → 90 D6
Pauk 41 G10
Paulis = Isiro . 57 D5
Paulistana ... 92 D5
Paulo Afonso .. 93 D6
Pavia 20 B2
Pavlodar 29 D8
Pavlograd =
  Pavlohrad ... 25 D4
Pavlohrad 25 D4
Pavlovo 24 B5
Pavlovsk 24 C5
Pawtucket 73 D10
Paxoí 23 E3
Payakumbuh .. 37 E2
Payne Bay =
  Kangirsuk .. 68 C4
Paysandú 94 C5
Paz, B. la 84 C2
Pazar 46 B5
Pazardzhik 22 C5
Peace → 70 C8
Peak Hill 63 B4
Peake 62 C2
' Peake Cr. → .. 62 A2
Pebane 59 B7
Pebas 90 D4
Peć 22 C3
Pechenga 28 C4
Pechenizhyn .. 17 D7
Pechora → .. 28 C6
Pechorskaya
  Guba 28 C6
Pecos → 78 E3
Pécs 16 E4
Pedder, L. 62 D4
Pedirka 62 A2
Pedra Azul ... 93 F5
Pedreiras 92 C5
Pedro Afonso . 93 D4
Pedro Juan
  Caballero .. 94 A5
Peebinga 62 B3
Peel →,
  Australia 63 B5
Peel →, *Canada* 70 B6
Peera Peera
  Poolanna L. . 62 A2
Pegasus Bay .. 65 E5
Pegu 41 J11
Pegu Yoma ... 41 H10
Pehuajó 94 D4

Peine 14 B6
Peip'ing =
  Beijing 35 C6
Peipus, L. =
  Chudskoye,
  Oz. 24 B2
Peixe 93 E4
Pekalongan ... 37 F3
Pekanbaru ... 37 D2
Pekin 77 E10
Peking = Beijing 35 C6
Pelagie, Is. ... 21 G4
Pelaihari 37 E4
Peleaga, Vf. ... 17 F6
Peleng 39 E2
Peljeŝac 20 C6
Pelly → 70 B6
Pelly Bay 68 B2
Pelly L. 70 B9
Peloponnese =
  Pelopónnisos □
  .... 23 F4
Pelopónnisos □ 23 F4
Peloro, C. 21 E5
Pelorus Sd. ... 65 D5
Pelotas 94 C6
Pelvoux, Massif
  du 13 D7
Pematangsiantar 37 D1
Pemba I. 57 F7
Pembroke,
  Canada 69 D3
Pembroke, *U.K.* 11 F4
Penang =
  Pinang 36 C2
Penápolis 94 A6
Peñarroya-
  Pueblonuevo 18 C3
Peñas, C. de .. 18 A3
Penas, G. de .. 95 F2
Pench'i = Benxi 35 B7
Pend Oreille L. . 80 A5
Pendembu 55 G2
Pendleton 80 C4
Penedo 93 E6
Penguin 62 D4
Peniche 18 C1
Penida 37 F5
Peninsular
  Malaysia □ .. 37 D2
Penmarch, Pte.
  de 12 C1
Pennines 11 D5
Pennsylvania □ 73 D7
Penola 62 C3
Penong 60 G5
Penrith 63 B5
Pensacola 74 D4
Pensacola Mts. 96 C4
Penshurst 62 C3
Penticton 71 D8
Pentland Firth . 10 B5
Penza 24 C6
Penzance 11 F4
Peoria 77 E10
Perabumulih .. 37 E2
Perche, Collines
  du 12 B4
Perdido, Mte. .. 19 A6
Perdu, Mt. =
  Perdido, Mte. 19 A6
Pereira 90 C3
Perekerten 62 B3
Pereyaslav-
  Khmelnytskyy 24 C3
Péribonca → . 69 D3
Perico 94 A3
Périgueux 12 D4

Perijá,
  Sierra de..... 90 B4
Perlas, Arch. de
  las 86 E4
Perm 29 D6
Pernambuco =
  Recife 92 D7
Pernatty
  Lagoon 62 B2
Pernik 22 C4
Perpendicular
  Pt. 63 B5
Perpignan 13 E5
Persepolis 44 D3
Pershotravensk 17 C8
Persian Gulf =
  Gulf, The ... 44 E2
Perth, *Australia* 60 G2
Perth, *U.K.* 10 C5
Perth Amboy .. 73 D8
Peru ■ 90 C3
Perúgia 20 C4
Pervomaysk ... 25 D3
Pervouralsk ... 29 D6
Pésaro 20 C4
Pescara 20 C5
Peshawar 42 B7
Peshkopi 22 D3
Pesqueira 92 D6
Petah Tiqwa .. 46 D3
Petauke 59 A6
Peter I.s Øy .. 96 A2
Peterborough,
  Australia .. 62 B2
Peterborough,
  Canada 69 D3
Peterborough,
  U.K. 11 E6
Peterhead 10 C6
Petersburg,
  Alaska, U.S.A. 71 C6
Petersburg, *Va.,*
  U.S.A. 73 F7
Petitsikapau, L. 69 C4
Petlad 43 H8
Peto 85 C7
Petone 65 D6
Petrich 22 D4
Petrikov =
  Pyetrikaw ... 17 B9
Petrograd =
  Sankt-
  Peterburg ... 24 B3
Petrolândia ... 93 D6
Petrolina 93 D5
Petropavl 29 D7
Petropavlovsk =
  Petropavl ... 29 D7
Petropavlovsk-
  Kamchatskiy 31 D13
Petrópolis 93 G5
Petroșani 17 F6
Petrovaradin .. 22 B2
Petrovsk 24 C6
Petrozavodsk .. 28 C4
Peureulak 36 D1
Pforzheim 14 D5
Phagwara 42 D9
Phalodi 42 F8
Phan Rang ... 36 B3
Phangan, Ko .. 36 C2
Phangnga 36 C1
Phatthalung .. 36 C2
Phetchabun ... 36 A2
Philadelphia .. 73 E8
Philippines ■ . 38 B2
Philippopolis =
  Plovdiv 22 C5
Phillip I. 63 C4

Phillott 63 A4
Phitsanulok . . . 36 A2
Phnom Dangrek 36 B2
Phnom Penh . . 36 B2
Phoenix 83 D6
Phra Nakhon Si
  Ayutthaya . . 36 B2
Phuket 36 C1
Phumiphon,
  Khuan 36 A1
Piacenza 20 B2
Pialba 63 A5
Pian Cr. → . . . 63 B4
Pianosa 20 C3
Piatra Neamț . . 17 E8
Piauí □ 92 D5
Piave → 20 B4
Pibor Post 53 G5
Pica 91 H5
Picardie 13 B5
Picardy =
  Picardie . . . 13 B5
Pichilemu 94 C2
Pico Truncado . 95 F3
Picton, Australia 63 B5
Picton, N.Z. . . . 65 D6
Pictou 69 D4
Picún Leufú . . . 95 D3
Piedmont =
  Piemonte □ . 20 B1
Piedras, R. de
  las → 91 F5
Piedras Negras 84 B4
Piemonte □ . . . 20 B1
Pierre Elliott
  Trudeau, Mt. . 70 B5
Piet Retief 59 D6
Pietermaritzburg 59 D6
Pietersburg . . . 59 C5
Pietrosul,
  Romania 17 E7
Pigüe 94 D4
Piketberg 58 E3
Piła 16 B3
Pilar, Brazil . . . 93 D6
Pilar, Paraguay 94 B5
Pilas Group . . . 38 C2
Pilcomayo → . . 94 B5
Pilibhit 42 E11
Pilica → 16 C5
Pílos 23 F3
Pilsen = Plzeň . 16 D1
Pimba 62 B2
Pimenta Bueno 91 F6
Pimentel 91 E3
Pinang 36 C2
Pinar del Río . . 86 B3
Pnarhisar 22 D6
Pińczów 16 C5
Pindiga 55 G7
Pindos Óros . . 23 E3
Pindus Mts. =
  Pindos Óros . 23 E3
Pine Bluff 79 B7
Pine Point 70 B8
Pinega → 28 C5
Pinerolo 20 B1
Pinetown 59 D6
Ping → 36 A2
Pingdong 35 D7
Pingliang 35 C5
Pingwu 35 C5
Pingxiang 35 D5
Pinhel 18 B2
Pini 37 D1
Piniós → 23 E4
Pinnaroo 62 C3
Pínnes, Ákra . . 23 D5
Pinrang 39 E1

Pinsk 17 B8
Pintados 91 H5
Pinyug 24 A6
Piombino 20 C3
Pioner, Os. 30 B7
Piorini, L. 90 D6
Piotrków
  Trybunalski . 16 C4
Pip 45 E5
Piquiri → 94 A6
Piracicaba 94 A7
Piracuruca . . . 92 C5
Piræus =
  Piraiévs 23 F4
Piraiévs 23 F4
Pirané 94 B5
Pirapora 93 F5
Pírgos 23 F3
Pirin Planina . . 22 D4
Piripiri 92 C5
Pirmasens . . . 14 D4
Pirot 22 C4
Piru 39 E3
Pisa 20 C3
Pisagua 91 G4
Pisciotta 21 D5
Pisco 91 F3
Písek 16 D2
Pishan 34 C2
Pising 39 F2
Pistóia 20 C3
Pisuerga → . . 18 B3
Pitarpunga, L. . 62 B3
Pitcairn I. 65 M17
Piteå 8 E12
Pitești 22 B5
Pithapuram . . . 40 J4
Pittsburg 79 A6
Pittsburgh 73 D5
Pittsworth 63 A5
Piura 90 E2
Placentia 69 D5
Placentia B. . . 69 D5
Plainview 78 B3
Pláka, Ákra . . 23 G6
Plakhino 28 C9
Plasencia 18 B2
Plata, Río de la 94 C5
Platani → 21 F4
Plato 90 B4
Platte → 77 F7
Plauen 15 C7
Pleiku 36 B3
Plenty, B. of . . 64 B7
Pleven 22 C5
Plevlja 22 C2
Płock 16 B4
Plöckenstein . . 15 D7
Ploiești 22 B6
Plovdiv 22 C5
Plumtree 59 C5
Plymouth 11 F4
Plzeň 16 D1
Po → 20 B4
Po Hai = Bo Hai 35 C6
Pobedy Pik . . . 29 E8
Pocatello 81 D7
Poços de Caldas 93 G4
Podgorica 22 C2
Podilska
  Vysochyna . . 17 D8
Podkamennaya
  Tunguska → . 30 C7
Podolsk 24 B4
Podor 55 E1
Pofadder 58 D3
Poh 39 E2
Pohnpei 64 J10

Poinsett, C. . . . 96 A12
Pointe-à-Pitre . . 87 C7
Pointe Noire . . . 56 E2
Poitiers 12 C4
Poitou 12 C3
Pokaran 42 F7
Pokataroo 63 A4
Pokrovsk =
  Engels 24 C6
Pola = Pula . . . 20 B4
Polan 45 E5
Poland ■ 16 B5
Polatsk 24 B2
Polcura 94 D2
Polesye = Pripet
  Marshes 17 B9
Poli 56 C2
Police 16 B2
Polillo Is. 38 B2
Políyiros 23 D4
Pollachi 43 P10
Polnovat 28 C7
Polonne 17 C8
Polonnoye =
  Polonne 17 C8
Poltava 24 D3
Polunochnoye . 28 C7
Polynesia 65 L15
Polynésie
  française =
  French
  Polynesia ■ . 65 M16
Pombal, Brazil . 92 D6
Pombal,
  Portugal . . . 18 C1
Pomézia 20 D4
Pomorski,
  Pojezierze . . 16 B3
Ponape =
  Pohnpei 64 J10
Ponca City . . . 78 A5
Ponce 87 C6
Pond Inlet 68 A3
Pondicherry . . 43 P11
Ponferrada . . . 18 A2
Ponnani 43 P9
Ponnyadaung . 41 F10
Ponoy → 28 C5
Ponta Grossa . 94 B6
Ponta Pora . . . 94 A5
Pontarlier 13 C7
Pontchartrain L. 79 D8
Ponte Nova . . . 93 G5
Pontevedra . . . 18 A1
Pontiac 72 C4
Pontianak 37 E3
Pontine Is. =
  Ponziane,
  Ísole 21 D4
Pontine Mts. =
  Kuzey
  Anadolu
  Dağları 46 B3
Pontivy 12 B2
Pontoise 12 B5
Ponziane, Ísole 21 D4
Poochera 62 B1
Poole 11 F6
Poona = Pune . 43 K8
Pooncarie 62 B3
Poopelloe L. . . 63 B3
Poopó, L. de . 91 G5
Popayán 90 C3
Popigay 30 B9
Popilta, L. 62 B3
Popio L. 62 B3
Poplar Bluff . . . 79 A8
Popocatépetl,
  Volcán 84 D5

Popokabaka . . . 56 F3
Poprád 16 D5
Porbandar 43 J6
Porcupine → . . 71 B5
Pordenone 20 B4
Pori 8 F12
Porkkala 9 G12
Porlamar 90 A6
Poroshiri-Dake . 32 F12
Porpoise B. . . . 96 A13
Porretta, Passo
  di 20 B3
Port Adelaide . 62 B2
Port Alberni . . . 71 D7
Port Alfred . . . 59 E5
Port Angeles . . 80 A2
Port Antonio . . 86 C4
Port Arthur,
  Australia . . . 62 D4
Port Arthur,
  U.S.A. 79 E7
Port-au-Prince . 87 C5
Port Augusta . . 62 B2
Port Augusta
  West 62 B2
Port Bergé
  Vaovao 59 H9
Port Bou 19 A7
Port Broughton 62 B2
Port-Cartier . . . 69 C4
Port Chalmers . 65 F4
Port Darwin . . . 95 G5
Port Davey . . . 62 D4
Port Dickson . . 37 D2
Port Elizabeth . 59 E5
Port Fairy 62 C3
Port-Gentil 56 E1
Port Harcourt . . 55 H6
Port Harrison =
  Inukjuak . . . 68 C3
Port
  Hawkesbury . 69 D4
Port Hedland . . 60 E2
Port Huron . . . 72 C4
Port Kembla . . 63 B5
Port Kenny . . . 62 B1
Port Lairge =
  Waterford . . . 11 E3
Port Laoise . . . 11 E3
Port Lincoln . . . 62 B2
Port Loko 55 G2
Port MacDonnell 62 C3
Port Macquarie . 63 B5
Port Moresby . 61 B8
Port Nelson . . 71 C10
Port Nolloth . . . 58 D3
Port Nouveau-
  Québec =
  Kangiqsualujjuaq
  . . . . 68 C4
Port of Spain . . 87 D7
Port Pegasus . 65 G2
Port Phillip B. . 63 C3
Port Pirie 62 B2
Port Safaga =
  Bûr Safâga . 52 C5
Port Said = Bûr
  Sa'îd 52 B5
Port Shepstone 59 E6
Port Stanley =
  Stanley 95 G5
Port Sudan =
  Bûr Sûdân . . 53 E6
Port Talbot . . . 11 F5
Port-Vendres . . 13 E5
Port Wakefield . 62 B2
Port Weld 36 D2
Porta Orientalis 22 B4

Portachuelo ... 91 G6
Portadown 11 D3
Portage La
  Prairie 71 D10
Portalegre 18 C2
Portile de Fier . 22 B4
Portimão 18 D1
Portland,
  N.S.W.,
  Australia 63 B4
Portland, *Vic.,*
  Australia 62 C3
Portland, *Maine,*
  U.S.A. 73 C10
Portland, *Oreg.,*
  U.S.A. 80 C2
Portland B. 62 C3
Portland Prom. 68 C3
Porto 18 B1
Pôrto Alegre . 94 C6
Porto Amboim
  = Gunza ... 56 G2
Pôrto de Móz .. 92 C3
Porto
  Empédocle .. 21 F4
Pôrto Esperança 91 G7
Pôrto Franco .. 92 D4
Porto Mendes . 94 A6
Pôrto Murtinho 91 H7
Pôrto Nacional 93 E4
Porto Novo ... 55 G5
Porto Santo .. 54 B1
Pôrto Seguro . 93 F6
Pôrto União .. 94 B6
Pôrto Válter .. 91 E4
Porto-Vecchio . 13 F8
Pôrto Velho ... 91 E6
Portoferráio .. 20 C3
Portoscuso 21 E2
Portovíejo 90 D2
Portree 10 C3
Portsmouth,
  U.K. 11 F6
Portsmouth,
  U.S.A. 73 F7
Porttipahtan
  tekojärvi 8 E13
Portugal ■ 18 C1
Porvenir 95 G2
Posadas 94 B5
Poshan =
  Boshan 35 C6
Poso 39 E2
Posse 93 E4
Possel 56 C3
Possession I. .. 96 B15
Poste Maurice
  Cortier 54 D5
Postojna 20 B5
Potchefstroom . 59 D5
Potenza 21 D5
Poteriteri, L. .. 65 G2
Potgietersrus .. 59 C5
Poti 25 E5
Potiskum 55 F7
Potomac → .. 73 E7
Potosí 91 G5
Pototan 38 B2
Potrerillos 94 B3
Potsdam 15 B7
Poughkeepsie . 73 D9
Pouso Alegre .. 93 E2
Považská
  Bystrica 16 D4
Povenets 28 C4
Poverty B. 64 C8
Póvoa de Varzim 18 B1

Powder → ... 76 B2
Powell L. 83 B7
Poyang Hu ... 35 D6
Požarevac 22 B3
Poznań 16 B3
Pozo Almonte . 91 H5
Pozoblanco ... 18 C3
Pozzuoli 21 D5
Prachuap Khiri
  Khan 36 B1
Prado 93 F6
Prague = Praha 16 C2
Praha 16 C2
Prainha,
  Amazonas,
  Brazil 91 E6
Prainha, *Pará,*
  Brazil 92 C3
Prairies 71 C9
Prapat 37 D1
Prata 93 F4
Prato 20 C3
Pravia 18 A2
Praya 37 F5
Preparis North
  Channel 41 K9
Preparis South
  Channel 41 K9
Přerov 16 D3
Preservation
  Inlet 65 G2
Presidencia
  Roque Saenz
  Peña 94 B4
Presidente
  Epitácio ... 93 G3
Presidente
  Hermes 91 F6
Presidente
  Prudente ... 93 G3
Prešov 16 D5
Prespa, L. =
  Prespansko
  Jezero 23 D3
Prespansko
  Jezero 23 D3
Presque Isle .. 73 A11
Preston 11 E5
Pretoria 59 D5
Préveza 23 E3
Příbram 16 D2
Prichard 74 D3
Prieska 58 D4
Prievidza 16 D4
Prilep 22 D3
Priluki = Pryluky 24 C3
Prime Seal I. .. 62 D4
Prince Albert .. 71 C9
Prince Albert
  Mts. 96 B15
Prince Albert
  Pen. 70 A8
Prince Albert Sd. 70 A8
Prince Charles I. 68 B3
Prince Charles
  Mts. 96 B10
Prince Edward
  I. □ 69 D4
Prince of Wales
  I., *Canada* ... 70 A10
Prince of Wales
  I., *U.S.A.* ... 71 C6
Principe da
  Beira 91 F6
Prins Harald
  Kyst 96 B8
Prinsesse Astrid
  Kyst 96 B7

Prinsesse
  Ragnhild Kyst 96 B8
Pripet → =
  Prypyat → .. 17 C10
Pripet Marshes 17 B9
Pripyat Marshes
  = Pripet
  Marshes 17 B9
Pripyats =
  Prypyat → .. 17 C10
Priština 22 C3
Privas 13 D6
Privolzhskaya
  Vozvyshennost
  .... 24 C6
Prizren 22 C3
Proddatur 43 M11
Progreso 85 C7
Prokopyevsk .. 29 D9
Prokuplje 22 C3
Prome = Pyè .. 41 H10
Propriá 93 E6
Prostějov 16 D3
Proston 63 A5
Provence 13 E6
Providence ... 73 D10
Providencia, I.
  de 86 D3
Provins 13 B5
Provo 81 E8
Prozna → 16 B3
Pruszków 16 B5
Prut → 17 F9
Pruzhany 17 B7
Prydz B. 96 A10
Pryluky 24 C3
Prypyat → ... 17 C10
Przemyśl 17 D6
Przhevalsk ... 29 E8
Psará 23 E5
Pskov 24 B2
Ptich =
  Ptsich → ... 17 B9
Ptsich → 17 B9
Puán 94 D4
Pucallpa 91 E4
Pudukkottai ... 43 P11
Puebla 84 D5
Pueblo 76 F2
Pueblo Hundido 94 B2
Puelches 94 D3
Puente Alto .. 94 C2
Puente-Genil .. 18 D3
Puerto Aisén .. 95 F2
Puerto
  Ayacucho ... 90 B5
Puerto Barrios . 85 D7
Puerto Bermejo 94 B5
Puerto
  Bermúdez ... 91 F4
Puerto Bolívar . 90 D3
Puerto Cabello . 90 A5
Puerto Cabezas 86 D3
Puerto Carreño 90 B5
Puerto Chicama 91 E3
Puerto Coig ... 95 G3
Puerto Cortés . 85 D7
Puerto
  Cumarebo .. 90 A5
Puerto del
  Rosario 54 C2
Puerto Deseado 95 F3
Puerto Heath .. 91 F5
Puerto La Cruz 90 A6
Puerto
  Leguízamo .. 90 D4
Puerto Lobos .. 95 E3
Puerto Madryn 95 E3

Puerto
  Maldonado .. 91 F5
Puerto Montt .. 95 E2
Puerto Morelos 85 C7
Puerto Natales 95 G2
Puerto Páez .. 90 B5
Puerto Pinasco 94 A5
Puerto
  Pirámides ... 95 E4
Puerto Plata .. 87 C5
Puerto Princesa 38 C1
Puerto Quellón 95 E2
Puerto Rico ■ . 87 C6
Puerto Sastre . 91 H7
Puerto Suárez . 91 G7
Puerto Wilches 90 B4
Puertollano ... 18 C3
Pueyrredón, L. . 95 F2
Pugachev 24 C6
Puget Sound . 80 B2
Puigcerdá 19 A6
Pukaki L. 65 F4
Pukapuka 65 L14
Pukekohe 64 B6
Pula 20 B4
Puławy 16 C5
Pullman 80 B5
Pulog 38 A2
Pułtusk 16 B5
Puna 91 G5
Puná, I. 90 D2
Punakha 41 D7
Punata 91 G5
Punch 42 C9
Pune 43 K8
Punjab □, *India* 42 D9
Punjab □,
  Pakistan 42 D8
Puno 91 G4
Punta Alta ... 94 D4
Punta Arenas . 95 G2
Punta de Díaz . 94 B2
Puntabie 62 B1
Puntarenas ... 86 E3
Punto Fijo 90 A4
Puquio 91 F4
Pur → 28 C8
Purace, Vol. .. 90 C3
Puralia =
  Puruliya 40 F6
Puri 40 H5
Purnia 40 E6
Purukcahu ... 37 E4
Puruliya 40 F6
Purus → 90 D6
Pusan 35 C7
Pushkino 24 C6
Putao 41 D11
Putaruru 64 C6
Puthein Myit → 41 K10
Putignano 21 D6
Puting, Tanjung 37 E4
Putorana, Gory 30 C7
Puttalam 43 Q11
Puttgarden 15 A6
Putumayo → .. 90 D5
Putussibau ... 37 D4
Puy-de-Dôme . 13 D5
Pweto 57 F5
Pwllheli 11 E4
Pyapon 41 J10
Pyasina → ... 30 B6
Pyatigorsk ... 25 E5
Pyè 41 H10
Pyetrikaw 17 B9
Pyinmana 41 H11
P'yŏngyang .. 35 C7
Pyrénées 19 A6
Pyu 41 H11

Q

Qādib 49 E5
Qā'emshahr . . . 44 B3
Qahremānshahr
= Bākhtarān . 46 D6
Qaidam Pendi . 34 C4
Qalāt 45 C6
Qal'at al Akhḍar 47 E4
Qal'eh Shaharak 42 B4
Qal'eh-ye Now 45 C5
Qamar, Ghubbat
al 49 D5
Qamruddin
Karez 42 D6
Qandahār 42 D4
Qandahār □ . . . 42 D4
Qapshaghay . 29 E8
Qâra 52 C4
Qarabutaq . . . 29 E7
Qarachuk 46 C5
Qaraghandy . . 29 E8
Qārah 47 E5
Qarataū 29 E8
Qarqan 34 C3
Qarqan He → . 34 C3
Qarqaraly 29 E8
Qarshi 29 F7
Qaşr-e Qand . 45 E5
Qasr Farâfra . 52 C4
Qatar ■ 44 E2
Qattâra,
Munkhafed el 52 C4
Qattâra
Depression =
Qattâra,
Munkhafed el 52 C4
Qāyen 44 C4
Qazaqstan =
Kazakstan ■ . 29 E7
Qazvin 46 C7
Qena 52 C5
Qeshm 44 E4
Qila Safed . . . 42 E2
Qila Saifullāh . 42 D6
Qilian Shan . . 34 C4
Qingdao 35 C7
Qinghai □ 34 C4
Qinghai Hu . . . 34 C5
Qinhuangdao . 35 C6
Qinzhou 35 D5
Qiqihar 35 B7
Qitai 34 B3
Qom 44 C2
Qomsheh 44 C2
Qondūz 45 B7
Qondūz □ 45 B7
Qostanay 29 D7
Qu Xian,
Sichuan,
China 35 C5
Qu Xian,
Zhejiang,
China 35 D6
Quambatook . . 62 C3
Quambone . . . 63 B4
Quan Long . . . 36 C3
Quandialla . . . 63 B4
Quang Ngai . . 36 A3
Quanzhou 35 D6
Quaqtaq 68 B4
Quaraí 94 C5
Quartu
Sant'Elena . . 21 E2
Quatsino 71 C2
Quba 25 E6
Qūchān 44 B4
Queanbeyan . . 63 C4
Québec 69 D3

Québec □ 69 D3
Queen
Alexandra Ra. 96 C15
Queen Charlotte
Is. 70 C6
Queen Charlotte
Str. 71 C7
Queen Elizabeth
Is. 66 B9
Queen Mary
Land 96 B11
Queen Maud G. 70 B9
Queen Maud
Land 96 B7
Queen Maud
Mts. 96 C16
Queenscliff . . 63 C3
Queensland □ . 61 E7
Queenstown,
Australia 62 D4
Queenstown,
N.Z. 65 F3
Queenstown,
S. Africa . . . 59 E5
Queimadas . . 93 E6
Quela 56 F3
Quelimane . . 59 B7
Quelpart =
Cheju Do . . . 35 C7
Quequén 94 D5
Querétaro . . . 84 C4
Quetta 42 D5
Quezon City . . 38 B2
Qui Nhon 36 B3
Quibaxe 56 F2
Quibdo 90 B3
Quiberon 12 C2
Quilán, C. 95 E2
Quilengues . . 58 A2
Quillabamba . 91 F4
Quillagua . . . 91 H5
Quillota 94 C2
Quilon 43 Q10
Quilpie 63 A3
Quimilí 94 B4
Quimper 12 B1
Quimperlé . . . 12 C2
Quincy 77 F9
Quines 94 C3
Quinga 59 H8
Quintanar de la
Orden 18 C4
Quintero 94 C2
Quinyambie . . 62 B3
Quipungo . . . 58 A2
Quirindi 63 B5
Quirinópolis . . 93 F3
Quissanga . . 59 G8
Quitilipi 94 B4
Quito 90 D3
Quixadá 92 C6
Qŭnghirot . . . 29 E6
Quondong . . . 62 B3
Quorn 62 B2
Qŭqon 29 E8
Qûs 52 C5
Quseir 52 C5
Qyzylorda . . . 29 E7

R

Raahe 8 F12
Raba 39 F1
Rába → 16 E3
Rabat, Malta . . 21 G5
Rabat, Morocco 54 B3
Rabaul 64 K10

Rābigh 47 G4
Race, C. 69 D5
Rach Gia 36 B3
Racibórz 16 C4
Racine 72 C2
Rădăuţi 17 E7
Radekhiv 17 C7
Radekhov =
Radekhiv . . 17 C7
Radhwa, Jabal 47 F4
Radom 16 C5
Radomsko . . . 16 C4
Radomyshl . . . 17 C9
Radstock, C. . . 62 B1
Rae 70 B8
Rae Bareli . . . 40 D3
Rae Isthmus . . 68 B2
Raetihi 64 C6
Rafaela 94 C4
Rafai 56 D4
Rafḥā 47 E5
Rafsanjān . . . 44 D4
Ragachow . . . 17 B10
Ragama 43 R11
Raglan 64 B6
Ragusa 21 F5
Raha 39 E2
Rahad al Bardī 53 F3
Rahaeng = Tak 36 A1
Rahimyar Khan 42 E7
Raichur 43 L10
Raigarh 40 G4
Railton 62 D4
Rainier, Mt. . . 80 B3
Raipur 40 G3
Ra'is 47 G4
Raj Nandgaon . 40 G3
Raja, Ujung . . 37 D1
Raja Ampat,
Kepulauan . 39 E3
Rajahmundry . 40 J3
Rajang → . . . 37 D4
Rajapalaiyam . 43 Q10
Rajasthan □ . . 42 F8
Rajasthan Canal 42 F8
Rajgarh 43 G10
Rajkot 43 H7
Rajpipla 43 J8
Rajshahi 41 E7
Rakaia 65 E5
Rakaia → . . . 65 E5
Rakan, Ra's . . 44 E2
Rakaposhi . . . 42 A9
Rakata, Pulau . 37 F3
Rakhiv 17 D7
Raleigh 75 B8
Ram Hd. 63 C4
Ramanathapuram
. . . . 43 Q11
Ramechhap . . 40 D6
Ramelau 39 F3
Ramgarh, Bihar,
India 40 F5
Ramgarh, Raj.,
India 42 F7
Rāmhormoz . . 47 E7
Ramnad =
Ramanathapuram
. . . . 43 Q11
Rampur 42 E11
Rampur Hat . . 40 E6
Ramree I. =
Ramree Kyun 41 H9
Ramree Kyun . 41 H9
Ramtek 43 J11
Ranaghat . . . 41 F7
Ranau 36 C5
Rancagua . . . 94 C2
Ranchi 40 F5

Randers 9 G10
Rangaunu B. . . 64 A5
Rangia 41 D8
Rangiora 65 E5
Rangitaiki → . 64 B7
Rangitata → . 65 E4
Rangon → . . . 41 J11
Rangoon 41 J11
Rangpur 41 E7
Ranibennur . . 43 M9
Raniganj 40 F6
Raniwara 43 G8
Rankin Inlet . . 70 B10
Rankins Springs 63 B4
Ranong 36 C1
Ransiki 39 E4
Rantau 37 E5
Rantauprapat . 37 D1
Rantemario . . 39 E1
Rapa 65 M16
Rapallo 20 B2
Rāpch 45 E4
Rapid City . . . 76 C3
Rarotonga . . . 65 M14
Ra's al Khaymah 44 E4
Ra's al-Unuf . . 52 B2
Ras Bânâs . . . 52 D6
Ras Dashen . . 57 B7
Râs Timirist . . 55 E1
Rasa, Punta . . 95 E4
Rashad 53 F5
Rashīd 52 B5
Rasht 46 C7
Rat Islands . . 71 C1
Ratangarh . . . 42 E9
Rathenow . . . 15 B7
Ratibor =
Racibórz . . . 16 C4
Ratlam 43 H9
Ratnagiri 43 L8
Raukumara Ra. 64 C7
Raurkela 40 F5
Rava-Ruska . . 17 C6
Rava Russkaya
= Rava-Ruska 17 C6
Rāvar 44 D4
Ravenna 20 B4
Ravensburg . . 14 E5
Ravi → 42 D7
Rawalpindi . . . 42 C8
Rawāndūz . . . 46 C6
Rawene 64 A5
Rawlins 81 E10
Rawson 95 E3
Ray, C. 69 D5
Rayadurg . . . 43 M10
Rayagada . . . 40 H4
Raymond 71 D8
Raz, Pte. du . . 12 B1
Razdel'naya =
Rozdilna . . . 17 E10
Razelm, Lacul . 22 B7
Razgrad 22 C6
Ré, I. de 12 C3
Reading, U.K. . 11 F6
Reading, U.S.A. 73 D8
Realicó 94 D4
Rebi 39 F4
Rebiana 52 D3
Rebun-Tō . . . 32 E12
Rechytsa 17 B10
Recife 92 D7
Reconquista . . 94 B5
Recreo 94 B3
Red →, La.,
U.S.A. 79 D8
Red →, N. Dak.,
U.S.A. 76 A6
Red Cliffs 62 B3

Red Deer

Red Deer 71 C8
Red Sea 48 C2
Red Tower Pass
= Turnu Roşu,
P. 17 F7
Redcar 11 D6
Redcliffe 63 A5
Redding 80 E2
Redditch 11 E6
Redon 12 C2
Redondela 18 A1
Redwood City . 82 B1
Ree, L. 11 E3
Reefton 65 E4
Regensburg ... 15 D7
Réggio di
Calábria 21 E5
Réggio
nell'Emília .. 20 B3
Reghin 17 E7
Regina 71 C9
Rehoboth 58 C3
Rehovot 46 E3
Rei-Bouba ... 53 G1
Reichenbach . 15 C7
Reidsville 75 A8
Reigate 11 F6
Reims 13 B6
Reina Adelaida,
Arch. 95 G2
Reindeer L. ... 71 C9
Reinga, C. ... 64 A5
Reinosa 18 A3
Reliance 70 B9
Remarkable, Mt. 62 B2
Remeshk 45 E4
Rendsburg 14 A5
Rengat 37 E2
Reni 17 F9
Renk 53 F5
Renmark 62 B3
Rennes 12 B3
Reno 80 F4
Reno → 20 B4
Rentería 19 A5
Republican → 76 F6
Repulse Bay . 68 B2
Requena, Peru . 90 E4
Requena, Spain 19 C5
Resadiye =
Datça 23 F6
Resht = Rasht . 46 C7
Resistencia .. 94 B5
Reşiţa 17 F5
Resolution I.,
Canada 68 B4
Resolution I.,
N.Z. 65 F2
Réthímnon 23 G5
Réunion ■ 51 J9
Reus 19 B6
Reutlingen ... 14 D5
Reval = Tallinn 24 B1
Revelstoke 71 C8
Rewa 40 E3
Rewari 42 E10
Rey Malabo .. 56 D1
Reykjavík 8 B2
Reynosa 84 B5
Rhein → 14 C4
Rhein-Main-
Donau-
Kanal → ... 15 D6
Rheine 14 B4
Rheinland-
Pfalz □ 14 C4
Rhin =
Rhein → ... 14 C4
Rhine =
Rhein → ... 14 C4

Rhineland-
Palatinate □ =
Rheinland-
Pfalz □ 14 C4
Rhode Island □ 73 D10
Rhodes =
Ródhos 23 F7
Rhodope Mts. =
Rhodopi
Planina 22 D5
Rhodopi Planina 22 D5
Rhön = Hohe
Rhön 14 C5
Rhondda 11 F5
Rhône → 13 E6
Rhum 10 C3
Riachão 92 D4
Riasi 42 C9
Riau □ 37 E2
Riau, Kepulauan 37 D2
Riau Arch. =
Riau,
Kepulauan .. 37 D2
Ribadeo 18 A2
Ribeirão Prêto . 93 G4
Riberalta 91 F5
Rîbniţa 17 E9
Riccarton 65 E5
Richland 80 B4
Richmond,
Australia ... 63 B5
Richmond, N.Z. 65 D5
Richmond,
Calif., U.S.A. 80 G2
Richmond, Va.,
U.S.A. 73 F7
Richmond Ra. . 63 A5
Ridder 29 D9
Ried 15 D7
Riesa 15 C7
Rieti 20 C4
Rig Rig 53 F1
Rīga 24 B1
Riga, G. of ... 24 B1
Rīgas Jūras Līcis
= Riga, G. of 24 B1
Rīgestān □ ... 42 D4
Rigolet 68 C5
Riiser-Larsen-
halvøya 96 A8
Rijeka 20 B5
Rimah, Wadi
ar → 47 F5
Rímini 20 B4
Rîmnicu Sărat . 17 F8
Rîmnicu Vîlcea 17 F7
Rimouski 69 D4
Rinca 39 F1
Rinconada 94 A3
Rinjani 37 F5
Rio Branco,
Brazil 91 E5
Río Branco,
Uruguay ... 94 C6
Río Cuarto ... 94 C4
Rio de Janeiro . 93 G5
Rio de
Janeiro □ ... 93 G5
Rio do Sul 94 B7
Río Gallegos .. 95 G3
Río Grande,
Argentina ... 95 G3
Rio Grande,
Brazil 94 C6
Rio Grande → 78
Rio Grande do
Norte □ 92 D6
Rio Grande do
Sul □ 94 B6

Rio Largo 93 D6
Río Mulatos ... 91 G5
Río Muni =
Mbini □ 56 D2
Rio Negro 94 B7
Rio Verde 93 F3
Ríobamba 90 D3
Ríohacha 90 A4
Ríosucio,
Caldas,
Colombia ... 90 B3
Ríosucio, Choco,
Colombia ... 90 B3
Rishiri-Tō 32 E12
Riva del Garda 20 B3
Rivadavia 94 B2
Rivera 94 C5
Riversdale 58 E4
Riverside 82 D4
Riverton,
Australia 62 B2
Riverton,
Canada 71 C10
Riverton, N.Z. . 65 G2
Riviera di
Levante 20 B2
Riviera di
Ponente ... 20 B2
Rivière-du-Loup 69 D4
Rivne 17 C8
Rívoli 20 B1
Rivoli B. 62 C3
Riyadh = Ar
Riyāḍ 47 F6
Rize 46 B5
Rizzuto, C. ... 21 E6
Roanne 13 C6
Roanoke 73 F6
Robbins I. 62 D4
Robertson 58 E3
Robertson I. ... 96 A4
Robertsport ... 55 G2
Robertstown .. 62 B2
Robinvale 62 B3
Roboré 91 G7
Robson, Mt. .. 71 C8
Roca, C. da .. 18 C1
Rocas, I. 92 C7
Rocha 94 C6
Rochefort 12 D3
Rochester,
Minn., U.S.A. 77 C8
Rochester, N.Y.,
U.S.A. 73 C7
Rock Hill 75 B7
Rock Island .. 77 E9
Rock Springs . 81 E9
Rockefeller
Plateau 96 C18
Rockford 77 D10
Rockhampton . 61 E9
Rocky Mount . 75 B9
Rocky Mts. ... 70 C7
Rod 42 E3
Rodez 13 D5
Ródhos 23 F7
Rodney, C. ... 64 B6
Roes Welcome
Sd. 68 B2
Rogachev =
Ragachow .. 17 B10
Rogatyn 17 D7
Rogoaguado, L. 91 F5
Rohri 42 F6
Rohtak 42 E10
Roi Et 36 A2
Rojas 94 C4
Rojo, C. 84 C5

Rokan → 37 D2
Rolândia 94 A6
Roma, Australia 63 A4
Roma, Italy ... 20 D4
Roman 17 E8
Romang 39 F3
Romania ■ ... 22 B5
Romanovka =
Basarabeasca 17 E9
Romans-sur-
Isère 13 D6
Romblon 38 B2
Rome = Roma 20 D4
Rome 74 B5
Romorantin-
Lanthenay .. 12 C4
Roncador, Serra
do 93 E3
Ronda 18 D3
Rondônia □ ... 91 F6
Rondonópolis . 93 F3
Ronge, L. la ... 71 C9
Ronne Ice Shelf 96 B3
Roodepoort ... 59 D5
Roorkee 42 E10
Roosevelt → . 91 E6
Roosevelt I. ... 96 B16
Roquetas de
Mar 19 D4
Roraima □ 90 C6
Roraima, Mt. . 90 B6
Rosa 57 F6
Rosa, Monte .. 13 D7
Rosario,
Argentina ... 94 C4
Rosário, Brazil . 92 C5
Rosario, Mexico 84 C3
Rosario,
Paraguay ... 94 A5
Rosario de la
Frontera ... 94 B3
Rosário do Sul 94 C6
Rosas, G. de . 19 A7
Roscommon .. 11 E2
Roseau, Domin. 87 C7
Roseau, U.S.A. 77 A7
Rosebery 62 D4
Roseburg 80 D2
Rosenheim ... 15 E7
Rosetown 71 C9
Rosetta =
Rashîd 52 B5
Roseville 80 F3
Rosewood ... 63 A5
Rosignano
Maríttimo ... 20 C3
Rosignol 90 B7
Roşiori-de-Vede 22 B5
Roslavl 24 C3
Roslyn 63 B4
Ross, Australia 62 D4
Ross, N.Z. ... 65 E4
Ross I. 96 B15
Ross Ice Shelf . 96 C16
Ross Sea 96 B15
Rossano Cálabro 21 E6
Rossland 71 D8
Rosslare 11 E3
Rosso 55 E1
Rossosh 24 C4
Rosthern 71 C9
Rostock 15 A7
Rostov, Don,
Russia 25 D4
Rostov, Yarosl.,
Russia 24 B4
Roswell 78 C1
Rotherham 11 E6
Roto 63 B4

144

Rotondo Mte. . 13 E8
Rotorua 64 C7
Rotorua, L. 64 C7
Rotterdam 14 C3
Rottweil 14 D5
Rotuma 64 L12
Roubaix 13 A5
Rouen 12 B4
Round Mt. 63 B5
Roussillon 13 E5
Rouyn 69 D3
Rovaniemi 8 E13
Rovereto 20 B3
Rovigo 20 B3
Rovinj 20 B4
Rovno = Rivne 17 C8
Rovuma ➤ .. 57 G8
Rowena 63 A4
Roxas 38 B2
Roxburgh 65 F3
Royal
Leamington
Spa 11 E6
Royan 12 D3
Rozdilna 17 E10
Rozhyshche ... 17 C7
Rtishchevo 24 C5
Ruahine Ra. ... 64 C7
Ruapehu 64 C6
Ruapuke I. 65 G3
Rub' al Khali . 48 D4
Rubio 90 B4
Rubtsovsk 29 D9
Rudall 62 B2
Rudolf, Ostrov . 28 A6
Rufa'a 53 F5
Rufiji ➤ 57 F7
Rufino 94 C4
Rufisque 55 F1
Rugby 11 E6
Rügen 15 A7
Ruhr ➤ 14 C4
Rukwa L. 57 F6
Rum = Rhum . 10 C3
Rumāḥ 47 F6
Rumania =
Romania ■ .. 22 B5
Rumbêk 53 G4
Rumia 16 A4
Rumoi 32 F12
Runanga 65 E4
Runaway, C. .. 64 B7
Rungwa 57 F6
Ruoqiang 34 C3
Rupa 41 D9
Rupat 37 D2
Rupert ➤ 69 C3
Rupert House =
Waskaganish 69 C3
Rurrenabaque . 91 F5
Rusape 59 B6
Ruschuk = Ruse 22 C5
Ruse 22 C5
Rushworth 63 C4
Russas 92 C6
Russellkonda .. 40 H5
Russkaya
Polyana 29 D8
Rustavi 25 E6
Rustenburg ... 59 D5
Ruteng 39 F2
Rutshuru 57 E5
Ruwenzori 57 D5
Ružomberok .. 16 D4
Rwanda ■ 57 E6
Ryazan 24 C4
Ryazhsk 24 C5
Rybache =
Rybachye ... 29 E9

Rybachye 29 E9
Rybinsk 24 B4
Rybinskoye
Vdkhr. 24 B4
Rybnitsa =
Rîbniţa 17 E9
Rylstone 63 B4
Rypin 16 B4
Ryūkyū Is. =
Ryūkyū-rettō 35 D7
Ryūkyū-rettō .. 35 D7
Rzeszów 16 C5
Rzhev 24 B3

S

Sa Dec 36 B3
Sa'ādatābād .. 44 D3
Saale ➤ 15 C6
Saalfeld 15 C6
Saar ➤ 13 B7
Saarbrücken . 14 D4
Saaremaa 24 B1
Šabac 22 B2
Sabadell 19 B7
Sabah □ 36 C5
Ṣabāḥ, Wadi ➤ 47 G7
Sabalān, Kūhhā-
ye 46 C6
Sábanalarga .. 90 A4
Sabang 36 C1
Sabará 93 F5
Saberania 39 E5
Sabhah 52 C1
Sabinas 84 B4
Sabinas Hidalgo 84 B4
Sablayan 38 B2
Sable, C.,
Canada 69 D4
Sable, C., U.S.A. 86 A3
Sable I. 69 D5
Sabrina Coast . 96 A12
Sabulubek 37 E1
Sabzevār 44 B4
Sabzvārān 44 D4
Săcele 17 F7
Sachsen □ 15 C7
Sachsen-
Anhalt □ 15 C7
Sacramento ... 80 F3
Sacramento ➤ 80 F3
Sacramento
Mts. 83 D10
Sadani 57 F7
Sadd el Aali .. 52 D5
Sado 33 G11
Sadon 41 E11
Safi 54 B3
Safid Kūh 42 B3
Saga, Indonesia 39 E4
Saga, Japan .. 32 C2
Sagala 55 F3
Sagar 43 M9
Sagil 34 A4
Saginaw 72 C4
Ṣagīr, Zāb aṣ ➤ 46 D5
Saglouc =
Salluit 68 B3
Sagua la Grande 86 B3
Saguenay ➤ . 69 D3
Sagunto 19 C5
Sahagún 18 A3
Sahand, Kūh-e 46 C6
Sahara 54 D6
Saharan Atlas =
Saharien,
Atlas 54 B5

Saharanpur ... 42 E10
Saharien, Atlas 54 B5
Sahiwal 42 D8
Sa'id Bundas . 53 G3
Saïda 54 B5
Sa'īdābād 44 D3
Sa'īdīyeh 46 C7
Saidpur 41 E7
Saidu 42 B8
Saigon = Phanh
Bho Ho Chi
Minh 36 B3
Saijō 32 C3
Saikhoa Ghat .. 41 D10
Saiki 32 C2
Sailolof 39 E4
St. Andrews .. 10 C5
St. Arnaud 62 C3
St-Augustin-
Saguenay .. 69 C5
St. Augustine . 75 E7
St. Austell 11 F4
St. Boniface .. 71 D10
St.-Brieuc 12 B2
St. Catharines . 69 D3
St.-Chamond .. 13 D6
St. Christopher-
Nevis ■ = St.
Kitts & Nevis 87 C7
St. Cloud 77 C7
St. Croix 87 C7
St.-Denis 12 B5
St.-Dizier 13 B6
St. Elias, Mt. .. 70 B5
St.-Étienne 13 D6
St.-Flour 13 D5
St. Francis, C. . 58 E4
St. Gallen =
Sankt Gallen 13 C8
St.-Gaudens .. 12 E4
St. George 63 A4
St.-Georges,
Fr. Guiana .. 92 B3
St. George's,
Grenada 87 D7
St. George's
Channel ... 11 F3
St. Georges Hd. 63 C5
St. Gotthard P.
= San
Gottardo, P.
del 13 C8
St. Helena ■ .. 51 H3
St. Helena B. .. 58 E3
St. Helens 62 D4
St. Helier 11 G5
St-Hyacinthe .. 69 D3
St. John 69 D4
St. John's,
Antigua 87 C7
St. John's,
Canada 69 D5
St. Johns ➤ .. 75 D7
St. Joseph ... 77 F7
St. Joseph, I. . 69 C1
St. Kilda, N.Z. . 65 F4
St. Kilda, U.K. . 10 C2
St. Kitts & Nevis 87 C7
St.-Laurent .. 92 A3
St. Lawrence ➤ 69 D4
St. Lawrence,
Gulf of 69 D4
St. Lawrence I. 71 B2
St. Leonard .. 69 D4
St.-Lô 12 B3
St-Louis 55 E1
St. Louis 77 F9
St. Lucia ■ ... 87 D7
St. Lucia, L. .. 59 D6

St. Maarten ... 87 C7
St.-Malo 12 B2
St-Marc 87 C5
St. Mary Pk. .. 62 B2
St. Marys 62 D4
St.-Mathieu, Pte. 12 B1
St. Matthews, I.
= Zadetkyi
Kyun 36 C1
St.-Nazaire ... 12 C2
St.-Omer 12 A5
St. Paul 77 C8
St. Peter Port .. 11 G5
St. Petersburg =
Sankt-
Peterburg .. 24 B3
St. Petersburg . 75 F6
St.-Pierre et
Miquelon □ . 69 D5
St.-Quentin ... 13 B5
St. Thomas I. .. 87 C7
St.-Tropez 13 E7
St. Vincent, G. . 62 C2
St. Vincent &
the
Grenadines ■ 87 D7
Saintes 12 D3
Saintonge 12 D3
Saipan 64 H9
Sairang 41 F9
Sairecábur,
Cerro 94 A3
Sajama 91 G5
Sajó 16 D5
Sakai 32 B4
Sakākah 47 E5
Sakakawea, L. . 76 B4
Sakarya =
Adapazarı ... 46 B2
Sakarya ➤ ... 25 E3
Sakata 33 G11
Sakhalin 31 D12
Sakon Nakhon . 36 A2
Sala 9 G11
Sala Consilina . 21 D5
Saladillo 94 D5
Salado ➤,
Buenos Aires,
Argentina ... 94 D5
Salado ➤,
La Pampa,
Argentina ... 94 D3
Salado ➤,
Santa Fe,
Argentina ... 94 C4
Salaga 55 G4
Salālah 49 D5
Salamanca,
Chile 94 C2
Salamanca,
Spain 18 B3
Salamís 23 F4
Salar de
Atacama .. 94 A3
Salar de Uyuni 91 H5
Salaverry 91 E3
Salawati 39 E4
Salayar 39 F2
Saldanha 58 E3
Sale, Australia . 63 C4
Salé, Morocco . 54 B3
Salekhard 28 C7
Salem, India .. 43 P11
Salem, U.S.A. . 80 C2
Salerno 21 D5
Salgótarján ... 16 D4
Salihli 23 E7
Salihorsk 17 B8
Salima 59 A6

Salina

Salina, *Italy* . . . 21　E5
Salina, *U.S.A.* . 76　F6
Salina Cruz . . . 85　D5
Salinas, *Brazil* . 93　F5
Salinas, *Ecuador* 90　D2
Salinas, *U.S.A.* 82　B2
Salinas Grandes 94　C3
Salinópolis . . . . 92　C4
Salisbury,
　Australia . . . 62　B2
Salisbury, *U.K.* 11　F6
Salisbury, *U.S.A.* 75　B7
Salliq . . . . 68　B2
Salluit . . . . 68　B3
Salmãs . . . . 46　C6
Salmon ⟶ . . . 80　C5
Salmon River
　Mts. . . . . 81　C6
Salon-de-
　Provence . . . 13　E6
Salonica =
　Thessaloníki . 23　D4
Salonta . . . . 16　E5
Salsk . . . . 25　D5
Salso ⟶ . . . . . 21　F4
Salt Creek . . . . 62　C2
Salt Lake City . 81　E8
Salta . . . . 94　A3
Saltillo . . . . 84　B4
Salto . . . . 94　C5
Salto ⟶ . . . . . 20　C4
Salton Sea . . . . 82　D5
Saltpond . . . . . 55　G4
Salûm . . . . 52　B4
Salûm, Khâlig el 52　B4
Salur . . . . 40　H4
Salvador . . . . . . 93　E6
Salwa . . . . 44　E2
Salween ⟶ . . . 41　J11
Salyan . . . . 25　F6
Salzach ⟶ . . . 15　D7
Salzburg . . . . . . 15　E7
Salzgitter . . . . . 14　B6
Salzwedel . . . . 15　B6
Sama . . . . 28　C7
Sama de
　Langreo . . . . 18　A3
Samales Group 38　C2
Samangán □ . . 45　B7
Samar . . . . 38　B3
Samara . . . . . . 24　C7
Samarinda . . . . 37　E5
Samarkand =
　Samarqand . 29　F7
Samarqand . . . 29　F7
Sāmarrā . . . . . . 46　D5
Sambalpur . . . . 40　G5
Sambar,
　Tanjung . . . . 37　E4
Sambas . . . . . . 37　D3
Sambava . . . . . 59　G10
Sambhal . . . . . 42　E11
Sambhar . . . . . 42　F9
Sambiase . . . . . 21　E6
Sambir . . . . 17　D6
Samoa ■ . . . . . . 65　L13
Samokov . . . . . 22　C4
Sámos . . . . 23　F6
Samothráki,
　Évros, Greece 23　D5
Samothráki,
　Kérkira,
　Greece . . . . . 23　E2
Sampacho . . . . 94　C4
Sampit . . . . 37　E4
Sampit, Teluk . 37　E4
Samra . . . . 47　F5
Samsun . . . . . . 46　B4
Samui, Ko . . . . 36　C2

Samut Prakan . 36　B2
Samut
　Songkhram ⟶
　. . . . . 36　B2
San . . . . 55　F4
San ⟶ . . . . 16　C5
San Agustin, C. 38　C3
San Andrés, I.
　de . . . . 86　D3
San Andrés
　Tuxtla . . . . . . 85　D5
San Angelo . . . 78　D3
San Antonio,
　Chile . . . . . . 94　C2
San Antonio,
　Spain . . . . . 19　C6
San Antonio,
　U.S.A. . . . . . 78　E4
San Antonio, C.,
　Argentina . . 94　D5
San Antonio, C.,
　Cuba . . . . . . 85　C8
San Antonio
　Oeste . . . . . . 95　E4
San Benedetto
　del Tronto . . 20　C4
San Bernardino 82　C4
San Bernardino
　Str. . . . . 38　B2
San Bernardo . 94　C2
San Bernardo, I.
　de . . . . 90　B3
San Borja . . . . 91　F5
San Carlos,
　Argentina . . 94　C3
San Carlos,
　Chile . . . . . . 94　D2
San Carlos, *Phil.* 38　B2
San Carlos,
　Amazonas,
　Venezuela . . 90　C5
San Carlos,
　Cojedes,
　Venezuela . . 90　B5
San Carlos de
　Bariloche . . . 95　E2
San Carlos del
　Zulia . . . . 90　B4
San Cristóbal,
　Argentina . . 94　C4
San Cristóbal,
　Mexico . . . . 85　D6
San Cristóbal,
　Venezuela . . 90　B4
San Diego . . . . 82　D4
San Diego, C. . 95　G3
San Felipe, *Chile* 94　C2
San Felipe,
　Venezuela . . 90　A5
San Felíu de
　Guíxols . . . . . 19　B7
San Fernando,
　Chile . . . . . . 94　C2
San Fernando,
　La Union, Phil. 38　A2
San Fernando,
　Pampanga,
　Phil. . . . . 38　A2
San Fernando,
　Spain . . . . . 18　D2
San Fernando,
　Trin. & Tob. . 87　D7
San Fernando,
　U.S.A. . . . . . 82　C3
San Fernando
　de Apure . . . 90　B5
San Fernando
　de Atabapo . 90　C5
San Francisco,
　Argentina . . 94　C4

San Francisco,
　U.S.A. . . . . . 82　B1
San Francisco
　de Macorîs . . 87　C5
San Francisco
　del Monte de
　Oro . . . . 94　C3
San Gil . . . . . . 90　B4
San Gottardo, P.
　del . . . . 13　C8
San Ignacio,
　Bolivia . . . . . 91　G6
San Ignacio,
　Paraguay . . . 94　B5
San Ildefonso,
　C. . . . . 38　A2
San Javier,
　Argentina . . 94　C5
San Javier,
　Bolivia . . . . . 91　G6
San Joaquin ⟶ 82　A2
San Jorge, B. de 84　A2
San Jorge, G. . 95　F3
San Jorge, G. de 19　B6
San José,
　Bolivia . . . . . 91　G6
San José,
　Costa Rica . . 86　E3
San José,
　Guatemala . . 85　E6
San Jose, *Phil.* 38　A2
San Jose, *U.S.A.* 82　B2
San Jose de
　Buenovista . . 38　B2
San José de
　Jáchal . . . . . . 94　C3
San José de
　Mayo . . . . . . 94　C5
San José de
　Ocune . . . . . 90　C4
San José del
　Guaviare . . . . 90　C4
San Juan,
　Argentina . . 94　C3
San Juan, *Phil.* 38　C3
San Juan,
　Puerto Rico . 87　C6
San Juan ⟶ . . 86　D3
San Juan, C. . . 56　D1
San Juan de los
　Morros . . . . . 90　B5
San Juan Mts. . 83　B9
San Julián . . . . 95　F3
San Justo . . . . 94　C4
San Leandro . . 82　B1
San Lorenzo . . 90　C3
San Lorenzo, I. 91　F3
San Lorenzo,
　Mt. . . . . 95　F2
San Lucas . . . . 91　H5
San Lucas, C. . 84　C2
San Luis . . . . . 94　C3
San Luis Obispo 82　C2
San Luis Potosí 84　C4
San Marino . . . 20　C4
San Marino ■ . 20　C4
San Martín, L. . 95　F2
San Matías . . . 91　G7
San Matías, G. 95　E4
San Miguel . . . 85　E7
San Miguel ⟶ 91　F6
San Miguel de
　Tucumán . . . 94　B3
San Narciso . . 38　A2
San Nicolás de
　los Arroyas . 94　C4
San-Pédro . . . . 55　H3
San Pedro de
　las Colonias . 84　B4

San Pedro de
　Lloc . . . . 91　E3
San Pedro de
　Macorís . . . . 87　C6
San Pedro del
　Paraná . . . . . 94　B5
San Pedro Sula 85　D7
San Pieto . . . . 21　E2
San Rafael,
　Argentina . . 94　C3
San Rafael,
　U.S.A. . . . . . 80　G2
San Ramón de
　la Nueva Orán 94　A4
San Remo . . . 20　C1
San Roque,
　Argentina . . 94　B5
San Roque,
　Spain . . . . . 18　D3
San Rosendo . . 94　D2
San Salvador,
　Bahamas . . . 86　B5
San Salvador,
　El Salv. . . . . . 85　E7
San Salvador de
　Jujuy . . . . 94　A4
San Sebastián,
　Argentina . . 95　G3
San Sebastián,
　Spain . . . . . 19　A5
San Severo . . . 20　D5
San Valentin,
　Mte. . . . . 95　F2
San Vicente de
　la Barquera . 18　A3
Sana' . . . . 49　D3
Sana ⟶ . . . . . 20　B6
Sanaga ⟶ . . . 56　D1
Sanana . . . . . . 39　E3
Sanandaj . . . . 46　D6
Sanco Pt. . . . . 38　C3
Sancti-Spíritus . 86　B4
Sancy, Puy de . 13　D5
Sandakan . . . . 36　C5
Sandanski . . . . 22　D4
Sanday . . . . . . 10　B5
Sandgate . . . . 63　A5
Sandía . . . . . . 91　F5
Sandıklı . . . . . 46　C2
Sandoa . . . . . . 56　F4
Sandomierz . . 16　C5
Sandoway . . . . 41　H10
Sandusky . . . . 72　D4
Sandwip Chan. 41　F8
Sandy C. . . . . 62　D3
Sandy L. . . . . . 71　C10
Sanford, *Fla.,*
　U.S.A. . . . . . 75　E7
Sanford, *N.C.,*
　U.S.A. . . . . . 75　B8
Sanford, Mt. . . 71　B5
Sanga ⟶ . . . . 56　E3
Sangamner . . . 43　K9
Sangar . . . . . . 31　C10
Sangasangadalam
　. . . . . 37　E5
Sangeang . . . . 39　F1
Sangerhausen . 15　C6
Sanggau . . . . . 37　D4
Sangihe, P. . . . 39　D3
Sangkapura . . 37　F4
Sangli . . . . 43　L9
Sangmélina . . . 56　D2
Sangre de Cristo
　Mts. . . . . 78　A1
Sanirajak . . . . 68　B2
Sankt Gallen . . 13　C8
Sankt Moritz . . 13　C8
Sankt-Peterburg 24　B3

Sankt Pölten .. 15 D8
Sankuru → .. 56 E4
Sanliurfa 46 C4
Sanlúcar de
  Barrameda .. 18 D2
Sannicandro
  Gargánico .. 20 D5
Sanok 17 D6
Sanshui 35 D6
Santa Ana,
  Bolivia 91 F5
Santa Ana,
  Ecuador 90 D2
Santa Ana,
  El Salv. 85 E7
Santa Ana,
  U.S.A. 82 D4
Santa Barbara . 82 C3
Santa Catalina I. 82 D3
Santa
  Catarina □ .. 94 B7
Santa Clara ... 86 B4
Santa Clotilde . 90 D4
Santa Coloma
  de Gramanet 19 B7
Santa Cruz,
  Argentina .. 95 G3
Santa Cruz,
  Bolivia 91 G6
Santa Cruz, Phil. 38 B2
Santa Cruz,
  U.S.A. 82 B1
Santa Cruz → . 95 G3
Santa Cruz de
  Tenerife .. 54 C1
Santa Cruz do
  Sul 94 B6
Santa Cruz I. .. 64 L11
Santa Elena ... 90 D2
Santa Eugenia,
  Pta. 84 B1
Santa Fe,
  Argentina .. 94 C4
Santa Fe, U.S.A. 83 C10
Santa Filomena 93 D4
Santa Inés, I. .. 95 G2
Santa Isabel =
  Rey Malabo . 56 D1
Santa Isabel,
  Argentina .. 94 D3
Santa Isabel,
  Brazil 93 E3
Santa Lucia
  Range 82 C2
Santa Maria,
  Brazil 94 B6
Santa Maria,
  U.S.A. 82 C2
Santa María → . 84 A3
Santa Maria da
  Vitória 93 E5
Santa Maria di
  Leuca, C. .. 23 E2
Santa Marta ... 90 A4
Santa Marta,
  Sierra Nevada
  de 90 A4
Santa Maura =
  Levkás 23 E3
Santa Rosa,
  La Pampa,
  Argentina ... 94 D4
Santa Rosa,
  San Luis,
  Argentina ... 94 C3
Santa Rosa,
  Bolivia 91 F5
Santa Rosa,
  Brazil 94 B6

Santa Rosa,
  U.S.A. 80 F2
Santa Rosa de
  Copán 85 E7
Santa Vitória do
  Palmar 94 C6
Santai 35 C5
Santana, Coxilha
  de 94 C5
Santana do
  Livramento .. 94 C5
Santander 18 A4
Sant'Antíoco .. 21 E2
Santarém, Brazil 92 C3
Santarém,
  Portugal 18 C1
Santiago, Brazil 94 B6
Santiago, Chile 94 C2
Santiago → .. 90 D3
Santiago de
  Compostela . 18 A1
Santiago de
  Cuba 86 C4
Santiago de los
  Cabelleros .. 87 C5
Santiago del
  Estero 94 B4
Santo Amaro .. 93 E6
Santo Ângelo . 94 B6
Santo Antonio . 93 F2
Santo Corazón 91 G7
Santo Domingo 87 C6
Santo Tomás . 91 F4
Santo Tomé ... 94 B5
Santo Tomé de
  Guayana =
  Ciudad
  Guayana 90 B6
Santoña 18 A4
Santoríni =
  Thíra 23 F5
Santos 94 A7
Santos Dumont 94 A8
Sanza Pombo . 56 F3
São Anastácio . 94 A6
São Bernado de
  Campo 93 G4
São Borja 94 B5
São Carlos ... 94 A7
São Cristóvão . 93 E6
São Domingos 93 E4
São Francisco . 93 F5
São
  Francisco → 93 E6
São Francisco
  do Sul 94 B7
São Gabriel ... 94 C6
São João da
  Madeira 18 B1
São João del
  Rei 93 G5
São João do
  Araguaia 92 D4
São João do
  Piauí 92 D5
São José do Rio
  Prêto 94 A7
São Leopoldo . 94 B6
São Lourenço . 93 G4
São
  Lourenço → 93 F2
São Luís 92 C5
São Marcos → 93 F4
São Marcos, B.
  de 92 C5
São Mateus .. 93 F6
São Paulo ... 94 A7
São Paulo □ .. 94 A7
São Roque, C.
  de 92 D6

São Sebastião, I.
  de 94 A7
São Tomé &
  Principe ■ .. 51 F4
São Vicente, C.
  de 18 D1
Saône → 13 D6
Saonek 39 E4
Saparua 39 E3
Sapele 55 G6
Saposoa 91 E3
Sapporo 32 F12
Sapulpa 79 B5
Saqqez 46 C6
Sar-e Pol 45 B6
Sar-e Pol □ ... 45 B6
Sar Planina .. 22 C3
Sarāb 46 C6
Sarada → 40 D3
Saragossa =
  Zaragoza .. 19 B5
Saraguro 90 D3
Sarajevo 20 C7
Saran, G. 37 E4
Sarandí del Yi . 94 C5
Sarangani B. .. 38 C3
Sarangani Is. .. 38 C3
Sarangarh 40 G4
Saransk 24 C6
Sarapul 29 D6
Sarasota 75 F6
Saratov 24 C6
Saravane 36 A3
Sarawak □ ... 37 D4
Saray 22 D6
Sarayköy 23 F7
Sarbāz 45 E5
Sarbīsheh ... 45 C4
Sarda → =
  Sarada → .. 40 D3
Sardalas 54 C7
Sardarshahr ... 42 E9
Sardegna □ .. 21 D2
Sardinia =
  Sardegna □ . 21 D2
Sardis 23 E7
Sargodha 42 C8
Sarh 53 G2
Sārī 44 B3
Sangöl 23 E7
Sarikamiş 46 B5
Sarikei 37 D4
Sark 11 G5
Şarköy 23 D6
Sarlat-la-Canéda 12 D4
Sarmi 39 E5
Sarmiento 95 F3
Sarnia 69 D2
Sarny 24 C2
Sarolangun ... 37 E2
Saronikós
  Kólpos 23 F4
Sarre = Saar → 13 B7
Sarreguemines 13 B7
Sarro 55 F3
Sarthe → 12 C3
Sartynya 28 C7
Sarvestān 44 D3
Sary-Tash 29 F8
Saryshagan .. 29 E8
Sasabeneh ... 49 F3
Sasaram 40 E5
Sasebo 32 C1
Saser 42 B10
Saskatchewan □ 71 C9
Saskatchewan →
  .... 71 C9
Saskatoon 71 C9
Saskylakh 30 B9

Sasovo 24 C5
Sassandra 55 H3
Sassandra → . 55 H3
Sássari 21 D2
Sassnitz 15 A7
Sassuolo 20 B3
Sasyk, Ozero .. 17 F9
Sata-Misaki .. 33 D2
Satadougou ... 55 F2
Satara 43 L8
Satmala Hills . 43 J9
Satna 40 E3
Sátoraljaújhely 16 D5
Satpura Ra. ... 43 J10
Satu Mare 17 E6
Satui 37 E5
Saturnina → .. 91 F7
Saudi Arabia ■ 47 F6
Sauerland 14 C4
Sault Ste. Marie,
  Canada 69 D2
Sault Ste. Marie,
  U.S.A. 72 A3
Saumlaki 39 F4
Saumur 12 C3
Saunders C. .. 65 F4
Sauri 55 F6
Saurimo 56 F4
Sava → 22 B3
Savage I. =
  Niue 65 L14
Savalou 55 G5
Savanna la Mar 86 C4
Savannah ... 75 C7
Savannah → . 75 C7
Savannakhet .. 36 A2
Savanur 43 M9
Savé 55 G5
Save → 59 C6
Sāveh 46 D7
Savelugu 55 G4
Savoie □ 13 D7
Savona 20 B2
Sawahlunto ... 37 E2
Sawai 39 E3
Sawai
  Madhopur .. 42 F10
Sawara 32 B7
Sawatch Mts. . 83 A9
Sawmills ... 59 B5
Sawu 39 F2
Sawu Sea ... 39 F2
Saxony, Lower
  =
  Niedersachsen □
  .... 14 B5
Say 55 F5
Sayán 91 F3
Sayan,
  Zapadnyy ... 30 D7
Saydā 46 D3
Sayghān 45 C6
Sayḥut 49 D5
Saynshand ... 35 B6
Sazanit 23 D2
Sázava → ... 16 D2
Sazin 42 B8
Scandicci ... 20 C3
Scandinavia .. 8 F10
Scarborough .. 11 D6
Scebeli,
  Wabi → 49 G3
Schaffhausen . 13 C8
Schefferville .. 69 C4
Schelde → ... 14 C3
Schenectady .. 73 C9
Schiermonnikoog
  .... 14 B4
Schio 20 B3

Schleswig	14	A5
Schleswig-		
Holstein □	14	A5
Schouten I.	62	D4
Schouten Is. =		
Supiori	39	E5
Schwäbische		
Alb	14	D5
Schwaner,		
Pegunungan	37	E4
Schwarzwald	14	D5
Schwedt	15	B8
Schweinfurt	14	C6
Schwenningen		
= Villingen-		
Schwenningen	14	D5
Schwerin	15	B6
Schwyz	13	C8
Sciacca	21	F4
Scilla	21	E5
Scilly, Isles of	11	G3
Scone	63	B5
Scotland □	10	C4
Scott Glacier	96	A12
Scott Inlet	68	A3
Scottsbluff	76	E3
Scottsdale	62	D4
Scranton	73	D8
Scunthorpe	11	E6
Scusciuban	49	E5
Scutari =		
Üsküdar	25	E2
Seaspray	63	C4
Seattle	80	B2
Sebastopol =		
Sevastopol	25	E3
Sebha =		
Sabhah	52	C1
Şebinkarahisar	46	B4
Sebta = Ceuta	18	E3
Sebuku	37	E5
Sebuku, Teluk	37	D5
Secretary I.	65	F2
Secunderabad	43	L11
Sedalia	77	F8
Sedan, Australia	62	B2
Sedan, France	13	B6
Seddon	65	D6
Seddonville	65	D5
Sedhiou	55	F1
Sedova, Pik	28	B6
Seeheim	58	D3
Seferihisar	23	E6
Segamat	37	D2
Segesta	21	F4
Seget	39	E4
Ségou	55	F3
Segovia =		
Coco →	86	D3
Segovia	18	B3
Segre →	19	B6
Séguéla	55	G3
Segura →	19	C5
Sehitwa	58	C4
Sehore	43	H10
Seine →	12	B4
Seistan	45	D5
Seistan,		
Daryācheh-ye	45	D5
Sekayu	37	E2
Sekondi-		
Takoradi	55	H4
Selaru	39	F4
Selçuk	23	F6
Sele →	21	D5
Selenga =		
Selenge		
Mörön →	35	A5
Selenge		
Mörön →	35	A5
Seletan, Tg.	37	E4
Sélibabi	55	E2
Selîma, El		
Wâhât el	52	D4
Selkirk	71	C10
Selkirk Mts.	71	C8
Selma	75	B8
Selpele	39	E4
Selu	39	F4
Selva	94	B4
Selvas	91	E5
Semani →	23	D2
Semarang	37	F4
Semey	29	D9
Semiozernoye	29	D7
Semipalatinsk =		
Semey	29	D9
Semirara Is.	38	B2
Semisopochnoi		
I.	71	C1
Semitau	37	D4
Semiyarka	29	D8
Semiyarskoye =		
Semiyarka	29	D8
Semmering P.	15	E8
Semnān	44	C3
Semnān □	44	C3
Semporna	38	D1
Semuda	37	E4
Sena Madureira	91	E5
Senador		
Pompeu	92	D6
Senaja	36	C5
Senanga	58	B4
Sendai,		
Kagoshima,		
Japan	32	D2
Sendai, Miyagi,		
Japan	33	G12
Senegal ■	55	F2
Senegal →	55	E1
Senge Khambab		
= Indus →	43	G5
Sengkang	39	E2
Senhor-do-		
Bonfim	93	E5
Senigállia	20	C4
Senj	20	B5
Senja	8	E11
Senlis	13	B5
Senmonorom	36	B3
Sennâr	53	F5
Senneterre	69	D3
Sens	13	B5
Senta	22	B3
Sentani	39	E6
Seo de Urgel	19	A6
Seoul = Sŏul	35	C7
Sepīdān	44	D3
Sept-Îles	69	C4
Sequoia		
National Park	82	B3
Seram	39	E3
Seram Laut,		
Kepulauan	39	E4
Seram Sea	39	E3
Serasan	37	D3
Serbia □	22	C3
Serdobsk	24	C5
Seremban	37	D2
Serenje	59	A6
Sereth =		
Siret →	17	F9
Sergino	28	C7
Sergipe □	93	E6
Sergiyev Posad	24	B4
Seria	36	D4
Serian	37	D4
Seribu,		
Kepulauan	37	F3
Sérifos	23	F5
Sermata	39	F3
Serny Zavod	29	F6
Serov	28	D7
Serowe	59	C5
Serpukhov	24	C4
Sérrai	22	D4
Serrezuela	94	C3
Serrinha	93	E6
Sertânia	92	D6
Serua	39	F4
Serui	39	E5
Serule	59	C5
Sesepe	39	E3
Sesfontein	58	B2
Sesheke	58	B4
Sète	13	E5
Sete Lagôas	93	F5
Sétif	54	A6
Seto	32	B5
Settat	54	B3
Setté-Cama	56	E1
Setúbal	18	C1
Setúbal, B. de	18	C1
Seulimeum	36	C1
Sevan, Ozero =		
Sevana Lich	25	E6
Sevana Lich	25	E6
Sevastopol	25	E3
Severn →,		
Canada	69	C2
Severn →, U.K.	11	F5
Severnaya		
Zemlya	30	B7
Severnyye Uvaly	24	B6
Severo-		
Yeniseyskiy	30	C7
Severodvinsk	28	C4
Sevilla	18	D2
Seville = Sevilla	18	D2
Sevlievo	22	C5
Seward	71	B5
Seward Pen.	71	B3
Sewer	39	F4
Seychelles ■	26	K9
Seymour	63	C4
Sfax	52	B1
Sfîntu Gheorghe	17	F7
Shaanxi □	35	C5
Shaba □	57	F4
Shabunda	57	E5
Shache	34	C2
Shackleton Ice		
Shelf	96	A11
Shackleton Inlet	96	C15
Shadrinsk	29	D7
Shāhābād	44	B4
Shahdād	44	D4
Shahdād,		
Namakzār-e	44	D4
Shahdadkot	42	F5
Shahgarh	42	F6
Shahhāt	52	B3
Shahjahanpur	42	F11
Shahr Kord	44	C2
Shahrig	42	D5
Shaikhabad	42	B6
Shajapur	43	H10
Shakhty	25	D5
Shakhunya	24	B6
Shaki	55	G5
Shala, L.	53	G6
Shalqar	29	E6
Sham, J. ash	44	F4
Shamil	44	E4
Shammar, Jabal	47	F5
Shamo = Gobi	35	B6
Shamo, L.	53	G6
Shamva	59	B6
Shan □	41	G12
Shandong □	35	C6
Shanghai	35	C7
Shangqiu	35	C6
Shangrao	35	D6
Shangshui	35	C6
Shannon	64	D6
Shannon →	11	E2
Shansi =		
Shanxi □	35	C6
Shantou	35	D6
Shantung =		
Shandong □	35	C6
Shanxi □	35	C6
Shaoguan	35	D6
Shaowu	35	D6
Shaoxing	35	C7
Shaoyang	35	D6
Shaqra',		
Si. Arabia	47	F6
Shaqrā', Yemen	49	E4
Sharjah = Ash		
Shāriqah	44	E3
Sharon	72	D5
Sharya	24	B6
Shashi,		
Botswana	59	C5
Shashi, China	35	C6
Shasta, Mt.	80	E2
Shatt al'Arab →	47	E7
Shaunavon	71	D9
Shawan	34	B3
Shawinigan	69	D3
Shcherbakov =		
Rybinsk	24	B4
Shchuchinsk	29	D8
Shebele =		
Scebeli,		
Wabi →	49	G3
Sheboygan	72	C2
Sheffield	11	E6
Shekhupura	42	D8
Shelburne	69	D4
Shelby	75	B7
Shelbyville	74	B4
Shellharbour	63	B5
Shenandoah →	73	E7
Shendam	55	G6
Shendî	53	E5
Shensi =		
Shaanxi □	35	C5
Shenyang	35	B7
Sheopur Kalan	42	G10
Shepetivka	17	C8
Shepetovka =		
Shepetivka	17	C8
Shepparton	63	C4
Sherbro I.	55	G2
Sherbrooke	69	D3
Sheridan	81	C10
Sherman	79	C5
Sherridon	71	C9
Shetland Is.	10	A6
Shibām	49	D4
Shigaib	53	E3
Shihchiachuangi		
=		
Shijiazhuang	35	C6
Shijiazhuang	35	C6
Shikarpur	42	F6
Shikoku	32	C3
Shikoku □	33	H10
Shikoku-Sanchi	32	C3
Shilabo	49	F3
Shiliguri	40	D7
Shillong	41	E8
Shilong	35	D6
Shimada	32	B6
Shimizu	32	B6

Shimoga 43 N9
Shimonoseki .. 32 C2
Shinano ⇁ ... 32 A6
Shīndand 42 C3
Shingū 32 C4
Shinyanga ... 57 E6
Shipehenski
Prokhod 22 C5
Shipki La 42 D11
Shīr Kūh 44 D3
Shirane-San ... 32 A6
Shīrāz 44 D3
Shire 59 B7
Shiretoko-Misaki 32 F13
Shiriya-Zaki .. 32 F12
Shīrvān 44 B4
Shirwa, L. =
Chilwa, L. ... 59 B7
Shivpuri 43 G10
Shizuoka 32 B6
Shklov =
Shklow 17 A10
Shklow 17 A10
Shkoder =
Shkodra ... 22 C2
Shkodra 22 C2
Shkumbini ⇁ . 23 D2
Shmidta, O. ... 30 A7
Sholapur =
Solapur 43 L9
Shoshone Mts. 80 F5
Shoshong 59 C5
Shreveport ... 79 C7
Shrewsbury .. 11 E5
Shrirampur .. 40 F7
Shu 29 E8
Shuangyashan 35 B8
Shule 34 C2
Shumagin Is. .. 71 C4
Shungnak 71 B4
Shūr ⇁ 44 D3
Shurugwi 59 B5
Shūsf 45 D5
Shūshtar 47 D7
Shwebo 41 F10
Shwegu 41 E11
Shweli ⇁ 41 F11
Shymkent ... 29 E7
Shyok 42 B11
Shyok ⇁ 42 B9
Si Kiang = Xi
Jiang ⇁ .. 35 D6
Si-ngan = Xi'an 35 C5
Si Racha 36 B2
Siah 47 G6
Siahan Range . 42 F4
Siaksriindrapura 37 D2
Sialkot 42 C9
Siantan, P. 37 D3
Siāreh 45 D5
Siargao 38 C3
Siasi 38 C2
Siau 39 D3
Šiauliai 24 B1
Šibenik 20 C5
Siberut 37 E1
Sibi 42 E5
Sibil 39 E6
Sibiti 56 E2
Sibiu 17 F7
Sibolga 37 D1
Sibsagar 41 D10
Sibu 37 D4
Sibuco 38 C2
Sibuguey B. ... 38 C2
Sibut 56 C3
Sibutu 38 D1
Sibutu Passage 38 D1
Sibuyan 38 B2

Sibuyan Sea .. 38 B2
Sichuan □ 34 C5
Sicilia 21 F5
Sicily = Sicilia . 21 F5
Sicuani 91 F4
Siddipet 43 K11
Sidéradougou . 55 F4
Sîdi Barrâni ... 52 B4
Sidi-bel-Abbès . 54 A4
Sidley, Mt. ... 96 B18
Sidon = Saydā 46 D3
Sidra, G. of =
Surt, Khalīj .. 52 B2
Siedlce 17 B6
Sieg ⇁ 14 C4
Siegen 14 C5
Siem Reap 36 B2
Siena 20 C3
Sieradz 16 C4
Sierra Colorada 95 E3
Sierra Gorda . 94 A3
Sierra Leone ■ 55 G2
Sífnos 23 F5
Sighetu-
Marmatiei ... 17 E6
Sighişoara 17 E7
Sigli 36 C1
Sigsig 90 D3
Sigüenza 19 B4
Siguiri 55 F3
Sihanoukville =
Kompong
Som 36 B2
Siirt 46 C5
Sikar 42 F9
Sikasso 55 F3
Sikhote Alin,
Khrebet ... 31 E11
Sikhote Alin Ra.
= Sikhote
Alin, Khrebet 31 E11
Síkinos 23 F5
Sikkim □ 40 D7
Sil ⇁ 18 A2
Silchar 41 E9
Silesia = Śląsk 16 C3
Silgarhi Doti . 40 C3
Silghat 41 D9
Silifke 46 C3
Siliguri =
Shiliguri 40 D7
Siling Co 34 C3
Silistra 22 B6
Silivri 22 D7
Sillajhuay,
Cordillera .. 91 G5
Silva Porto =
Kuito 58 A3
Simanggang .. 37 D4
Simav 23 E7
Simbirsk 24 C6
Simeria 17 F6
Simeulue 37 D1
Simferopol ... 25 E3
Sími 23 F6
Simikot 40 C3
Simla 42 D10
Simplon P. 13 C8
Simpson Desert 60 F6
Simunjan 37 D4
Sinabang 37 D1
Sinadogo 49 F4
Sinai = Es Sînâ' 52 C5
Sinai, Mt. =
Mûsa, G. ... 47 E3
Sinaloa de
Levya 84 B3
Sīnāwan 54 B7
Sincelejo 90 B3

Sincorá, Serra
do 93 E5
Sind □ 42 F6
Sind Sagar
Doab 42 D7
Sindangan ... 38 C2
Sines 18 D1
Sines, C. de .. 18 D1
Singa 53 F5
Singapore ■ .. 37 D2
Singaraja 37 F5
Singida 57 E6
Singitikós
Kólpos 23 D5
Singkaling
Hkamti ... 41 E10
Singkawang .. 37 D3
Singleton 63 B5
Singora =
Songkhla .. 36 C2
Sinjai 39 F2
Sinjār 46 C5
Sinkat 53 E6
Sinkiang Uighur
= Xinjiang
Uygur
Zizhiqu □ .. 34 B3
Sinni ⇁ 21 D6
Sinnuris 52 C5
Sinop 46 B3
Sintang 37 D4
Sintra 18 C1
Sinŭiju 35 B7
Siocon 38 C2
Siófok 16 E4
Sioma 58 B4
Sion 13 C7
Sioux City ... 77 D6
Sioux Falls .. 76 D6
Sioux Lookout . 71 C10
Siping 35 B7
Sipura 37 E1
Siquijor 38 C2
Siracusa 21 F5
Sirajganj 41 E7
Sirdaryo =
Syrdarya ⇁ . 29 E7
Siret ⇁ 17 F9
Sirohi 43 G8
Sironj 43 G10
Síros 23 F5
Sirsa 42 E9
Sisak 20 B6
Sisaket 36 A2
Sisophon 36 B2
Sīstān va
Balūchestān □ 45 E5
Sitapur 40 D3
Sitges 19 B6
Sitía 23 G6
Sitka 71 C6
Sittang Myit ⇁ 41 J11
Sittwe 41 G9
Siuri 40 F6
Sīvand 44 D3
Sivas 46 C4
Siverek 46 C4
Sivrihisar ... 46 C2
Sîwa 52 C4
Siwalik Range . 40 D4
Siwan 40 D5
Sjælland 9 G10
Sjumen =
Šumen 22 C6
Skadarsko
Jezero 22 C2
Skagerrak 9 G9
Skagway 71 C6
Skala-Podilska . 17 D8

Skala
Podolskaya =
Skala-Podilska 17 D8
Skalat 17 D7
Skardu 42 B9
Skarzysko-
Kamienna ... 16 C5
Skeena ⇁ ... 70 C6
Skegness 11 E7
Skeldon 90 B7
Skellefte älv ⇁ 8 F12
Skellefteå ⇁ . 8 F12
Skíathos 23 E4
Skien 9 G9
Skierniewice .. 16 C5
Skikda 54 A6
Skipton 62 C3
Skíros 23 E5
Skole 17 D6
Skópelos 23 E4
Skopje 22 C3
Skvyra 17 D9
Skye 10 C3
Skyros = Skíros 23 E5
Slamet 37 F3
Śląsk 16 C3
Slatina 22 B5
Slave ⇁ 70 B8
Slavgorod ... 29 D8
Slavonski Brod 20 B7
Slavuta 17 C8
Slavyansk =
Slovyansk ... 25 D4
Slawharad ... 17 B10
Sleaford B. ... 62 B2
Sleeper Is. 68 C2
Sligeach = Sligo 11 D2
Sligo 11 D2
Sliven 22 C6
Slobodskoy ... 24 B7
Slobozia 22 B6
Slonim 17 B7
Slough 11 F6
Slovak Rep. ■ . 16 D5
Slovakia =
Slovak Rep. ■ 16 D5
Slovakian Ore
Mts. =
Slovenské
Rudohorie .. 16 D4
Slovenia ■ 20 B5
Slovenija =
Slovenia ■ .. 20 B5
Slovenská
Republika =
Slovak Rep. ■ 16 D5
Slovenské
Rudohorie .. 16 D4
Slovyansk ... 25 D4
Sluch ⇁ 17 C8
Słupsk 16 A3
Slutsk 17 B8
Smara 54 C3
Smarhon 17 A8
Smederevo .. 22 B3
Smith Arm ... 70 B7
Smithton 62 D4
Smithtown ... 63 B5
Smoky Bay .. 62 B1
Smolensk 24 C3
Smolikas, Óros 23 D3
Smolyan 22 D5
Smorgon =
Smarhon ... 17 A8
Smyrna = İzmir 23 E6
Snake ⇁ 80 B4
Snake I. 63 C4
Snake River
Plain 81 D7

Sneek

Sneek 14 B3
Sněžka 16 C2
Snøhetta 8 F9
Snowdon 11 E4
Snowdrift 70 B8
Snowtown 62 B2
Snowy → 63 C4
Snowy Mts. ... 63 C4
Snyatyn 17 D7
Snyder 78 C3
Soalala 59 H9
Sobat, Nahr → 53 G5
Sobral 92 C5
Soc Trang 36 C3
Soch'e =
  Shache .. 34 C2
Sochi 25 E4
Société, Is. de la 65 L15
Society Is. =
  Société, Is. de
  la 65 L15
Socompa,
  Portezuelo de 94 A3
Socorro 90 B4
Socotra 49 E5
Soda Plains .. 42 B11
Söderhamn ... 8 F11
Sodiri 53 F4
Sodo 53 G6
Sofia = Sofiya . 22 C4
Sofia → 59 H9
Sofiya 22 C4
Sogamoso ... 90 B4
Sognefjorden . 8 F9
Sohâg 52 C5
Soissons 13 B5
Sokal 17 C7
Söke 23 F6
Sokhumi 25 E5
Sokodé 55 G5
Sokol 24 B5
Sokółka 17 B6
Sokolo 55 F3
Sokołów
  Podlaski 17 B6
Sokoto 55 F6
Solano 38 A2
Solapur 43 L9
Soledad 90 B6
Soligalich =
  24 B5
Soligorsk =
  Salihorsk ... 17 B8
Solikamsk ... 28 D6
Solimões =
  Amazonas → 92 C3
Solingen 14 C4
Sóller 19 C7
Sologne 12 C4
Solok 37 E2
Solomon Is. ■ . 64 K10
Solomon Sea . 61 B9
Solon 35 B7
Solor 39 F2
Solothurn 13 C7
Šolta 20 C6
Solţānābād .. 44 B4
Solunska Glava 22 D3
Solwezi 59 A5
Soma 23 E6
Somali Rep. ■ . 49 F4
Somalia =
  Somali Rep. ■ 49 F4
Sombor 22 B2
Sombrerete .. 84 C4
Sombrero 87 C7
Somerset East . 59 E6
Somerset I. ... 70 A10
Someş → ... 17 E6
Sommariva ... 63 A4

Somme → ... 12 A4
Somosierra,
  Puerto de ... 18 B4
Somport, Puerto
  de 12 E3
Sóndrio 20 A2
Sonepur 40 G4
Song Cau 36 B3
Songea 57 G7
Songhua
  Jiang → ... 35 B8
Songkhla 36 C2
Songpan 34 C5
Sonipat 42 E10
Sonmiani 42 G5
Sono → 93 D4
Sonora → 84 B2
Sonsonate 85 E7
Soochow =
  Suzhou 35 C7
Sopi 39 D3
Sopot 16 A4
Sopron 16 E3
Sør-Rondane .. 96 B8
Sorata 91 G5
Sorel 69 D3
Sorgono 21 D2
Soria 19 B4
Sorkh, Kuh-e .. 44 C4
Soroca 17 D9
Sorocaba 94 A7
Soroki =
  Soroca 17 D9
Sorong 39 E4
Soroti 57 D6
Sørøya 8 D12
Sorrento 63 C3
Sorsogon 38 B2
Sosnowiec ... 16 C4
Souanké 56 D2
Soúdhas, Kólpos 23 G5
Sŏul 35 C7
Sound, The =
  Øresund 9 G10
Sources,
  Mt. aux 59 D5
Soure 92 C4
Souris 71 D9
Souris → 71 D10
Sousa 92 D6
Sousel 92 C3
Sousse 52 A1
South Africa ■ 58 E4
South
  Australia □ .. 62 B2
South Bend ... 72 D2
South
  Carolina □ .. 75 C7
South China Sea 36 C4
South Dakota □ 76 C4
South East C. . 62 D4
South Horr 57 D7
South I. 65 E3
South
  Invercargill .. 65 G3
South Korea ■ 35 C7
South Magnetic
  Pole 96 A13
South
  Nahanni → .. 70 B7
South Natuna Is.
  = Natuna
  Selatan,
  Kepulauan .. 37 D3
South Orkney Is. 96 A4
South Pagai, I.
  = Pagai
  Selatan, P. .. 37 E2
South Platte → 76 E4

South Pole .... 96 C
South
  Ronaldsay .. 10 B5
South
  Saskatchewan →
  .... 71 C9
South Shetland
  Is. 96 A4
South Shields . 11 D6
South Taranaki
  Bight 64 C6
South Uist 10 C3
South West C. . 62 D4
Southampton . 11 F6
Southampton I. 68 B2
Southbridge .. 65 E5
Southend-on-
  Sea 11 F7
Southern Alps . 65 E4
Southern Indian
  L. 71 C10
Southern
  Ocean 96 A9
Southern
  Uplands 10 D5
Southport 63 A5
Southwest C. . 65 G2
Soutpansberg . 59 C5
Sovetsk,
  Kaliningd.,
  Russia 24 B1
Sovetsk, Kirov,
  Russia 24 B6
Sôya-Misaki .. 32 E12
Soyo 56 F2
Sozh → 17 C10
Spain ■ 18 C4
Spalding 62 B2
Spanish Town . 86 C4
Sparta = Spárti 23 F4
Spartanburg .. 75 B7
Spárti 23 F4
Spartivento, C.,
  Calabria, Italy 21 F6
Spartivento, C.,
  Sard., Italy .. 21 E2
Spátha, Ákra . 23 G4
Spencer, C. ... 62 C2
Spencer G. 62 B2
Spenser Mts. . 65 E5
Spey → 10 C5
Speyer 14 D5
Split 20 C6
Spokane 80 B5
Spoleto 20 C4
Sporyy Navolok,
  Mys 28 B7
Spratly I. 36 C4
Spree → 15 B7
Springbok 58 D3
Springfield, N.Z. 65 E4
Springfield, Ill.,
  U.S.A. 77 F10
Springfield,
  Mass., U.S.A. 73 C9
Springfield, Mo.,
  U.S.A. 79 A7
Springfield,
  Ohio, U.S.A. . 72 E4
Springfield,
  Oreg., U.S.A. 80 C2
Springfontein . 59 E5
Springhill 69 D4
Springhurst .. 63 C4
Springs 59 D5
Squamish 71 D7
Srbija =
  Serbia □ 22 C3
Sre Umbell ... 36 B2

Srebrnica 20 B7
Sredinny Ra. =
  Sredinnyy
  Khrebet 31 D14
Sredinnyy
  Khrebet 31 D14
Srednevilyuysk 31 C10
Šrem 16 B3
Sremska
  Mitrovica ... 22 B2
Sri Lanka ■ ... 43 R12
Srikakulam ... 40 H4
Srinagar 42 B9
Stade 14 B5
Stadlandet ... 8 F9
Stafford 11 E5
Stakhanov ... 25 D4
Stalingrad =
  Volgograd .. 25 D5
Staliniri =
  Tskhinvali ... 25 E5
Stalino =
  Donetsk ... 25 D4
Stalinogorsk =
  Novomoskovsk
  .... 24 C4
Stalowa Wola . 17 C6
Stamford 73 D9
Stanislav =
  Ivano-
  Frankivsk ... 17 D7
Stanke Dimitrov 22 C4
Stanley,
  Australia 62 D4
Stanley, Canada 71 C9
Stanley, Falk. Is. 95 G5
Stanovoy
  Khrebet 31 D10
Stanovoy Ra. =
  Stanovoy
  Khrebet 31 D10
Stanthorpe ... 63 A5
Stara Planina .. 22 C4
Stara Zagora .. 22 C5
Starachowice .. 16 C5
Staraya Russa . 24 B3
Starbuck I. 65 K15
Stargard
  Szczeciński .. 16 B2
Staritsa 24 B3
Starogard
  Gdański 16 B4
Starokonstantinov
  =
  Starokonstyantyniv
  .... 17 D8
Starokonstyantyniv
  .... 17 D8
Staryy
  Chartoriysk .. 17 C7
Staryy Oskol .. 24 C4
State College .. 73 D7
Staten, I. =
  Estados, I. de
  Los 95 G4
Statesville 75 B7
Stavanger 9 G9
Staveley 65 E4
Stavropol 25 D5
Stawell 62 C3
Steenkool =
  Bintuni 39 E4
Stefanie L. =
  Chew Bahir .. 53 H6
Stefansson Bay 96 A9
Steiermark □ .. 15 E8
Steinkjer 8 F10
Stellenbosch .. 58 E3
Stendal 15 B6

Steornabhaigh
= Stornoway   10   B3
Stepanakert =
Xankändi   ...   25   F6
Stephens Creek   62   B3
Stepnoi = Elista   25   D5
Stepnyak   29   D8
Sterlitamak   ...   29   D6
Stettin =
Szczecin   16   B2
Stettiner Haff   ..   15   B8
Stettler   71   C8
Steubenville   .   72   D5
Stevenage   11   F6
Stewart   70   B6
Stewart, I.   95   G2
Stewart I.   65   G2
Steyr   15   D8
Stillwater, N.Z.   65   E4
Stillwater,
U.S.A.   78   A5
Štip   22   D4
Stirling   10   C5
Stockerau   15   D9
Stockholm   ...   9   G11
Stockport   11   E5
Stockton   82   B2
Stockton-on-
Tees   11   D6
Stoke on Trent   11   E5
Stokes Pt.   62   D3
Stolac   20   C6
Stolbovoy,
Ostrov   30   B11
Stolbtsy =
Stowbtsy   ...   17   B8
Stolin   17   C8
Stonehaven   ...   10   C5
Stonewall   ...   71   C10
Stony Tunguska
=
Podkamennaya
Tunguska   →   30   C7
Stora Lulevatten   8   E11
Storavan   8   E11
Store Bælt   9   G10
Store Creek   ..   63   B4
Storm B.   62   D4
Stormberge   ..   59   E5
Stornoway   10   B3
Storozhinets =
Storozhynets   17   D7
Storozhynets   ..   17   D7
Storsjön   8   F10
Storuman   ...   8   E11
Stowbtsy   17   B8
Strahan   62   D4
Stralsund   15   A7
Strand   58   E3
Stranraer   11   D4
Strasbourg   ..   13   B7
Stratford,
Canada   ...   69   D2
Stratford, N.Z.   .   64   C6
Strathalbyn   ..   62   C2
Straubing   15   D7
Streaky B.   ...   62   B1
Streaky Bay   ..   62   B1
Strelka   30   D7
Strezhevoy   ..   29   C8
Strimón   →   ..   23   D4
Strimonikós
Kólpos   23   D5
Stromboli   21   E5
Stronsay   10   B5
Stroud Road   .   63   B5
Strumica   22   D4
Stryy   17   D6
Strzelecki Cr.   →   62   A2

Stuart Ra.   62   A1
Stung Treng   ..   36   B3
Stutterheim   ...   59   E5
Stuttgart   14   D5
Styria =
Steiermark □   15   E8
Suakin   53   E6
Subansiri   →   ..   41   D9
Subi   37   D3
Subotica   16   E4
Suceava   17   E8
Suchou =
Suzhou   35   C7
Süchow =
Xuzhou   35   C6
Sucre   91   G5
Sudair   47   F6
Sudan ■   53   E4
Sudbury   69   D2
Sûdd   53   G4
Sudeten Mts. =
Sudety   16   C3
Sudety   16   C3
Sudirman,
Pegunungan   39   E5
Sueca   19   C5
Suez = El
Suweis   52   C5
Suez, G. of =
Suweis, Khalîg
el   52   C5
Sugluk = Salluit   68   B3
Suhār   44   E4
Suhbaatar   ...   35   A5
Suhl   14   C6
Suihua   35   B7
Sukadana,
Kalimantan,
Indonesia   ...   37   E3
Sukadana,
Sumatera,
Indonesia   ...   37   F3
Sukaraja   37   E4
Sukarnapura =
Jayapura   ...   39   E6
Sukhona   →   ..   28   C5
Sukhumi =
Sokhumi   ...   25   E5
Sukkur   42   F6
Sukkur Barrage   42   F6
Sula, Kepulauan   39   E3
Sulaiman Range   42   D6
Sulawesi □   ...   39   E2
Sulawesi Sea =
Celebes Sea .   39   D2
Sulima   55   G2
Sulina   17   F9
Sulitjelma   8   E11
Sullana   90   D2
Sultanpur   40   D4
Sulu Arch.   ...   38   C2
Sulu Sea   38   C2
Suluq   52   B3
Sulzberger Ice
Shelf   96   B17
Sumalata   39   D2
Sumatera □   ...   37   D2
Sumatra =
Sumatera □   .   37   D2
Sumba   39   F1
Sumba, Selat .   39   F1
Sumbawa   37   F5
Sumbawa Besar   37   F5
Sumbe   56   G2
Šumen   22   C6
Sumgait =
Sumqayıt   ...   25   E6
Summerside   ..   69   D4
Šumperk   16   D3

Sumqayıt   25   E6
Sumter   75   C7
Sumy   24   C3
Sunbury   63   C3
Sunda, Selat   ..   37   F3
Sunda Str. =
Sunda, Selat   37   F3
Sundarbans,
The   41   G7
Sundargarh   ..   40   F5
Sunderland   ...   11   D6
Sundsvall   ...   8   F11
Sungaigerong   37   E2
Sungailiat   37   E3
Sungaipakning   37   D2
Sungaipenuh .   37   E2
Sungaitiram   ...   37   E5
Sungari =
Songhua
Jiang   →   ...   35   B8
Sungguminasa   39   F1
Sunghua Chiang
= Songhua
Jiang   →   ...   35   B8
Sungurlu   46   B3
Sunnyvale   ...   82   B1
Suntar   30   C9
Supaul   40   D6
Superior   77   B8
Superior, L.   ...   69   D2
Suphan Dağı   .   46   C5
Supiori   39   E5
Sūr, Lebanon ..   46   D3
Sūr, Oman   ...   45   F4
Sura   →   24   B6
Surabaja =
Surabaya   ...   37   F4
Surabaya   37   F4
Surakarta   37   F4
Surat, Australia   63   A4
Surat, India   ...   43   J8
Surat Thani   ..   36   C1
Suratgarh   42   E8
Surgut   29   C8
Suriapet   43   L11
Surigao   38   C3
Surinam ■   ..   92   B2
Suriname =
Surinam ■   ..   92   B2
Suriname   →   ..   92   A2
Surt   52   B2
Surt, Khalîj   ..   52   B2
Suruga-Wan   .   32   B6
Süsangerd   ...   47   E7
Susanville   80   E3
Susquehanna   →
....   73   E7
Susques   94   A3
Susunu   39   E4
Susurluk   23   E7
Sutherland Falls   65   F2
Sutlej   →   42   E7
Suva   64   L12
Suva Planina .   22   C4
Suvorov Is. =
Suwarrow Is.   65   L14
Suwałki   17   A6
Suwarrow Is. .   65   L14
Suweis, Khalîg
el   52   C5
Suzdal   24   B5
Suzhou   35   C7
Suzu-Misaki   ..   32   A5
Svealand □   ..   9   G10
Sverdlovsk =
Yekaterinburg   29   D7
Svetlogorsk =
Svyetlahorsk   17   B9
Svetozarevo ..   22   B3

Svishtov   22   C5
Svislach   17   B7
Svyetlahorsk   .   17   B9
Swabian Alps =
Schwäbische
Alb   14   D5
Swakopmund .   58   C2
Swan Hill   62   C3
Swansea,
Australia   63   B5
Swansea, U.K.   11   F5
Swatow =
Shantou   35   D6
Swaziland ■   ..   59   D6
Sweden ■   ...   9   G10
Sweetwater   ..   78   C3
Swellendam   ..   58   E4
Świdnica   16   C3
Świdnik   17   C6
Świebodzin   ...   16   B2
Świecie   16   B4
Swift Current ..   71   C9
Swindon   11   F6
Swinemünde =
Świnoujście .   16   B2
Świnoujście   ..   16   B2
Switzerland ■   .   13   C8
Sydney,
Australia   63   B5
Sydney, Canada   69   D4
Sydra, G. of =
Surt, Khalîj   ..   52   B2
Syktyvkar   28   C6
Sylhet   41   E8
Sylt   14   A5
Sym   29   C9
Syracuse   73   C7
Syrdarya   →   ..   29   E7
Syria ■   46   D4
Syrian Desert =
Ash Shām,
Bādiyat   ...   47   D4
Syzran   24   C6
Szczecin   16   B2
Szczecinek   ...   16   B3
Szczytno   16   B5
Szechwan =
Sichuan □   ..   34   C5
Szeged   16   E5
Székesfehérvár   16   E4
Szekszárd   ...   16   E4
Szentes   16   E5
Szolnok   16   E5
Szombathely ..   16   E3

T

Tabacal   94   A4
Tabaco   38   B2
Ţābah   47   F5
Tabarka   54   A6
Ţabas,
Khorāsān, Iran   44   C4
Ţabas,
Khorāsān, Iran   45   C5
Tabatinga, Serra
da   93   E5
Tablas   38   B2
Table B. =
Tafelbaai   ..   58   E3
Table Mt.   58   E3
Tábor   16   D2
Tabora   57   F6
Tabou   55   H3
Tabrīz   46   C6
Tabūk   47   E4

Tacheng	34	B3
Tacloban	38	B2
Tacna	91	G4
Tacoma	80	B2
Tacuarembó	94	C5
Tademaït, Plateau du	54	C5
Tadjoura	49	E3
Tadmor	65	D5
Tadoussac	69	D4
Tadzhikistan = Tajikistan ■	29	F8
Taegu	35	C7
Taejŏn	35	C7
Tafalla	19	A5
Tafelbaai	58	E3
Tafermaar	39	F4
Taft	38	B3
Taga Dzong	41	D7
Taganrog	25	D4
Tagbilaran	38	C2
Tagish	70	B6
Tagish L.	70	B6
Tagliamento →	20	B4
Taguatinga	93	E5
Tagum	38	C3
Tagus = Tejo →	18	C1
Tahakopa	65	G3
Tahan, Gunong	36	D2
Tahat	54	D6
Tāherī	44	E3
Tahiti	65	L16
Tahoe, L.	80	F3
Tahoua	55	F6
Tahta	52	C5
Tahulandang	39	D3
Tahuna	39	D3
Taï	55	G3
Tai Hu	35	C7
Taibei	35	D7
T'aichung = Taizhong	35	D7
Taidong	35	D7
Taieri →	65	G4
Taihape	64	C6
Tailem Bend	62	C2
Taimyr Peninsula = Taymyr, Poluostrov	30	B7
Tain	10	C4
Tainan	35	D7
Taínaron, Ákra	23	F4
T'aipei = Taibei	35	D7
Taiping	36	D2
Taitao, Pen. de	95	F1
Taiwan ■	35	D7
Taïyetos Óros	23	F4
Taiyuan	35	C6
Taizhong	35	D7
Ta'izz	49	E3
Tajikistan ■	29	F8
Tajo = Tejo →	18	C1
Tājūrā	52	B1
Tak	36	A1
Takada	32	A6
Takaka	65	D5
Takamatsu	32	B4
Takaoka	32	A5
Takapuna	64	B6
Takasaki	32	A6
Takatsuki	32	B4
Takaungu	57	E7
Takayama	32	A5
Takefu	32	B5
Takengon	39	D1
Takeo	36	B2
Tåkestän	46	D7
Takhār □	45	B7
Takum	55	G6
Talara	90	D2
Talas	29	E8
Talaud, Kepulauan	38	D3
Talaud Is. = Talaud, Kepulauan	38	D3
Talavera de la Reina	18	C3
Talayan	38	C2
Talbragar →	63	B4
Talca	94	D2
Talcahuano	94	D2
Talcher	40	G5
Taldy Kurgan = Taldyqorghan	29	E8
Taldyqorghan	29	E8
Ṭalesh, Kūhhā-ye	46	C7
Tali Post	53	G5
Talibon	38	B2
Taliwang	37	F5
Tall 'Afar	46	C5
Talladega	74	C4
Tallahassee	75	D5
Tallangatta	63	C4
Tallarook	63	C4
Tallinn	24	B1
Talodi	53	F5
Taltal	94	B2
Talwood	63	A4
Talyawalka Cr. →	62	B3
Tamale	55	G4
Tamanrasset	54	D6
Tamarang	63	B5
Tamaské	55	F6
Tambacounda	55	F2
Tambelan, Kepulauan	37	D3
Tambo de Mora	91	F3
Tambora	37	F5
Tambov	24	C5
Tamburâ	53	G4
Tâmchekket	55	E2
Tamega →	18	B1
Tamenglong	41	E9
Tamgak, Mts.	55	E6
Tamil Nadu □	43	P10
Tammerfors = Tampere	8	F12
Tamo Abu, Pegunungan	37	D5
Tampa	75	F6
Tampere	8	F12
Tampico	84	C5
Tamrida = Qādib	49	E5
Tamsagbulag	35	B6
Tamu	41	E10
Tamworth	63	B5
Tana →, Kenya	57	E8
Tana →, Norway	8	D13
Tana, L.	53	F6
Tanahbala	37	E1
Tanahgrogot	37	E5
Tanahjampea	39	F2
Tanahmasa	37	E1
Tanahmerah	39	F6
Tanami Desert	60	D5
Tanana	71	B4
Tanana →	71	B4
Tananarive = Antananarivo	59	H9
Tánaro →	20	B2
Tandag	38	C3
Tandil	94	D5
Tandil, Sa. del	94	D5
Tando Adam	42	G6
Tandou L.	62	B3
Tane-ga-Shima	33	D2
Taneatua	64	C7
Tanen Tong Dan	41	J12
Tanezrouft	54	D5
Tanga	57	F7
Tanganyika, L.	57	F5
Tanger = Tangier	54	A3
Tanggula Shan	34	C4
Tangier	54	A3
Tangshan	35	C6
Tanimbar, Kepulauan	39	F4
Tanimbar Is. = Tanimbar, Kepulauan	39	F4
Tanjay	38	C2
Tanjore = Thanjavur	43	P11
Tanjung	37	E5
Tanjungbalai	37	D1
Tanjungpandan	37	E3
Tanjungpinang	37	D2
Tanjungredeb	37	D5
Tanjungselor	37	D5
Tanout	55	F6
Tanta	52	B5
Tantung = Dandong	35	B7
Tanunda	62	B2
Tanzania ■	57	F6
Taolanaro	59	K9
Taoudenni	54	D4
Taourirt	54	B4
Tapa Shan = Daba Shan	35	C5
Tapah	37	D2
Tapajós →	92	C3
Tapaktuan	37	D1
Tapanui	65	F3
Tapauá →	91	E6
Tapeta	55	G3
Tapi →	43	J8
Tapirapecó, Serra	90	C6
Tapuaenuku, Mt.	65	D5
Tapul Group	38	C2
Taquari →	91	G7
Tara, Australia	63	A5
Tara, Russia	29	D8
Tara →, Montenegro, Yug.	22	C2
Tara →, Russia	29	D8
Tarabagatay, Khrebet	29	E9
Tarābulus, Lebanon	46	D3
Tarābulus, Libya	52	B1
Tarakan	37	D5
Taralga	63	B4
Taranaki □	64	C6
Tarancón	19	B4
Taranga Hill	43	H8
Táranto	21	D6
Táranto, G. di	21	D6
Tarapacá	90	D5
Tararua Ra.	64	D6
Tarashcha	17	D10
Tarauacá	91	E4
Tarauacá →	91	E5
Tarawera	64	C7
Tarawera L.	64	C7
Taraz	29	E8
Tarbela Dam	42	B8
Tarbes	12	E4
Tarcoola	62	B1
Tarcoon	63	B4
Taree	63	B5
Tarfaya	54	C2
Tarifa	18	D3
Tarija	94	A4
Tariku →	39	E5
Tarim Basin = Tarim Pendi	34	C3
Tarim He →	34	C3
Tarim Pendi	34	C3
Taritatu →	39	E5
Tarkhankut, Mys	25	D3
Tarko Sale	28	C8
Tarkwa	55	G4
Tarlac	38	A2
Tarma	91	F3
Tarn →	12	D4
Tarnobrzeg	16	C5
Tarnów	16	C5
Tarnowskie Góry	16	C4
Taroom	63	A4
Taroudannt	54	B3
Tarragona	19	B6
Tarrasa	19	B7
Tarso Emissi	52	D2
Tarsus	46	C3
Tartagal	94	A4
Tartu	24	B2
Tarṭūs	46	D3
Tarutung	37	D1
Tasāwah	52	C1
Taschereau	69	D3
Tash-Kömür	29	E8
Tash-Kumyr = Tash-Kömür	29	E8
Tashauz = Dashhowuz	29	E6
Tashi Chho Dzong = Thimphu	41	D7
Tashkent = Toshkent	29	E7
Tashtagol	29	D9
Tasman B.	65	D5
Tasman Mts.	65	D5
Tasman Pen.	62	D4
Tasmania □	62	D4
Tatabánya	16	E4
Tatar Republic □ = Tatarstan □	29	D6
Tatarbunary	17	F9
Tatarsk	29	D8
Tatarstan □	29	D6
Tateyama	32	B6
Tathra	63	C4
Tatra = Tatry	16	D4
Tatry	16	D4
Tatta	43	G5
Tatuī	94	A7
Tat'ung = Datong	35	B6
Tatvan	46	C5
Taubaté	94	A7
Tauern	15	E7
Taumarunui	64	C6
Taumaturgo	91	E4
Taungdwingyi	41	G10
Taunggyi	41	G11
Taungup	41	H10
Taungup Pass	41	H10
Taungup Taunggya	41	H9
Taunton	11	F5

Taunus 14 C5
Taupo 64 C7
Taupo, L. 64 C6
Tauranga 64 B7
Tauranga Harb. 64 B7
Taurianova .. 21 E6
Taurus Mts. =
  Toros Dağları 46 C3
Tavda 29 D7
Tavda → 29 D7
Taveta 57 E7
Tavira 18 D2
Tavoy 36 B1
Tawau 36 D5
Tawitawi 38 C2
Tay → 10 C5
Tayabamba .. 91 E3
Taylakova 29 D8
Taylakovy =
  Taylakova ... 29 D8
Taymā 47 F4
Taymyr, Oz. ... 30 B8
Taymyr,
  Poluostrov .. 30 B7
Taytay 38 B1
Taz → 28 C8
Taza 54 B4
Tazovskiy ... 28 C8
Tbilisi 25 E5
Tchad = Chad ■ 53 E2
Tchad, L. 53 F1
Tch'eng-tou =
  Chengdu 35 C5
Tchibanga 56 E2
Tch'ong-k'ing =
  Chongqing .. 35 D5
Tczew 16 A4
Te Anau, L. ... 65 F2
Te Aroha 64 B6
Te Awamutu .. 64 C6
Te Kuiti 64 C6
Te Puke 64 B7
Te Waewae B. . 65 G2
Tebakang 37 D4
Tébessa 54 A6
Tebicuary → . 94 B5
Tebingtinggi . 37 D1
Tecuci 22 B6
Tedzhen =
  Tejen 29 F7
Tefé 90 D6
Tegal 37 F3
Tegina 55 F6
Tegucigalpa ... 85 E7
Tehachapi ... 82 C3
Tehrān 44 C2
Tehuantepec .. 85 D5
Tehuantepec, G.
  de 85 D5
Tehuantepec,
  Istmo de 85 D6
Tejen 29 F7
Tejo → 18 C1
Tekapo, L. 65 E4
Tekeli 29 E8
Tekirdağ 22 D6
Tekkali 40 H5
Tel Aviv-Yafo .. 46 D3
Tela 85 D7
Telanaipura =
  Jambi 37 E2
Telavi 25 E6
Telekhany =
  Tsyelyakhany 17 B7
Teles Pires → . 91 E7
Telford 11 E5
Télimélé 55 F2
Tellicherry 43 P9
Telsen 95 E3

Teluk Anson .. 37 D2
Teluk Betung =
  Tanjungkarang
  Telukbetung . 37 F3
Teluk Intan =
  Teluk Anson . 37 D2
Telukbutun ... 37 D3
Telukdalem ... 37 D1
Tema 55 G4
Temax 85 C7
Temerloh 37 D2
Temir 29 E6
Temirtau,
  Kazakstan .. 29 D8
Temirtau, Russia 29 D7
Temma 62 D3
Temora 63 B4
Tempe 83 D7
Temple 78 D5
Temuco 94 D2
Temuka 65 F4
Tenali 40 J3
Tenasserim .. 36 B1
Tenda, Col di .. 20 B1
Tendaho 49 E3
Tenerife 54 C1
Teng Xian 35 C6
Tengah □ 39 E2
Tengah
  Kepulauan . 37 F5
Tengchong ... 34 D4
Tenggara □ ... 39 E2
Tenggarong .. 37 E5
Tengiz, Ozero . 29 D7
Tenkasi 43 Q10
Tenke 57 G5
Tenkodogo ... 55 F4
Tennessee □ .. 74 B4
Tennessee → .. 72 F1
Tenom 36 C5
Tenryū-
  Gawa → ... 32 B5
Tenterfield 63 A5
Teófilo Otoni . 93 F5
Tepa 39 F3
Tepic 84 C4
Teplice 16 C1
Ter → 19 A7
Téra 55 F5
Téramo 20 C4
Terang 62 C3
Terebovlya ... 17 D7
Terek → 25 E6
Teresina 92 D5
Terewah, L. ... 63 A4
Terhazza 54 D3
Teridgerie
  Cr. → 63 B4
Termez =
  Termiz 29 F7
Términi Imerese 21 F4
Termiz 29 F7
Térmoli 20 C5
Ternate 39 D3
Terni 20 C4
Ternopil 17 D7
Ternopol =
  Ternopil 17 D7
Terowie, N.S.W.,
  Australia 63 B4
Terowie,
  S. Austral.,
  Australia 62 B2
Terracina 20 D4
Terralba 21 E2
Terranova =
  Ólbia 20 D2
Terrassa =
  Tarrasa 19 B7

Terre Haute ... 72 E2
Terschelling .. 14 B3
Teruel 19 B5
Teryaweyna L. . 62 B3
Teshio-
  Gawa 32 F12
Tesiyn
  Gol......... 34 A4
Teslin 70 B6
Tessalit 54 D5
Tessaoua 55 F6
Tetas, Pta. ... 94 A2
Tete 59 B6
Teterev → ... 17 C10
Teteven 22 C5
Tetiyev 17 D9
Tétouan 54 A3
Tetovo 22 C3
Teuco → 94 B4
Teun 39 F3
Teutoburger
  Wald 14 B5
Tévere → 20 D4
Tewantin 63 A5
Texarkana ... 79 C6
Texas 63 A5
Texas □ 78 D4
Texas City ... 79 E6
Texel 14 B3
Teyvareh 45 C6
Tezpur 41 D9
Thabana
  Ntlenyana ... 59 D5
Thabazimbi ... 59 C5
Thailand ■ ... 36 A2
Thailand, G. of 36 B2
Thakhek 36 A2
Thal 42 C7
Thala La 41 C11
Thallon 63 A4
Thames 64 B6
Thames → ... 11 F7
Thane 43 K8
Thanh Pho Ho
  Chi Minh ... 36 B3
Thanjavur 43 P11
Thar Desert ... 42 F7
Tharad 43 G7
Thargomindah 63 A3
Tharrawaddy .. 41 J10
Thásos 23 D5
Thaton 41 J11
Thaungdut ... 41 E10
Thayetmyo ... 41 H10
Thazi 41 G11
The Alberga → 62 A2
The Coorong .. 62 C2
The Frome → . 62 A2
The Grampians 62 C3
The Great Divide
  = Great
  Dividing Ra. . 61 E8
The Hague = 's-
  Gravenhage . 14 B3
The
  Hamilton → 62 A2
The
  Macumba → 62 A2
The Neales → 62 A2
The Pas 71 C9
The Rock 63 C4
The Salt L. 62 B3
The
  Stevenson → 62 A2
The
  Warburton → 62 A2
Thebes = Thívai 23 E4
Theebine 63 A5

Thermaïkós
  Kólpos 23 D4
Thermopylae P. 23 E4
Thessaloníki .. 23 D4
Thessaloniki,.
  Gulf of =
  Thermaïkós
  Kólpos 23 D4
Thetford 11 E7
Thetford Mines 69 D3
Thevenard 62 B1
Thiel Mts. 96 C2
Thiers 13 D5
Thies 55 F1
Thika 57 E7
Thimphu 41 D7
Thionville 13 B7
Thíra 23 F5
Thistle I. 62 C2
Thívai 23 E4
Thomas, L. ... 62 A2
Thomasville,
  Ga., U.S.A. .. 75 D6
Thomasville,
  N.C., U.S.A. . 75 B7
Thompson 71 C10
Thomson's Falls
  = Nyahururu 57 D7
Thrace 22 D6
Three Hummock
  I. 62 D3
Three Points, C. 55 H4
Thun 13 C7
Thunder Bay .. 69 D2
Thung Song .. 36 C1
Thunkar 41 D8
Thüringer Wald 14 C6
Thurles 11 E3
Thurloo Downs 63 A3
Thurso 10 B5
Thurston I. 96 B2
Thylungra 63 A3
Tia 63 B5
Tian Shan 34 B3
Tianjin 35 C6
Tianshui 35 C5
Tiaret 54 A5
Tiassalé 55 G4
Tibati 53 G1
Tiber =
  Tévere → .. 20 D4
Tiberias, L. =
  Yam Kinneret 46 D3
Tibesti 52 D2
Tibet =
  Xizang □ ... 34 C3
Tibooburra ... 62 A3
Tiburón 84 B2
Tìchît 55 E3
Ticino → 20 B2
Tiddim 41 F9
Tidjikja 55 E2
Tidore 39 D3
Tiel 55 F1
Tierra de
  Campos 18 A3
Tierra del
  Fuego, I. Gr.
  de 95 G3
Tiétar → 18 C2
Tieyon 62 A1
Tiflis = Tbilisi . 25 E5
Tifu 39 E3
Tighina 17 E9
Tignish 69 D4
Tigre → 90 D4
Tigris = Dijlah,
  Nahr → 47 E6
Tigyaing 41 F11

Tîh, Gebel el	52	C5	Tmassah	52	C2	Tonga ■	65	L13	Tougué	55	F2
Tijuana	84	A1	Toamasina	59	H9	Tonga Trench	65	L13	Toul	13	B6
Tikamgarh	43	G11	Toay	94	D4	Tongareva	65	K15	Toulepleu	55	G3
Tikhoretsk	25	D5	Toba	32	B5	Tongchuan	35	C5	Toulon	13	E6
Tikrīt	46	D5	Toba Kakar	42	D6	Tonghua	35	B7	Toulouse	12	E4
Tiksi	30	B10	Tobago	87	D7	Tongjiang	35	B8	Toummo	52	D1
Tilamuta	39	D2	Tobelo	39	D3	Tongking, G. of			Toungoo	41	H11
Tilburg	14	C3	Tobermory	10	C3	= Tonkin, G.			Touraine	12	C4
Tillabéri	55	F5	Toboali	37	E3	of	35	D5	Tourane = Da		
Tílos	23	F6	Tobol →	29	D7	Tongoy	94	C2	Nang	36	A3
Tilpa	63	B3	Toboli	39	E2	Tongren	35	D5	Tourcoing	13	A5
Tilsit = Sovetsk	24	B1	Tobolsk	29	D7	Tongsa Dzong	41	D8	Touriñán, C.	18	A1
Timaru	65	F4	Tobruk =			Tongue →	76	B2	Tournai	14	C2
Timbedgha	55	E3	Tubruq	52	B3	Tonk	42	F9	Tournon	13	D6
Timboon	62	C3	Tobyl =			Tonkin, G. of	35	D5	Tours	12	C4
Timbuktu =			Tobol →	29	D7	Tonlé Sap	36	B2	Towamba	63	C4
Tombouctou	55	E4	Tocantinópolis	92	D4	Toompine	63	A3	Towang	41	D8
Timimoun	54	C5	Tocantins □	93	E4	Toora	63	C4	Townsville	61	D8
Timişoara	16	F5	Tocantins →	92	C4	Toowoomba	63	A5	Toyama	32	A5
Timmins	69	D2	Tochigi	32	A6	Topeka	77	F7	Toyohashi	32	B5
Timok →	22	B4	Tocopilla	94	A2	Topki	29	D9	Toyonaka	32	B4
Timon	92	D5	Tocumwal	63	C4	Topol'čany	16	D4	Toyooka	32	B4
Timor	39	F2	Tocuyo →	90	A5	Topolobampo	84	B3	Toyota	32	B5
Tinaca Pt.	38	C3	Todeli	39	E2	Torata	91	G4	Tozeur	54	B6
Tindouf	54	C3	Todenyang	57	D7	Torbalı	23	E6	Trá Li = Tralee	11	E2
Tingo Maria	91	E3	Todos os			Torbat-e			Trabzon	46	B4
Tinjoub	54	C3	Santos, B. de	93	E6	Heydārīyeh	44	C4	Trafalgar, C.	18	D2
Tinnevelly =			Togba	55	E2	Torbat-e Jām	45	C5	Trail	71	D8
Tirunelveli	43	Q10	Togian,			Torbay	11	F5	Tralee	11	E2
Tinogasta	94	B3	Kepulauan	39	E2	Tordesillas	18	B3	Trancas	94	B3
Tínos	23	F5	Togliatti	24	C6	Torgau	15	C7	Trang	36	C1
Tintinara	62	C3	Togo ■	55	G5	Torino	20	B1	Trangan	39	F4
Tioman, Pulau	37	D2	Toinya	53	G4	Torit	53	H5	Trangie	63	B4
Tipongpani	41	D10	Tojikiston =			Tormes →	18	B2	Trani	20	D6
Tipperary	11	E2	Tajikistan ■	29	F8	Torne älv →	8	E12	Transantarctic		
Tīrān	44	C2	Tojo	39	E2	Torneå = Tornio	8	E12	Mts.	96	C3
Tirana	22	D2	Tokala	39	E2	Torneträsk	8	E11	Transilvania	17	F7
Tiranë = Tirana	22	D2	Tōkamachi	32	A6	Tornio	8	E12	Transilvanian		
Tiraspol	17	E9	Tokanui	65	G3	Tornquist	94	D4	Alps =		
Tire	23	E6	Tokar	53	E6	Toro, Cerro del	94	B3	Carpaţii		
Tirebolu	46	B4	Tokarahi	65	F4	Toroníios			Meridionali	17	F7
Tiree	10	C3	Tokat	46	B4	Kólpos	23	D4	Transylvania =		
Tîrgovişte	22	B5	Tokelau Is.	65	K13	Toronto,			Transilvania	17	F7
Tirgu-Jiu	17	F6	Tokmak	29	E8	Australia	63	B5	Trápani	21	E4
Tirgu Mureş	17	E7	Tokushima	32	B4	Toronto, Canada	69	D3	Traralgon	63	C4
Tirich Mir	42	A7	Tokuyama	32	B2	Toropets	24	B3	Trasimeno, L.	20	C4
Tîrnăveni	17	E7	Tōkyō	32	B6	Tororo	57	D6	Traun	15	D8
Tírnavos	23	E4	Tolaga Bay	64	C8	Toros Dağlan	46	C3	Travemünde	15	B6
Tirodi	43	J11	Tolbukhin =			Tôrre de			Travers, Mt.	65	E5
Tirol □	14	E6	Dobrich	22	C6	Moncorvo	18	B2	Travnik	20	B6
Tirso →	21	E2	Toledo, Spain	18	C3	Torre del Greco	21	D5	Trébbia →	20	B2
Tiruchchirappalli	43	P11	Toledo, U.S.A.	72	D4	Torrejón de			Trebič	16	D2
Tirunelveli	43	Q10	Toledo, Montes			Ardoz	18	B4	Trebinje	20	C7
Tirupati	43	N11	de	18	C3	Torrelavega	18	A3	Treinta y Tres	94	C5
Tiruppur	43	P10	Tolga	54	B6	Torremolinos	18	D3	Trelew	95	E3
Tiruvannamalai	43	N11	Toliara	59	J8	Torrens, L.	62	B2	Tremp	19	A6
Tisa →	22	B3	Tolima	90	C3	Torrente	19	C5	Trenčín	16	D4
Tisdale	71	C9	Tolitoli	39	D2	Torreón	84	B4	Trenque		
Tisza = Tisa →	22	B3	Tolo	56	E3	Torres	84	B2	Lauquen	94	D4
Tit-Ary	30	B10	Tolo, Teluk	39	E2	Torres Vedras	18	C1	Trent →	11	E6
Titicaca, L.	91	G5	Toluca	84	D5	Torrevieja	19	D5	Trento	20	A3
Titograd =			Tomakomai	32	F12	Tortosa	19	B6	Trenton	73	D8
Podgorica	22	C2	Tomar	18	C1	Tortosa, C. de	19	B6	Trepassey	69	D5
Titov Veles	22	D3	Tomaszów			Torūd	44	C3	Tres Arroyos	94	D4
Titova-Mitrovica			Mazowiecki	16	C4	Toruń	16	B4	Três Corações	93	G4
= Kosovska-			Tombé	53	G5	Tosa-Wan	32	C3	Três Lagoas	93	G3
Mitrovica	22	C3	Tombouctou	55	E4	Toscana □	20	C3	Tres Montes, C.	95	F1
Titovo Užice	22	C2	Tombua	58	B2	Toshkent	29	E7	Tres Puentes	94	B2
Titule	57	D5	Tomelloso	18	C4	Tostado	94	B4	Tres Puntas, C.	95	F3
Tivaouane	55	F1	Tomingley	63	B4	Tosya	46	B3	Três Rios	93	G5
Tívoli	20	D4	Tomini	39	D2	Toteng	58	C4	Treviso	20	B4
Tiwī	45	F4	Tomini, Teluk	39	E2	Totma	24	A5	Triabunna	62	D4
Tizi-Ouzou	54	A5	Tomorit	23	D3	Totten Glacier	96	A12	Trichinopoly =		
Tiznit	54	C3	Tomsk	29	D9	Tottenham	63	B4	Tiruchchirappalli		
Tjirebon =			Tonantins	90	D5	Tottori	32	B4		43	P11
Cirebon	37	F3	Tonawanda	73	C6	Touba	55	G3	Trichur	43	P10
Tlaxcala	84	D5	Tondano	39	D2	Toubkal, Djebel	54	B3	Trida	63	B4
Tlaxiaco	84	D5	Tonekābon	44	B2	Tougan	55	F4	Trier	14	D4
Tlemcen	54	B4	Tong Xian	35	C6	Touggourt	54	B6	Trieste	20	B4

Triglav 20 A4
Tríkkala 23 E3
Trikora, Puncak 39 E5
Trinidad, *Bolivia* 91 F6
Trinidad,
  Colombia ... 90 B4
Trinidad, *Cuba* 86 B3
Trinidad,
  Uruguay 94 C5
Trinidad, *U.S.A.* 78 A1
Trinidad, I. 95 D4
Trinidad &
  Tobago ■ .. 87 D7
Trinity ─► 79 E6
Trinity B. 69 D5
Trinity Range .. 80 E4
Trinkitat 53 E6
Tripoli =
  Tarābulus,
  Lebanon 46 D3
Tripoli =
  Tarābulus,
  Libya 52 B1
Trípolis 23 F4
Tripura □ 41 F8
Trivandrum ... 43 Q10
Trnava 16 D3
Troglav 20 C6
Trois-Rivières . 69 D3
Troitsko
  Pechorsk ... 28 C6
Trollhättan 9 G10
Tronador 95 E2
Trondheim 8 F10
Trondheimsfjorden
  .... 8 F10
Trout L. 70 B7
Trouville-sur-
  Mer 12 B4
Troy, *Turkey* .. 23 E6
Troy, *Ala.,*
  U.S.A. 74 D5
Troy, *N.Y.,*
  U.S.A. 73 C9
Troyes 13 B6
Trucial States =
  United Arab
  Emirates ■ .. 44 F3
Trujillo,
  Honduras ... 85 D7
Trujillo, *Peru* . 91 E3
Trujillo, *Spain* . 18 C3
Trujillo,
  Venezuela ... 90 B4
Truk 64 J10
Trundle 63 B4
Truro, *Canada* . 69 D4
Truro, *U.K.* 11 F4
Truskavets 17 D6
Trutnov 16 C2
Tsaratanana . 59 H9
Tsarevo =
  Michurin .. 22 C6
Tsau 58 C4
Tselinograd =
  Astana 29 D8
Tsetserleg 34 B5
Tshabong 58 D4
Tshane 58 C4
Tshela 56 E2
Tshikapa 56 F4
Tshofa 57 F5
Tshwane 58 C4
Tsihombe 59 K9
Tsimlyansk Res.
  =
  Tsimlyanskoye
  Vdkhr. 25 D5
Tsimlyanskoye
  Vdkhr. 25 D5

Tsinan = Jinan 35 C6
Tsinghai =
  Qinghai □ .. 34 C4
Tsingtao =
  Qingdao 35 C7
Tskhinvali 25 E5
Tsna ─► 24 C5
Tsu 32 B5
Tsuchiura 32 A7
Tsugaru-Kaikyō 32 F12
Tsumeb 58 B3
Tsumis 58 C3
Tsuruga 32 B5
Tsurugi-San .. 32 C4
Tsuruoka 33 G11
Tsyelyakhany . 17 B7
Tual 39 F4
Tuamotu Arch.
  = Tuamotu Is. 65 L16
Tuamotu Is. ... 65 L16
Tuamotu Ridge 65 M17
Tuao 38 A2
Tuapse 25 E4
Tuatapere 65 G2
Tubarão 94 B7
Tubau 37 D4
Tübingen 14 D5
Tubruq 52 B3
Tubuai Is. 65 M16
Tucacas 90 A5
Tucson 83 D7
Tucumcari ... 78 B2
Tucupita 90 B6
Tucuruí 92 C4
Tucuruí, Reprêsa
  de 92 C4
Tudela 19 A5
Tudmur 46 D4
Tuen 63 A4
Tuguegarao .. 38 A2
Tukangbesi,
  Kepulauan .. 39 F2
Tūkrah 52 B3
Tuktoyaktuk ... 70 B6
Tukuyu 57 F6
Tula, *Mexico* .. 84 C5
Tula, *Russia* .. 24 C4
Tulak 45 C5
Tulancingo ... 84 C5
Tulare 82 B3
Tulcán 90 C3
Tulcea 17 F9
Tulchyn 17 D9
Tuli, *Indonesia* 39 E2
Tuli, *Zimbabwe* 59 C5
Tullamore,
  Australia 63 B4
Tullamore,
  Ireland 11 E3
Tulle 12 D4
Tullibigeal ... 63 B4
Ṭulmaythah ... 52 B3
Tulsa 79 A6
Tulua 90 C3
Tulungagung .. 37 F4
Tum 39 E4
Tumaco 90 C3
Tumatumari ... 90 B7
Tumba, L. 56 E3
Tumbarumba . 63 C4
Túmbes 90 D2
Tumby Bay ... 62 B2
Tumeremo ... 90 B6
Tumkur 43 N10
Tump 42 F3
Tumpat 36 C2
Tumu 55 F4
Tumucumaque,
  Serra 92 B3

Tumut 63 C4
Tuncurry 63 B5
Tunduru 57 G7
Tundzha ─► ... 22 D6
Tunga Pass .. 41 C10
Tungabhadra ─►
  .... 43 M11
Tungaru 53 F5
Tunguska,
  Nizhnyaya ─► 30 C6
Tunis 54 A7
Tunisia ■ 54 B6
Tunja 90 B4
Tunuyán ─► .. 94 C3
Tunxi 35 D6
Tupelo 74 B3
Tupinambaranas 90 D7
Tupiza 94 A3
Tupungato,
  Cerro 94 C3
Túquerres 90 C3
Tura 30 C8
Turabah 47 E5
Tūrān 44 C4
Turayf 47 E4
Turda 17 E6
Turek 16 B4
Turfan = Turpan 34 B3
Turfan
  Depression =
  Turpan Hami 34 B3
Tŭrgovishte ... 22 C6
Turgutlu 23 E6
Turhal 46 B4
Turia ─► 19 C5
Turiaçu 92 C4
Turiaçu ─► ... 92 C4
Turin = Torino 20 B1
Turkana, L. ... 57 D7
Turkestan =
  Türkistan ... 29 E7
Turkey ■ 46 C3
Türkistan 29 E7
Turkmenistan ■ 29 F6
Turks & Caicos
  Is. ■ 87 B5
Turku 9 F12
Turnagain, C. . 64 D7
Turneffe Is. ... 85 D7
Turnhout 14 C3
Tŭrnovo =
  Veliko
  Tŭrnovo 22 C5
Turnu Măgurele 22 C5
Turnu Roşu, P. 17 F7
Turpan 34 B3
Turpan Hami . 34 B3
Turukhansk .. 30 C6
Tuscaloosa ... 74 C4
Tuscany =
  Toscana □ .. 20 C3
Tuticorin 43 Q11
Tutóia 92 C5
Tutong 36 D4
Tutrakan 22 B6
Tuttlingen 14 E5
Tutuala 39 F3
Tutuila 65 L13
Tuvalu ■ 64 K12
Tuxpan 84 C5
Tuxtla Gutiérrez 85 D6
Tuy 18 A1
Tuz Gölü 46 C3
Ṭūz Khurmātū . 46 D6
Tuzla 20 B7
Tver 24 B4
Tweed Heads . 63 A5
Twillingate 69 D5
Twin Falls ... 81 D6

Twofold B. 63 C4
Tyachiv 17 D6
Tychy 16 C4
Tyler 79 C6
Tyre = Sūr ... 46 D3
Tyrol = Tirol □ 14 E6
Tyrrell ─► 62 C3
Tyrrell, L. 62 C3
Tyrrhenian Sea 21 E4
Tyumen 29 D7
Tzaneen 59 C6
Tzukong =
  Zigong 35 D5

U

U.S.A. = United
  States of
  America ■ .. 67 F10
Uarsciek 49 G4
Uato-Udo 39 F3
Uatumã ─► .. 90 D7
Uaupés 90 D5
Uaupés ─► ... 90 C5
Ubá 93 G5
Ubaitaba 93 E6
Ubangi =
  Oubangi ─► . 56 E3
Ubauro 42 E6
Ube 32 C2
Ubeda 18 C4
Uberaba 93 F4
Uberlândia ... 93 F4
Ubon
  Ratchathani . 36 A2
Ubort ─► 17 B9
Ubundu 57 E5
Ucayali ─► ... 90 D4
Uchiura-Wan . 32 F12
Udaipur 43 G8
Udaipur Garhi . 40 D6
Udgir 43 K10
Udhampur ... 42 C9
Udi 55 G6
Údine 20 A4
Udmurtia □ .. 28 D6
Udon Thani .. 36 A2
Udupi 43 N9
Ueda 32 A6
Uele ─► 57 D4
Uelzen 14 B6
Ufa 29 D6
Ugab ─► 58 C2
Ugalla ─► ... 57 F6
Uganda ■ ... 57 D6
Ugljane 20 B5
Ugolyak 30 C10
Uibhist a Deas
  = South Uist 10 C3
Uibhist a Tuath
  = North Uist 10 C3
Uíge 56 F2
Uinta Mts. ... 81 E8
Uitenhage ... 59 E5
Ujjain 43 H9
Ujung Pandang 39 F1
Ukerewe I. ... 57 E6
Ukhrul 41 E10
Ukhta 28 C6
Ukraine ■ ... 25 D3
Ulaanbaatar .. 35 B5
Ulaangom 34 A4
Ulan Bator =
  Ulaanbaatar . 35 B5
Ulan Ude 30 D8
Ulcinj 22 D2

Ulhasnagar ...	43	K8
Ulladulla	63	C5
Ullapool	10	C4
Ulm	14	D5
Ulmarra	63	A5
Ulonguè	59	A6
Ulster ☐	11	D3
Ulubat Gölü ...	23	D7
Uludağ	23	D7
Ulungur He →	34	B3
Uluru = Ayers		
Rock	60	F5
Ulutau	29	E7
Ulverstone	62	D4
Ulyanovsk =		
Simbirsk ...	24	C6
Ulyasutay	34	B4
Umala	91	G5
Uman	17	D10
Umaria	40	F3
Umarkot	43	G6
Umba	28	C4
Umbrella Mts. .	65	F3
Ume älv → ...	8	F12
Umeå	8	F12
Umera	39	E3
Umm al		
Qaywayn ...	44	E3
Umm Bel	53	F4
Umm Lajj	47	F4
Umm Ruwaba .	53	F5
Umnak I.	71	C3
Umniati → ..	59	B5
Umtata	59	E5
Umuarama ...	93	G3
Una →	20	B6
Unalaska	71	C3
Uncía	91	G5
Underbool	62	C3
Ungarie	63	B4
Ungarra	62	B2
Ungava B.	68	C4
Ungava Pen. ..	68	B3
Ungeny =		
Ungheni	17	E8
Ungheni	17	E8
União da Vitória	94	B6
Unimak I.	71	C3
United Arab		
Emirates ■ ..	44	F3
United		
Kingdom ■ .	11	E5
United States of		
America ■ ..	67	F10
Unnao	40	D3
Unst	10	A6
Ünye	46	B4
Upata	90	B6
Upemba, L. ...	57	F5
Upington	58	D4
Upper Hutt ...	65	D6
Upper Volta =		
Burkina		
Faso ■	55	F4
Uppsala	9	G11
Ur	47	E6
Uracara	90	D7
Ural =		
Zhayyq → .	29	E6
Ural	63	B4
Ural Mts. =		
Uralskie Gory	28	D6
Uralla	63	B5
Uralsk = Oral .	24	C7
Uralskie Gory .	28	D6
Uranquinty ..	63	C4
Urawa	32	B6
Uray	29	C7
Urbana	72	D1

Urbino	20	C4
Urbión, Picos de	19	A4
Urcos	91	F4
Urda	25	D6
Urdzhar	29	E9
Ures	84	B2
Urfa = Sanliurfa	46	C4
Urganch	29	E7
Urgench =		
Urganch ...	29	E7
Uribia	90	A4
Urla	23	E6
Urmia =		
Orūmīyeh ...	46	C6
Urmia, L. =		
Orūmīyeh,		
Daryācheh-ye	46	C6
Uroševac	22	C3
Uruana	93	F4
Urubamba	91	F4
Urubamba → .	91	F4
Uruçuí	92	D5
Uruguai → ...	94	B6
Uruguaiana ...	94	B5
Uruguay ■ ...	94	C5
Uruguay → ..	94	C5
Urumchi =		
Ürümqi	34	B3
Ürümqi	34	B3
Usakos	58	C3
Usedom	15	B8
Ush-Tobe	29	E8
Ushant =		
Ouessant, I. d'	12	B1
Ushuaia	95	G3
Üsküdar	25	E2
Usman	24	C4
Usoke	57	F6
Uspallata, P. de	94	C3
Uspenskiy ...	29	E8
Ussuriysk	31	E11
Ust-Aldan =		
Batamay ...	31	C10
Ust Ilimpeya =		
Yukti	30	C8
Ust Ishim	29	D8
Ust-		
Kamenogorsk		
= Öskemen .	29	E9
Ust-Karenga .	31	D9
Ust Kuyga	31	B11
Ust Muya	30	D9
Ust Olenek ...	30	B10
Ust Port	28	C9
Ust Tsilma	28	C6
Ust Urt =		
Ustyurt,		
Plateau	29	E6
Ust Vorkuta ...	28	C7
Ústí nad Labem	16	C2
Ustica	21	E4
Ustinov =		
Izhevsk	28	D6
Ustye	30	D7
Ustyurt, Plateau	29	E6
Usu	34	B3
Usuki	32	C2
Usumacinta →	85	D6
Usumbura =		
Bujumbura ..	57	E5
Uta	39	E5
Utah ☐	81	F8
Utete	57	F7
Utiariti	91	F7
Utica	73	C8
Utrecht	14	B3
Utrera	18	D3
Utsunomiya ...	32	A6

Uttar Pradesh ☐	42	F11
Uttaranchal ☐...	40	C2
Uttaradit	36	A2
Uummannarsuaq		
= Farvel, Kap	68	C6
Uusikaupunki .	8	F12
Uvat	29	D7
Uvinza	57	F6
Uvira	57	E5
Uvs Nuur	34	A4
Uwajima	32	C3
Uyuni	91	H5
Uzbekistan ■ ..	29	E7
Uzerche	12	D4
Uzh →	17	C10
Uzhgorod =		
Uzhhorod ...	17	D6
Uzhhorod	17	D6
Uzunköprü	22	D6

V

Vaal →	58	D4
Vaasa	8	F12
Vác	16	E4
Vach → =		
Vakh →	29	C8
Vadodara	43	H8
Vadsø	8	D13
Vaduz	13	C8
Váh →	16	E4
Vahsel B.	96	B5
Vaigach	28	B6
Vakh →	29	C8
Val d'Or	69	D3
Valahia	22	B5
Valandovo	22	D4
Valcheta	95	E3
Valdayskaya		
Vozvyshennost		
....	24	B3
Valdepeñas ...	18	C4
Valdés, Pen. ...	95	E4
Valdez	71	B5
Valdivia	95	D2
Valdosta	75	D6
Valença	93	E6
Valença do Piauí	92	D5
Valence	13	D6
Valencia, Spain	19	C5
Valencia,		
Venezuela ...	90	A5
Valencia ☐	19	C5
Valencia, G. de	19	C6
Valencia de		
Alcántara ...	18	C2
Valencia I.	11	F1
Valenciennes ..	13	A5
Valentim, Sa. do	92	D5
Valera	90	B4
Valjevo	22	B2
Vall de Uxó ...	19	C5
Valladolid,		
Mexico	85	C7
Valladolid, Spain	18	B3
Valle de la		
Pascua	90	B5
Valledupar	90	A4
Vallejo	80	F2
Vallenar	94	B2
Valletta	21	G5
Valls	19	B6
Valognes	12	B3
Valona = Vlóra	23	D2
Valozhyn	17	A8
Valparaíso	94	C2

Vals, Tanjung .	39	F5
Valsad	43	J8
Valverde del		
Camino	18	D2
Van	46	C5
Van, L. = Van		
Gölü	46	C5
Van Gölü	46	C5
Van Rees,		
Pegunungan	39	E5
Vanadzor	25	E5
Vancouver,		
Canada	71	D7
Vancouver,		
U.S.A.	80	C2
Vancouver I. ..	71	D7
Vänern	9	G10
Vanga	57	E7
Vangaindrano .	59	J9
Vännäs	8	F11
Vannes	12	C2
Vanrhynsdorp .	58	E3
Vanua Levu ..	64	L12
Vanuatu ■ ...	64	L11
Vapnyarka	17	D9
Varanasi	40	E4
Varangerfjorden	8	D13
Varaždin	20	A6
Varberg	9	G10
Vardak ☐	45	C7
Vardar =		
Axiós → ...	23	D4
Varese	20	B2
Varna	22	C6
Varzaneh	44	C3
Vasa Barris →	93	E6
Vascongadas =		
País Vasco ☐	19	A4
Vasht = Khāsh	42	E2
Vasilevichi	17	B9
Vasilkov =		
Vasylkiv ...	17	C10
Vaslui	17	E8
Västerås	9	G11
Västervik	9	G11
Vasto	20	C5
Vasylkiv	17	C10
Vatican City ■ .	20	D4
Vatomandry ...	59	H9
Vatra-Dornei .	17	E7
Vättern	9	G10
Vaupés =		
Uaupés → .	90	C5
Vawkavysk	17	B7
Vaygach, Ostrov	28	C6
Vedea →	22	C5
Vega	8	E10
Vegreville	71	C8
Vejer de la		
Frontera	18	D3
Vélez	90	B4
Vélez Málaga .	18	D3
Vélez Rubio ...	19	D4
Velhas →	93	F5
Velika Kapela .	20	B5
Velikaya → ...	24	B2
Veliki Ustyug .	24	A6
Velikiye Luki ..	24	B3
Veliko Tŭrnovo	22	C5
Velikonda Range	43	M11
Velletri	20	D4
Vellore	43	N11
Venado Tuerto	94	C4
Vendée ☐	12	C3
Vendôme	12	C4
Venézia	20	B4
Venézia, G. di .	20	B4

Venezuela ■ .. 90 B5
Venezuela, G. de 90 A4
Vengurla 43 M8
Venice =
  Venézia 20 B4
Venkatapuram . 40 H3
Ventotene 21 D4
Ventoux, Mt. . 13 D6
Ventspils 24 B1
Ventuarí ⇢ .. 90 C5
Ventura 82 C3
Venus B. 63 C4
Vera, *Argentina* 94 B4
Vera, *Spain* ... 19 D5
Veracruz 84 D5
Veraval 43 J7
Verbánia 20 B2
Vercelli 20 B2
Verde ⇢ 95 E3
Verden 14 B5
Verdun 13 B6
Vereeniging .. 59 D5
Verga, C. 55 F2
Verín 18 B2
Verkhnevilyuysk 30 C10
Verkhniy
  Baskunchak . 25 D6
Verkhoyansk . 31 C11
Verkhoyansk Ra.
  =
  Verkhoyanskiy
  Khrebet .. 31 C10
Verkhoyanskiy
  Khrebet .. 31 C10
Vermilion 71 C8
Vermont □ 73 C9
Vernon, *Canada* 71 C8
Vernon, *U.S.A.* 78 B4
Véroia 23 D4
Verona 20 B3
Versailles 12 B5
Vert, C. 55 F1
Verviers 14 C3
Veselovskoye
  Vdkhr. 25 D5
Vesoul 13 C7
Vesterålen ... 8 E11
Vestfjorden ... 8 E10
Vesuvio 21 D5
Vesuvius, Mt. =
  Vesuvio 21 D5
Veszprém 16 E3
Vetlugu ⇢ ... 28 D5
Vettore, Mte. .. 20 C4
Veys 47 E7
Vezhen 22 C5
Viacha 91 G5
Viamão 94 C6
Viana 92 C5
Viana do
  Alentejo 18 C2
Viana do Castelo 18 B1
Vianópolis 93 F4
Viaréggio 20 C3
Vibo Valéntia . 21 E6
Vicenza 20 B3
Vich 19 B7
Vichy 13 C5
Vicksburg 79 C8
Victor 43 J7
Victor Harbor . 62 C2
Victoria, *Canada* 71 D7
Victoria, *Chile* . 95 D2
Victoria, *Guinea* 55 F2
Victoria = Labuan,
  Malaysia 36 C5
Victoria □ 62 C3

Victoria, L.,
  Africa 57 E6
Victoria, L.,
  Australia 62 B3
Victoria Beach . 71 C10
Victoria de
  Durango =
  Durango 84 C4
Victoria Falls . 59 B5
Victoria I. 70 A8
Victoria Ld. .. 96 B14
Victoria
  Taungdeik .. 41 G9
Victoria West . 58 E4
Victorica 94 D3
Vicuña 94 C2
Vidin 22 C4
Vidisha 43 H10
Viedma 95 E4
Viedma, L. 95 F2
Vienna = Wien . 15 D9
Vienne 13 D6
Vienne ⇢ 12 C4
Vientiane 36 A2
Vierzon 12 C5
Vietnam ■ 36 A3
Vigan 38 A2
Vigévano 20 B2
Vigia 92 C4
Vigo 18 A1
Vijayawada ... 40 J3
Vikeke 39 F3
Vikna 8 F10
Vila da Magania 59 B7
Vila de João
  Belo = Xai-Xai 59 D6
Vila do Bispo .. 18 D1
Vila Franca de
  Xira 18 C1
Vila Machado . 59 B6
Vila Nova de
  Gaia 18 B1
Vila Real 18 B2
Vila Real de
  Santo António 18 D2
Vila Velha 93 G5
Vilaine ⇢ 12 C2
Vilanculos ... 59 C7
Vileyka 17 A8
Vilhelmina 8 F11
Vilhena 91 F6
Vilkitskogo,
  Proliv 30 B8
Vilkovo =
  Vylkove 17 F9
Villa Ahumada . 84 A3
Villa Ángela .. 94 B4
Villa Bella ... 91 F5
Villa Bens =
  Tarfaya 54 C2
Villa Colón ... 94 C3
Villa de María . 94 B4
Villa Dolores . 94 C3
Villa Hayes .. 94 B5
Villa María ... 94 C4
Villa Mazán ... 94 B3
Villa Montes .. 94 A4
Villa Ocampo . 94 B5
Villacarrillo .. 18 C4
Villach 15 E7
Villagarcía de
  Arosa 18 A1
Villaguay 94 C5
Villahermosa . 85 D6
Villajoyosa ... 19 C5
Villalba 18 A2
Villanueva de la
  Serena 18 C3

Villanueva y
  Geltrú 19 B6
Villarreal 19 C5
Villarrica, *Chile* 95 D2
Villarrica,
  Paraguay ... 94 B5
Villarrobledo .. 19 C4
Villavicencio . 90 C4
Villaviciosa .. 18 A3
Villazón 94 A3
Villena 19 C5
Villeneuve-
  d'Ascq 13 A5
Villeneuve-sur-
  Lot 12 D4
Villingen-
  Schwenningen 14 D5
Vilnius 24 C2
Vilyuy ⇢ 31 C10
Vilyuysk 31 C10
Viña del Mar . 94 C2
Vinaroz 19 B6
Vindhya Ra. .. 43 H10
Vineland 73 E8
Vinkovci 20 B7
Vinnitsa =
  Vinnytsya .. 17 D9
Vinnytsya 17 D9
Virac 38 B2
Viramgam 43 H8
Viranşehir ... 46 C4
Virden 71 D9
Vire 12 B3
Vírgenes, C. .. 95 G3
Virgin Is. *(U.K.*
  -U.S.A.) ■ .. 87 C7
Virginia □ 73 F6
Virginia Beach . 73 F8
Virovitica 20 B6
Virudunagar . 43 Q10
Vis 20 C6
Visalia 82 B3
Visayan Sea .. 38 B2
Visby 9 G11
Višegrad 20 C7
Viseu, *Brazil* .. 92 C4
Viseu, *Portugal* 18 B2
Vishakhapatnam 40 J4
Viso, Mte. ... 20 B1
Vistula =
  Wisła ⇢ ... 16 A4
Vitebsk =
  Vitsyebsk .. 24 B3
Viterbo 20 C4
Viti Levu 64 L12
Vitigudino ... 18 B2
Vitória, *Brazil* . 93 G5
Vitoria, *Spain* . 19 A4
Vitória da
  Conquista .. 93 E5
Vitsyebsk 24 B3
Vittória 21 F5
Vittório Véneto 20 B4
Vivero 18 A2
Vize 22 D6
Vizianagaram . 40 H4
Vjosa ⇢ 23 D2
Vladikavkaz .. 25 E5
Vladimir 24 B5
Vladimir
  Volynskiy =
  Volodymyr-
  Volynskyy .. 17 C7
Vladivostok .. 31 E11
Vlissingen ... 14 C2
Vlóra 23 D2
Vltava ⇢ 16 C2
Vogelsberg ... 14 C5

Voghera 20 B2
Vohibinany ... 59 H9
Vohimarina ... 59 G10
Vohimena,
  Tanjon' i ... 59 K9
Vohipeno 59 J9
Voi 57 E7
Voiron 13 D6
Vojvodina □ .. 22 B2
Volga ⇢ 25 D6
Volga Hts. =
  Privolzhskaya
  Vozvyshennost
  .... 24 C6
Volgodonsk .. 25 D5
Volgograd 25 D5
Volgogradskoye
  Vdkhr. 24 C6
Volkhov ⇢ ... 24 A3
Volkovysk =
  Vawkavysk .. 17 B7
Volochanka .. 30 B7
Volodymyr-
  Volynskyy ... 17 C7
Vologda 24 B4
Vólos 23 E4
Volovets 17 D6
Volozhin =
  Valozhyn ... 17 A8
Volsk 24 C6
Volta ⇢ 55 G5
Volta, L. 55 G5
Volta Redonda 93 G5
Volterra 20 C3
Volturno ⇢ .. 20 D4
Volzhskiy 25 D5
Voríai
  Sporádhes . 23 E4
Vorkuta 28 C7
Voronezh 24 C4
Voroshilovgrad
  = Luhansk .. 25 D4
Voroshilovsk =
  Alchevsk ... 25 D4
Vosges 13 B7
Vostok I. 65 L15
Vouga ⇢ 18 B1
Voznesensk .. 25 D3
Voznesenye .. 28 C4
Vrangelya,
  Ostrov 31 B15
Vranje 22 C3
Vratsa 22 C4
Vrbas ⇢ 20 B6
Vrede 59 D5
Vredenburg .. 58 E3
Vršac 22 B3
Vryburg 58 D4
Vryheid 59 D6
Vukovar 20 B7
Vulcan 17 F6
Vulcaneşti ... 17 F9
Vulcano 21 E5
Vulkaneshty =
  Vulcaneşti .. 17 F9
Vung Tau 36 B3
Vyatka = Kirov 28 D5
Vyatskiye
  Polyany ... 24 B7
Vyazma 24 B3
Vyborg 28 C3
Vychegda ⇢ . 28 C5
Vychodné
  Beskydy ... 17 D5
Vylkove 17 F9
Vynohradiv ... 17 D6
Vyshniy
  Volochek .. 24 B3
Vyškov 16 D3

Wa 55 F4
Waal → 14 C3
Wabash → ... 72 F1
Waco 78 D5
Wad Banda ... 53 F4
Wad Hamid ... 53 E5
Wâd Medanî .. 53 F5
Waddington, Mt. 71 C7
Waddy Pt. 63
Wadi Halfa 52 D5
Wafrah 47 E6
Wager B. 68 B2
Wager Bay 68 B1
Wagga Wagga 63 C4
Waghete 39 E5
Wah 42 C8
Wahai 39 E3
Waiau → 65 E5
Waibeem 39 E4
Waigeo 39 E4
Waihi 64 B6
Waihou → ... 64 B6
Waikabubak ... 39 F1
Waikari 65 E5
Waikato → ... 64 B6
Waikerie 62 B2
Waikokopu 64 C7
Waikouaiti 65 F4
Waimakariri → 65 E5
Waimate 65 F4
Wainganga → 43 K11
Waingapu 39 F2
Wainwright,
    Canada 71 C8
Wainwright,
    U.S.A. 71 A3
Waiouru 64 C6
Waipara 65 E5
Waipawa 64 C7
Waipiro 64 C8
Waipu 64 A6
Waipukurau ... 64 D7
Wairakei 64 C7
Wairarapa, L. .. 65 D6
Wairoa 64 C7
Waitaki → 65 F4
Waitara 64 C6
Waiuku 64 B6
Wajima 32 A5
Wajir 57 D8
Wakasa-Wan .. 32 B4
Wakatipu, L. .. 65 F3
Wakayama 32 B4
Wakefield 65 D5
Wakema 41 J10
Wakkanai 32 E12
Wakool 63 C3
Wakool → 62 C3
Wakre 39 E4
Wałbrzych 16 C3
Walcha 63 B5
Wałcz 16 B3
Wales □ 11 E4
Walgett 63 A4
Walgreen Coast 96 B1
Walhalla 63 C4
Walla Walla ... 80 B4
Wallachia =
    Valahia 22 B5
Wallal 63 A4
Wallaroo 62 B2
Wallerawang .. 63 B5
Wallis & Futuna,
    Is. 64 L13
Wallowa Mts. .. 80 C5
Wallsend 63 B5
Wallumbilla ... 63 A4

Walvisbaai 58 C2
Wamba 57 D5
Wamena 39 E5
Wamulan 39 E3
Wana 42 C6
Wanaaring ... 63 A3
Wanaka 65 F3
Wanaka L. 65 F3
Wanapiri 39 E5
Wanbi 62 B3
Wandoan 63 A4
Wangal 39 F4
Wanganella ... 63 C3
Wanganui 64 C6
Wangaratta ... 63 C4
Wangary 62 B2
Wangerooge .. 14 B4
Wangiwangi .. 39 F2
Wanxian 35 C5
Warangal 43 L11
Waratah 62 D4
Waratah B. 63 C4
Warburton ... 63 C4
Ward 65 D6
Ward → 63 A4
Wardha 43 J11
Wardha → ... 43 K11
Warialda 63 A5
Wariap 39 E4
Warkopi 39 E4
Warmbad,
    Namibia ... 58 D3
Warmbad,
    S. Africa 59 C5
Warner Mts. .. 80 E3
Warracknabeal 62 C3
Warragul 63 C4
Warrego → .. 63 B4
Warren 63 B4
Warrenton ... 58 D4
Warrenville ... 63 A4
Warri 55 G6
Warrina 62 A2
Warrington, U.K. 11 E5
Warrington,
    U.S.A. 74 D4
Warrnambool . 62 C3
Warsa 39 E5
Warsaw =
    Warszawa ... 16 B5
Warszawa ... 16 B5
Warta → 16 B2
Warthe =
    Warta → ... 16 B2
Waru 39 E4
Warwick 63 A5
Wasatch Ra. .. 81 E8
Wash, The ... 11 E7
Washim 43 J10
Washington .. 73 E7
Washington □ . 80 B3
Washington, Mt. 73 B10
Wasian 39 E4
Wasior 39 E4
Waskaganish .. 69 C3
Wasserkuppe .. 14 C5
Watangpone .. 39 E2
Waterbury ... 73 D9
Waterford ... 11 E3
Waterloo,
    S. Leone 55 G2
Waterloo, U.S.A. 77 D8
Waterton-Glacier
    International
    Peace Park .. 81 A6
Watertown ... 73 C8
Waterville ... 73 B11
Watford 11 F6
Watling I. = San
    Salvador 86 B5

Watrous 71 C9
Watsa 57 D5
Watson Lake .. 70 B7
Watsonville ... 82 B2
Wattiwarriganna
    Cr. → 62 A2
Watuata =
    Batuata 39 F2
Watubela,
    Kepulauan .. 39 E4
Watubela Is. =
    Watubela,
    Kepulauan .. 39 E4
Wauchope 63 B5
Waukegan ... 72 C2
Waukesha 72 C1
Wausau 77 C10
Wauwatosa ... 72 C2
Waverley 64 C6
Wâw 53 G4
Wâw al Kabîr .. 52 C2
Waxahachie .. 79 C5
Wayabula Rau . 39 D3
Wayatinah 62 D4
Waycross 75 D6
Wazirabad 42 C9
We 36 C1
Weda 39 D3
Weda, Teluk .. 39 D3
Weddell I. 95 G4
Weddell Sea .. 96 A4
Wedderburn .. 62 C3
Wee Waa 63 B4
Weemelah 63 A4
Weiden 15 D7
Weifang 35 C6
Weimar 15 C6
Weipa 61 C7
Weir → 63 A4
Wejherowo ... 16 A4
Welbourn Hill . 62 A1
Welkom 59 D5
Wellesley Is. .. 60 D6
Wellington,
    Australia 63 B4
Wellington, N.Z. 65 D6
Wellington, I. .. 95 F1
Wellington, L. . 63 C4
Wels 15 D8
Welshpool ... 11 E5
Wemindji 69 C3
Wenatchee 80 B3
Wenchi 55 G4
Wenchow =
    Wenzhou ... 35 D7
Wendesi 39 E4
Wensu 34 B3
Wentworth ... 62 B3
Wenut 39 E4
Wenzhou 35 D7
Werda 58 D4
Werder 49 F4
Weri 39 E4
Werra → 14 C5
Werribee 63 C3
Werrimull 62 B3
Werris Creek .. 63 B5
Wersar 39 E4
Weser → 14 B5
Wesiri 39 F3
West Bengal □ 40 F7
West Beskids =
    Západné
    Beskydy 16 D4
West Falkland . 95 G4
West Fjord =
    Vestfjorden . 8 E10
West Ice Shelf . 96 A11
West Nicholson 59 C5

West Palm
    Beach 75 F7
West Pt. 62 C2
West Virginia □ 72 E5
West Wyalong . 63 B4
Westall Pt. 62 B1
Westbury 62 D4
Westerland ... 14 A5
Western
    Australia □ .. 60 F3
Western Dvina
    =
    Daugava → . 24 B1
Western Ghats 43 N9
Western
    Sahara ■ ... 54 D2
Western Samoa =
    Samoa ■ ... 65 L13
Westerwald ... 14 C4
Westland Bight 65 E4
Weston 36 C5
Weston-super-
    Mare 11 F5
Westport,
    Ireland 11 E2
Westport, N.Z. . 65 D4
Westray 10 B5
Wetar 39 F3
Wetaskiwin .. 71 C8
Wetzlar 14 C5
Wewak 61
Wexford 11 E3
Weyburn 71 D9
Weymouth ... 11 F5
Whakatane ... 64 B7
Whale → 68 C4
Whale Cove .. 70 B10
Whales, B. of .. 96 B16
Whangamomona
    .... 64 C6
Whangarei ... 64 A6
Whangarei Harb. 64 A6
Wheeling 72 D5
White →, Ark.,
    U.S.A. 79 C8
White →, Ind.,
    U.S.A. 72 E2
White Cliffs .. 62 B3
White I. 64 B7
White Nile = Nîl
    el Abyad → .. 53 E5
White Russia =
    Belarus ■ .. 24 C2
White Sea =
    Beloye More 28 C4
Whitecliffs ... 65 E4
Whitehaven ... 11 D5
Whitehorse ... 70 B6
Whitemark ... 62 D4
Whitfield 63 C4
Whitianga 64 B6
Whitney, Mt. .. 82 B3
Whittlesea ... 63 C4
Wholdaia L. .. 70 B9
Whyalla 62 B2
Whyjonta 62 A3
Wichita 78 A5
Wichita Falls .. 78 C4
Wick 10 B5
Wickham, C. .. 62 C3
Wicklow Mts. .. 11 E3
Wieluń 16 C4
Wien 15 D9
Wiener Neustadt 15 E9
Wiesbaden ... 14 C5
Wilcannia 62 B3
Wildspitze 14 E6
Wilhelm, Mt. .. 61 B8
Wilhelm II Coast 96 A11

Wilhelmshaven   14   B5
Wilkes-Barre . .   73   D8
Wilkie   71   C9
Willandra
  Billabong
  Creek ~➤   . . .   63   B4
Willemstad . .   87   D6
William Creek .   62   A2
Williams Lake .   71   C7
Williamsburg .   73   F7
Williamsport .   73   D7
Williamstown .   63   C3
Williston   76   A3
Willowmore . . .   58   E4
Willunga   62   C2
Wilmington,
  Australia . . .   62   B2
Wilmington,
  Del., U.S.A. .   73   E8
Wilmington,
  N.C., U.S.A. .   75   B9
Wilpena Cr. ~➤   62   B2
Wilson   75   B9
Wilson ~➤   62   A3
Wilsons
  Promontory .   63   C4
Wimmera ~➤ . .   62   C3
Winchester . .   11   F6
Wind River
  Range   81   D9
Windau =
  Ventspils . . .   24   B1
Windhoek   58   C3
Windsor,
  Australia . . .   63   B5
Windsor, N.S.,
  Canada   69   D4
Windsor, Ont.,
  Canada   69   D2
Windward Is. . .   87
Wingen   63   B5
Wingham   63   B5
Winisk ~➤   69   C2
Winneba   55   G4
Winnipeg   71   D10
Winnipeg, L. . .   71   C10
Winnipegosis L.   71   C9
Winona   77   C9
Winston-Salem   75   A7
Winterthur   13   C8
Winton,
  Australia . . .   61   E7
Winton, N.Z. . .   65   G3
Wirrulla   62   B1
Wisconsin □ . .   77   C10
Wisła ~➤   16   A4
Wismar   15   B6
Witbank   59   D5
Wittenberg   15   C7
Wittenberge . . .   15   B6
Wkra ~➤   16   B5
Włocławek   16   B4
Włodawa   17   C6
Wodonga   63   C4
Wokam   39   F4
Wolfsberg   15   E8
Wolfsburg   15   B6
Wolin   16   B2
Wollaston, Is. .   95   H3
Wollaston Pen.   70   B8
Wollongong . . .   63   B5
Wolseley   62   C3
Wolverhampton   11   E5
Wondai   63   A5
Wongalarroo L.   63   B3
Wônsan   35   C7
Wonthaggi   63   C4
Woocalla   62   B2
Woodburn   63   A5
Woodenbong .   63   A5

Woodend   63   C3
Woodland   80   F3
Woodroffe, Mt.   60   F5
Woods, L. of the   71   D10
Woodstock . . .   69   D4
Woodville   64   D6
Woolamai, C. . .   63   C4
Woolgoolga . . .   63   B5
Woombye   63   A5
Woomera   62   B2
Worcester,
  S. Africa   58   E3
Worcester, U.K.   11   E5
Worcester,
  U.S.A.   73   C10
Workington . .   11   D5
Worms   14   D5
Worthing   11   F6
Wosi   39   E3
Wou-han =
  Wuhan   35   C6
Wour   52   D2
Wousi = Wuxi .   35   C7
Wowoni   39   E2
Woy Woy   63   B5
Wrangel I. =
  Vrangelya,
  Ostrov   31   B15
Wrangell   71   C6
Wrangell Mts. .   71   B5
Wrath, C.   10   B4
Wrexham   11   E5
Wright   38   B3
Wrigley   70   B7
Wrocław   16   C3
Września   16   B3
Wu Jiang ~➤ . .   35   D5
Wuhan   35   C6
Wuhsi = Wuxi .   35   C7
Wuhu   35   C6
Wukari   55   G6
Wuliaru   39   F4
Wulumuchi =
  Ürümqi   34   B3
Wum   55   G7
Wuntho   41   F10
Wuppertal   14   C4
Würzburg   14   D5
Wutongqiao . .   34   D5
Wuwei   34   C5
Wuxi   35   C7
Wuyi Shan . . .   35   D6
Wuzhi Shan . . .   35   E5
Wuzhong   35   C5
Wuzhou   35   D6
Wyandotte   72   C4
Wyandra   63   A4
Wyangala Res.   63   B4
Wyara, L.   63   A3
Wycheproof . . .   62   C3
Wynbring   62   B1
Wyndham,
  Australia   60   D4
Wyndham, N.Z.   65   G3
Wynnum   63   A5
Wynyard   62   D4
Wyoming □ . . .   81   D10
Wyong   63   B5

X

Xai-Xai   59   D6
Xainza   34   C3
Xangongo   58   B3
Xankändi   25   F6
Xánthi   22   D5
Xapuri   91   F5

Xi Jiang ~➤ . . .   35   D6
Xiaguan   34   D5
Xiamen   35   D6
Xi'an   35   C5
Xiang Jiang ~➤   35   D6
Xiangfan   35   C6
Xiangtan   35   D6
Xiao Hinggan
  Ling   35   B7
Xiapu   35   D6
Xichang   34   D5
Xigazê   34   D3
Xinavane   59   D6
Xing'an   35   D6
Xingren   35   D5
Xingtai   35   C6
Xingu ~➤   92   C3
Xining   34   C5
Xinjiang Uygur
  Zizhiqu □ . . .   34   B3
Xinjin   35   C7
Xinxiang   35   C6
Xinyang   35   C6
Xinzhu   35   D7
Xique-Xique . .   93   E5
Xisha Qundao =
  Hsisha
  Chuntao   36   A4
Xixabangma
  Feng   40   C5
Xizang □   34   C3
Xuanhua   35   B6
Xuchang   35   C6
Xuzhou   35   C6

Y

Ya'an   34   D5
Yaapeet   62   C3
Yabelo   53   H6
Yablonovy Ra. =
  Yablonovyy
  Khrebet   30   D9
Yablonovyy
  Khrebet   30   D9
Yacuiba   94   A4
Yadgir   43   L10
Yagoua   56   B3
Yahuma   56   D4
Yakima   80   B3
Yakutat   71   C6
Yakutsk   31   C10
Yala   36   C2
Yalinga   56   C4
Yalong Jiang ~➤   34   D5
Yalova   22   D7
Yalta   25   E3
Yalutorovsk . .   29   D7
Yam Ha Melah
  = Dead Sea .   47   E3
Yam Kinneret .   46   D3
Yamagata   33   G12
Yamaguchi . . .   32   B2
Yamal,
  Poluostrov . .   28   B8
Yamal Pen. =
  Yamal,
  Poluostrov . .   28   B8
Yamantau, Gora   29   D6
Yamba, N.S.W.,
  Australia   63   A5
Yamba,
  S. Austral.,
  Australia   62   B3
Yâmbiô   53   H4
Yambol   22   C6

Yamdena   39   F4
Yamethin   41   G11
Yamma-Yamma,
  L.   62   A3
Yamoussoukro   55   G3
Yampil   17   D9
Yampol =
  Yampil   17   D9
Yamuna ~➤ . . .   40   E3
Yamzho Yumco   34   D4
Yana ~➤   31   B11
Yanac   62   C3
Yanbu 'al Baḥr   47   F4
Yancannia   62   B3
Yanco Cr. ~➤ . .   63   C4
Yandoon   41   J10
Yangambi   56   D4
Yangch'ü =
  Taiyuan   35   C6
Yangchun   35   D6
Yangjiang   35   D6
Yangon =
  Rangoon   41   J11
Yangquan   35   C6
Yanji   35   B7
Yanna   63   A4
Yanqi   34   B3
Yantabulla   63   A4
Yantai   35   C7
Yanykurgan . . .   29   E7
Yao   53   F2
Yaoundé   56   D2
Yapen   39   E5
Yapen, Selat . .   39   E5
Yaqui ~➤   84   B2
Yar-Sale   28   C8
Yaraka   61   E7
Yaransk   24   B6
Yardea P.O. . . .   62   B2
Yaremcha   17   D7
Yarensk   28   C5
Yarí ~➤   90   D4
Yarkand =
  Shache   34   C2
Yarkhun ~➤ . . .   42   A8
Yaroslavl   24   B4
Yarram   63   C4
Yarraman   63   A5
Yarranvale   63   A4
Yarras   63   B5
Yartsevo   30   C7
Yaselda   17   B8
Yasinya   17   D7
Yass   63   B4
Yatağan   23   F7
Yathkyed L. . . .   70   B10
Yatsushiro   32   C2
Yauyos   91   F3
Yavari ~➤   90   D4
Yavatmal   43   J11
Yavoriv   17   D6
Yavorov =
  Yavoriv   17   D6
Yawatahama . .   32   C3
Yazd   44   D3
Yazd □   44   C3
Yazdān   45   C5
Yazoo ~➤   79   C8
Ye Xian   35   C6
Yebyu   41   K12
Yecla   19   C5
Yedintsy =
  Edinița   17   D8
Yeelanna   62   B2
Yegros   94   B5
Yei   53   H5
Yekaterinburg .   29   D7
Yekaterinodar =
  Krasnodar . .   25   D4

Yelarbon	63	A5
Yelets	24	C4
Yelizavetgrad =		
Kirovohrad . .	25	D3
Yell	10	A6
Yellow Sea . . .	35	C7
Yellowhead Pass	71	C8
Yellowknife . . .	70	B8
Yellowknife →	70	B8
Yellowstone →	76	B3
Yellowstone		
National Park	81	C8
Yelsk	17	C9
Yemen ■	49	E3
Yenangyaung .	41	G10
Yenbo = Yanbu		
'al Baḩr	47	F4
Yenda	63	B4
Yenice	23	E6
Yenisey →	28	B9
Yeniseysk	30	D7
Yeniseyskiy		
Zaliv	28	B9
Yenyuka	31	D10
Yeola	43	J9
Yeovil	11	F5
Yerbent	29	F6
Yerevan	25	E5
Yermak	29	D8
Yershov	24	C6
Yerushalayim =		
Jerusalem . .	47	E3
Yessey	30	C8
Yeu, I. d'	12	C2
Yevpatoriya	25	D3
Yeysk	25	D4
Yezd = Yazd . .	44	D3
Yiannitsa	23	D4
Yibin	35	D5
Yichang	35	C6
Yichun	35	B7
Yilan	35	D7
Yinchuan	35	C5
Yingkou	35	B7
Yingtan	35	D6
Yining	34	B3
Yinmabin	41	F10
Yishan	35	D5
Yíthion	23	F4
Yiyang	35	D6
Yog Pt.	38	B2
Yogyakarta	37	F4
Yokadouma	56	D2
Yokkaichi	32	B5
Yoko	53	G1
Yokohama	32	B6
Yokosuka	32	B6
Yola	53	G1
Yonago	32	B3
Yongji	35	C6
Yonibana	55	G2
Yonkers	73	D9
Yonne →	13	B5
York, U.K.	11	E6
York, U.S.A.	73	E7
York, C.	61	C7
Yorke Pen.	62	B2
Yorkton	71	C9
Yos Sudarso,		
Pulau	39	F5
Yosemite		
National Park	82	B3
Yoshkar Ola .	24	B6
Youghal	11	F3
Young	63	B4
Younghusband,		
L.	62	B2
Younghusband		
Pen.	62	C2
Youngstown . .	72	D5
Yozgat	46	C3
Ysyk-Köl, Ozero	29	E8
Yu Jiang →	35	D6
Yu Shan	35	D7
Yuan Jiang →	35	D6
Yuanling	35	D6
Yuanyang	34	D5
Yuba City	80	F3
Yūbari	32	F12
Yucatán □	85	C7
Yucatán, Canal		
de	85	C7
Yucatán,		
Península de	85	D7
Yucatan Str. =		
Yucatán,		
Canal de	85	C7
Yuci	35	C6
Yugoslavia ■ . .	22	B3
Yukon →	71	B3
Yukon		
Territory □ . .	70	B6
Yukti	30	C8
Yuma	82	D5
Yumen	34	C4
Yun Xian	35	C6
Yungas	91	G5
Yunnan □	34	D5
Yunta	62	B2
Yurgao	29	D9
Yuribei	28	B8
Yurimaguas . .	91	E3
Yuryung Kaya .	30	B9
Yushu	34	C4
Yuzhno-		
Sakhalinsk . .	31	E12
Yvetot	12	B4

Z

Zabid	49	E3
Zābol	45	D5
Zābol □	45	D6
Zābolī	45	E5
Zabrze	16	C4
Zacapa	85	E7
Zacatecas	84	C4
Zacoalco	84	C4
Zadar	20	B5
Zadetkyi Kyun	36	C1
Zafra	18	C2
Żagań	16	C2
Zagazig	52	B5
Zagorsk =		
Sergiyev		
Posad	24	B4
Zagreb	20	B6
Zāgros, Kūhhā-		
ye	44	C2
Zagros Mts. =		
Zāgros,		
Kūhhā-ye . .	44	C2
Zāhedān	45	D5
Zahlah	46	D3
Zaïre =		
Congo → . .	56	F2
Zaïre = Congo,		
Dem. Rep. of		
the ■	56	E4
Zaječar	22	C4
Zakhodnaya		
Dzvina =		
Daugava → .	24	B1
Zākhū	46	C5
Zákinthos	23	F3
Zakopane	16	D4
Zalaegerszeg .	16	E3
Zalău	17	E6
Zaleshchiki =		
Zalishchyky .	17	D7
Zalew Wiślany .	16	A4
Zalingei	53	F3
Zalishchyky . .	17	D7
Zambeze → . .	59	B7
Zambezi =		
Zambeze →	59	B7
Zambezi	58	A4
Zambia ■	59	B5
Zamboanga . .	38	C2
Zamora, Mexico	84	D4
Zamora, Spain	18	B3
Zamość	17	C6
Zanaga	56	E2
Zanesville	72	E4
Zanjān	46	C7
Zanjān □	46	C7
Zante =		
Zákinthos . .	23	F3
Zanzibar	57	F7
Zaouiet El-Kala		
= Bordj Omar		
Driss	54	C6
Zaouiet Reggane	54	C5
Zap Suyu =		
Kabīr, Zab		
al →	46	C5
Zapadnaya		
Dvina	28	D4
Zapadnaya		
Dvina → =		
Daugava → .	24	B1
Západné		
Beskydy	16	D4
Zaporizhzhya .	25	D4
Zaporozhye =		
Zaporizhzhya	25	D4
Zara	46	C4
Zaragoza	19	B5
Zarand	44	D4
Zaranj	42	D2
Zaria	55	F6
Zaruma	90	D3
Żary	16	C2
Zarzis	52	B1
Zaskar Mts. . .	42	C10
Zavāreh	44	C3
Zawiercie	16	C4
Zāyandeh → .	44	C3
Zaysan	29	E9
Zaysan, Oz. . .	29	E9
Zbarazh	17	D7
Zdolbuniv	17	C8
Zduńska Wola .	16	C4
Zeebrugge	14	C2
Zeehan	62	D4
Zeerust	59	D5
Zeila	49	E3
Zeitz	15	C7
Zelenograd . .	24	B4
Zémio	57	C5
Zemun	22	B3
Zenica	20	B6
Žepce	20	B7
Zêzere →	18	C1
Zgorzelec	16	C2
Zhabinka	17	B7
Zhailma	29	D7
Zhambyl = Taraz	29	E8
Zhangaqazaly .	29	E7
Zhanghua	35	D7
Zhangjiakou . .	35	B6
Zhangye	34	C5
Zhangzhou . . .	35	D6
Zhanjiang	35	D6
Zhanyi	34	D5
Zhaotong	34	D5
Zhashkiv	17	D10
Zhayyq →	29	E6
Zhdanov =		
Mariupol . . .	25	D4
Zhejiang □ . .	35	D7
Zhengzhou . .	35	C6
Zhenjiang	35	C6
Zhenyuan	35	D5
Zhezqazghan .	29	E7
Zhigansk	30	C10
Zhijiang	35	D5
Zhilinda	30	B9
Zhitomir =		
Zhytomyr . . .	17	C9
Zhlobin	17	B10
Zhmerinka =		
Zhmerynka . .	17	D9
Zhmerynka . .	17	D9
Zhodino =		
Zhodzina . . .	17	A9
Zhodzina	17	A9
Zhongdian . . .	34	D4
Zhumadian . .	35	C6
Zhuzhou	35	D6
Zhytomyr	17	C9
Zibo	35	C6
Zielona Góra .	16	C2
Zigey	53	F2
Zigong	35	D5
Zigui	35	C6
Ziguinchor . .	55	F1
Zile	46	B3
Žilina	16	D4
Zillah	52	C2
Zimbabwe ■ .	59	B5
Zimnicea	22	C5
Zinder	55	F6
Zion National		
Park	83	B6
Zipaquirá . . .	90	C4
Ziway, L.	53	G6
Zlatograd	22	D5
Zlatoust	29	D6
Zlin	16	D3
Zlītan	52	B1
Zmeinogorsk .	29	D9
Znojmo	16	D3
Zolochev =		
Zolochiv . . .	17	D7
Zolochiv	17	D7
Zomba	59	B7
Zongo	56	D3
Zonguldak . .	46	B2
Zorritos	90	D2
Zouar	52	D2
Zouérate	54	D2
Zrenjanin	22	B3
Zuetina = Az		
Zuwaytīnah .	52	B3
Zufar	48	D5
Zug	13	C8
Zugspitze	14	E6
Zula	53	E6
Zumbo	59	B6
Zungeru	55	G6
Zunyi	35	D5
Zürich	13	C8
Zuwārah	52	B1
Zvishavane . .	59	C6
Zvolen	16	D4
Zwettl	15	D8
Zwickau	15	C7
Zwolle	14	B4
Żyrardów	16	B5
Zyryan	29	E9
Zyryanovsk =		
Zyryan	29	E9
Żywiec	16	D4

THE WORLD

0 1138 0153772 2
Wentworth - Alumni Library

RECEIVED
ALUMNI LIBRARY

SEP 1 4 2001

Wentworth Institute of Technology
550 Huntington Avenue
Boston, Ma 02115-5998

THIS BOOK MAY NOT LEAVE THE LIBRARY!

Alaska (U.S.A.)

GREENLAND (Den.)

ICE

CANADA

IREL

UNITED STATES

NORTH

PO

ATLANTIC

MOR

Tropic of Cancer

W. SAHARA

Hawaiian Is. (U.S.A.)

MEXICO

CUBA

OCEAN

MAURITAN

BELIZE
HAITI / DOM. REP.

GUATEMALA HOND. JAMAICA

CAPE VERDE IS.

SEN.

EL SAL. NICARAGUA

G.

G.B.

COSTA RICA

GUINE.

PANAMA

VENEZUELA

S.L.

LIBERI

PACIFIC

COLOMBIA

GUY. SUR.
F./GUIANA

Equator

ECUADOR

PERU

BRAZIL

BOLIVIA

SOUT

FRENCH POLYNESIA

OCEAN

ATLANT

Tropic of Capricorn

PARAGUAY

OCEA

CHILE

URUGUAY

ARGENTINA

S

Anta